Constructing the Infrastructure for the Knowledge Economy

Methods and Tools, Theory and Practice

Constructing the Infrastructure for the Knowledge Economy

Methods and Tools, Theory and Structure

Edited by

Henry Linger and Julie Fisher
Monash University
Melbourne, Australia

Wita Wojtkowski and W. Gregory Wojtkowski
Boise State University
Boise, Idaho

Jože Zupančič
University of Maribor
Kranj, Slovenia

and

Kitty Vigo and Josie Arnold
Swinburne University of Technology
Melbourne, Australia

Kluwer Academic / Plenum Publishers
New York, Boston, Dordrecht, London, Moscow

Proceedings of 12th International Conference on Information Systems and Development, held in Melbourne, Australia, August 29–31, 2003.

ISBN 0-306-48554-0
ISBN E-book 0-306-48555-9

233 Spring Street, New York, New York 10013

http://www.kluweronline.com

10 9 8 7 6 5 4 3 2 1

A C.I.P. record for this book is available from the Library of Congress

Printed in the United States of America

COMMITTEES

Conference and Program co-Chairs

Henry Linger
Julie Fisher

Organising Committee Members

Henry Linger
Julie Fisher
Kitty Vigo
Josie Arnold

Proceedings Editors

Henry Linger
Julie Fisher
Gregory Wojtkowski
Wita Wojtkowski
Jož e Zupanèiè
Kitty Vigo
Josie Arnold

The Program co-Chairs would like to thank all those who assisted with the process of reviewing papers. All papers were independently double blind referred with an Associate Editor making the final recommendation to the Program co-Chairs. The final determination of paper acceptance was made by the Program co-Chairs based on reviewer and Associate Editor assessments.

International Program Committee

Witold Abramowitz
Gary Allen
Josie Arnold
Juris Borzovs
Frada Burstein
Julie Fisher
John Gammack
Shirley Gregor
Janis Grundspenkis
Helen Hasan
Juhani Iivari
Lech Janczewski
Marius Janson
Roland Kaschek
Marite Kirikova
Gábor Knapp
Henry Linger
Björn Lundell
Leszek A. Maciaszek
Sal March
Gábor Magyar
Judy McKay
Mike Metcalfe
Robert Moreton
Anders G. Nilsson
Jacob Norjberg
Annet Nothingam
Tore Orvik
Malgorzata Pankowska
Anne Persson
Graham Pervan
Jaroslav Pokorny
Graeme Shanks
Larry Stapleton
Eberhard Stickel
Uldis Sukovskis
Jacek Unold
Olegas Vasilecas
Kitty Vigo
Benkt Wangler
Leoni Warne
Gregory Wojtkowski
Wita Wojtkowski
Stanislaw Wrycza
Jož e Zupanèiè

Associate Editors

External Reviewers

PREFACE

This publication is the outcome of the 12th International ISD Conference held in Melbourne in 2003. The theme for the 2003 conference was "Constructing the Infrastructure for the Knowledge Economy: Methods & Tools, Theory & Practice." Many of the papers reflected this theme covering a range of topics from traditional systems development through to emerging technologies. The International ISD Conference evolved from the first Polish-Scandinavian Seminar on Current Trends in Information Systems Development Methodologies, held in Gdansk, Poland in 1988. The International Conference is dedicated to IS development and compliments the network of general information systems conferences (ICIS, ECIS, AMCIS, PACIS, ACIS).

The development of information systems has paralleled technological developments and the deployment of that technology in all areas of society, including government, industry, community and in the home. More recently the convergence of information and communications technologies has presented a challenge for the ISD profession in terms of accommodating mobility, access, interoperability, distribution, connectivity, media and the diversity and volume of information.

IS development, both as a professional and academic discipline, has responded to this challenge through methodologies, tools and theory development. As a practice-based discipline, ISD has always promoted a close interaction between theory and practice that has been influential in setting the ISD agenda. This agenda has largely focused on the integration of people, processes and technology and the context in which this occurs.

This year, the conference provided an opportunity to bring to Melbourne participants from the first Polish and Scandinavian ISD workshop which evolved into the ISD conference we know today. The Faculty of Information Technology, Monash University, provided the financial support that allowed us to invite Juhani Iivari, Nillson Anders, Stanislav Wrycza and Karlheinz Kautz who all participated in the inaugural Workshop. We took the unique opportunity of their participation in the conference to hold an open forum. Together with Wita Wojtkowski, Robert Morton, Shirley Gregor and Dubravka Cecez-Kecmanovic, they discussed the issues confronting ISD today drawing on the historical perspective to inform the discussion.

Clive Finkelstein, Piero Mussio and Dubravka Cecez-Kecmanovic were keynote speakers who set the tone of the conference. We would like to thank all authors, and participants for contributing to what we believe was a successful and memorable conference. Many of the participants at this year's conference have travelled from Europe to attend the conference reflecting the origins of the conference and its importance and we would like to thank these participants for their continuing support.

The conference call for papers attracted a high number of very good quality papers. Of the 85 papers submitted we accepted 51, representing an acceptance rate of 60%. All papers were double-blind refereed by at least two independent reviewers and an Associate Editor. The reviewers and Associate Editors did an excellent job providing very detailed reviews on all the papers submitted. Their diligence and attention to detail has ensured the high quality of the papers presented at the conference.

We would also like to thank and acknowledge the work of those behind the scenes, Josie Arnold and Kitty Vigo (Swinburne University) for managing the web site, Marion Easton for her excellent efforts in managing the paper review process and corresponding with authors, Irene Thavarajah and Julie Austin who provided the back-up administrative support so competently. Finally our thanks go to the School of Information Management and Systems for the financial and other support provided.

Henry Linger
Julie Fisher
Conference co-Chairs
ISD 2003

CONTENTS

KEYNOTES

1. ISD DISCOURSES AND THE EMANCIPATION OF MEANING 1
Dubravka Cecez-Kecmanovic

2. E-DOCUMENTS AS TOOLS FOR THE HUMANIZED MANAGEMENT OF COMMUNITY KNOWLEDGE 27
Piero Mussio

3. ENTERPRISE INTEGRATION USING ENTERPRISE ARCHITECTURE 43
Clive Finkelstein

THEORETICAL FOUNDATIONS

4. THE FORMULATION OF DESIGN THEORIES FOR INFORMATION SYSTEMS 83
Shirley Gregor and David Jones

5. JUSTIFYING ISD KNOWLEDGE CLAIMS 95
Mike Metcalfe

6. THE RO THEORY, DISCOVERY OF BUI, AND IS: BEGINNING OF THEORETICAL FOUNDATIONS 103
Sergey Ivanov

7. THE DYNAMICS OF AN INFORMATION SYSTEM IN LIGHT OF CHAOS THEORY 115
Jacek Unold

ISD METHODS

8. INFORMATION SYSTEMS DEVELOPMENT METHODOLOGIES IN PRACTICE 127
Bo Hansen, Karlheinz Kautz, and Dan Jacobsen

9. SOFTWARE DEVELOPMENT METHODOLOGY EVALUATION MODEL 141
Damjan Vavpotič, Marko Bajec, and Marjan Krisper

10. REPRESENTING PART-WHOLE RELATIONS IN CONCEPTUAL MODELLING: A COMPARISON OF OBJECT-ORIENTED AND ENTITY RELATIONSHIP MODELLERS 155
Graeme Shanks, Elizabeth Tansley, Simon Milton and Steve Howard

11. EXISTENCE DEPENDENCY AND INFORMATION STRUCTURE 169
C. N. G. (Kit) Dampney and Janet Aisbett

12. TOWARDS A GENERIC MODEL FOR AGILE PROCESSES 179
Anne Fuller and Peter Croll

13. CONTINUOUS INTEGRATION AS A MEANS OF COORDINATION: A CASE STUDY OF TWO OPEN SOURCE PROJECTS 187
Jesper Holck and Niels Jørgensen

14. ON BUSINESS RULES APPROACH TO THE INFORMATION SYSTEMS DEVELOPMENT 199
Irma Valatkaite and Olegas Vasilecas

15. BUSINESS FUNCTIONS PROTOTYPING VIA XSLT 209
Karel Richta

16. OLD TRICK,NEW DOGS: LEARNING TO USE CRUD MATRICES EARLY IN OBJECT-ORIENTED INFORMATION SYSTEM DEVELOPMENT 223
Ilona Box

17. FROM VERNACULAR TO RATIONAL DESIGN IN SOFTWARE ENGINEERING: CONSEQUENCES OF THE DESIGNER'S CHANGING ROLE 237
Paul R. Taylor

REQUIREMENTS FOR ISD

18. PICTURING PROBLEMS 251
Mike Metcalfe

19. USING COGNITIVE MAPPING FOR PROBLEM ANALYSIS IN INFORMATION REQUIREMENTS DETERMINATION 267
Judy McKay and Peter Marshall

20. A QUALITY MODEL FOR THE EVALUATION OF SOFTWARE REQUIREMENTS SPECIFICATIONS 281
Jennifer L. Gasston

21. A QUALITATIVE METHOD FOR IDENTIFYING FACTORS THAT INFLUENCE USER SATISFACTION 293
Bernard J. Terrill and Andrew Flitman

22. DOMAIN MODEL DRIVEN APPROACH TO CHANGE IMPACT ASSESSMENT 305
Darijus Strašunskas and Sari Hakkarainen

23. TRACKING BUSINESS RULES FROM THEIR SOURCE TO THEIR IMPLEMENTATION TO SUPPORT IS MAINTENANCE 317
Marko Bajec, Damjan Vavpotič, and Marjan Krisper

24. PROCESS OF REQUIREMENTS EVOLUTION IN WEB-ENABLED EMPLOYEE SERVICE SYSTEMS 331
Pradip K. Sarkar and Jacob Cybulski

25. DISTRIBUTING USABILITY: THE IMPLICATIONS FOR USABILITY TESTING 341
Lejla Vrazalic

26. INTEGRATING SECURITY DESIGN INTO INFORMATION SYSTEMS DEVELOPMENT 355
Murray E. Jennex and Margaret Lowe

27. INTEGRATING SECURITY PROPERTIES WITH SYSTEMS DESIGN ARTEFACTS 367
Khaled Md. Khan

KNOWLEDGE MANAGEMENT

28. KNOWLEDGE CREATION THROUGH SYSTEMS DEVELOPMENT 379
Helen Hasan

29. FROM PHILOSOPHY TO KNOWLEDGE MANAGEMENT AND BACK AGAIN 393
Jeremy Aarons

30. KNOWLEDGE MANAGEMENT STRATEGIES: LEADERS AND LEADERSHIP 405
Suzanne M. Zyngier and Frada Burstein

31. TRUST, CONTROL, AND DESIGN: A STUDY OF COMPUTER SCIENTISTS 417
Supriya Singh and Christine Satchell

32. BUILDING AN OPEN DOCUMENT MANAGEMENT SYSTEM WITH COMPONENTS FOR TRUST 431
Gábor Knapp, Gábor Magyar, and Gergely Németh

33. KNOWLEDGE REUSE IN PROJECT MANAGEMENT 443
Jillian Owen, Frada Burstein, and William P. Hall

34. DEVELOPING KNOWLEDGE MANAGEMENT SYSTEMS IN BPM CONTEXT 455
Pin Chen

35. MODELLING EMERGENT PROCESSES IN KNOWLEDGE-INTENSIVE ENVIRONMENTS 469
I. T. Hawryszkiewycz

36. ENABLING PROBLEM DOMAIN KNOWLEDGE TRANSFORMATION DURING OBJECT ORIENTED SOFTWARE DEVELOPMENT 481
Oksana Nikiforova and Marite Kirikova

WEB AND INTERNET BASED SYSTEMS

37. WEB DEVELOPMENT: THE DIFFERENCES, SIMILARITIES AND IN-BETWEENS 495
Karlheinz Kautz and Sabine Madsen

38. SEARCHING FOR A METHODOLOGY FOR SMART INTERNET TECHNOLOGY DEVELOPMENT 507
Jenine Beekhuyzen, Liisa von Hellens, Michelle Morley, and Sue Nielsen

39. A PROPOSED TAXONOMY OF MEDIA COLLECTIONS AND ITS IMPLICATIONS FOR DESIGN AND MANAGEMENT OF MULTIMEDIA DATABASES 519
Valerie J. Hobbs and Diarmuid J. Pigott

40. XML DATA WAREHOUSE POSSIBILITIES AND SOLUTIONS 531
Jaroslav Pokorny

41. "WEB PRESENCE": FORMULATING A "WICKED" RESEARCH PROBLEM 543
Sherre Roy and Paul Ledington

42. AUTOMATIC TOPIC MAP CREATION USING TERM CRAWLING AND CLUSTERING HIERARCHY PROJECTION 555
Witold Abramowicz, Tomasz Kaczmarek, and Marek Kowalkiewicz

43. DISCOVERING WWW USER INTERFACE PROBLEMS VIA USER SURVEYS AND LOG FILE ANALYSIS 569
Jason Ceddia, Judy Sheard, and Renee Gedge

44. E-GOVERNMENT SERVICES: ONE LOCAL GOVERNMENT'S APPROACH 581
Peter Shackleton, Julie Fisher, and Linda Dawson

45. WEB AUCTIONS: AN IMPACT ANALYSIS FOR BALTIC REGION SMES 593
Stanis³aw Wrycza

46. EXPERIENCES IN USING A WEB-BASED GDSS TO COORDINATE DISTRIBUTED GROUP DECISION-MAKING PROCESSES 605
Patrick P. Cao, Jocelyn C. San Pedro and Frada Burstein

47. WHISPERS FROM A DISCOURSE: DIGITAL TELEVISION IN AUSTRALIA 617
Cate Dowd

EDUCATION

48. WALKING THE WALK OF ETEACHING AND E-LEARNING: ENCHANCING TEACHING AND LEARNING USING THE NEW TECHNOLOGIES 629
Josie Arnold

49. EFFECTIVE TEACHING OF GROUPWARE DEVELOPMENT: A CONCEPTUAL MODEL 643
Adel M. Aladwani

50. APPLICATION OF SYSTEM ENGINEERING METHODS IN INFORMATION SYSTEMS CURRICULA DEVELOPMENT 649
Albertas Caplinskas and Olegas Vasilecas

CASE STUDIES

51. CONSIDERATIONS IN SYSTEMS DEVELOPMENT OF APPLICATIONS FOR MOBILE DEVICES: A CASE STUDY 661
Linda Dawson and Julie Fisher

52. OUTSOURCING: AN INFORMATION SYSTEMS DEVELOPMENT CASE STUDY IN AN INDONESIAN SME 675
Mira Kartiwi and Helen Hasan

53. CURRENT STATUS AND TRENDS IN CUSTOMER RELATIONSHIP MANAGEMENT: THE CASE OF SLOVENIA 683
Boštjan Kos and Jož e Zupanèiè

54. INFORMATION SYSTEM DEVELOPMENT FOR DEMOLITION MATERIAL MANAGEMENT 695
Chunlu Liu and Sung Kin Pun

55. A DISTRIBUTED LOGISTIC SUPPORT COMMUNICATION SYSTEM 705
V. Gruhn, M. Hülder, R. Ijioui, F.-M. Schleif, and L. Schöpe

ISD DISCOURSES AND THE EMANCIPATION OF MEANING

Dubravka Cecez-Kecmanovic[1]

ABSTRACT

In this paper I'd like to expose the view of Information Systems Development (ISD) processes as discursive practices, the view that puts the politics of meaning making and interpretation at centre stage. Such a view aims to assist deconstruction of discursive regimes instituted by ISD processes and methodologies, the production of representations and legitimation of meaning (through business process models, information requirements specifications, databases, knowledge bases, procedures, rules, etc.) within a particular social, political and economic context and power relations. To achieve this aim I will propose a discursive framework for examining ISD that highlights particular distinctions among ISD processes as organisational discourses: on one hand, ISD are seen as sites of domination, hegemonic consent, and colonisation of meaning, and on the other, as sites of dissensus discourses, multiple value and interest positions, and the struggle for democratic change and emancipation of meaning. By drawing from three published examples of ISD research, I will illustrate the nature of these distinctions and the type of analysis enabled by the proposed discursive ISD framework and will also demonstrate the relevance of new insights thus gained.

1. INTRODUCTION

Information Systems (IS) have become one of the most critical, if not the most important, enabler and inhibitor of organisational transformation, growth and survival. Information Systems Development (ISD) processes, including information systems planning, analysis, design, implementation, and maintenance, have become sites of continuous social action through which organisational meanings are produced and the construction of reality sustained. ISD, therefore, in its most elemental articulation, entails

---

[1] Dubravka Cecez-Kecmanovic, School of Information Systems, Technology and Management, Faculty of Commerce and Economics, University of New South Wales, Sydney, NSW 2052

meaning making and interpretation, knowledge production and the construction of reality. Given how little we know about such interpretive work that is fundamental to ISD, it is not surprising that IS are more often criticised as inhibitors than praised as enables of organisational transformation, growth and survival.

In this paper I'd like to raise some concerns regarding two sides of the *ISD—organization* relationship: how organizational discourses influence and construct ISD and conversely, how discourses mediated or enabled by ISD (re)construct actors and organizations. These concerns have their origin in understanding organizations as discursively constructed (Alvesson and Karreman, 2000) and the idea that discourse is the foundation of the social construction of reality (Berger and Luchmann, 1966). More specifically, I am concerned how IS, like other artefacts and material objects, individual and collective identities, social and power relationships, are constructed by organizational discourses operating within particular historical and societal contexts. Furthermore, I am interested in investigating how discursive ISD practices bring particular IS 'into being'. Do IS models really 'represent' reality, as many ISD textbooks and IS developers and researchers assume? How ISD approaches and methodologies enable some and disable other discourses and thereby reproduce dominant power structures, social relations and organisational meanings?

Investigation of these questions and the assumptions underlying ISD processes, as Hirschheim and Klein (1989, 1994) convincingly argued, is essential for understanding different ISD approaches and methodologies, the nature of developed systems, as well as the resulting changes in organisational practices. In their landmark paper, Hirschheim and Klein (1989) proposed a four-paradigm ISD framework, based on Burrell and Morgan's sociological paradigms (1979) – functionalist, social relativist, radical structuralist and neo-humanist. By adopting particular lines of distinction Hirschheim and Klein's (1989) framework draw attention to differences in the ontological and epistemological assumptions behind alternative views of ISD in both practice and research.

The ISD paradigms highlighted the difference (and conflicts) between the predominant functionalist ISD approach and emerging alternative approaches (Hirchheim et al., 1995). Similar to other social sciences, ISD paradigms are seen as a basis for conflict and exclusion (paradigmatic incommensurability). On the other hand, in the IS research generally, there are calls for pluralism and the use of multiple paradigms (Landry and Banville, 1992). While defining the alternatives, paradigms have been used to reify concepts and approaches (Deetz, 1996). They have a tendency to constrain the debate and prevent us from seeing other important differences in the ISD practice and research. As ISD processes change and research agendas evolve, there is a need to revisit lines of distinction underlying these paradigms and perhaps bring in new ways of seeing ISD processes by exploring other dimensions of difference. This paper explores an alternative view of ISD as discursive organisational practices, the view that puts the politics of meaning making, representations and (re)construction of reality at centre stage.

The purpose of this paper is to propose the discursive framework for ISD processes and demonstrate how such framework enables new insights into and distinctions among various ISD practices. By drawing from three published examples of ISD research, the paper demonstrates how the discursive framework draws attention to i) ISD discourses as forms of regulation, domination and colonization of meaning (hegemonic discourses), ii) ISD practices as sites of confrontation of values and interest and negotiation of meaning (participatory discourses), and iii) ISD practices as sites of struggles for transformative, democratic social change and emancipation of meaning (emancipatory discourses). The proposed discursive framework is not intended so much as an alternative way of classifying ISD, but rather as a way of exposing some interesting contrasts and stimulating new and potentially more productive debates regarding relevant ISD issues, research questions, and methods.

To achieve these objectives the paper first investigates ISD processes from a language perspective and then presents a brief discussion about ISD as organisational discourses. This is followed by three examples of ISD from the literature. The new discursive ISD framework that identifies four types of ISD discourses (hegemonic, covert hegemonic, participatory and emancipatory) is developed in the next sections. The framework is explained and discussed by drawing from the three examples of ISD research. The final section summarises major contributions and implications of the proposed discursive framework.

2. LANGUAGE AND ISD

In the process of ISD we conduct requirements analysis: we talk to the users of the future IS and apply various methods and techniques to describe how business processes operate and how they can be changed and improved, e.g. made more efficient, productive, or reliable. We then model information flows and processes and define *information requirements*, which together with the model of business processes serve as specifications for the design of the envisaged IS. We use, for instance, entity-relationship diagrams to represent entities and their characteristics, as well as how one type of entity is related to other types. In such a way we claim to represent or map a relevant domain of 'reality' which is going to be served by the IS. In other words, we represent a reality and the desired content and functions of IS as a future part of this reality.

When we apply ISD methodologies we are primarily concerned with the correctness of representation, that is, how accurately entity-relationship models, and consequently database structures, map the reality. The reality, that is processes, objects, their attributes and relationships are assumed to exist and naturally occur. Thus our task in information modelling is to identify those processes, objects, their attributes and relationships and map them as accurately as possible (and practicable). We do realise that any modelling is accurate to a degree as it involves selection (of important from unimportant), abstraction (of some objects, attributes and relationships), and description (naming, documenting). But what we do not recognise is that by doing so – by selecting, abstracting and describing – we project a particular way of *seeing* the reality. And like all seeing, modelling is also *seeing as* (Deetz, 2000); what one is modelling or *what one is seeing as* depends on values and preferences.[2] As information modelling and requirements

---

[2] The following quote from Deetz (2000) cleverly illustrates the point:

"The teacher presents four boxes to a child. In each there is a picture—a tree, cat, dog, and squirrel respectively. The child is asked which one is different. A child worthy of first grade immediately picks the three, as do most of us. The child knows how to divide plans from animals. Hidden from our ordinary thinking, but equally important, the child knows that the plant/animal distinction is the preferred distinction to apply, that this is the type of object reproduction that is preferred. The perception and choice is both true *and* good. It could not be made if the child had not implicitly considered both senses of right—i.e., true and preferred. To successfully complete the task, the child must both know which distinction is to be preferred in application to the indeterminate (not yet objectified things) to see it as that object and to discern which box is

specification imply *certain* values and interests, the subsequent design of data structures, databases and programs necessarily implant these values and interests. Those in organisations who have the power and expertise to define the purpose, role and tasks of IS and specify information requirements have in fact the privilege of implanting into IS their seeing of reality, that is, their value-laden distinctions and models. In other words, their views, values and interest become inscribed into IS software design. As Bowker and Star (1994) wittily note:

> ... values, opinions, and rhetoric are frozen into codes, electronic thresholds and computer applications. ... we can say that in many ways, software is *frozen organisational discourse*. (p. 187; emphases added)

What remains imperceptible in this process (one might say conveniently so) is that by naming entities and relationships found in the 'reality' we analyse, we participate in the act of (re)constituting these entities and relationships. By distinguishing some objects and labelling them as a particular class of entities and identifying some of their attributes as well as some of their relationships with other classes of objects, we participate in a more fundamental process of object constitution through language. We identify some objects, but not others. We specify some attributes and not others. We map some relationships and not others. While doing so we claim that they naturally "exist" and therefore should be mapped. When "mapped", these entities, attributes and relationships stand for the reality observed and thereby reconstruct it. As these maps become transformed into data structures and databases, and coded into application software, the reconstructed reality is built into IS design (that is frozen into codes and computer applications) and subsequently "made real" through system's implementation and operation.

Objects (organisational units, costs, revenue, tasks, employees), however, in real life situations can be seen (and constructed) in many different ways depending on a point of view and alternative value positions and interest. When, for instance, in the case of a Decision Support System (DSS) development in a Government Department (the first example to be discussed below), employees' time was defined as either "time devoted to customer-related work" or "other time", this did not seem as something of concern, just a way of recording employees' time. However, when the DSS developer collected and entered the employees' time data into DSS, their work and their time have been defined as either *customer-related* or *other*. Named as *other* types of work, quality improvement, staff development and training, organising, coordinating and similar activities, were devalued and their relevance to the provision of services to customers denied. By making such a distinction the DSS developer, in cooperation with managers, redefined employees' work in a way that reflected managers' *seeing* of employees as "providers of services to clients" (consistent with their economic rationalist agenda of the Department restructure). Employees, however, had no chance to put forward their own, alternative seeing of their work, as the distinction between *customer-related* and *other time* was treated as natural and inevitable. Implemented in DSS such a distinction redefined the essence of employees' work and in turn affected their individual and collective identity, and sense of worth and contribution to the Department.

---

to be circled if the plant/animal distinction is used." While the first task is "a question of values", the second task "since it is a function of the first, has embedded in it this value element". (p. 734)

By implanting the distinction between *customer-related* or *other time* into the DSS, managers inscribed their values and preferences into the system which subsequently served to justify decisions and change the reality (retrench staff and transform the Department). Alternative views of employees' work, as might have been seen by different stakeholders, including alternative definitions of work types and times recorded in the DSS, would have enabled different (re)constructions of reality and could have opened other avenues for transforming the Department.

Without expending the above argument any further I'd like briefly to make my point that ISD methodologies in general and information requirements specification in particular, are based on the representational conception of language. Interestingly enough ISD thinking and practice have not as yet come to grips with a serious critique of such a conception of language carried out in various disciplines, including linguistics, sociology, cultural studies, social psychology, education and organisational studies (see eg. Denzin, 1992; Kincheloe and McLaren, 1994; Deetz, 1996; Gee, 1996; Carspecken, 1999). Researchers in these disciplines have long come to understand that language cannot be assumed to mirror reality, nor can it be taken as a neutral and objective medium for describing the "real world". Having such an understanding of language in mind I propose that business process models, information models and database structures are not simply "descriptions" of the real world but serve to construct it. They are not neutral and objective representations but instead value-leaden distinctions and interest-based re-constructions. These propositions in turn raise some interesting questions regarding the use of language in ISD: How ISD methodologies create discourses that reproduce dominant organisational meanings and sustain the construction of reality? How the meanings constructed and promoted in business process analysis, requirements specification and databases design, come to be taken-for-granted as natural and inevitable? How power discourses undermine the multiple meanings (constructed by different groups) by legitimating some and invalidating others, and thus implant a single, "correct" set of meanings into IS? Can ISD discourses disrupt prevailing organisational meanings, contest dominant socio-cultural productions and thereby advance the struggle for emancipation of meaning?

3. INFORMATION SYSTEMS AS ORGANIZATIONAL DISCOURSES

Following the "linguistic turn" in social sciences (sociology in particular) scholars in organisation studies are increasingly paying attention to discursive nature of organisations. Organisations are conceptualized as discursively constructed collections of texts (Alvesson and Karreman, 2000; Keenoy et al., 2000; Hardy et al., 2000; Grant et al., 1997). Such a view emphasizes the "talked" and the "textual" nature of social interaction through which social reality is reproduced and organisations recreated. The key questions that such a view opens up are:

- how this reality is constructed and sustained and
- how organisations are (re)produced by historically situated discourses.

In answering these questions one cannot avoid the role of IS. Namely, any information system – be it a transaction based IS, MIS, DSS, executive IS or computer-mediated communication – is a system of texts, consisting of more or less structured data such as data sets in databases, models in DSS, or natural language messages in email or groupware interactions. In other words, as a system of texts an information system represents a form of organizational discourse, and thus a means of organizing social reality. Like other discourses, IS bring certain objects into being. As I have indicated above, the IS do not simply 'mirror' reality, translating, for instance, objects and their relationships into database structures. Rather, IS (re)construct objects and relationships, "identify" some objects and not others, institute some rules and procedures, thereby implying certain views, values and norms (and disregarding others). Through their implementation and recurrent use IS become a powerful ordering force, a means for the production, distribution and consumption of organisational meanings. As discourses that (re)organize and (re)produce social texts by employing ever more powerful Information and Communication Technologies (ICT), IS play an increasingly important role in the social (re)construction of reality.

From a discursive theory approach (Alvesson and Karreman, 2000; Keenoy et al., 2000; Hardy et al., 2000; Grant et al., 1997; Lemke, 1993,1995), ISD can be seen as a site of ongoing discursive struggles through which organisational meanings are reconstructed, imposed, contested and negotiated. ISD processes can thus be conceptualised as discursive practices by different groups of actors who struggle to shape "presentations" of reality (frame problems and ways the future IS would resolve them) in particular ways, according to their views, interests and values, and thereby achieve certain political effects. What is particularly interesting is to understand how such discursive practices, that is ISD processes, are ideologically shaped by the relations of power and dominant discourses.

An information system is not created in a vacuum, nor does it originate from a blanc sheet of paper when an analyst gets out there and starts talking to users and documenting their requirements (despite the fact that this is what we teach our students). When we approach ISD as a discourse practice we immediately realize how it is embedded in global and local contexts (eg. ISD approaches and methodologies taught in Universities and those practiced in a company), as well as how it is connected to other organisational discourses preceding, parallel to or following ISD. To help us explore some of these issues in more details I'd like to propose a theoretical framework that distinguishes some broad types of ISD discursive practices in organisations. The purpose of such a framework is to make us aware not only of different characteristics of ISD practices but also, and perhaps more importantly, of their implications for the construction and reproduction of meanings, individual and collective identities, social and power structures. But before I present the framework I'd like first to introduce three interesting and to a degree exemplary cases of ISD that will enable me to link the proposed concepts and theoretical positions to practice and our real life experiences.

4. EXAMPLES OF ISD

4.1. Case #1: DSS Development in a Government Department

The first case is an action research project that involved the development and implementation of a Decision Support System (DSS) for Human Resource Services (HRS) section of a large Government Department (Molineux, 1998). As one of semi-autonomous businesses line, HRS was created to provide non-payroll related human resource services to other business lines ("clients") and corporate entity of the Department. These services included performance management, occupational health and safety, employment equity and diversity, industrial relations, workforce planning, HR strategy and development. As part of a broader rationalization strategy, HRS service provision to clients within the Department was to become "externally contestable" within two years. In other words, HRS's charges for services had to be competitive as the business lines would be able to choose their supplier from outside the Department. For HRS that meant a major change: moving from "a monopoly supplier in a fairly stable environment into a full competition in a quite dynamic environment" (Molineux, 1998, p. 234). Such a change required a significant alteration in staff attitudes, especially in relation to clients and meeting their needs. Managers, who also had to change their approach to and methods of managing staff, feared that HRS is leading to a crisis point.

The author carried out the action research project in which he provided expertise in the application of Dynamic Systems Modelling that was the basis for the development of the DSS (Molineux, 1998). The objective of the DSS was to assist management teams in understanding the dynamic relationships between the demand and supply of services and making policy and staffing decisions to transform HRS into leaner, and more efficient and effective service provider. DSS played a key role in implementing "the economic rationalist model of contestability" (p. 238) in HRS.

The project started with a cost attribution survey administered in Nov 1996 in a Region (the Department had offices nation-wide). The chronological sequence of events is presented in Table 1. The survey collected data about *client-related* and *other* (non-client-related) work by staff. Staff volunteered to monitor and record how they spent their time in a fortnight period. The participation rate was 67%. Data from the survey plus data about staff supply, expenses and revenue using the new charging out methodology (already available in the Department) were used to develop the DSS. Based on the collected data DSS calculated that staff utilization rate was very low, 32.8%.

The DSS was presented first to regional managers (Dec 1996) and then to the National HR manager and the executive (Feb 1997). As a result a National level DSS was developed and the National time recording and billing IS was designed to support new working practices and feed data into the DSS. To gather more accurate and up-to-date data about staff utilisation of time, the second cost attribution survey was conducted in March 1997, with staff participation rate of 76% this time. Based on this survey data DSS showed 44% time utilization rate (the increase compared to the first survey was attributed to staff familiarity with the survey and its purpose).

Once implemented DSS played a key role in staff rationalization in the Department. As the author noted, DSS ensured that "the general approach of contestability was accepted as a necessity for HRS to survive" (Molineux, 1998, p. 243). The DSS implementation was a significant success as its output was "highly valued and relied on by the executive, particularly the National manager" (p. 243). DSS was used to justify decisions to cut staff: the first one third staff cut in March 1997 (which resulted in 32% of staff accepting voluntary redundancy in July) and the second 26% staff cut in 1998.

The author also indicates that there were obstacles in achieving given objectives:

> A key obstacle was the fact that much of the change was being directed by events nationally.... Many staff did not work in the private sector and were unfamiliar with balance sheets and other financial documents... Another obstacle was the disillusionment of many HRS staff members, which it was thought may influence early successes. (Molineux, 1998, p. 239)

Table 1. Events leading to the implementation of the DSS to support HRS managers' decision making

Nov 1996	Cost attribution survey in a Region (staff recorded times for client-related work in a fortnight period) with 67% staff participation rate
Dec 1996	Presentation of DSS to Regional managers; DSS provided time utilization by staff (based on the survey), business expenses, revenue calculated based on charging out services, staff utilization rate (~33%) and profit/loss calculation
Feb 1997	DSS demonstration to the National HR manager and the executive, which led to the decision to develop the National level DSS
March 1997	DSS justified staff reduction of approximately 1/3 (voluntary redundancies offered to staff); Second cost attribution survey with 76% participation rate; based on this survey DSS calculated staff utilization rate of 44%
May-June 1997	Design of the National time recording and billing IS to support new working practices and feed the National level DSS
June 1997	Workshops with staff to "explain the vision and direction of HRS and introduce the time and billing system and train staff to use it".
1 July 1997	New National time recording IS alive; All staff recorded their client attributable time with some problems experienced due to lack of training in some regions; charging out services to clients initially had many errors; The author offered a high level job in the Department (National level)
July 1997	Staff reductions took place (25% accepted voluntary redundancy packages)
Aug 1997	DSS provided to the National manager 5 different scenarios and predictions based on varying expenses, revenue, demand and supply variables;
Oct 1997	DSS provided to the executive meeting further 7 scenarios which was followed by several more scenarios indicating a probable crises on the horizon due to higher then needed staff numbers (DSS showed that only 170 out of existing 240 were sustainable, assuming winning all the externally contestable contracts)
March 1998	The decision to reduce staff to 170 (reduction of 26%) was made.

Staff involvement was considered necessary for several reasons. Firstly, it was HRS staff who provided HR services to clients and whose work had to be dramatically changed. Secondly, only HRS staff could provide data about the ways services were provided and time allocated (collected by the two surveys). And thirdly, the new approach to HRS service provision and transformation of business processes in the Department depended on staff acceptance of change. As the author explains:

> Staff involvement was critical and the National manager visited all staff several times in 1997 to ensure direct involvement of staff. New skills were developed and a customer focus established. (Molineux, 1998, p. 244).

Furthermore, the author emphasises that the training of staff was "critical for to the modelling project [DSS] to get accurate data for use in projections of future scenarios." (Molineux, 1998, p. 241).

4.2. Case #2: Procurement of an Integrated Payroll/Personnel IS in a Hospital

The second case deals with the acquisition of an integrated IS in a Hospital (Waring, 1999). Waring conducted an action research project (for 6 months) to assist the Hospital in procurement and acquisition of the IS to serve both Finance and Personnel department. Senior management was pressured on one hand, by increasing demands for information from National Health Services (NHS) and on the other, by inability to provide required information due to low data quality, inflexibility and incompatibility of existing systems. In 1997 Senior management created a Project team (consisting of the Project manager, three members from Finance and three from the Personnel department) to find solution for an integrated payroll/personnel IS (IPPIS). Senior management did not want to make the decision: "IS belongs to the users so they should determine which was procured".

Finance and Personnel departments had different problems and agendas. Dissatisfied with their old payroll DB (disconnected from personnel DB), the Finance department was primarily interested in the Payroll IS. They had "a 'closed' gate-keeping culture" and their involvement in the Team was strictly focused on tasks and procedures. They attempted to dominate discourse and take control of the project arguing that:

> The payroll is vital and mistakes can cost the Hospital thousands of pounds. (Waring, 1999, p. 7)

The Personnel department, on the other hand, had a more open culture with staff more 'laid back'. They were concerned with data quality, production of a wide range of reports, and the functioning of both departments, and the necessary changes resulting from IPPIS implementation. They were also interested in broader organisational issues and team building. The author noted that the representatives of the IT department were conspicuously missing. With their reputation of speaking "techno-babble", the IT department was seen as a barrier to successful procurement of IS, and therefore deliberately omitted from the Project team and excluded from the process.

Companies were invited to give demonstrations of their packages (individual personnel and payroll IS and/or IPPIS). The Project team also visited other hospitals which implemented different packages. These visits and demonstrations gave them insight into some business and organisational problems that they had not considered before. After a visit to a hospital that implemented an integrated IS they concluded that:

> ... the IPPIS was not the problem itself but the way it has been implemented. (Waring, 1999, p. 9)

The situation however was complicated by the sudden merger with another Hospital, which resulted in the inclusion of additional team members from its Personnel department and going through the tender process again. The situation in the Project team became 'tense' with raising uncertainties regarding the future operations of all the departments and implications for staff. At this point the author was invited to:

> facilitate discussions... and [help staff] understand what integration meant to them and its implications for their respective departments. (Waring, 1999, p. 10)

As different departments had different interests, histories, cultures, information needs and IT experiences, it was not surprising that they had considerably different expectations from the IPPIS. The Project manager wanted all user departments to understand what an integrated IS meant for them and how it would affect their work. But:

> ... nowhere was any guidance on how departments with different cultures might negotiate and consider their own particular concerns...articulating requirements was a problem from the beginning and anticipating future difficulties was almost impossible. (Waring, 1999, p. 11)

The researcher introduced IDEFINE, a graphical language tool to describe existing and future operations and systems. After training team members were able to document their views and articulate their interests:

> Once trained everyone diagrammed their own system as it currently stood and discussed it with the staff who were not present at the Project team meetings. (p. 11)

> IDEFINE was instrumental in enabling discourses as it gave all participants in the project a 'common language' through which to communicate. The language ... allowed everyone to see how everyone else worked within their departments – something that had never happened before. (Waring, 1999, p. 13)

The researcher had no interest in any particular solution or package. Her role was to help staff apply IDEFINE and facilitate the process, including:

Articulation of different views and interests; exposition of biases, hidden issues and illegitimate claims; Argumentation process and conduct of *rational discourse;* Identification and examination of essential organisational problems that existed irrespective of IS and new ones related to implementation of the new IPPIS, integration of payroll and personnel services, new working practices etc.; Meaningful interaction with vendors and clear specification of requirements and the future IS implementation.

The use of commonly understood graphical language (IDEFINE) enabled staff from different departments (and later on Unions as well) to develop some shared understanding of changes in working practices, explore conflicting situations and negotiate integrated solutions before the contract with the software vendor had been signed.

Case #3: ISD Practices in Colruyt

The third case of research into ISD practices comes from the longitudinal case study of Colruyt, Belgium's third largest retail company (Janson and Cecez-Kecmanovic, 2003; Cecez-Kecmanovic and Janson, 2002). Since the Company's inception in 1965 its owner and members of upper management introduced flexible organisational structure, distributed decision-making and employees' participation. What made participative decision-making in Colruyt particularly successful was personal responsibility and initiative at all levels, Company-wide sharing of information and broad consultation with all members interested in and affected by decisions. Such approach to decision-making was enabled and assisted by creative deployment of IT and innovative ISD processes. This is illustrated with two examples.

How the Company operates is illustrated by the following quotes from the late Jo Colruyt, Company founder and its former president, and a manager (quoted in Janson and Cecez-Kecmanovic, 2003):

> Power decentralization has the enormous advantage arising from organizational flexibility to instantly adjust the organization to new situations. Hundreds of employees obtain the power to take initiative. They will experience this in their personal life, and consider it an enrichment of their professional life. (Collruyt, p. 4)

> One has to respect employees' rights to make their own decisions. One cannot just force decisions taken somewhere else on one's subordinates...one has to ensure the availability of information and informing employees about information sources. (Manager, p. 5)

Due to such philosophy and practice, the needs for a Company-wide communication system that would enable dissemination and sharing of information were recognised as soon as the Company became too big to rely on face-to-face communications. To meet Company needs the IS department developed and implemented an information system for information dissemination (ISID), a predecessor of groupware, in the early 80s. ISID, still extensively used, supports bottom-up initiatives for problem solving and broadly based participation in decision-making. One of its important roles is to assist employees and the IS department in initiating, discussing and deciding about new IS developments.

A particular feature of ISD as practiced by the IS Department in Colruyt is the location of most their "work analysts" in major user departments. These analysts regularly participate in users' exploration of various problems whether or not related to IS. In such a way analysts are in a position to advise users regarding possibilities to solve problems, for instance, with better use of existing IS or with modified IS. Furthermore, through their continual collaboration, analysts and users develop mutual understanding that enable them to work on new innovative IS solutions for identified problems. The history of ISD in Colruyt shows that most IS were developed due to initiatives of workers and managers typically concerned with quality of services to customers, efficient organisation and operations of stores and warehouses, improvement of working conditions and productivity of employees (Janson and Cecez-Kecmanovic, 2003).

ISD processes follow a pattern similar to other decision-making processes: one or more individuals recognize a problem the solution of which may require an IS, an organizational process change, or a combination of both. When the potential users and the analyst conclude that a new IS is needed, a request for assistance is then submitted to the IS department and publicly announced via ISID. A system developer from the IS department, after an in-depth consultation with the initiators and other potential users, analyses the problem and develops a cost-benefit analysis. Based on the information so created the analyst then decides whether to advise major or minor IS development.

Major IS developments are prioritised by a steering group comprising members of top management and the chief information officer. Minor IS developments are at the discretion of the IS department, which has a budget for this purpose. In either case, solving the users' problem through close cooperation between users and IS analysts is a common practice. Apart from face-to-face meetings, all phases of ISD are supported by ISID. All major documents and decisions are shared, any suspected negative impacts and future implications discussed. Users participate throughout ISD processes as part of their regular work processes and feel ownership of IS thus developed.

Participatory culture is developed and nurtured through Company-sponsored seminars (during working hours) on any topic of interest to the members: self-development, self-realization, communicative abilities, collective well-being, cooperative work, etc. The late Jo Colruyt stressed the importance of seminars:

> Many employees attending [such] seminars require the Company to change its orientation. The Company is the people and when they change the Company has to change. Members of top management have to attend these training sessions also, so that they know what ideas exist among the employees...otherwise they cannot relate to employees. (Jo Colruyt, p. 4)

Drawing on the Company documents, Janson and Cecez-Kecmanovic (2003) quote an employee opinion about the training:

> Many courses are available on the topic [of communication & relationships]. Participating in these seminars remains one of my best experiences. I learned to better understand myself, something that I consider very important: to know oneself, confront oneself, and ask questions of oneself. I learned to understand my emotions and understand how they played an important role in my relations, communications and [human] contacts. This process of learning with and about myself made it possible to obtain better insights into other people, understand others, achieve open dialog, learn better the wishes and goals of others, and to love others better. (Worker, p. 4)

Training seminars, attended by everyone from top managers down to the lowest ranking clerks, are found to be integral to working processes in Colruyt and essential for building its participatory culture.

The three cases of ISD illustrate – each in its own peculiar way – the relevance of concerns I am raising in this address. I will refer to these cases in my analysis of different ISD discourses as defined by the framework I am proposing in the following sections.

5. EXPLORING DIFFERENCES AMONG ISD DISCOURSES

By exploring ISD as discursive practices I aim to focus attention to social constructions through language, including the use of ISD methodologies to specify IS requirements, and to the role of IS developers and researchers in these constructions. Furthermore, by understanding discursive practices of ISD I believe we would be able to better understand and explain the resulting IS and the their role and impact on the (re)creation and maintenance of meanings and social realities, power and social structures. To examine differences in ISD discourses I propose two orthogonal dimensions: the *consensus–dissensus* dimension and the *system–lifeworld* dimension. The first "consensus–dissensus" dimension[3] is taken from Deetz's discursive framework which identifies four research orientations in organisational studies (1994, 1996). In the ISD context this dimension refers to "consensus–dissensus" ISD discourse within an

[3] The idea to investigate the "consensus–dissensus" dimension comes from Deetz' (1994, 1995, 1996) framework that identifies different research orientations in Organization Science. His framework involves two contrasting dimensions: "local/emergent" vs "elite/apriori" dimension and "consensus" vs "dissensus" dimension. These two dimensions produced four discourses—*normative*, *interpretive*, *critical* and *dialogic*—each denoting a particular orientation to organisations, a set of specific assumptions and dimensions of interest shaping the research approach.

organisation and in the wider IS community. This dimension enables us making a distinction between ISD practices that are compliant with and imbedded in dominant organisational discourses, existing social orders and power structures, called, following Deetz (1994), "consensus" discourses; and ISD practices that object the dominant discourses and disrupt existing social orders and power structures, called "dissensus" discourses.

The other dimension that I propose is the "system–lifeworld"[4] dimension concerned with the substantive and interventionist aspects of ISD. Like society, organisations can be seen as simultaneously systems and lifeworld of their members (Cecez-Kecmanovic, et al., 2002). The system's pole of this dimension focuses on organisation's material and intellectual production, its economic foundation, administrative and management structure, information structures and databases, rules and regulations, and the like. It draws attention to ISD intervention in these systems and resulting contribution to organisational performance, functionality, efficiency and effectiveness, that is, *system integration aspects.*

The opposite, *lifeworld* pole of this dimension focuses on the symbolically created universe of daily social activities of organisational members, and the taken-for-granted, shared, background stock of knowledge, that involves vast and unexpressed sets of beliefs, convictions, tacit assumptions, and values. Members draw upon this knowledge to make sense of situations, other actors, and their linguistic acts, and to take actions. The lifeworld dimension draws attention to the ISD impact on lifeworld reproduction, and the resulting social integration, cultural reproduction and socialisation of organisational members.

5.1. The Consensus–Dissensus Dimension of ISD Discourses

This dimension draws attention to differences among ISD discourses in relation to existing social orders and power structures. The distinction made along this dimension highlights sets of assumptions about the social-organisational context and the role of IS in this context. Consensus or dissensus, as Deetz (1996) remarks, should not be understood as agreement and disagreement but rather as presentation of unity or of difference, the continuation or disruption of any prevailing discourses"[5] (p. 197).

The consensus ISD discourses describe the approach by many IS developers and researchers who assume unity of interests and take existing (dominant) social orders and power structures as natural and unproblematic. They apply ISD methodologies to understand the current social order, rules and norms, and operations of power, and to the needs of key actors (managers), the guardians of the social order, in order to be able to design and implement IS to meet their needs. They do not question existing structures of

---

[4] Following Habermas' (1987) system/lifeworld distinction, organisations may be conceived as both systems and socio-cultural lifeworld of its members. The socio-cultural lifeworld is the symbolically created, taken-for-granted universe of daily social activities of organisational members, which involves language, social structures, and cultural tradition as the background knowledge that members share. While material production refers to the system aspect of an organisation, cultural reproduction, social integration and socialisation refer to the lifeworld of its members (Habermas, 1987).

[5] Deetz also notes that the consensus-dissensus dimension has some similarity with Burrell and Morgan's (1979) distinction between an interest in "change" vs. "regulation". However, as Deetz explains, the change-regulation dimension emphasises group or class conflict, while the consensus-dissensus dimension emphasises domination and its reproduction through discourses.

domination, coercive use of power, or oppressive social relations nor do they challenge dominant discourses and "natural" orders. The IS so designed result from and are embedded in dominant discourses, typically determined by economic rationalist, managerialist or technocratic ideologies. By engaging in consensus discourses and designing IS to fulfil the identified information needs, IS practitioners reproduce (unwittingly perhaps) existing social orders and strengthen power structures.

An additional set of assumptions apply to ISD processes themselves and the application of ISD methodologies within consensus discourses. First, developers and researchers assume that particular languages, such as DFD, ER or UML, used to describe business processes and specify information requirement, are value neutral and unambiguous. Such languages, it is assumed, have a representational role and the developers use them to 'mirror' reality in databases and software programs. For instance, a classical database systems textbook explicitly states that one of the goals of object oriented databases is "to maintain a direct correspondence between real-world and database" (Elmasri and Navathe, 2000, p. 362). Second, the application of ISD methodologies is assumed to embody characteristics of scientific methods and thereby ensure an "objective" analysis and "correct" mapping of reality into IS. Consequently, IS researchers and developers as neutral experts and facilitators of reality mapping are concerned with accuracy, completeness and efficiency of representations.

On the other hand, ISD processes that assume multiple and diverse organisational discourses, and involve actors with conflicting interests, values and needs exemplify dissensus discourses. The dissensus ISD discourses are therefore considered inevitably entangled in the conflicts and tensions between different groups of actors (called stakeholders) and their struggle for domination. ISD practices and research in the dissensus pole raise awareness of and pay attention to the diversity of organisational discourses. Unlike consensus discourses, dissensus ISD discourses assume power as productive. By involving multiple stakeholders, by challenging apparent order and by potentially disrupting dominant discourses, they aim to play a transformating and liberating role in organisations.

Language in dissensus ISD discourses is not considered a neutral and objective conduit of description of the "real world". Rather, language is perceived as a medium for argumentation and struggle for meanings. The "mirror" metaphor "gives way to the 'lens' … metaphor noting a shifting analytic attempt to see what could not be seen before" (Deetz, 1996, p. 197). Language enables articulation of different views and multiple meanings and recreation of reality through ISD. IS developers and users, and also different user groups, are seen as necessarily involved in negotiation of meanings, co-creation of inter-subjective meanings, and in the emergence and resolution of conflicts. While recognizing conflicting interests and values, ISD developers and researchers aim to establish an open dialogue and assists the emergence of inter-subjectively created meanings, including specifications of information and data structures in IS. Consequently, it is assumed that information requirements specifications do not "map the reality" but rather result from argumentation, meaning negotiation and co-creation. IS researchers and developers are seen as historically and socially situated social actors, who play a role in organisational discourses and meaning making through ISD. They are active agents of change who are necessarily positioned.

5.2. The "System–Lifeworld" Dimension of ISD Discourses

The "system–lifeworld" dimension draws attention to differences regarding the conceptions of organisations and organisational processes as target domains of ISD interventions. Organisations may be conceived as both systems and socio-cultural lifeworld of its members, which is reflected in the system–lifeworld dimension. Those ISD discourses that focus on the functioning of systems, such as production systems, financial systems, distribution systems, supply chain management, decision making processes, typically seeking to improve functionality, efficiency and effectiveness of these systems, are at the system's pole of the system–lifeworld dimension. Such ISD discourses are concerned with concrete facticities, for instance, organisational units, physical artefacts (machinery, buildings, technology), resources, process and structures, which need to be controlled and managed to achieve certain goals (systems' rationalisation). As management is charged with responsibility to control the systems and achieve the given goals, IS practitioners and researchers, often see IS as serving managers or other actors with formal status and authority to achieve their goals.

ISD as systems discourse is an arena of purposeful action in Weberian sense and instrumental rationality: IS as instruments of scientific-rational control are conceived as means to achieve given ends. It is a discourse focused on hard facts – production plans, productivity, efficiency, service quality, delivery times, client-related times, and the like – that leaves no space for "soft" issues. The privileged language of functionality establishes a monopoly of facts (a fixed language game). ISD discourses are assumed to deal with representations of the 'object world': eg. models of business processes or information structure models that consist of truth claims about this world. While there may be attempts by some participants to make different claims about how things are, the proper application of the ISD methodologies, it is assumed, will ensure that 'correct representations' of systems are captured. Furthermore, technical language of requirements engineering, database structures and design, servers and clients, privileges IS developers and their claims to truth. More broadly speaking the application of IT in business/management domain is considered an advancement of scientific-rational control. Similarly, ISD methodologies are seen as guided by pseudo-scientific principles.

Alternatively, ISD discourses may be located in the lifeworld pole of the "systems–lifeworld" dimension. Such ISD discourses are grounded in understanding organisations as communities and are focused on social integration, cultural reproduction, and socialisation of members. IS are viewed as part of social fabric of an organisation as community and as a medium for social interaction through which social reality is (re)constructed. The role of IS is conceived as contributing to shared social goals and social integration. While generally the ISD lifeworld discourses are much broader than organisations-as-systems and they do include systems' aspects. The major difference emphasised by the systems-lifeworld dichotomy is the way of dealing with systems issues. While in systems discourse participants – developers and users – aim (and sometimes compete) to establish their truth claims as the only legitimate ones (and thereby control the re-production of reality in IS), in lifeworld discourse participants seek mutual understanding, and aim to cooperatively establish acceptable claims to truth, legitimacy and sincerity. In other words, ISD processes are an arena of communicative action, cooperation and communicative rationality (Habermas, 1984).

The application of ISD methodologies within the lifeworld discourse involves not only models, techniques and procedures for IS analysis and design, but also ways of locating ISD in a broader social, historical and cultural context. This is achieved by conducting ISD as argumentation processes and nurturing communicative practices that involve "multiple language games" and emergent meanings. In this type of ISD discourses communicative competence of actors, both developers and users, is of key importance. The lifeworld discourses involving communicatively competent participants are a prerequisite for ISD as enabler of social change with emancipatory potential.

6. THE DISCURSIVE FRAMEWORK FOR INVESTIGATING *ISD*

By combining the two dimensions discussed above I suggest a grid which distinguishes four types of ISD discourses (as ideal types in Weber's sense) (Figure 1). On the left hand side, defined by consensus discourses, ISD discourses are embedded in and are part of a *hegemonic* field characterized by oppressive works of power and domination, legitimized by the existing social order taken as natural. The notion of hegemony, as defined by Gramsci (1986), denotes the ability of some groups, assumed to be naturally superior, to exercise power and control over other people. People are not usually "forced to concede power or control to another group, rather they believe that their own interests are best served by that other group being in power" (Tietze, et al. 2003, p. 149). As a wilful consent to domination, hegemony is achieved through socio-cultural productions and socialisation processes.

6.1. Hegemonic ISD Discourses

The hegemonic field defined by consensus pole has two domains: the **hegemonic ISD discourses** (consensus-system) and **covert hegemonic ISD discourses** (consensus-lifeworld), depending on the degree to which hegemony is covert. Furthermore, establishment of hegemonic ISD discourses is often linked with the production of ideology: managerialist ideology, economic rationalism or technologic imperatives. Through hegemonic ISD discourses organisational members are made to consent to the dominant views of systems, including systems goals, identification and framing of systems' problems (their economic viability, functionality, efficiency, etc.), and the resulting specification of information requirements for information systems that will resolve these problems and contribute to systems' goals. IS development methodologies play an important role in establishing and maintaining ISD hegemonic discourses by determining and allowing a particular language game. They prescribe the language of systems, performance, functionality, as well as objects, attributes and relationships, and models that represent systems and information requirements. They also prescribe ways the language can be used. As a consequence the participants, including those adversely affected by the future IS, consent to and adopt dominant meanings established through ISD and eventually inscribed in the designed IS.

The covert hegemonic ISD discourse goes one step further in ensuring participants' consent: it uses the rhetoric of social concerns, community and employees' interests to achieve domination in a more subtle form and win voluntary consent of those it manipulates and deceives. As a result meanings are colonized while those subjected to manipulation feel comfortable in the relationships of domination and subordination.

Lifeworld

COVERT HEGEMONIC ISD
- A site of hegemonic consent, coercive manipulation and colonization of meaning
- A process of subtle implants of hegemonic/ideological meanings
- Risks: latent resistance and covert obstruction

EMANCIPATORY ISD
- A site of struggle for democratic change and emancipation of meaning
- A process of transformative social action
- Risks: slipping into cultural domination and subtle manipulation

Consensus discourse ← → **Dissensus discourse**

HEGEMONIC ISD
- A site of legitimate domination and consensus discourse that establish 'correct' meanings
- A process focused on techniques, procedures and methods as mechanisms of control
- Risks: passive or active resistance and obstruction

PARTICIPATORY ISD
- A site of confrontation of multiple, conflicting discourses and different systems of meaning
- A process of argumentation and negotiation of meanings
- Risks: increasing tensions and conflicts; escalation of political fights

Systems

Figure 1. Differences in ISD discourses (Adapted from Cecez-Kecmanovic, 2003)

Going back to the Case #1, the development and implementation of DSS may be explained within the hegemonic ISD field in the discursive framework (Figure 1). DSS development was explicitly conceived as driven by the dominant discourse imposed by the ideology of economic rationalism and inevitability for the HRS's services to become externally contestable. Such ideology was never questioned, nor has the approach to transform service provision by the HRS. The DSS discourse was embedded in and became part of the established ideological hegemony. This is evident in the way data were collected and the "system" modelled in the DSS: the key concept of "employees' time spent on client-related work" as opposed to "other time" (recorded via surveys) was the direct consequence of the ideology of economic rationalism. It was only the view of employees as "service providers to clients" and the concern for the time spent on service provision that figured in the modelling of the HRS's work in DSS. Based on the voluntarily provided data by staff and other assumptions about the clients, demand for services and expected charging rates, the DSS calculated existing and predicted future "time utilization rates". The DSS was taken as a true, correct representation of the system and hence its reports were the basis for serious decision about staff cuts.

The dominant discourse of economic rationalism was considered inevitable and was presented as the only option for the HRS to survive external contestability and become economically viable. No other options were ever discussed. Staff was never involved in any such discussion. The hegemonic ISD discourse ensured that the resulting DSS was fully embedded in dominant discourse and also used to strengthen the economic rationalist agenda.

The researcher/designer of DSS worked hard to understand the planned changes and what the top executive wanted. He then stimulated staff to participate in surveys (without them fully understanding the purpose) to collect data for DSS. As he assumed that managers' objectives are the legitimate Department objectives, he defined the success of the DSS in terms of contributing to these objectives. The researcher/designer sees his role in embracing and upholding the dominant discourse, which in this case happen to be the ideology of economic rationalism.

This case is an honestly presented example of a DSS development through action research that legitimated domination through the consensus discourse. The dominant ISD discourse worked well. The DSS was considered a great success. The dominant economic rationalist and managerialist discourse established "correct" meanings, which, embedded in DSS, reconstructed reality, the nature of employees' work, their contribution to the Department, their identity and sense of value. Staff was reported to be disillusioned but "voluntarily" participated in this process, subjected themselves to instrumentalisation and consented to manipulation. From the description in the paper it seems that this case demonstrates characteristics of an overt hegemonic ISD discourse, with potentially some elements of the covert hegemonic type. However the latter cannot be determined as the paper does not report whether and to what extend the National manager who "visited all staff several times in 1997 to ensure direct involvement of staff" referred to staff wellbeing, their interest and their needs.

Another interesting insight from the discursive approach to ISD would be better understanding of potential resistance to domination and its conversion into a harmful action. While hegemonic consent may seem almost a perfect solution for a manager to achieve his/her objectives, the problem is that it is never completely established. While in the Molineux (1998) paper resistance was not explicitly discussed, some descriptions indicate that existed, perhaps in a disguised form. Any hegemonic ISD discourse involves an inherent risk of resistance and in particular covert forms of resistance by those subjected to domination. It would be interesting to examine whether and in what ways hegemonic ISD discourses provoke resistance and harmful actions by staff negatively affected by the resulting IS, and how such actions contribute to IS failures.

6.2. Participatory and Emancipatory ISD Discourses

On the right-hand side of Figure 1, defined by dissensus discourses, ISD is conceived and conducted as transformative and liberatory social practice. When primarily focused on systems concerns, ISD discourses are called **participatory**. When in addition, ISD involves broad participation and also focuses on social integration and lifeworld issues, seeking emancipation, it is called here **emancipatory ISD**. The distinction between the two is not clear-cut but rather a matter of degree.

Participatory ISD discourses cover a range of approaches characterised by involving "users, developers and technology itself in a process of technological development" (Asaro, 2000, p. 257). Participatory ISD methodologies explicitly "represent" users in various stages of ISD in order to get better presentation of different views, to create higher quality information requirements and to overcome resistance and validate IS design proposals (Hirschheim and Klein, 1994). The key characterisation of the participatory ISD practices can be derived from the dissensus–systems domain within the discursive framework. By focusing on "systems", participatory ISD discourses remain concerned with business systems' functionality, systems' rationality goals (productivity, efficiency and effectiveness), and with IS development to improve functionality and achieve given goals. However, what makes them different from hegemonic discourses is involvement of multiple user groups that typically have different views and interests. While the tension levels and intensity of conflicts among different user groups may very, participatory ISD in the proposed framework are seen as sites of confrontation of multiple, conflicting discourses and different systems of meaning needing elaborate processes of argumentation and meaning negotiation (Figure 1). I refer to the Case #2 presented above to illustrate participatory ISD discourses.

In Case #2, the procurement process for an Integrated Payroll/Personnel IS involved multiple and conflicting discourses. The researcher conducting the action research sow her role as facilitator in the procurement process. She made explicit attempts to assist different actors and groups to make their views and understanding of the focal processes (finance, especially payroll related, personnel and operations of the Hospital, related finance and personnel processes and others) visible and known to each other and to the wider community. She assisted the establishment of a dialogue between different groups with different interests, views and local cultures.

The focus was clearly on operations, flows, coordination, integrated functions, control, effective reporting, etc., that is, on systems' aspects. The particular use of common graphical language (IDEFINE) to describe operations and processes in each department enabled

- articulation of different views and different systems of meaning
- comparison of different practices and negotiation of meanings
- open dialogue that challenged various authorities and power structures
- collective and individual critical self-reflection
- negotiation regarding changes in work processes and agreement about future operations of the IS internally and
- precise and comprehensive specifications for the Vendor.

Despite attempts by some groups to dominate discourse and take control of the procurement process, the IPPIS analysis, information requirements specification and system procurement had characteristics of a participatory ISD discourse. The IPPIS analysis and procurement process revealed incompatible work practices, operational differences, entrenched conflicting views and interests, as well as different systems of meaning. It also revealed inherent conflicts and tendencies by some groups to dominate. According to the Project manager, throughout the process tensions grew and caused *"a great deal of upset for those participating in the debates"*. Escalation of political fights, which is a recognised risk of participatory discourses, was prevented by successful facilitation of the argumentation process and negotiations of meanings. That a workable agreement was finally reached may be attributed to a large extent to the researcher's role and successful facilitation.

Participatory ISD discourses as exemplified by this case, remain focused on systems' issues and rarely call into question set goals of systems' performance. Given different interests in the functioning of systems, participatory ISD discourses are sites of conflict between capital and work, between the technology and organisational/social systems, between dominant and subordinate cultures, between different meaning systems. Typical for participatory discourses is the use of a privileged language of systems by various groups in their struggle for power and domination. In the Hospital case, finance and personnel professional language were included while IT language was deliberately excluded, thereby strengthening the position of the finance and personnel departments at the expense of the IT department.

While this case exemplifies participatory ISD discourses, it should be noted that the author identified some emancipatory potential due to "the opportunity for individual department and collective self-determination… and some critical self-reflection" (Waring, 1999, p. 15).

Emancipatory ISD discourses, as determined by the lifeworld–dissensus domain of the framework (Figure 1), describe ISD processes as transformative social actions focused on social and cultural integration while concerned with functioning of systems. Situated historically, socially and politically, ISD discourses are seen as sites of struggle for democratic social change and emancipation of meanings. The need for emancipatory ISD approaches and the proposals for emancipatory ISD methodologies have been both praised (Hirschheim 1994; Hirschheim et al. 1995; Asaro, 2000) and condemned (Wilson, 1997). Resisting here the attraction of engaging in the debate, I will discuss some interesting insights from considering the ISD practices described in the Case #3 as emancipatory discourses.

Case #3 describes ISD in the Colruyt Company conceived as a form of organisational development that involves all employees, not only managers, in improving services to clients, improving working conditions and satisfaction in work, increasing Company competitiveness and its financial viability. The focus of ISD discourses and organisational development however is not only on systems issues (functionality, profitability, quality of customer services, and the like). Systems issues are always related to lifeworld issues. The values underlying ISD discourses include concerns for individual wellbeing – material, social and emotional, for the quality of work environment and enjoyment in work, personal autonomy and freedom, just and fair work relations and relations with customers. Drawing on Company documents Janson and Cecez-Kecmanovic (2003) quote a bookkeeper:

> I enjoy my work and being part of the Company. Most of my colleagues consider it normal that we commit ourselves 100% to the job. This relates to my being considered a human being and a Company member within Colruyt. These feelings arise on account of the Colruyt culture: one of open relationships.

A distinguishing feature of ISD discourses in Colruyt is their focus on systems issues but considered integral to lifeworld issues. For instance, service to customers, store functioning and check-out procedures, the use of check-out IS, are discussed together with workers multi-skilling, improvement of skills, the meaning of work, enjoyment of work, personal commitment to work, and personal satisfaction. ISD discourses are embedded in other Company discourses typically related to employees' personal development, education, career paths, excellence in job, as well as collective achievements, Company successes, and future developments. These discourses are promoted and invigorated through the on-going seminars, which is echoed in the discussions and documents distributed via ISID. They have a huge impact on individual and collective identity and their sense of community (assumed to be broader than the Company itself).

It is important to note however, that these discourses are far from being harmonious. Similar to the Hospital case, here too, conflicts of interests, views and meanings are inherent and endemic. In fact, democratic workplace and participatory decision-making processes, as evidenced in Colruyt, stimulate and enable expressions of different interests, positions and views. Employees are trained to express themselves and properly argue their proposals and preferences. Being communicatively competent is considered condictio sine qua non for practicing participatory decision-making. Quotes from two clerks illustrate this point (Janson and Cecez-Kecmanovic; 2003):

> [Company environment] can be equated with a sea populated by many fish including sharks. He who wants to swim has to learn to get along with both. [But], on second thought even sharks can be likable.

> I realized quickly that good relations [with colleagues] were necessary. I acquired self-confidence, I believed in myself, and that led to better and more relations with colleagues. The knowledge I acquired taught me not to stay quiet when something was amiss, but instead to discuss matters. It was and still creates a wonderful feeling.

In addition the Unions add to the dissensus discourses. Suspicious of the Company management real interests and agendas the Union claimed that the seminars indoctrinate and covertly manipulate employees:

> [they] cause [people] to think Colruyt, to live Colruyt, to sleep Colruyt. It is always the same [thing]. What I have heard is that employees who don't [attend] seminars are not liked very much. (Socialist Union)

The Union also pointed to dehumanising effects of technology and attacked specifically IS that have been developed, they claim, with full participation and support of those negatively affected. The authors reported that the workers themselves were critical of the Unions, accusing them for being biased and self-interested.

ISD discourses in Colruyt, like other organisational discourses, are characterised by dissensus. While the Company has a distinct and strong culture it actually does not mean less variety in discourses or absence of conflicting views. Quite the contrary, the Colruyt culture encourages employees to speak up, to argue their view and to present their proposals/solutions publicly (via ISID). Different views or proposals regarding an IS are typically exposed and subjected to criticism, through involvement of all interested or affected employees. As a result ISD discourses are not limited in any way: they address both systems and lifeworld issues; they include employees with different interests, knowledge, experience and roles; they also address broader organisational issues (beyond particular process or function). Top management often plays the role of devil's advocate and seeks to expose critical or weak points of a proposed IS, but do not make a decision about it. It is therefore not easy for the IS solutions to be justified and withstand the critique of the wide audience (informed via ISID) and management. Furthermore, an ISD process may take comparatively longer time (in particular the analysis and information requirements stage) but IS implementation is typically faster and straightforward. As the users are actively involved (sometimes as major proposers) from the very beginning, user resistance is unknown phenomenon in Colruyt. The success rate if IS in Colruyt has been exceptionally high.

As this analysis demonstrates, the dissensus—lifeworld ISD discourses in Colruyt are sites of competing significations and struggle for transformative social action and democratic change. These discourses are named emancipatory[6] due to their inherent emancipatory potential which, it should be noted, is realised only to a degree, depending on the concrete historical, social and cultural conditions and limitations. The source of emancipatory potential in these discourses is the productive use of power, openness to and continuous struggle among different views and interest positions, public exposure of apparent natural orders and concealed social relations of inequality and oppression, improvement of working conditions, emancipation of meaning and resistance to domination and ideological manipulation.

These same features of emancipatory ISD discourses that enable transformative social action, democratic change and emancipation entail hidden dangers of slipping into cultural domination and subtle manipulation. (This was illustrated by the Union's concerns regarding the culture and the use of technology in Colruyt.) In other words, the emancipatory ISD discourses involve the risks of degenerating into covert hegemonic discourses. Authors (Janson and Cecez-Kecmanovic, 2003) found that communicative competence of all employees, including IS specialists, prevents manipulation and indoctrination and guards against such risks.

7. CONCLUSION

In this paper I intended to raise some important concerns about ISD practices and the roles of IS developers and researchers. Firstly, I questioned the widely accepted assumption that by designing IS ("describing" business processes and 'modelling' information requirements) developers are "mapping" the reality into databases and programs. Instead, as I demonstrated, by identifying and naming objects, their attributes and relationships as "given in reality", developers in fact participate in a more fundamental act of reality re-constitution. Secondly, objects (organisational units, costs, revenue, tasks, employees) can be seen (and constructed) in different ways depending on a point of view, interest and value positions. By selecting and naming *some* objects and presenting them in a *particular way*, IS developers reproduce the lines of distinction that produce some things as alike and others as different and thereby help reproduce a particular view of the reality, permeated by certain values and interests. Thirdly, I argued that the dominant set of assumptions about ISD processes precludes IS developers and researchers from understanding how modelling reality in ISD processes involves struggles for meaning and how the resulting IS become engaged into the (re)production of organisational meanings and the construction of reality.

---

[6] Emancipation is used here cautiously to denote seeking the power to control ones own life and achieve greater autonomy and human agency. As Kincheloe and McLaren (1998) remark "no one is ever completely emancipated from the socio-political context that has produced him or her" (p. 282).

These concerns motivated me to explore theorizing ISD as manifestations of discourses and power relations of the social and political context that produce them. By adopting a discursive theory perspective of organisations (Alvesson and Karreman, 2000) and understanding discourses as the foundation of the social construction of reality (Berger and Luchmann, 1966) I situated ISD processes within organizational discourses. I proposed considering IS as discursively constructed and ISD processes as discursive practices and sites of struggles through which organisational meanings are imposed, contested and negotiated.

In order to assist the exploration of ISD processes as discursive practices I proposed the discursive framework by combining two dimensions of contrast: the *consensus-dissensus* dimension and the *systems-lifeworld* dimension. The grid thus formed distinguishes *hegemonic, covert hegemonic, participatory* and *emancipatory* ISD discourses. These four types of ISD discourses are discussed by referring to the illustrative cases of empirical studies of ISD selected from the literature. Each discourse type identifies a distinct nature of ISD, determined by the relation toward dominant organisational discourses and by its domain and nature of intervention (systems or lifeworld).

The paper demonstrates how discursive framework assists in rasing awareness of the ideological imperatives and power struggles behind ISD practices and epistemological assumptions that inform ISD research. The application of the proposed discursive ISD framework in the selected empirical ISD studies draws attention to ISD roles in and implications for the construction and reproduction of meanings, social order, power structures, individual and collective identities or in other words the (re)construction of social reality. As the analysis of these studies shows the discursive framework enables deconstruction of discursive regimes instituted by ISD approaches and methodologies, which play a key role in the production of representations and legitimation of meanings (through models, tools and techniques).

It is important to mention that the investigation of ISD discourses was inspired and encouraged by two exceptional sources. First, it was Hirschheim and Klein's (1989) renowned work on ISD paradigms based on Burrell and Morgan's (1979) sociological paradigms (functionalist, social relativist, radical structuralist and neo-humanist). The second was Deetz's (1996) critique and rethinking of these paradigms and his insightful discussion on four organisational discourses. The discursive ISD framework proposed in this paper is not intended as an alternative ISD paradigm framework, but rather as an attempt to expose some new and interesting distinctions in ISD practices and stimulate novel and potentially more productive debates regarding relevant ISD issues, themes, and research questions.

I'll conclude with a hope that the discursive ISD framework may inform a critical postmodern research into ISD processes, methodologies and practices that exposes what appears natural and questions what appears obvious. Furthermore, the framework may assist both researchers and practitioners in understanding how organizational discourses construct IS and how in turn discourses mediated or enabled by IS (re)construct actors and organizations. Lastly, and most importantly, by furthering our understanding, informed by the proposed discursive ISD framework, we can empower ourselves to dig more deeply into the complexity of the construction of meanings via ISD and, I do hope, work together toward the emancipation of meaning and a transformative ISD praxis.

REFERENCES

Alvesson, M. and Karreman, D., 2000, Taking the linguistic turn in organisational research, *The Journal of Applied behavioral Science,* **36**, 2: 136–158.

Alvesson, M. and Willmott, H., 1992, On the idea of emancipation in management and organization studies, *Academy of Management Review*, **17**, 3: 432–464.

Asaro, P.M., 2000, Transforming society by transforming technology: the science and politics of participatory design, *Accounting, Management and Information Technology,* **10**: 257–290.

Berger, P. and Luckmann, T.L., 1966, *The Social Construction of Reality: A Treatise on the Sociology of Knowledge*, Doubleday, Garden City, NY.

Bowker, G. and Star, S.L., 1994, Knowledge and infrastructure in international information management: Problems of classification and coding, in: *Information Acumen. The Understanding and Use of Knowledge in Modern Business*, L. Bud-Frierman, ed., Routledge, London, pp. 187–213.

Burrell, G. and Morgan, G., 1979, *Sociological Paradigms and Organizational Analysis*, Heinemann, London.

Carspecken, P.F., 1999, *Four Scenes for Posing the Question of Meaning and Other Essays in Critical Philosophy and Critical Methodology*, New York, Peter Lang.

Cecez-Kecmanovic, D., 2003, ISD as discursive practices—revisiting research paradigms, SISTM research paper, Faculty of Commerce and Economics, UNSW, Australia.

Cecez-Kecmanovic, D. and Janson, M., 2002, Information Systems and rationalisation of organisations: An exploratory study. The European Conference on Information Systems ECIS 2002, Gdansk, Poland, pp. 57–67.

Cecez-Kecmanovic, D., Janson, M. and Brown, A., 2002, The rationality framework for a critical study of Information Systems, the *Journal of Information Technology*, **17**: 215–227.

Deetz, S., 1995, *Transforming Communication, Transforming Business: Building Responsive and Responsible Workplaces*, Hampton Press, Cresskill, NJ.

Deetz, S., 1996, Describing differences in approaches to organization science: Rethinking Burrell and Morgan and their legacy, *Organization Science*, **7**, 2: 191–207.

Deetz, S., 2000, Putting the community into organizational science, *Organization Science* **11**,6: 733–738.

Denzin, N.K., 1994, The art and politics of interpretation, in: *Handbook of Qualitative Research,* N.K. Denzin and Y.S. Lincoln, eds., Thousand Oaks, CA, Sage, pp. 500–515.

Gee, J., 1996, *Social Linguistics and Literacies: Ideology in Discourse* (2nd ed.), London, Taylor & Francis.

Gramsci, A., 1986, *Selections from Prison Notebooks* (ed. and trans. Q. Hoare and G. Smith), New Left Books, London.

Grant, D., Keenoy, T. and Oswick, C., 1997, Organizational discourses: Text and context, *Organization*, **4**,2: 147–157.

Habermas, J., 1984, *The Theory of Communicative Action – Reason and the Rationalisation of Society* (Vol I), Beacon Press, Boston, MA.

Habermas, J., 1987, *The theory of Communicative Action – The Critique of Functionalist Reason* (Vol II), Beacon Press, Boston, MA.

Hardy, C., Palmer, I. and Phillips, N., 2000, Discourse as a strategic resource, *Human Relations,* **53**, 9: 1227–1247.

Hirchheim, R.A. and Klein, H.K., 1989, Four paradigms of Information System Development, *Communication of the ACM,* **32**, 10: 1199–1216.

Hirchheim, R.A. and Klein, H.K., 1994, Realizing emancipatory principles in Information Systems Development: The case for ETHICS, *MISQ*, **18**,1: 83–109.

Hirschheim, R., Klein, H.K. and Lyytinen, K., 1995, *Information Systems Development and Data Modelling: Conceptual and Philosophical Foundations*, Cambridge University Press.

Janson, M. and Cecez-Kecmanovic, D., 2003, Information Systems and the participatory ethos, *The European Conference on Information Systems ECIS 2003*, Naples, Italy.

Keenoy, T., Marshak, R.J., Oswick, C., and Grant, D., 2000, The discourse of organizing, *The Journal of Applied Behavioural Science,* **36**,2: 133–145.

Kincheloe, L.J. and McLaren, P., 1994, Rethinking critical theory and qualitative research, in: *Handbook of qualitative research*, N.K. Denzin and Y.D. Linkoln, eds, Sage, London, pp. 279–313.

Landry, M. and Banville, C., 1992, A disciplined methodological pluralism for MIS research, *Accounting, Management, and Information Technology*, **2**, 2: 77–97.

Lemke, J., 1993, Discourse, dynamics, and social change, *Cultural Dynamics*, **6**: 243–275.

Lemke, J., 1995, *Textual Politics: Discourse and Social Dynamics*, London, Taylor & Francis.

Molineux, J., 1998, The application of a Dynamic System Model to the process of contestability in the Human Resources section of the ATO, in: the Proceedings of the 4th Australia and New Zealand Systems Conference on Creative Systems Practice, Sydney, NSW, Australia, pp. 234–247.
Tietze, S., Cohen, L. and Musson, G., 2003, *Understanding Organizations through Language*, London, Sage.
Waring, T.S., 1999, The challenge of emancipation in Information Systems implementation: A case study in an NHS Trust Hospital, *Critical Management Studies* Conference, Manchester.
Wilson, F.A., 1997, The truth is out there: The search for emancipatory principles in Information Systems design, *Information Technology and People*, **10**,3: 197–204.

E-DOCUMENTS AS TOOLS FOR THE HUMANIZED MANAGEMENT OF COMMUNITY KNOWLEDGE

Piero Mussio*

ABSTRACT

e-Documents appear as a new media, complementing the traditional documents in recording, evolving and making available community knowledge. The process of interaction between members of the community and e-documents appears as a new and complex field that is constrained by present day design and implementation technologies. These constraints result in e-documents that become fences that drive the community members to follow unfamiliar reasoning strategies, to adopt unreliable procedures and to reach undesired goals. To dissolve the fence, the design and implementation of interactive, multimodal, hypermedia e-documents require new models and new metrics of interpretation. This paper proposes a model-based approach to the study of the expert-document interaction process and frames the phenomena that characterize this process.

INTRODUCTION

The pervasive diffusion of computer based, multimodal, and hypermedia systems determines an evolution in the documentation styles, notations and procedures of experts. Before the computer age, communities of experts progressively developed documentation styles, notations and procedures to record the community's knowledge on a permanent physical media. This enabled the community's knowledge to be available to members when and where they require it and in the shape required to perform their current activities.

In a computer-based system, documents exist 'virtually' as the result of an interpretation of a program by a computer. These documents are here called *electronic documents* (e-documents). e-Documents can be accessed when and where required and perceived by community members since the program generates some physical representations, for

* Piero Mussio, Dipartimento di Scienze dell'Informazione, Università degli Studi di Milano, Milano, Italy
mussio@dico.unimi.it

Constructing the Infrastructure for the Knowledge Economy
Edited by H. Linger *et al.*, Kluwer Academic/Plenum Publishers, 2004

example images on a screen. This dependence on a machine offers some advantages: e-documents become dynamic, proactive and interactive entities, able to adapt their own behavior to the experts' requirements and needs. However, community members are not computer experts and often not even computer literate. The open problem is how e-documents are shaped and allowed to behave and interact so that community members can properly perceive, understand, distribute and manage documents.

From a computer science perspective, the experience gained in the use of computer based, interactive, multimodal, hypermedia systems is defining an important shift in computing paradigms. Several researchers try to characterize this shift: Shneidermann claims "Old computing is about what computers can do, new computing about what humans can do".[1] From a different point of view, Wegner and co-authors find Turing Machines inadequate to describe interactive computing processes, and propose Persistent Turing Machine to account for these new types of processes.[2] This paper focuses on the study of interactive systems used by communities of experts to achieve their tasks. These interactive systems are seen as electronic documents, tools which experts use to develop their activities but also to record and share their common knowledge. e-Documents appear as a new media, complementing the traditional documents in recording, evolving and making available the community knowledge.

The process of interaction between experts and e-documents appears as a new and complex field that is constrained by present day design and implementation technologies. These constraints result in e-documents that become fences that drive the community members to follow unfamiliar reasoning strategies, to adopt unreliable procedures and to reach undesired goals. The use of such e-documents in the execution of real tasks may make the achievement of the tasks difficult, or even impossible. As a consequence, e-documents of great technological value have failed because they have not been able to overcome these hurdles. The design and implementation of interactive, multimodal, hypermedia e-documents require new models and new metrics of nteraction, which are under development.

This paper describes some steps toward responding to this request. It proposes a model-based approach to the study of the expert-document interaction process and to frame the phenomena that characterize this process. Model-based design method[3] of electronic documents are also considered.

The paper is organized as follows: first – section 2 – a view on pre-electronic document use is discussed and contrasted in section 3 with the use of e-documents. Then in section 4, the process of interaction between users and e-documents is discussed, adopting the PCL model for HCI to frame several phenomena which affect this process and that have been recognized and studied separately so far. Last, section 5 outlines some guidelines on the design of e-documents aimed at reaching a quality of interaction adequate to the user needs. Section 6 concludes the paper.

2. PRE-ELECTRONICS DOCUMENT

In the pre-electronic world, a document is a physical artifact, constituted by a physical support modified by some human activity that some humans use as a tool of study, consultation or research in achieving a task. In the following we call the humans using the document as a source of knowledge *users of the document* (or *users* for short). Users interpret the document by applying their cognitive criteria and recognizing sets of elementary tokens on the support as functional or perceptual units that we call *characteristic structures* (**cs**), or *structures* for short. Examples of **cs** are letters in an alphabet, symbols or icons in technical languages. Users associate to each **cs** a meaning: the association of a **cs** with a meaning is called *characteristic pattern (cp)* or *patterns* for short. Users recognize complex *structures* formed by more simple ones (words formed by letters, plant maps formed by icons etc.) and attribute them a meaning stemming from the meaning of the components *structures*. The document itself is interpreted as a meaningful entity, a complex *pattern*.

In our work, we restrict our attention to documents intentionally created to record and diffuse scientific or technical knowledge. Communities of experts in different disciplines develop notations to represent on a permanent support (ie to materialize) abstract or concrete concepts, observational data, prescriptions, procedures, strategies to reach a goal, and results of activities.

The document notation stems from the community activities and experiences and is defined by

1. a finite set of elementary structures (the notation alphabet);
2. a set of lexical, syntactic and layout rules to organize the structures in the alphabet into more complex ones, up to a whole document;
3. methods to organize, shape and materialize structures on suitable supports, e.g. write on paper, engrave in stones, etc; and
4. interpretation correspondences which allow users to link elementary and complex structures with concepts so that a document can be organized to convey the intended meaning or, once existing, to be adequately interpreted.

Community members develop and evolve the notation to make it easier to express constructs arising in problems, make the documents more suggestive, improve the ability to subordinate detail and to achieve economy in reasoning (adapted from Iverson (1980); also see reference 5 for a discussion). However, expressing a concept through the community notation is not without a cost because "every notation highlights some kind of information at the expense of obscuring other kinds".[6] Users from other communities with different skills and interpretation abilities, may associate the same *structure* to a different meaning and therefore ascribe a different meaning to the whole document. Other problems that can arise include the fact that certain users can only understand some parts of the document and in the extreme, they do not even recognize the artifact at hand as a document.

The community does not in general explicitly state the notation elements (alphabet, rules, materialization methods and interpretation correspondences) even if its members use them consistently in authoring or interpreting the document. When made explicit, the notation elements are seldom defined according to computer science formalisms, and are always situated in the specific context. Engineering mechanical drawings are examples of documents authored and interpreted using precise but not formalized rules.[7] Anatomical tables are examples of scientific indexical images.[8] built on implicitly defined alphabets and rules. An interpreted radiography, used in this paper as a running example, is a document generated by a machine in which physicians recognize and annotate several *structures* to which they associate a meaning.

The *interaction* between the members of the community and documents is based on human activities, such as reading and annotating a document. Members of the community adapt their behaviors to better exploit the notation. For example they develop in time specialized *reading patterns*, sequences of reading modes and events, which allow efficient reading of a document in relation to the current aims and tasks of the reader. Reading patterns characterize user reading activity and hence the user-document interaction while users navigate and manipulate documents. Reading patterns depend on user culture, skills and goals but also on document notation, activity performed and context.[9]

In conclusion, community members define and evolve a notation and act as *authors* to produce complex *structures*, the documents, on some physical support. A document materializes the intended meaning in the form the authors consider to be more appropriately understood by the member of their community. Humans, as *users*, read (perceive and interpret) and annotate the document following their reading patterns and according to their current goals. Their understanding is constrained by the depth of their knowledge of the notation adopted by authors. *Pre-electronic documents*, once constructed, do not evolve in time (if one neglects aging) and can be considered as closed, time-invariant systems, which during the *user/document interaction* play a passive role. On the contrary, both the *notation* in which a document is expressed and the *reading patterns* through which it is read, *co-evolve* in time, in that using the documents change the way users perform their activity, and as they change, they adapt the notation to their new strategies.

3. ELECTRONIC DOCUMENT

In the electronic world, documents become '*electronic*', in that they are no more recorded on a permanent support, but exist '*virtually*' as the result of the interpretation of a program by a computer.[10] Users can perceive e-documents because the computational process generates some physical representations. For example images on a screen, in which texts, pictures and graphs appear. These physical representations exist and are perceivable only while the electronic machinery maintains them in existence. The e-document is less persistent than paper-based one, but this dependence on a computer offers some advantages. Interactive computers allow e-documents to be managed and adapted by their users more easily than paper-based ones; e-documents can evolve during their usage and adapt to their users. With the advent of the web, the e-document evolves to "a unit consisting of dynamic, flexible, non linear content, represented as a set of linked information items, stored in one or more physical media or networked sites; created and used by one or more individuals in the facilitation of some process or project".[11] However, e-documents appear to users as single entities even when their content is distributed in different, geographically remote repositories. Moreover, the physical representation results from a mapping of the content of the document into output events perceivable by users (e.g. the images on the screen or a speech through a microphone). The process of creating the content of a document is separated by the process of its materialization (physical representation), which may be multimodal. The materialization can be adapted to the culture, skills and abilities of the current user, without altering its content.

To make these considerations concrete, let us introduce a scenario, drawn from a first analysis of physicians collaborating to achieve a diagnosis.[12] In the scenario, a pneumologist and a radiologist, incrementally gain insight into the case at hand by successive interpretations and annotations of chest radiographies, performed in (possibly) different places and at (possibly) different times. They are supported by two interactive prototypes, *B-Radio* and *B-Diagno*.

B-Radio and *B-Diagno* are e-documents in that the two physicians use them to pursue goals and perform tasks which in the past were done using paper-based documents. For example, the physicians use the two e-documents to permanently track the diagnostic process by recording the observational data, the activities they perform, their observations and the results that they progressively obtain.

Some aspects of the user/e-document interaction are similar to those of the user/document interaction. A radiologist explores a screen, such as the one shown in Fig.1, applying reading patterns suited to her current task. She looks at the screen and recognizes several *structures* which she interprets as *patterns,* assigning them a meaning which depends on the context. For example, the user can interpret the screen shown in Fig. 1 because she recognizes several *structures* on the top of the screen, as the tools to interact with Internet Explorer, the browser managing the process. Under it, a set of *structures* form a header which, if correctly interpreted, informs her that *B-Radio* is the active e-document. Two *structures* lie under the header, an equipment area on the right, and a working area on the left. In the equipment area, the radiologist identifies four menus (four *patterns*), denoting repositories of entities to be worked (images and annotations) and equipment to work on the entities. In the working area, tools are represented by icons, and data as raster or vector images, materializing the *structures* of interest. Each image represents an entity to be worked on and is associated with a handle, a tool-box and some identifiers. These four entities form an *annotation bench*. The toolbox shows the tools required for the execution of the current task. The identifiers identify the physician performing the task, the patient to which the data refers to, and the image (set of data) referred to that patient.

Other aspects of the interaction with e-documents are new. New forms of interaction arise, because users navigate and interact with the document by operating on the computer I/O devices (the mouse, the key board, etc.) and the document responds to these user actions. Users look at the screen and specify their commands to the system by performing some input operations in relation to the *patterns* they recognize in it. In direct manipulation environments, users act on the input device, feel as if they were directly operating on the *pattern*, for example they feel as if moving the mouse they directly drag the pointer on the screen. For this reason, a pair <*operation*, *pattern*> is a user *action*.

e-Documents react to *actions* because they are *active, pro-active and evolutive*. They are *active* in that they are able to interpret the user actions and execute the associated computations. e-Documents are *pro-active* in that they fire some computational activities without an explicit user command. For example they interpret some action or some results of user actions to foresee some plausible users needs and support them by adequate computational activities or even to adapt or evolve the system to satisfy them. They are *evolutive* in that their content, structure, materialization and set of associated tools are modified, enriched or reduced by the interaction. Due to these capabilities, e-documents can self-*adapt* to the current context of activity in several way.

Users in turn adapt themselves to the new documentation style: not only do they develop new reading patterns but they also develop *interaction patterns*, sequences of actions, specialized to achieve some goal, which they can execute without any specific thinking.[13, 14]

These concepts are illustrated in both Fig. 1 and 2. In Fig. 1, the image on the bench represents an intermediate result obtained by the radiologist who recognized some *structures* of medical interest that need to be signaled to the pneumologist. She surrounds them by a closed line to make them evident. The image resumes the state of the radiography interpretation activity after the radiologist

1. has obtained the data of his interest (a radiography of the patient, whose surname is Rossi) performing some suited action pattern
2. has recognized some *structures* interpreted as denoting a pleural effusion
3. has selected from the toolbox the tool for free hand drawing of close curves, the tenth button from left (whose icon is a close curve)

B-Radio has reacted to this last action pattern, presenting him a cursor, the cross. The radiologist then uses a mouse to steer the cross to surround the *patterns* of interest, and *B-Radio* stores data characterizing the traced line. After closing the curve, the radiologist selects the a button ('a') in the top menu, initiating the annotation activity and *B-Radio* makes available to her an annotation window in which the radiologist can type his classification of the *structures* ('Pleural effusion') and comments ('Potential pneumonia') as shown in Fig. 2. When the radiologist clicks the 'add' button to record his annotation, *B-Radio* closes the annotation window; adds to the framed area an icon of a pencil as an anchor to the annotation and pro-actively transforms the framed area into a *user-defined widget*, by associating it to a pop-up menu. To achieve the last point, *B-Radio* interprets the radiologist annotation and establishes the menu title and items, interpreting rules based on context and past experience records the new widget among the tools available to the users.

In this way, *B-Radio* evolves the functionality of the annotation bench associated with Mr. Rossi's radiography. Fig. 3a shows the radiologist exploiting the new widget by clicking the 'Density Evaluation' button after having selected a graph as the mode of presentation of the results. As a reaction, *B-Radio* computes the gray level histogram of the framed area, materializes it in the form required by the user (the graph in Fig. 3b), and permanently associates it to the annotation. This updates the knowledge/information about Mr. Rossi's case.

B-Radio and B-Diagno are *self-adaptive.* They are not identical because they have to support physicians, who share a common cultural kernel, but developed different experiences, and specializations, performing different types of tasks to achieve a diagnosis. Hence, each e-document adapts every shared set of data (a tool, an annotation, an image) interpreting and materializing it according to

a) the notation and skill of the different users - the radiologist and the pneumologist
b) the constraints of the different context.

Moreover, each one is *adapted* to the specific environment in that it makes available specialized data and tools not available in the other environment.

For example, when the pneumologist requires the annotated radiography of patient Rossi, *B-Diagno* associates the radiologist defined widget and annotations in *B-Radio* to a new behavior and new tools suited for pneumologist activity. When the pneumologist selects the pencil, *B-Diagno* displays the text of the annotation performed by the radiologist and a new menu, a set of links to the available records of data on patient Rossi (Fig. 4a). The pneumologist selects 'Radiological interpretation' to query details of the

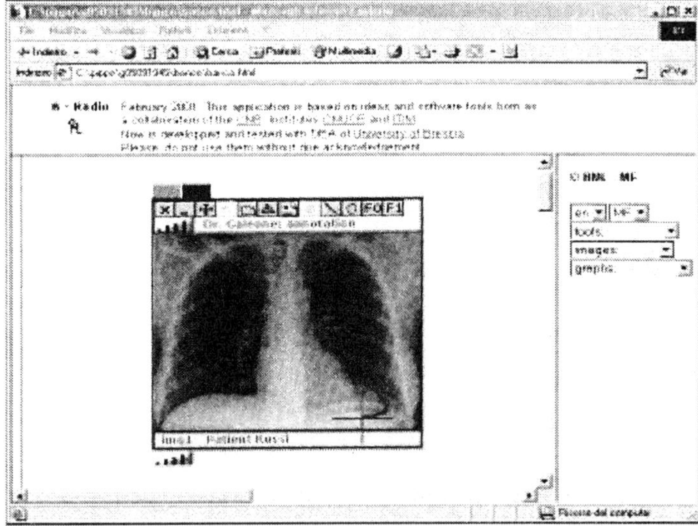

Figure 1. *B-Radio* Web page. The radiologist is analyzing chest radiography.

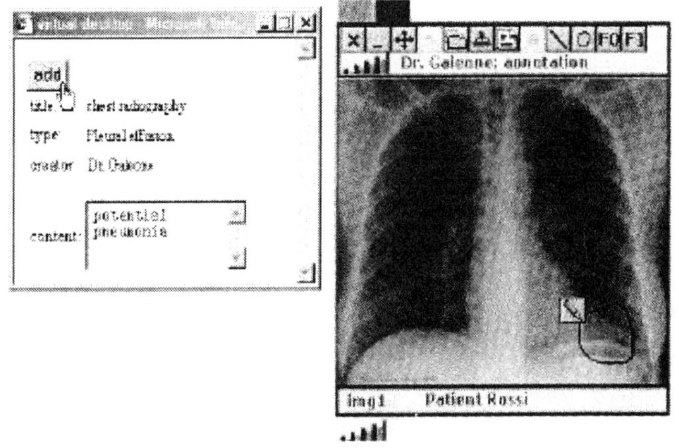

Figure 2. In *B-Radio* the radiologist is annotating the surrounded area.

radiologist's interpretation of the radiograph (Fig. 4a). *B-Diagno* presents the data related to the density of the pleural effusion - i.e. represented as a gray level histogram in Fig. 3b, accessed in a form better suited to her activity. She can obviously add her diagnosis to the document as a separate annotation (Fig. 4b) or add it to the radiologist's annotations.

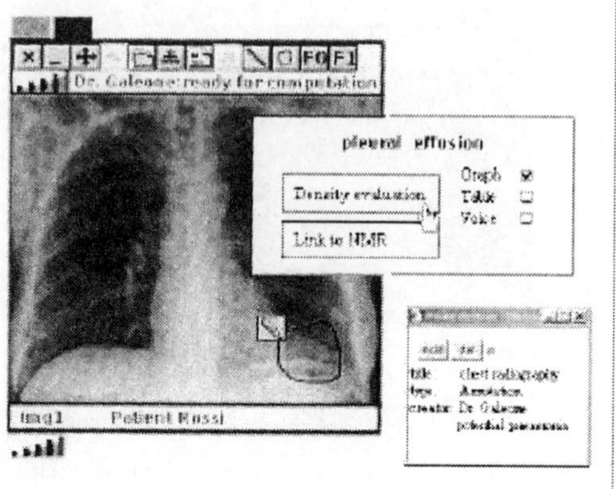

Figure 3a. In B-Radio the radiologist obtains the density evaluation of the pleural effusion using the button 'density evaluation'.

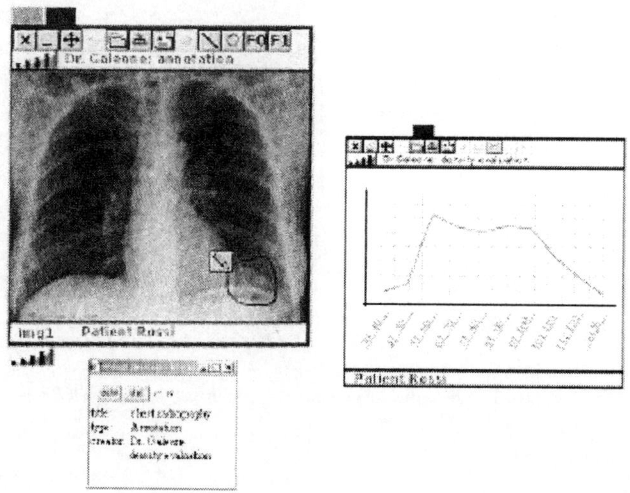

Figure 3b. In B-Radio the radiologist obtains the density evaluation of the pleural effusion using the button 'density evaluation'.

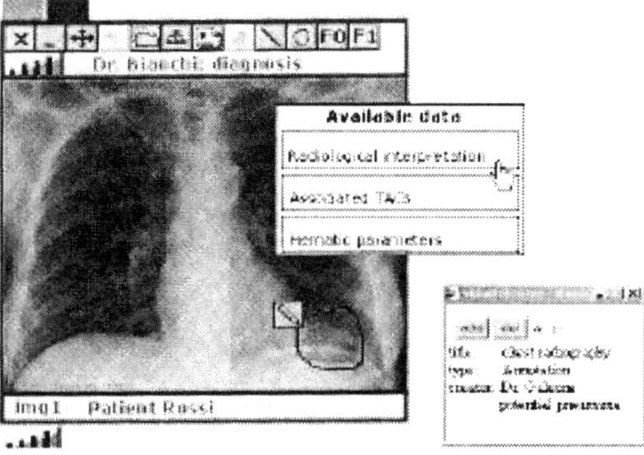

Figure 4a. Working in B-Diagno the pneumologist obtains the radiological interpretation and gives her diagnosis.

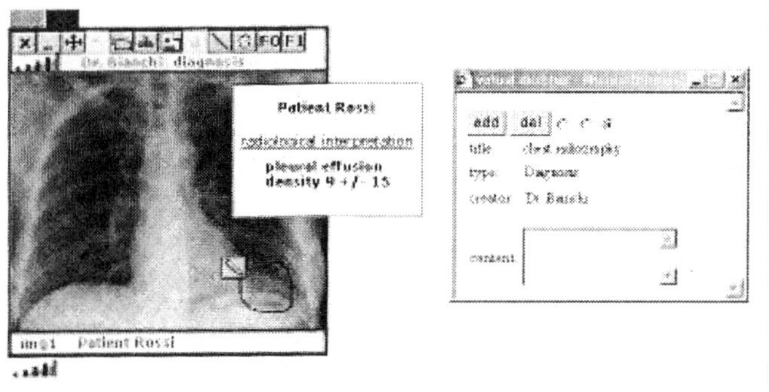

Figure 4b. Working in B-Diagno the pneumologist obtains the radiological interpretation and gives her diagnosis.

4. A VIEW ON USER E-DOCUMENT INTERACTIVE PROCESS

The scenario illustrates how users can develop their interaction with e-documents. In contrast to pre-electronic documents, an e-document is a system which has a virtual existence in that it exists as the result of the interpretation of a system of programs by a computer; is: dynamic in that its content (state) evolves; is open in that it interacts with the environment and its dynamics is influenced by the interaction; is developmental in that it can permanently evolve its organization and content from an initial state under the influence of the interaction process.

These new characteristics of the e-document forces users to evolve from readers to co-authors in that they are not only required to interpret the document (recognize and understand patterns) but also to navigate the document and determine its evolution with their decisions. To interpret this new role, the user has to develop new reading and interaction patterns. To achieve his/her tasks, users need to "concentrate on what they want to achieve instead of how the underlying program actually produces it".[15] We adopt the model of HCI recently proposed the Pictorial Computing Laboratory[16] in order to adequately model the user/e-document interaction process and characterize the phenomena which determine the development of the e-document.

This model recognizes the interaction between users and e-document as a *syndetic* process in which systems of different nature (the cognitive human and the 'mechanical' machine) cooperate to achieve a task.[17] The different systems interact by communicating, interpreting and materializing sequences of messages at successive instants of time. If we restrict to the case of WIMP (Windows, Icons, Menus, Pointers) interaction,[10] the messages exchanged are the whole images which appear on the computer screen and are formed by text, icons, graphs, pictures, windows as in Fig. 1.

There are two *interpretations* of each element on the screen and each action during the interaction. One interpretation is performed by the user depending on her role in the task as well as her culture, experience, and skills. The second interpretation is internal to the system, associating the image with a computational meaning, as determined by the programs implemented in the system.[5] The user identifies some *structures* on the screen and interprets them as *patterns*, deriving the whole message meaning. On the basis of this interpretation, she decides what to do next, and manifests her intention by an *action*. The system perceives the operation as an input event OPERATION (OP), and relates this event to a known STRUCTURE, that is itself related to a COMPUTATIONAL PROCESS. The system computes its response to the human activity by executing a COMPUTATIONAL PROCESS on the new data, the computer interpretation of the OPERATION on the STRUCTURE. The results of this computational activity are materialized as new STRUCTURE which modify the IMAGE on the screen that the system maintains.

The interaction is *adequate* if

1. the STRUCTURE recognized by the human on the screen, i.e. in the current IMAGE, matches the STRUCTURE known by the system and
2. the interpretation by the user is consistent with the COMPUTATIONAL PROCESS, i.e. the reaction of the e-document is the one expected by the user and understandable by her.

5. PHENOMENA REALTED TO E-DOCUMENT INTERACTION

The existence of a syndetic process based on two different interpretations give rise to several phenomena, which must be identified and described in order to design and implement quality e-documents. Most of these phenomena are known and studied in the current literature, but they are discussed separately and from different points of view, typically Usability Engineering, Software Engineering and Information System Development. The aim is to frame the phenomena in an unique model to understand their influence on the HCI process to derive an approach to e-document design and development which overcomes the hurdles they create as well as exploiting the possibilities they offer.

The phenomena studied so far are:

5.1. Communication Gap Between Designers and Users

A communicational gap exists between users and designers because designers and users have different cultural backgrounds, skills and acquired capabilities.[5] Therefore, designers and users adopt different approaches to abstraction since, for instance they may have different notions about the details that can be abridged. Moreover, users reason heuristically rather than algorithmically, using examples and analogies rather than deductive abstract tools. Users document their activities, prescriptions, and results through their own notations, articulating their activities according to their traditional tools rather than computerize ones. The communication gap is important for HCI design because, as highlighted by the PCL model, there are two interpretations of each image on the screen and of each action performed to modify it. The first interpretation is performed by the user, the second by the system.

The system interpretation reflects the designer understanding of the task, implemented in the programs that control the machine. Hence, the interactive system usually is customized to the culture, skill and articulation of the designer. Users often find hurdles in mapping the events occurring in the interaction process onto their culture, skill and specific forms of articulation.[18] When discordance occurs, users are unable to follow their own strategies in solving their tasks and may reach incomplete or wrong results or may be lost in the virtual space.

5.2 User Diversity

In the scenario presented in this paper, pneumologists and radiologists are physicians who share common knowledge, but perform different types of activities and use different tools to collaborate to achieve a common task. They also develop and use different dialects of a common medical notation to document their results. This is a common case as in general users do not constitute a uniform populations, but form communities that are characterized by specific (sub)cultures, goals, notations, tools, activities, and responsibilities. In some cases, user diversity arise because of specific abilities (physical and/or cognitive), and context of activity. As a consequence, specialized user dialects stem from the existence of users communities which develop peculiar abilities, knowledge and notations. Often, these notations are dialects of a more general one, because the notation arises from different practical situations and environments.

For example, technical mechanical drawings are organized according to rules which are different in Europe and in USA.[7] Explicative annotations are written in different national languages. Often the whole document (drawing and text) is organized according to guidelines developed in each single company. The correct and complete understanding of a technical drawing depends on the recognition of the original standard as well as on the understanding of the national (and also company developed) dialects. Notably, users belonging to different communities may (mis)understand the same document at different level of details.

In HCI, it is well known that "using the system changes the users, ...".[19] Actually, using the e-document (the *system* in Nielsen's quotation) users change their way of interpreting the interaction, gaining insight in the e-document materializations and dynamics, and develop new reading and interaction patterns. After a while the human become a different user than she was before.

In addition, the user/e-document interaction may be inadequate if the users interact with e-documents that are developed by experts of different culture and skills.

5.3. Shielding Technologies

Technology may become a shield, which impede users to perceive correctly their working situation, to reason on their problems and to follow adequate resolution strategies. In fact, every tools has a *grain*, a tendency to (implicitly) push the user toward certain kind of use.[22] And every technology favors the production of tools with some *grain*. The *grain* makes it easier for the users to perform certain activity and difficult or impossible to perform other tasks. As a result, users to try to achieve their tasks by choosing strategies which are apparently easily executable, but which do not really fit their need. As a consequence, they make more errors, require greater cognitive efforts and achieve inappropriate goals. Many examples of this phenomenon can be found in the literature. Illustrating the needs for an adequate enterprise architecture, Filkestein comments on the tendency of current IT technologies toward the construction of specialized, non-integrated tools, each one supporting a specific IT activity.[23] The technology shields the holistic nature of the enterprise since the tools force the users to operate in a non integrated way within the enterprise that is an integrate system. At a lower level of abstraction, Dix et alt.[22] illustrate how different programming paradigms facilitate different policies in dialogue control. Loop-based code facilitate pre-emptive system dialog while notification-based make this difficult.

5.4. Co-Evolution of Systems and Users

As the user becomes experienced in interacting with the e-document, it induces the evolution of the e-document usage procedures. As indicated by Nielsen "using the system changes the users, and as they change they will use the system in new ways".[19] These new uses of the e-document force users to ask for adaptation of the system to match the evolution of the working environment. Designers are traditionally in charge of managing this evolution, adapting the e-document to its new usages. We called this phenomenon co-evolution of users and systems. Co-evolution stems from two main sources: a) user creativity, i.e. users may devise novel ways to exploit the system in order to satisfy some needs not considered in the specification and design phase; and b) user acquired habits, i.e. users may follow some interaction strategy to which they are (or become) accustomed to.[14]

Co-evolution implies tailoring that, according to,[20] is "the activity of modifying an existing computer system in the context of its use, rather than in the development context." All these activities are made difficult by the communication gap. One way to overcome the gap, is for users themselves to tailor the system to meet their needs. Tailoring stems from the need to continuously adapt the system and is seen as the indirect long-term collaboration between developers and users.

In Bourguin et alt.[21] it is observed that co-evolution of users and systems implies a more general phenomenon: the new uses of the system also determine the evolution of the user culture and of her models and procedures of task evolution. On the other hand, the requests from users force the evolution of the whole technology supporting this interaction. In this view, two different cycles of co-evolution exits and influence each other: an inner one, involving the user and the e-document and a more general one involving the organizational context in which users explicate their activities and the technology of e-document creation. The two cycles are not necessarily virtuous cycles as shielding technologies and communication gap can interfere with these cycles.

5.5. Implicit Information and Tacit Knowledge

Pre-electronic documents are created following user defined notation. Using these notations, a relevant part of the information carried by the document is embedded in its visual organization and shape materialization. We call this part of the information carried by the document *implicit information*. For example, in the documents of scientific communities, the use of bold characters and specific styles indicates the parts of the documents - paper title, abstract, section titles - which synthesize its meaning.[24] Strips of images, for example illustrating procedures or sequences of actions to be performed, are organized according to the reading habits of the expected reader: from left to right for western readers, from right to left for eastern ones. Furthermore, some icons, textual words, or images may be meaningful only to the experts in some discipline: for example, icons representing cells in a liver simulation may have a specific meaning only for hepatologists,[25] while a radiography may be meaningful to physicians but not to other experts.

Implicit information is significant only to users who posses the knowledge to interpret it. Most of this knowledge is not made explicit nor codified but is *tacit knowledge* that users possess and use to carry out tasks and to solve problems. But it is knowledge that they are unable to express verbally and they may even be unaware that they possess it. It is a common experience that in many fields users exploit their tacit knowledge since they are often more able to do than to explain what they do. Tacit knowledge is related to the specific work domain and it is also exploited by users to interpret the messages from the software system. Tacit knowledge is also often affected by perceptual mechanisms depending on mood, culture, motivation, and even emotion.[26] Users exploit tacit knowledge in interpreting a document as well as in organizing it when they author it. User defined notations allow users to exploit their tacit knowledge and the documents constructed in these notations incorporate this knowledge as a part of the implicit information.

e-Documents are in general designed without explicitly taking into account the problem of implicit information, user articulation skills and tacit knowledge. The e-document that is produced can therefore be interpreted at high cognitive costs. Often, the e-document become a *fence* for the users because

1. it is organized and materialized around the designer's culture
2. the imbedded tools impose reading and interaction patterns that are aliens to the user
3. uncontrolled *grains* implicitly influence the interaction process.

The fence drives the users (often gently) toward unfamiliar reasoning strategies, resulting into inefficient procedures and undesired goals. The use of such systems makes the achievement of real tasks difficult or even impossible.

6. SUGGESTIONS FOR HUMANIZED MANAGEMENT OF COMMUNITY KNOWLEDGE

The research reported in this paper aims to dissolve the fence in order to overcome the pathologies inherent in interaction processes and to exploit the possibilities offered by e-documents. The research starts from our experience in developing e-documents to support scientific and technical experts in their work.[5, 12, 25, 27] Our aim is to allow experts to steer the interaction process according to their reasoning styles, becoming masters of the interaction. Interacting with the e-document, users determine the evolution of the e-document itself and the community knowledge stored in it. On the whole, users are in control of the accumulation and evolution of the community's knowledge. This situation is what we call *humanized management* of community knowledge.

Experts in these communities use different technical methods, languages, goals, tasks, ways of thinking, and documentation styles. The pre-electronic notations they developed emerge from their practical experiences in their specific domain and from their working practice. Using the notation, experts produce documents which convey implicit information suited to an interpretation based on their tacit knowledge. Documents are concrete and situated in the specific context, in that they are based on icons, symbols and words that resemble and schematize the tools and the entities that are to be operated in the working environment. The documents produced in time record the community knowledge, and can be properly understood, retrieved, browsed and navigated by users, who have the experience to know the notation and acquire the tacit knowledge necessary to interpret it. To allow humanized management of community knowledge, e-documents should be;

1. concrete
2. situated in a specific context (in the same way as pre-electronic documents were)
3. carry the same implicit information that pre-electronic documents carried.

This formulation suggests the first principle of e-document design: 'recognize e-documents users as expert in their domain of activity'. Recognizing users as domain experts means recognizing their notations, dialects and working strategies as reasoning and communication tools. It also implies that they are not experts in computer science.

The designer should also recognize user diversity: experts in a community develop several different dialects of their notation. Recognizing user diversity calls for the ability to represent a meaning of a concept with different materialization, e.g. text or image or sound, and to associate with the same materialization a different meaning according, for example, to the context of interaction. For example the same radiography is interpreted in different ways by a radiologist and a pneumologist. These two domain experts are however collaborating to get a common goal. For this, they use a same set of data, which is represented according to their specific skills. This is a common case as experts often work in a team to perform a common task. The team might be composed by members of different sub-communities, each sub-community with different expertise. Each sub-community should need an appropriate computer environment, suitable to them to manage their own view of the activity to be performed.

On the other side, it must also be recognized that e-documents are different from traditional documents in that they are an interactive, evolutive, dynamic systems, and that user and e-document form a syndetic, co-evolutive system. Supporting co-evolution requires that e-documents developed for a community can be tailored by its members to the newly emerging requirements.[20]

Taking into account all these observations, we start the development of e-documents from the notations usually exploited by the experts in their application domain.[12, 25, 27] We evolve these notations into interaction visual languages, whose sentences are the images appearing on the screen during the interaction. In each interaction phase, these images are valid documents in the user's work site and they can be understood by the user's community at this site. Therefore, the interaction visual language allows users to understand and control the interaction process. The evolution from the user notation to the interaction visual language is obtained by enriching the symbols that represent concepts and relations of the language used by the user in his/her working environment, so as to fully exploit the power of the computing system. Thus the methodology is particularly focused on the so-called "language augmentation" phase, where the traditional notation is enriched by new elements and functions for interactive computing.[27]

7. CONCLUSIONS

In the interactive computer age, documents become electronic, because they;

1. are no longer only recorded on permanent supports, but also exists 'virtually' as the result of their interpretation by a computer program
2. can interact with their users
3. can evolve during their usage, under the influence of the interaction.

Users are no longer only readers of the documents, but become co-authors of the document, determining its current state and influencing its evolution through their interaction. In the paper, e-documents are seen as a new medium, subject to two interpretations: the one of the user, the co-author, and the one of the author , the designer of the computer program. Co-evolution is a primary phenomenon determining the management and the evolution of community knowledge, but it can be polluted by the communicational gap and grain, which steer the interaction process through uncontrolled paths. In this case, the technology conditions the development of community knowledge. Our aim on is to allow a humanized management of community knowledge. Current technologies seem powerful enough to support us. We only need to learn how to use them.

ACKNOWLEDGEMENTS

The author wishes to thank the members of the PCL group. In particular Daniela Fogli and Marco Padula for the stimulating discussions during the development of this work and Giuseppe Fresta for the design and implementation of the prototypes presented in the paper. The support of EUD-Net Thematic Network (IST-2001-37470) is also acknowledged.

REFERENCES

1. B. Schneiderman, Leonardo's Laptop: Human needs and the New Computing Technologies, Invited Talk, Opening Session, UACHI Conference, Crete, June 03, www.cs.edu/hcil/nnewcomputing.
2. P. Wegner, D. Goldin, Computation beyond Turing machines, *Communications of the ACM*, 46 (4), 100–102 (2003).
3. B. Lawson, *How Designers Think* (Architectural Press, Oxford, 1997).
4. K. E. Iverson, Notation as a tool of thought, *Communications of the ACM*, 23(8), 444–465 (1980).
5. P. Carrara, D. Fogli, G. Fresta, P. Mussio, Toward overcoming culture, skill and situation hurdles in human-computer interaction. *Int. Journal Universal Access in the Information Society*, 1(4), 288–304 (2002).
6. M. Petre, T. R. G. Green, Learning to Read Graphics: Some Evidence that 'Seeing' an Information Display is an Acquired Skill. *Journal of Visual Languages and Computing*, 4 (1), 55-70 (1993).
7. ISO Standard: ISO 5456 Technical Drawing Projection Methods.
8. P. Codognet, An historical Account of Indexical Images: from Ancient Art to Web, Proc. 1999 Symp. On Visual Languages, IEEE Comp. Society.
9. K. Hornbæk, E. Frøkjær, Reading Patterns and Usability in Visualization of Electronic Documents, *ACM TOCHI*, Vol. 10, No. 2 (2003).
10. J. Preece, *Human-Computer Interaction* (Addison-Wesley, 1994).
11. L. Shamber, What is a document? Rethinking the concept in uneasy times. *Journal of the ASIS*, 47 (9), 669–671 (1996).
12. M. F. Costabile, D. Fogli, G. Fresta, P. Mussio., A. Piccinno, Computer Environments for Improving End-User Accessibility, in: N. Carbonell and C. Stephanidis (Eds), *"Universal Access - Theoretical Perspectives, Practice, and Experience", LNCS 2615*, 129-140 (2002).
13. D. J. Majhew. *Principles and Guideline in Software User Interface Design* (Prentice Hall, 1992).
14. S. Arondi, P. Baroni, D. Fogli, P. Mussio. Supporting co-evolution of users and systems by the recognition of Interaction Patterns. Proceedings of the International Conference on Advanced Visual Interfaces (AVI 2002), Trento, May 2002, 177–189.
15. B. Bieber, F. Vitali, H. Ashman, V. Balasubramanian, H. Oinas-Kukkonen, Fourth Generation Hypermedia: Some Missing Links for the WWW. *Int. Journal Human Computer Studies*, 47, 31–65 (1997).
16. P.Bottoni, M. F. Costabile, P. Mussio, Specification and Dialogue Control of Visual Interaction through Visual Rewriting Systems, *ACM Trans. on Programming Languages and Systems*, Vol. 21, No. 6, 1077–1136, (1999).
17. P. Barnard, J. May, D. Duke, D. Duce, Systems, Interactions, and Macrotheory. *ACM Trans. on Human-Computer Interaction*, 7(2), 222–262.
18. J. Nielsen, *Usability Engineering* (Academic Press, San Diego, 1994) p. 219.
19. J. Nielsen, *Usability Engineering* (Academic Press, San Diego, 1994).
20. A. I. Mørch, N. D. Mehandjiev, Tailoring as Collaboration: The Mediating Role of Multiple Representations and Application Units, *Computer Supported Cooperative Work*, 9, 75–100 (2000).
21. G. Bourguin, A. Derycke, J C. Tarby, Beyond the Interface: Co-evolution inside Interactive Systems - A Proposal Founded on Activity Theory, Proc. IHM-HCI (2001).
22. A. Dix, J. Finlay, G. Abowd, R. Beale, *Human Computer Interaction* (Prentice Hall, London, 1998).
23. C. Filkenstein, Enterprise Integration Using Enterprise Architecture, Keynote Address, ISD 2003, Melbourne, Aug. 2003.
24. J. Borchers. *A pattern approach to interaction design* (John Wiley & Sons, 2001).
25. P. Mussio, M. Pietrogrande, M. Protti, Simulation of Hepatological Models: a Study in Visual Interactive Exploration of Scientific Problems, *Journal of Visual Languages and Computing*, 2, 75–95 (1991).
26. D. A. Norman,. Emotion and design: Attractive things work better. *Interactions Magazine*, ix (4), 36-42 (2002).
27. A. Bianchi, M. D'Enza, M. Matera, A. Betta, Designing Usable Visual Languages: the Case of Immune System Studies, Proc. IEEE Int. Symposium on VL99, September 1999.

ENTERPRISE INTEGRATION USING ENTERPRISE ARCHITECTURE

Clive Finkelstein*

ABSTRACT

The paper first introduces the concepts of Enterprise Architecture based on the *Zachman Framework for Enterprise Architecture*. The evolution of enterprises into the Information Age is discussed, together with the evolution of Systems Development Methodologies – resulting in redundant data and redundant processes. To be effective in addressing the problems of non-integrated databases and processes that exist in most enterprise today, Enterprise Integration requires both Business Integration and Technology Integration.

The importance of Metadata for Enterprise Integration is discussed. The Information Engineering methodologies from 1976 through the 1980s have evolved into Enterprise Engineering methods to achieve Business Integration using Enterprise Architecture. The concepts of XML and Web Services are introduced in the paper, with examples. These technologies are used to achieve the Technology Integration component of Enterprise Integration using Enterprise Architecture. Based on the Enterprise Engineering methods, these technologies are also used for rapid delivery of Enterprise Architecture.

1. THE EVOLUTION OF ENTERPRISE ARCHITECTURE

Enterprise Architecture was developed by John Zachman while with IBM in the 1980s, after observing the Building and Airplane construction industries and the IT industry. He saw similarities between the construction of Buildings, Airplanes and the Information Systems used by an Enterprise.

---

* Clive Finkelstein, Managing Director, Information Engineering Services Pty Ltd,, *PO Box 246, Hillarys WA 6923 Australia,* Phone +61-8-9402-8300 • Fax +61-8-9402-8322 • ABN: 70 005 224 920; ACN: 005 224 920, Email *cfink@ies.aust.com* • Web Site *http://www.ies.aust.com/~ieinfo/*

These industries manage the design, construction and maintenance of complex products by considering the needs of different people. The Owner in the Building industry uses Architect's Drawings to determine if the building will address specific requirements. For Airplane manufacture, this is achieved by the high-level Work Breakdown Structure of the plane. A Model of Business is needed for Information Systems. Figure 1 illustrates this.

DIFFERENT PERSPECTIVES

Buildings	Airplanes	Enterprise
Architect's Drawings	OWNER Work Breakdown Structure	Model of Business
Architect's Plans	DESIGNER Engineering Design	Model of Info System
Contractor's Plans	BUILDER Manufacturing Engineering Design	Technology Model

Figure 1. The Owner, Designer and Builder are interested in different representations or diagrams from their perspectives, in design and construction of buildings, airplanes, and enterprise systems.

The *Designer*, however, needs a different set of diagrams: *Architect's Plans* for the building; sets of *Engineering Design* diagrams for the plane; or *Information System Models* for the enterprise.

The Builder relies on still different types of diagrams: *Contractor's Plans* for construction of the building; *Manufacturing Engineering Design* for plane construction; or *Technology Models* for information systems.

In addition, there are a number of different questions – called *Primitives or Interrogatives* or *Abstractions* – that need to be considered. These are illustrated by Figure 2.

WHAT is needed is important to know. This is represented in Figure 3 by *Material*, such as *Bill of Materials* for buildings and planes, and *Data Models* for Information Systems. HOW these are used is indicated by *Functions*, such as *Functional Specifications* for buildings and planes, and *Functional Models* for Information Systems. WHERE is also important, as indicated by *Location* – in *Drawings* for building and plane construction and in *Network Models* for Information Systems.

Bringing these concepts together, the result is a Matrix of five Rows and three Columns as shown in Figure 3. These represent the perspectives for each of:

- The *Planner*, who is interested in *What*, *How* and *Where*

- The *Owner*, who is also interested in *What*, *How* and *Where*
- The *Designer*, who is interested in *What*, *How* and *Where*
- The *Builder*, who is interested in *What*, *How* and *Where* ... and
- The *Subcontractor*, who also is interested in *What*, *How* and *Where*

DIFFERENT ABSTRACTIONS

WHAT	HOW	WHERE
Material	Function	Location
Bill of Materials	Functional Specifications	Drawings
Data Models	Functional Models	Network Models

Figure 2. Different questions (called Primitives or abstractions) also need to be considered in the design and construction of buildings, airplanes and enterprise systems

	WHAT	HOW	WHERE
Planner			
Owner			
Designer			
Builder			
Subcontractor			
Final Structure			

Figure 3. There are fact five perspectives that each need to be considered, from the Perspective of: the Planner; Owner; Designer; Builder; and Subcontractor.

The last Row addresses the *Final Structure:* the final product to be produced. Further, different documentation, models or representations may also be utilized in each cell of the Zachman Framework as shown by Figure 4.

	What *Data*	How *Function*	Where *Location*
PLANNER Objectives/Scope	List of Things	List of Processes	List of Locations
OWNER Conceptual	Enterprise Model	Activity Model	Business Logistics
DESIGNER Logical	Logical Data Model	Process Model	Distrib. Architect.
BUILDER Physical	Physical Data Model	System Model	Technol. Architect.
SUBCONTRACTOR Out-of-Context	Data Definition	Program	Network Architect.
FUNCTIONING ENTERPRISE	Data	Function	Network

Figure 4: Different model representations exist in each of 15 cells to address the perspective of each row and the focus of each column

For example, reading down Column 1 – WHAT (*Data*) we see that:

- The cell formed by intersection of the Objectives / Scope row (of interest to the Planner) and the Data column shows that a "List of Things" is relevant to this cell.
- The cell intersected by the Owner row and Data column is the "Enterprise Model" – also called the Strategic Model.
- The cell for the Designer row and the Data column shows that "Logical Data Model" documentation is appropriate for this cell.
- The Builder row and Data column cell contains the "Physical Data Model"
- The Subcontractor row and Data column cell contains physical "Data Definition" scripts for installation of databases.

Reading down Column 2 – HOW (*Process*) and Column 3 – WHERE (*Network*), we also see in Figure 4 that each row in these columns has various representations in the cells for these columns as well. Several types of models may also be relevant to each cell.

For all things that we consider in business or day-to-day life – whether for buildings, for planes or for complex enterprise systems – there are in fact six independent variables. These are based on six Primitive Interrogatives: *What, How, Where, Who, When, Why.*

There are therefore a further three columns: WHO; WHEN; and WHY in the complete *Zachman Framework for Enterprise Architecture*. These questions are shown in Figure 5 by all six columns in the Zachman Framework for Enterprise Architecture.

	What Data	How Function	Where Location	Who People	When Time	Why Future
PLANNER Objectives/Scope	List of Things	List of Processes	List of Locations	Organization Structure	List of Events	List of Goals Objectives
OWNER Conceptual	Enterprise Model	Activity Model	Business Logistics	Work Flow	Master Schedule	Business Plan
DESIGNER Logical	Logical Data Model	Process Model	Distributed Architecture	Human Interface	Process Structure	Business Rules
BUILDER Physical	Physical Data Model	System Model	Technology Architecture	Presentation Interface	Control Structure	Rule Design
SUBCONTRACTOR Out-of-Context	Data Definition	Program	Network Architecture	Security Interface	Timing Definition	Rule Specifications
FUNCTIONING ENTERPRISE	Data	Function	Network	Organization	Schedule	Strategy

Figure 5. The complete Zachman Framework for Enterprise Architecture is based on a further three columns, for a total of six columns and five rows – making up 30 cells. Each cell may contain various types of models, as illustrated in this figure.

Figure 4 has in fact been expanded in Figure 5 to show examples of typical model contents for each cell. For example, the How column (Col 2) shows that an *Activity Model* is relevant to the Owner row (Row 2). As a further illustration, Col 2 Row 3 – a cell of interest to the Designer – shows that a *Process Model* is relevant for this cell.

In summary, the Framework rows therefore indicate different Views (or Perspectives) of people in the Enterprise, from the Perspectives of the: *Planner, Owner, Designer, Builder,* and *Subcontractor*. The Framework columns also address different primitive questions (also called interrogatives or abstractions) of *WHAT, HOW, WHERE, WHO, WHEN* and *WHY.*

1.1. Using the Zachman Framework for Enterprise Architecture

The focus of Enterprise Architecture ideally should be based on *Rows 1 and 2*, from the perspectives of the *Planner* and the *Owner*. These perspectives focus on the future as indicated by Column 6 (Why): representing Business Plans for the enterprise.

Clear directions can then be provided to Row 3 (for the *Designer*), Row 4 (for the *Builder*) and Row 5 (for implementation by the *Subcontractor*).

John Zachman makes the case that by addressing the six Primitives (the Interrogatives or questions of *What, How, Where, Who, When* and *Why*) very complex Composites (such as Buildings, Planes, or Enterprise Systems) can be developed. He indicates that answers to these questions (the primitives – *What, How, Where, Who, When* and *Why*) can be used to capture the knowledge that is needed to construct any complex object.

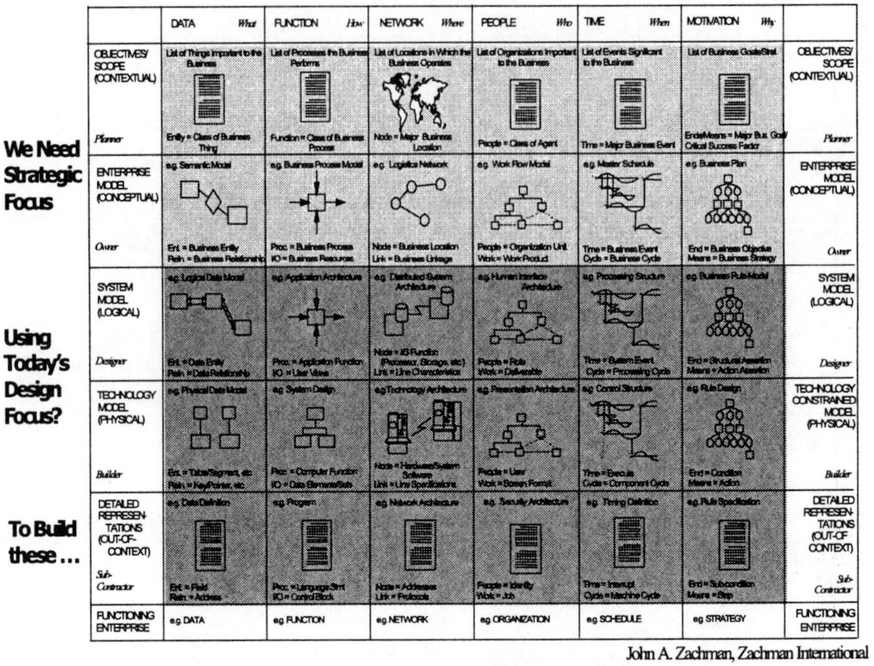

We Need Strategic Focus

Using Today's Design Focus?

To Build these...

	DATA *What*	FUNCTION *How*	NETWORK *Where*	PEOPLE *Who*	TIME *When*	MOTIVATION *Why*	
OBJECTIVES/ SCOPE (CONTEXTUAL) *Planner*	List of Things Important to the Business Entity = Class of Business Thing	List of Processes the Business Performs Function = Class of Business Process	List of Locations in Which the Business Operates Node = Major Business Location	List of Organizations Important to the Business People = Class of Agent	List of Events Significant to the Business Time = Major Business Event	List of Business Goals/Strat. Ends/Means = Major Bus. Goal/ Critical Success Factor	OBJECTIVES/ SCOPE (CONTEXTUAL) *Planner*
ENTERPRISE MODEL (CONCEPTUAL) *Owner*	e.g. Semantic Model Ent. = Business Entity Reln. = Business Relationship	e.g. Business Process Model Proc. = Business Process I/O = Business Resources	e.g. Logistics Network Node = Business Location Link = Business Linkage	e.g. Work Flow Model People = Organization Unit Work = Work Product	e.g. Master Schedule Time = Business Event Cycle = Business Cycle	e.g. Business Plan End = Business Objective Means = Business Strategy	ENTERPRISE MODEL (CONCEPTUAL) *Owner*
SYSTEM MODEL (LOGICAL) *Designer*	e.g. Logical Data Model Ent. = Data Entity Reln. = Data Relationship	e.g. Application Architecture Proc. = Application Function I/O = User Views	e.g. Distributed System Architecture Node = I/S Function (Processor, Storage, etc) Link = Line Characteristics	e.g. Human Interface Architecture People = Role Work = Deliverable	e.g. Processing Structure Time = System Event Cycle = Processing Cycle	e.g. Business Rule Model End = Structural Assertion Means = Action Assertion	SYSTEM MODEL (LOGICAL) *Designer*
TECHNOLOGY MODEL (PHYSICAL) *Builder*	e.g. Physical Data Model Ent. = Table/Segment, etc. Reln. = Key/Pointer, etc.	e.g. System Design Proc. = Computer Function I/O = Data Elements/Sets	e.g. Technology Architecture Node = Hardware/System Software Link = Line Specifications	e.g. Presentation Architecture People = User Work = Screen Format	e.g. Control Structure Time = Execute Cycle = Component Cycle	e.g. Rule Design End = Condition Means = Action	TECHNOLOGY CONSTRAINED MODEL (PHYSICAL) *Builder*
DETAILED REPRESEN-TATIONS (OUT-OF-CONTEXT) *Sub-Contractor*	e.g. Data Definition Ent. = Field Reln. = Address	e.g. Program Proc. = Language Stmt I/O = Control Block	e.g. Network Architecture Node = Addresses Link = Protocols	e.g. Security Architecture People = Identity Work = Job	e.g. Timing Definition Time = Interrupt Cycle = Machine Cycle	e.g. Rule Specification End = Sub-condition Means = Step	DETAILED REPRESEN-TATIONS (OUT-OF-CONTEXT) *Sub-Contractor*
FUNCTIONING ENTERPRISE	e.g. DATA	e.g. FUNCTION	e.g. NETWORK	e.g. ORGANIZATION	e.g. SCHEDULE	e.g. STRATEGY	FUNCTIONING ENTERPRISE

John A. Zachman, Zachman International

Figure 6. The Zachman Framework for Enterprise Architecture shows we have traditionally taken a Designer's focus in building down from Row 3. We have not typically taken the perspectives of the Planner or the Owner into account.

The complete Zachman Framework for Enterprise Architecture is illustrated now in Figure 6 showing representative models for each of the 30 cells. Traditionally, in building Enterprise Systems we have taken a bottom-up view. We have looked at the existing systems – whether manual or automated – represented by the bottom row of the framework.

From a bottom-up view, we have looked at ways in which current manual or automated systems have been implemented. We then examined ways to improve these systems: either by automating manual systems; or by using new technology to improve existing automated systems. We have taken a design focus from the perspective of Row 3 (Designer) and then moved down again to Rows 4 and 5 (Builder and Subcontractor): using different technologies to bring about the desired improvements.

However this approach is quite technical. Traditionally, it has been difficult to include the perspectives of the Owner (at Row 2) or the Planner (at Row 1).

		What Data	How Function	Where Location	Who People	When Time	Why Future
Horizontal Slice	PLANNER Objectives/Scope	List of Things	List of Processes	List of Locations	Org Structure	List of Events	List of Goals/Obj
	OWNER Conceptual	Enterprise Model	Activity Model	Business Logistics	Work Flow	Master Schedule	Business Plan
	DESIGNER Logical	Logical Data Model	Process Model	Distrib. Architect.	Human Interface	Process Structure	Business Rules
	BUILDER Physical	Physical Data Model	System Model	Technol. Architect.	Presn Interface	Control Structure	Rule Design
	SUBCONTRACTOR Out-of-Context	Data Definition	Program	Network Architect.	Security Interface	Timing Definition	Rule Specs
	FUNCTIONING ENTERPRISE	Data	Function	Network	Organization	Schedule	Strategy

Figure 7. An enterprise-wide approach is shown as a horizontal band across the width of each cell. A high-level view of the models represented within each cell is shown as a narrow "slice" for the enterprise-wide band at the top of each cell.

1.2. Identifying Reusable, Priority Areas for Early Delivery

John Zachman notes that by taking a top-down approach, Building construction and Airplane design have developed interchangeable parts that can be reused. He gives the example of standard doors and windows in buildings. He points out that: *"the Boeing 737, 747, 757 and 767 airplanes were designed so they all use a standard undercarriage. But it is hard to achieve reusability if each component is built from scratch each time."* He adds that *"the IT industry has tried to build reusable code or components by using Object-Oriented methods. But we have not been particularly successful to date. We do use O-O to build reusable components for screen design and other systems components. But we have not been very successful using O-O methods in identifying many reusable activities and processes within an enterprise."* John states that *"enterprise reusability is only achieved effectively by taking an enterprise-wide approach: not in detail across the enterprise, but broadly to encompass the whole enterprise"*.

This is illustrated in Figure 7 as horizontal "slices" in each cell. For example, a high-level view of the Business Plans for an enterprise is shown by the horizontal slice at the top of each cell for Col 6 (Why) with Row 1 (Planner), and Col 6 (Why) with Row 2 (Owner). Strategic Planning uses the method of Goal Analysis in Col 6 to identify these horizontal slices as a high-level *"List of Goals/Objectives"* and high-level *"Business Plans"*.

Similarly, these high-level plans can be used to identify high-level data that is required to implement those plans within the enterprise. Col 1 (Data) with Row 1

(Planner) in Figure 7 shows a *"List of Things"* as a high-level horizontal slice in that cell. Col 1 (Data) with Row 2 (Owner) further represents this data as an *"Enterprise Model"*. A high-level horizontal slice of an Enterprise Model – called a *Strategic Model* – is appropriate, and applies to this cell. *Strategic Modelling* is the method used to develop a Strategic Model as the horizontal slice for these two cells.

Furthermore, horizontal slices in Col 2 (How) for Row 1 (Planner) and for Row 2 (Owner) represent a high-level *"List of Processes"* and high-level *"Activity Models"*. A data model can be used to identify a List of Processes in Col 2, Row 1 as a *List of Activities.* This list is then used to identify and define Activity Models in Col 2, Row 2. Activities can be identified from data models, for further documentation as Activity Models. Other methods are used for Col 3 (Where), Col 4 (Who) and Col 5 (When): each for Rows 1 and 2.

The high-level focus of the horizontal "slice" at the top of each cell enables priority areas to be identified that need to be implemented first.

Reusability Definition

	What Data	How Function	Where Location	Who People	When Time	Why Future
PLANNER Objectives/Scope	List of Things	List of Processes	List of Locations	Org Structure	List of Events	List of Goals/Obj
			Reusability Definition			
OWNER Conceptual	Enterprise Model Key	Activity Model Key	Business Logistics Key	Work Flow Key	Master Schedule Key	Business Plan Key
DESIGNER Logical	Logical Data Model	Process Model	Distrib. Architect.	Human Interface	Process Structure	Business Rules
BUILDER Physical	Physical Data Model	System Model	Technol. Architect.	Presn Interface	Control Structure	Rule Design
SUBCONTRACTOR Out-of-Context	Data Definition	Program	Network Architect.	Security Interface	Timing Definition	Rule Specs
FUNCTIONING ENTERPRISE	Data	Function	Network	Organization	Schedule	Strategy

Figure 8. Rows 1 and 2 are used for Reusability Definition. A number of cells are Key to identifying enterprise-wide Reusability Opportunities.

Rows 1 and 2 – from the perspectives of the Planner and the Owner – are critical. These two rows are used to identify reusability opportunities within an enterprise. Figure 8 highlights these two rows of the Zachman Framework. A number of cells in these rows are also vitally important. *Business Plans* in Col 6 (Why) are *Key* to setting directions for the future. Col 4 (Who) identifies the *Organization Structure* in Row 1. This is also *Key,* as it enables key managers to identify relative priorities based on the Business Plans. Col 5 (*When*) shows that a *List of Events* and the *Master Schedule* are also Key. Recent Enterprise Architecture projects have shown that the use of Business Events is a powerful way to identify enterprise-wide Reusability Opportunities.

The Business Plans from Col 6 are used to develop a high-level *Strategic Model* in Col 1 (Data). This is a *Key* cell as it is vital in identifying high-level data and information that are needed to manage the progress of the enterprise towards the future. Activity Models in Col 2 (How) are also vital: these Activity Models are *Key* to identifying critical activities that should be carried out by the enterprise in the future. Col 3 (Where) is important, as the Business Logistics of the enterprise are also *Key.*

John Zachman discusses that *"Enterprise Architecture is used for the management of Enterprise Change."* In fact, *"if Enterprise Architecture is not used",* he says, *"there are only three Options for Managing Enterprise Change: by Trail and Error; by Reverse Engineering; or by Going Out of Business!"*

2. THE EVOLUTION OF ENTERPRISES INTO THE INFORMATION AGE

We are at a dramatic and historical point of convergence: in technology and in business. The Internet and associated technologies today enable the customers, suppliers and business partners of an enterprise all to work together at electronic speeds. These technologies are transforming organizations. Processes that took days or weeks to complete previously by using mail, fax and courier communication ... now take hours, minutes, and sometimes even seconds. This is the direct consequence of Technology.

Technology alone is not the answer. To achieve any degree of success in Enterprise Integration requires that Technology Integration be used within a coherent, integrated enterprise, through Business Integration. But we still have a long way to go in most enterprises to realize Business Integration.

To appreciate what still has to be achieved, we need to review what I call the *"Process Engineering Bible".* I describe the book in this way as it has had a dramatic effect in the way that organizations function. To consider its impact, we need to review its message. But first:

- What is its title?
- Who was the author?
- When was it published?

Perhaps we can identify the book by first considering its author:

- Was it Michael Hammer or James Champy: of *Reengineering the Corporation*[1] fame? No, it was neither of them.
- Was it Ken Orr,[2] Ed Yourdon[3] or Tom de Marco[4]: of *Software Engineering* fame? No, it was not them either.
- Well, was it Peter Drucker: of *Management*[5] and *Strategic Planning*[6] fame? No, not him.
- Was it Edwards Demming: of *Quality Control* fame? No, not him either.

- Was it Alfred Sloan, or Henry Ford? No, the book I am referring to was published long before all of these eminent people.

So which book am I talking about? As soon as I give you the author and its title – with its publication date – its significance will become apparent. The reference is as follows:

- Adam Smith, *Wealth of Nations,* (1776)[7]

This was one of the most influential books at the start of the Industrial Age. It described the evolution from the Agricultural Age to the Industrial Age. It was the foundation for most industrial enterprises in the late 18th Century and into the 19th Century.

2.1. Transition from the Agricultural Age to the Industrial Age

To understand the importance of Adam Smith's *Wealth of Nations*, we will review part of the first chapter. Box 1 provides an extract from Chapter 1 of Book One. Its language is unusual today. I have included part of the initial paragraphs; to help readability I have added comments in brackets to indicate the terminology that we use today to describe the same concepts.

Box 1: Extract from Adam Smith's "Wealth of Nations"

EXTRACT FROM BOOK ONE: *"Of the Causes of Improvement In the Productive Powers Of Labour, and of the Order According to which its Produce is Naturally Distributed Among the Different Ranks of the People."*

CHAPTER 1: *"Of the Division of Labour"*

"... To take an example, therefore, from a very trifling manufacture; but one in which the division of labour has been very often taken notice of, the trade of the pin-maker ... a workman ... could scarce ... make one pin in a day, and certainly could not make twenty. (In today's terminology he is referring to: *serial operation.*)

But in the way in which this business is now carried on, not only the whole work is a peculiar trade, but it is divided into a number of branches, of which the greater part are likewise peculiar trades. (In today's terminology this refers to: *object-oriented methods.*)

One man draws out the wire, another straights it, a third cuts it, a fourth points it, a fifth grinds it at the top for receiving the head; to make the head requires two or three distinct operations (object-oriented encapsulation)*; to put it on is a peculiar business, to whiten the pins is another; it is even a trade by itself to put them into the paper; and the important business of making a pin is ... divided into about eighteen distinct operations ...* (object-oriented methods)

I have seen a small manufactory of this kind where ten men only were employed ... they could, when they exerted themselves, make among them about twelve pounds of pins in a day ... upwards of forty-eight thousand pins in a day. Each person, therefore ... might be considered as making four thousand eight hundred pins in a day. (object-oriented reusability)

But if they had all wrought separately and independently... they certainly could not each of them have made twenty, perhaps not one pin in a day (serial operation) *... ; that is, certainly, not ... the four thousand eight hundredth part of what they are at present capable of performing, in consequence of a proper division and combination of their different operations.* (object-oriented reusability) ... "

The principles that Adam Smith advocated broke complex processes into simpler process steps. He showed by using technologies available in his day – an illiterate workforce – that people could be trained to carry out each step repetitively. In this way they were able to achieve much higher levels of productivity that if one worker carried out each step in turn. Smith showed that component steps could also be combined in different ways for new, improved processes. These are the same concepts that we still use today for *Reusability*, using *Object-Oriented methods*.

Adam Smith's breakthrough was the foundation for late 18th Century – early 19th Century Industrial Enterprises. With the focus mainly on manufacturing physical items, this period also saw the same concepts applied to knowledge-based processes for Bank Loans and for Insurance Policy Applications. Instead of manufacturing steps, a Loan Application or a Policy Application approval process was broken down into discrete steps to be carried out by different people: each skilled in assessing an aspect of the relevant application. Each process step was carried out in a defined sequence: the step was completed before the next step in sequence was started. The result was the definition of *serial processes*.

As the Application Form was routed to each person in the Approval Process, details of the relevant applicant and the current status of the process were recorded in hand-written ledgers; these were called the Applicant Ledger, or the Customer Ledger. Each person involved in carrying out a process step kept an individual record of every Applicant or Customer that worker had processed, and the stage the Applicant had reached in the Approval Process.

The 20th Century saw an improvement in these process steps with introduction by Henry Ford of the *Assembly Line* method of automobile manufacture. The vehicle being built physically moved along each section of the assembly line, where different components were added in each step of the assembly process.

This period also saw the introduction of *parallel processes*: two or more processes could be carried out concurrently, with each process step executed independently of other process steps. An example is the parallel construction of the body of the automobile, while the engine is also constructed. Each parallel process path is thus independent of the other parallel paths, until they need to converge. Only when the automobile has to be driven off the assembly line does the engine have to be fitted into the car.

By the middle of the 20th Century, the Industrial Enterprise had evolved into a complex series of manual processes. The pace of progress had seen most enterprises evolve to use increasingly complex business processes, with rapidly growing transaction volumes to be manually processed. And what was the result?

"These enterprises found they were operating in a continual state of Manual Chaos!"

Then the computer came on the scene in the second half of the 20th Century

2.2. Transition from the Industrial Age to the Information Age

Starting from the late 1950s – through the 60s, 70s, and right up to today – we have seen manual processes being automated by computer. What was the result? The processes were automated, but we took the existing manual processes and then automated them essentially AS-IS: without much change. That is, the automated processes were being executed as for the manual processes, but faster, and more accurately.

"In so doing, we moved from Manual Chaos ... instead to Automated Chaos!"

Enterprises tried to hide this automated chaos. Through to the mid-90s, most enterprises could confine their automated chaos in the back office. Instead they presented a calm, in-control, front-office appearance to the outside world. They tried to emulate the graceful swan, gliding effortlessly across the surface of a glass-like lake with no apparent effort. The furious paddling activity – trying to move ahead – was hidden below the surface.

But with rapid acceptance of the Internet in the second half of the 90s the chaos moved from the back office ... onto the front doorstep of enterprises: through their web sites.

"Customers could visit these enterprises by the click of a mouse. But they could just as quickly leave with the click of a mouse if they did not find what they needed!"

The reason they left is not because of what the automated processes could do; rather, they left because the processes did not provide what the customers needed.

This was because redundant processes and redundant data, by their definition, are non-integrated. Another term for non-integration is *Disintegration.* That is, by automation most enterprises had evolved from non-integrated manual processes to *disintegrated automated processes.*

The problem is much worse than this! Most automated processes today assume that the technologies of the past still apply. The manual processes that they automate required paper-based forms that were mailed, or later faxed. So their automated counterparts are based on forms that are also printed to be mailed or faxed. On receipt at their destination, the data in these forms are manually reentered into relevant systems: with manual work; with extra staffing to do that reentry; with delays; with errors; and with associated costs.

We will later see how printed forms can be automatically converted into electronic forms using the Extensible Markup Language (XML), and then transmitted electronically to receiving applications within an enterprise, or between enterprises. This is Enterprise Application Integration (EAI). It replaces mail transmission and manual reentry, paper-based systems that were designed for completion over weeks or days. These are replaced instead with electronic systems that can inter-communicate within minutes or seconds – anywhere in the world.

The problem is that automated systems that assume inter-communication with printed forms and manual reentry over weeks and days do not work well when asked to inter-communicate with electronic forms that bypass the need for manual reentry – and that complete in minutes, or seconds. What is the basic reason for this dichotomy?

"Today we have 21st Century Enterprises that utilize 21st Century Technologies ... yet most enterprises today still use 18th Century Disintegrated Business Processes!"

The business processes – originally designed based on principles set by Adam Smith in 1776 – have not evolved to take advantage of the technologies we have available today. This is a Business problem; not a Technology problem. It requires business decisions. It requires business expertise. These are the basic ingredients for Business Integration.

This paper shows how Business Integration is realized by Enterprise Architecture. But the architects of an enterprise cannot be found in its IT Department. This leads us to two important principles:

1. Enterprise Architects are the senior managers who set the directions for the future, based on processes designed for that future and its technologies. For the future cannot be based on 18th Century business processes that no longer respond to the rapid-change environment of today ... and even greater change tomorrow.
2. The future will be based on business processes that use the technologies of today and tomorrow to complete in minutes and seconds what previously took days and weeks ... with strategic directions set by senior management, and with business experts and IT experts working together in a design partnership

Using Enterprise Architecture and Enterprise Engineering, business experts and IT experts together identify reusable business activities, reusable business processes and integrated databases for Business Integration. These take advantage of the latest technologies for Technology Integration. And what is the result?

Integrated 21st Century Enterprises with Integrated 21st Century Processes!

Enterprise Architecture and Enterprise Engineering achieve Business Integration in the enterprise for more effective Technology Integration. Before we examine these further, we first need to review the evolution of *Systems Development Methodologies* in the Information Age.

3. THE EVOLUTION OF SYSTEMS DEVELOPMENT METHODOLOGIES

Methodologies evolved from the start of the Information Age to help us examine current manual processes so we could automate them. From rudimentary methodologies in the 1960s, by the 1970s these had evolved into the Software Engineering methods. Michael Jackson,[8] Ken Orr, Ed Yourdon, Tom de Marco and others were key originators of the *Software Engineering* methodologies: also called the *Structured Methods.*

3.1. The Evolution of Software Engineering

These methods analyzed current manual processes, documenting them with Data Flow Diagrams (DFDs) and Functional Decomposition Diagrams (FDDs). The structure of modular programs to automate these processes was documented using Structure Charts (SCs). Programs were then written in various programming languages to execute the automated processes.

As discussed, in automating manual processes *AS-IS*, we moved from manual chaos to automated chaos. This was due to the fact that common manual processes, used in various parts of the enterprise, had often evolved in quite different ways. For example, a process to manually accept an order (an *Order Entry Process*) may be carried out differently according to how the order was received: by mail; or by phone; or instead from a salesperson. The Order Entry Process may also be carried out differently depending on the specific products or services that were ordered. The result was the evolution of different manual processes, all intended to achieve the same objective: *Accept an Order for Processing*. When these manual processes were automated, we found we also had many automated Order Entry Processes, all intended to Accept an

Order for Processing. We had lost sight of the principle of *Reusability*, first identified by Adam Smith in Box 1.

This added to the automated chaos: when a change had to be made to a process, the same change had to be made to every version of that process throughout the enterprise. Every program that automated the different versions of the process had to be changed, often in slightly different ways.

> *The result was also chaos: Program Maintenance Chaos!*

With Software Engineering, each DFD that was defined for a process identified the data that it needed: as *Data Stores*. Each different version of the same process resulted in a different data store version of required data. Redundant data versions were implemented for each automated process. In fact, we earlier saw this problem start to emerge with the 19th Century industrial enterprise: we discussed that Insurance and Bank workers each kept a separate hand-written Applicant Ledger or Customer Ledger to answer queries. What was the result?

> *With these redundant data versions, we moved to Data Maintenance Chaos!*

Whenever a change had to be made to data values for maintenance purposes, such as by changing a customer's address, every version of that address had to be changed. This was redundant data maintenance processing. It required redundant staffing to do this redundant work. And because redundant data maintenance programs were developed independently, these data maintenance workers also had to be trained in the different operating procedures that were used for data entry by each redundant data maintenance program. This resulted in redundant training.

> *All of these are redundant costs that are regularly incurred by every enterprise today: in redundant data maintenance costs for redundant data value changes; and also in redundant staffing and redundant training to carry out this redundant work. These are all redundant costs. They negatively affect the bottom line – in reduced profits for Commercial enterprises, or in reduced cost-effectiveness for Government or Defence enterprises.*

3.2. The Evolution of Information Engineering

In this same period – from the late 60s through the early 70s – Edgar Codd, a Research Fellow at IBM San Jose Labs, developed the Relational Model from mathematical set theory.[9] This was the foundation of the *Relational Data Base* technology that we still use today. The first *Relational Data Base Management* (RDBMS) systems were released by IBM Corporation (IBM DB2 RDBMS) and by Oracle Corporation (Oracle RDBMS) in the late 70s and early 80s.

From the mid 70s, three approaches emerged to apply concepts of the Relational Model to the methods that were used for *Data Base Design*. One approach was developed in UK and Europe; another approach was developed in the USA; and a third approach was developed independently in Australia. Each addressed development of Data Modelling methods, using *Normalization* to eliminate redundant data versions.[10–13]

The Australian approach also evolved into integrated methods for information, using a rigorous engineering discipline, called: *Information Engineering (IE)*. Originally developed by Clive Finkelstein,[14] IE was popularized world-wide throughout the 1980s by James Martin.[15] Further books showed the use of Business-Driven Information Engineering.[16, 17] This evolved into what is today called: *Enterprise Engineering*. This paper provides an overview of the latest Enterprise Engineering methods used for Enterprise Architecture.

3.3. The Evolution of Object-Oriented Methods

In the late 1980s, the concepts of Object-Oriented (O-O) development and the Unified Modelling Language (UML) were developed by Grady Booch,[18, 19] James Rumbaugh[20] and Ivar Jacobson.[21, 22] Object-Oriented methods based on UML were found to be very effective in developing reusable code. They use a number of diagrams to model various aspects for O-O development. Relevant diagrams are: *Class Diagrams; State Transition Diagrams: Use-CASE Diagrams: Sequence Diagrams; Collaboration Diagrams;* and *Activity Diagrams.*

Booch, Rumbaugh and Jacobson established Rational Corporation to develop associated UML modelling tools. They popularized UML and the Rational Software tools, which became widely used in the late 1990s. When IBM purchased Rational Corporation in early 2003 Rational and its various software tools became a subsidiary of IBM.[23]

3.4. Enterprise Engineering Evolution for Enterprise Architecture

Following the earlier introduction to Enterprise Architecture, we will look at systems development problems. The typical approach used to design and build enterprise systems with traditional systems development methods is summarized below:

- Systems Requirements have typically been defined by IT staff, by interviewing users to determine their operational business needs.
- The designs that are established are then based on Technology, with Application Design, Database Design and Object Design reflecting that technology.
- The technology is used to deliver the desired business benefits.
- These designs are then implemented to meet desired business Performance Requirements.

This traditional approach to Systems Development has been *Technology-Dependent*, as illustrated in Figure 9.

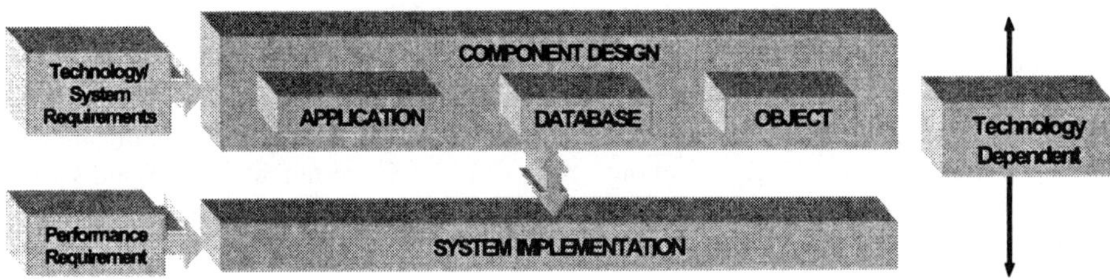

Figure 9. Traditional Systems Development methods interview users to determine operational business needs. Specific technologies have then been used to develop the required systems. This approach is Technology-Dependent.

This traditional approach to Systems Development has resulted in problems:

- The *Business Needs* have been difficult to determine. If these needs are not understood or expressed clearly, the designed systems may not address the real needs of the users and management.
- The systems that are developed are typically not aligned with corporate goals that set directions for the future. This is one of the main problems with systems development today.
- But the strategic directions are not clear; yet they must be understood if IT is to design flexible systems that support the strategic directions.

In fact, problems with traditional development methods are much greater than suggested above. The business needs have traditionally been decided by reviewing the operational processes of the business. These processes were determined based on strategic plans typically defined many years ago, sometimes even a decade ago.

Yet in the early 90s we had no idea – not even in our wildest predictions of the future – that we would today be able to communicate instantly with customers, suppliers and business partners anywhere in the world, through the Internet. The environment that we accept today as the norm was way beyond our most fanciful imagination a decade ago.

The strategic plans defined in the 90s did not anticipate that these organizations would today communicate with each other in seconds. They assumed communication would be as it had always been, by mail – or later by fax – with responses received days or weeks later. The most rapid response these business processes assumed was at best in hours. The business processes we still use today were never designed to respond in seconds. This point is critical: *"The traditional systems development approach – interviewing users based on existing business processes and then identifying their future needs – does not work well in periods of rapid change, such as today."* I will make this point even stronger. *"If we base our needs for the future on operational processes that we still use today – we are implicitly assuming that the future will be similar to the past. This is dangerous; very few industries and enterprises can say today that their future will be like their past. Most know that the future will be different. The only certainty we have is that the processes we need then will be quite different from the processes we use today."*

This brings us to a very important principle for change:

> ***We must design for tomorrow based not on operational processes still used today. We have to design for tomorrow by using new activities and processes tailored for the environment of the Internet – which represents our present and our future – so that enterprises can respond in seconds or minutes, not in days or weeks.***

Enterprise Engineering is designed to provide support for a future where *the only thing that remains constant … is change itself.* Businesses must change, to compete with other organizations in their relevant markets. This is true for Commercial organizations, which compete with other organizations. It is true for Government Departments that compete with other departments for government funding. And it is also true for Defence, which competes with hostile Defence forces, and also with friendly Defence forces for limited resources.

Competition today demands systems that can change easily to support rapid business change. Many of these business changes may need significant change or redevelopment of systems. Yet most of those systems were not designed for change. Existing systems may need massive modification to support essential business changes. Often it is faster to throw the existing systems away and start over again: developing new systems from scratch. This can be slow and very costly.

The advantages and benefits of Technology were not clear in the early 90s to many senior managers. It was sometimes difficult to get funding approval for new projects and funding for the resources that are vital for success. But the Internet and the Year 2000 problem in the late 90s both demonstrated to management the dramatic impact that Technology can have on the enterprise.

We discussed earlier that we have taken a bottom-up view with traditional methods in building systems for the enterprise. We looked at the existing systems – whether manual or automated – as represented by the bottom row of the Zachman Framework for Enterprise Architecture.

From a bottom-up view, we looked at ways in which current manual or automated systems have been implemented. We then examined ways to improve these systems: either by automating manual systems; or by using technology to improve existing automated systems.

As discussed with Figure 6, we have taken a design focus from the perspective of Row 3 (Designer) using traditional methods, and then moved down again to Rows 4 and 5 (for Builder and Subcontractor): using technologies to bring about the desired improvements. We saw that this approach is quite technical. Traditionally, it has been difficult to include the perspectives of the Owner (at Row 2) or the Planner (at Row 1).

How can we address these problems and involve the Planner and the Owner in setting directions for the future? We will now consider solutions to these problems that have resulted from the traditional approach to Systems Development:

- The Systems that are to be developed for the future must support the corporate goals. This is the most common systems development problem today.
- We must therefore determine the goals for the future. But goals are expressed in business terms, not in systems terms. How can we determine what to implement?
- We earlier discussed that IT Departments must be aware of strategic directions so they can design for the future. This is difficult, as most IT Departments do not participate in Strategic Planning.
- Yet we have seen that IT must build systems based on strategic plans if those systems are to be aligned with corporate goals. They must be based on activities and processes designed for the future, not the past.
- If this is done, Technology can then offer competitive advantage: it can be used to help achieve the strategic plans and corporate goals, with new activities and processes that respond in seconds or minutes – not in days or weeks.

Enterprise Engineering resolves many of these problems with Systems Development today.[24] It enables Business Experts and IT experts to work together in a Design Partnership – using Enterprise Engineering along with CASE (Computer Aided Software Engineering) Modelling Tools. Enterprise Engineering is supported by: *Enterprise Architecture; Business Re-Engineering; Forward Engineering;* and *Reverse Engineering.* These business-driven methods are used by Business Experts and IT Experts to:

- Build Systems for the future that can support the corporate goals.

- Identify goals for the future in business terms, so that IT can determine what to implement in systems terms.
- Enterprise Engineering provides strategic business planning methods so that the IT Department can participate in Strategic Planning with management.
- Enterprise Engineering enables IT to build systems based on the Strategic Plans so that those systems are aligned with corporate goals.
- Technology can then offer competitive advantage – used to help achieve the strategic plans and corporate goals.

We will now examine the Business-Driven Enterprise Engineering methodologies in more detail. These methods support all phases of the Systems Development Life Cycle (SDLC). Figure 10 illustrates that Phases above the line are *Technology-Independent* methods and focus on the business. They apply to Rows 1 – 3 (Planner, Owner and Designer) of the Zachman Framework. These methods are *Strategic Business Planning, Data Modelling* and *Function Modelling*:

- The *Strategic Directions* set by management provide input to *Strategic Business Planning*. These are addressed in Col 6 of the Zachman Framework.
- These plans indicate the *Information Requirements* of management that are input to *Data Modelling* in Col 1: Strategic; Tactical; and Operational Data Modelling.
- Plans and data models define *Information Usage* as input to *Function Modelling:* for *Activity Modelling; Scenario Modelling;* and *Process Modelling* in Col 2.

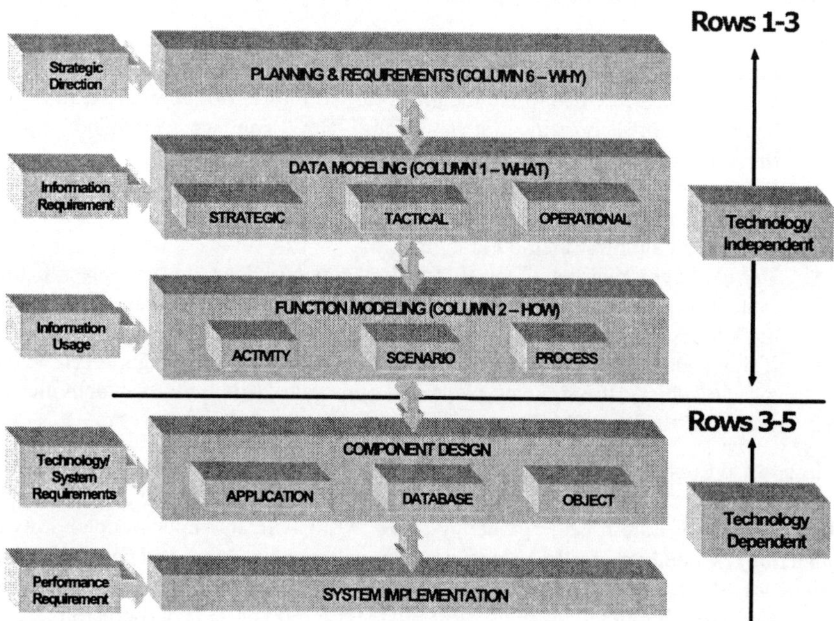

Figure 10. Enterprise Engineering supports all rows of the Zachman Framework, with rapid implementation of priority Enterprise Architecture areas.

The above phases of Figure 10 define Technology-Independent business requirements and address Enterprise Architecture Rows 1-3. Phases below the line in Figure 10 are *Technology-Dependent* and address the Enterprise Architecture Rows 3-5 (for Designer, Builder and Subcontractor). These methods address *Component Design* and *Systems Implementation*:

- *Technology and Systems Requirements* of the business provide input to Systems Design. Internet technologies and Object-Oriented methods in this phase are used for Application Design, Data Base Design and Object Design of systems to be deployed on corporate Intranets and/or the Internet.
- Identified *Performance Requirements* then provide the input required by the Systems Implementation phase.

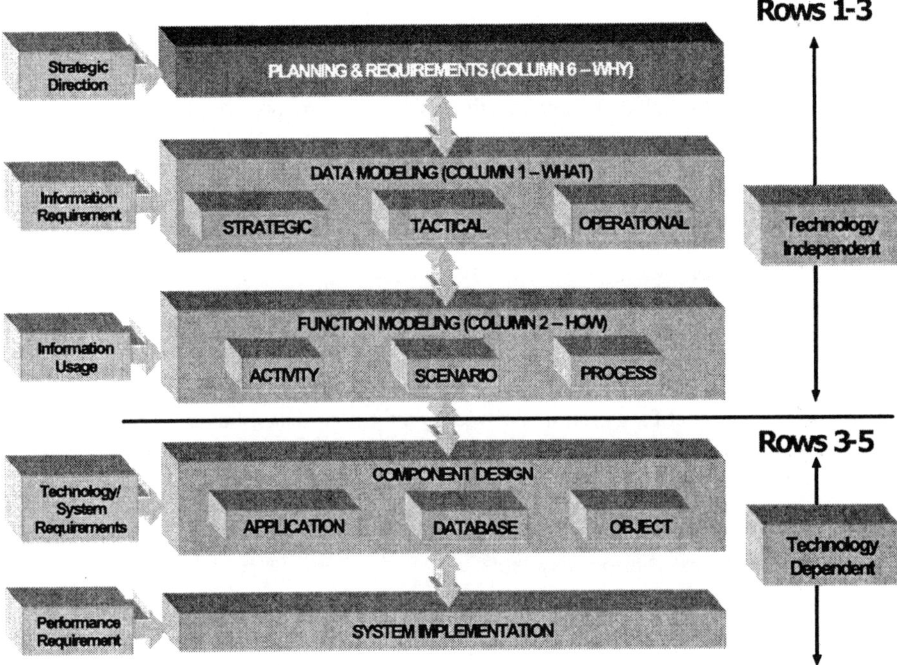

Figure 11: Strategic Business Planning Methods Address Enterprise Planning and Requirements for the Future

Figure 11 shows the first Enterprise Engineering phase: *Strategic Business Planning.* This identifies *Planning & Requirements* in the figure above. It determines the needs of the enterprise for the future. These Strategic Plans are represented by Column 6 (Why) in the Zachman Framework.

Strategic Business Planning (in Col 6) uses the Enterprise Engineering method of *Goal Analysis* to determine Strategic Plans for the future. Goal Analysis is used to:

- Identify goals from existing Strategic Plans, so that a clear understanding can be reached of the business needs of the enterprise.
- Help develop business goals (where they do not yet exist) – or refine any goals that already exist – to ensure that business results are clearly stated.
- Help develop project goals from business goals – or refine any project goals that already exist – to ensure that the business results and the project results can be clearly expressed and define what the project must achieve.
- Consider alternative technologies to be used for implementation. Some of these technologies include: Enterprise Application Integration (EAI); Enterprise Portals; XML and Web Services.

These strategic planning methods all provide input to systems development. Knowledge of Strategic Business Planning methods and terminology through Goal Analysis helps IT experts and Business experts understand the business goals and priorities for Strategic and Tactical Business Plans. It helps in determining the business and technical critical issues. Goal Analysis helps IT experts and Business experts to communicate with senior managers who are the Corporate and Technical Decision-makers.

Knowledge of strategic business planning methods and terminology through the use of Goal Analysis also helps IT experts and Business experts provide technology input to the business plans:

- Goal Analysis is used to guide an organization's Technology agenda. It identifies priorities for early delivery. In conjunction with the other Enterprise Engineering methods, it supports a powerful rapid-delivery capability for large organizations.
- After Goal Analysis, Strategic Modelling methods use Business Plans to develop a Strategic Model. This is then used to develop a Strategic Information Systems Plan (SISP) for project planning.
- For Enterprise Architecture, this SISP is called the *Enterprise Architecture Plan (EAP).* Project Plans can be derived directly from data models, using the method of Entity Dependency Cluster Analysis. This will enable us to derive required Project Plans for Enterprise Architecture implementation. We then use Technology for significant Competitive Advantage.
- Finally, Goal Analysis, when used with Enterprise Engineering, leads to the early delivery of priority systems.

Looking at the Data Modelling phase in more detail in Figure 12, Strategic Business Planning identifies the *Information Requirements* of management and provides input to this phase:

- Strategic Business Plans provide input to Strategic Modelling, to develop a strategic data model, called a *Strategic Model.*
- Analysis of the Strategic Model produces a Strategic Information Systems Plan, called an Enterprise Architecture Plan – EAP – as discussed above.
- The Strategic Model, the EAP and Tactical Business Plans all provide input to tactical data modelling, to develop *Tactical Models*.
- The EAP, Tactical Models and Operational Business Plans also provide input to operational data modelling, to develop *Operational Models.*

- *Data Modelling* and *Business Normalisation* methods are used to develop Strategic Data Models, Tactical Data Models and Operational Data Models.

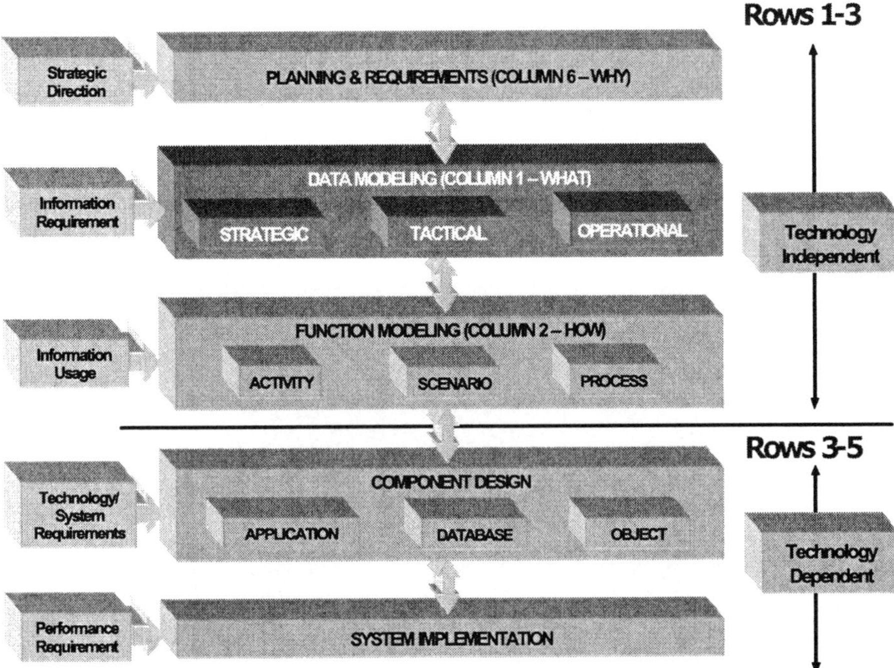

Figure 12. Data Modelling Methods identify Strategic, Tactical and Operational Data and Information needed for the Future based on the Business Plans.

Data Modelling is used to develop a Strategic Model from Strategic Plans for the rapid development of high-level business data models. These data models are used to develop project plans to deliver high-priority and high Return-on-Investment (ROI) systems early.

Data modelling also helps to identify various alternatives, leading to business benefits. This provides business justification for Technology alternatives, funding approval for the Technology and resources for implementation.

The Enterprise Architecture Plan (EAP) is one deliverable from Strategic Modelling and Strategic Data Model Analysis. This establishes clear project plans for priority projects. It leads to detailed development of approved projects. Tactical and operational data models then define data bases in detail, ready for implementation.

Function Modelling in Figure 13 addresses Col 2 (How) of the Zachman Framework. It is based on the *Information Usage* of management, as determined by the Strategic Plans defined by Goal Analysis (in Col 6 – Why). *Information Requirements* of management (from data models in Col 1 - What) also provide input to Function Modelling.

Function Modelling includes the methods of:

- *Activity Modelling:* that indicates *What has to be Done* to provide the required information to management. Activity models address Col 2 (How) in Rows 1 and 2 (for Planner and Owner).
- *Process Modelling:* that indicates *How Processes are to be Carried Out*, based on required Activities. This address Col 2 (How) in Rows 2 and 3 (for Owner and Designer).
- *Scenario Modelling:* that indicates *Who is Involved* in Activities and Processes. It identifies people from the Organization Structure (in Col 4 – Who, Row 1 – Planner).

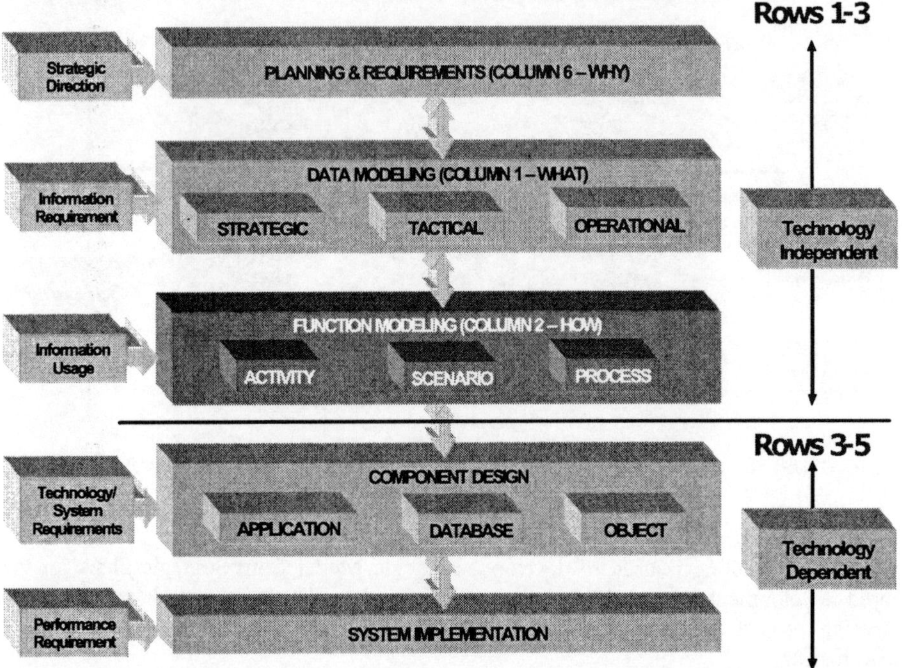

Figure 13. Function Modelling is used to model business activities, business processes and business scenarios that ensure the enterprise can change rapidly to accommodate business changes in competition or in the environment.

Function Modelling is used to model business activities as Activity Models (also using Activity Based Costing), and as Process Models that define business processes. It aligns activities and processes to strategic plans to support corporate goals, project goals and system goals. It is used for development of approved projects, to define business objects for Object-Oriented (O-O) development, for XML development, and for XML Repositories. Function Modelling ensures systems can change rapidly.

In the discussion of the Component Design Phase of Enterprise Engineering above, we saw the typical approach that has been used to design and build enterprise systems previously with traditional systems development methods. This used the following steps:

- *Systems Requirements* were typically defined by IT staff, based on interviewing users to find out their operational business needs.
- The designs that were established were based on Technology, with Application Design, Database Design and Object Design reflecting that technology. The technology was then used to deliver the desired business benefits.
- These designs were then implemented to meet desired business *Performance Requirements*.
- We discussed that these traditional approaches to Systems Development are all *Technology-Dependent*.
- We saw that using traditional Systems Development methods in the rapid change environment of today is dangerous: these methods are based on the operational processes used today: these processes typically reflect the past, not the future.

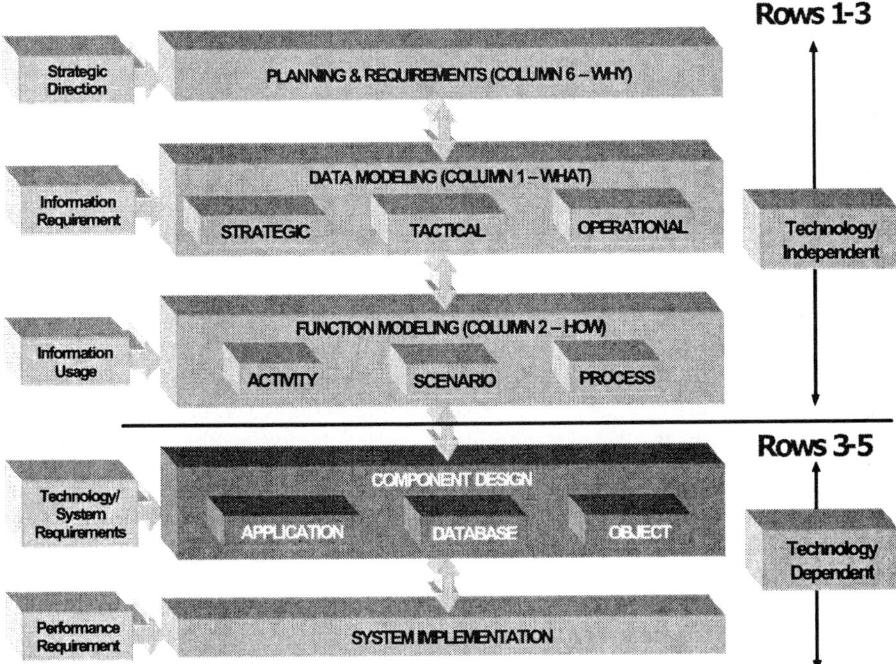

Figure 14. Component Design can be completed with a better understanding of the business needs for the future, from the earlier Enterprise Engineering Phases.

However by using the prior *Technology-Independent* phases of Enterprise Engineering, Figure 14 shows that the business needs for the future are now clearly defined from Strategic Plans and Business Plans as a result of:

- *Goal Analysis:* to define Strategic Business Plans for the future.
- *Data Modelling:* to develop Strategic, Tactical and Operational Data Models.
- *Function Modelling:* using Activity Modelling and Activity Based Costing, Process Modelling and Scenario Modelling.

The business priorities are now clearly defined from business needs and project plans. The data models are now fully developed at strategic, tactical and operational levels to address future needs. Activity models and process models are now fully developed, with business processes defined as business objects for future needs and environments. Technology is used for rapid development, with technologies such as Enterprise Portals, EAI, XML, and Web Services. This is summarized in Box 2.

Box 2: Enterprise Engineering for Enterprise Architecture

The use of Enterprise Engineering methods for Enterprise Architecture results in rapid definition of a Strategic Model for an enterprise – typically over 2 days – in a facilitated modelling session with business experts of relevant project areas of the enterprise.

From a Strategic Model defined in a 2-day facilitated modelling session, a Strategic Information Systems Plan (SISP) is developed as an Enterprise Architecture Plan (EAP): typically in a total of 4 weeks. This includes the 2-day facilitated modelling session for development of the strategic model. The EAP identifies priority Enterprise Architecture areas for rapid delivery and implementation.

The EAP is developed using Data Model Entity Dependency Cluster Analysis and Project Planning methods. These Project Plans are the basis for later development of: Tactical and Operational Data Models (in Col 1); and Activity Models and Process Models (in Col 2) of the Zachman Framework. This leads to rapid implementation of priority systems for the priority project areas. With this analysis and the technologies, priority project areas can typically be delivered into production in 3 month increments.

We will complete this section with a summary of business-driven Enterprise Engineering.

4. SUMMARY OF ENTERPRISE ENGINEERING

Enterprise Engineering supports all phases of the Systems Development Life Cycle (SDLC). Phases above the line of Figure 14 are *Technology-Independent* and focus on the business. These are Strategic Business Planning, Data Modelling and Function Modelling:

- The Strategic Directions set by management provide input to Strategic Business Planning (Col 6).
- These plans indicate the Information Requirements of management and provide input to Data Modelling (Col 1).
- Based on the Organization Structure (Col 4, Row 1), managers identify priority areas for early delivery.
- The business plans, data models and priorities identify Information Usage and are input to Function Modelling: for Activity Modelling; Scenario Modelling; and Process Modelling (Col 2).

The phases above the line in Figure 14 each define *Technology-Independent* business requirements that address Enterprise Architecture Rows 1-3.

The Designer (Row 3) takes a transitional perspective. The identified needs of the Planner and Owner (Rows 1 and 2) are expressed so they can be implemented by the Builder and Subcontractor (Rows 4 and 5) using relevant technology.

The phases below the line in Figure 14 are all *Technology-Dependent*. They address Enterprise Architecture Rows 3-5: as determined in Row 3. These are the Component Design and Systems Implementation phases:

- Technology and Systems Requirements of the business provide business input to Systems Design. Internet technologies are used in this phase for Application Design, Data Base Design and Object Design of systems to be deployed on corporate Intranets and/or the Internet.
- Identified Performance Requirements then provide input required by the Systems Implementation phase.

Summarizing Enterprise Engineering used with the Zachman Framework, the preferred way to implement for the needs of future follows:

- The focus of Enterprise Architecture ideally should be based on *Rows 1 and 2*, from the perspectives of the *Planner* and the *Owner*. These perspectives focus on the future as indicated by Column 6 (Why): which represents the Business Plans for the future.
- Clear directions can then be provided to Row 3 (for the *Designer*), Row 4 (for the *Builder*) and Row 5 (for implementation by the *Subcontractor*).
- The result is development of flexible systems based on the needs of the future, to be implemented rapidly using Object-Oriented methods and Internet technologies and tools.

5. USING ENTERPRISE ARCHITECTURE FOR ENTERPRISE INTEGRATION

At the start of this paper we discussed *that Enterprise Integration* depends on *Business Integration* and also *Technology Integration*. Business Integration is achieved through the use of Enterprise Architecture and related Enterprise Engineering methods. Technology Integration is achieved with the use of XML, EAI, Web Services and Enterprise Portals. We will now discuss some of the implications of Business Integration. We will then look at technologies that assist with Technology Integration.

5.1. The Importance of Metadata

Enterprise Integration is critically dependent on clear definition of the *Metadata* used in an enterprise. We will see below that knowledge of metadata is critical for both Business Integration and Technology Integration. When asked to define the meaning of metadata, most IT experts respond with a definition of: *"data about data"*, or *"information about information"*.

These definitions are meaningless to non-technical business managers: they do not even begin to explain the meaning of metadata; let alone its vital importance for Enterprise Integration, Business Integration and Technology Integration. Yet clear definition of the metadata of an enterprise – referred to as *Enterprise Metadata* – is vital for success in each of these integration endeavors. A better definition of metadata is provided by the following non-technical analogy in Box 3.

Box 3: A Non-Technical Introduction to Metadata

Consider how we communicate by phone. As all countries are interconnected by the global phone network, we can dial any number at random and a phone will likely ring somewhere in the world. However if the person who answers it speaks a different language, communication may not be possible. But by using an Interpreter for each pair of languages (or instead a Translation Dictionary), we are able to communicate regardless of the spoken language.

Now consider that different "language" or terminology may be used in various parts of a business. We call this "jargon". For example, Finance people and Engineering people may not understand each other because they use different terms to refer to their areas of knowledge.

Consider also that different terms can mean the same thing in various parts of the business, such as "Customer", "Client" and "Debtor". These words are synonyms: they are used respectively by the Sales Department and Order Entry Department; by the Credit Control Department; and also by the Finance Department. Each synonym refers to a buyer of products or services from an enterprise. To communicate most effectively, a common term must be agreed and its exact meaning defined and documented – so all know what that term means.

Metadata documents an organization's terminology and meaning. It documents the enterprise language typically as an *Enterprise Glossary of Terminology*. This glossary is the enterprise equivalent of a Translation Dictionary as discussed above.

As we discussed in relation to Adam Smith, enterprises have historically evolved with different terminology in various parts of the organization. The need for a common language for communication in an enterprise was not recognised. Consider the problems that arose as computers were introduced to automate processes and data. We discussed that this introduced problems of data redundancy, data maintenance redundancy and process redundancy. To achieve Business Integration and Technology Integration common terminology – as *Enterprise Metadata* – must be used.

Data Modelling is used to identify metadata and define what each term means. These definitions are captured by data modelling tools and stored in a Repository. Agreed common terms, with other enterprise terminology, constitute the *Enterprise Glossary* that we discussed above. The Enterprise Glossary is the Language Dictionary of a business: similar to the Translation Dictionaries used with different spoken languages.

We discussed that Data Modelling methods are used within Enterprise Engineering. They define metadata. Their use is vital to achieve Business Integration. Their use is also vital to implement Enterprise Architecture.

To illustrate the problems that arise from a lack of definition of Enterprise Metadata, we will consider a hypothetical enterprise in Box 4: XYZ Corporation. XYZ is a Sales and Distribution organization that purchases products and services from its suppliers, to sell to its customers.

We can see in Box 4 that common data exists redundantly throughout XYZ: as *customer name* and *customer address* in the CUSTOMER table; as *client name* and *client address* in the CLIENT table; again as *debtor name* and *debtor address* in the DEBTOR table; as *supplier name* and *supplier address* in the SUPPLIER table; and as *creditor name* and *creditor address* in the CREDITOR table.

Box 4: XYZ Case Study Example

Both the *Sales Department* and the *Order Entry Department* of XYZ accept orders from "Customers". They keep details of customers in a database table that is called CUSTOMER. Details recorded about each customer include: *customer number* – for identification – as well as *customer name, customer address* and *customer account balance.*

The *Credit Control Department* keeps similar details, but it uses different terminology to that used by the Sales and Order Entry Departments. Instead, it refers to people who buy products and services from XYZ on credit as "Clients", not Customers. Details about each client are recorded in a CLIENT table, such as *client id, client name, client address, client account balance* and *client credit limit.*

The Accounts Receivable section in the *Finance Department* uses terminology that is different yet again from that used by the Sales, Order Entry or Credit Control Departments. It calls the people who pay for orders: "Debtors". Details recorded in a DEBTOR table include *debtor code, debtor name, debtor address* and *debtor account balance.*

If an organization that deals with XYZ as a Customer, Client or Debtor is also a Supplier, then the *Purchasing Department* uses different terminology yet again: it refers to these organizations as "Suppliers". Details are kept in a SUPPLIER table, including *supplier number, supplier name, supplier address* and *supplier account balance.* This balance is different to *customer account balance*: the amount owed by a customer to XYZ. Instead *supplier account balance* is the amount owed by XYZ to the supplier.

Payment of the *supplier account balance* by XYZ is managed by the Accounts Payable section in the Finance Department. Their terminology differs yet again from the other departments: suppliers who have to be paid by XYZ are called "Creditors". Their details are *creditor code, creditor name, creditor address* and *creditor account balance* – kept in a CREDITOR table.

This redundant data presents no problem if its values do not change. Such non-volatile data in database tables need ever be changed. But if data values are volatile and can change – such as for *name* or more likely for *address* – then every redundant version must be changed. We discussed this problem earlier. For example, if a Customer phones the Order Entry Department to notify them that it has changed its address, then the CUSTOMER, CLIENT, DEBTOR, SUPPLIER and CREDITOR tables must all be changed correctly to record the new address in each of *customer address, client address, debtor address, supplier address* and *creditor address* respectively.

We have seen above that different "language" or terminology is used in various parts of the business. We call this "jargon". Sales, Order Entry and Credit Control managers and staff, Finance and Purchasing managers and staff may not understand each other because they all use different terms to refer to their areas of knowledge.

Yet each of these terms all represent the same organization that deals with XYZ: as a "Customer" – used by the Sales Department and Order Entry Department; as a "Client" – used by the Credit Control Department; as a "Debtor" or a "Creditor" – used by the Finance Department; and as a "Supplier" – used by the Purchasing Department. These synonyms all identify a buyer of products and services from XYZ, or a supplier to XYZ.

To communicate most effectively, a common term must be agreed and its exact meaning defined and documented – so all know what that term means. The above example considers various roles that an organization takes in dealing with XYZ: as a Customer; a Client; a Debtor; a Supplier; and a Creditor. A common term that could be used through all of XYZ may be ORGANIZATION, with common details such as *organization number, organization name* and *organization address.*

5.2. Technologies for Enterprise Integration

Very effective technologies are now becoming available for Enterprise Integration. As we discussed at the start of this chapter, these achieve *Technology Integration*, based on the use of XML (Extensible Markup Language), Enterprise Application Integration (EAI) and Web Services. Enterprise Portals also offer easy access to enterprise resources. We will introduce these technologies in this paper.

XML is totally dependent on knowledge of metadata. A prerequisite to the effective use of XML is Data Modelling: to define metadata that XML requires. Many data modelling tools today automatically generate XML Document Type Definition (DTD) and XML Schema Definition (XSD) definition files from defined metadata.

We discussed XYZ Corporation earlier. Consider now two other organizations: ABC Inc and DEF Enterprises who buy products from XYZ. In doing business with its Customer: ABC Inc, XYZ carries out the following business activities:

- The XYZ Sales Department accepts Sales Orders from its Customer ABC to be processed by the XYZ Order Entry Department. This is the *Order Entry Management* activity.
- Before an order can be processed, the XYZ Credit Control Dept first checks the available credit for its Client ABC based on its current values of *client account balance* and *client credit limit*, and the total amount of the requested order. This activity is called *Credit Control Management* to authorize Order Entry Processing.
- After the Order Entry Department has fully processed the order, the Accounts Receivable section in the XYZ Finance Department uses the *Customer Invoice Management* activity to issue an invoice. This increases the *debtor account balance* of Debtor ABC by the total amount of the order.
- The new *debtor account balance* is used to update the redundant versions of the same amount due to XYZ: the *customer account balance* for Customer ABC in the Sales and Order Entry Departments; and the *client account balance* for Client ABC for the Credit Control Department. This activity is required for data maintenance synchronization of these redundant versions of *account balance.* It is the *Accounts Receivable Management* activity.

Because of the different terminology and identification used by each area of XYZ, it is not always clear they are dealing with the same organization: ABC. For example, Customers of XYZ are identified in the Sales and Order Entry Departments by *customer number*: ABC therefore has a unique Customer Number. Clients are identified in the Credit Control Department by *client id*, with a unique Client ID for ABC. Debtors are identified in the Finance Department by *debtor code*, again with a unique Debtor Code for ABC. But due to the lack of Business Integration, ABC Inc now appears to XYZ as three quite separate organizations: as a Customer; as a Client; and as a Debtor. Let us examine how XML handles this situation.

XML indicates the context of relevant data by surrounding that data with "tags" that define its meaning. For example, sales orders from ABC appear in XML as: <Customer>*ABC Inc*</Customer> … where <Customer> is called an XML start tag and </Customer> is called an XML end tag. XML tags are used to surround and identify relevant data content: shown here and in Figure 15 in *italics*. In this example, clearly ABC Inc is a customer.

Using XML, Sales Orders from ABC appear as:
<Customer>*ABC Inc*</Customer>

- *<Customer>* is a start tag and *</Customer>* is an end tag. These XML tags surround and identify relevant data content. Clearly ABC, Inc is a customer

The Credit Control and Finance Departments use different terminology. They only recognize ABC by their relevant terms:
<Client>ABC Inc</Client> for the Credit Control Department
<Debtor>ABC Inc</Debtor> for Accounts Receivable in the Finance Department

---

Figure 15. XML start and end tags surround and describe relevant data content

Similarly, by using relevant tags for the Credit Control and Finance Departments, we can see in Figure 15 that they also do business with ABC – by using their terminology – as: <Client>*ABC Inc*</Client> and as <Debtor>*ABC Inc*</Debtor>. The start and end tags clearly indicate the terminology that is used in each department. We can see from these XML data fragments that each department is dealing with the same enterprise: ABC.

Let us now discuss the relevant activities and the corresponding documents that are exchanged between Customer ABC and its Supplier XYZ.

- The ABC Purchasing Activity produces *Purchase Orders* that are sent to XYZ as its Supplier. These Purchase Orders can be sent by mail, fax or email.
- When received by the XYZ Order Entry Department they are processed as *Sales Orders* by the XYZ Order Entry Management activity, as discussed above.
- On Sales Order acceptance after Credit Control Management processing by the XYZ Credit Control Department, XYZ sends an *Order Acknowledgement* back to ABC, followed later by a *Delivery Advice* or *Advance Shipping Notice* (ASN). These documents are received by the ABC Purchase Order Acceptance activity.
- Finally the Accounts Receivable section in the XYZ Finance Department sends a *Customer Invoice* to its Debtor: ABC. It is received by the ABC Accounts Payable in their Finance Department as a *Supplier Invoice* – from its Supplier XYZ.
- All these documents are exchanged between the two companies: the *Purchase Order* originating the order at ABC; the *Order Acknowledgement* of receipt by XYZ, sent back to ABC; the *Delivery Advice* or *Advance Shipping Notice;* and later the *Invoice* that are sent by XYZ to ABC. Each of these documents must be reentered by XYZ or by ABC staff into the relevant XYZ or ABC processing systems.

5.3. Some XML Basic Concepts

An example of the Purchase Order that is exchanged between both companies is shown in Figure 16. This Purchase Order (PO) is issued by *"Smith and Co":* a subsidiary of ABC. It is a Purchase Order expressed in XML. We will use this PO to discuss some of the basic concepts of XML,[25] documented in Box 5.

ABC PO Format - Smith and Co

```
<PurchaseOrder>
  <Party Type="Buyer">
  <Reference>AB24567</Reference>
    <Name>Smith and Co</Name>
    <Street>123 High St</Street>
    <Town>Epping Forest</Town>
    <PostCode>E15 2HQ</PostCode>
  </Party>
  <Party Type="Supplier">
    ...
  </Party>
  <OrdNo>1234</OrdNo>
  <OrderItem>
    ...
  </OrderItem>
  <Tax Type="VAT" Percent="17.5">
    ...
  </Tax>
  ...
</PurchaseOrder>
```

Figure 16. Example of an XML Purchase Order (Source: Software AG)

Box 5: Basic XML Concepts

XML is text, in any written language. It is human-readable and machine-readable. Each start tag, such as <Name>, is an XML element. It must be followed by an end tag, such as </Name>. Both tags surround the data content: Figure 16 shows that this content is "Smith and Co".
A tag or XML element is a single word with no spaces, where the first character of the tag is a letter or an underscore: it cannot be a number or any special character other than an underscore. Distinct from HTML which is case-insensitive, XML is case-sensitive. For this reason <NAME>, <Name> and <name> are three different XML elements or tags.
An XML element start tag can also contain XML attributes, separated from the start tag and each other by a space. Each attribute name is followed by an "=" and then a value surrounded by single or double quotes. For example, <Party Type="Buyer"> in Figure 16 or <Tax Type="VAT" Percent="17.5"> are XML attributes of the <Party> and <Tax> XML elements.

5.4. The Need for XML Transformation

Consider now that Smith and Co is no longer a subsidiary of ABC Inc, but is a subsidiary of DEF Enterprises. The Purchase Order instead would use the XML PO format that is utilized by DEF. This is shown in Figure 17: side-by-side with the same PO in the XML format that is used by ABC. This Purchase Order is *OrderNo: 1234.*

DEF PO Format – Smith and Co

```
<PurchaseOrder OrderNo="1234">
  <Buyer BuyerNo="AB24567"
     Name="Smith and Co">
    <Address1>123 High St</Address1>
    <Address2>Epping Forest</Address2>
    <Zip>E15 2HQ</Zip>
  </Buyer>
  <Supplier>
    ...
  </Supplier>
  <OrderItem>
    ...
  </OrderItem>
  <Tax>
    <TaxType>VAT</TaxType>
    <TaxPercent>17.5</TaxPercent>
    ...
  </Tax>
  ...
</PurchaseOrder>
```

ABC PO Format - Smith and Co

```
<PurchaseOrder>
  <Party Type="Buyer">
  <Reference>AB24567</Reference>
    <Name>Smith and Co</Name>
    <Street>123 High St</Street>
    <Town>Epping Forest</Town>
    <PostCode>E15 2HQ</PostCode>
  </Party>
  <Party Type="Supplier">
    ...
  </Party>
  <OrdNo>1234</OrdNo>
  <OrderItem>
    ...
  </OrderItem>
  <Tax Type="VAT" Percent="17.5">
    ...
  </Tax>
  ...
</PurchaseOrder>
```

- ***Different organizations can define same data in different ways***
- ***Enterprise Application Integration uses XML to resolve differences***

Figure 17. A Purchase Order in two different XML formats (Source: Software AG)

We see in Figure 17 that the DEF PO format on the left shows Purchase Order Number as an attribute of *<PurchaseOrder OrderNo="1234">*. On the right it is shown as an XML element *<OrdNo>1234</OrdNo>*.

The Buyer Number identification and name on the left for DEF are shown as attributes of Buyer: *<Buyer BuyerNo="AB24567" Name="Smith and Co">*. On the right for ABC each is an XML element: *<Reference>AB24567</Reference> <Name>Smith and Co</Name>*.

On the right the address is *<Street>123 High St</Street> <Town>Epping Forest</Town> <PostCode>E15 2HQ</PostCode>*. On the left the address uses quite different element names: *<Address1>123 High St</Address1> <Address2>Epping Forest</Address2> <Zip>E15 2HQ</Zip>*.

Finally we can see that XML attributes for *<Tax>* are used by ABC, as: *<Tax Type="VAT" Percent="17.5">*. In contrast, the format on the left uses child elements of *<Tax>*. These are: *<TaxType>VAT</TaxType> and <TaxPercent>17.5</TaxPercent>*, surrounded by *<Tax>* ... *</Tax>* as their parent element.

From Figure 17 we see that these Purchase Order formats in XML are quite different to each other, yet both contain exactly the same PO data content. Both ABC and DEF are customers of XYZ, which likely uses yet another XML format for its Sales Order. As noted in the figure, different organizations can all define the same data in different ways. Each of the customers of XYZ may have quite different PO formats.

So what should XYZ do? Should it require every customer to use a standard format, such as the XYZ Sales Order format? This would be very convenient for XYZ. But it is unlikely to be so convenient for its customers. Rather than change their PO formats so they could buy from XYZ, it is easier for them not to buy. Instead they can buy from a supplier other than XYZ. If XYZ mandated that only its XML Sales Format be used, it would quite likely lose many customers and their orders.

Because each customer most likely has its own PO format in XML, to keep their business XYZ must be able to accept every different format. It therefore must be able to transform each format into its own Sales Order XML format. This is one of the advantages of XML: it is very easy to do data transformation using XML.

Extensible Style Language Transformation[26] (XSLT) is used to transform from one XML format to another. The XSLT language specifies in XML the transformation that is to be carried out, processed by an XSLT processor – called an XSLT Transformation Engine.[27]

Each document to be exchanged between XYZ and ABC previously has had to be printed and then mailed – or faxed – as we discussed above. It has then been manually reentered by the receiving company into its relevant system for processing.

XML messaging allows these enterprise applications to be integrated. Not surprisingly, this is called *Enterprise Application Integration.* EAI is used across enterprise boundaries between XYZ and ABC as inter-enterprise application integration. Used within an enterprise, such as in XYZ, it is intra-enterprise application integration.

A transformation front-end is added to each system for EAI between the various systems. In normal processing workflow, these are the ABC Procurement System, the XYZ Order Entry System, the XYZ Order Acknowledgement system, the ABC Acknowledgement Receipt system, the XYZ Delivery Advice system or XYZ Advance Shipping Notice system, the ABC Delivery Receipt system or ABC Advance Shipping Notice system, the XYZ Customer Invoicing system and the ABC Accounts Payable system.

6. INTRODUCTION TO WEB SERVICES

As we discussed earlier, today each program and each software component is still largely hand-coded from scratch. Yet much of the hand-coded logic in most programs is implied by the database structure that the program is designed to use. Code generators today can use standard code patterns to automatically generate 80%–90% of program code that was previously 100% manually coded. Using these code generators, we are starting to see the automatic generation of programs in a variety of languages. But object-oriented programming has not yet fully delivered on its promise of interchangeable and reusable code modules. Of course it is true that object-oriented programmers can develop reusable code modules. But it takes considerable time and skill to achieve this result. We discussed in that this has limited our ability to reuse much code.

Because of different hardware and operating system platforms, we still have considerable problems in integrating code modules within and between enterprises. These different platforms and programming languages use various Application Program Interfaces (APIs). Programs or code modules written in one language with a particular API cannot be easily integrated with other programs or code modules on different platforms. To address this problem, Remote Procedure Call (RPC) technologies that use CORBA (Common Object Request Broker Architecture), COM (Common Object Model) and other approaches have enabled tightly-coupled integration of code across dissimilar platforms in real-time.

But the complexity of RPC approaches for different APIs has meant that code module integration and reuse is still time-consuming and difficult. Web Services and associated XML technologies have recently been developed to address real-time program and code module integration. We will discuss Web Services and related XML technologies in this paper.

Furthermore, most enterprises have a common problem: different business processes and procedures are used to do the same thing, where a common standard procedure could be used instead. For example, we discussed problems experienced in updating a changed customer address in each of the different versions of Customer data in an enterprise. The customer address may need to be changed in the Customer table (for the Sales and Order Entry Departments), the Client table (for the Credit Control Department), and the Debtor table (for the Accounts Receivable section of the Finance Department).

These tables must be changed using special address-change maintenance programs written for each separate Department. The same details must be updated in every table where the customer's address exists redundantly. This is redundant work. It also requires redundant staffing to enter these redundant data changes. These programs may each use change procedures that do not all operate the same way. This also means redundant training, if the programs used for address-update all have different data entry operating procedures.

This address data should be able to be updated using a common customer-address-update process, used as a standard process throughout the enterprise. This will lead to the design of common, reusable business processes using Web Services, and common Web Service processes and workflows.

So now let us now consider the concepts, components and potential of Web Services in the IT industry.

6.1. Concepts and Components of Web Services

Web Services have recently emerged to address the problems of software integration discussed above. Early work carried out independently by various companies over the period 1999-2000 culminated in the submission by IBM, Microsoft and Ariba of initial Web Services specifications for consideration by the World Wide Web Consortium (W3C) in September, 2000. Web Services are based on XML. The IBM AlphaWorks web site[28] describes Web Services as follows:

> *"Web services are self-describing, self-contained, modular applications that can be mixed and matched with other Web services to create innovative products, processes, and value chains. Web services are Internet applications that fulfill a specific task or a set of tasks that work with many other web services in an interoperable manner to carry out their part of a complex work flow or a business transaction. In essence, they enable just-in-time application integration and these web applications can be dynamically changed by the creation of new web services. Various applications that are available on the Internet can be accessed and invoked at run time without prior knowledge and programming requirements to enable business processes and decision-making at Web speeds. IBM's Web Services Toolkit provides a runtime environment as well as demo/examples to design and execute web-service applications to find one another and collaborate in business transactions without programming requirements or human intervention."*

Many companies are currently working on specifications for interoperable Web Services.[29]

To combine or integrate different application programs before, each API to be used by code modules in those programs was defined for the specific language and operating system used. It generally meant that all programs had to use the same language and operating system.

This programmatic integration of code modules and applications using language-specific and operating-system-specific APIs has made program integration very difficult in the past. Code modules integrated using Remote Procedure Call (RPC) technologies such as COM or CORBA interfaces have been used as we discussed earlier, but they are tightly-coupled. Because of this tight coupling, a change that is made in one component can affect other components; their level of integration is fragile. While they are effective, these technologies have been very complex and time-consuming. They have therefore been expensive to use and maintain.

In contrast, Application Program Interfaces can also be defined using XML. An API can be specified in an XML language called *SOAP (Simple Object Access Protocol),* shown in Figure 18. This offers the advantage that it can be used with any programming language and operating system that understands XML. As SOAP is much simpler, integrated code modules can be loosely-coupled. Changes in one component do not affect other components as we saw with tightly-coupled RPC approaches; instead, program integration is more flexible. Because of this, SOAP is less expensive to use and maintain.

The definition of APIs using SOAP is one required component of Web Services. The services that can be carried out by the code module or program must also be described. This is specified using another language based on XML, called *WSDL (Web Services Description Language).* WSDL identifies the SOAP specification that is to be used for the code module API. It identifies the input and output SOAP message tags that are also required for input to and output from the module or program. Each WSDL specification is then used to describe the particular Web Services to be accessed via the Internet, or from a corporate Intranet, by publishing it to a relevant Internet or Intranet Web Server.

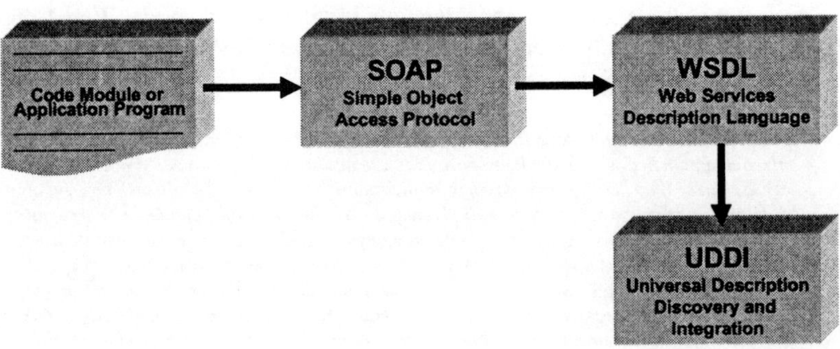

Figure 18. Web Services are implemented using SOAP (Simple Object Access Protocol), WSDL (Web Services Description Language) and UDDI (Universal Description, Discovery and Integration).

But SOAP and WSDL alone are not sufficient. Unless Web Services are published in an electronic "Yellow Pages" directory that is accessible within an enterprise (via its Intranet) or available world-wide (via the Internet), no one would know of the existence of the available Web Services. Another XML language is used to achieve this: called *UDDI (Universal Description, Discovery and Integration).* This is used for publication in a UDDI directory, which enables the Web Services to be found by others. SOAP, WSDL and UDDI are related to each other as shown in Figure 18.

6.2. Intranet and Internet Web Services for Integration

To understand their power, ease-of-use and flexibility, we will look at two examples that illustrate how Web Services can be used internally within an enterprise, and externally between enterprises. The first example uses Web Services within an enterprise, via the Intranet. The second example then considers Web Services between enterprises, across the Internet.

6.3. Intranet Web Services Integration Example

We will use the earlier problem that we discussed arising from redundant data, requiring data entry to make required changes to each redundant data version. We saw that this resulted in redundant work and redundant staffing to do that work. It also often resulted in redundant training for the staff: to use different data entry procedures for each data maintenance process. These were all manual procedures that were used to make the required data changes. They were slow, error-prone and expensive. And until all required changes were made, other problems were encountered because the different versions of the data were not synchronized.

We saw that EAI can assist here. Web Services also offer a great deal of benefit. Each data entry maintenance program used to change a redundant table can be defined so that the data changes are expressed as Web Services, using SOAP. In this instance, integration with Web Services is achieved in real-time

For example, a Web Service using SOAP – called *CreateNewCustomer* (say) – invokes the *Create Customer* logic and business rules by the Customer data entry program used in the Sales and Order Entry Departments. *ReadCustomer, UpdateCustomer* and *DeleteCustomer* Web Services can also be defined, to invoke the corresponding *Read, Change* or *Delete* logic and business rules in the Customer data entry program. Similarly *CreateNewClient, ReadClient, UpdateClient* and *DeleteClient* Web Services can be defined with SOAP to invoke the corresponding logic and rules in the Client data entry program for the Credit Control Department. And so also, SOAP Web Services can be defined to invoke the Debtor data entry program logic and rules in the Accounts Receivable section of the Finance Department.

We discussed if a Customer Address change was made manually by the Order Entry Department, an *Address Change Notification Form* was also printed. This form was sent to the Credit Control and Accounts Receivable sections; they could make the relevant manual data changes to the Client and Debtor tables that they also maintain. We discussed that these manual changes were slow, error-prone and expensive. In the past, the only way to avoid this manual updating was to completely replace the separate redundant tables by an integrated table for use by all. In addition, all of the previous application programs that used the redundant tables also have had to be replaced by new, integrated programs that used the integrated table. This approach, requiring table replacement and application program redevelopment, was expensive and complex.

Instead, these data changes can be expressed as Web Services for each redundant table. Each Web Service is specified using WSDL. This identifies the defined SOAP specifications and relevant SOAP input and output messages. When the WSDL specifications are published to the Intranet Web Server, the *Address Change Notification Form* that was previously printed is replaced by SOAP and WSDL defined Web Services. Each WSDL specification identifies the relevant SOAP messages needed to invoke data change logic and business rules in the Customer, Client or Debtor tables as illustrated in Figure 19.

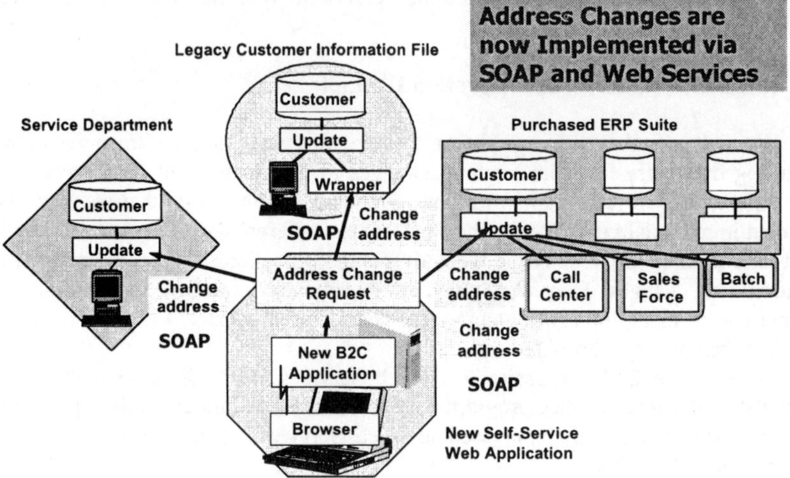

Figure 19: Address Change Notification using SOAP and Web Services avoids the need for Manual Reentry. (Source: adapted from Gartner Group)

The slow, error-prone manual procedures for data entry are now replaced by real-time, dynamic Web Service transactions. These are sent via the Intranet as SOAP messages that invoke the relevant Web Service in each table needed to keep the redundant data up-to-date. The result is the immediate synchronization of all related data changes to all relevant tables. Using Web Services, redundant tables can remain, and can continue to be updated by their separate data entry programs. This updating is now done faster and automatically using SOAP messages and Web Services in real-time, rather than having the costly redevelopment and replacement of the tables and programs with integrated tables and programs. The earlier redundant data problem has now been replaced by a replicated data environment: maintained up-to-date and synchronized in real time.

6.4. Internet Web Services Integration Example

The second Web Services example shows their use outside the enterprise. In this case we will look at the ordering of products or services from an Online Store (called an *e-Tailer*) via the Internet. The Store accepts orders online, for payment by credit card. The credit card must first be approved by the relevant Bank. If the card is valid and credit is available, payment is credited to the Store's Bank account. The Store then orders the requested products or services from its Supplier, and arranges with a Logistic (Shipping) Company for the goods to be picked up from the Supplier and delivered directly to the Customer. This is called "drop-shipping".

In the past, this scenario was carried out by the Store using mail, phone or fax to communicate with the Bank, the Supplier and the Shipping Company. This took time and often introduced errors or delays. To improve customer service, the Store replaced this mail, phone and fax communication with online coordination with the Bank, the Supplier and the Shipping Company. But this presented severe problems in the past using Remote Procedure Call technologies. For example, the Bank may use CORBA for online credit card authorization and payment, the Logistic Company may use COM, and the Supplier may use yet another RPC approach. These different RPC interfaces add dramatically to complexity and to the time required by the Store to implement this online coordination.

Now let us consider this scenario using Web Services, as shown in Figure 20. The Bank defines its *CreditCardApproval* and *CreditCardPayment* Web Services using SOAP. It publishes these interfaces, plus SOAP input and output message formats, to its Internet Web Server using WSDL. It registers these credit card Web Services (defined by SOAP and WSDL) using UDDI (Universal Description, Discovery and Integration) to the UDDI Registry[30]. Similarly the Supplier and the Shipping Company also register their respective Web Services using SOAP, WSDL and UDDI.

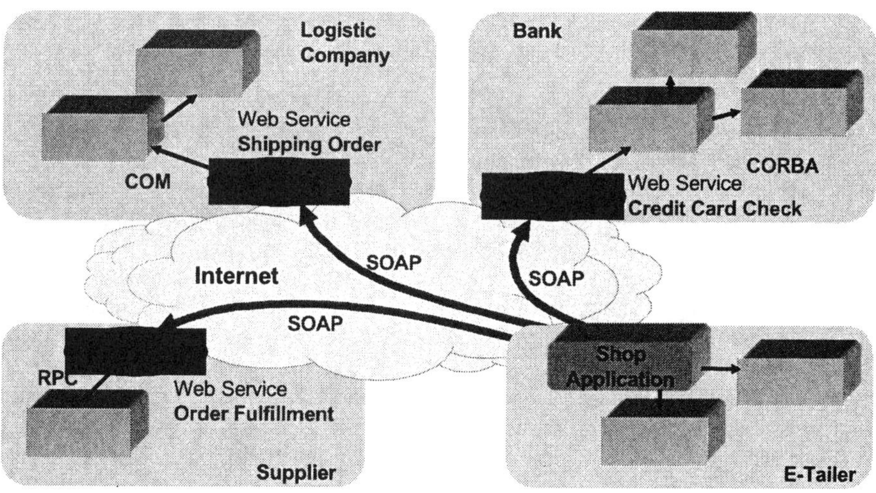

Figure 20. Invocation of Remote Web Services for Credit Card Approval, Order Fulfillment and Shipping using SOAP (Source: Software AG)

To locate Banks, Suppliers and Shipping Companies that offer relevant Web Services, the Store visits the UDDI Registry. It issues UDDI *"Find"* requests to locate Web Services that satisfy its requirements. Using the SOAP, WSDL and UDDI specifications published by relevant companies, the Store prepares the SOAP interface, and input and output messages. It sends these SOAP messages to the URL Internet address of the relevant Web Servers, as published in the UDDI Registry via UDDI and WSDL by the selected Bank, Supplier and Shipping Company.

This Web Services approach has many benefits. A standard way is used to integrate with Web Services offered by any organization, regardless of where they are located world-wide. This has clear advantages of greater simplicity and ease-of-use, which in turn lead to benefits of faster implementation and lower cost.

The Store can select any Bank, Supplier and Shipping Company that meets its needs for Web Services. For example, if a Customer is located overseas, a Supplier and Shipping Company near the Customer can easily be used. This offers the benefit of lower cost – so producing greater profit – or the lower cost can be passed on to the Customer as lower prices.

Each of the Web Services companies gain benefits also. Web Services can be easily published for world-wide access. Depending on the value of a Web Service to users world-wide, each Web Service can be charged on a per-use basis. Each "per-use" price may be a micro-payment of less than a dollar, for example. But such Web Services – which previously have been inaccessible; locked away in legacy application programs – can also generate additional revenue.

7. SUMMARY OF ENTERPRISE INTEGRATION USING ENTERPRISE ARCHITECTURE

Adam Smith's book, *Wealth of Nations* (1776), was influential for the Industrial Age. It described the evolution from the Agricultural Age to the Industrial Age. It was the foundation for most industrial enterprises in the late 18th Century and into the 19th Century.

- By the middle of the 20th Century, the Industrial Enterprise had evolved into a complex series of manual processes. The pace of progress had seen most enterprises evolve to use increasingly complex business processes, with rapidly growing transaction volumes to be manually processed. These enterprises found *... they were operating in a continual state of Manual Chaos!*
- From the late 1950s, manual processes were automated by computer. We took the existing manual processes and then automated them essentially AS-IS: without much change. In so doing, we moved from Manual Chaos ... *to Automated Chaos!*
- With rapid acceptance of the Internet in the second half of the 90s the chaos moved from the back office ... onto the front doorstep of enterprises: through their web sites. Customers could visit these enterprises by the click of a mouse. But they could just as quickly leave ... *if the processes did not provide what the customers needed.*

- The problem is that we have 21st Century Enterprises that use 21st Century Technologies ... *yet most enterprises today still use 18th Century Disintegrated Business Processes!*
- The business processes – originally designed based on principles set by Adam Smith in 1776 – have not evolved to take advantage of the technologies we have today. *We need integrated 21st Century Enterprises together with integrated 21st Century Processes!*
- We discussed the problem of redundant data versions in most enterprises. When data values change, all redundant versions must be updated to synchronize with that change. With redundant data, we moved to *Data Maintenance Chaos!*
- We also discussed evolution of Systems Development Methodologies: Software Engineering; Information Engineering; and Object-Oriented methods. We saw that in spite of these methods, process changes that require procedural program changes resulted in *Program Maintenance Chaos!* Our procedural programming methods were not designed to accommodate change easily, and object-oriented methods could not identify enterprise-wide reusable code.
- We saw that many Data Maintenance and Program Maintenance problems are resolved by *Business Integration.* We learned that Business Integration is best achieved by using Enterprise Architecture.
- We saw that Data Modelling methods are used within Enterprise Engineering. They define metadata. Their use is vital to achieve Business Integration. Their use is also vital to implement Enterprise Architecture.
- We discussed Enterprise Architecture and concepts of the *Zachman Framework for Enterprise Architecture.* The architects of an enterprise are not in its IT Department:

    1. Enterprise Architects are the senior managers who set the directions for the future, based on business plans and strategies, and on processes designed for that future and its technologies.
    2. The future will be based on business processes that use the technologies of today and tomorrow ... with strategic directions set by senior management, and with business experts and IT experts working in a design partnership.

- We discussed the need for Enterprise Reusability. The Zachman Framework for Enterprise Architecture – from the perspectives of the Planner and the Owner rows – are critical for reusability. These two rows identify reusability opportunities within an enterprise.
- We discussed some of the concepts of Enterprise Engineering, used to identify reusability opportunities based on business plans ... for rapid delivery of priority areas into production typically in three month increments.
- We must design for tomorrow based on business plans for the future. We should use activities and processes tailored for the environment of the Internet – which represents our present and our future – so that enterprises can respond rapidly.
- We completed the paper with a brief overview of some of the technologies that are used for Enterprise Integration. We discussed the use of XML to bypass the need for manual reentry of purchase orders and other related documents, with data transformation for Enterprise Application Integration (EAI).

REFERENCES

1. Michael Hammer and James Champy, *Reengineering the* Corporation, (Nicholas Brealey Publishing, London, 1993).
2. Ken Orr, *Structured Systems Development*, (Yourdon Press, New York, NY, 1977).
3. Ed Yourdon and Larry Constantine, *Structured Design: Fundamentals of a Discipline of Computer Program Systems Design*, (Prentice-Hall, Englewood Cliffs, NJ, 1978).
4. Tom De Marco, *Software Systems Development*, (Yourdon Press, New York, NY, 1982)
5. Peter Drucker, *Management: Tasks, Responsibilities,* (Practices, Harper & Row, New York, NY, 1974).
6. Peter Drucker, *Management: Challenges for the 21st Century*, (HarperCollins, New York, NY 1999).
7. Adam Smith, *An Inquiry into the Nature and Causes of the Wealth Of Nations*, (1776). Often called just "*Wealth of Nations*". The text of Book One is available from the link: http://arts.adelaide.edu.au/person/DHart/ETexts/Liberalism/AdamSmith/WealthOfNations1776/Book1.html
8. Michael Jackson, *Principles of Program Design*, (Academic Press, New York, NY, 1975).
9. Edgar Codd, A Relational Model for Large Shared Data Banks, *CACM*, 13 (6), 377–87 (1970).
10. R. Fagin, Normal Forms and Relational Database Operators, Proc ACM SIGMOD International Conference on Management of Data (1979).
11. Chris Date, *Introduction to Data Base*, Volumes 1 and 2, (Addison-Wesley, Reading, MA, 1982).
12. W. Kent, A Simple Guide to Five Normal Forms in Relational Database Theory, *CACM*, 26 (2) (1983).
13. Chris Date, *An Introduction to Database Systems – Volume 1*, 4th Edition, (Addison-Wesley, Reading, MA, 1986).
14. Clive Finkelstein, Information Engineering, six InDepth articles, *Computerworld* (May–June 1981).
15. Clive Finkelstein and James Martin, Information Engineering, two-volume Technical Report, Savant Institute, Carnforth, UK (Nov 1981).
16. Clive Finkelstein, *An Introduction to Information Engineering*, (Addison-Wesley, Sydney, NSW, 1989).
17. Clive Finkelstein, *Information Engineering: Strategic Systems Development*, (Addison-Wesley, Sydney, NSW, 1992).
18. Grady Booch, *Object-Oriented Analysis and Design with Applications*, 2nd Edition, (Addison-Wesley, Reading, MA, 1994).
19. Grady Booch, Ivar Jacobson, and James Rumbaugh, *The Unified Modeling Language User Guide*, (Addison-Wesley, Reading, MA, 1998).
20. James Rumbaugh, Grady Booch and Ivar Jacobson, *The Unified Modeling Language Reference Manual*, Addison-Wesley Object Technology Series, (Addison-Wesley, Reading, MA, 1998).
21. Ivar Jacobson, Grady Booch, Ivar Jacobson and James Rumbaugh, *The Unified Software Development Process*, (Addison-Wesley, Reading, MA, 1999).
22. Grady Booch, James Rumbaugh and Ivar Jacobson, *The Complete UML Training Course*, (Prentice-Hall, Englewood Cliffs, NJ, 2000).
23. Further information about Rational, within IBM, is available from the Rational web site at: http://www.rational.com/.
24. Enterprise Engineering methods draw on the Information Engineering methods described in the earlier books above by Clive Finkelstein. Enterprise Engineering includes Enterprise Architecture enhancements. It also addresses Internet technologies for rapid delivery, including: XML; Enterprise Application Integration (EAI); Web Services; Service-Oriented Architectures and Enterprise Portals.
25. Introductory articles and white papers on XML can be found at the World Wide Web Consortium (W3C) at http://www.w3c.org and the Organization for Advancement of Structured Information Standards (OASIS) at http://www.xml.org.
26. Extensible Style Language Transformation (XSLT) and Extensible Style Language (XSL) specifications and white papers are available from W3C – http://www.w3c.org and from OASIS – http://www.xml.org.
27. Links to many XSLT Transformation Engines are at W3C – http://www.w3c.org and at OASIS – http://www.xml.org.
28. The IBM Alphaworks web site is at http://www.alphaworks.ibm.com/.
29. The Web Services Interoperability Group (WS-I) was founded by IBM, Microsoft, BEA and others in 2002. Its goal is to achieve seamless Web Services interoperability between all vendors in WS-I.
30. The Public UDDI Registry is at http://www.uddi.org/, accessible across the Internet from any browser. Private UDDI Registries can also be implemented in an enterprise, accessible via its Intranet.

THE FORMULATION OF DESIGN THEORIES FOR INFORMATION SYSTEMS

Shirley Gregor and David Jones*

1. INTRODUCTION

Our aim in this paper is to explore in some detail how design theories for information systems can be understood and explicated. Information Systems (IS) as a discipline is concerned with action – the design, construction and use of software and systems involving people, technology, organizations and societies. In acting in building information systems it is preferable not to approach every new development problem afresh. We would like some guiding knowledge that transfers from one situation, in which action is taken, to another. Generalized knowledge of this type can be referred to as *design theory*.

There has been some work on the nature of information systems design theories (ISDTs) but some questions have not been dealt with satisfactorily and there are issues that need untangling. What are the things that we are talking about building? Are we interested in design theory for tools and methodologies in addition to complete information systems? How is design theory articulated? Is it about the attributes of the artefact when constructed, the process that brings it into being, or is there more? What is the relationship between design theory and other types of theory? Should the word theory be used at all? Is it a special type of traditional theory? Is specification of 'micro theories' or 'kernel' theories a necessary part of design theory? Our paper provides an elaboration of design theory that goes some way towards answering these questions in what we believe is a more comprehensive manner than has been done previously.

Questions about design theory are significant for the Information Systems discipline. The development of design theories provides a response to calls for theory that is unique to our discipline, separate from our various referent disciplines (Weber, 1997). Knowledge about Information Systems development methodologies and specific applications systems are recognized as core knowledge for the discipline (Baskerville and Myers, 2002, following Davis, 2000). These core knowledge areas have vital relevance to industry. The shortcomings in the extant literature on design theory means, however, that researchers have little in the way of accepted guidelines for presenting or accumulating

* Shirley Gregor, School of Business and Information Management, Australian National University, Canberra 0200 Australia. David Jones, Faculty of Informatics and Communication, Central Queensland University, Rockhampton 4702 Australia.

knowledge on the design or development of information systems artefacts in research papers, theses and practitioner articles.

In the remainder of this paper we investigate the nature and possible component parts of an ISDT. The scope of the paper does not extend to a detailed discussion of the manner in which the knowledge for an ISDT is acquired and justified, though these epistemological issues will be addressed in further work.

2. DESIGN AND THEORIZING

In this paper we adopt a wide rather than a narrow view of theory. The word theory is used to encompass what might be termed elsewhere conjectures, models, frameworks, or "body of knowledge". Our ontological position recognizes theory as having an existence separate from the subjective understanding of individuals, an inhabitant of the World 3 of Habermas (1984) and Popper (1986). Theory and theoretical knowledge are invented by human beings rather than being discovered. We invent concepts, models and schemes to make sense of experience and, further, we continually test and modify these constructions in the light of new experience. Theoretical terms are abstractions, human inventions that are simply convenient devices for managing and expressing the relations among observables. Concepts and ideas are invented but correspond to something in the real world (World 1). A computer program as an electronic artefact exists in World 1, yet the articulation of the algorithm or design principles that are represented in the program belongs to World 3. Though there may be a degree of interpersonal agreement about the objects in Worlds 1 and 3, each of us experiences these in a different way in terms of our own subjective understanding (World 2).

There are limits on what we class as theory. Theory is about abstraction and generalisation about phenomenon, interactions and causation. We do not regard a collection of facts, or knowledge of an individual fact or event, as theory. "Data are not theory" (Sutton and Shaw, 1995, p. 374), though data may form the foundation for theoretical development. Thus, a description of the method used in one case for the construction of an artefact is not theory.

Taking a broad view of theory it is possible to identify five inter-related categories of theory based on the primary type of question at the foundation of a research project (Gregor, 2002a, 2002b). These five categories are summarized in Table 1.

Thus, in this paper we are concerned with theory of Type V – theory for design and action. We recognize design theory as a prescriptive[1] type of theory that can build on and incorporate the other types of theory. It gives guidelines or principles that can be followed in practice.

There are diverging views on the status of design theory and its relationship to other types of theory. The classic work that treats design theory (science) as a special prescriptive type of theory is Herbert Simon's *The Sciences of the Artificial* (1996) first published in 1969.

Simon (1996, p. xii) notes that in an earlier edition of his work he described a central problem that had occupied him for many years,"How could one construct an empirical theory?" :

[1] The term "prescriptive" is used rather than the term "normative" as the latter can have connotations of a moral dimension, that is a normative "should" rather than a prescriptive or imperative "how to". Though important, matters relating to ethical and moral issues are beyond the scope of this paper.

> I thought I began to see in the problem of artificiality an explanation of the difficulty that has been experienced in filling engineering and other professions with empirical and theoretical substance distinct from the substance of their supporting sciences. Engineering, medicine, business, architecture and painting are concerned not with the necessary but with the contingent – not with how things are but with how they might be – in short, with design.

Simon contrasts design science with natural science, which is concerned with knowledge about natural objects and phenomena. Design science must take account of natural science as an artefact is a meeting-place or interface between the inner environment of the artefact and the outer environment in which it performs, both of which operate in accordance with natural laws. Simon discussed design science in the contexts of economics, the psychology of cognition, and planning and engineering design, but not Information Systems. It has taken some time for Simon's ideas to filter through to Information Systems and they are still not unequivocally accepted in this discipline.

Weber (1987), for example, recognized difficulties with design work in Information Systems. He saw the "lure of design and construction" as a factor inhibiting the progress of Information Systems as a discipline and called for theory that gave Information Systems a paradigmatic base.

Table 1. Categories of Theory

Theory category		Research question	IS Examples
I.	Analyzing and Describing	What is?	Taxonomy of information systems development models (Kwon and Zmud, 1987)
II.	Understanding	How and why?	Structurational model of technology (Orlikowski, 1992)
III.	Predicting	What will be?	Organizational size as a predictor of innovativeness, without justification (Rogers, 1995)
IV.	Explaining and Predicting – "traditional theory"	What is, how, why and what will be?	Theory of representation (Weber, 1997)
V.	Design and Action	How to do something?	Design of executive information systems (Walls, Widmeyer, and El Sawy, 1992) Design of systems supporting emergent knowledge processes (Markus, Majchrzak, and Gasser, 2002)

In 1992, Simon's ideas were adopted and applied to consideration of ISDT by Walls et al. (1992). Recently the ideas of these authors have enjoyed some currency as shown in the specification of a design theory for knowledge management systems by Markus et al. (2002). The explication of ISDT by Walls et al. (1992) is probably the most complete and thorough to date, and is discussed in more detail further in this paper.

Since 1992, however, there have been varying and rather scattered approaches to the problem and articulation of design theory in Information Systems and allied fields. March and Smith (1995) followed Simon's ideas closely, with an important difference. They saw design science products comprised of four types: constructs, models, methods, and implementations, but excluded theories. Jarvinen (2001) expresses similar views.

Other discussion of related work in the Information Systems literature is scattered and appears under different labels. Associated research has been referred to as engineering type research (Cecez-Kecmanovic, 1994), as a constructive type of research (Iivari, Hirschheim and Klein 1998), as prototyping (Baskerville and Wood-Harper, 1998), and a systems development approach (Lau, 1997; Burstein and Gregor, 1999). Gregor examined different types of theory in Information Systems (2001, 2002a) and design theory in particular (2002b), but did not explore the formulation of design theory in detail.

Relevant work appears in other disciplines, including management accounting (Kasanen, Lukha, and Siitonen, 1993), accounting information systems (David, Gerard, and McCarthy, 2000) and education (Savelson et al., 2003). The design patterns approach has enjoyed some prominence and considers the sharing of design knowledge drawn from practice rather than theory (Alexander, Ishikawa, and Silverstein, 1977). Schön (1983) links the development of professional knowledge to "reflection–in–action", though he focussed more on the epistemology of practice, placing technical problem solving within a broader context of reflective enquiry.

The conclusion drawn from the extant literature is that while considerable attention has been paid to the concept of design theory, there is a lack of consensus as to its nature and comparatively little discussion as to how it should be formulated, in Information Systems or elsewhere. This challenge is addressed in the following sections.

3. FORMULATING INFORMATION SYSTEMS DESIGN THEORY

In discussing ISDT we should first consider the nature of the artefacts about which we are theorizing. We are considering systems that involve humans, technology, organizations and society. The essence of these artefacts is that they are systems in which there is human use of information and communication technologies. It is this property that distinguishes ISDTs from other types of design theory: for example, in architecture, medicine, or management. A further characteristic of the nature of the artefacts we are considering is that they are not static. An information system, given its encapsulation of humans, technology, organizations and society, will evolve. This evolution will be driven by the changes in its component systems, organizations, people and technology, and the external environment with which it interacts.

In discussing the formulation of an ISDT we extend the work of Walls et al. (1992), who largely relied on Dubin (1978) as a basis for specifying theory. Dubin's view of theory is that of the traditional Type IV category (Table 1), with units of analysis, laws of interaction and so on. Though these ideas are still relevant to an ISDT they do not go far enough in specifying what should be considered in an ISDT. In expanding on the work of Walls et al. (1992) we have gleaned further ideas from Heidegger (1993) and from using more of Simon's ideas.

Heidegger (1993, p. 313) seeks to identify the essence of modern technology. This process commences with an examination of the instrumentalist view of technology as suggested by Aristotle and his four explanations for change, commonly known as the four causes.

> For centuries philosophy has taught that there are four causes: (1) the *causa materialis*, the material out of which, for example, a silver chalice is made; (2) the *causa formalis*, the form, the shape into which the material enters; (3) the *causa finalis*, the end, for example, the sacrifical rite in relation to which the required chalice is determined as to

its form and matter; (4) the *causa efficiens*, which brings about the effect that is the finished, actual chalice, in this instance the silversmith."

Heidegger showed that these four causes differ from one another yet belong together in considering the nature of the artefact. The coming together of the four causes in the chalice is seen as example of poiçsis, the arising of something from out of itself, as for example, in the bursting of a blossom into bloom. We will build on this idea to explicitly consider all four causes as part of an ISDT.

Heidegger (1993) goes on to argue that while an instrumental view of technology may be correct it is not the true essence of modern technology. Modern technology, as opposed to previous technology modifies and challenges the natural order. It controls and reorders the natural order rather than simply using it. Heidegger uses the comparison between a windmill, which harnesses the wind but doesn't change it, and a hydro-electric dam, which captures and changes the river. The objects within the natural order are modified to become a standing reserve for technology. The water of the river becomes the power source for hydro-electric power generation. The way in which these objects are perceived is framed with a different perspective provided by modern technology. This "enframing" (ge-stell) offered by modern technology and its capacity to overwhelm and restrict all other ways of revealing is the essence and danger of modern technology. Hence this view provides an argument for supplementing the four causes, the instrumental view of technology, with consideration of the revealing which the ISDT offers.

From the above we suggest that an ISDT should have six aspects: the four explanations of Aristotle, plus the microtheories justifying the design (Simon, 1996; Walls et al., 1992), plus the idea of entailments or enframing (Heidegger, 1993). Thus, an ISDT would have an embodiment that takes the form:

1. In order for a system to meet a particular goal or satisfy certain requirements:
2. it could take a certain form or shape,
3. it can consist of certain material components,
4. it could be constructed by a certain process involving certain agents.
5. The justification for the design, for the links between goal, form, process, and materials, depends on certain micro theories.
6. The design has certain entailments or implications, in terms of emergence, evolution or constraints.

We argue that a theory that is fully formulated should incorporate consideration of all six aspects, even if some aspects are in vestigial form. It is probable that if we examine specific ISDT we will find that some aspects are paid much more attention than others, with other aspects of the design perhaps implicitly assumed. Partial ISDTs may focus on one element, for example the process by which a particular type of information system can be built. We argue, however, that all six aspects must be present in some form in order for an ISDT to exist. For example, the principles for building a system to achieve some end may be hypothesized, but unless some feasible method for bringing the design into being using existing materials is also envisaged, then a design theory does not exist. Using this criteria, Vanevaar Bush's ideas for the Memex (Bush 1945), was not a design theory.

Formulation of an ISDT in this form can lead to testable research hypotheses. A specific example is taken from a review of explanations from knowledge-based systems (Gregor and Benbasat, 1999), which is used as an illustration throughout the next section.

> The inclusion of a suitable explanation facility (a design feature) will lead to improved performance, learning and more positive user perceptions of intelligent support system (design goals). (adapted from Gregor and Benbasat, 1999)

Such hypotheses may not always be able to be tested in any simple or direct fashion. Landauer (1987) points out the difficulties of attempting to test the effectiveness of one total system against that of another.

Each of the six aspects of a design theory is discussed in the following section.

4. THE SIX ASPECTS OF AN INFORMATION SYSTEMS DESIGN THEORY

The six proposed aspects of an ISDT are discussed in more detail.

4.1 The purpose, end or goal (the *causa finalis*)

This aspect is "what the system is for", the set of meta-requirements that specifies the type of system to which the theory applies. These requirements can only be understood in terms of the environment in which the system is to operate; just as, in order to understand the purpose of the silver chalice, we need to understand the religious ritual in which the chalice is to be used.

This aspect of the theory formulation allows different theories to be categorized, compared and extended. For example, a contribution to an ISDT for decision support systems would be expected to show that it filled some gap in existing ISDT, offered an ISDT that was superior in some way to existing ISDT, or extended an existing ISDT.

As an example, the review article by Gregor and Benbasat (1999) began by demonstrating that there was a lack of understanding and agreement about how explanation functions in knowledge-based systems (the class of systems) should be constructed. These functions are included in intelligent systems with the aim of improving performance with the system, learning from the system, and user perceptions of the system (design goals). Some explanation was given of the context in which such systems are used.

4.2 The form, shape or features (the *causa formalis*)

This aspect refers to the structure or organization of the design product. The shape of the design is seen in the properties, functions, features or attributes that the system possesses when constructed. For example, a design theory for a word processor could show how a completed system included file manipulation features, text manipulation features and so on and how these features were interrelated.

Simon (1996) presents the view that complex systems might be expected to be constructed as a hierarchy of levels, or in a boxes-within-boxes form. A powerful technique for designing such a complex structure is to discover viable ways of decomposing it into semi-independent components corresponding to its many functional parts. The design of each component can then be carried out with some degree of independence of the design of others, since each will affect the others largely through its functioning and independently of the details of the mechanisms that accomplish the function. The decomposition of the complete design into functional components will not be unique, and there may exist alternative feasible decompositions of radically different kinds.

Information systems are obviously examples of complex systems that benefit from decomposition into sub-systems or component parts in both design and construction, as is recognized in many systems development methodologies. Thus, we expect that design theory can be used on a number of levels – for a system as a whole and for the sub-systems within the system.

From our continuing example with knowledge-based systems, a design principle at one level is that these systems should include an explanation function, under certain conditions. The design theory for the explanation function itself is at a lower level and includes principles such as "Explanations should be provided automatically if this can be done relatively unobtrusively" (Gregor and Benbasat, 1999, p. 497).

4.3 The material components (the *causa materialis*)

This aspect concerns the physical entities involved in the class of information systems under consideration – for example, people, hardware, networks, the physical environment. The properties of these entities are relevant to the design theory in accordance with theories of natural science and human behaviour.

Our continuing example (Gregor and Benbasat, 1999) recognizes the limitations placed on explanations from knowledge-based systems by available technology (somewhat implicitly) in terms of presentation formats recognized (text or multimedia). Similarly, the article encompasses consideration of human users with discussion of different usage by expert compared with novice users. Knowledge of differences, however, is not translated into design guidelines for different types of users.

4.4 The means or process (the *causa efficiens*)

This aspect concerns the means by which the design is brought into being – a process involving agents and actions. Simon (1996, p. 130) believed that process and product were inextricably linked.

> What we ordinarily call "style" may stem just as much from these decisions about the design process as from alternative emphases on the goals to be realized through the final design ... both the shape of the design and organization of the design process are essential components of a theory of design.

It may be argued that a particular process, methodology or tool has usefulness in building IS across a wide range. For example, Truex, Baskerville, and Klein (1999) make the claim that organizations that are not stable, but continuously adapting to their environment, need system development methods that assume that systems should be under constant development, can never be fully specified, and are subject to constant adjustment and adaptation.

Conversely, the construction of an information system of a particular type could be done in more than one way. The characteristics of the different methods will normally have implications for the "emergence"/long term life of the system as well as a range of other tradeoffs in terms of cost, efficiency and so on. In any case, an ISDT should explicitly address what method (or methods) can be used to construct a design.

Examination of the article by Gregor and Benbasat (1999) shows it is lacking in this respect. A fuller ISDT for explanation facilities would include some of the methods that are required to build them; for example, knowledge acquisition techniques for gaining knowledge from experts to justify explanations or participative design methods such as those used by De Greef and Neerincx (1995) to ensure explanations match user needs.

4.5 Micro theories or "binding knowledge"

This aspect provides the justificatory knowledge for linking goals, shape, processes, and materials. Some knowledge is needed of how material objects behave so as to judge their capabilities for a design. For example, the bandwidth of communication channels limits designs of e-commerce systems by placing limits on data carried within a time period. Knowledge of human cognitive capacities heavily influences principles of human-computer interaction design. Simon (1996) refers to these theories as "micro theories" and Walls et al. (1992) as "kernel theories". Walls et al. (1992) see kernel theories as informing design products and design processes separately. Here we argue that they are a linking mechanism for a number, or all, of the other aspects of the design theory.

The nature and degree of reliance on micro theories is arguable. Theories might come from natural science, social science (Simon, 1996) or practitioner-in-use theories (Sarker and Lee (2002). Simon argues that it is possible to have a design theory with an incomplete understanding of the micro-theories on which it is based, believing that building a theory of a system:

> Does not depend on having an adequate micro theory of the natural laws that govern the system components.
> Such a micro theory might be simply irrelevant. (p. 19)

He argues that the relationship between design science and natural science can follow what he observes in the practice of the natural sciences. We do not have to know, or guess at, all the internal structure of the system components, but only that part of it that is crucial to the abstraction in the design theory. An example is given of the first time-sharing computer systems, where only fragments of theory were available to guide initial designs.

The phenomena that arise out of the creation of design science artefacts can be the targets of natural science research (March and Smith, 1995). In any new discipline people often do things for which theory has no explanation and provides no foundation, and theory evolves only after practice has demonstrated that something works (Glass, 1996). Natural science explanations of how and why an artefact works may lag years behind the application of the artefact (March and Smith, 1995).

Our example article on explanation facilities argues for a theoretical base that includes Toulmin's model of argumentation (Toulmin, 1958). It is shown that explanations that conform to Toulmin's model of argumentation, in that they provide adequate justification for the knowledge offered, should be more persuasive and lead to greater trust, agreement, satisfaction, and acceptance – of the explanation and possibly also of the system as a whole. Toulmin's theory provides a link between design principles and goal, but it also suggests a link between process and goal – the process of constructing explanations should include the gathering of what is regarded as adequate justificatory evidence for each explanation.

4.6 Entailments – emergence, *poiçsis,* enframing

The sixth and final aspect of design theory is consideration of the possible entailments of the design. This is probably the most difficult aspect to both delineate in a meta-theoretical sense and to deal with in a specific ISDT. A reason Popper and the Greek thinkers were against technology and an "instrumentalist" view of science was from a sense of ignorance of the effects our interventions might have on nature (O'Hear, 1989).

A relatively prosaic view of this aspect is that it means designing for flexibility and continuing evolution of a system in the face of an uncertain future. Simon (1996) considered that with complex systems and design of an evolving artefact, flexibility and adaptability could be enabled by feedback loops to refine design.

O'Hear (1989, p. 220) writes of an "evolutionary trajectory" rather than "a design" and notes the attempt to predict the direction or outcome of a particular technological innovation in advance is bound to be uncertain. It is possible that all that can be done is to be aware of the possibilities of emergence, poiçsis and enframing from technological designs.

Our example article on explanations is completely deficient in this respect. No consideration is given to the possibility that the nature of explanations could vary over time, or with the experiences of a particular user. Some thought on this aspect could lead to a richer design theory for more flexible explanatory capabilities.

5. CONCLUDING REMARKS

In view of the limited discussion that has occurred to date on the formulation of design theory specifically for Information Systems, some of the ideas expressed here may be regarded as rather novel and are likely to lead to further debate, which is to be encouraged. The thinking of the authors has changed in the course of writing this paper and may evolve again with further work.

What we propose here draws on work mainly from Simon (1996) and Heidegger (1993) but synthesizes thoughts from these authors in arriving at the six aspects of a design theory proposed. Neither of these authors attempted to specify clearly how a design theory should be expressed.

A number of issues have not been addressed in the paper. One issue is the level of theory dealt with. The ISDT we have used as examples could be regarded as "mid-range". They deal with a class or category of systems. It is possible that we may be able to discover "grand" theories of design or design principles that cover a large set of systems. For example, design process guidelines such as "Most theories of IS implementation are too narrow and mechanistic; IS implementation can only be understood as part of the broader social and organizational context" (Klein and Myers, 1999, p. 80) are at a high level of generalization. Should we be looking for more, very general, guidelines of this nature?

A second issue is the manner in which the theory formulation is represented. Representation languages could include ordinary language, mathematics, drawings, models and diagrammatic tools (Simon, 1996). Simon posits that problem representation influences design and that special forms of logic may be needed to capture reasoning about imperatives. Here we have proposed that design theory can be formulated in ordinary propositional form (possibly supplemented by diagrammatic representations) and specified six aspects of the theory that should be described. Similar but different ideas can be found in the literature on design patterns, where the key ingredients of a pattern are listed (Alexander et al., 1977). Additionally, Jarvinen (2001) suggests theory development could be expressed in terms of advancement from an initial, somewhat problematic state of knowledge, to another "better" state through the construction/design of some artefact. Research of this type should provide a description of these two states of knowledge (before and after the artefact was constructed). These works have not attempted to elucidate theory specification to the degree we have here, but there is a possibility that expressing design theory in their terms could lead to different outcomes. This possibility is beyond the scope of the current paper, but could be investigated in further work.

A third issue is the idea of entailments in a design theory, in terms of poiçsis and enframing, which remains problematic and deserves much further attention than has been possible here.

We believe, however, that our paper is useful in considering the formulation of design theory separately from consideration of the epistemological issues of how such theory can be developed and tested, though both matters are necessarily linked. A clearer idea of how a design theory can be formulated provides a basis for further work on evaluating contributions to knowledge of this type. Many Information Systems researchers are doing work of the ISDT type, as shown by Morrison and George (1995), but have little guidance on how to express what they are doing. Work towards clearer theory formulation should help with the further aim of building a cumulative body of knowledge.

REFERENCES

Alexander, C., Ishikawa, S., and Silverstein, M., 1977, *A Pattern Language: Towns, Buildings, Construction*, Oxford University Press.

Baskerville, R. and Wood-Harper, A.T., 1998, Diversity in information systems action research methods, *European Journal of Information Systems*, 7: 90–107.

Baskerville, R.L. and Myers, M.D., 2002, Information systems as a reference discipline, *Management Information Systems Quarterly*, 26(1): 1–14.

Burstein, F., and Gregor, S., 1999, The Systems development or engineering approach to research in information systems: an action research perspective, in: *Proceedings of the 10th Australasian Conference on Information Systems*, B. Hope and P. Yoong, eds., Victoria University of Wellington, New Zealand, pp. 122-134.

Bush, V., 1945, As we may think. *The Atlantic Monthly*.

Cecez-Kecmanovic, D., 1994, Engineering type information systems research: A discussion on its position and quality, Proceedings of the 5th Australian Information Systems Conference, Monash Department of Information Systems, Caulfield, Vic., 767-770.

David, J., Gerard, G., and McCarthy, W., 2000, *Design Science: Building the Future of Accounting Information Systems*, SMAP.

Davis, G., 2000, Information systems conceptual foundations: looking backward and forward, in: *Organizational and Social Perspectives on Information Technology*, R. Baskerville, J. Stage, and J. DeGross, eds., Kluwer, Boston.

De Greef, H. P., and Neerincx, M. A., 1995, Cognitive support: designing aiding to supplement human knowledge, *International Journal of Human-Computer Studies*, 42, 531–571.

Dubin, R., 1978, *Theory Building*. (Rev. ed.), Free Press, London.

Gregor, S., 2002a, A theory of theories in Information Systems, in *Information Systems Foundations: Building the Theoretical Base*, S. Gregor and D. Hart, eds., Australian National University, Canberra, pp. 1–20.

Gregor, S., 2002b, Design theory in information systems. *Australian Journal of Information Systems*, Special Issue: 14-22.

Gregor, S., 2001, Theory formulation in e-commerce: Puzzles and opportunities, in *Developing a dynamic, integrative, multi-disciplinary research agenda in e-commerce/e-business*, S. Elliot, K. Andersen, and P. Swatman, eds., International Federation of Information Processing, pp 3–19.

Gregor, S., and Benbasat, I., 1999, Explanations from intelligent systems: Theoretical foundations and implications for practice, *Management Information Systems Quarterly*, 23(4): 497–530.

Glass, R., 1996, The relationship between theory and practice in software engineering, *Communications of the ACM*, 39(11), 11–13.

Habermas, J., 1984, Theory of communicative action, in: *Vol 1: Reason and the Rationalization of Society*, Heinemann, London.

Heidegger, M., 1993, The question concerning technology, in: *Basic Writings*, Harper, San Fransisco, pp 311–341, translated from Martine Heidegger, 1954, *Vortrage and Aufsatze*, Gunther Neske Verlag, Pfullingen, pp 13–44.

Iivari, J., Hirschheim, R., and Klein, H. K., 1998, A paradigmatic analysis contrasting information systems development approaches and methodologies, *Information Systems Research*, June: 164–193.

Jarvinen, P., 2001, *On Research Methods*. Opinpajan Kirja, Tampere, Finland.

Kasanen, E., Lukha, K., and Siitonen, A., 1993, The constructive approach in management accounting research, *Journal of Management Accounting Research*: 243–264.

Klein, H. K., and Myers, M. D., 1999, A set of principles for conducting and evaluating interpretive field studies in Information Systems, *MIS Quarterly*, March: 67–93.

Kwon, T. H., and Zmud, R. W., 1987, Unifying the fragmented models of information systems implementation, in *Critical Issues in Information Systems Research*, R.J. Boland and R.A. Hirschheim, eds., Wiley.

Landauer, T.K., 1987, Relations between cognitive psychology and computer system design, in *Interfacing thought*, J.M. Carroll, ed., MIT Press.

Lau, F., 1997, A review on the use of action research in information systems studies, in *Information Systems and Qualitative Research*, L. A. Liebenau and J. DeGross, eds., Chapman & Hall, London, pp. 31–68.

March, S.T., and Smith, G.F., 1995, Design and natural science research on information technology, *Decision Support Systems*, 15: 251–266.

Markus, M., Majchrzak, L.A., and Gasser, L., 2002, A design theory for systems that support emergent knowledge processes, *MIS Quarterly*, 26: 179–212.

Morrison, J., and George, J.F., 1995, Exploring the software engineering component in MIS research, *Communications of the ACM*, 38(7): 80–91.

O'Hear, A., 1989, *Introduction to the Philosophy of Science*, Clarendon Press, Oxford.

Orlikowski. W., 1992, The duality of technology: Rethinking the concept of technology in organizations, *Organization Science*, 3(3): 398–427.

Popper, K., 1986, *Unended Quest an Intellectual Autobiography*, Fontana, Glasgow.

Rogers, E., 1995, *Diffusion of Innovations*. The Free Press, New York.

Sarker, S., and Lee, A., 2002, Using a positivist case research methodology to test three competing theories-in-use of business process reengineering, *Journal of the AIS*, 2(7).

Savelson, R., Phillips, D.C., Towne, L., and Feuer, M., 2003, On the science of education design studies, *Educational Researcher*, 32(1): 25–28.

Schön, D., 1983, *The Reflective Practitioner*. Basic Books.

Simon, H., 1996, *The Sciences of the Artificial*. (3rd edn.). MIT Press, Cambridge, MA.

Sutton, R.I., and Shaw, B.M., 1995, What theory is not, *Administrative Sciences Quarterly*, 40(3): 371–384.

Toulmin, S., 1958, *The Uses of Argument*. Cambridge University Press, Cambridge.

Truex, D., Baskeville, R., and Klein, H., 1999, Growing systems in emergent organizations, *Communications of the ACM*, 42(8): 117–123.

Walls, J. G., Widmeyer, G. R., and El Sawy, O. A., 1992, Building an information system design theory for vigilant EIS, *Information Systems Research*, 3(1): 36–59.

Weber, R., 1987, Toward a theory of artefacts: a paradigmatic base for information systems research, *Journal of Information Systems*, Spring: 3-19.

Weber, R., 1997, *Ontological Foundations of Information Systems*. Coopers & Lybrand, Melbourne.

JUSTIFYING ISD KNOWLEDGE CLAIMS

Mike Metcalfe[1]

ABSTRACT

This paper is a revisit of Churchman's "The Design Of Inquiring Systems" from the perspective of Argumentative Inquiry. It will argue that Churchman's five guarantors of "truth" can be interlocked with the idea that knowledge (objective or interpreted) is created and validated through argumentation. The implications of this is that Churchman's guarantors, the ancient art of argument and perspectival thinking become three stands woven together to provide interpretive ISD with a workable definition of distinguishing "myth" from "fact".

1. THE PROBLEM

For those of us who interpret information systems development (ISD) beyond objective knowledge to include a search for justified stakeholders' perspectives, there is a requirement to have and apply some "guarantors of truth." We need a means of justifying knowledge claims in order to be able to distinguish 'myth' from the rationally justified. We struggle to be able to determine what in discipline is unsupported hunches and what is "knowledge" validated reasoning and empirics to the satisfaction of a knowledgeable community. Without some "guarantors of truth" ISD is in danger of repeating the horrors that followed the Nazi persecution of "Jewish physics" and Stalin's enforcement of "Marxist biology." In both cases myth was allowed to suppress the truth and millions of people died as a consequence. Writers are now calling for "Feminist algebra," and "New Age Physics" (Stove, 1998). Some justified middle ground between only recognising objective physical knowledge and the "anything goes" of post-modernism may be appropriate for a discipline responsible for designing life-support and community wealth-creating technologies.

This paper will explore the argument that *Churchman's hierarchy of five guarantors of "truth" can be interlocked with the idea that knowledge (objective or interpreted) is*

[1] University of South Australia, mike.metcalfe@unisa.edu.au

Constructing the Infrastructure for the Knowledge Economy
Edited by H. Linger *et al.*, Kluwer Academic/Plenum Publishers, 2004

created and validated through argumentation. This is thought to provide a usefully different interpretation (perspective) on Churchman's ideas. Stating this argument raises inquiry questions about what is argumentative inquiry and what results when it is used to review Churchman's hierarchy of inquiry systems. The word "truth" is being interpreted very liberally to include the objective one truth AND the interpretive approach of accepted knowledge claim that are rationally justified explanations of the world. I believe this aligns with Churchman's definition of truth. Some readers may prefer "guarantors of knowledge" with a reminder that if it is "myth" it is not "knowledge". Post-modern "knowing" is being excluded.

First, a brief review of argumentative inquiry will be presented. This is followed by a review of Churchman's book using argument as a perspective (lens, theory, intellectual frame). Last the implications of this perspective will be discussed.

2. ARGUMENTATIVE INQUIRY

The dialectic, reasoned, rhetorical or argumentative inquiry process is about the only non-violent mechanism humans have to construct, refine, apply or challenge diverse perspectives. People who claim to have a new idea or perspective are asked to justify their claims by providing supporting evidence while others are allocated the competitive task of thinking of ways to counter this evidence. Structures for organisational inquiry that use argument have developed over the centuries, typified by the English justice system. This process of organisational argument goes to heart of democratisation of community groups, commercial organisations, government and science. In science, the main supporting evidence for a knowledge claim (argument) is repeatable observations. However, in complex social situations like courts, government and interpretive IS research, repeatability is not possible because self-conscious human beings, unlike molecules, learn. Given the need to present a convincing argument and a lack of repeatability (the smoking gun evidence), interpretive researchers have turned to perspectival thinking. That is, again unlike what is possible when researching into molecules experiences, interpretive research convince by seeking interlockers' (participants, stakeholders etc) perspectives on the problem under consideration.

The ethnography of human inquiry shows it to be a social activity and, as such, alternative perspectives will exist. Ignoring these, treating them as unfortunate noise or simply not appreciating that they exist, means forgoing an opportunity to use these forces as motivation to better understand a situation – see Mason and Mitroff (1981) and Linstone (1999). Put the other way around, an inquiry into a complex social situation can be viewed as the end result of an argument between vested interests, which is dependent of what ideas are raised, who got a voice and how well they are communicated. Inquiry as argument aligns with what Crosswhite and Walton call persuasive dialogue reasoning: that is, it assumes you are trying to convince cynical, yet competent, opponents of your claim or vision, prior experience or preferences. Yet the priority is learning not persuasion per se. The philosophical basis comes from Socrates, Plato and Aristotle's dialectic reasoning, re-visited through Popper, (1972) Walton (1998), Eemeren et al (1987), Perelman and Olbrechts-Tyteca (1969) and Crosswhite (1996). The "guarantor" that argument will produce justified knowledge is the establishment of effective competitive rules of verbal competition (or questioning) between the participants. For some communities, this competition has to be encouraged but very mildly, in others it needs to be restrained and depersonalised.

Tracy and Glidden-Tracey (1999) propose three elements that are related to conducting inquiry as a reasoned argument: "(a) focus on underlying assumptions, (b) avoidance of compartmentalizations of inquiry components, and (c) iterative comparisons of assumptions across components." This emphasis on revealing underlying assumptions is an integral part of argumentation and something that makes this approach particularly relevant to human inquiry. Tracy and Glidden-Tracey go on to say that to argue before a critical audience for a specific approach from among identifiable options requires careful thought and more careful articulation of assumptions. This aligns with the extensive management literature on the use of argument in both problem formulation and decision-making. For example, Niederman and DeSanctis's (1995) empirical experiments suggest that the argument approach leads to a greater combination of both coverage of critical issues and higher satisfaction with the inquiry exercise, leading to a greater commitment to implementation. Meyers and Seibold (1989) also summarise the extensive empirical research on analysing argumentative processes in everyday commerce, while Fischer and Forrester report on research being undertaken on the role of argument in government policy formulation. They both report that it was helpful in drawing out issues and in improving understanding between parties.

As research reports are about communication, the argumentation approach doubles up in this role, both as a report writing strategy and as a means of improving social interaction. Users are more likely to be committed to a new design if they have been involved in a reasonable argumentative process or if their questions are anticipated by reporting the arguments or evidence. If nothing else, the perceptions of the purpose and context of the inquiry will be better communicated. The management literature supporting the role of argument to assist communication is even more extensive than the decision-making literature. Meyers and Seibold (1989) summarise it by saying that, from the discipline's beginnings in late nineteenth-century as forensics pedagogy, the study of argument has been a rich intellectual tradition in the field of communication.

A further attraction of the argument approach is that it makes bias explicit. Pretending to be impartial where repeat experiments were not possible has stressed scientific inquiry and is unconvincing in the political competition of modern communities. Much time and emotion is saved if each actor openly states his or her preference, or claim, up-front, rather than pretending to present impartial questions and then be asked to justify this claim in a public arena. Argument opens the door for perspectival inquiry. An argument requires more than one perspective (bias), which inform each other.

3. CHURCHMAN'S HIERARCHY

The title of Churchman's book (1971) is problematic[2]. It is officially, "The Design of Inquiring Systems". He suggests an alternative, "The Design Of An Inquiring Society" which hints at his grander intentions. But the introduction makes it clear he is exploring the extent to which research can be mechanised, something very 1970's and something his Nobel Prize competitor Herbert Simon also focused upon. Churchman seems to be

[2] With thanks to Chris Stewart to alerting me to this.

trying to identify the how much we can mechanise human-like inquiry so as to automate the generation of knowledge. He is doing this as a way to bring out the issues, and to improve our appreciation of human inquiry. His is a multiple approach as opposed to Simon's mono decision tree approach. Churchman identifies 3 ways of seeing the world that need to be capable of being mastered by humans inquiry skills. These are: 1) the world as composed of atoms (from Democritus), 2) the world composed of purposeful entities (Aristotle) and 3) where events in the world are only known with a certain degree of probability (Carneades). He then attempts to identify the hierarchical function of human thinking into a convenient 5 layers of strategic thinking that can deal with these three views. These he gets from his own background – the history of the theory of knowledge.

The base strategy he labels as Leibnizian. This is reasoning, logic, mathematics, an in-the-head inquiry; *arguing with oneself.* It is presented as form of inquiry that could be done by someone in a sensory-deprivation tank. It processes memory facts rather than sensory inputs. Given the mind's need to consider thoughts in a linear fashion, inquiry is a completely mental process of associating a string of propositions using 'if-then' functions as in: If Socrates is a man, and all men are mortal, then Socrates is mortal. After some processing in this way, a whole series of facts can be thought of as connected by a sort of network of related facts. Socrates is connected to mortalily, Ancient Greece, public debate and so on. Ancient Greece is connected to Plato, the Iliad, democracy and so on... The quality of the network (nodes and connections) is only as good as the quality of the reasoning that formed the connection links. Churchman calls this reasoning the guarantors of truth at this level of inquiry. This sort of inquiry is increasingly becoming programmable into computers, and the resulting net of facts storable in a relational database. However, while very effective for mathematics, this form of inquiry is not expected to be a vibrant source knowledge for solving 'wicked' problems.

As well as being able to do this form of within-the-head inquiry, Churchman draws on the thinking of Locke to suggest the next level of strategy for thinking about human inquiry. This includes using sensory input (sight, touch, smell, hearing). This is "out there" inquiry, outside the head. In the simple Lockian form, we wander about the planet absorbing sense data which we store in our memory as more "fact nodes" which our Leibnizian reasoning can then link together with whatever else it already has. In this way, we continually expand the network (web) of our knowledge. Experience becomes our web of fact nodes and connections, some known with less certainty than others. The guarantor of the quality of the empirical nodes on the web is the accuracy of the sensory input, for example the precision of an observation. Therefore, convincing others of the accuracy of our experiences becomes based upon the accuracy of our observations; *an argument over precision.* Cohen (1994) argues the unique quality of science is its pride in rigor, the "precision of empirics", inquiry becomes gathering sense data very carefully.

This leads to Churchman's next strategic level of thinking about inquiry, which is based on Kant's a priori ideas. Here we see reasoning, past experience and the present object-under-study interacting upon each other. Observations have to be explained, what we see depends on how we look and how we have previously rationalised the world. If human are perceived in atomistic terms rather than purposeful ones, then how we look and what is found, will differ. As Churchman seems to be heading towards the importance of shifting perspectives (paradigms, worldviews) as the core of human inquiry, Kant's work is seen as an introduction to this point. *Observations have to be argued over;* 'X' is proved to be true or it is not. The scientific tradition of constructing

Table 1. Churchman's guarantors

Name	Guarantor	Comments
Singer	Sweeping in new perspectives	It is ethically required to allow in justifications of new perspectives on a problem.
Hegel	Argument between different perspectives	Argument for differing perspectives on the same object under study.
Kant	A priori and argument	Arguing how experience or theory affects what is observed, as in Kuhn's and Chamber's theory laden observation.
Lockian	Empirics	Outside of self, through the senses, argument over precision of observation.
Leibnitz	Logic, Reasoning	Reasoning with oneself, within the head, machine-like application of rules of logic.

of experiment to specifically include or exclude options in repeatable situations is a very powerful form of inquiry. It is a combination of reasoning and empirics. However, it is limited to only those cases where situations can be repeated with controllable variables, such as with the physical world.

This strategic level of thinking about inquiry seamlessly merges into the next higher level which Churchman calls the Hegelian design of inquiry. This is more explicit about *arguing for perspectives.* Now, however, two perspectives are argued against each other. It is not 'that X is (or is not) proven' but that X is preferable to Y. Where X and Y are alternative perspectives. This includes Hegel's separation of the object under study from the perspective being taken. For example, the object under study may be the physical world. Possible perspectives are 1) atomistic 2) teleological and 3) probabilistic.

At the fifth and final strategic level of thinking about human inquiry, Churchman calls Singerian inquiry. This sees seeking new justified perspectives, or at least encouraging all perspectives be given an opportunity to be argued for as an ethical imperative. Stakeholder's worldviews need to be *'swept in' to the arguments* about the object under study if there is to be ethical inquiry.

4. THE ARGUMENT PERSPECTIVE

Churchman's strategic levels of appreciating human inquiry, while clearly presented in a perspectival way, can also be perceived through an argumentative inquiry lens. At the bottom level, the Leibnizian view of inquiry as reasoning has a ring of being argumentative if only with oneself or with historical "facts" in terms reminiscent of predicate logic. The Lockian view can be seen as argumentative but here the argument is with the precision of the empirics. "Is the gas pure enough?" "What was the sample size"? Moving up the hierarchy, the Kantian view is one of combining theory, reasoning and empirics (this occurs because), which is clearly argumentative in the Popperian sense involving a universal audience.

Hegel and Singer introduce the perspectival thinking which is seen to also align with argument. To accept that an argument is possible is to accept there are at least two perspectives. From Kant to Hegel, an epistemological split may be seen. Is the argument one to prove the indisputable truth of some fact or is to justify one of many possible perspectives on the same object under study. Even if one perspective dominates, like a popular scientific law, this can still be seen as only the argument that is most generally accepted at some particular point in time.

Thus the argument perspective seems to fit very well over Churchman's hierarchy but by integrating perspectival and argumentative thinking.

5. IMPLICATIONS

Clearly this is a big topic to explain in a limited space. But this paper has attempted to start the process of weaving together the argument and perspectival thinking approaches around Churchman's seminar work in "The Design Of Inquiring Systems". It used the age old argumentative inquiry approach to review Churchman's ideas, especially in terms of the guarantors of truth. The purpose was to revitalise the discussion about what we know and what is unjustified myth; our discipline needs discipline about its knowledge claims.

The author feels that interpretive ISD still needs some validation methods, given he is part-realist, and suspects ISD as a discipline, like mathematics or biology, has to be at least part-realist, but to also respect rational justified perspectives on the physical world. Argument provides the link between physical realism and respecting interlocutor's perspectives. In the physical domain the evidence to support an argument can be repeatable observation. Repeatability is often not possible in the social world yet argument is, but here the argument is not for the accuracy of observations but rather to justify a perspective through argument. The all-important guarantor of truth is provided by requiring that knowledge claims have to be justified, challenged, before a universal and knowledgeable audience, one that has the power to accept or reject any claim. Maybe then we will have some confidence that the 'cathedrals' built by our discipline will fall down or not.

REFERENCES

Churchman, C W., 1971, *The Design of Inquiring Systems*, Wiley, New York.

Cohen, H. F., 1994, *The Scientific Revolution: A Historiographical Inquiry*, University of Chicago Press, Chicago.

Crosswhite, J. 1996, *Rhetoric of Reason*. University of Wisconsin Press.

Eemeren, F. H., Grootendorst, R and Kruiger, T. 1987, *Handbook of Argumentation Theory,* Foris Publications, Dordrecht.

Linstone, H. A., 1999, *Decision Making for Technology Executives: Using Multiple Perspectives to Improve Performance,* Artech House, Norwood, MA.

Mason, R. O. and Mitroff, I., 1981, *Challenging Strategic Planning Assumptions*, John Wiley and Sons, New York.

Meyers, R. A. and Seibold, D. R., 1989, *Perspectives on Group Argument, Communications Yearbook*, 14: 268–302.

Niederman, F and DeSanctis, G., 1995, The Impact of the Structured Argument Approach on Group Problem Formulation, *Decision Sciences*, 26(4): 451–475.

Perelman, C. and Olbrechts-Tyteca, L., 1969, *The New Rhetoric: A treatise on argumentation,* University of Notre Dame.
Popper K. R., 1972, *Conjectures and Refutations.* Routledge and Paul, London.
Stove D, 1998, *Anything Goes,* Maclay Press: New South Wales.
Tracey T. J. G. and Glidden-Tracey C. E., 1999, *Integration Theory,* Research Design, Measurement and Analysis, *Counselling Psychologist*, 27(3): 299-324.
Walton, D. 1998, *The New Dialectic.* Toronto University Press, Toronto.

THE RO THEORY, DISCOVERY OF BUI, AND IS

Beginning of theoretical foundations

Sergey Ivanov[1]

1. INTRODUCTION

This brief, but in-depth, analysis and propositions have been an ambitious endeavor of the author to review, analyze, understand, obtain and discover scientifically-based foundations for the organizational theories Dr. Elliott Jaques has put forward during the past fifty-five years of research. This endeavor has lasted for over two years, having started with the author's interest to work on a doctoral dissertation based on the Requisite Organization theory at the School of Business and Public Management of The George Washington University, a well-known school in Washington, DC that has allowed bizarre, original, and non-traditional ideas to be investigated and worked on for doctoral theses.

The author spent first year and a half studying the scientific principles and foundations for the Requisite Organization theory as without an accurate understanding of the logic, data, and propositions, it would have been impossible to offer a respectable summary of critiques, and during the past six months, concurrently, the author has read and re-read varied sources, such as books, articles, including personal interviews with a variety of gurus and experts in the field of organizational sciences in an attempt to present a most accurate summary of critiques of the theory to the present day.

The author is eternally grateful to Dr. Elliott Jaques, who personally tutored and taught the deepest foundations for the Requisite Organization theory (and other theories as well) – Dr. Jaques' phone rang several times a week, sometimes a day, for the past two years, with the author's putting his best efforts, though not always best, into understanding what is there to critique based on testable scientific principles, until Dr. Jaques' passing away on March 8, 2003. Dr. Jaques spent an immeasurable amount of time with the author; thus, a critic of this paper may well accuse the author of being biased, but it is for the intelligent reader to judge this paper and its intentions, ideally having read the paper.

The author is tremendously thankful to Dr. Jaques for his schooling, which, if it were judged by Dr. Jaques' consulting hours, would have run the author several times the cost

---

[1] Sergey Ivanov, The George Washington University, Washington, D.C., 20052, U.S.A.

of the entire Ph.D. program, which is quite expensive as George Washington is a private institution. Nonetheless, the author's intention is to be fair to the science, scientific method and testable scientific principles, which were one of the main lessons Dr. Jaques instructed; thus, this article, the author hopes, is a fair and accurate representation of the state of the current thought of organizational theorists regarding the Requisite Organization theory, previously known as Stratified Systems Theory, and its implications for the development of the IS theory.

2. WHAT CONSTITUTES THE REQUISITE ORGANIZATION THEORY

> *A theory is good theory if it satisfies two requirements: It must accurately describe a large class of observations on the basis of a model that contains only a few arbitrary elements, and it must make definitive predictions about the results of future observations.*
> (Hawking 1988)

The Requisite Organization theory is a good theory according to the definition and argument put forth by Stephen Hawking because it precisely describes the managerial organizations worldwide and makes definitive predictions about future developments of these organizations and their behavior, thus, making the theory testable and refutable as a result of comparison of predicted and later-on observed behavior.

The Requisite Organization theory (Jacques 1996) was previously known by another name, Stratified Systems Theory (SST), which itself was derived and based on the General Theory of Bureaucracy (Jacques 1976), also developed by Dr. Elliott Jaques in the late 70s.

The General Theory of Bureaucracy and Stratified Systems Theory have both been re-thought, re-worked and "re-versioned" into the new theory, from now on to be called the Requisite Organization Theory,[2] as depicted on the Figure 1.

As evident from Figure 1, Dr. Elliott Jaques has developed several theories addressing different phenomena observed. This paper mostly concentrates on the foundations for the Requisite Organization theory, and the preceding theories' concepts included in the present organizational theory. This paper, though, does exclude the discussion of foundations for the Theory of Life, Concepts for Information Complexity, Time and Space; however, some of the concepts for the latter theories are included and discussed in the paper as they relate to the Jaques organizational theory, the Requisite Organization theory, to be called the RO theory in this paper. Also, in the figure, the boxes with uninterrupted filled lines imply a completed theory, and the boxes with interrupted lines imply unfinished theories.[3]

According to Stephen Hawking, who is one of the world's leading theoretical physicists today, a good theory should contain only on a few arbitrary elements. Indeed, the Requisite Organization theory is founded on only two fundamental concepts: time and information complexity.

---

[2] This is an important fact to state regarding these theories, as there is a wide confusion which is the present theory, and whether they are different or same. So, in order to prevent the reader from being confused, the author thought it would be important to explain the evolution and present state of Dr. Elliott Jaques theories.

[3] The development of the theories of Information Complexity and Time and Space, has unfortunately been interrupted by the sudden death of Dr. Elliott Jaques on Saturday, March 8, 2003 (at the age of 86).

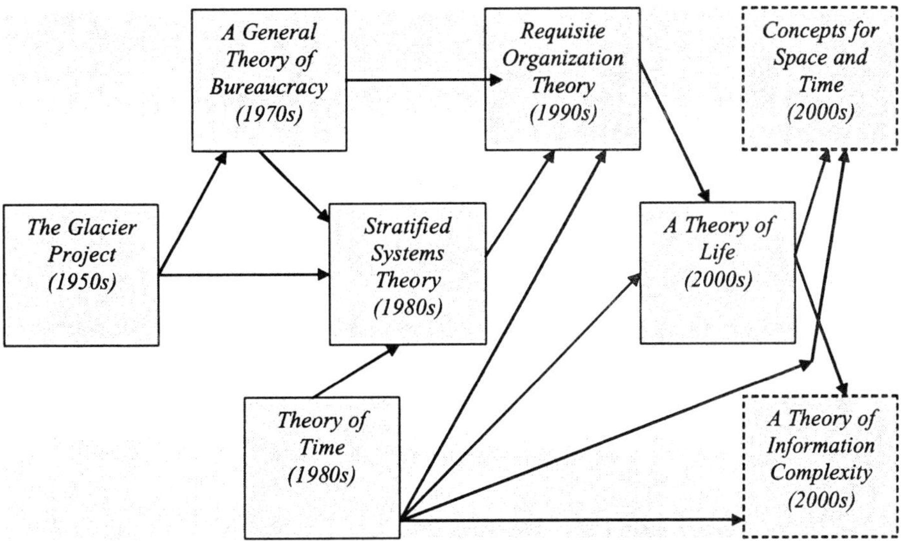

Figure 1. Theories' Historical Development

Figure 2 depicts how the two basic elements, time and information complexity, give rise to the RO theory.

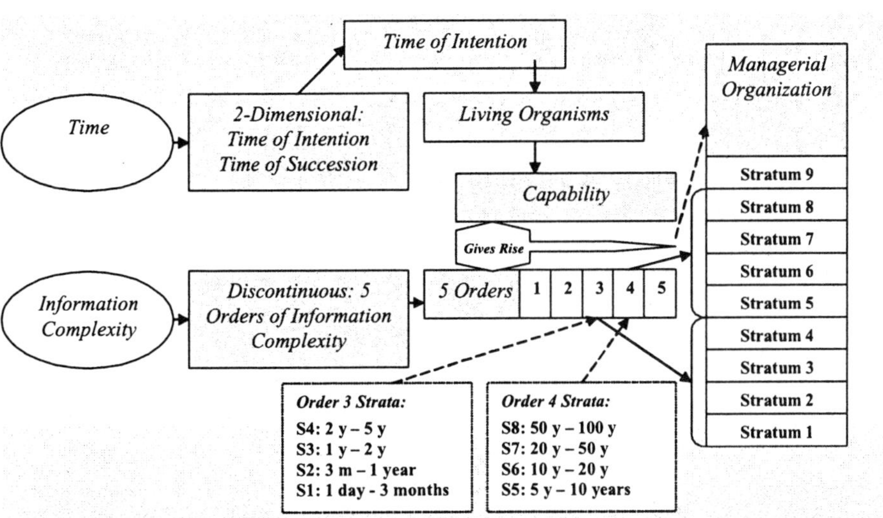

Figure 2. The RO theory's Foundations

The first fundamental proposition and assumption founded on data is that time is two-dimensional, consisting of the time of succession (the normal passing clock-time) and time of intention – to achieve what by when into the future. Intentionality is the main fundamental characteristic that gives rise to living organisms, and distinguishes the physical objects from the living organisms. The premise is that the regular physical objects do not intend to achieve "what by when" – they instead dwell in the four-dimensional world, the three space coordinates and one of time, the time of the clock (succession). All living organisms, instead, reside in the five-dimensional world, same three space coordinates, but two time dimensions, the time of succession (clock) and the time of intention – all living organisms are "going" somewhere – trying to achieve, as Dr. Jaques would say, "what by when" – certain desired results by a certain deadline.

To achieve certain desired results by a definitive deadline requires that the living organism juggles the complexity of information to make decisions, such as which road to take out of the many options available. The information that the living organism receives is coming in from the outside world dynamically, in always changing states, movements and directions. Each living organism (and species) processes this dynamically-arriving information based on the internal capability of the organism to deal with the information complexity. The capability of the living organism is defined by its ability to plan goals into the longest time (of intention) into the future, such as get food within an hour, buy a house within a year, and so on – these times vary greatly with the species' evolutionary development.

Humans are presently the only known species[4] who have the highest capability to plan events into the longest possible future, to deal with the changing worldly events. All other known species mature within only the first order of information complexity; only humans have spread across the five orders of complexity of information. (Jacques 2002b) Most human adults operate in Order 3 information complexity, which means that they are capable to plan events between 1 day and 5 years into the future. Extraordinary humans reside in the next order of capability, Order 4, and are capable of executing goals lasting between 5 to 100 years into the future. The RO theory's main proposition is that the discontinuous capability of humans has given rise to the discontinuous levels of Managerial Organizations.

Furthermore, there are four discontinuous and objectively noticeable strata within each order of information complexity. So far the evidence (data) has shown that all living organisms, not depending on the species, deal in distinctly four different ways with the rising complexity of information in each order, to be recursively repeated in the next order: in declarative, cumulative, serial and parallel modes, as depicted in Figure 3.

These strata are discontinuous, with the species maturing from the lowest stratum to the highest, depending on the internal growth of capability, which so far has not been found to be dependent on any social factor, such as education, status in the society, and so on. The vast majority of human adults mature to Order 3, and lesser numbers to Order 4, still being differentiated by the in-born (as the data presently shows) capability. The humans are the only known species to have spread through several orders of information complexity, (Jacques 2002a) thus, creating the managerial type of organization consisting of roles at different strata to achieve objectives, largely to organize the members of the species to a useful and productive endeavor for the survival of the species – most work in

[4] All other known species mature within only the first order of information complexity; only humans have spread across the five orders of complexity of information.

human societies is organized in various types of managerial hierarchies, in which a member derives a living from filling a role in this type of an organization. The managerial organization consists of roles, and according to the RO theory, each role should be a stratum apart, the manager's role one stratum higher than the subordinates, where each person's capability matches the role's stratum.

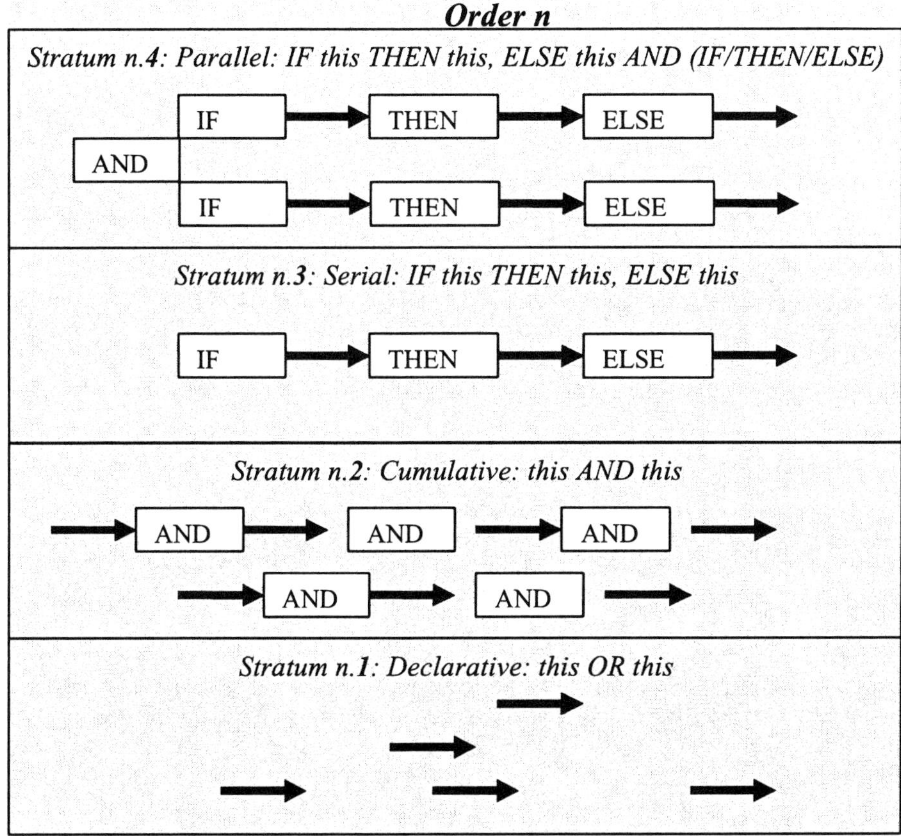

Figure 3. Modes of Information Processing in Each Order

Each role can be measured precisely using the time-span of the role measuring instrument, obtaining the ratio-scale data for the size (level) of the role. There is no precise measuring instrument to measure each person's capability, though several evaluative methods have been developed by Jaques and Cason. (1994) The methods allow evaluating the capability of a human to determine which stratum the member has matured to, and the high, middle or low level within the stratum. Furthermore, the data collected by Jaques shows that capability matures in stable and predictable patterns based on the in-born acceleration rate and the time of succession, thus, predictable at any time of succession into the future when the person would mature from the lower stratum to the next higher one, and if the acceleration rate is high enough, determines the highest order of information complexity and the highest stratum within this order the person can mature to given s/he lives up/survives to a certain age.[5]

Having identified the main cause for the rise of the Managerial Organization (discontinuous capability of humans to deal with information complexity), Dr. Jaques identified major parts and relationships between the various parts of this type of an organization, such as manager, subordinate, roles, authorities, accountabilities, and others. (Jacques 2002c)

3. DISCOVERY OF BASIC UNIT OF INFORMATION

Dr. Jaques, in his unpublished paper "Orders of Complexity of Information and the Worlds We Construct" (Jacques 2002b) has identified and elaborated the differences between the orders of information complexity, and how the living organisms handle complexity. His paper preludes to a major discovery of a basic unit of information, which Dr. Jaques was very excited to share with the author in April 2002. The basic unit of information is a tangible, something with can be pointed to that objectively exists. For example, the statement, "pick up this stick" (assuming that there is a stick lying on a floor), contains two basic units of information (2 BUI)[6]:

pick up → 1 BUI
this stick → 1 BUI

The statement "pick up this stick"[7] is communicated to the reader via the written language, this essay, which would be communicated among the species of the first order of complexity of information via signaling. (Jacques 2002a) Thus, humans physically manipulate various tangible things via different orders of information complexity; the greater the capability of a member is, the greater s/he influences the tangibles from the abstract levels of information, intangibles, which are a collection of tangibles (such as, trash) – second order, related systems of intangibles – third order, continuously changing intangibles – fourth order, and related systems of continuously changing intangibles – fifth order, based on the matured capability.[8]

---

[5] The current predictability rates do not account for the time of succession differentials noticeable when traveling at high velocities, such as the speed of light; gravitational effects are also discounted, and so on; these effects should be accounted in the further development of the RO theory, but at the present time all these high-velocity/gravitational variables play an unnoticeable role, as presently evidenced by the data collected by Jaques.

[6] The discovery of the basic unit of information was made by Dr. Elliott Jaques in April 2002; Dr. Jaques has shared this discovery with the author of this paper when they both met in Washington, DC, in April 2002.

[7] The reason that the author has chosen the statement "pick up this stick" is personally very special to the author – in the early morning (9 AM) in a Washington hotel's room, Dr. Elliott Jaques tried to teach the author his latest discovery, and to convey it, he would throw his walking stick on the floor asking the author to pick it up and count the number of BUIs, eventually quite irritably as the author was slow picking up the ideas.

[8] Even though the BUI is discovered, and can objectively be pointed to, the sudden death of Dr. Elliott Jaques has stopped his research into the nature of information complexity, and finding the measuring instrument to measure the complexity with ratio scale values.

4. WHY THE REQUISITE ORGANIZATION THEORY IS A GOOD THEORY

The RO theory, according to Stephen Hawking's definition, complies with the requirement of being a 'good' theory. Besides having only two arbitrary elements (time of intention and complexity of information), the RO theory makes definitive predictions for all Managerial Organizations, which could be tested objectively and scientifically by anyone interested. Some of the predictions include:

If the CEO's role is stratum *n*, and the incoming CEO's capability is *n-m* (one or more strata below), the company will suffer dramatically – there will be an outflow of people, the new CEO might possibly be fired, or the company would be reduced in size to match the capability of the new CEO, such as instead of being the stratum *n* company, it would become *n-m*. Furthermore, a market test could be constructed: if the new CEO's capability is a stratum or more higher than the previous, the market value of the company will rise, and the shares of stock will rise in value and price, and the opposite would happen if the new CEO's capability is below the requirement of the role.

Other predictions include that if the manager's role is one stratum higher than the subordinate's, and the capabilities of manager and subordinate match the complexities of their roles (the level of work measured by the time-span measuring instrument), this would constitute an effective manager-subordinate relationship, with both, the manager and subordinate reporting feeling just right towards their working relationship[9]. There are a wide variety of other tests that could be invented by intelligent users of the RO theory to test logical corollaries of the RO theory, such as role-based pay, and many others.

Furthermore, the RO theory is ethical, respectful and humane treating humans in the society. The theory explains why all humans are not born equal based on their in-born capability, which is objectively and accurately observable, thus, preventing discrimination based on "common-sense-half-truths," and particularly stops race, gender, social status, sexual-orientation, and other socially invented characteristics to differentiate and restrict certain persons' access to societal resources and working roles proper for their current developed capability. Thus, in order to qualify for a certain organizational role, all a person would have to demonstrate would be the skills and knowledge required, and capability matching the complexity of the role, rather than intuitive feelings of the interviewers whether or not the interviewee would work out based on non-stated criteria of their opinions, which are often inaccurate, demoralizing and destructive, especially when the "wrong person" enters the "wrong role" – both, organization and people suffer, including the person whose capability does not match the role s/he is put in.

Thus, in summary, the RO theory is a scientific theory, based on very few arbitrary elements, with definitive boundaries and predictions, which are testable objectively. Furthermore, the RO theory allows ratio-scale measurements of the size of the role (level of work) via the time-span measurement instrument (Jacques 1964) and an accurate objective evaluation of the capability of the member of the human species. (Jacques & Cason 1964) The theory has a univocal vocabulary, thus, allowing the discussion of the same phenomenon using the same terminology, and overall, is refutable if it does not withstand the empirical tests.

---

[9] This area of the RO theory is presently being tested by the author in an attempt to validate and possibly advance the RO theory in elaborating further the nature of the manager-subordinate relationship.

5. GORMAN'S DATA ELEMENT

Michael Gorman, one of the leading database theorists and practitioners at the present time, has been developing methodology for large enterprise data sharing, attempting to resolve the problem that large government departments and large corporations have many different databases, with business- and mission-critical data, but same information maybe and generally is saved in different fields with different names, different datatypes, and furthermore with different table[10] structures, and different relationships between tables. In his article, "A Column By Any Other Name Is Not a Data Element," Gorman (2002) states the problem and attempts to differentiate and identify the actual data elements, which are represented in columns of a relation. Gorman (2002) defines data elements as "context independent business fact semantic templates." He then proposes to use a CASE (Computer-Aided Software Engineering) tool to identify the business facts, and draw columns for already identified data elements, to ensure that information could be shared later among a wide variety of databases an enterprise employs (also using a variety of different DBMSs).

The CASE tool that Gorman promotes is the one that his company, Whitemarsh Information Systems, has developed – the tool is called "Metabase." This tool is based on Gorman's methodology to identify and abstract to and from different levels of information, identify data elements, and use the repository to generate SQL DDL and an actual application using another GUI CASE tool, Clarion, which generates the application from a SQL dictionary.

The problem with Gorman's approach, even though it is the most precise, elegant and creative methodology offered to the public at the present time, is that it is not based on science. Gorman' genius has understood that different types of meta data reside at different levels of abstraction. He identifies the following four layers in developing a database application: (Goman 2003)

Specified Context Data Model Layer → analogous to a high level conceptual design.
Implemented Technology Schema Layer → 3rd Normal form ERD logical data model.
Operational Vendor DBMS Schema Layer→ analogous to a physical data model.
Application View Schema Layer → business application view schemas in conformance with common business language terms.

Unfortunately these levels of abstraction are arbitrary and are not based on actually existent orders of abstractions discovered by Dr. Elliott Jaques, and furthermore, it is not clear how Gorman's data element is related to the Basic Unit of Information, the tangible, discovered by Jaques in 2002. It is the premise of this paper that any methodology will fail if it is not based on a solid theory, and Gorman's lacks the fundamental theory to justify the abstracting data elements to and from the levels Gorman has identified; they are arbitrary and imprecise, unless found to be related to the science of information complexity and the BUI.

---

[10] The author is describing the problem as it relates to the Relational Databases, but same conclusions could be carried over to other types of databases.

6. ABSTRACTION-BASED DATA MODELING TECHNIQUE AND NATURALLY OCCURRING INTENTIONAL RELATIONSHIPS

A possible (and likely the only one) solution to reconcile Gorman's approach and the RO theory is to map properly the BUI, data elements and other 'things of interest' to the Orders of Information Complexity discussed earlier in this paper. Databases describe naturally occurring intentional relationships between things of interest in a certain domain. Each relationship is a result of an intention, a business purpose encompassing the events of interest so that to gain efficiency, accessibility and other benefits of information readily available via the database technology. The organizational purpose originates in one of the higher-strata of information complexity, and relates information at different levels of information complexity, starting with abstract information types (higher abstraction level) and ending with tangibles (actual point-able data recorded in databases).

Figure 4 describes the intentionality rising from Managerial Organizations:

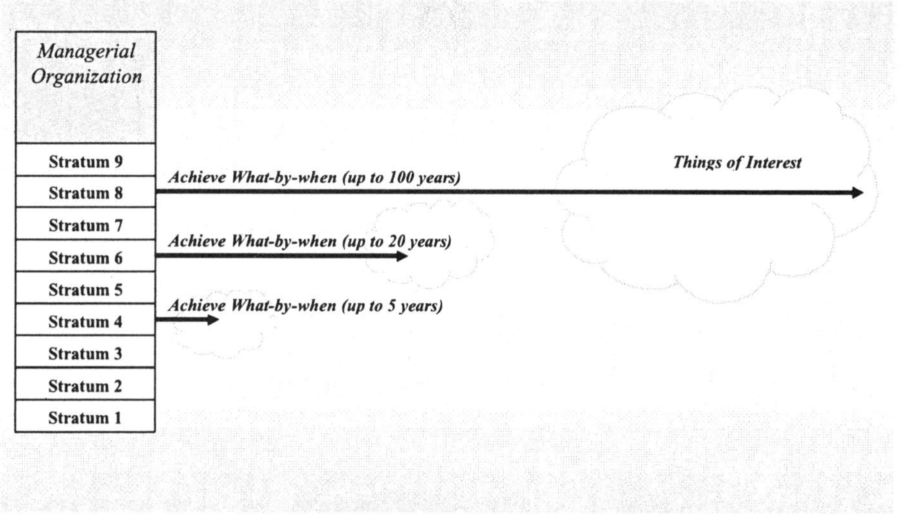

Figure 4. Intentionality

The "Things of Interests" (in the figure above) comprise tangible as well as more abstract achievement points, creating an explicit set of specific things the organization needs to account for, while achieving its goals. For example, an organization may need to save the customer information, billing information, and all types of other things the company needs to conduct its business and deliver on its long-term (often called strategic) goals.

The 1st order of Complexity of Information, according to Jaques, consists of manipulation of tangible information – each tangible is called a Basic Unit of Information, including both, nouns and verbs. The nouns are BUI foundations for Gorman's 2nd Order of Complexity of Information, Basic Data Element, which in the 3rd Order of Complexity of Information becomes a Basic Data Schema, or 3rd Normal Form ERD. Similarly, verb BUIs could be promoted to classes of behavior (2nd Order of Complexity of Information) and collection of classes of behavior (3rd Order of Complexity of Information), as a beginning for theoretical foundations for the behavior object-modeling, and a new approach to modeling the business model. Gorman's methodology accomplishes and includes hierarchical relationships among different abstract types of information to be mapped and used throughout developing the database model, thus, more accurately describing the naturally-occurring relationships in a computer model, preserving the hierarchy (relationships) between the abstract levels as well as relationships on the same level of complexity (relational design), giving a possible theoretical foundation to the abstraction-based data modeling technique that Gorman has developed. The abstraction-based data modeling technique[11] allows accurate mapping of things of interest among various abstract levels of information complexity an organization needs to record in the database(s).

The mappings of Jaques' BUI and Gorman's Data Element in Figure 5 this paper offers pending comments and critiques from peers:

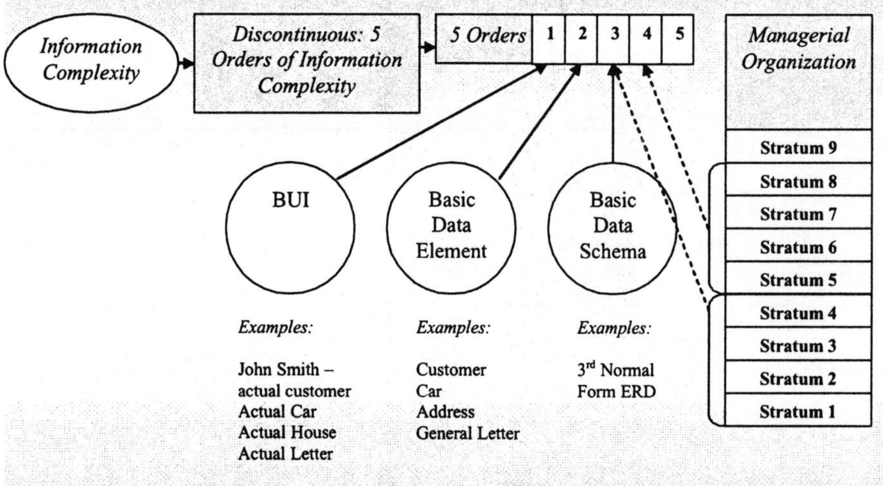

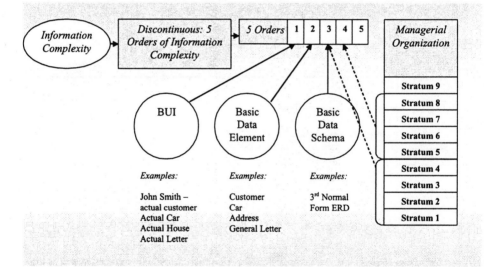

Figure 5. Relating Basic Unit of Information and Basic Data Element

7. COMPLEXITY DIRECTIONS

Complexity is one of the problems-to-be-resolved, remaining a highly obscure and difficult issue to tackle. Presently, there does not exist a measuring instrument to measure

[11] The abstraction-based data modeling technique has been developed by Michael Gorman, and is still in development pending the author's attempt to incorporate it into the scientific research on information complexity offered by Dr. Elliott Jaques, thus, attempting to create a scientific theoretical foundation for the abstraction -based data modeling.

the complexity of the system precisely – it just hasn't been invented yet! The author strongly believes that a successful IS theory must include a means to measure complexity of information for its proper modeling; so that a precise and accurate data model could be designed based on the scientific principles of the IS theory.

Dr. Jaques has given some insights into the nature of complexity. He believed that complexity depends on the number of variables and the rate of their occurrence. This paper additionally demonstrates that possibly identification BUI, data elements, time of intention and time of succession may possibly lead to discovering a measuring instrument to measure the complexity of intentional endeavors; thus, the heading of this section hints that complexity is directional, based on the time of intention.

8. SUMMARY AND CONCLUSION

This paper discussed the RO theory, which is the only testable and scientific theory in existence at the present time regarding the Managerial Organization, the discovery of the Basic Unit of Information, Gorman's methodology to enterprise data sharing and data element (abstraction-based data modeling technique), in an attempt to begin the discussion and formulation of testable principles for the IS theory of tomorrow, which must be based on testable and scientific principles. Gorman has offered a very creative idea for a data element and its use in propagation through various levels of abstraction to design, develop, and share data among various enterprise database applications. His method is called abstraction-based data modeling technique. Further development of this methodology is needed to describe the propagation of BUIs to Data Elements through the Orders of Information Complexity (abstraction levels). Furthermore, Dr. Elliott Jaques' research into the nature of information complexity allows a scientific mapping between the Basic Unit of Information, Data Element, and precise mapping between classes of information in different orders of information complexity. Thus, the combination of the RO theory with the abstraction-based data modeling methodology offers new insights into the nature of complexity, and development of a scientific IS theory of tomorrow.

REFERENCES[12]

Gorman, Michael, 2002, *A Column by Any Other Name Is Not A Data Element.* Bowie, MD: Whitemarsh.

Gorman, Michael, 2003, *A Metadata Architecture For DoD Data Management.* Bowie, MD: Whitemarsh.

Hawking, Stephen W., 1988, *A Brief History of Time: From the Big Bang to Black Holes.* New York, NY: Bantam Books.

Jaques, Elliott, 1964, *Time-Span Measurement Handbook*: Cason Hall.

Jaques, Elliott, 1976, *A General Theory of Bureaucracy.* London, UK: Heinemann Educational Books.

Jaques, Elliott, 1996, *Requisite Organization.* Arlington, Virginia: Cason Hall & Co.

Jaques, Elliott, 2002a, *The Life and Behavior of Living Organisms: a General Theory.* Westport, CT: Praeger Publishers.

Jaques, Elliott, 2002b, *Orders of Complexity of Information and the Worlds We Construct.* Gloucester, MA: Unpublished.

Jaques, Elliott, 2002c, *The Psychological Foundations of Managerial Systems.* San Antonio, TX: Conference of Psychology.

Jaques, Elliott & Cason, Kathryn, 1994, *Human Capability.* Rockville, MD: Cason Hall.

[12] For a complete list of references, please contact the author at sergey@gwu.edu. If you would like to reach the author by mail, please write to Sergey Ivanov, 20101 Academic Way, Suite 321, Ashburn, VA 20147, USA.

THE DYNAMICS OF AN INFORMATION SYSTEM IN LIGHT OF CHAOS THEORY

Jacek Unold*

1. INTRODUCTION

The area of information systems is variously perceived to have real or imaginary links with information technology and therefore an information system (IS) is often seen to be about technology. However, this area is multidisciplinary and although information technology (IT) is certainly relevant, so are human and organizational aspects (e.g., Vidgen et al., 2002). All information systems, from manual to informal to computer-based, are designed, operated and used by people in a variety of organizational and environmental settings and contexts. The ubiquitous processes of globalization and virtualization are constantly changing our understanding of the human factor involved in the operation of information systems. No longer can we perceive the "people" component of IS as independent individuals. The users of local, regional and global telecommunication networks create a specific form of a "virtual crowd", accessing the same sources of information and reacting to the same sets of stimuli.

The article concentrates on the nature of a social subsystem of an information system. It analyzes the nature of information processes of collectivity within an IS and introduces a model of IS dynamics. The model is based on the assumption that a social subsystem of an information system works as a *nonlinear dynamic system*, and therefore chaos theory is applicable in this area. The model of IS dynamics is verified on the indexes of the stock market. It arises from the basic assumption of the technical analysis of the markets, that is, the index chart reflects the play of demand and supply, which in turn represents the crowd sentiment on the market.

* Jacek Unold, The Wroclaw University of Economics, Komandorska 118/120, 53-345 Wroclaw, Poland, unold@han.ae.wroc.pl; phone: (48-71) 36-80-379; fax: (48-71) 36-80-369.

Constructing the Infrastructure for the Knowledge Economy
Edited by H. Linger *et al.*, Kluwer Academic/Plenum Publishers, 2004

2. INFORMATION SYSTEM IN AN ORGANIZATION

All organizations have information systems. S. Benson and C. Standing (2002, 5) identify the following components of an IS: *people, data/information, procedures, hardware, software, communications.*

According to R. Vigden et al (2002, 2), an information system is a set of interacting components- *people, procedures,* and *technologies* – that together collect, process, store, and distribute information to support control, decision-making and management in organizations.

In the next approach, D. Avison and G. Fitzgerald (2003, 19) define an IS as a system which assembles, stores, processes and delivers information relevant to an organization (or to society), in such a way that the information is accessible and useful to those who wish to use it, including managers, staff, clients and citizens. The authors stress that an information system is a human activity (social) system, which may or may not involve the use of computer systems. This definition is very useful in that it emphasizes the human and organizational aspects of information systems, and makes clear that not all information systems use IT. The area of IS might include simple *manual* (paper-and-pencil) information systems, *informal* (word-of-mouth) information systems or *computer-based* information systems.

In the same work, D. Avison and G. Fitzgerald (2003, 5, 6) outline two examples of an IS, at somewhat different ends of the spectrum. One is a payroll system, which was one of the first applications to be computerized. The other example system is very different. It is an electronic auction house, such as eBay. It is relatively new (eBay started in 1995) and exciting, and uses the World Wide Web as its user interface. Yet, essentially, it is just an information system. It matches buyers with sellers utilizing an auction concept. The electronic auction enables buyers and sellers to be geographically distributed across the world. The electronic auction is an IS, comprising people, rules, procedures, technology, software, communications and allied services. Such electronic houses reflect the shift from marketplace to marketspace in modern business environment.

Despite slightly different approaches and definitions, *people* are required for the operation of all information systems. These people resources include end users and IS specialists. IS specialists are people who develop and operate information systems. End users (also called users or clients) are people who use an IS and the information it produces. There are different types of user in any system, and they need to be recognized and addressed. The term "stakeholders" is sometimes used as a surrogate for users, but it was introduced into the IS literature to represent a broader set of people who have involvement, influence in, or are affected by the development, use, implementation, and impact of IS. In their stakeholder analysis of a new IT-based trading mechanism in the Dutch flower markets, A. Kambil and E. van Heck (1998) limit the concept of stakeholder to buyers, sellers and intermediaries. Such an understanding of this concept will be used in further analysis.

3. THE CONCEPT AND DETERMINANTS OF IS DYNAMICS

The next concept, which has to be discussed is that of *dynamics* and *IS dynamics.* One of the meanings of the word *dynamics* (gr. *dynamikos* – strong, forceful) refers to the motivating or driving forces, physical or moral, in any field (Webster's, 2002, 445). By the dynamics of an organization we understand the dynamics of its information system, considering the subjectivity and crucial role of its social subsystem (stakeholders). Such a notion of dynamics represents changes in the various types of knowledge, in the learning, and unlearning processes (Eden and Spender, 1998, 15). In this approach, the basic ideas and determinants of the IS dynamics are: *knowledge*, *learning* and *unlearning*. The research shows that *collective knowledge* cannot be understood without paying attention to the communication processes going on among the group's members (Weick and Roberts, 1993, 358). It follows that *information processes of collectivity* are another determinant of the IS dynamics, and learning and unlearning processes constitute a specific category of those processes.

According to B. Turniansky and A. P. Hare (1998, 112), *organizational learning* is a metaphor to focus attention on the ways an organization *adapts* to its environment. Organizational learning occurs when knowledge, acquired and developed by individual members, is embedded in "organizational memory". This process can be identified at four levels of learning: individuals, groups, organizations, and populations of organizations. S. Cook and D. Yanow (1993) present "a cultural perspective" of organizational learning, which is understood as the acquiring, sustaining, or changing of intersubjective meanings through the collective actions of the group. This concept directly refers to the generic notion of dynamics, understood as the ability to act. Hence, *collective behavior* is the next determinant of the IS dynamics.

The central concept embracing individual and collective knowledge, both explicit and implicit, is that of the "activity system" (Eden and Spender 1998, 15). The key to the nature of activity system is the dynamics, which leads to changes in various types of knowledge and its information processes (including learning and unlearning). This concept points to the next determinant of the IS dynamics: *collective mind*. The collective mind is located in the practice of the activity system. Any entity that has capacities for generating and absorbing information, for feedback and self-regulation, possesses mind. K. E. Weick and K. H. Roberts (1993, 377) suggest that the key feature, which distinguishes the different forms or types of organization, is the degree to which they facilitate or inhibit the development of collective mind. Many authors use the notions of collective mind and organizational culture interchangeably (Eden and Spender, 1998).

The notion of collective mind offers a means to contemplate *organizational intelligence*. It is interesting that an organism (system) does not even need a brain in order to be intelligent. Intelligence is a property that emerges when a certain level of organization is reached, which enables the system to process the information (Wheatley, 1999, 98).

The concepts of *collective mind* and *organizational intelligence* add a crucial qualitative dimension to the systems analysis. They add the missing internal social dimension to the technical or mechanistic dimension, which is the focus of classical theory of systems and organizations.

4. SELF-ORGANIZATION IN AN INFORMATION SYSTEM

The discussion of organizational intelligence and other determinants of system dynamics leads to the issue of alternative organizational forms. Further analysis will help identify the basic characteristics of a social subsystem of an IS. Modern literature identifies four basic forms (Turniansky and Hare, 1998, 101):

- the bureaucratic organization,
- the post-bureaucratic, interactive organization,
- team-based organization,
- self-organization.

The fourth category, self-organization, is especially important for further analysis. The challenges of the future – globalization and virtualization of business activity – are indicating that organizations will probably have to move much closer to the model of a *complex adaptive system*. Some of the characteristics of complex adaptive systems (Freedman, 1992), which are relevant to this discussion include:

a) they consist of a network of agents acting in a self-managed way without centralized control;
b) the environment in which the agents find themselves is constantly changing and evolving since it is produced by their interactions with other agents;
c) organized patterns of behavior arise from competition and cooperation among the agents;
d) this cooperation produces structures arising from interactions and interdependencies.

The processes in a complex adaptive system are those of mutual adjustment and self-regulation. The structure that emerges is not simply an aggregation of individual actions, but has unique properties not possessed by individuals alone. Self-organization can not be imposed from outside, but operates from within the system itself. Organization is not designed into the parts, but is generated by the interaction of those parts as a whole. The self-organizing form has implications for organizational learning and creativity. Self-organizing systems are characterized by system resiliency rather than stability. When such a system has to deal with new information (*information shock*), it reconfigures itself to adapt to the new situation. At the same time, the life of a complex adaptive system depends on the access to new information. In a seemingly paradoxical way, openness to the environment, to information from outside, leads to higher levels of system autonomy and identification. Another principle fundamental to self-organizing systems is *self-reference*. In response to environmental disturbances that signal the need for change, the system changes in a way that remains consistent with itself in that environment.

The chosen research area for this analysis is an information system of a stock market or, to be more specific, its social subsystem. Modern stock exchange operates analogously to the electronic auction house, cited previously as an example IS. Its social subsystem can be referred to as a group of stakeholders, limited to buyers and sellers, which is analogous to the cited example of the Dutch flower markets. What is important, unlike other collectivities, the behavior of a stock market collectivity is reflected by relatively simple and concrete indicators. These are: price changes shown by the index chart, and some "mechanical" indicators of collective activity, such as volume (the total number of shares changing hands during a session) and total turnover (money engaged on either side during a session).

Our initial analysis shows that such defined social subsystem of a stock market's IS reveals all the attributes of a complex adaptive system. This system consists of a network of agents (here: investors) acting in a self-managed way without centralized control (attribute a). The environment in which the investors operate changes and evolves constantly, which is a result of continuous fluctuations in economy and the market situation. The investors try to follow these changes, which produces interactions among them, reflected by individual orders placed during a session (b). The daily activity of the market is based on competition and cooperation among the investors, which leads to a consensus, reflected by the prevailing market trend. This trend proves the existence of organized patterns of collective behavior (c). The analysis of the fourth attribute (d) points to the emergence of a natural dynamic structure of such a system, which is linked to the organized patterns of behavior. Recapitulating, these phenomena reflect the dynamics of the information system of a stock market.

5. IS COMPLEXITY AND CHAOS THEORY

The analysis of self-organization leads to the issue of system complexity. Unlike traditional science, which studies "ideal" phenomena, complexity theory studies the phenomena most common in the real world: turbulence and disequilibrium, self-organization, adaptation, system learning. These are some of the "emergent behaviors" which crop up again and again not only in biological systems, but also in technological, computational and economic systems. These behaviors are characteristic of nonlinear, complex adaptive systems (Battram, 1999, 16).

Complexity theory offers a range of new insights into the behavior of social and economic systems. The idea of self-organization and emergence can be used to identify and explain the dynamics of individual and collective behavior on the stock market. Thousands of independent and difficult to observe transactions, carried out by individual participants of the market, generate the emergence of specific and predictable patterns of collective behavior. These phenomena can only be identified on the higher (collective, not individual) level of social organization. S.Kauffman's (1995) famous phrase "order for free" describes this process of "crystallization", also known as the emergence of complexity in complex adaptive systems.

There are four classes of behavior, which occur time and time again in complexity science (Battram, 1999, 139): stasis, order, complexity at the edge of chaos, chaos. Order means predictability and stereotypical behavior, in other words, it is the area of determinism. Complexity exists at the "edge of chaos", poised between order and chaos. It is a point in a complex system when ordered behavior gives way to turbulent behavior and when order makes the transition to complexity. This is the beginning of indeterminism.

Nonlinear, complex adaptive systems evolve toward a certain point, which is very difficult to define. This point is called an *attractor*. The concept of the attractor comes from chaos theory, which is now part of complexity science. It is a complex mathematical concept, which explains the behavior of dynamical systems using the idea of "phase space" – an imaginary mathematical space, which represents all the possibilities in a situation. In other words, the attractor depicts where the system is heading, based on the rules of motion in the system. The chaotic behavior of the system weaves into a pattern, which is called a *strange attractor* and it reflects the order inherent in chaos (Fig. 1).

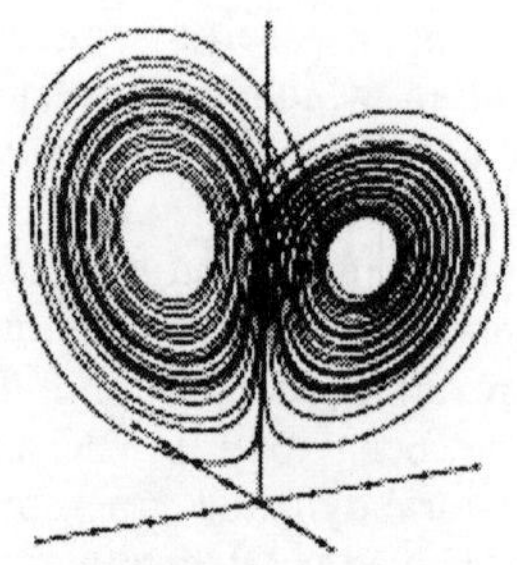

Figure 1. Strange attractor

The strange attractor is not the shape of chaos but that of wholeness. When we concentrate on individual moments or fragments of experience, we see only chaos. But if we look at what is taking shape, we see order. Order always displays itself as patterns that develop over time. Therefore, long-term dynamics of a system is defined by its attractors, then, the shape of the attractor defines the type of the dynamics. The shape of the entire system is predictable or predetermined but how this shape takes form is through individual acts of free agency.

Nonlinear, complex adaptive systems generate *fractals.* (Peters, 1996). Fractals are infinitely complex objects, contained in a finite space. They are *self-similar*. Attractors and fractals can be the basis of a new approach to organizational change and systems dynamics. According to A. Battram (1999, 148, 154), the attractor is a powerful metaphor, which can assist new thinking in "possibility space" – the metaphorical equivalent of phase space. In this approach, values, goals, theories, commitment, leadership: all can be considered as attractors bringing people together. At the same time, fractals have direct application for how we understand organizations and information systems. According to M. Wheatley (1999, 128), all organizations are fractal in nature. It is hard to find an organization that is not deeply patterned with self-similar behaviors evident everywhere. And in true fractal fashion, this self-similarity does not restrict individuals from diverse and unique actions. It is obvious that the same applies to any IS.

These recurring patterns of behavior are what many call the culture of the organization. This means a strong link between the concept of fractal with the idea of collective mind (see the sameness of organizational culture and collective mind in section 3).

The chaos theory researchers study moving shapes, which reflect the dynamics of the whole system. A similar approach can be applied in the modeling of the dynamics of the information system in an organization. The need for embracing the wholeness means a withdrawal from the analysis of individual behavior and concentration on the collective behavior within the social subsystem of an IS.

6. STRANGE ATTRACTOR AS A MODEL REPRESENTATION OF I.S. DYNAMICS

The crowd is created by information capable of uniting single individuals into a group. The group, then, lives its own life, a life, which depends on the exchange of information with the environment. The most significant symptom of this phenomenon is the collectivity's fluctuation during this exchange, and it reflects its dynamics. According to the theory of cycles such stable fluctuations between a system and its subsystem can be presented in a model form as a bounded cycle (Plummer, 1998) (Fig.2).

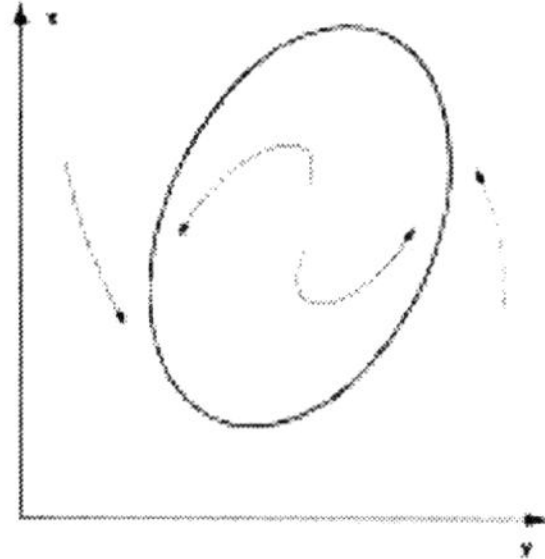

x - crowd sentiment
y - prices

Figure 2. Formation mechanism of a spiral of the collectivity adaptation process: a bounded cycle
Source: Adapted from (Plummer, 1998)

The bounded cycle is one of the basic forms of an attractor. It is also a basic mechanism through which complex adaptive systems react to the fluctuations of the environment. Because this cycle is stable, it does not represent all adaptive processes. In reality, the flow of information is not a continuous process. So when unexpected information appears (*information shock*), the collectivity tries to conform to the new conditions by `changing its dynamic structure. It is expressed by a sudden "jump" from the cycle path. As far as financial market collectivities are concerned, a jump in both *prices* (y) and *moods* (x) occurs (Fig. 3).

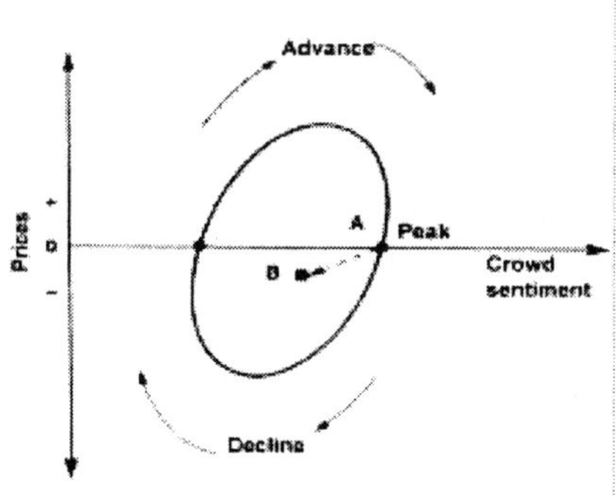

x - crowd sentiment
y – prices

Figure 3. Formation mechanism of a spiral of the collectivity adaptation process - information shock and "jump" from the cycle path
Source: Adapted from (Plummer, 1998)

Some time later, the collectivity tries to return to the basic cycle path and this phenomenon can be expressed by a *spiral of the adaptation process* (Fig. 4).

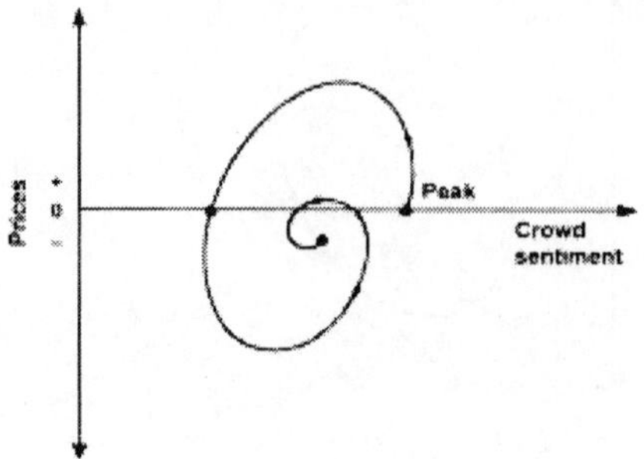

x - crowd sentiment
y - prices

Figure 4. Formation mechanism of a spiral of the collectivity adaptation process - spiral of the adaptation process.
Source: Adapted from (Plummer, 1998)

The spiral in Fig. 4 represents a new, modified, form of the attractor presented in Fig. 2. This spiral is a metaphorical equivalent of a *fractal attractor*. As will be proven in the next section, the identified spiral movement is isomorphic and self-similar. It means that, according to chaos theory, the spiral is really a fractal, so the metaphor has a deep theoretical grounds. The mechanism described above confirms one of the basic assumptions of complexity science: fluctuations and change are essential to the process by which order is created (Wheatley, 1999, 19).

The identification of an attractor in the analyzed IS carries far reaching theoretical and methodological consequences. The presented analysis refers to the dynamics of the collectivity of stock market investors. This collectivity has been recognized as a social subsystem within an IS of a certain organization, that is, the stock market. The fact that the identified attractor – a spiral – has a fractal structure implies self-similarity and recurrence of the system behavior. Recurring patterns of behavior in an organization are called organizational culture, and the notion of *organizational culture* is used interchangeably with the concept of *collective mind* (Eden and Spender, 1998, 15). Thus, the identification of a *fractal attractor* in the analyzed IS confirms, on the grounds of chaos theory, the phenomenon of rationality of collective behavior and defines the model representation of the IS dynamics – a spiral movement.

7. LOGARITHMIC SPIRAL AS A MATHEMATICAL DIMENSION OF IS DYNAMICS

In the next step the observations concerning the nature of adaptive processes of collectivity will be supplemented with the issue, What kind of a spiral represents these phenomena?

There are many different spiral movements, so it is necessary to define a mathematical base for this specific model curve, which reflects collectivity dynamics. This base can be found in the world of nature, because a collectivity also forms a natural system (Frost and Prechter, 1999). In isomorphic growth, a new unit grows in proportion to the old one and still retains the same shape. This is exactly the process of growth in a spiral shell. It appears that this spiral is logarithmic and is based on the Golden Section (Golden Ratio), which is described by the Fibonacci ratio Φ=1.618. Nature uses the Golden Ratio and the Golden Spiral (logarithmic spiral) in its most intrinsic building blocks and in its most advanced patterns, in forms as miniscule as atomic structure and DNA molecules, to those as large as planetary orbits and galaxies. The tail of a comet curves away from the sun in the Golden Spiral. Distant galaxies, hurricane clouds, ocean waves and whirlpools swirl in logarithmic spirals, as do many other natural phenomena.

The fact that a collectivity also forms a natural system is a basic premise allowing us to look for analogies in the behavior of *collectivity* and *natural phenomena*. This natural law, permeating the Universe and described by the Fibonacci ratio Φ=1.618, should refer to the dynamics of collective behavior as well. Since adaptations to the exchange of information spiral, and financial markets reflect psychology and the dynamics of the crowd, the spiral identified in price formations also should be logarithmic. The case study confirms that, indeed, the top of each successive wave of higher degree on the index chart is the touch point of the logarithmic expansion, as presented in Fig. 5.

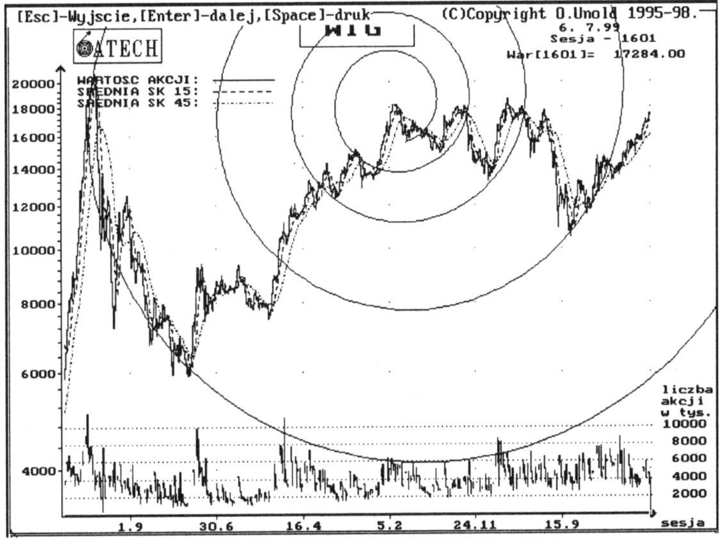

Figure 5. Logarithmic spiral on the Warsaw Stock Exchange Index (WIG)
Source: author's research

The next diagram confirms that the phenomena described in this analysis are identified in any market behavior, both on the emerging Polish stock market and the developed French one (Fig. 6). This analysis has been conducted on the indexes of the leading stock markets (Dow Jones in USA, FTSE in the UK, DAX in Germany,

Hangseng in Hong Kong), and each case shows the logarithmic nature of the market trend expansion (Unold, 2003). This observation allows for the generalization of market behavior, identified as a research example of IS dynamics.

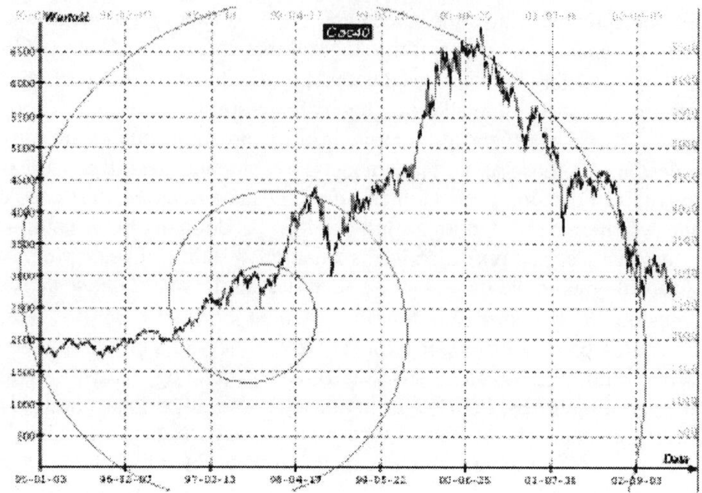

Figure 6. Logarithmic extension of the trend on the French stock exchange (CAC40): January 1995 – April 2003
Source: author's research

8. CONCLUSIONS

The dynamic growth of Information Technology (IT) has accelerated the birth of the Global Information Society. This new technological potential, however, cannot change traditional ways of thinking and reasoning, because people themselves do not change that fast. There is a danger that this dichotomy will create a huge gap between a society and the new IT world. To overcome this threat, we have to develop methods and tools, which will help analyze and fully understand the very nature of human decision processes.

The research project presented in this article provides an approach to help us understand these social phenomena. It examines the nature of the social subsystem of an IS and introduces a model of IS dynamics. The model assumes that the social subsystem is a nonlinear dynamic system, and therefore we can utilize the basic elements of chaos theory. The research area is the collectivity of stock market investors, constituting the "people" component of the chosen IS, which is the IS of a stock exchange. The proposed model reveals the basic mechanism forming a spiral of collective adaptation process. This spiral is a metaphorical equivalent of a fractal attractor, although deeply grounded on the theoretical level, because the spiral is isomorphic and self-similar. This observation is confirmed in the practical part of the research – the logarithmic extension is identified in any trend on any stock market.

The revealed nature of IS dynamics shows that the decision-making process of collectivity is adaptive and follows specific patterns found in nature. Therefore, unlike the decision-making process of an individual, it can be expressed mathematically and is predictable. In other words, individual behavior – which is often irrational and unpredictable - composes, analogous to the uncertainty principle, an adaptive, spiral, and, thus, predictable process of collective decision-making.

The achieved outcome also confirms the possibility of a deterministic approach to certain qualitative factors encountered in an information system. These parameters, considered indeterministic so far, refer to the dynamics of group behavior within an IS. This should help increase the efficiency of management through better understanding, and even predicting the behavior of large groups of people. Besides the domain of IS, the potential beneficiaries include the areas of finance, communications, marketing, cyberspace, distant learning, and politics. The disclosure of a mathematical expression of IS dynamics (Φ=1.618) is the first significant step in this direction.

REFERENCES

Avison, D., Fitzgerald, G., 2003, *Information Systems Development: Methodologies, Techniques and Tools*, McGraw-Hill, New York.

Battram, A., 1999, *Navigating Complexity*, The Industrial Society, London.

Benson, S., Standing, C., 2002, *Information Systems: A Business Approach*, John Wiley & Sons, Milton.

Cook, S. D. N., Yanov. D., 1993, Culture and organizational learning, *Journal of Management Inquiry*, 2.

Eden, C., Spender, J. C., 1998, *Managerial and Organizational Cognitio:. Theory, Methods and Research*, Sage Publications, London.

Freedman, D. H., 1992, Is management still a science? *Harvard Business Review*, Nov.–Dec.

Frost, A., Prechter, R., 1999, *Elliot Wave Principle,* John Wiley & Sons, New York.

Kambil, A., van Heck, E., 1998, Re-engineering the Dutch flower auctions: A framework for analyzing exchange organizations automation, *Information Systems Research*, 9.

Kauffman, S., 1996, *At Home in the Universe*, Oxford University Press, Oxford.

Peters, E. E., 1996, *Chaos and Order in the Capital Markets. A New View of Cycle, Prices, and Market Volatility*, John Wiley & Sons, New York.

Turnianski, B., Hare, A. P., 1998, *Individuals in Groups and Organizations*, Sage Publication, London.

Unold, J., 2003, *Information Systems Dynamics and Adaptive Rationality* (in Polish), The Wroclaw University of Economics Press, Wroclaw.

Vigden, R., Avison, D., Wood, B., Wood-Harper, T., 2002, *Developing Web Information Systems*, Butterworth-Heinemann/Elsevier Science, Oxford.

Webster's Encyclopedic Unabridged Dictionary of the English Language (2002), Portland House.

Weick, K. E., Roberts K. H., 1993, Collective mind in organization: heedful interrelating on flight decks. *Administrative Science Quarterly*, 38.

Wheatley, M. J., 1999, *Leadership and the New Science. Discovering Order in a Chaotic World*, Berrett Koehler Publishers, San Francisco.

INFORMATION SYSTEMS DEVELOPMENT METHODOLOGIES IN PRACTICE

Bo Hansen, Karlheinz Kautz, and Dan Jacobsen*

1. INTRODUCTION

This article contributes to the ongoing discussion about the practical use of ISD methodologies. Many anecdotes exist, but there is little empirical documentation about the actual use of development methods (Nandhakumar and Avison, 1999).

There are many arguments for adopting and using ISD methodologies. Avison and Fitzgerald (1995) mention accurately recording of requirements, making it possible to monitor progress, providing a system within an appropriate time limit and at an acceptable cost, securing well documented systems easy to maintain, making it possible to identify changes as early as possible, and making it possible to deliver a system which is liked by the relevant parties.

Fitzgerald (1998a) extends this list to also include: a framework for the use of techniques and resources at the right time in the development process, the possibility for developers to specialize and thus to differentiate the remuneration, and also the possible standardization of the process and thereby the facilitation of the interchangeability of developers among projects.

In spite of these arguments various studies report that the methodologies are often not used as intended and that systems developers in projects either question the purpose of the methods and techniques specified in the methodologies or express a need for a different kind of support for their development work. One continuously reappearing issue is that the methods are used in a very pragmatic way and therefore the methods' underlying philosophy has no wider implication for the development situation (Curtis et al., 1988), (Bansler and Bødker, 1993), (Fitzgerald, 1998a), (Madsen and Kautz, 2002).

To contribute to the scientific documentation of methodology utilization, we provide here an empirically grounded study of the practical use of development methods in three projects within a large Danish software development company.

* Bo Hansen, Karlheinz Kautz, and Dan Jacobsen, Copenhagen Business School, Department of Informatics, Howitzvej 60, DK-2000 Frederiksberg, Denmark

This article is structured as follows: Section 2 presents the literature findings that helped us understand and conceptualise this study and section 3 describes our research method. In section 4 the case company is shortly introduced and in section 5 our main results from the analysis are presented. Section 6 contains a discussion of these results and emphasises our main findings, and finally section 7 summarises on our study.

2. BACKGROUND

Research on applying ISD methodologies suggests there is a disparity between the way methods are formally described and the way in which methods are used in practice.

Truex et al. (2000) argue that the basic assumptions underlying the concept of ISD methodologies must be addressed. They question that ISD is a manageable, linear, unique, repeatable and rational process and propose an alternative set of amethodical assumptions. They also suggest that both views must be kept in mind when engaging in the development of information systems. Stolterman (1992) supports the statement that the assumption underlying the perceived need for system development methodologies is that a developer's basic approach to developing systems is irrational and that this irrationality must be addressed to let the process follow the ideal of rationality. Robey and Markus (1984) propose a political view on ISD methodologies and describe how the activities in traditional system development life cycles can be seen as rituals supporting the view that systems development is a rational process. In line with these conclusions Nandhakumar and Avison (1999) report how an ISD methodology had the purpose as a symbol to support the fiction of systems development as a controllable process, but in use was too structured and rational to be of any help in the development process. Likewise it has been reported that the use of a methodology serves as a social defence against engaging in the real and complicated task of developing information systems (Wastell, 1996).

Bansler and Bødker (1993) found that developers selected some parts and techniques from a method and combined these with other tools to allow the use of the method to fit their needs thereby circumventing the limitations of the method. Fitzgerald (1998a) also found that different methods are used in a pragmatic way resulting in a unique instantiation of the method for each development project. He explains this as the adoption of techniques of the method but without any adoption of the philosophy on which the method is built. Madsen and Kautz (2002) report that techniques from a method were used but the framework for the development process proposed by this method was not. They explain the departure from the method in this particular case by a conflict between the iterative process proposed by the used methodology and the customers' demand for a fixed price contract.

Kautz and McMaster (1994) analysed the introduction of a structured methodology and identified eight different factors that had an impact on the adoption of the methodology. The adoption failed and use of the methodology was abandoned due to the antecedents to the introduction making adoption difficult, an unclear mission of the introduction, a lack of management support, hostile characteristics of the organization culture, doubts about the usability and validity of the methodology, insufficient training and insecurity with the methodology, no systematic monitoring of the introduction process, and a change process with no participation by the methodology users in the decisions taken.

Finally, Curtis et al. (1988) found that the productivity of the developers and quality of developed systems were affected by limited domain knowledge, fluctuating requirements and communication breakdowns. They argue that system development processes and methods do not support learning about a domain, understanding the fluctuating nature of requirements and realizing the impact of the environmental and organizational context, in which systems development takes place.

3. RESEARCH METHOD

Our research relies upon a case study carried out in three development projects in a large Danish software company. The data collection is based on twelve semi-structured qualitative interviews with developers and project managers and representatives of the method support department.

We chose a research method, which reflects our intention of investigating how the world behaves instead of investigating if the world behaves in a specific way. This emergent strategy leaves us with no specific hypothesis and suggests we adapt an open method.

With the collected data from the interviews we performed an analysis based on the Grounded Theory methodology (Glaser and Strauss, 1967), (Strauss and Corbin, 1998). The Grounded Theory framework describes a way to search relevant topics and relations through three sequential steps, as we here will present the way we implemented them. After an initial individual reading of the data material, the following three phases were collaboratively performed by two of the researchers.

Open coding is the initial step in which the data or text is opened and the different meanings of the participants statements is sought. All text material is read and interesting quotations are categorized and marked with labels explaining the meanings they express. The result of this process is a large set of different codes or concepts presenting the thoughts, ideas, and meanings the text material represents.

Axial coding is the process, in which appropriate categories are found that describe relations between the different codes or concepts. The underlying meanings behind the different concepts are identified and are categorized in main and subcategories, which in combination constructs patterns or sets of axis explaining the data material.

In selective coding based on the categories these patterns are combined into a coherent image of the data. This image is constructed around the main categories and therefore represents an entire framework of the relevant parts of the topics in focus for the investigation.

In spite of our open and emergent strategy, we agree with Walsham (1995) in his warning against ignoring any existing theory and therefore we let ourselves and our study be informed by relevant literature.

It is important to keep in mind that the chosen research method relies heavily on the data material which is the participants' interpretation of the phenomenon under investigation and on the researchers' perception and interpretation of this interpretation, but in line with Strauss and Corbin (1998) we acknowledge and cannot avoid such a situation when examining phenomena in social contexts where "[...] interpretations must include the perspectives and voices of the people whom we study".

4. CASE DESCRIPTION

This study was conducted in a large Danish software company. The company's customers are both private and public organizations. The company has a quality assurance program and a general development process, which have been ISO-9001 certified. A method support department is responsible for describing and introducing methodologies as well as consulting the projects in the choice of methodology and to assist in quality assurance.

Two types of projects can be identified. The first type is maintenance projects, which maintain and extend or improve the functionality of systems already in use. The second type deal with the development of new systems or the re-implementation of older systems using new technology.

4.1. The method support department

The company has several formal methodologies described in guidelines and developed by the method support department, which comprise both structured and object oriented techniques based on a waterfall model inspired overall development scheme, and ideally project management chooses from these when a new project is constituted. A move towards component based development has been decided by management approximately five years ago and a CASE tool for supporting this has been introduced by the department along with guidelines describing a customized version of the methodology accompanying the tool. It is the decision of the project management of the individual projects if they want to acquire the services from the department. Two method consultants were interviewed for our research.

4.2. Project A

Project A develops a re-implementation of an administrative system which uses component based mainframe- and web-technology. The project consists of 15 people, of which 4 have been interviewed counting 1 project manager, 1 product architect and 2 developers.

Preceding this project another project had initiated an analysis of the system to be developed, but the efforts were abandoned due to the complexity. The component architecture of the system was devised on a "work camp", where a selection of the team members came to an agreement on the architecture of the system. To assist the development of the web-front-end, the project has used prototyping and developed a prototype through an iterative process, which has resulted in a final prototype that has been approved by a group of users.

Although the CASE tool for component based development is officially used in the project to some extent in conjunction with a web-development application, an alternative approach not part of the organization's formal method portfolio inspired by the extreme programming approach XP (Beck, 1999) has been chosen. The approach consists of a number of heuristics that the participants describe as their development methodology. Using these heuristics the project develops the system in incremental steps of about one to two weeks implementing one small part of the system at a time. The project has decided not to use any consultancy from the method support department.

4.3. Project B

Project B enhances an administrative system used by several customers. The system consists of a large ERP solution combined with a business rule system and mainframe components. During initiation of the project the project manager and a few project members performed an initial analysis and decided on a development plan constituted by 17 sub-projects divided over two years having 3–4 projects run simultaneously with 20 team members altogether. Five interviews were conducted in this project.

To assist in developing the architecture of the system, the project used a consultant from the method support department to help adapting an architecture-paradigm which had been developed by the method support department, but not been used before. In one of the sub-projects in which three of the interviews were carried out, a method inspired by object oriented analysis and design had been chosen which one of the experienced developers had used before, but which had not been the official method approved by project management for that project. The method was used with some adjustments to fit the particular needs of the project where the user requirements for the sub-project had already been defined and the design requirements were dictated by the decision to use the ERP system as a component. No method consultant was used in this sub-project.

4.4. Project C

Project C re-develops an administrative system based on a client-server architecture. The project, which is close to being finished, employs 20 people, of whom one has been interviewed. At the time when the project was initiated, it was decided to adapt the component based CASE tool and to use the accompanying methodology. The methodological guidelines describe the activities that should be performed during development – from modeling the application domain to designing components in the CASE tool. The design guidelines are closely linked to the tool and describe how components should be created and give advice on how the functionality of the tool can be used to specify these components. No method consultant was used in this project.

5. RESULTS

On the basis of our analysis of the empirical data we conclude that the practical use of system developments methodologies is affected by processes and factors belonging to the following five categories: universality, confidence, experience, co-determination, and introduction. In the following we will describe each of these categories in detail and present how we have found that the practical use of methodologies is affected in the projects.

5.1. Universality

Our study shows that the idea of having one universally applicable methodology is not shared among the respondents. They argue that existing systems, which have been developed using a specific methodology and therefore their architecture and documentation were influenced by the prescribed methods, cannot be re-modelled, changed or enhanced without paying respect to that methodology.

When developing large systems based on the waterfall model, which is promoted in the company for its generality the developers have experienced problems with sequential methods because the initial analysis tends to be incorrect or inaccurate when the development runs over a longer period of time. The application domain is changing faster than it is possible to design and develop large and complicated systems. One systems developer pointed out:

> Yes... Hmm... we gave that up! We found that we couldn't analyse this area thoroughly, because before we were done with that it has changed too much. Hmm... So actually we ditched the waterfall method and said: It won't do it! We'll never finish this if we do it the 'right' way!

The complexity of the big systems is also affecting the usability and the usage of the sequential methodology in the development projects. Some projects are so complex that the cognitive abilities of the developers are not adequate to comprehend all the dimensions at any one time. In some situations this might lead the project to a paralytic state where the analysis just goes on and on without ever finishing. As one of the project leaders expressed it:

> Because there are so many details in this... So if you try to embrace the whole area detailed [...] you'll be dead before you finish.

To avoid these situations some of the projects have adopted other methodologies than the official ones or supplemented them with alternative techniques. In project A none of the official methodologies is used at all and instead prototyping techniques are applied to make the process iterative. Also the use of end users as consultants for the developers is practised. This helps the project to make a correct design, but also the end users learn new things about the domain as the systems evolve – another indication of the difficulties with the complete up-front analysis tactic.

Another reason why the one-size-fits-all-methodology is not feasible concerns the developers' experience that different tools and platforms advocate different methodologies. Software development in the company using the CASE tool always means applying the accompanying development guidelines. These however cannot be used without the tool. In project B where the platform is an ERP solution combined with a business rule system and mainframe components, this directly affects the chosen methodology as according to the project members no one of the formal methodologies fits this development setup. Therefore the project developed its own approach.

Finally, the application of the methods and techniques is influenced by the development tools. In project C where the development is taking place using the for the CASE tool prescribed guidelines, the developers experience problems because the development tool is not capable of handling certain modelling techniques. This directly affects the development process in that the developers are forced very early in the development process to begin the actual physical modelling – instead of starting with a more abstract business model as would be more sensible and as intended by the methodology underlying the guidelines.

5.2. Confidence

The developers explicated a need to feel confident about the progress their development work. Project C used a methodology prescribing the development of early prototypes to help the developers sketch the business model of the system. These prototypes were not intended to represent any final system parts, and thus the customers are not presented with any user interfaces. The developers disliked this situation. They felt a need to please the customers and offered them a prototype where those could see the actual progress and got the possibility to recognize small parts of the final system. This would give the developers an indication or feedback that they were on the right track which created security for both sides. A project manager confirmed this by stating that seeing the customers applaud contributes to the drive of a project to sustain the development efforts.

The need for confidence was also brought up in the context of the larger, mission critical systems developed by the company. These are often under time pressure and the developers sometimes abridge the use of the prescribed methodologies. Typically the developers would like to collect and analyse more comments from the end users, but when the schedule does not allow this, the developers with a high degree of uncertainty develop solutions as they assume the end users want them. Not being able to use the techniques they themselves have agreed upon, is experienced as unsafe and frustrating.

Confidence is also an issue for management in the company and leads to a more symbolic use of the methodologies. In the project which was using the not official prototyping approach, plans and communication upwards in the company were adjusted with the help of some of the official techniques to what the project leaders thought management needed with respect to feeling safe about the project's performance and continuity. Providing management with some security is also the motivation for other projects, which use the CASE tool, but which do only so in a very superficial way. These projects also hope to achieve some goodwill from management because they apply the prescribed standards.

5.3. Experience

The 3rd identified theme concerns the developers' experience with regard to both the development process and the application domain. The experienced developers express that they can use their domain knowledge in many situations instead of the prescribed methods and that their ability to overview the application domain enables them to analyse and design the systems without having to go through formal step by step guides.

Another finding relates to the experienced developers' ways of using the tools and techniques that they are in fact using. The use of the methodology is not characterized as a general adoption of the underlying philosophy, but more as a toolbox where appropriate techniques and methods can be found. One architect explained:

> [...] we use just as many methods as everybody else... It is just that we are so old and experienced developers, so we just kind of do it without needing a nice template around it [...]

This pragmatic use of the methodology has implications for the adoption of new methodologies as well. When the developers are not adopting the philosophy of a methodology their general way of working is not changing when a new methodology is introduced – only more tools and techniques are put in their tool box.

On the other hand the less experienced developers express a need for explicated methodologies, which can help them learn the company's development practices. Some state that they are frustrated because it is difficult to know how to handle certain development situations. They have to rely fully on the experienced developers who thus have an important role and possess power with regard to the education of new developers.

5.4. Co-determination

Our study suggests that the use of methodologies in the development also is related to the developers' desire for co-determination and involvement.

In project A where we found a high degree of co-determination with regard to method selection – the project utilizing the prototyping approach – the expressed motivation and eagerness for the project to succeed was much higher than in the other projects. The developers felt a responsibility, which resulted in an esprit-de-corps and a willingness to work very hard. It lead to an attitude where they wanted to show the rest of the organization that their way of doing things was good and worked well.

In the project the developers' urge to participate in the planning and implementation of their work conditions lead to a methodological change as the project adopted a new methodology, which does not stem from the method support department. The developers explain that they had heard of XP and that they wanted to try this approach. An architect stated:

> So we needed to try it. You know, it is just as much for our own... for fun! Otherwise we wouldn't bother!

The less formalized structure of XP appealed to the developers and played an important role in their reasoning for using that particular methodology, which underlines the developers' desire for more freedom in their work.

5.5. Introduction

Finally, the introduction of a methodology in general plays an important role with regard to the adoption of the prescribed methods. In the company a focus exists on the formal quality system and every project has to comply to the formal requirements from the ISO certification. With regard to the choice of development methods the formal requirements are less distinct and it is very much up to the projects to choose between the available methodologies. But having said this a wish from both the management and the method support department exists for the projects to adopt the component based development methodology. Of the three projects only one was actually following this methodology. One of the reasons for this lack of adoption is, that management did not fully back up its introduction. One project leader argued:

> [...] the management did not treat it as a shift of paradigm, which it really was. It is actually a shift of paradigm to begin using this [...]

The introduction of the new methodology was not taken seriously enough and the developers were not offered the necessary education and training. The new tools were installed on the workstations and some courses were arranged, but there was no other information about why the new methodology was introduced and which advantages its use would have.

In project B the project manager and a systems architect decided to adopt parts of another methodology to define the systems architecture. In the beginning the project experienced problems with regard to how to use these techniques in practice. The purpose of the different techniques was not clear and therefore the developers' enthusiasm to use them was low. The project had however a close co-operation with the method support department and when the problems of understanding the techniques arose the method experts could easily assist and thus the adoption became less problematic. Also the method experts benefited from this close co-operation because it became clearer, which part of the method documentation was unclear and more generally which parts of the methodology needed improvement.

6. DISCUSSION – RELATING THE THEMES

The five themes are not independent, but are highly interrelated. In the following discussion we relate some of them to each other in more depth by linking them to the existing literature from the IS field and emphasise one main finding in each subsection.

6.1. Universality, Complexity, Experience, Freedom of Choice: Methodologies are adjusted in action; no universally applicable methodology exists

We have found the idea of having one universally applicable methodology flawed. This finding is in line with other researchers' suggestions. Brooks (1987) describes that a methodology "silver-bullet" does not exist because of the complexity of information systems and their being part of many different interconnected systems. Truex et al. (2000) share this perspective and present the argument that systems development is not a rational process that can be controlled by formal structures, and that many methodologies actually include certain phases, steps or techniques to find and eliminate errors stemming from the use of the methodology itself. They further state that the development process is locally situated and cannot be disengaged from the specific context in which it exists.

We also show that varying experience of the developers has an impact on the utilization of methodologies, which leads to the application of different methodologies in different projects. These findings are also reported by others. Stolterman (1992) shows that developers used methodologies only to some extent. They were able to do so because they "just knew" what to use. Bansler and Bødker (1993) find that some developers do not use a methodology as specified; they believed that some of the techniques would not give them any new information because they knew the application area and the resulting system well. Fitzgerald (1997; 1998a) reports about variance of systems developers in their use of methodologies depending on their experience. When the developers are inexperienced they tend to follow the methods more rigorously, but after having gained some experience they tend to manage more by themselves and follow the methodologies to a lesser extent. After gaining even more experience and insight into the problem areas, they see why and where methodologies can help them, and they again use the offerings of the methodologies.

In our study the developers express that there is a close relation between the choice of development platform and the choice of methodology, which indicates that different methodologies are needed in different technical settings. The developers experience restrictions and limitations grounded especially in the implementation of methodologies in development tools. Like our respondents Stolterman (1992) notices how developers become irritated when a certain approach does not credit them with an own will and ability to judge and adjust methodologies to specific development situations and that they demand a certain element of freedom of choice. These results are in agreement with Orlikowski and Robey (1991) who present a study where tools constrained the development work and confined the developers by inappropriately restricting the design approach and vocabulary to concepts known to the tools. Also Nandhakumar and Avison (1999) report how a software tool forced the developers to improperly use specific techniques, and they confirm both the link between the choice of development tool and the choice of methodology and the experienced restrictions, which we found. All these findings render the claim of methodology universality void.

Finally, this is also supported by the fact that developers' curiosity and interest in new developments combined with their experience with inappropriate methodologies has an impact on the utilization of methodologies. This is in line with Fitzgerald (1998b) who states in his study that working with new software technologies is a significant motivator among developers. Our findings suggest that developers get inspired and like to apply new methodologies they find outside their organization. Thus they introduce new methodologies into their work, which occasionally leads to the adoption of new practices. Experimenting with new methodologies, which is necessary to assess their qualities, is clearly in conflict with the idea of only using one all-purpose methodology, but is one of the developers' driving forces for their work.

6.2. Confidence, Complexity, Symbolism: Methodologies are used symbolically

Our study provides examples of the use of methodologies with the purpose of making different parties more confident with regard to project progress. We confirm Wastell's (1996) finding that, when developers are confronted with the challenge of developing large and complex information systems, a methodology can act as a means to provide them with comfort and confidence and to give them the belief that they are capable of the task. Wastell (1996) found also that developers sometimes use the prescribed methods just because they are supposed to do so. The system they develop does not really benefit from the methods, but the developers do "the right thing" and therefore feel secure. Nandhakumar and Avison (1999) support this finding. Robey and

Markus (1984) as well as Stolterman (1992) give further examples of the symbolic or political use of methodologies in that they find certain processes are only performed to give the overall development process a rational appearance.

6.3. Complexity, Change, Confidence: Methodology utilization moves towards incremental methodologies

Our study suggests that there is a move towards using methodologies proposing an incremental workflow and away from the sequentially organized methodologies. This is in line with many other studies, which give various reasons for this trend.

We found that the size and complexity of the systems can become so large that developers are not able to cognitively comprehend them, and thus it is necessary to break them down in smaller parts or to start working with a smaller subset, e.g. in the form of prototyping and prototypes. The same argument is seen to be valid for the customers or end users, they cannot comprehend the total system at once either (Brooks, 1987; Curtis et. al., 1988). Like Fitzgerald (1998b) we find that the rapid changes in the application domain and the changing nature of the business environment make it inappropriate to base development on the traditional life cycle approaches.

We extend that argument and provide empirical evidence of how an iterative approach might give the developers and the clients a sense of control and comfort meaning that the continuous deliverances or tests of prototypes directly illustrate progress to both parties. This point is further developed when also considering the extra motivation we have observed among the participants when they are able to see that their work can be helpful to the clients. Unlike others (Bjerknes and Mathiassen, 2000; Madsen and Kautz, 2002) we have not found that this shift towards the adoption of incremental methodologies might not be seen as entirely positive from the customers' point of view. These authors report that many customers want control over the process and therefore prefer fixed price contracts and only a few deliveries, which can be a problem when working with incremental methodologies.

6.4. Explicitness, Experience, Involvement: Methodology adoption depends on management support, explications and co-operation

Explicitness is an important issue regarding the utilization, and thereby adoption of and education in new methodologies. Our study suggests that it is problematic to educate staff in methodologies when these are not made explicit. In some of the investigated projects the methodology documentation was very sparse and thus new employees had to rely on their more experienced colleagues. These are often more reluctant to adopt new methodologies, and thus the diffusion is slowed down as there is a close connection between the developers' experience and their ability and willingness to adopt new methodologies. The experienced developers tend to use their own knowledge and choose the techniques that they have tried before instead of adopting new methodologies.

Like Kautz and McMaster (1994) we have shown that poor management support makes it hard to diffuse new methodologies in an organization especially when no clear mission statement is communicated or when the necessary resources are not made available for the introduction process.

Another important issue is the co-operation with the method support department. We show that when the users and the designers of the methodology work closely together during method implementation, both parties benefit from the process. The developers understood the meaning of the provided techniques and the method designers improved their comprehension of the developers' needs and thus redesigned parts of the method to better comply to the expressed needs and developed new ways of teaching and explaining the methodology. Similar effects of co-operation and involvement are described by Kautz and McMaster (1994), who reported that involvement brings responsibility along and thereby supports adoption, a finding, which we too show.

7. CONCLUSION

In summary, our work provides an empirical study investigating the utilization of ISD methodologies in practice. It confirms and extends the existing body of knowledge in the field and offers an empirical documentation identifying five themes and their interplay and relationship, which affect the application of ISD methodologies and which can serve as a basis for further research. The themes are described through the concepts of universality, confidence, experience, co-determination, and introduction. They emphasize that methodologies are adjusted in action and that no universally applicable methodology exists; that methodologies are used symbolically; that methodology utilization moves towards incremental methodologies; and that methodology adoption depends on management support, explications and co-operation.

REFERENCES

Avison, D. E., and Fitzgerald, G., 1995, *Information Systems Development: Methodologies, Techniques and Tools*, McGraw-Hill, Maidenhead, UK

Bansler, J., and Bødker K., 1993, A reappraisal of structured analysis: design in an organizational context, *ACM Transactions on Information Systems*, **11**:2: 165–193.

Beck, K., 1999, Embracing change with extreme programming, *IEEE Computer*, October: 70–77

Bjerknes, G., and Mathiassen, L., 2000, Improving the customer-supplier relation in it development, Proceedings of the 33rd Hawaii International Conference on Systems Sciences.

Brooks, F. B. jr., 1987, No silver bullet – essence and accidents of software engineering, *Computer*, **20**:4: 10–19.

Curtis, B., Krasner, H., and Iscoe, N., 1998, A field study of the software design process for large systems, *Communications of the ACM*, **31**:11.

Fitzgerald, B., 1997, The use of systems development methodologies in practice: a field study, *The Information Systems Journal*, **7**:3: 201–212.

Fitzgerald, B., 1998a, An empirical investigation into the adoption of systems development methodologies, *Information and Management*, **34**: 317–328.

Fitzgerald, B., 1998b, An empirically-grounded framework for the information systems development process, Proceedings of ICIS (International Conference on Information Systems), Helsinki, Finland

Glaser, B. G., and Strauss, A. L., 1967, *The Discovery of Grounded Theory - Strategies for Qualitative Research*, Aldine De Gruyter, New York.

Kautz, K., and McMaster, T., 1994, Introducing structured methods: an undelivered promise? – a case study, *Scandinavian Journal of Information Systems*, **6**:2: 59–78.

Madsen, S., and Kautz, K., 2002, Applying system development methods in practice – the rup example, Proceedings of 11th International Conference on Information Systems Developments, Methods & Tools - Theory & Practice, Riga, Latvia.

Nandhakumar, J., and Avison, D. E., 1999, The fiction of methodological development: a field study of information systems development, *Information Technology & People*, **12**:2: 176–191.

Orlikowski, W. J., and Robey, D., 1991, Information technology and the structuring of organizations, *Information Systems Research*, **2**:2: 143–169.

Robey, D., and Markus M. L., 1984, Rituals in information system design, *MIS Quarterly*, **8**:1: 5–15.

Stolterman, E., 1992, How system designers think about design and methods. some reflections based on an interview study, *Scandinavian Journal of Information Systems*, **4**.

Strauss, A., and Corbin, J., 1998, *Basics of Qualitative Research*, SAGE Publications, London, UK.

Truex, D., Baskerville, R. and Travis, J., 2000, Amethodical systems development: the deferred meaning of systems development methods, *Accting., Mgmt. & Info. Tech.*, **10**: 53–79.

Walsham, G., 1995, Interpretive case studies in is research: nature and method, *European journal of Information Systems*, **4**:2: 74–81.

Wastell, D. G., 1996, The fetish of technique: methodology as a social defense, *Information Systems Journal*, **6**: 25–49.

SOFTWARE DEVELOPMENT METHODOLOGY EVALUATION MODEL

Damjan Vavpotič, Marko Bajec, and Marjan Krisper*

ABSTRACT

In the paper we present software development methodology evaluation model that helps a software development company to find out what is the most suitable methodology for its needs. The purpose of the evaluation model is not to prescribe the use of a certain methodology, but merely to suggest what kind of methodology is suitable for a certain type of organization or project. In the paper we discuss requirements and guidelines for the evaluation model, and design and function of the model.

1. INTRODUCTION

In recent years many new software development methodologies emerged. Even though every methodology advocates its proficiency in some aspect and claims to have some advantage over the other, they are quite different in the field they cover. Some methodologies are process oriented, other people oriented, some are specialized for a certain type of application, other are more general, some are designed only for small projects, other are appropriate only for large projects, etc. Since it takes a lot of time and money for a company to change a development methodology, once it has been accepted, it is essential that the selection is done correctly. The problem is, however, how to choose a methodology that fits best the requirements of an organization and its type of projects.

This problem has been addressed, one way or another, many times before.[1, 2] Fitzgerald,[3] for instance, found out that 60 per cent of companies do not use methodologies at all and that only six per cent reported following a methodology rigorously. Of course, there are many reasons why organizations avoid or misuse

* Damjan Vavpotič, Marko Bajec, Marjan Krisper, University of Ljubljana, Faculty of Computer and Information Science, Tržaška 25, 1000 Ljubljana, Slovenia.

development methodologies. One of them is the fact that they typically can not afford to spend enough time and resources to closely examine and evaluate different types of methodologies. In many cases the selection of methodology is only based on an advice of a consultant company trying to sell its own one. In this paper we introduce a methodology evaluation model that organizations could use to consider wider range of methodologies, and thus select a methodology that meets their requirements and expectations. This model is currently being introduced into Slovenian government institutions.

The evaluation model can be used in two ways. The organizations that do not use any formal methodology, can use the model to select the most appropriate methodology according to their requirements and characteristics, while the organizations, that already use some formal methodology can revaluate the appropriateness of this methodology. The purpose of the evaluation model is not to prescribe the use of a certain methodology, but merely to suggest what kind of methodology is suitable for a certain type of organization or project.

The paper is organized as follows. Section 2 describes guidelines that were used for creation of the evaluation model. In section 3 the conceptual design of the evaluation model is discussed, focusing on essential elements of the model. Section 4 introduces the characteristics of methodologies and projects/organizations. These characteristics form two frameworks: methodology characteristics framework and project/organization characteristics framework. Both frameworks are integrated into the evaluation model. In section 5 the implementation and function of the evaluation model is described in detail. Finally, in section 6 an example of practical application of the evaluation model is presented. We conclude the paper with a proposal for further work and possible improvements of the evaluation model.

2. GUIDELINES AND REQUIREMENTS

Before we could start creating the evaluation model we had to define basic guidelines, requirements and scope of the model.

First we defined the scope of the model. We limited the evaluation model to software development methodologies that are used for in-house software development. That means that we did not consider special methodologies like e.g. ERP system development methodologies, methodologies specialized mainly for project management, etc. We considered mostly methodologies that can be found or implemented in typical software development organizations. The following types of software development methodologies were to be included in the evaluation model: Rapid development methodologies like Extreme programming, Rapid application development, Adaptive software development, SCRUM, Feature driven development, etc. Object oriented methodologies like Rational Unified Process, Object oriented software process, OPEN, etc. Data and/or process oriented methodologies like Information Engineering, Custom Development Method, Structured Systems Analysis and Design Method, etc. Other custom methods implemented by different organizations and government institutions.

Although it is possible to extend the scope of the model we believe that we captured the most frequent methodologies used by software development organizations.

Next question was how to define and where to find rules that would enable us to evaluate suitability of certain methodology for certain project/organization. We decided that the rules shall be based on knowledge that already exists and can be found in the methodology publications. To this end, we carefully studied several methodologies, books and research papers addressing this topic.[4–10] A lot of methodology publications contain various theses and rules about software development. Usually these theses and rules have been well tested and proved on practical cases. Although we can not say that a certain rule can be applied in every case of software development, these rules can serve us as general guidelines for methodology selection.

Next we defined the requirements for the evaluation model:

- The evaluation model should be easily extendable as we expect the knowledge base will grow gradually. Besides adding new rules into the knowledge base the model should also enable us to easily add new methodologies and new types of projects/organizations.
- The evaluation model should enable us to experiment with different characteristics i.e. to include/exclude a certain characteristic from evaluation and also to assign certain weight to certain characteristic. This way we could test suitability of certain methodology for certain project/organization using only selected characteristics and also properly weight characteristics regarding their importance.
- Another requirement for the evaluation model is transparency. The result of the evaluation model should not only be an estimation which methodology is better than another but also an explanation why a certain methodology is better than another for a certain project/organization.
- The model should work with incomplete information. E.g. even if we do not (can not) enter all characteristics of a certain methodology or project we should still be able to evaluate this methodology or project. The characteristics that we do not know should act as neutral i.e. they should not influence the evaluation neither in positive nor negative manner.

Another question was which technology (tool) we shall use to implement the evaluation model. What we needed was a simple tool with good customization capabilities. We decided to use MS Excel. Before we choose Excel we also considered other possibilities. One possibility was to use specialized decision making tools (e.g. DEX[11, 12]). We found such tools too confining as we also wanted to experiment with the structure of the model. Another possibility was to create the decision model using relational database containing rules and characteristics. Such solution would offer great customization capabilities, but would be rather complicated. So Excel came out as the simplest tool with good capabilities for customization. One of the advantages of Excel was also it includes a relatively capable program language (Visual Basic for Applications) that was used to create parts of the evaluation model. It also enables us to easily create diagrams, formulas, etc.

3. CONCEPTUAL DESIGN OF THE METHODOLOGY EVALUATION MODEL

As mentioned the purpose of the evaluation model is to evaluate how appropriate a certain methodology is for a certain kind of project/organization. So basically we have to answer the following questions: What are the characteristics of a certain methodology? What are the characteristics of a certain project/organization? What is the influence of a certain project/organization characteristic on a certain methodology characteristic and vice versa? Which characteristics of methodology or project/organization are more/less important? Based on these questions we designed the evaluation model that is comprised of the following conceptual elements (see Figure 1):

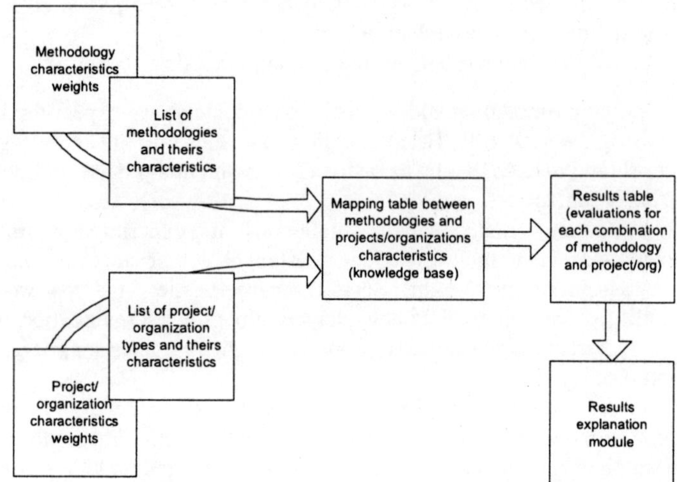

Figure 1. Conceptual design of the methodology evaluation model

- The first element is a list of different methodologies and respective characteristics. This list contains predefined methodologies and also enables us to add new (custom) methodologies to compare them with others.
- Complementary to the list of methodologies is the list of project / organization types and theirs characteristics. This list also contains some predefined types of projects/organizations and can be used to add new (custom) projects/ organizations.
- The core element of the model is a mapping table. This table contains rules (evaluations) of how a certain methodology characteristic suits a certain project / organization characteristic or vice versa. The mapping table contains general rules (knowledge base) and is not dependent on any methodology or project. The rules defined in this table are derived from methodology publications. The mapping table is not fixed i.e. it can be expanded by adding new rules.
- An important element is also results table that shows evaluations of methodologies and projects. Results are presented in a two-dimensional table that shows evaluation for each combination of methodology and project/ organization.
- Next element is results explanation module. Using results explanation module we can examine the cause for certain result (evaluation) in the results table. Results explanation module determines which combinations of methodology and project/organization characteristics have most positive influence and which have most negative influence on certain result.

- The evaluation model also includes weights for methodology characteristics and project/organization characteristics. By setting a certain weight user can change the importance of a certain characteristic. These weights can be configured and stored so that evaluations with different weight configurations can be compared.

4. IDENTIFICATION OF THE METHODOLOGY EVALUATION MODEL CHARACTERISTICS

To create the evaluation model we had to identify the most important characteristics of methodologies and projects/organizations. These characteristics form two frameworks: methodology characteristics framework and project/organization characteristics framework.[13] The purpose of this paper is not to fully explain these frameworks but only to present the basic structure of both frameworks as they are integral parts of the evaluation model.

Methodologies characteristics were identified based on different methodology evaluation frameworks,[2, 6] methodologies description,[6, 9, 14–19] etc. We partitioned these characteristics into flowing five groups that are further divided into different characteristics and sub-characteristics:

- Process characteristics: Primary workflows (requirements, analysis, design, implementation, testing, deployment, maintenance and growth), Supporting workflows (configuration management, project management, environment, human resource management), Development time distribution, Process life-cycle(s), Development perspective and load (top-down, bottom-up, frontloaded, backloaded, balanced), Process roles (stakeholder roles, development roles, analytical roles, test roles, management roles), Use of prototypes
- Notation characteristics: Types of supported notation (object oriented notation - UML, process/structure notation, data modeling notation, business modeling notation), Notation description, Support for distributed environment
- Recommended tools and development languages: Recommended/prescribed tools for activities support (requirements, analysis and design, project management, configuration management, report generation, functional testing, non-functional testing), Recommended/prescribed development languages (Java, other OO languages, structural languages, other)
- Target applications: Types of target applications (IS, web, special applications), Architecture (2-tier, 3-tier, standalone), Target DBMS type (relational, hierarchical, object), Connectivity and legacy system support
- Support and training: Training for different roles (developer, designer, analyst, project manager, tester, other), Available support (courses, literature, on-line support), Consistency of concepts (methodology, tools, languages)

These (sub)characteristics (together there are 61) form methodology characteristics framework that we use to classify methodologies.

Next step was to find the most important project characteristics. These characteristics are essential in establishing a link between different methodologies and various kinds of projects. Based on project evaluation frameworks,[20, 21] different sources[1, 2, 8, 9, 14, 19] and experience we derived the following six groups of characteristics:

- Complexity and size of a planned system: System size, System complexity and architecture, Criticality of the system, System history, Planned future
- Project type: Project priorities, Predictability, Time, Cost
- Type of a planned system: Types of target applications (IS, web, special applications), Architecture (2-tier, 3-tier, standalone), DBMS type (relational, hierarchical, object), Connectivity and legacy system support
- Development environment: Development team size, Development team location, Number of development organizations, Number of all organizations involved in development
- Human factor and organization type: Development team experience in SW development, Development team experience in formal methodologies, Similar problem domain experience, Willingness to learn, Cooperation, Discipline, Type of the organization
- Customer characteristics: Quality of customer organization / business processes, Customer problem domain knowledge, Customer cooperation, Customer requirements regarding methodology and documentation

These (sub)characteristics (together there are 35) form project/organization characteristics framework that is used to classify projects/organizations.

Presented frameworks are not meant to be fully comprehensive and we are aware that these are only some of the characteristics that can be identified. E.g. one of important aspects of methodologies that we do not cover in our methodology characteristics framework is methodology paradigm (scientific vs. systems paradigm as described in methodology framework defined by Avison[6]). We did not include this aspect because we compare only methodologies with similar paradigm (i.e. scientific paradigm). So in our case this aspect is not useful for differentiation between (these similar) methodologies.

We tried to include the characteristics that could be clearly identified and used to distinguish between different methodologies or projects/organizations. Although we know that it is possible to identify many more characteristics we believe these characteristics should be sufficient for the needs of the evaluation model.

5. IMPLEMENTATION AND FUNCTION OF THE EVALUATION MODEL

The evaluation model is implemented in MS Excel. It is comprised of four basic spreadsheets that implement: a mapping table (contains the rules for evaluation), a list of methodologies, a list of projects/organizations and a spreadsheet that holds the results of the evaluation.

There are also three additional spreadsheets that enable us to weight the characteristics of methodologies and projects. Figure 2 shows a generic example of the four spreadsheets and also how the results are computed. To simplify the explanation weight spreadsheets are excluded from the example. Evaluation model also includes a results explanation module. Figure 2 is explained in detail in the following paragraphs.

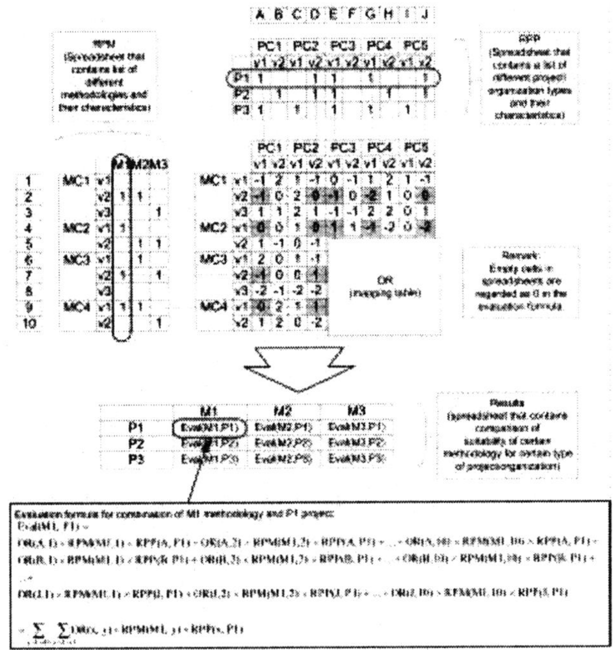

Figure 2. Evaluation of a result for combination of methodology M1 and project P1

5.1. Mapping table

As we already mentioned the rules of the methodology evaluation model are based on methodology publications. These rules are captured in a mapping table that is comprised of:

- Methodology characteristics and possible values for each characteristic. Characteristics are arranged vertically in the mapping table. Each characteristic has two or more corresponding values listed. E.g. description of implementation workflow is one of methodology's characteristics (scope of the methodology). This characteristic can take three different values: methodology doesn't cover implementation workflow at all, methodology covers implementation workflow but in less detail and depth – more is left for the developers to interpret, methodology covers implementation workflow down to the smallest detail.
- Project/organization characteristics and possible values for each characteristic. These characteristics are arranged horizontally in the mapping table with corresponding values listed. E.g. criticality of a system to be developed is one of project's characteristics that can take four different values: system failure can result in a loss of comfort, system failure can result in a loss of discretionary money, system failure can result in a loss of essential money, and system failure can result in a loss of life.

- An evaluation (rule) for each combination of methodology characteristic value and project/organization characteristic value. These evaluations are based on methodology publications. There are five different evaluations that can be assigned to a certain combination of methodology characteristic value and project/organization characteristic value: very suitable (2), suitable (1), neutral (0), unsuitable (-1), very unsuitable (-2). E.g. based on Cockburn[7] we defined the following rule: "In case the methodology doesn't cover implementation workflow at all it is very unsuitable for development of a system which's failure can result in a loss of life." So we evaluate this combination of values as very unsuitable (-2) in the mapping table. Next we should define similar rules for every combination of methodology characteristic value and project/organization characteristic value.

Figure 3 illustrates the preceding example. It shows a part of a mapping table that contains rules for every possible combination of methodology characteristic value and project/organization characteristic value.

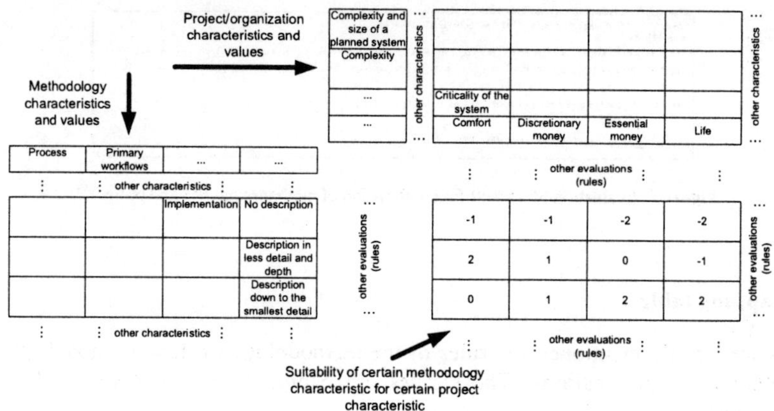

Figure 3. Part of the mapping table (example)

Rules are contained in a mapping table that is implemented in spreadsheet named OR. It is comprised of 61 different methodology characteristics with over 180 possible values and 35 different project/organization characteristics with nearly 100 possible values. To evaluate all combinations of methodology and project/organization characteristics in the mapping table we would have to create about 18000 (180 x 100) rules (evaluations). Of course it is not possible (nor necessary) to find a correlation between each and every methodology and project/organization characteristic. Till now we defined about 2650 rules i.e. about 15% of all rules. All defined rules are based on methodology publications.

Figure 2 shows an example of OR spreadsheet. Horizontally the spreadsheet contains five different project/organization characteristics ("PC1"..."PC5"). In our case every project characteristic has two different values ("v1" and "v2"). Vertically are four different methodology characteristics ("MC1"... "MC4"). Methodology characteristics "MC2" and "MC4" have two different values ("v1" and "v2") and "MC1" and "MC3" three different values ("v1", "v2" and "v3"). The core of the spreadsheet contains evaluations (rules) for each combination of methodology characteristic value and project characteristic value.

5.2. List of methodologies

The list of methodologies is implemented in a spreadsheet named RPM and includes instances of methodologies like RUP, CDM, XP, FDD, IE, OOSP, etc. These methodologies can also serve as a reference when evaluating custom methodology of an organization. RPM spreadsheet is comprised of 61 methodology characteristics and related values which are arranged vertically in the spreadsheet. These characteristics have already been discussed in section 4. Instances of methodologies are arranged horizontally with proper values selected. User can add own methodologies to this list. An example of RPM spreadsheet is shown on Figure 2.

5.3. List of projects/organizations

The list of projects/organizations is implemented in a spreadsheet named RPP. User can add his own project/organization to the list and properly select its characteristics. RPP spreadsheet is comprised of 35 project/organization characteristics and related values which are arranged horizontally in the spreadsheet. These characteristics have already been discussed in section 4. Instances of projects/organizations are arranged vertically with suitable values selected. Figure 2 shows an example of RPP spreadsheet.

5.4. Results

Results (evaluations) are computed in Results spreadsheet. This spreadsheet contains final evaluations for every combination of methodology instance and project/organization instance. Results spreadsheet enables us to easily compare results and to determine which methodologies are more or less appropriate for a certain project/organization. Each result is calculated according the following evaluation formula:

$$Eval(Mx, Py) = \sum_{\substack{y=1\rightarrow\text{number of}\\ \text{methodology}\\ \text{characteristics}}} \sum_{\substack{x=1\rightarrow\text{number of}\\ \text{project}\\ \text{characteristics}}} OR(x,y) \times RPM(Mx,y) \times RPP(x,Py)$$

In the formula *Eval* is an evaluation (result) of combination of a certain methodology instance (characteristics of a certain methodology in column *Mx* in RPM spreadsheet) and a certain project/organization instance (characteristics of a certain project in row *Py* in RPP spreadsheet). Figure 2 shows an example of *Eval* formula for methodology M1 and project P1.

Note that preceding evaluation formula (*Eval*) is a simplification of evaluation formula actually used in the evaluation model. Formula actually used in the evaluation model also includes weights for project/organization characteristics and weights for methodology characteristics.

5.5 Results explanation module

Another essential part of the evaluation model is the explanation module. It provides explanation for selected evaluation in Results spreadsheet. The explanation module computes positive or negative contribution of each individual combination of methodology characteristic and project/organization characteristic for selected methodology and project/organization.

The explanation module uses the same spreadsheets as evaluation model i.e. mapping table (OR), list of methodologies (RPM), list of projects/organizations (RPP) and evaluations (Results). To explain the evaluations (form Results spreadsheet) the explanation module uses the same procedure as the evaluation model to compute these evaluations. The only difference is that it does not compute a final evaluation for selected methodology and project/organization, but only a partial evaluation (contribution) for one combination of methodology characteristic and project/organization characteristic for selected methodology and project/organization. The computed contributions are presented in an ordered list so the most important characteristic combinations (with greatest positive or negative contribution) can be easily identified.

6. TESTING THE EVALUATION MODEL

Although work on the evaluation model is still in progress, we carried out simple practical tests of the evaluation model. Reader should note that these tests are not intended to provide complete and solid proof that the model is sound and perfect. They are only means to test whether we are moving in the right direction or not. In this paragraph we present a test on three real life projects and six different methodologies that gave us interesting results.

The following methodologies have been evaluated:

- New custom methodology that was developed for a certain SW development organization developing IS using OO languages (mostly Java). Methodology is based on philosophy of lightweight methodologies.
- Old methodology that was used by the same SW development organization and relies mostly on the skills and experiences of the developers. Development was done mostly in an ad hoc, trial and error manner.
- Rational Unified Process – standard variant.
- Rational Unified Process – small projects variant.
- Custom Development Method – Fast Track (small projects variant) developed by Oracle to be used together with its DBMS and development tools like Designer and Developer, but it can also be used with other development tools.
- Extreme Programming (XP).

The above methodologies have been evaluated in combination with the following projects/organizations:

- SW development organization that utilizes the first two methodologies from the preceding list. Its typical projects are small to medium sized with up to six developers.

- Faculty portal project was a small/medium sized project employing five developers using Oracle's DBMS and web development tools.
- Bank project was medium sized project. Two organizations participated in the development of a part of a bank system. It was important that the system performed as planned without unexpected errors.

Table 1 shows the results of the evaluation (Results spreadsheet). Methodologies are presented in columns and projects/organizations in rows. Evaluation for each combination of methodology and project/organization is computed in the table.

Table 1. Results of the evaluation

	New SW dev. org. methodology	Old SW dev. org. methodology	RUP	RUP Small	CDM light	XP
SW devel. organization	9070	5737	6320	8807	8468	8808
Faculty portal project	8790	5639	4932	8069	8535	8590
Bank project	6689	1990	8640	8070	8205	6442

The first row in the table (see Table 1) shows results for the software development organization. We can see that new custom methodology created for this organization is as expected evaluated as the most suitable. More interesting are the evaluations of RUP Small and XP. Both methodologies received a fairly high evaluation and should be considered as a good alternative (in fact the new custom methodology also includes many elements of RUP, some of XP and also some of CDM). We can also see that the old development methodology was evaluated as rather unsuitable compared to other methodologies. To test these results we conducted a small survey among the potential users of the new custom methodology after presenting it to them. All of them agreed that the new methodology would bring advantages and is better that the old one.

The second row shows evaluations for Faculty portal project. It is a project of a similar size as typical organization's projects in the first case, so the results are also similar. In practice an "ad hoc" methodology with elements of CDM was used on this project.

The third row shows somewhat different project. It is a medium sized bank project. This project is the largest and the most complex of the three. We can see that RUP comes out as the most suitable option, but we should also consider CDM light, and RUP Small. In practice "ad hoc" development with elements of CDM was used on this project. One of the companies that worked on this project is currently trying to introduce CDM light to work on similar projects.

To fully test and also improve the model are developing web-based application that would allow government institutions and other interested organizations to test and explore the model. We will allow users of the web application not only to add new methodologies and projects but also to experiment with rules and new characteristics. We believe the feedback that we will get from the users will play an important role in identifying deficiencies, improving and testing the model.

7. CONCLUSIONS AND FUTURE WORK

In the paper we presented an evaluation model that helps an organization to find out what is the most suitable methodology for its types of projects. The model is based on the evaluation of the characteristics that are on the one hand important for methodologies and on the other for projects or organizations. For instance companies that develop software for critical systems will typically require complex and rigorous methodology. On the contrary software development companies that develop small business applications advocate the use of more simple and light methodologies.

The model that is described in the paper can be used in two ways. The organizations that do not use any formal methodology, can use the model to select the most appropriate methodology according to their requirements and characteristics, while the organizations, that already use some formal methodology can revaluate the appropriateness of this methodology.

The evaluation model is part of an ongoing research. Since it has not been yet fully tested our future work will be based on application of the model on real examples. To this end we are developing a simple web-based application that will allow organizations to evaluate and find out the most suitable methodology for their needs. The feedback that we will get from the users will help us to identify deficiencies of the model and to improve it.

REFERENCES

1. A. Cockburn, Selecting a project's methodology, *IEEE Software* **17**(4), 64–71 (2000)
2. The Object Agency, Comparison of Object-Oriented Development Methodologies (Object Agency inc., 1995); http://www.toa.com/smnn?mcr.html.
3. B. Fitzgerald, An empirical investigation into the adoption of system development methodologies, *Information & Management* **34**, 317–328 (1998).
4. S. Ambler, *Process patterens: Building Large-Scale Systems Using Object Technology* (Cambridge University Press, 1998).
5. S. Ambler, *Agile Modeling.: Effective Practices for eXtreme Programming and the Unified Process* (John Wiley & Sons, Inc., 2002).
6. D. Avison and G. Fitzgerald, *Information Systems Development: Methodologies, Techniques and Tools*, Third Edition (McGraw-Hill Education, 2003).
7. A. Cockburn, *Agile software development* (Addison-Wesley, 2002).
8. Fowler, M., The new methodology, Thoughtworks report (March 2001); http://martinfowler.com/articles/newMethodology.html.
9. S. McConnell, *Rapid development: Taming Wild Software Schedules* (Microsoft Press, 1996).
10. G. Miller, Sizing Up Today's Lightweight Software Processes, *IT Professional* **3**(3), 46–49 (2001).
11. M. Bohanec, V. Rajkovic, DEX: An Expert System Shell for Decision Support, *Sistemica* **1**(1), 145–157 (1990).
12. M. Bohanec and V. Rajkovic, Multi-attribute decision modeling: Industrial applications of DEX. *Informatica* 23, 487–491 (1999).
13. D. Vavpotic and M. Bajec, M. Krisper, Characteristics of software development methodology evaluation model, in: *Business information technology management: facilitating global IS alliances* (BitWorld, Ecuador, 2002).
14. K. Beck, *Extreme Programming Explained: Embrace Change* (Addison-Wesley, 1999).
15. J. Highsmith, *Adaptive software development: a collaborative approach to managing complex systems* (Dorset House Publishing, 2000).
16. I. Jacobson, G. Booch, and J. Rumbaugh, *The unified software development process* (Addison-Wesley, 1999).
17. P. Kruchten, *The Rational Unified Process, An Introduction*, Second Edition, (Addison Wesley, 2000).
18. Rational Unified Process, RUP 2001.03, electronic edition (Rational Software, 2001).

19. L. Rising and N. Janoff, The Scrum software development process for small teams, *IEEE Software* **17**(4), 26–32 (July/August 2000).
20. B. W. Boehm et al., *Software Cost Estimation with Cocomo II*, First Edition (Prentice Hall PTR, 2000).
21. D. Garmus and D. Herron, *Measuring the software process: A practical guide to functional measuring* (Yourdon Press, Prentice Hall, New Jersey, 1996).
22. B. Boehm, *Making RAD work for your project*, Computer **32**(3), 113–114 (1999).
23. CDM Classic 2.6 & CDM Fast Track 1.2 (Oracle Method Group, 2000).
24. W. Scacchi, Process Models in Software Engineering, *Encyclopedia of Software Engineering*, Second Edition, 993–1005 (Wiley, New York, 2002).
25. I. Warren, *The Renaissance of Legacy Systems Method*, (Springer-Verlag, London, 1999).

REPRESENTING PART-WHOLE RELATIONS IN CONCEPTUAL MODELLING

A comparison of object-oriented and entity relationship modellers

Graeme Shanks, Elizabeth Tansley, Simon Milton, and Steve Howard[1]

1. INTRODUCTION

The idea that one thing may be part of another thing seems fundamental to the way humans perceive and understand phenomena. Part-whole (or meronymic) relations have been of interest to philosophers concerned with ontology (eg. Bunge, 1977; Weber, 1997; Chisholm, 1996) and psychologists concerned with human cognition (eg. Winston et al., 1987).

The representation of part-whole relations is a fundamental issue in conceptual modelling. Information systems researchers have long been concerned with finding better ways to model these and other constructs as a basis for building better information systems. Part-whole relations feature in early work on database abstractions (Smith and Smith, 1977), in entity relation modelling (Teory et al., 1986) and in more recent work on conceptual modelling (Storey, 1991). They have also been fundamental to object-oriented conceptual modelling approaches (eg. Opdahl et al., 2001) including the de facto standard Unified Modelling Language (UML) (Rumbaugh et al., 1999).

Part-whole relations remain problematic in the context of conceptual modelling in information systems for a number of reasons:

- Important theoretical issues surrounding these representations remain unresolved. For example the transitivity and symmetry of part-whole relations remains unclear (Winston et al., 1987). A much deeper understanding of part-whole relations is needed as a basis for conceptual modelling (Wand and Weber, 2002).

[1] Graeme Shanks, Monash University, Melbourne, Australia, 3800. Elizabeth Tansley, Central Queensland University, Queensland, Australia. Simon Milton, University of Melbourne, Melbourne, Australia 3010. Steve Howard, University of Melbourne, Melbourne, Australia 3010.

- Different ways of representing part-whole relations have been proposed. Composite things are sometimes represented explicitly as entities (eg. Kilov and Ross, 1994, 96-97) and sometimes implicitly as relationships between the components of the composite (eg. Chen, 1976, 31). Few empirical studies of alternative representations of part-whole relations have been undertaken.

In addition, explicit representation of part-whole relations has been included in object-oriented approaches to conceptual modelling for some time while the entity relationship approach does not include a specific symbol for part-whole relations. Object-oriented modellers seem to be more concerned with representing the complex structure of things and their interaction. Many of the constructs in object-oriented modelling languages seem to originate from object-oriented programming concepts, and implementation concerns are important. In contrast, the entity relationship modellers seem to be more concerned with supporting the conceptual design of databases with completeness and flexibility assuming importance (Moody and Shanks, 2002).

Previous experimental research (Shanks et al., 2002) has shown that conceptual models (using UML) that use a class construct to represent a composite enable end users to better understand the semantics associated with the composite than conceptual models that use an association to represent the composite. In this paper we describe exploratory research we undertook to determine the similarities and differences in the perceptions of experienced entity relationship modellers and experienced object-oriented modellers about the representation of part-whole relations. Our research was motivated in three ways:

- Improving systems development by improving conceptual modelling practice (Moody and Shanks, 1998);
- Testing theoretical work that predicts how part-whole relations should be best represented and learning about the strengths and weaknesses of different conceptual modelling practices;
- Contributing to improved conceptual modelling practice by better understanding the differences between object-oriented and entity relationship modellers' representation of part-whole relations.

The paper is structured as follows. The next section presents the theoretical background to the research and the questions we answered. The following section describes the research method we used. The next section presents the results. The following section discusses some implications of the research for research and practice and the paper concludes with a discussion of the limitations of the paper and some directions for future research.

2. THEORY AND RESEARCH QUESTIONS

Appendix 2 shows four pairs UML class models that represent part-whole relations. In each pair of models, the model on the left shows composites represented explicitly using the UML class construct, while the model on the right shows the composite represented implicitly using the UML association construct. The theory we use is based on an ontological theory proposed by Bunge (1977) and adapted for information systems by Wand and Weber (Weber, 1997). Wand et al. (1999) argue that representing composites using the UML class construct is better as follows:

2.1. The world consists of things that possess properties.

Things and properties are the two atomic constructs needed to describe the world. Every thing in the world possesses one or more properties. Properties themselves cannot have properties and cannot simply exist by themselves: they must attach to a thing. Two types of properties that exist in the world are intrinsic properties, which depend on one thing only, and mutual properties, which depend on two or more things.

2.2. Things may associate to form composite things

A thing is a composite if and only if it is formed from the combination of at least two other things. Otherwise, it is a simple thing. Every composite thing possesses emergent properties - properties not possessed by the components of the composite.

In the context of Bunge's ontology a composite must be represented as a UML class construct. It cannot be represented as a UML association as it must possess at least one emergent property and associations cannot have properties, as they are themselves mutual properties. Only things have properties. A conceptual model that contravenes ontological principles will suffer from "construct overload" where different real world concepts are represented by the same modelling construct. Users of the model must employ tacit knowledge to determine the semantics of the model (Wand and Weber, 1993). For example, in the first pair of models in Appendix 2, it is unclear if "Book" is a thing or a mutual property in the right hand model.

Shanks et al. (2002) have shown that representing part-whole relations as UML classes is important as it allows users to better understand the models. However, it is unclear if experienced object-oriented and entity relationship modellers agree. We selected experienced modellers for the study in order to ensure that the subjects have sufficient experience to understand the *practical* use of the modelling tools they use from a range of domains. Further, we wanted to, as much as possible, avoid formal educational influences from their experiences in tertiary education. We also sought people experienced in one of the two modelling languages dominant in industry. We therefore ask the following exploratory research questions:

Question 1: How will experienced object-oriented and entity relationship modellers evaluate conceptual model fragments that represent part-whole relations as UML class constructs and UML association constructs?

Question 2: Will experienced object-oriented and entity relationship modellers represent a composite as a UML class construct or a UML association construct in a small modelling exercise?

3. RESEARCH METHOD

A laboratory setting was chosen for this exploratory study as we sought to (a) manipulate in specific ways the representations we used, (b) control for extraneous factors that might confound any impacts of alternative representations, and (c) retain the complete attention of the experienced practitioners who participated in the study. We structured the study into two separate tasks, a conceptual model fragment task and a conceptual modelling task. The conceptual model fragment task was designed to elicit the views of experienced conceptual modellers about alternative representations of part-whole relations (Q1). The conceptual modelling task was designed to determine the preferred representation of part-whole relations by experienced conceptual modellers (Q2).

3.1 Conceptual Model Fragment Task

3.1.1. Materials

Three sets of materials were developed for the study. The first was a summary of the UML symbols used in the diagrams provided to participants in the study. The second comprised a personal profile questionnaire to gain information about participant's backgrounds. The third comprised four pairs of UML conceptual model fragments representing familiar domains. In each pair of models, one was ontologically sound and represented a composite as a UML class while the other was ontologically unsound and represented a composite as a UML association.

The first pair of model fragments represented a school class, as shown in Figure 1.

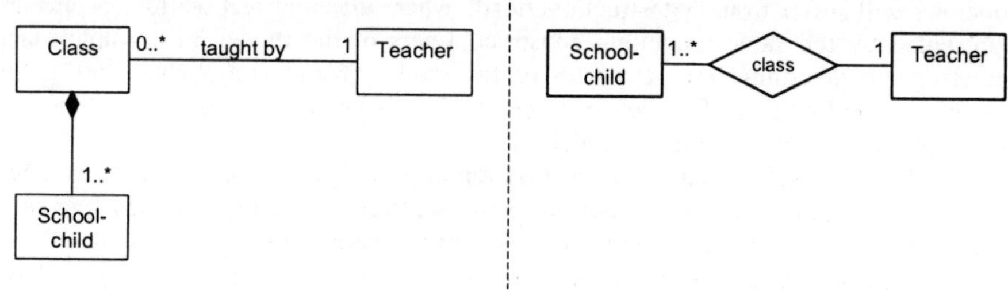

Figure 1. School model

The fragment on the left is considered ontologically sound because the composite thing (the school class[2]) is represented as an object class and not as an association. The fragment on the right is ontologically unsound because the school class is represented by an association/relationship. Assume that the composite thing school class possesses the emergent property number of children. Bunge's ontology forbids the attachment of properties to relationships or associations, therefore it cannot be attached to the school class in the right-hand fragment. This property is called emergent because it does not belong to the child thing but only emerges when the composite thing school class is formed.

Similar discussions apply to the following fragment pairs, as shown in Figure 2 to Figure 4.

---

[2] The word *class* here refers to a group of school children, not a UML object type.

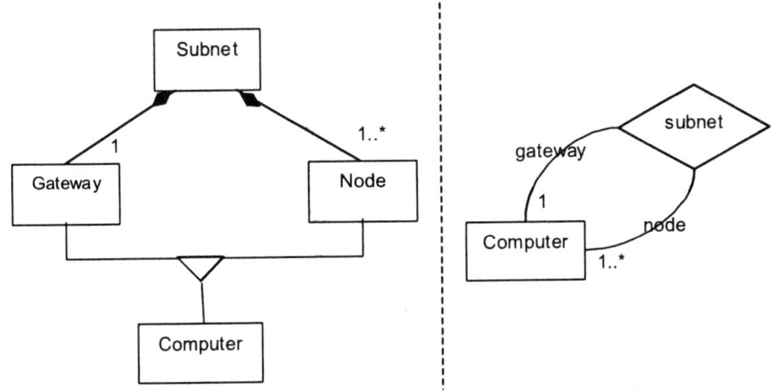

Figure 2. Subnet model

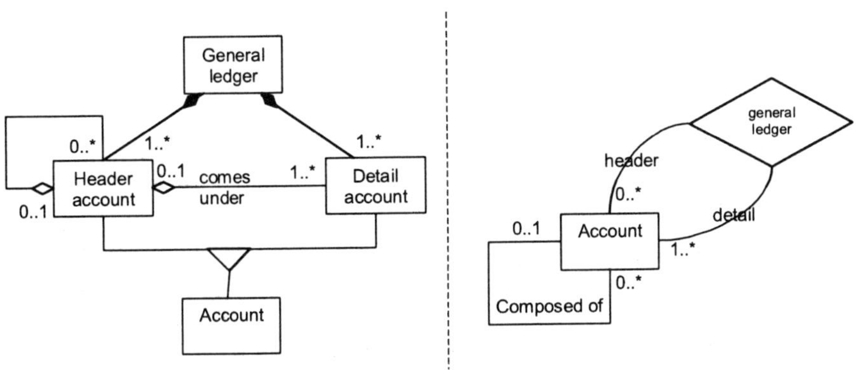

Figure 3. General ledger model

3.1.2. Participants

Six experienced conceptual modellers participated in the study, three with extensive object-oriented modelling experience and three with extensive entity relationship modelling experience. All had at least a Bachelor's degree.

3.1.3. Procedure

Participants were run independently one-by-one through the task. Participants had no contact with each other. When they arrived, they were asked to complete a consent form and a personal profile questionnaire and given the document that explained the UML symbols. They were then shown the first pair of UML model fragments and asked to comment on the strengths and weaknesses of each representation. The participants were encouraged to "think aloud" and voice their thoughts as they proceeded. The researcher prompted for further comments as required. This process was repeated for each pair of model fragments. The session was tape recorded to facilitate later transcription and data analysis.

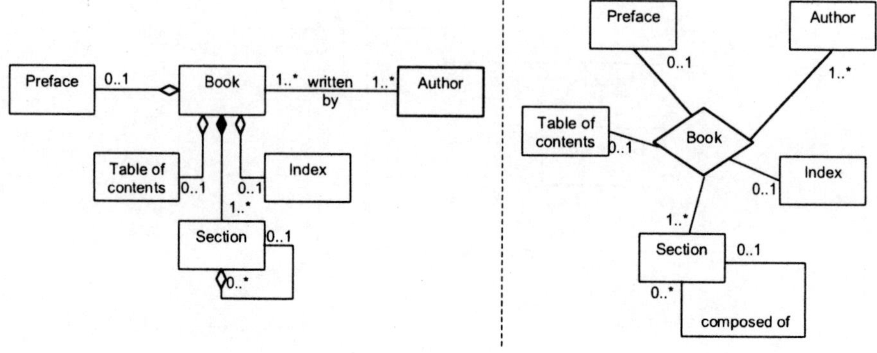

Figure 4. Book model

3.2 Conceptual Modelling Task

3.2.1. Materials

Three sets of materials were developed for the study. The UML symbol summary and personal profile questionnaire are described in the conceptual model fragment task above. The third comprised a description of a small domain to be represented as a UML conceptual model (see Appendix 1). The domain was selected to include part-whole relations.

3.2.2. Participants

The same six participants as for the conceptual modelling task participated in this task.

3.2.3. Procedure

Participants were again run one-by-one through the task, immediately after completing the conceptual model fragment task. They were given the description of the domain and asked to design a UML conceptual model of the domain. Participants were asked to comment on the strengths and weaknesses of their conceptual models, "thinking aloud" as they proceeded. The session was tape-recorded to facilitate later transcription and data analysis.

4. RESULTS

4.1. Data Model Fragment Task

In general both the experienced object-oriented and entity relationship modellers preferred the ontologically sound representations to the ontologically unsound representations of the model fragments. Overall, the ontologically sound representations were found to be clearer representations that made more sense. They provided more information about the domain and the inherent structure in the domain was explicit. The ontologically unsound representations were more compact and concise but had poor navigability and were potentially misleading. Detailed analysis of comments made by each of the two types of participant follows, together with an analysis of the similarities and differences between the two types of participant.

4.1.1. Experienced Entity Relationship Modeller Comments

All experienced entity relationship modellers found the ontologically sound representation of the "School Model" clear and superior. One modeller found the sound model to be generalisable while two of the modellers commented that the sound version was better but should have a many to many association between teacher and class for "historical accuracy". The unsound representation was found to be more compact but "hiding" too much information.

Two of the modellers found the sound representation of the "Subnet Model" to be "more explicit" and clearer. One modeller commented "Don't have to remember details, can understand it, straightforward". Another commented "there's more information on the paper, less has to go in your head". The third modeller commented "I can't use either of these diagrams, they just don't mean anything to me" indicating a lack of familiarity with the domain.

All three of the modellers found the sound representation of the "General Ledger Model" more descriptive, easier to understand. One commented that the sound model "maps directly to implementation" while another commented: "I would have to do less in my head" with the sound representation. The unsound model was found to more compact but with less information about the domain.

All three modellers found the sound representation of the "Book Model" very clear and more explicit than the unsound representation. One modeller commented that it was a "neater diagram, I can see what I am doing". One commented that he didn't like the unsound representation because it was difficult to navigate: "the only way I can navigate this is to start in the middle and work outwards".

4.1.2. Experienced Object-Oriented Modeller Comments

Two of the three experienced object-oriented modellers found the ontologically sound representation of the "School Model" preferable and "making perfect sense". One modeller did not like either representation and commented that the sound representation may not be suitable for class scheduling, indicating a connection to class behaviour as well as structure.

Two of the modellers found the sound representation of the "Subnet Model" preferable although one suggested including inheritance. The third modeller was uncertain about the domain the model was trying to represent and unable to comment on the models.

There was considerable disagreement concerning the "General Ledger Model". One of the modellers found the sound representation preferable as it "made more sense" and "gave more information". Another modeller preferred the unsound model as it "simplifies things a bit and contains all the information". The third modeller was critical of both models but found the unsound model to be more concise and contain less information.

All three modellers agreed that the sound representation of the "Book Model" was superior. One commented: "clearly would model it this way ... have a tendency to like aggregating objects". Another commented that the sound representation made more obvious "the structure of the book and what's related to what. Two commented on the use of strong aggregation in the sound model clarifying that the section would be deleted when the book was deleted.

4.1.3. Similarities and Differences

Clearly, there was strong agreement amongst both types of modeller that the ontologically sound representation was preferable. Although the unsound representation was more concise it contained less information and was more difficult to navigate. Entity relationship modellers focused on issues such as generalisability and historical accuracy as desirable characteristics of a conceptual model. In contrast, object-oriented modellers focused on class behaviour and structure as a means of cascading deletions. Entity relationship modellers seem to focus on the models as conceptual models of the domain whereas object-oriented modellers seem to focus more on the behavioural aspects of the domain and its possible implementation in a programming language.

4.2 Conceptual Modelling Task

The models produced by the six modellers were examined, and the constructs used by each modeller were catalogued. Table 1 shows which modelling constructs were used by each modeller to represent different aspects of the problem domain.

Table 1. Summary of conceptual model features

Participant	**ER modeller 1**	**ER modeller 2**	**ER modeller 3**	**OO modeller 1**	**OO modeller 2**	**OO modeller 3**
Conceptual model features						
Lichtenberg explicitly modelled	yes	yes	no	yes	yes	yes
Lichtenberg composed of states	association	association	n/a	weak aggregation	strong, directed aggregation	association
States composed of regions	association	association	association	weak aggregation	strong, directed aggregation	weak aggregation
Region composed of electorates	association	association	association	weak aggregation	strong, directed aggregation	association

Table 1. (continued)

Participant	ER modeller 1	ER modeller 2	ER modeller 3	OO modeller 1	OO modeller 2	OO modeller 3
Conceptual model features						
Explicitly models 6 states	no	no	no	yes	yes	yes
State has system of local government	not modelled	not modelled	not modelled	weak aggregation	no	not modelled
Electorates have political candidates	not modelled	not modelled	association	yes	strong, directed aggregation	n/a
Electorates have boundaries	not modelled	not modelled	n/a	weak aggregation	weak, directed aggregation	association class
Boundaries modelled as...	free text	free text	not modelled	class	class	class
Council governs a region	association	council not shown	council not shown	weak aggr with stereotype	strong, directed aggregation	association
Political candidates	not modelled	not modelled	class	class	not modelled	class
Political candidates are...	n/a	n/a	related to electorate	supertype of electoral cand	n/a	supertype of electoral cand.
Council has one mayor	association	not modelled	mayor not shown	weak aggregation	assoc with role name	association
Council has aldermen/ elected candidates	not directly	not modelled	n/a	association	weak aggregation with role name	weak aggregation
Mayor/aldermen subtypes of member	yes	flagged	n/a	weak aggregation	role name & OCL	yes
Full hierarchy or generalisation	both	both	hierarchy	Hierarchy	hierarchy	hierarchy
Historical accuracy	yes	yes (in transcript)	yes (term)	yes (in transcript)	no	no
Region name unique within state	not modelled	not modelled	no	no	no	no
Electorate# unique within region	not modelled	not modelled	no	no	yes	no
Alternative way to model	hierarchy or generalisati on	hierarchy or generalisati on	Using aggregation s	none	subtyping/ inheritance	none

An analysis of the similarities and differences between conceptual models produced by experienced entity relationship modellers and object-oriented modellers, as illustrated in this table, is presented below.

4.2.1. Use of Aggregation

The entity relationship modellers used associations to represent the structure of Lichtenberg into states, regions and electorates. In contrast, the object-oriented modellers used some form of aggregation. In general, throughout the models, object-oriented modellers used aggregation frequently whereas entity relationship modellers used association rather than aggregation.

The use of aggregation in some circumstances was confusing. For example, one object-oriented modeller used weak aggregation to represent "council has one mayor" (council being the aggregate). The motivation for doing so appeared to be desired object behaviour. Another object-oriented modeller was asked why he used strong aggregation and indicated that strong aggregation implied that the component object should not be abstracted. When one object-oriented modeller was questioned about the use of weak aggregation, he indicated, "...if you deleted the council you'd delete candidates which obviously isn't what you want to do [so weak aggregation was used instead of strong aggregation]".

4.2.2. Main Focus of the Modellers

Object behaviour and system implementation appeared to be the dominant concern of the OO modellers. In contrast, entity relationship modellers seemed more concerned with characteristics of the conceptual model including stability, flexibility and understandability.

Two of the entity relationship modellers expressed a paramount concern about the stability of the hierarchy structure from the country down to electorates, and accordingly presented two alternative representations: one that was more understandable but susceptible to a change in the hierarchy structure and another which was highly flexible but very obtuse in meaning and harder to implement. Long-term stability and avoiding duplication appeared to be the predominant concerns of the entity relationship modellers.

4.2.3. Explicit Representation of Constraints and History

All three object-oriented modellers explicitly restricted the number of states to 6. The entity relationship modellers, however, modelled the relationship as 1 to many. One entity relationship modeller commented that, "The fact there are six of them [is irrelevant]... There are three numbers in computing, nought one and many". All three entity relationship modellers were conscious of the need for historical accuracy, for example, the need to be able to recall who was mayor of a given region in 1993. They included provision in their model for historical accuracy, for example, a "term of office" class. Only one object-oriented modeller discussed the need for historical accuracy

This indicates a greater interest in flexibility, stability and historical aspects of conceptual modelling in entity relationship modellers, with a contrasting focus on details and implementation by object-oriented modellers.

4.2.4. Alternative Representations

An unanticipated by-product of the study was that two of the three entity relationship modellers developed two possible representations *without prompting*. These two modellers were particularly concerned with the stability of the state-region-electorate hierarchy, and their alternative representations catered for the possibility of change in the hierarchy structure. The object-oriented modellers did not consider developing alternative representations, but viewed modelling as an iterative evolving process with periodic revisions to conceptual models.

5. IMPLICATIONS OF THE RESEARCH

Our results have implications for both practice and research and come directly from pursuing the research questions stated earlier. For practice we have further support for the representation of composites as UML classes rather than UML associations. Experienced modellers found the representation of composites as UML classes to be clear, explicit and easy to understand. In contract, while the representation of composites as UML associations was more concise it was more difficult to navigate and contained less information.

An important contribution of this research is the comparison of results between the two modelling communities. To this end, our results suggest that while experienced entity relationship modellers represent composites as UML classes they model part-whole relations using associations rather than the explicit aggregation symbol available in UML. This suggests that entity relationship modellers required further training in the concept of part-whole relations and their representation. Experienced entity relationship modellers focus on the flexibility, stability and understandability of their conceptual models.

We found that experienced object-oriented modellers also represent composites as UML classes and make extensive use of the explicit aggregation symbol available in UML. However, they focus more on the implementation aspects of the system they are modelling. This suggests that object-oriented modellers require further training in the design of conceptual models and the desirable qualities of conceptual models.

In terns of research, our results add strength to the growing body of empirical research that supports the usefulness of ontological theories as a means of predicting the strengths and weaknesses of conceptual modelling languages and practices.

6. LIMITATIONS AND FUTURE RESEARCH DIRECTIONS

Like most laboratory-based research, the tasks in our study are limited in scope and somewhat artificial. Further research might be field-based including case studies and action research to further examine conceptual modelling practices in more realistic situations. Specifically, this research might explore the differences between the two communities of modellers further in the context of industrial practice. It will also clarify the extent to which, and the contexts in which, ontologically sound models are found in practical situations. An important facet to the latter opportunity is the examination of implementation issues in selection of ontologically sound over ontologically unsound models.

ACKNOWLEDGEMENTS

A University of Melbourne grant funded this research. We thank Ron Weber and Paul Taylor for helpful comments on our research.

APPENDIX – Conceptual Modelling Task

The country of Lichtenberg is divided into 6 states (also known as principalities). Each state observes the same system of local government. States are divided into a number of regions, each region having a unique name within the state. Each region is then divided down into electorates. Each electorate is identified by a number that is unique within the encompassing region. Electorate boundaries are identified in very loose terms, such as, "West boundary: to McLaren Street; North boundary: to McKenzie Creek", and so on.

At election time, one political candidate is elected in each electorate by popular vote. That candidate becomes the elected member for the electorate. The council that governs a region is composed of all the elected members from that region. One and only one elected member will be the mayor of that council. The remaining elected members on council are referred to as Aldermen or Alderwomen.

Draw a UML class diagram to represent elected members, councils, electorates, states, and so on. State and federal governments are outside the scope of this problem.

Sample Solution

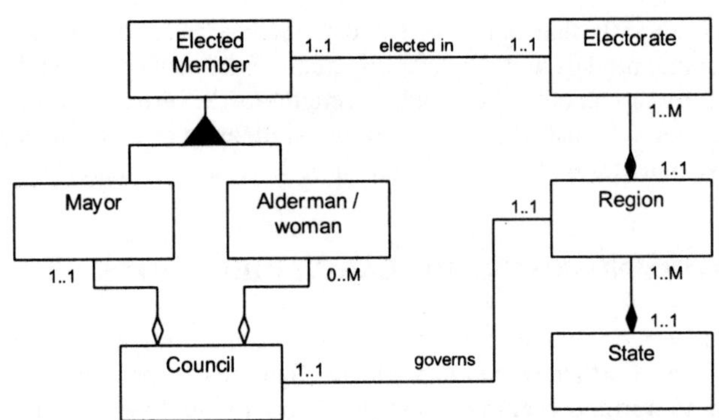

REFERENCES

Bunge, M., 1977, *Treatise on Basic Philosophy: Volume 3: Ontology I: The Furniture of the World*, Reidel, Boston.

Chisholm, R. M., 1996, *A Realistic Theory of Categories: An Essay on Ontology*, Cambridge University Press, Cambridge.

Floyd, C., 1986, A comparative evaluation of system development methods, in: *Information System Design Methodologies: Improving the Practice* T. W. Olle, H. G. Sol and A. A. Verrijn-Stuart, (eds), North-Holland, Amsterdam, 19–54.

Moody, D.L. and Shanks, G., 1998, Improving the quality of entity-relationship models: An action research programme, *The Australian Computer Journal,* 30, 129–138.

Moody, D. and Shanks, G., 2002, Improving the Quality of Entity Relationship Models: Experience in Research and Practice, *Information Systems Journal.*

Opdahl, A. L., Henderson-Sellers, B. and Barbier, F., 2001, Ontological analysis of whole–part relationships in OO-models, *Information and Software Technology,* 43, 387–399.

Rumbaugh, J., Jacobson, I. and Booch, G., 1999, *The Unified Modelling Language Reference Manual*, Addison-Wesley, Reading, Mass.

Shanks, G, Tansley, E., Nuredini, J., Tobin, D. and Weber, R., 2002, Representing Part-Whole Relationships in Conceptual Modelling: An Empirical Evaluation, Proc. International Conference on Information Systems, Barcelona.

Smith, J. M. and Smith, D. C. P., 1977, Database abstractions: Aggregation, *Communications of the ACM,* 20:6, 405–413.

Storey, V., 1991, Meronymic relationships, *Journal of Database Administration,* 2:3, 22–35.

Teorey, T. J., Yang, D. and Fry, J. P., 1987, A logical design methodology for relational databases using the extended entity-relationship model, *ACM Computing Surveys,* 18:2, 197–222.

Wand, Y., Storey, V., Weber, R., 1999, An ontological analysis of the relationship construct in conceptual modeling, *ACM Transactions on Database Systems*, 24, 494–528.

Wand, Y. and Weber, R., 1993, On the ontological expressiveness of information systems analysis and design grammars, *Journal of Information Systems*, 3, 217–237.

Wand, Y. and Weber, R., 2002, Information systems and conceptual modelling: A research agenda, *Information Systems Research*, 13.

Weber, R., 1997, *Ontological Foundations of Information Systems*, Coopers and Lybrand Monograph.

Winston, M. E., Chaffin, R., and Herrman, D., 1987, A taxonomy of part-whole relations, *Cognitive Science*, 11, 417–444.

EXISTENCE DEPENDENCY AND INFORMATION STRUCTURE

C. N. G. (Kit) Dampney and Janet Aisbett[1]

1. INTRODUCTION

The technologies providing connectivity, storage, communication bandwidths and graphics user interfacing continue to improve. Security and privacy are being comprehensively addressed. Middleware, integrated development environments, visual tools, and componentry enable more sophisticated applications and interconnectivity over diverse computing environments. This enables better data transfer capability. But what about information?

Information is perceived in the mind, with its meaning partly carried in the data, partly implied by its context, and partly interpreted according to the shared experience and agreement of the receiver and sender (Searle, 1995). In information transfer by face-to-face communication, a mere 20% of the meaning is carried in the words alone (e.g. Ragnuthan, 1996). Meaning is also conveyed by cues from facial expression, turns of phrase and the context extant in the locale. Beyond that, grammatical structures of natural language help constrain the several meanings that words alone might convey. Researchers in computational linguistics, for example, continue to discover sophisticated constructs that imply deeper meanings (e.g. Miltsakaki et al., 2002).

Understanding information structure is a focus for research in fields including linguistics, knowledge representation, and information systems. This paper contends that a very simple construct, *existence dependency*, provides the basis for meaningful information structures. These structures, we argue, reflect natural constraints well codified in mathematics that assist induce and constrain meaning across large problem domains. Existence dependency governs patterns or meta-structure that can guide an information systems design. We illustrate our argument by showing how existence dependency relates to structures from mathematical categorical theory, and to diagrams in the Unified Modelling Language (UML).

[1] University of Newcastle, University Drive, Callaghan, NSW Australia 2308.

1.1. Ubiquity of Existence Dependency

The important role of existence dependency in structuring information has been widely recognised. Existence dependency is expressed variously as:

- *functional dependency* (mandatory many-to-one or mandatory one-to-one relationship) between entities from an entity-relationship modeling perspective,
- *arrows* of a category in a category theoretic formalization of the entity relationship model (Dampney and Johnson, 1993),
- *referential integrity*, *inclusion constraints* and *existence constraints* in relational database (e.g. Elmasri and Navanthe, 1989) according to whether a conceptual or physical emphasis is being made, and
- a partial order on object types or classes defining a fundamental relation type that describes aggregation in object oriented approaches (Snoeck and Dedene, 1998).

Existence dependency has been recognized and used implicitly in practice as *business normalisation* since the 1970s (Finkelstein, 1989).

1.2. Terminology and Notation

Object is used in category theory (CT) in a general way. In UML the meaning of *object* depends on context, either meaning *object type* at the analysis stage (alternatively *object class* at the design stage) or *object instance*. A *CT object,* depending on context, corresponds to either a UML object type or class or a UML object instance. CT objects in this paper will correspond to a UML object type or class. The term *model* is similarly overloaded. *Model* may correspond a) to a theory of UML object types, b) to a logical representation of UML object classes on the computer, and c) a model relating a theory to a representation which satisfies the theory. An entity relationship diagram, in whatever mathematics denotes it, can correspond to all three at once.

Existence dependency relationships, by their nature, are acyclic between object types. Recursive relationships exist, where existence dependency traverses a finite chain, a hierarchy or more generally a lattice. For simplicity we omit *recursive* existence dependencies in this paper. There may also be mutual existence dependency between objects, which can be mostly resolved by considering mutually dependent object as a single object.

We can then suppose existence dependencies form an acyclic graph which can be aligned to favour one direction. Conventions in use align existence dependencies left to right (Finkelstein, 1989) or bottom to top (Snoeck and Dedene, 1998). To complicate matters, the arrow notation for dependency can be drawn in either direction, from dependent to independent or vice-versa.

We resolve arrow direction for existence dependency to correspond to function notation, because simple existence dependencies satisfy the properties of mathematical functions. (More sophisticated existence dependencies arise when we allow more complex objects required to properly represent generic roles). Existence dependency will therefore be denoted B →A, meaning *"The existence of an object B depends on the existence of an object A"*. In terms of representation on a computer, B →A expresses the fact that the existence of an instance of an object type B depends on the existence of some instance of an object type A.

As new entities form, so the direction of growth is in the opposite direction to existence dependency. The same argument applies to specialization hierarchy, where refinement of subtypes and inheritance of attributes is in the opposite direction to dependency. The formation of new entities and refinement of type is conceptualized by actions causing new entities to come into existence.

Both existence dependency and action flow/refinement are useful metaphors. In the diagrams in this paper, the direction of existence dependency is from top to bottom, with the lowest level forming the base objects. The action flow direction bottom-to-top can be seen as a metaphor for growth, in keeping with, say, building construction or natural flora. An example is provided in Figure 1(a), which can be viewed as a lattice partially order by existence dependency.

2. INFORMATION CONSTRUCTS THAT *NATURALLY* CONSTRAIN PROBLEM DOMAIN DEFINITION

The mathematics of category theory (notably Barr and Wells, 1999), the maturation of programming language semantics (Jacobs, 1999), an ontological foundation of information systems (Weber, 1997), empirical investigation of very large information system models (e.g. Dampney et al., 2001), and the development of UML (e.g. Rumbagh et al., 1999) and its challenger OML (Firesmith et al., 1998) have brought the elements of information systems analysis and design into a clearer focus. In previous and related research we have demonstrated the application of existence dependency by formulating it in category theory. Category theory itself is a prodigious synthesis within mathematics – it is a universal algebra synthesizing the constructs of many branches of mathematics.

This gives us ground for a deep conjecture –

> *that the natural constructs discovered by category theory are in keeping with the natural constructs that we humans use to perceive and describe our reality, and which are apparent in information structures.*

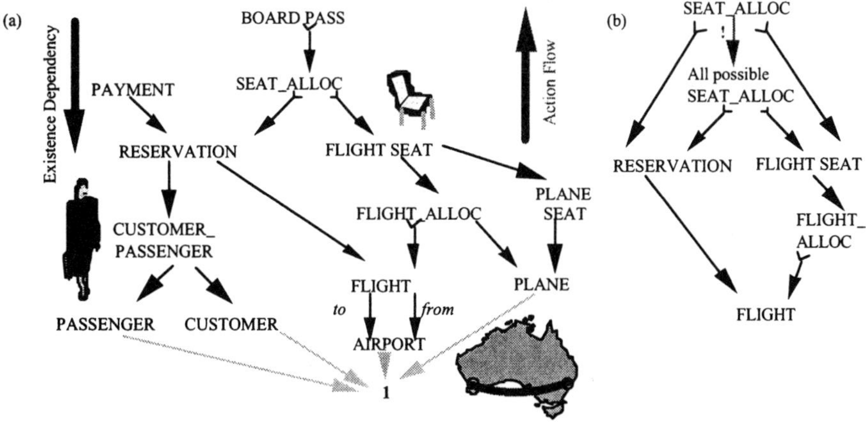

Figure 1. (a) Existence dependency lattice describing information structures of a FLIGHT_SEAT_ RESERVATION system entity relationship model. For simplicity all flights are single segment. Grey arrows to singleton entity "1" represent the context which is assumed to be constant; (b) "All possible SEAT_ALLOC", The limit of FLIGHT SEAT and RESERVATION over FLIGHT

The conjecture needs to be considered in the light of arguments put forward in mathematical philosophy (e.g. Stefanik, 1994) and by philosophers in general (e.g. van Fraasen, 2002). Around this philosophical issue is the tension between information systems as a natural ontology (Colomb and Weber, 1998) or as a computer-based artefact.

In this section we describe some of the natural constructs from category theory and their interpretation in information systems. Category Theory uses *diagrams* made up of arrows and objects to express the mathematics.

2.1. Commuting Diagrams of Existence Dependencies

Fundamental to category theory is the *commuting diagram* construct which can capture the concept of consistent (existence) dependency (Dampney and Johnson, 1995; Dampney et al., 1994).

Consider multiple paths of existence dependencies between two objects, such as SEAT_ALLOC to FLIGHT in Figure 1(a) or 1(b). Where existence dependency of an object on another is the same along all paths, we say it is *consistent*. Catgeory theorists say the diagram made up of the objects and arrows *commutes*. If, as in the arrival and departure AIRPORTS in Figure 1(a), there are multiple existence dependencies between objects, then we have inconsistent existence dependencies. In summary, commuting (alternatively non-commuting) diagrams express consistent (alternatively distinct) *roles* of a target object in the information structure of an entity relationship model.

2.2. Limits that Form Commuting Diagrams and Induce Further Meaning

Category theory *limits* can be used to induce new categorical objects and add problem-domain semantics to the model. Limits (alternatively co-limits) are associated with a commuting diagram, as the unique object that forms the commuting diagram with unique arrows from all other objects (alternatively, to all other objects). Figure 1(b) illustrates the limit object "all possible SEAT_ALLOC". Previous practical work of Dampney and collaborators suggests that the meaning of such limit objects is relevant and natural (see Dampney and Johnson, 1995; Dampney et al., 2001).

Attributes or properties that in a UML diagram are part of the class definition can be represented in category theory as maps between categorical objects representing the class (entity) and the attribute type.

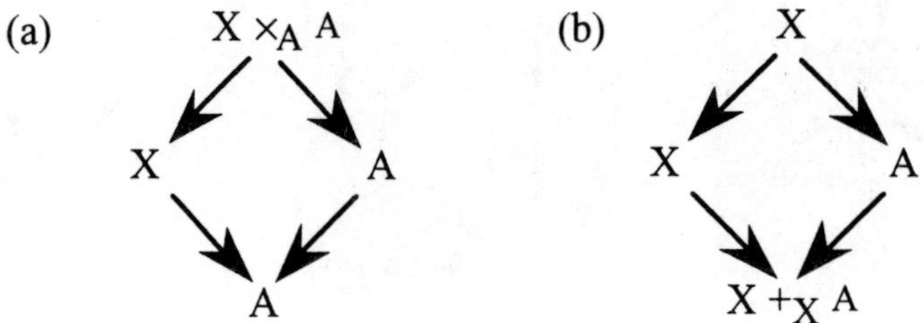

Figure 2. Constructing tables and formal concepts using limits – see text for detail

For example, if a map $p_A{:}X \rightarrow A$ associates entities X with their values on an attribute set A, then the limit $A \times_A X$ formed over p_A and the identity map $A \rightarrow A$ is essentially the table of (entity, attribute value) pairs. The colimit $A +_X X$ formed from p_A and the identity map $X \rightarrow X$ is essentially the partitioning of X into classes according to attribute value. $A +_X X$ corresponds to a *concept* in the theory of formal concept analysis (e.g. Davey and Priestley, 2002).

2.3. Fibrations and Fibres

Category theory fibration has proven to be a useful abstraction technique both in theory and practice (Colomb et al., 2001; Dampney et al., 2001). Fibration, roughly speaking, is a general way of replacing the functions representing existence dependencies between object types with a more abstract mapping (a functor) between clusters of object types. This effectively hides fine structure. A fibration, it can be shown, preserves (in)consistent dependency, and thus preserves role. Role is thus seen as fundamental in information structures, an issue addressed again in Figure 3.

Fibres are intimately linked with topology in mathematics. Information structures extended to deal with attributes can thus be formulated by sub-objects with characteristic attribute values. These sub-objects form category theory topoi (Michael Johnson, personal communication 2001) that Jacobs (1999, p.43) identify as fibres over their objects. UML object types thus refine to attributes. Aisbett and Gibbon (2001) present a topological formalization of knowledge representation that extends and refines attributes as understood in information structures.

2.4. Context Implicit in the (Omitted) Terminal Object

For the kinds of categories involved here, there is an object, the terminal object "**1**", to which every other object has a unique function.[2] The existence of all the other objects depend on the terminal object, which is the *context* of the problem domain. The convention in E-R modeling is to leave out any entity which describes context that is constant over the given problem domain. The convention eliminates the apparently obvious, and it reduces clutter in the model. For the model in Figure 1, such an entity would include the single airline company involved and all else that is constant.

However, context is a major issue. Conveying meaning becomes problematic when context changes across the problem domain and its domain of discourse.

2.5. Analysis of Meta-Models (Patterns) and Knowledge Models

Natural constructs of limits and co-limits have application to meta-models, that is, proposed patterns of information structure. The analogy is natural language grammar specifying permitted and thus disambiguated patterns of parts of speech. This analogy also sheds light on a continuing fundamental challenge in information modeling – the confusion of ontological and computer representational issues. An example is the well-known design pattern for representing role generically.

---

[2] In the *Sets category*, every instance of every object type has a mapping to the single instance in the terminal object type.

Consider Figure 3. The problem is that (a) does not retain the essential and obvious ontological constraint that an action will be dependent on the party (parties) performing the action and suffering the action.

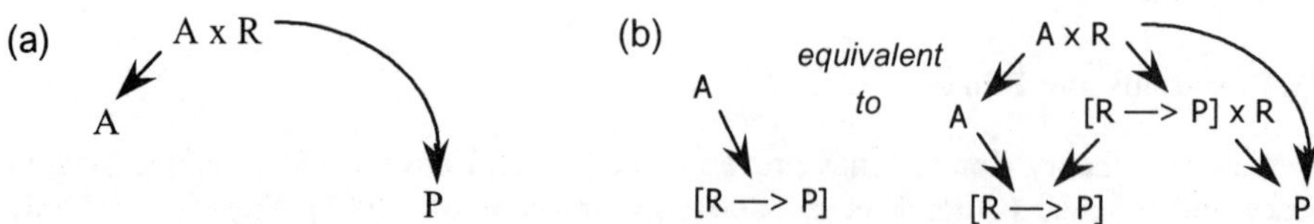

Figure 3. The (a) logical computer representation and (b) ontological representation of the pattern of an act A dependent on the various roles R of people P

The problem is caused because insufficient information structure is represented. The issue is addressed by describing the dependency as in Figure 3(b), together with the natural invariant specified by the commuting diagram between A x R and P. This invariant defines the category as *Cartesian closed*, which in turn leads on to an important intersection with the denotational semantics used in formal programming language specification.

The category theory constructs, more generally, are thus seen as constructs for knowledge models that enable richer ontologies.

2.6. Dynamics Inferred from Existence Dependencies

The dual of existence dependency is action flow. Permitted action sequences can be partly inferred from an object's participation as the target of existence dependencies (Dampney, 1987), and more completely codified by Snoeke and Dedene (1998). Dampney (1998) described dynamics using 2-categories based on Katis et al (1997), based in turn on a broad literature arising from Milner's (1992) seminal research. Further research by Johnson (2001) formalizes the extension of static information structure to dynamic behaviour in the theory.

This suggests that our information system analysis and design methods should link static structure and dynamics. Such links are described in the following section

3. THE EXISTENCE DEPENDENCY CONSTRUCT – A BASIS FOR UML DESIGN AND ANALYSIS METHODS

This section illustrates, using the toy Entity Relationship model in Figure 1(a), how existence dependency can play a core role in the accepted UML methods. Entity Relationship models are easily normalized so that all relationships are existence dependencies and the model thus forms a lattice of existence dependencies.

3.1. Use Case and Dependency Diagrams.

Use cases such as described in Figure 4, are interactions between external actors and the information system. The use cases are not part of the problem domain's conceptual information structure, but at the design stage each use case can be specified by adding a User Interface (UI) object to the existence dependency lattice of the problem domain. Objects at the base of the model first come into existence (are created) followed by objects dependent on them, such that all existence dependencies are satisfied.

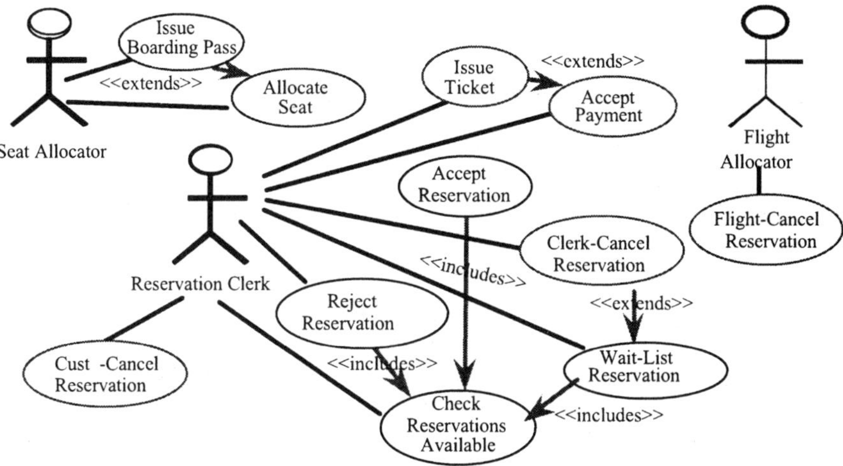

Figure 4. Use Cases for the simplified FLIGHT_SEAT_RESERVATION system.

Actions on objects are conceptualized as events and originate with a human or system actor external to the system. Some events do not create a new object, but modify an object, which is represented by updating some, possibly optional, attribute(s).

Actions on an object must also satisfy whatever constraints there may be on the object and the objects that contain it or that it contains within an existence dependency lattice. For example, to create RESERVATION, the FLIGHT, CUSTOMER and PASSENGER must all exist. There will also be additional constraints effecting actions that impact RESERVATION THAT might include:-

- credit worthiness of the CUSTOMER – ability to pay for RESERVATION;
- the available SEATs on the FLIGHT – ability to allocate a SEAT to the RESERVATION.

3.2. Deriving State Transition Diagrams

Existence dependencies provide a starting point for specifying the behaviour of an object using a state-transition diagram (figure 5) that shows the permitted sequencing of events. Actions on an object will change its state. The existence dependency lattice constrains the possible sequencing of actions. For example a SEAT cannot be allocated to a RESERVATION until the RESERVATION is created. Once created a RESERVATION can be paid – this independence in the sequencing between PAYMENT and SEAT ALLOCation is implied by the existence dependencies. Similarly a FLIGHT cancellation must necessarily cause a RESERVATION cancellation.

3.3. Deriving Collaboration Diagrams

The following collaboration diagram specifies the CREATE RESERVATION use case. The sequencing of actions follows the dependency lattice under RESERVATION. A User interface object is added above the problem domain information structure as illustrated in Figure 6.

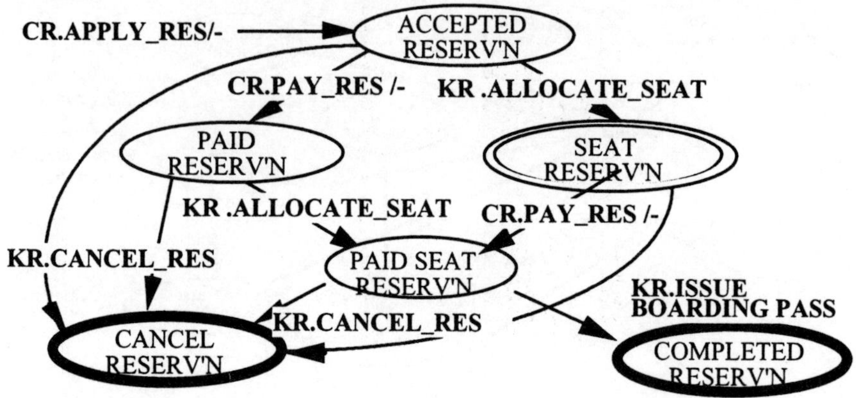

Figure 5. Simplie version of a State-transition diagram of the FLIGHT_SEAT_RESERVATION system.

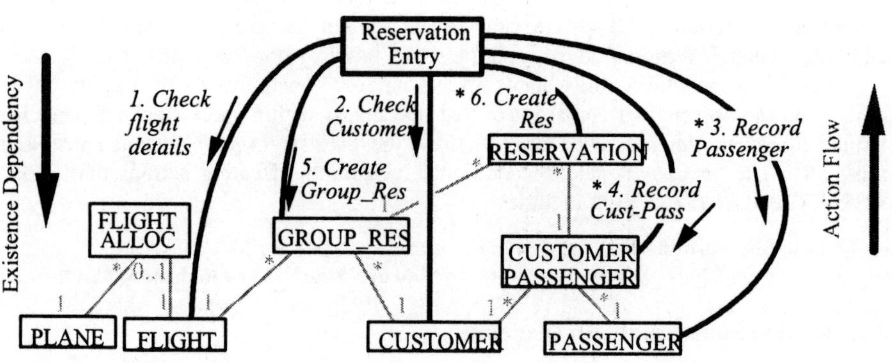

Figure 6. Collaboration model for the external action *create_reservation.*

3.4. Deriving Activity Diagrams

The activity diagram is a useful tool for specifying permitted work-flow (e.g. Fowler, 1997). Permitted sequence of activities dependent on objects closely follow the existence dependency diagram. This idea was used by Finkelstein since the 1980s. Figure 7 shows the dependency model rotated to emphasize the flow of activities from left to right to be associated with existence dependency.

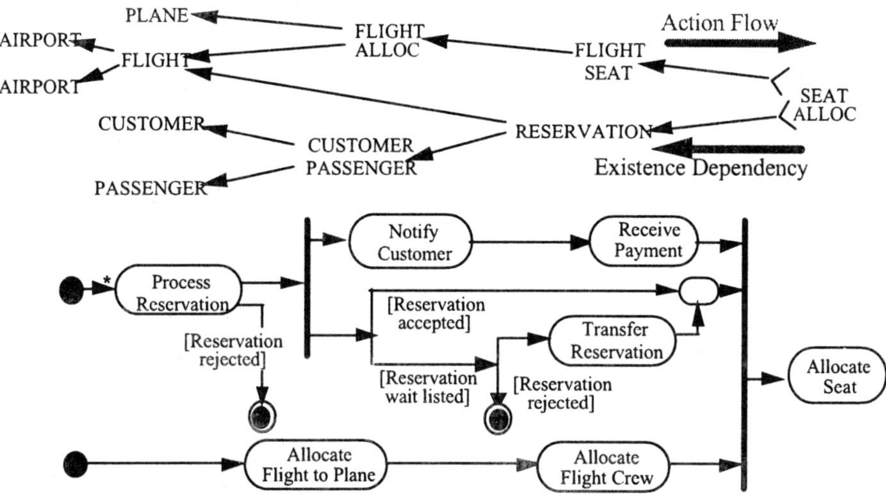

Figure 7. Activity diagram for FLIGHT processes (some detail omitted) aligned with the dependency diagram

4. CONCLUSIONS

The concept of existence dependency is proposed as an important fundamental construct for information structures. It is the basic component of several other constructs.

Meta-models provide the basic patterns or templates that constitute information structure. Analogous to language grammars, meta-models provide the rules for combining parts of concept representation. Metaphorically, they allow us to go beyond simply lining up nouns with entities and verbs with relationships, to having a framework to form clauses and sentences

Existence dependency diagrams are a means of reconciling and bringing together the various analysis and design methods that form part of the Unified Modelling Language.

Dependency suggests that decomposition to relatively independent components does not occur, at least for reasonably structured information systems. Rather, decomposition occurs at the information system meta-model level; that is, in the components of analysis and design, viz. the object, state, transitions, relationship, use-case, interactions etc. At the level of information systems the components may be tightly intertwined with each other, and the relationships between them require as much specification as the components themselves.

REFERENCES

Aisbett, J. and G. Gibbon, 2001, A general formulation of conceptual spaces as a meso level representation, *Artificial Intelligence*, 133, 189–232.

Barr, M and C. Wells, 1999, *Category Theory for Computer Scientists*, Prentice Hall.

Colomb, R. M. and R. Weber, 1998, Completeness and quality of an ontology for an information system, in: *Formal Ontology in Information Systems (International Conference on Formal Ontology in Information Systems,* N. Guarino, ed., IOS-Press (Amsterdam, Oxford, Tokyo, Washington, DC), pp.207–217.

Colomb, R. M, C. N. G. Dampney, and M. S. J. Johnson, 2001, Use of category-theoretic fibration as an abstraction mechanism in informationsystems, *Acta Informatica*, 38, 1–44

Dampney, C. N. G, 1987, Specifying a semantically adequate structure for information systems and databases, Proceedings of the 6th. International Conference on the Entity-Relationship Approach, New York, 143–164.

Dampney, C. N. G., 1998, The event as a fundamental construct of information systems, *Proceedings of Ninth Australasian Conference on Information Systems,* University of New South Wales, Sydney, pp. 120–133.

Dampney, C. N. G., M. S. J. Johnson, P. Dazeley and V. Reich, 1994, A higher order "commuting diagram" structure that supports very large information system data and process architecture, *International Federation for Information Processing Transactions*, North Holland, A54, pp. 211–222.

Dampney, C. N. G. and M. S. J. Johnson, 1995. Application of consistent dependency to corporate and project information models. *Lecture Notes in Computer Science*, Springer-Verlag, 1021, pp445—446.

Dampney, C. N. G., G. Pegler and M. S. J. Johnson, Harmonising Health Information Models - a critical analysis of current practice, *Health Informatics Conference 2001 Proceedings*.

Davey, B. A. and H. A. Priestley, 2002, *Introduction to Lattices and Order,* (second edition), Cambridge University Press.

Elmasri and Navanthe, 1989, *Database Systems,* Benjamin/Cummings Publishing Company Inc.

Finkelstein, C., 1989, *An Introduction to Information Engineering: From Strategic Planning to Information Systems*, Addison Wesley.

Firesmith, D., B. Henderson-Sellers, and I. Graham, 1998, *Open Modelling Language Reference Manual,* Cambridge University Press.

Fowler, M., 1997, *UML Distilled: applying the standard object modeling language,* Addison-Wesley.

Johnson, M. S. J. and C. N. G. Dampney, 1993, Category theory and information systems engineering, *Proceedings of AMAST93,* University of Twente, pp. 95–103.

Johnson, M. S. J. and C. N. G. Dampney, 1994, On the value of commutative diagrams in information modelling, *Springer Workshops in Computing*, Nivat et al, eds., Springer, London. pp. 47–60.

Johnson, M. and R. Rosebrugh, 2001, Update algorithms for the sketch data model, Proceedings of the Fifth International Conference on Computer Supported Cooperative Work in Design, London, Ontario, 367–376.

Katis, P., N, Sabadini and R. F. C. Walters, 1997a;b, Span (Graph): A categorical algebra of transition systems; Representing place/transition nets, *in Span(Graph)*, Johnson, M. S. J., ed., pp. 307–321; pp 322-336.

Milner, R., 1980, A Calculus of Communicating Systems, *Lecture Notes in Computer Science 92*, Springer-Verlag.

Miltsakaki, E., C. Creswell, K. Forbes, R. Prasad, A. Joshi and B. Webber, 2002, The discourse anaphoric properties of connectives, Proceedings of the 4th Discourse Anaphora and Anaphor Resolution Colloquium (DAARC 2002), Lisbon.

Raghuram, S., 1996, Knowledge creation in the telework context, *International Journal of Technology Management*, 11, 7/8, 859–870.

Rumbaugh, J., I Jacobson, and G. Booch, 1999, *The Unified Modelling Language Reference Manual*, Addison-Wesley.

Searle, J., 1995, *The Construction of Social Reality*, New York, Free Press.

Stefanik, R., 1994, *Structuralism, Category Theory and Philosophy of Mathematics*, Washington : MSG Press.

Snoeck, M. and G. Dedene, 1998, Existence Dependency: The key to semantic integrity between structural and behavioural aspects of object types, *IEEE Transactions on Software Engineering*, 24, 4.

van Fraasen, B. C., 2002, *The Empiricist Stand*, Yale University.
(See also http://www.geometry.net/detail/philosophers/van_fraassen_bas.php)

Weber, R., 1997, *Ontological Foundations of Information Systems*, Coopers & Lybrand Accounting Research Methodology Monograph No 4.

TOWARDS A GENERIC MODEL FOR AGILE PROCESSES

Anne Fuller and Peter Croll*

1. INTRODUCTION

The development of the information systems software typically follows standard Software Engineering (SE) practices. SE is a discipline founded on improving development methods to eliminate or mitigate the many risks associated with software projects[1] and traditional SE methodologies have generally been classified as following a particular process model e.g. a Waterfall, Spiral or the V process model.[2] This ability to apply a particular process model to a method has enabled researchers to theorize about methods in a generic sense and allowed the results of research centered on a particular method to be extrapolated to other methods fitting the same model.

The rise of the internet has been accompanied by a major change in the information system and software development landscape. Monolithic development efforts have been replaced by smaller, leaner projects producing web-based software in an environment where volatile requirements are the norm, and delivery expected in weeks or months rather than years. The various methods classified as Agile share a number of features aimed at meeting the needs of many of today's software projects.

The changing nature of both the development environment and the software itself has meant that SE today is riskier than ever, thus any methods must be both cognizant of and address these risks.[3] Despite the reported successes, there is concern that the Agile methods lack the discipline to allow them to be more widely utilized.[4,5] We are currently involved in a project that will attempt to demonstrate that the Agile methods do provide effective risk management. We would prefer to reason generically and provide a mapping between common risk elements and a model rather than consider each Agile process individually. However the software processes/methodologies classified as Agile adhere to a set of principles rather than follow a common process and there remains many "significant differences".[6] Thus it is difficult to produce a generic model of an Agile process[7] with sufficient granularity to be useful for this purpose. Consequently, while the model developed unifies the elements common to all Agile processes, it is not itself

---

* University of Wollongong, Wollongong, Australia

process oriented. That is the model does not attempt to describe any Agile process as such. Rather, the model illustrates the essential components of an Agile process and attempts to show that being "Agile" is a specific combination of practices.

2. AGILE AND RAD

Poinsignon[8] attributes Rapid Application Development (RAD) as being "the very first Agile method" and McTaggart[9] describes Agile methods as "lightweight RAD". Dynamic Systems Development Method (DSDM) is an Agile method specifically developed as a framework for RAD projects[11] while Zeichick[12] refers to extreme programming (XP) as an "Agile rapid-application development process". Thus our initial research included an investigation of RAD models.

RAD processes are sometimes modeled as a series of "mini-waterfalls", indicating their iterative nature.[13] However Beynon-Davies[14] believes that RAD "does not appear to be an information systems methodology in the accepted sense of the term", citing its lack of a prescriptive approach for this opinion. Instead of describing a RAD process, he provides a list of common components. Another non-process oriented, but more coarse grained view describes four fundamental characteristics of a RAD process: people, tools, methodology and management.[14]

Without making any assertions regarding the relationship between RAD and Agile, we propose to follow a similar approach. Our model describes Agile processes in terms of their common elements rather than attempting to provide a generic description of any procedures followed. Interestingly, as we will show, these elements can be classified according to the previously mentioned fundamental characteristics.

3. AGILE DEVELOPMENT

Beginning with RAD, the last decade or so has seen the emergence of many development methodologies aimed at streamlining the development process. The "Agile" methods also surfaced during this period, although the term was not in general use prior to the famous meeting at Snowbird, Utah in February, 2001.[15] Much has since been written about the outcomes of this meeting, the Agile Manifesto and its accompanying 12 supporting practices, and this paper is not intended to provide a comprehensive overview of Agile principles. Further information regarding the Agile movement may be found at www.Agilealliance.org.

Abrahamsson et al.[16] define Agile software development as "incremental, cooperative, straightforward and adaptive", and this definition is then used as a basis for the analysis of several Agile methods. However this definition is too abstract for our purposes. A more detailed model of what constitutes an Agile process is required.

A survey of the literature reveals many differences between the various Agile methods and we must return to the Agile Manifesto and its 12 supporting principles in order to see any commonality. The first eWorkshop on Agile Methods in April 2002 also agreed to use the values and principles of the Manifesto and as the working definition of Agile development.[17] These then provided our basis for developing the Jigsaw Model described in the following section.

4. JIGSAW MODEL

Sixteen elements typifying an Agile process have been identified. These are, in no particular order, teams, communication, trust, reflection, self organising, shared vision, sustainablepace, iterations, refactoring, continuous testing, adaptation, working software, customer involvement, simplicity, programmer estimation and early delivery.

Figure 1, models Agile processes as a jigsaw, comprised of 16 separate pieces representing each these 16 elements.

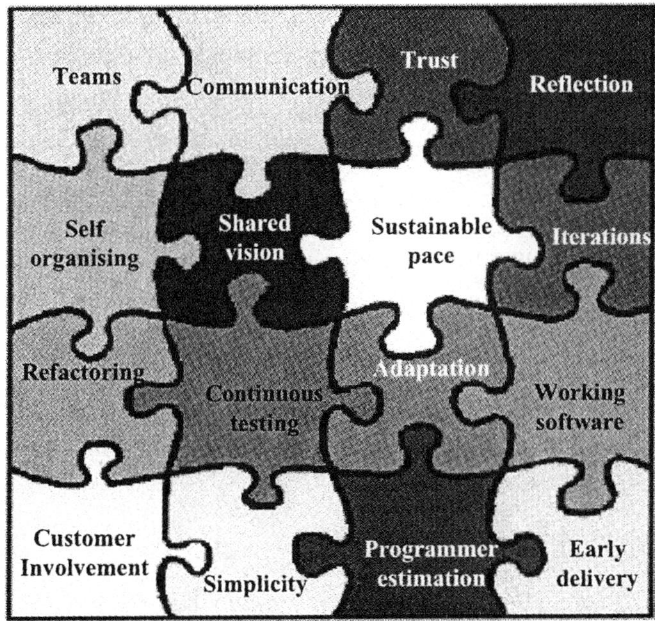

Figure 1: Jigsaw Model of Agile Processes

Many of these elements are drawn directly from the manifesto and its supporting principles. The correspondence is illustrated in Table 1.

The relationship between the other four elements, the manifesto and its principles may be less obvious. Continuous testing of the software product may be considered part of "continuous attention to technical excellence". Having programmers estimate the time required for a particular task is part of trusting your people to get the job done and is common to a greater or lesser degree in the various Agile methods.

A "shared vision" is a mechanism for communicating and understanding the overall goals of the project and all methods have some similar concept e.g. XP has its system metaphor, SCRUM its sprint. Cohn and Schwaber[18] have argued that a shared vision is essential for project success.

A team, as in "a group organized to work together"[19] is a concept common to most development methodologies. However the Agile team can be viewed using the alternative meaning:"a group on the same side, as in a game".[19] Teamwork underpins much of the Agile approach e.g. Cockburn[20] describes software development as a "cooperative game of invention and communication".

Table 1. Correspondence between the Agile Manifesto Supporting Principles and elements of the Jigsaw Model

Agile Principle	Jigsaw Model Element
Our highest priority is to satisfy the customer through early and continuous delivery of valuable software	Early delivery
Welcome changing requirements, even late in development. Agile processes harness change for the customer's competitive advantage.	Adaptation
Deliver working software frequently, from a couple of weeks to a couple of months, with a preference to the shorter timescale.	Iterations
Business people and developers must work together daily throughout the project.	Customer Involvement
Build projects around motivated individuals. Give them the environment and support they need, and trust them to get the job done.	Trust
The most efficient and effective method of conveying information to and within a development team is face-to-face conversation.	Communication
Working software is the primary measure of progress.	Working software
Agile processes promote sustainable development. The sponsors, developers, and users should be able to maintain a constant pace indefinitely.	Sustainable pace
Continuous attention to technical excellence and good design enhances agility.	Refactoring
Simplicity--the art of maximizing the amount of work not done--is essential.	Simplicity
The best architectures, requirements, and designs emerge from self-organizing teams	Self Organising
At regular intervals, the team reflects on how to become more effective, then tunes and adjusts its behavior accordingly.	Reflection

5. WHY MODEL AGILE DEVELOPMENT AS A JIGSAW?

We have chosen a jigsaw firstly as an allegory for the way many traditionalists view Agile processes: they have all the pieces, but can't put them together to see the overall picture. Don Wells[21] makes a similar suggestion regarding XP and adds "individually the pieces make no sense, but when combined together a complete picture can be seen". Secondly, if any one of the pieces is missing then the Agile picture is incomplete. Thus if a process only includes 15 of these 16 elements then it's not completely Agile. For example, Beck and Fowler[22] caution against adopting just some of the practices (of XP) to mix and match with more traditional approaches, and go on to give the example illustrated in Figure 2. In Beck and Fowler's example the project manager continues to be responsible for task estimation. Removing the programmer estimation piece from the jigsaw leaves the agile model incomplete. Something is clearly missing from the picture of the process, in this case it is benefits arising from the "sense of ownership" programmers have "if they did the breakdown and estimates themselves".[22]

A third reason for using a jigsaw is that each piece has a unique shape illustrating that, while each Agile process has their own methods, provided the method fulfils the requirement of the particular element i.e. has the same overall shape, then it fits into the picture. This also implies that any piece can be replaced with a piece (or pieces) with the same outline. For example the length of the iterations varies from as little as one week (XP) to 6 – 8 weeks (DSDM).

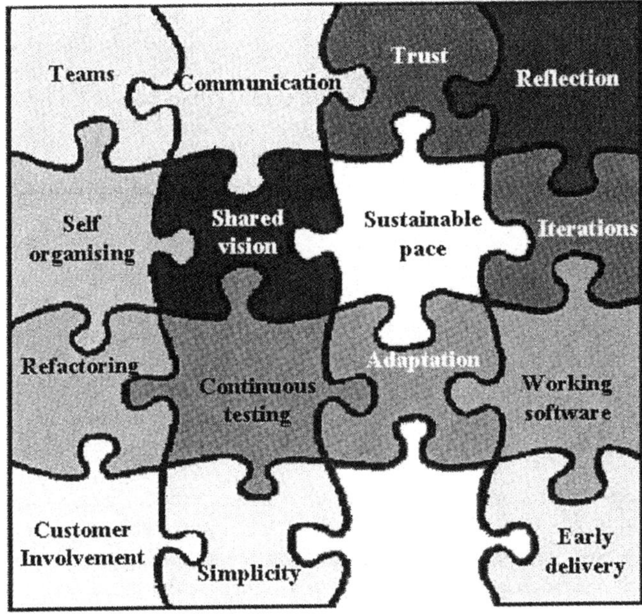

Figure 2. Jigsaw model of an incomplete process.

Finally, although we could probably have modeled these aspects of Agile methods another way, the game metaphor is common in Agile processes, e.g. XP's planning game, the SCRUM methodology and its sprints. Thus the jigsaw symbolism seemed particularly appealing.

It should be noted that the relative positions of the pieces in the current model convey no meaning. In addition, individual elements of the jigsaw model may be intended to provide greater coverage than implied by Table 1. For example, the "adaptation" element does not only model the capacity to respond to change but also represents the idea that an Agile process may be adapted to better suit a given situation. In fact adaptation appears common and is discussed in a number of experience reports.[23,24]

As already discussed, our search for an Agile model began with RAD. In fact the model of RAD as being comprised of four basic components, people, tools, methods and management became our starting point. All the pieces of the jigsaw can be classified as fitting one of these categories. Currently the tools/methods separation is somewhat arbitrary. While refactoring is generally acknowledged to be a design tool,[6,25] it could be argued that the other elements could be either tools or methods. It is possible that this is one way in which Agile and RAD diverge, and that at the generic level of this model there is no actual difference between a tool and a method.

6. FUTURE WORK

This paper has discussed a preliminary version of the jigsaw model. However, before the model is used to reason generically about Agile processes and risk management, its appropriateness is to be further validated by extending the model to DSDM and XP. This is expected to result in two finer grained jigsaw models detailing ways in which the various tools and methods applicable to these specific processes map to elements of the model presented here. There are two reasons for choosing XP and DSDM. Among the published Agile methods, only XP and DSDM have substantial records of successful industrial application.[15] These two methods also represent opposite ends of the Agile planning spectrum,[26] thus results should be able to be extrapolated to other methods.

The ultimate aim of the project is to show that the Agile methods do address common software development risks by mapping elements of the Software Engineering Institute's Risk Identification list [27] to elements of the Jigsaw Model.

7. CONCLUSION

We have developed an initial version of a generic model describing the defining elements of an Agile process. These elements are represented as pieces of a jigsaw, illustrating two essential notions. All pieces of the jigsaw must be present for the process modeled to be completely Agile and, if any piece is replaced, the outline of the replacement must be the same. This allows the different processes to adopt different methods, but provided the methods achieve the same goal, i.e. have the same shape, then the jigsaw can be completed, and the process is Agile.

A model such as this provides researchers with a tool for reasoning about Agile processes in a generic sense, rather than being constrained to state the limitations of their conclusions to the particular processes investigated. It can also be used to determine whether or not a process is indeed Agile.

REFERENCES

1. Tom Roberts, Why Can't We Implement This SDM? *IEEE Software*, Nov/Dec, 70–75 (1999)
2. Bob Hughes and Mark Cotterell, *Software Project Management*, 3rd Edition, (McGraw Hill, 2002)
3. A. Fuller, P. Croll and O. Garcia, Why Software engineering is riskier than ever. Proceedings of the 2nd Asia, Pacific Conference on Quality Software (APAQS 2001). (2001)
4. S. Rakitin, Manifesto Elicits Cynicism, *Computer*, Dec. 2001, 4 (2001)
5. Mark C. Paulk, Extreme Programming from a CMM Perspective. *IEEE Software* 18(6): 19–26 (2001)
6. Martin Fowler, The New Methodology, (February, 2003) http://www.martinfowler.com/articles/newMethodology.html originally published as "Put Your Processes on a Diet," *Software Development*, vol. 8, no. 12, Dec. 2000
7. S. Thomas, An Agile Comparison (December, 2002) http://www.balagan.org.uk/work/agile_comparison.htm,
8. Eric Poinsignon, Introduction to Agile Method Movement, *CERN-CNL-2002-002*, Vol. XXXVII, issue no 2, (February, 2003) http://ref.cern.ch/CERN/CNL/2002/002/SDTagile/
9. Murdoch McTaggart, RADical Software Development, *Application Development Advisor*, Nov-Dec 2001, www. appdevadvisor.co.uk (2001)
10. James Martin, *Rapid Application Development*, (Macmillan Publishing Co.,1991)

11. DSDM Consortium, *History of DSDM* (February, 2003) http://www.dsdm.org/en/about/history.asp
12. Alan Zeichick, eXtreme Programming: Developing Agility with Intel Processors and Development Tools, (February, 2003) http://w ww.devx.com/Intel/Article/6832
13. CASEMaker Inc., What is RAD? (October, 2002) www.casemaker.com/download/products/totem/rad_wp.pdf
14. Paul Beynon-Davies, Rapid Application Development (RAD), (February 2003) http://www.comp.glam.ac.uk/SOC_Server/research/gisc/RADbrf1.htm
15. Jim Highsmith, History: The Agile Manifesto, http://agilemanifesto.org/history.html (2001)
16. P. Abramsson, O. Salo, J. Ronkainen and J. Warsta, *Agile Software Development Methods: Review and Analysis*, Espoo 2002, (VTT Publications 478, 2002)
17. Fraunhofer USA, Summary of the First workshop on Agile Methods, (2002)
18. M. Cohn and K. Schwaber The Need for Agile Project Management, *Agile Times Newsletter*, 1/1, 10–12 (2003)
19. The Online Dictionary, http://dictionary.reference.com
20. A. Cockburn, *Agile Software Development* (Addison Wesley 2002)
21. Don Wells, What is Extreme Programming? (February, 2003) http://www.extremeprogramming.org/what.html
22. Kent Beck and Martin Fowler, *Planning Extreme Programming*, (Addison Wesley, 2001)
23. M. Lippert and S. Roock, Adapting XP to Complex Applicatoin Domains. ESEC/FSE 2001, Proceedings of Joint 8th European Software Engineering Conference (ESEC) and 9th ACM SIGSOFT Symposium on the Foundations of Software Engineering (FSE-9) (2001)
24. J. Pelrine, Modelling infection scenarios – a fixed price eXtreme Programming success story, *OOPSLA 2000*, 23–24 (2000)
25. Bob Martin, Rigorous refactoring or BFUD, *Agile Times Newsletter*, 1/1, 6 (2003),
26. B. Boehm, Get Ready for Agile Methods, with Care, *IEEE Computer*, Vol. 35, No. 1, 64–69 (2002)
27. M. J. Carr, S. L. Konda, I. Monarch, F. C Ulrich. and C. F. Walker, Taxonomy-Based Risk Identification, Software Engineering Institute Technical Report, CMU/SEI-TR-6, ESC-TR-93-183 (1993)

CONTINUOUS INTEGRATION AS A MEANS OF COORDINATION

A case study of two open source projects

Jesper Holck and Niels Jørgensen*

1. INTRODUCTION

Open source software development challenges traditional views on software development; an apparently anarchistic bunch of hackers, working for free, produce widely used software. In this paper we investigate the role played by continuous integration with regard to coordinating the efforts of hundreds of developers in two open source projects, FreeBSD and Mozilla.

1.1. Characteristics of open source development

Previous research on open source development shows a number of characteristics that may make these projects more difficult to manage and coordinate than more traditional software development projects:

Few specifications: Many of the documents traditionally regarded as essential for coordination seem to be missing from most open source projects, including plans and schedules (Mockus et al., 2002).

Geographical distribution: A study of Linux contributors showed them to "come from a truly worldwide community spanning many organizations" (Dempsey et al., 2002), and a recent on-line survey of 2,784 open source participants (Ghosh et al., 2002) showed that "most of the developers feature networks that consist of rather few people." Integration may be particularly difficult for geographically distributed projects (Herbsleb and Grinter, 1999).

Volunteers: Most developers contribute to the projects in their free time – even though as many as 40% are paid for (some of) their work (Hars and Ou, 2001; Jørgensen, 2001) – and so are presumably less likely to accept to be ordered around and perform tedious tasks.

* Jesper Holck, Copenhagen Business School, Department of Informatics, Howitzvej 60, DK-2000 Frederiksberg, Denmark, jeh.inf@cbs.dk. Niels Jørgensen, Roskilde University, Computer Science, Universitetsvej 1, DK-4000 Roskilde, Denmark, nielsj@ruc.dk.

Constructing the Infrastructure for the Knowledge Economy
Edited by H. Linger *et al.*, Kluwer Academic/Plenum Publishers, 2004

Self-directed egoists: This characterization of open source developers given in (Raymond, 2000) may be crude, but is not too distant from the results from empirical studies. According to Lakhani et al. (2002), the two most important motivations for participating in an open source project were "intellectually stimulating" and "improves skill." For only 20% of the developers, "work with team" was a key motivator.

1.2. Continuous integration

We define continuous integration loosely as a process where changes are added frequently, typically at least daily, to a development version of the software, which is kept in a working state as it evolves gradually to production release.

Continuous integration in this sense is used in open source as well as commercial projects. Our definition comprises the approach of a fixed, daily cycle that produces a new development release, as in projects at Microsoft (Cusumano and Selby, 1997) and Mozilla, as well as less structured approaches as in FreeBSD, where new development releases are created many times each day. Continuous integration may be of particular interest in open source projects, because the approach does not require work to be organized on the basis of a project plan stipulating successive phases of requirement specification, design, implementation, and testing, and so may be well suited to the open source characteristics postulated above in subsection 1.1.

Several development methods label certain activities as continuous integration, including eXtreme Programming, where it is one of 12 recommended best practices (Beck, 2000), and Unified Process (Jacobson et al., 1999). Studies of commercial projects using daily builds, and thus some form of continuous integration, indicate several advantages, including reduced integration risk (errors are found early) and motivation (you see a working system) (Cusumano and Selby, 1997; Ebert et al., 2001; Olsson and Karlsson, 1999). Continuous integration can be seen as a way to avoid 'big bang' integration, where all modules are combined in one go, and which usually results in large numbers of errors, hard to isolate and correct because of the vast expanse of the program (Pressman, 1992).

However, to our best knowledge there have been no publicized studies that establish an overall picture of possible properties of continuous integration, whether for commercial or open source projects. For example, how well does the approach scale? Beck assumes that XP's reliance on continuous integration is a major reason why XP is *not* well suited for projects with many concurrent developers (Beck, 2000).

Continuous integration may supplement a phased approach, 'continuous' then referring to the way integration takes place during a phase of integration and test; and it may be part of iterative methods with (as in XP) or without (as in FreeBSD and Mozilla) processes prescribing that modules and their interfaces are designed and documented, at least to some extent, prior to implementation.

A study of integration in software development should relate integration to the broader issue of coordination. Maybe the most important means of coordination in traditional software engineering are the architectural design and the project plan (see e.g. Hoffer et al., 2002; Pressman, 1992). By dividing the code into separate modules and specifying the interfaces of each, the architectural design simplifies coordination of programmers working on separate modules, as it avoids the need for detailed knowledge of each other's work. In this way, the architectural design serves as a vehicle for managing the usability dependency (one module's output is another module's input) mentioned in (Malone and Crowston, 1994). By breaking down the project into a task network, the project plan ensures that tasks are performed in the right order, in this way handling the prerequisite constraint dependencies (task A must be finished before task B can begin), also mentioned in (Malone and Crowston, 1994). It is our hypothesis that continuous integration can serve as a means of coordination, to some degree replacing the coordination role of the architectural design and task network documents.

1.3. Our study

Our study is a multiple, explorative case study in the sense of (Yin, 1998). We have pulled statistical data from FreeBSD's and Mozilla's repositories in October 2002, studied the projects developers' mailing lists, and drawn on a survey of 72 FreeBSD developers, performed in November 2000 which was also the basis for (Jørgensen, 2001).

The paper is organized as follows: Section 2 introduces the projects and the organization of their repositories into branches. Sections 3-5 describe how continuous integration effects the life cycle of a change, from initialization (section 3), over source code development (section 4), to commit and post-commit test (section 5). Section 6 concludes.

2. THE "TRUNK" IN FREEBSD AND MOZILLA

FreeBSD and Mozilla (see Table 1 for basic facts) organize their source code repository (from now on: the *repository*) around a main branch (the *trunk*) into which most changes are inserted, and one (Mozilla) or more (FreeBSD) additional branches hosting the projects' production releases.

Table 1. Basic facts on FreeBSD and Mozilla

Name	FreeBSD	Mozilla
Product	Server operating system	Web browser
Major product qualities	Robustness, security	Independence, open interfaces, user interface
Major platforms	Intel x86, Alpha, SPARC, PC-98	Windows, Linux, MacOS
Approximate size of trunk	29,000 files, 11 million lines	40,000 files, 6 million lines
Activity on trunk in October 2002	118 persons *committed* 2,063 changes	107 persons *committed* 2,856 changes
50% of these commits made by	12 developers	7 developers
Project management	9 person elected *Core Team* (*The FreeBSD core team*)	11 person *Mozilla.org Staff* (*Mozilla roles and responsibilities*, 2002)

The repositories are stored at central locations, reachable via the Internet (www.freebsd.org and www.mozilla.org). Developers contribute to the projects by continually and in parallel updating (changing, adding, and deleting) repository files; a process controlled by means of CVS augmented with extra tools. Each file change (*commit*) creates a new version; all old file versions remain accessible, thereby making it always possible to go back to an older version of a file if problems or errors are introduced.

The software product that results from *building* with the newest versions of all files is called the *development version*; because files are updated continuously, the development version will also be constantly evolving. The aggregation of all files related to the development version is called the *trunk*.

Because both projects maintain production releases, and so need to isolate new development on a file from file versions part of production releases, there is a need to make branches in the repository. At a certain time a branch is created as a (logical) copy of the most recent file versions from the trunk; hereafter, changes to the trunk will not directly influence the branch, and vice versa. A developer must specify the branch he wants to use when downloading or committing source files.

In addition to development and production versions, both projects' software is available in a number of versions, adapted to a wide range of different platforms (the table only shows the most important). As a consequence, developers not only need to differentiate between releases (residing on different branches), but must also be able to commit changes intended for specific platforms; this is implemented using conditional compilation rather than branching.

3. INITIALIZATION OF WORK ON A CHANGE

3.1. Work breakdown

As mentioned in section 1, an important aspect of coordinating a large software project is how work is broken down into parts, and in this section we will describe how this is done in the two projects. Both projects have a notion of code ownership, in the sense that most files have a *maintainer* (FreeBSD) or *module owner* (Mozilla), often responsible for entire directories or applications.

> The maintainer owns and is responsible for that code. This means that he is responsible for fixing bugs and answering problems reports [...] (Kamp, 1996).

Code ownership does not prevent dependencies between concurrent work on different tasks involving the same files; work on a task involving files "owned" by someone else is by no means excluded. Rather, code ownership is a mechanism for coordination via a consensus process:

> [A commit should happen] only once something resembling consensus has been reached (*The FreeBSD committers' big list of rules*).

In both projects there is work on tasks that involve large numbers of files, giving rise to dependencies with concurrent work on other tasks involving the same files. An example of a very large task is the recent work in FreeBSD on Symmetric Multi-Processing (SMP), which enables the operating system to utilize multiple processors. Work was organized as a project in itself, headed by a project manager, and was broken down into small changes, added incrementally to the trunk. This approach was due in part to 'big bang' integration problems experienced in another open source operating system:

> ... they [BSD/OS] went the route of doing the SMP development on a branch, and the divergence between the trunk and the branch quickly became unmanageable. [...] We are completely standing the kernel on its head, and the amount of code changes is the largest of any FreeBSD kernel project taken on thus far. To have done this much development on a branch would have been infeasible *(FreeBSD SMP project manager, November 2000).*

Changes related to SMP in FreeBSD have been added incrementally over several years. This has been a difficult task, and for several months during the fall in 2000, this work severely "destabilized" the trunk, causing build failures and other errors due to dependencies with other, concurrent work on the trunk. The decision in FreeBSD to avoid working on a separate branch can be viewed as a preference to deal with these dependencies on the fly, rather than after accumulating changes on a separate branch, which was seen as entailing a risk of "big bang" integration problems.

3.2. Design

Neither FreeBSD nor Mozilla requires design to precede coding, in the sense of writing, discussing, or approving written design documents prior to coding. Some documentation of the design of the systems' basic architecture is accessible, though.

Indeed in practice, for the individual change there is typically no design document. 31 of the 72 committers surveyed in FreeBSD responded that they had never distributed a design document (defined as a separate document, distinct from a source file).

The lack of an established practice of using design documents as a coordination mechanism should, however, be viewed in the context of the projects being largely maintenance-oriented. FreeBSD has inherited a largely unaltered, basic architectural design from its predecessors, the first versions of which were developed in the late 1970s (*About FreeBSD's technological advances*).

Mozilla, being a much younger project with roots that back no further than to the mid-90s, is more in need of providing its own design documentation. For example, the project has developed its own component model (XPCOM) and uses a software layer originally developed by Netscape that provides a platform-independent interface to multithreading (NSPR). These and other complex, project-specific parts of Mozilla are described at an introductory level (*Hacking Mozilla*) as well as in more detail in a series of publicly available documents (*Core architecture*).

4. SOURCE CODE DEVELOPMENT

Before committing his contribution, the work of a developer can be divided into code, review, and a test with local copies of the repository files.

4.1. Code

Extensive coding guidelines exist in both projects. These indicate a strong emphasis on quality in a broad sense, including security and internationalization, not merely quality in the sense of avoiding broken builds and simple programming errors.

The developers' contribution will be highly visible once committed:

- The repositories are browsable, providing easy public access to all sources files.

- In both projects, an automatic mail message is sent to other developers immediately upon commit of a change.

This visibility encourages developers to strive to produce code that will be perceived to be of high quality. In responding to the statement "Knowing that my contributions may be read by highly competent developers has encouraged me to improve my coding skill", 57% of the 72 FreeBSD committers surveyed said "yes, significantly", and 29 % "yes, somewhat". One committer added: "Embarrassment is a powerful thing."

The visibility of the code is in part due to the project being open source, but also to the approach of continuous integration: A large number of developers are working with the most recent version of the trunk, and monitor the changes being made because their work depends on them.

4.2. Review

Both projects require changes to be submitted to review prior to commit. If the developer is a committer, this review may be the only occasion where others are involved in approving the developer's work prior to commit.

FreeBSD's Committer's Guide rule 2 is "discuss any significant change before committing" (*The FreeBSD committers' big list of rules*), and 86% of the committers surveyed said that they actually received feedback on their latest change when submitting it to review.

Mozilla has detailed rules requiring all changes to be reviewed by another committer, and in most cases to be "super-reviewed" as well:

> This 'super-review' will look at the quality of the code itself, its potential effects on other areas of the tree, its use of interfaces, and otherwise its adherence to Mozilla coding guidelines and is done by one or more of a designated group of strong hackers (Eich and Baker, 2003).

4.3. Test

Both projects explicitly and strongly state the requirement that the developer's change must not break the build. To meet this requirement, before committing, the developer has to test his contribution locally, using copies of the most recent files in the repository; an activity similar to the integration test found in traditional software engineering (Pressman, 1992).

The build process is fully automated, but correcting a broken build can be highly challenging, since the failure may be due to dependencies to files or modules outside of the area of the developer's primary expertise.

4.3.1. The Basic "Don't Break the Build" Rule

In FreeBSD, the rule is stated as follows:

> If your changes are to the kernel, make sure you can still compile [the kernel]. If your changes are anywhere else, make sure you can still [compile everything but the kernel] (*The FreeBSD committers' big list of rules*).

In Mozilla, the committer must also run a set of simple tests. The underlying rationale is explained as follows:

> The program has to be stable enough to serve as a platform to code new features. You can't verify new features if the program is crashing at startup or has major runtime flaws. Being able to pull a tree and build it is useless unless you can execute the program long enough [to] create and debug new code. (Yeh, 1999)

It is noteworthy that breaking the build (making the development version unusable) will not only obstruct the use of the trunk to test changes already committed (see section 5 below), but also other developers' work in the pre-commit test stage, as they cannot do this with an already broken development version.

4.3.2. Interpretation of the basic rule

A major challenge is for the projects to strike a balance that avoids broken builds, but leaves room for relevant exceptions:

> I can remember one instance where I broke the build every 2-3 days for a period of time; that was necessary [due to the nature of the work]. That was tolerated – I didn't get a single complaint *(Interview with FreeBSD committer, November 2000).*

Interpretation of the "don't break the build"-rule is particularly called for with respect to the effort a developer should invest to prevent broken builds on *any* platform. Recall from section 2 that FreeBSD and Mozilla are developed for many platforms, of which 4 and 3, respectively, are particularly prioritized. Due to platform differences, a build may succeed on one and fail on another. However, most developers have only access to a single platform, so in practice it will be very difficult to perform trial builds on each prioritized platform before check-in.

In part the problem of broken builds on other platforms is solved by making a set of central build machines available, to which sources can be uploaded and subjected to a trial build, prior to commit; however, this is tedious and is not enforced as a general rule in either project. As a middle road, Mozilla provides so-called portability guides with rules and recommendations for producing cross-platform software (e.g. Williams, 1998).

Thus, while FreeBSD and Mozilla in principle delegate to the developer the responsibility to integrate his change, in practice a major challenge is to strike a reasonable balance, accepting to some degree that developers from time to time break the build and thus disrupt other developers' work. Indeed, requiring in an absolute sense that committed changes are free of errors would be absurd and defy the purpose of using the trunk for community testing, as discussed below.

5. COMMIT AND POST-COMMIT TEST

The final stages a change goes through are *commit*, *community test*, and *stabilization*.

5.1. Commit

A commit of a change is the act of uploading to the trunk the set of file modifications that constitute the change.

Committers have write privileges to the entire repository, and it is up to the committer to decide when the change is sufficiently tested for commit. The ability to commit without awaiting approval is highly motivating:

> I don't feel I'm at the whim of a single person. *(FreeBSD developer, November 2000).*
>
> [...] there is a tremendous satisfaction to the "see bug, fix bug, see bug fix get incorporated" so that the fix help others' cycle. *(FreeBSD developer, November 2000).*

This may apply also to developers whose work is paid for by a company:

> I use FreeBSD at work. It is annoying to take a FreeBSD release and then apply local changes every time. When [...] my changes [...] are in the main release [...] I can install a standard FreeBSD release [...] at work and use it right away. *(FreeBSD developer, November 2000).*

5.2. Community testing

After being committed to the trunk, the change is tested. This is not a systematic test of the specific change, but a build verification and a use test.

5.2.1. Build verification

In FreeBSD, there is an automated routine for building the trunk twice a day on the major processor architectures, so-called Tinderbox-builds, the result of which are shown on a webpage (http://www.rtp.freebsd.org/~des). However, there is no established process for acting on the automatic messages, and most build errors will be detected by currently active developers, reporting the problem to one or more mailing lists, even before the Tinderbox-builds are run.

In Mozilla, there is a well-defined process for a daily verification effort using a cluster of build machines (representing all targeted platforms). At 8 AM (PST) each working day, the build machines download the newest source code, build it, and execute a small number of regression tests.

During Mozilla's build verification, developers that have committed changes since the previous day's verification are said to be "on the hook":

> If you are on the hook, your top priority is to be available to the build team to fix bustages. [...] You are findable. You are either at your desk, or pageable, checking e-mail constantly, or on IRC so that you can be found immediately and can respond to any problems in your code (*Hacking Mozilla with Bonsai*).

Due to a fear of "big bang" integration problems, Mozilla's repository is closed until successful termination of build verification, meaning that no commits (except if part of the corrective effort) are allowed until all three prioritized platforms pass the test; this may last from 2 to several hours. The reason for "closing the tree" for all platforms is given in (Yeh, 1999):

> During the development of Netscape Navigator and Netscape Communicator it was argued many times that [...] we should care less about a particular set of platforms and fix regressions on these "second-class" platforms later. We tried this once. The reason why we don't have Netscape Communicator on Win16 was the result of putting off the recovery of that platform until later. After a couple of weeks recovery became impossible. [...] The problems will stack up [...] as the codebase moves forward and it never catches up.

5.2.2. Use test

Use testing corresponds to Raymond's "parallel debugging" (Raymond, 2000) and results in a stream of bug reports, the primary source of new requirements (see section 3). Use testing is performed in part by non-developers; this is especially prioritized by Mozilla, where semi-stabilized versions of the trunk are released for this purpose (e.g. release 1.2 of November 26, 2002); and in part by developers, where use testing may coincide with work on other changes in the pre-commit test stage (see section 4).

5.3. Stabilization

A change is production released when it becomes part of a production release of the project's software. We discuss the process leading to major production releases (for example, FreeBSD's 5.0 of January 2003, and Mozilla's 1.0 of June 2002). In addition, the projects create minor production releases (FreeBSD 4.6, 4.7, etc.; Mozilla 1.1, 1.2, etc.).

Production releases are created by first declaring a period of stabilization, effectively restricting which changes that are allowed to be committed. During stabilization, changes are subjected to community testing in the same manner as in the previous stage, but only necessary changes are allowed, most notably bug-fixes. In FreeBSD, the stabilization period for 5.0 lasted for two months, the first month being less strict with new features being allowed on a case-by-case basis at the release engineering team's discretion, the second more strict with commits allowed only if they were bug-fixes.

When the software is considered sufficiently stable, it is declared a production release. Thus, the stabilization period is sufficient for changing "work in progress" to "production release"; there is no need for separate stages or teams dedicated to releasing, as the software is already in a working state.

In Mozilla, the stabilization period prior to the 1.0 release can be considered to have lasted more than 8 months, beginning with the 0.9.6 release (in November 2001) upon which the "the trunk is closed to all but a relative few bug fixes, and everyone is focused on testing." (Eich, 2002)

There is indication of pressure from Mozilla developers to relax commit restrictions:

> [...] we're not looking for new features; we want stability, performance [...], tolerably few bugs [...]. Features cost us time [...] those implementing the features [...] could instead help fix 1.0 bugs [...]. If you think you must have a feature by 1.0, please be prepared to say why to drivers, and be prepared to hear "we can't support work on that feature until after 1.0 has branched" in reply. (Eich, 2002)

To allow for the resumption of new development on the trunk, the final 2 months of stabilization for Mozilla's 1.0 release took place on a separate branch (created April 2002). This isolation of bug-fixing from new development is in some sense a departure from strict adherence to continuous integration, and indicates the following dilemma associated with stabilization:

- Creating a separate stabilization branch allows for resumption of new development, which is otherwise halted when "destabilizing" changes are prohibited on the trunk.
- However, a separate stabilization branch makes it necessary for bug-fixes to the trunk to also be made to the branch (and vice versa); it doubles the tasks related

to managing a branch (assigned to branch drivers in Mozilla), and divides the pool of user/developers between the branches:

> This branch [Mozilla 1.0] obviously entails overhead in driving, merging, reviewing, and testing. (Eich, 2002)

Because of this dilemma, decisions regarding if and when to branch are both important and difficult. Both projects follow a model where major releases are (almost) simple snapshots of the development branch, and branches are only made in order to stabilize upcoming releases. This is very much in line with branch-by-purpose model recommended by Walrad and Strom (2002).

6. CONCLUSION

Our case study of FreeBSD and Mozilla as viewed from the perspective of coordination indicates a number of possible advantages, disadvantages, and challenges associated with continuous integration. At a basic level, it appears that the processes actually work in the two projects studied: in spite of distributed developers, volunteering for tasks, and without design documents, FreeBSD and Mozilla produce widely used software. Where traditional software engineering projects rely on explicit task assignment and detailed design documents for coordination, these projects rely on continuous integration.

Advantages may include:

- Continuous integration may be highly motivating: developers are to a large degree free to choose which task they want to work on and can commit changes without awaiting approval – it feels unbureaucratic and lets the developer see the result of his work quickly become part of the project's software (section 4).
- To produce a software version which is mature enough for production release, the projects 'stabilize' their development version; this is a relatively painless process because the software is already in a working condition, and unexpected delays due to integration problems are avoided.

While extensive freedom for developers to choose what to work on may be unusual in commercial projects, the motivational advantage of seeing changes integrate quickly may be independent of whether a project is open source or commercial. Also, both kinds of projects can benefit from the reduced risk of unexpected production release delays.

Disadvantages may include:

- The combination of the requirements for the trunk to be "buildable" and for all new development to be committed to the trunk makes heavy demands on developers. With the source code in the trunk changing constantly, implementing a change is like hitting a moving target, and requires that local source code be synchronized frequently.
- If a commit breaks the build, work on the project is disrupted. Developers will not be able to test local source code changes with the newest source code in the trunk; this may be just a nuisance, but may also block further work on code changes. Also, users and developers are prevented from community testing the newest software version.

These disadvantages are independent of project type, although in typical commercial projects, broken builds do not effect user-testers outside of the project organization.

The challenges posed by continuous integration include the following:

- The need to implement measures that reduce the risk of new commits breaking the build. Measures taken in FreeBSD and Mozilla include coding guidelines and code exposure (section 4.1), demands for review before commit (section 4.2), urging developers to avoid broken builds (section 4.3), demands (in Mozilla) that committers be available (section 5.2), central test facilities (section 5.2), and Mozilla's closing of the tree while testing (section 5.2).
- There is a potential conflict between stabilization and new development. If stabilization is insulated on a separate branch, developer resources for testing and managing will be divided between community testing and stabilization. On the other hand, a prolonged stage of stabilization on the trunk will have the cost of holding back new development (section 5).
- An additional challenge is how to define and interpret the "don't break the build"-rule (section 4). Indication that strict compliance with this rule may not be optimal was evident in both projects, one reason being that most developers do not have convenient access to all platforms on which they should (ideally) test their changes before committing.

Establishing a project culture, whether the project is open source or commercial, with strong encouragement to produce high quality code, but also with tolerance and mutual support is perhaps the major challenge; indeed, the approach of continuous integration may provide a basis for developing such a culture, since the quality of the project's most recent source code becomes a common point of continuous, project-wide focus.

REFERENCES

About FreeBSD's technological advances. Retrieved Dec. 1, 2002, from http://www.freebsd.org/features.html

Beck, K., 2000, *Extreme Programming Explained*, Addison Wesley, Boston, USA.

Core architecture. Retrieved Dec. 1, 2002, from http://www.mozilla.org/catalog/architecture/

Cusumano, M. A., and Selby, R. W., 1997, How Microsoft builds software, *CACM,* **40**(6): 53–61.

Dempsey, B., Weiss, D., Jones, P., and Greenberg, J., 2002, Who is an open source developer? A qualitative profile of a community of open source Linux developers, *CACM,* **45**(2): 67–72.

Ebert, C., Parro, C. H., Suttels, R., and Kolarczyk, H., 2001, Improving validation activities in a global software development. Paper presented at the 23rd International Conference on Software Engineering (ICSE '01), Toronto, Canada.

Eich, B., 2002, Mozilla 1.0 manifesto. Retrieved Nov. 15, 2002, from http://www.mozilla.org/roadmap/mozilla-1.0.html

Eich, B., and Baker, M., 2003, Mozilla "super-review". Retrieved April 21, 2003, from http://www.mozilla.org/hacking/reviewers.html

The FreeBSD committers' big list of rules. Retrieved Dec. 1, 2002, from: http://www.freebsd.org/doc/en/articles/committers-guide/rules.html

The FreeBSD core team. Retrieved April 21, 2003, from http://www.freebsd.org/doc/en/articles/contributors/staff-core.html

Ghosh, R. A., Glott, R., Krieger, B., and Robles, G., 2002, Part 4: Survey of developers, *FLOSS final report.*

Hacking Mozilla. Retrieved Dec. 1, 2002, from http://www.mozilla.org/hacking/

Hacking Mozilla with Bonsai. Retrieved Dec. 1, 2002, from http://www.mozilla.org/hacking/bonsai.html

Hars, A., and Ou, S., 2001, Working for free? Motivations of participating in open source projects. Paper presented at the 34th Hawaii International Conference on System Sciences, Hawaii.

Herbsleb, J. D., and Grinter, R. E., 1999, Splitting the organization and integrating the code: Conway's law revisited. Paper presented at the International Conference on Software Engineering (ICSE '99).

Hoffer, J. A., George, J. F., and Valacich, J. S., 2002, *Modern System Analysis and Design*. Prentice Hall, Upper Saddle River, New Jersey, USA.

Jacobson, I., Booch, G., and Rumbaugh, J., 1999, *The Unified Software Development Process*. Addison Wesley, Indianapolis, USA.

Jørgensen, N., 2001, Putting it all in the trunk: Incremental software development in the FreeBSD open source project, *Information Systems Journal,* **11**(4): 321–336.

Kamp, P.-H., 1996, Source tree guidelines and policies. Retrieved Dec. 1, 2002, from http://www.freebsd.org/doc/en/books/developers-handbook/policies.html

Lakhani, K. R., Wolf, B., Bates, J., and DiBona, C., 2002, The Boston Consulting Group hacker survey. Retrieved May 8, 2003, from http://www.osdn.com/bcg/

Malone, T. W., and Crowston, K., 1994, The interdisciplinary study of coordination, *ACM Computing Surveys,* **26**(1): 87–119.

Mockus, A., Fielding, R. T., and Herbsleb, J. D., 2002, Two case studies of open source software development: Apache and Mozilla, *ACM Transactions on Software Engineering and Methodology,* **11**(3): 309–346.

Mozilla roles and responsibilities, 2002. Retrieved April 18, 2003, from: http://www.mozilla.org/about/roles.html

Olsson, K., and Karlsson, E.-A., 1999, *Daily Build - the Best of Both Worlds: Rapid Development and Control.* Swedish Engineering Industries, Lund, Sweden.

Pressman, R. S., 1992, *Software Engineering - a Practitioner's Approach* (3rd, international ed.). McGraw-Hill, New York, USA.

Raymond, E. S., 2000, The cathedral and the bazaar, v. 3. Retrieved April 8, 2003, from http://www.catb.org/~esr/writings/cathedral-bazaar/cathedral-bazaar/

Walrad, C., and Strom, D., 2002, The importance of branching models in SCM, *IEEE Computer,* **35**(9): 31–38.

Williams, D., 1998, C++ portability guide, version 0.8. Retrieved Dec. 1, 2002, from http://www.mozilla.org/hacking/portable-cpp.html

Yeh, C., 1999, Mozilla tree verification process. Retrieved April 11, 2003, from http://www.mozilla.org/build/verification.html

Yin, R. K., 1998, *Case Study Research: Design and Methods.* Sage Publications, Newbury Park, USA.

ON BUSINESS RULES APPROACH TO THE INFORMATION SYSTEMS DEVELOPMENT

Irma Valatkaite and Olegas Vasilecas*

1. INTRODUCTION

Business rules approach to information systems (IS) development emerged as the response to the growing need of business organizations to manage their knowledge explicitly and map it effectively to business IS in order to support daily business operations.

Business rules are at the heart of the business: they state core business policies, control and influence the behavior of people and systems in the organization. Therefore it is vital to find the rules and ensure that the rules are appropriate. In the process of finding the right rules set the consensus from all the business stakeholders is obtained on what the rules should be and conflicting policies are reconciled. As the business changes the rules set must be properly maintained and adapted to the new conditions.[15] These activities carry the label of business modeling and answer the question of "what" – what the business is.

The second question is "how" – how to use the knowledge obtained in the first step? There are two ways how to put business rules to work. First one is simply to use business rules for guidance of people in the business. The second one comprises the technology using which a substantial subset of discovered and agreed business rules can be automated in information (or program) systems. Here one must deal with information (or program) system modeling and development activities.

In this paper we focus on the second way. We analyze IS modeling using business rules approach. For that purpose we look at what business rules are, what types of business rules can be enforced in business IS, and what technologies can be employed for business rules implementation. A business IS development framework is proposed which defines methods to analyze, model and structure business knowledge, and map the resulting business rules model to the implementation level.

---

* Information Systems Laboratory, Vilnius Gediminas Technical University, Vilnius, Lithuania.

2. BUSINESS RULES

2.1. Definition

Business rules definition is twofold.[3, 11] From a business perspective ("Zachman[23] row-2") business rule is a statement that defines or constrains some aspect of the business; it is intended to assert the business structure, or to control or influence the behavior of the business. The final business rules set must comprise only atomic business rules. Atomic business rules are such that cannot be broken down or decomposed further into more detailed business rules because, if reduced any further, there would be loss of important information about the business.

From an IS perspective ("Zachman[23] row-2") business rule is a statement which constrain certain business aspect, define the business structure, and control business processes. In IS it is implemented as facts registration (as data) and constraints applied during registration process.

1.1. Motivation

Why business rules?

The motivation behind this approach is rather straightforward:

1. The concept of a business rule is not a new one, and business representatives use it to describe business processes of their organizations. Thus business representatives are capable of using the concept by themselves while identifying business rules.
2. Business rules are the method to structure business knowledge. Since it is easily comprehensible and convenient for both business representatives and system analysts, it constitutes an excellent basis for communication.
3. Business rules structure closely resembles the structure of production rules thus it is possible to represent business rules using some formal logic-based modeling language.
4. Business rules in a formal representation language allow using this representation for automatic implementation.
5. Business rules are expected to change more frequently than the rest of business objects, and tend to evolve over time as a result of new business requirements. Therefore it is reasonable to identify business rules as a separate component and deal with it respectively at logical and physical levels.

1.2. Taxonomies

Ellen Gottesdiener[6] states: "There is no agreed-upon taxonomy for business rules, nor does there need to be." While it is questionable whether there should be a single agreed taxonomy, it is indeed true that it does not exist yet. Different authors or research groups presented various taxonomies, as shown in Table 1.

Table 1. Various Business Rules Taxonomies

Source	Business rules taxonomy
Business Rules Group (1995, revised in 1997 and 2000) 0	- term (a type of structural assertion) - fact (terms linked together; another type of structural assertion) - derivation (facts derived from other facts) - constraint (also called action assertions)
Graham (1998) 0	- attribute assertion (range constraints, enumeration constraints, type constraints) - operational assertion (pre-condition, post-condition, invariance condition) - class invariant
Morgan (2002) 0	- basic constraint - list constraint - classification - computation - enumeration
Ross (2001) 0	- rejecter (constraint) - producer (subcategories: computation and derivation rules) - projector (stimulus/response rule which include enabler rules, copier rules and executive (trigger) rules)
Ross (2001) 0	- term - fact - computation - constraint - inferred knowledge - action business rule
von Halle (1997) 0	- definition - fact - constraint - derivation - inference
von Halle (2002) 0	- terms - facts And 5 type of rules: - mandatory constraint - guideline - action enabler - computation - inference
Date (2000) 0	- constraint - state constraint - transition constraint - stimulus/response - derivation - computation - inference
Odell 0	- constraint (state constraint, transition, event/action or/and stimulus/response, operation, structure) - Derivation (computations, inference) Notes: rules can be global, local, and / or temporal
Sobiesky, Krovvidy, McClintock, Thorpe 0	- definitions - basic integrity constraints - general declarative constraints - procedural constraints - inferential - derivation
Gottesdiener 0	- term definitions - facts relating terms - constraints - action enablers - derivations - inferences

The list is quite extensive, it covers the opinions of business rules researchers working in this field. However, from an implementation perspective the business rules categories can be divided into two broad types:

1. Terms, facts, and state integrity constraints can be considered as structural assertions, which introduce the definitions of business entities and describe the connections between them. Since they can be captured by a conceptual model of the problem domain, e.g., by an Entity-Relationship (ER) or a UML class model, they can be regarded not as business rules but rather as concepts in the business vocabulary (or ontology).
2. Other categories can be considered as dynamic assertions which fall into the following main types:
   - dynamic constraints restrict the admissible transitions from one state of the system to another;
   - derivation rule is a statement of knowledge that is derived from other knowledge by an inference or a mathematical calculation;
   - reaction rules are concerned with the invocation of actions in response to events, they state the conditions under which actions must be taken.

The rules of the last category (dynamic assertions) directly fall under ECA paradigm (when *event* occurs, if *condition* is true, then *action*) from active databases field.[1] As it is shown in,[20] dynamic assertions smoothly map to the ECA paradigm:

1. All business rules operate on data (are data driven) and are triggered by data state transitions. Therefore each business rule has an event, which may be stated explicitly or assumed implicitly. For the latter case an implicit event is formulated as the appropriate data state transition.
2. Some business rules have an explicit condition, some do not. The missing condition can always be substituted with a default condition stated as *TRUE*.
3. All dynamic assertions have a defined action – it is at the heart of reaction and derivation rules. Dynamic constraints may not have the explicit action, since they can state what transition from one data state to another is not admissible. The action for this type of rules could be defined as corrective actions or presenting the appropriate instructions to the business user.

3. IMPLEMENTING BUSINESS RULES

Any information system implementing business rules must adhere to the following requirements: it must be developed and deployed quickly, be easy to modify and maintain, and have a long and useful life. The most important factor is speed – how fast IS can be developed and how fast the changes of business rules can be incorporated.[9]

As it is surveyed in,[2] to achieve flexibility and adaptability, several different approaches were traditionally used where the most common include:

1. parameterization: parameters may be set in a configuration file or in a database, and can be managed through a configuration utility. Doing so, the application can be adapted to different environments and situations just by parameter settings.

2. database triggers and stored procedures: most applications rely on a persistent data store that is usually based on relational database technology. Relational Database Management Systems (RDBMS) provide triggers that have ability to execute actions, immediately before/after particular events occur. This characteristic makes triggers convenient for implementation of business rules. Since the implementation of the business rules resides in the database itself, modifications are application independent and can be performed without accessing the application logic.

Modern ways of business rule implementation follow the business rule approach and manipulate business rules in an explicit manner. Within the context of the business rules approach, a business rule represents an important meta-element that needs to be captured, formalized and implemented apart from the other elements constituting the application architecture. Today, several development tools are available, based on business rule-oriented technologies. Considering how they represent, implement and execute business rules, they can be classified as follows:

1. Database-independent tools: business rules are implemented within a database, using triggers and stored procedures. However, they are generated automatically and managed by the development and not database tool.
2. Server-based tools: business rules that are created by a development tool become middle-tier application services and reside on an application server.
3. Rule-based systems: instead of specifying constraints on specific data elements or tables, a logic-oriented approach captures the higher-level business logic and rules associated with different situations. At run-time special engines are used to process the rules and to generate appropriate responses.

4. BUSINESS IS DEVELOPMENT FRAMEWORK USING BUSINESS RULES APPROACH

Taking into account the above mentioned considerations and available technologies, we propose a framework for business IS development using business rules approach (the framework metamodel is shown in Figure 1).

The chosen implementation technology is *database independent tools* because it offers a number of advantages but uses the proven and well-known technologies thus allowing a cut in the development time.

Automatic implementation is at the heart of the framework because "having the rules doesn't really help that much if you don't have an automated way to enforce them".[7] OMG group stresses the automatic implementation issue as well in their Request For Information on Business Rules.[11]

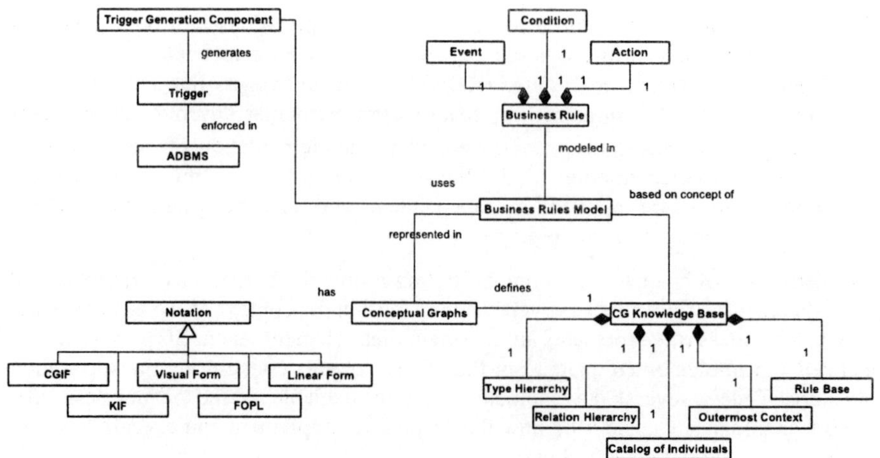

Figure 1. Business IS Development Framework Mctamodel

The major business IS development framework components are the following:

4.1 Conceptual model of the business rules and business domain

The uniform and consistent conceptual model of the domain is the commonly agreed necessity of all software engineering disciplines. We propose to model business domain with explicit attention to business rules using conceptual graphs (CG)[17] as the modeling language. The major advantages of CG are:

- the conceptual domain model is a basis and a common reference point for communication of systems analysts and business representatives because of the characteristics of CG. Moreover, since CG is a conceptual modeling language based on linguistics, psychology, and philosophy,[4] it is possible to get a nearly natural language representation of modeled business rules, thus having a possibility to check if business rules were modeled using proper CG constructs.
- it is possible to check the correctness and consistency of the model using CG operations. However, it is a future research topic and currently no work is carried out towards this goal.
- since CG has a textual notation (Linear Form, Conceptual Graphs Interchange Format, Knowledge Interchange Format) it is possible to use the model as input for some automatic generation or inference mechanism. In the proposed framework the textual model format in CGIF is used as input for automatic rules implementation component (trigger generation mechanism).

The possible ways to model business rules using CG and also advantages of this approach are presented in Valatkaite and Vasilecas[19] and Von Halle.[21] In the latter it is proposed to model business IS using the CG element Knowledge Base that consists of the following elements:

1. Concept Hierarchy – to represent entities (or terms)

2. Type Hierarchy – to represent relations
3. Catalog of Individuals – to represent facts
4. Outermost Context – to represent system boundaries
5. Rule Base – a proposed extension to the Knowledge Base to represent business rules

The Rule Base element is designed specifically for business rules modeling. The approach presented covers the business rules of dynamic assertions type by employing the rule metamodel based on ECA paradigm. The rule metamodel (or rule pattern) to use is shown in Figure 2.

Rule is: <INITIATOR> yields <RESULT>
Where:
INITIATOR is (database event / user input / another rule firing event)
RESULT is conditional action: if <CONDITION> then <ACTION>
CONDITION is any number of data state checks
ACTION is any number of data state transitions

Figure 2. A rule metamodel

The structural assertions must be modeled using other CG Knowledge Base elements – Concept Hierarchy and Relation Hierarchy thus forming business IS ontology.

4.2 Active databases for business rules implementation

Business rules are implemented within active databases, using triggers and stored procedures. The ability of active databases (triggers) to demonstrate reactive behavior makes active databases convenient for implementation of business rules. For example, by using "before-insert" trigger the record can be checked (and refused if violates any business rule) before it is actually inserted. Since the implementation of the business rules resides in the database itself, modifications are application independent and can be performed without accessing the application logic. There are several advantages of using database triggers to enforce business rules:[2]

- The business rules are independent from the application logic, since they are stored in the database.
- The business rules reside on the database server (on the one single place). Therefore, they are not dispersed over a number of clients.
- Modifications of business rules can be performed remotely (remote accessibility is one of the most important features of the database servers).
- The place where the particular business rules are implemented is easier to be found, since we know the actions that initiate them.
- Adding a new business rule does not require application code to be changed.

4.3 Trigger generation component

As it was already mentioned, the automatic implementation is at the heart of the proposed framework. Implementation of business rules (as triggers) is performed and managed automatically by the special trigger generation component thus achieving the required flexibility and automated business rules implementation. As shown in the detailed view of the framework components in

Figure 1, trigger generation component translates business rules model to trigger specification. The generation algorithm presented in Valatkaite and Vasilecas[18] makes use of CGIF format of business rules model and maps its constructs to appropriate PL/SQL blocks (Oracle 8i is used as target active databases management system). The current state of trigger generation component has a number of limitations. The major one is that the generation algorithm is defined only for CGIF format as input although conceptual graphs have a number of other textual notations. The goal is to have a trigger generation component independent from model language and target ADBMS. This can be achieved with the special preprocessors, which would be responsible for mapping modeling languages notations to the business rules repository and the generation component would use repository data as input instead of conceptual model itself. Moreover, this architecture will enforce synchronization of business rules conceptual model, repository and implementation.

4.4 Business rules repository

A repository must adhere to the principles of component architecture. The goal is to have a repository with the following characteristics:

- strictly defined visual interface for rules inserting / editing;
- automatic trigger generation component to ensure the consistency between the rules in repository and their implementation in active databases management system;

The second characteristic is not a mandatory part of repository itself. However, such component facilitates the usage of repository.

5. CONCLUSIONS AND FUTURE RESEARCH

In this paper we have surveyed the state of the art in business rules research. The given survey is by no means complete since we have focused on an implementation perspective giving just hints on business rules research within business perspective.

Our analysis has revealed that although business rules have been researched for more than a decade, there is no consensus yet about the taxonomies or technologies for a business rules implementation. While it is commonly agreed that business rules approach brings a lot of advantages, the modeling languages, tools, and methodologies are only beginning to emerge.

We have analyzed the proposed taxonomies of business rules and found that despite the different naming and structuring conventions it is possible to divide business rules into structural assertions and dynamic assertions, where the latter can be mapped to ECA paradigm.

Based on this we have proposed the business information systems development framework using business rules approach. The major components of the framework are: active databases for the business rules implementation, an automatic business rules implementation component (trigger generation component), and conceptual graphs as the modeling language for business rules. These technologies enable to achieve the required flexibility and the speed of an implementation of business IS and give a good response to the requirements for business rules systems as formulated by OMG.

Nevertheless, a large bulk of work still remains to be done. Especially to provide for systems that implement components of proposed framework in a robust, efficient and well-defined way, and to gather practical experience such that users may employ the automatic generation of active databases triggers.

REFERENCES

1. ACT-NET Consortium: The Active Database Management Systems Manifesto: A Rulebase of ADBMS Features, *ACM Sigmod Record*, Vol. 25(30), 40–49 (1996).
2. M. Bajec, R. Rupnik, and M. Krisper, Using Business Rules Technologies To Bridge The Gap Between Business And Business Applications, in: Proceedings of the IFIP 16th World Computer Congress 2000, Information Technology for Business Management (G Rechnu, Ed), Beijing, China, 2000, pp. 77–85
3. Business Rules Group. Defining Business Rules ~ What Are They Really? (formerly known as the "GUIDE Business Rules Project Final Report," November 1995), Business Rules Group, (3rd Ed.), July 2000. (Available at www.businessrulesgroup.org.)
4. M. Chein, M. L. Mugnier, Conceptual Graphs: Fundamental Notions. *Revue d'Intelligence Artificielle*, Vol. 6, No.4, 365–406 (1992).
5. C. J. Date, *What Not How: The Business Rules Approach to Application development*, (Reading. Mass.: Addison-Wesley Longman).
6. E. Gottesdiener, Top Ten Ways Project Teams Misuse Use Cases – and How to Correct Them, Part I: Content and Style Issues, The Rational Edge, June 2002, URL: http://www.therationaledge.com/content/jun_02/ t_misuseUseCases_eg.jsp.
7. E. Gottesdiener, Business RULES Show Power, Promise, *Application Development Trends*, Volume 4, Number 31, March 1997: see: http://www.ebgconsulting.com/publications.html#business_rules
8. I. Graham, *Requirements Engineering and Rapid Development*, (Addison-Wesley, 1998).
9. N. Lin, Alternatives For Rule-based Application Development, *Business Rules Journal*, Vol. 3, No. 10 (October 2002), URL:http://www.BRCommunity.com/a2002/n007.html.
10. T. Morgan, *Business Rules and Information Systems: Aligning IT with Business Goals*, (Addison-Wesley, 2002).
11. Object Management Group. Business Rules in Models: Request for Information. URL: http://cgi.omg.org/cgi-bin/doc?ad/2002-9-13 (2002)
12. J. Odell, Business Rules, *Object Magazine*, February, 1995 republished in: *Wisdom of the Gurus: A Vision for Object Technology*, Charles Bowman, ed., (SIGS Books, 1996) and in: *Advanced Object-Oriented Analysis & Design using UML*, (SIGS Books, 1998).
13. R. G. Ross, The Business Rules Classification Scheme, *DataToKnowledge Newsletter*, Volume 29, Number 5, (2001). See: http://www.brcommunity.com/a2001/b086.html
14. R. G. Ross, and G.S.W. Lam, RuleSpeakTMSentence Templates: Developing Rule Statements Using Sentence Patterns, Business Rule Solutions, (2001). Downloadable via: http://www.brsolutions.com/rulespeak_download.shtml
15. R. G. Ross, *The Business Rule Book: Classifying, Defining and Modeling Rules*, 2nd edition, (Database Research Group, Boston, MA, 1997).
16. J. Sobieski, S. Krovvidy, C. McClintock, and M. Thorpe, KARMA: Managing Business rules from Specification to Implementation, paper presented at American Association of Artificial Intelligence Conference, Innovative Applications of AI track, Portland, Or, 7/96. Business Rule Summit, February 26–28, 1996, Miller Freeman Inc., 600 Harrison Street, San Francisco, CA 94107

17. J. F. Sowa, *Knowledge Representation: Logical, Philosophical, and Computational Foundations*, (Brooks/Cole, Pasific Grove et al., 2000).
18. I. Valatkaite and O. Vasilecas, Deriving active database triggers from business rules model with conceptual graphs, *Lithuanian Mathematical Journal*, Vilnius, MII, t. 42, special issue "Proceedings of the XLIII conference of Lithuanian Mathematical Society", 289–293, (2002, in Lithuanian).
19. I. Valatkaite and O. Vasilecas, Application Domain Knowledge Modeling Using Conceptual Graphs, in: *Information Systems Development: Advances in Methodologies, Components and Management.* Kirikova, M. ed. (Kluwer Academic/Plenum Publishers, 2002), pp. 193–202.
20. I. Valatkaite and O. Vasilecas, A Conceptual Graphs Approach for Business Rules Modeling. Accepted by Seventh East-European Conference on Advance in Databases and Information Systems (ADBIS), September 3–6, 2003, Dresden, Germany. To be published in *Lecture Notes of Computer Science*, Springer-Verlag, 2003.
21. B. Von Halle, *Business Rules Applied: Building Better Systems Using the Business Rules Approach*, (John Wiley & Sons, 2002).
22. B. Von Halle, The business rule roadmap, *Database Programming and Design*, 10(10), 13–15, (1997).
23. J. A. Zachman, A Framework for Information Systems Architecture, *IBM Systems Journal*, vol. 26, no. 3, IBM Publication G321-5298 (1987).

BUSINESS FUNCTIONS PROTOTYPING VIA XSLT*

Karel Richta[†]

1. INTRODUCTION

At the present time, there is no doubt that the languages based on XML-family of formats belong to the most discussed topics of the information industry (XML is an abbreviation for eXtensible Markup Language, see e.g. XML, 2003; W3C, 2003). The primary goal of the XML format was to provide the text marking mechanism for documents, and use this technique in information exchange between resources. XML-data are intended to be generated and consumed by applications. Consequently, the XML language has recently emerged as a new approach for information representation.

The required structure of an XML-document can described by the document type definition (DTD is an abbreviation for Document Type Definition) or by XML-schema (OMG, 2003; XML, 2003). There is a trend in the information industry to conceive collections of XML-data as a database (Pokorný, 2000). Using the terminology usual in databases, it is possible to view XML as a language for data modeling. A set of well-formed XML-documents is then a database and the associated DTD or XML-schema is its database schema (Pokorný, 2001).

XML-data have to be presented in some legible format. World Wide Web Consortium (W3C, 2003) developed the extensible stylesheet language XSL for this purposes (XSL is an abbreviation for eXtensible Stylesheet Language). The specification of XSL consists of three parts: XSL Transformations (XSLT) is a language for the description of a transformation of XML-documents, the XML Path Language (XPath) is an expression language used by XSLT to access or refer to parts of an XML-document, and the third part is XSL Formatting Objects: an XML vocabulary for specifying

* This work has been partially supported by the research program no. MSM 212300014 "Research in the Area of Information Technologies and Communications" of the Czech Technical University in Prague (sponsored by the Ministry of Education, Youth and Sports of The Czech Republic), and it also has been partially supported by the grant No. 201/03/0912 "XML Documents Searching and Indexing" of the Grant Agency of The Czech Republic.

† Karel Richta, dept. of Computer Science & Engineering, Faculty of Electrical Engineering, Czech Technical University (Czech Institute of Technology), Prague 2, Karlovo nám. 13, 121 35, Czech Republic; also dept. of Software Engineering, Faculty of Mathematics & Physics, Charles University, Prague 1, Malostranské nám. 25, 118 00, Czech Republic.

formatting semantics. An XSL stylesheet specifies the presentation of a class of XML-documents by describing how an instance of the class is transformed into an XML-document that uses the formatting vocabulary. The principle of XSLT processing is understandable from the Figure 1.

This paper will examine possible usage of XSLT language for business function modeling. The typical present application supposes some information stored inside a database (e.g. relational one, see Figure 2). The state of any information system can also be described by a set of XML-documents (at least by the XML representation of relational data). Any other XML-document can be the part of information processing. When we have such a set of XML-documents, we need to manipulate them for various business purposes, similarly as the usual business functions do with a database.

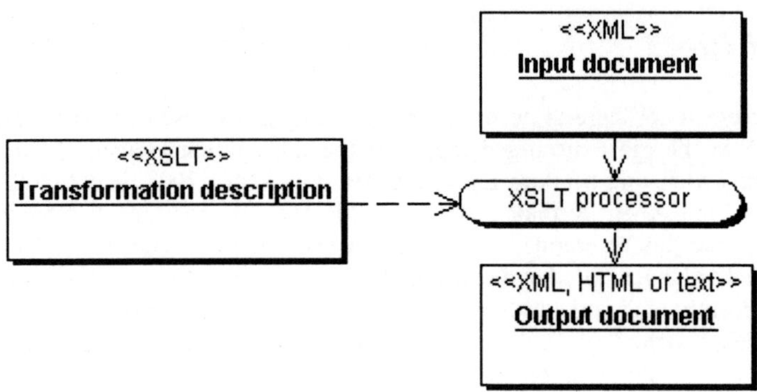

Figure 1. The principle of XSLT processing

So, an information system specification consists of at least two parts: the definition of the information system state and the definition of information system behavior. Both parts can be formally specified – see e.g. Frappier and Habrias (FME, 2002). The definition of the information system state is usually defined with the help of a conceptual data model. The behavior describes system services, and consists of a definition of services signature and a set of business rules (constraints, axioms). The signature serves as the definition of user commands syntax. The rules specify the semantics. Any structure satisfying axioms is a so-called model of a specification. The meaning of a specification can be defined as the isomorphic class of all acceptable models – it means the class of models, which are exchangeable by each other. The exact definition of a specification can be found in (Dershowitz and Jouannaud, 1989).

The most important point is that the rigorous specifications can serve as an unambiguous and strict interface between customer, software analyst, designer, and programmer. The results of negotiations between customer (somebody, who needs software for solving a certain problem), and a software producer can be declared as a more or less formal specification of a given problem.

The basic problem here is the specification level. The more the specification is precise, the more it is not legible, and opposite. In (Bisová and Richta, 2000) the function specification in Unified Modeling Language is discussed (UML – see pages of Object Management Group – OMG, 2003), and how to derive XML syntax and system documents from the system specification in UML. The basic set of UML diagrams concerns the syntax. The semantic part of a specification in UML can be defined with the

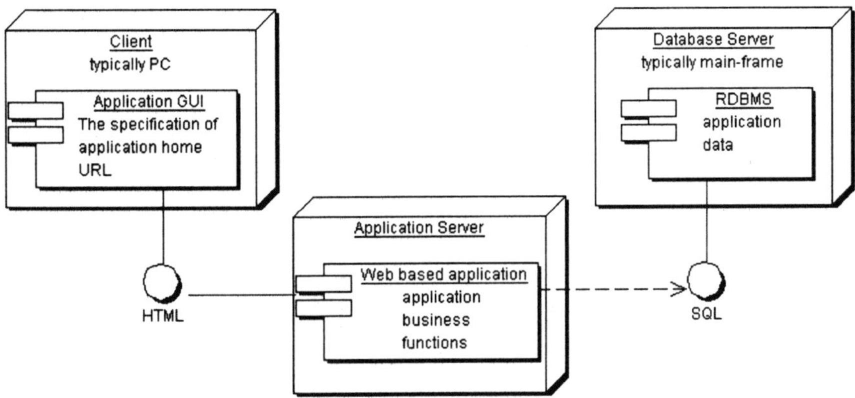

Figure 2. The typical current Web based application

help of OCL (Object Constraint Language) or in any other suitable specification language. Formerly we use VDM/SL (Vienna Definition Method / Specification Language, see Agerholm, FME, 2002) as a specification language in (Richta, 2000). In present we try to use algebraic specification instead (Badawy and Richta, 2002; Richta, 2001).

Required business functions have to be specified. An acceptable format can be UML specification, where the semantics is specified by OCL constraint definitions. Any correct implementation of such a specification can be viewed as the solution of the problem. In the following we shortly introduce the idea how the specification in UML/OCL can be converted into XML-like format, and used as XSLT meta-code for the description of arbitrarily complex business rules.

The specification can be prototyped – the problem is how to construct an appropriate prototype for a given function specification. We have to design a completing procedure, which for the given specification completes the appropriate implementation. If the procedure succeeded, we receive a prototype, which simulates the specification.

These problems need to be addressed; the paper discusses a suggestion on how to construct a prototype with the help of XSLT (all definitions concerning XML and XSLT can be found on W3C pages). The key problem in prototyping is to produce a prototype in a short time and at a sufficient level of efficiency for testing. A very simple method is to transform the information system specification into XSLT code (XSL-transformation). The input documents are to be converted into XML format and expressed as XML-documents. The required structure is expressed as a DTD or XML-Schema. The semantic part of a specification is converted into XSLT code and used as a rewriting system (Dershowitz and Jouannaud, 1989). The prototyped behavior is done through rewriting.

Any user requirement is transformed into the XML-term that is rewritten with the help of XSLT into a canonical form – the meaning of the requirement.

2. THE STATE OF INFORMATION SYSTEM

The *state* of information system is usually described by a conceptual data model. Such a model describes the domain consisting of all necessary aspects – databases used, files opened, etc. The conceptual data model is usually created during a detailed analysis of business requirements. Let us suppose for example very simple application called Employee Manager, which is used for employee list elaboration (see Figure 3).

The state of Employee Manager can be represented by employees' table, i.e. by the relational table EMP:

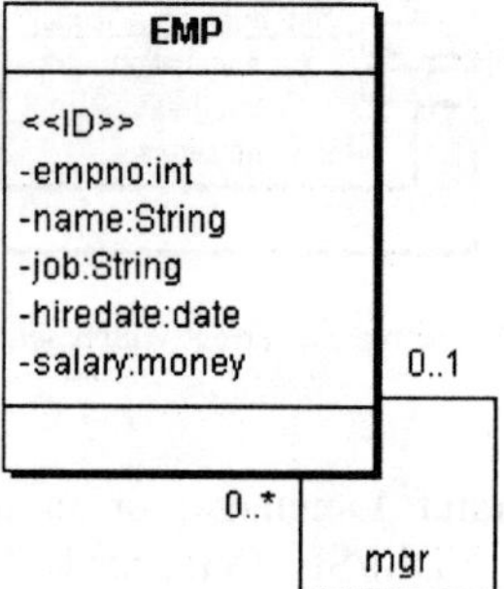

Figure 3. The employees' data

```
create table EMP ( empno int primary key,
  name String,
  job String,
  hiredate date,
  salary money,
  mgr int references EMP(empno)
);
```

The actual state can also be represented as an XML-document. The set of all possible states constitutes a domain of XML-documents that is definable by DTD or XML-Schema. E.g., the employees' data can be described by the following DTD:

```
<!ELEMENT employees (employee)*>
<!ELEMENT employee (name,hiredate,salary)>
<!ATTLIST employee
   EMPNO ID #REQUIRED
   MGR IDREF #IMPLIED>
<!ELEMENT name (#PCDATA)>
<!ELEMENT hiredate (#PCDATA)>
<!ELEMENT salary (#PCDATA)>
```

The actual state of the employees' data can be represented according to this DTD by the following XML-document:

```
<?xml version="1.0"?>
<!DOCTYPE employees SYSTEM "emp.dtd">
<employees>
  <employee EMPNO="E7344" MGR="E7999">
    <name>John Smythe</name>
    <hiredate>22.2.2000</hiredate>
    <salary>20000.00</salary>
  </employee>
  <employee EMPNO="E7999">
    <name>Peter King</name>
    <hiredate>12.6.2000</hiredate>
    <salary>50000.00</salary>
  </employee>
</employees>
```

3. PRESENTATION OF THE SYSTEM STATE

The Employee Manager has to display the actual state of employees (i.e. either the content of EMP table or the content of the suitable XML-document). In the relational environment, the appropriate SQL code can be:

```
SELECT empno, name, hiredate, salary FROM emp;
```

In the XML representation, the XML-document representing the actual content is to be converted into user-friendly format, e.g. into HTML-document, that can be viewed by any HTML browser. The conversion can be described by XSLT transformation. We use here a very simple format, in the real application some sort of HTML-table or HTML-form will be used.

```
<xsl:stylesheet version="1.0"
     xmlns:xsl="http://www.w3.org/1999/XSL/Transform"
     xmlns="http://www.w3.org/TR/xhtml1/strict">
<xsl:output method="html" indent="yes"/>

<xsl:template match="employees">
 <html>
   <head><title><xsl:text>EMPLOYEES</xsl:text></title></head>
   <body>
     <h1> <xsl:text>EMPLOYEES</xsl:text> </h1>
     <xsl:for-each select="employee">
       <h2><xsl:apply-templates select="@EMPNO"/></h2>
       <xsl:apply-templates/>
     </xsl:for-each>
   </body>
 </html>
</xsl:template>

<xsl:template match="name">
```

```
  <h3><xsl:apply-templates/></h3>
</xsl:template>

<xsl:template match="hiredate">
  <p><b>Hiredate: </b><xsl:apply-templates/></p>
</xsl:template>

<xsl:template match="salary">
  <p><b>Salary: </b><xsl:apply-templates/></p>
</xsl:template>

</xsl:stylesheet>
```

The current state of EMP table can be transformed by XSLT processor into HTML code. As an illustration we had convert it into the following HTML page (strictly speaking into XHTML 1.0 code):

```
<html xmlns="http://www.w3.org/TR/xhtml1/strict">
  <head>
    <title>EMPLOYEES</title>
  </head>
  <body>
    <h1>EMPLOYEES</h1>
    <h2>E7344</h2>
    <h3>John Smythe</h3>
    <p><b>Hiredate: </b>22.2.2000</p>
    <p><b>Salary: </b>20000.00</p>
  <h2>E7999</h2>
    <h3>Peter King</h3>
    <p><b>Hiredate: </b>12.6.2000</p>
    <p><b>Salary: </b>50000.00</p>
  </body>
</html>
```

4. THE INFORMATION SYSTEM BEHAVIOR DESCRIPTION

The *behavior* of an information system can be modeled as a mapping from state to state. Such a mapping can be interpreted as a mapping from one XML-document into another one. The appropriate transformation of XML-documents can again be described by an XSLT transformation. E.g., the Employee Manager contains one business function for the report of employee salaries (Figure 4).

This function serves for employees' table exploitation. It means the meaning of this function is a mapping from any state of employees' table into a list of couples <name,salary> for each employee. More formally, in the case of RDBMS data storage, this function can be assessed via SQL command:

```
SELECT 'Name: '||empno, 'Salary: '||salary FROM emp;
```

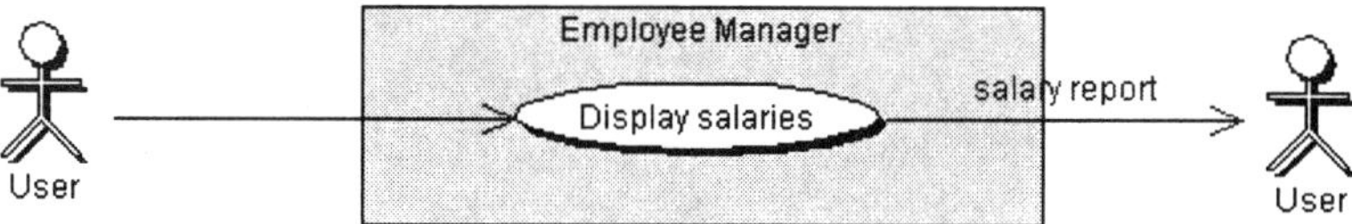

Figure 4. Use case model for salary report

In the case of XSLT, the same function can be implemented by the following XSLT code:

```
<xsl:stylesheet
xmlns:xsl="http://www.w3.org/1999/XSL/Transform">
<xsl:output method="xml" indent="yes"/>
  <xsl:template match="employee">
    <xsl:text>Name:</xsl:text><xsl:value-of select="name"/>
    <xsl:text>Salary:</xsl:text><xsl:value-of
select="salary"/>
  </xsl:template>
</xsl:stylesheet>
```

The main idea of this paper is to give a picture of the derivation of XSLT code from a function specification in UML/OCL format, as the Figure 5 shows.

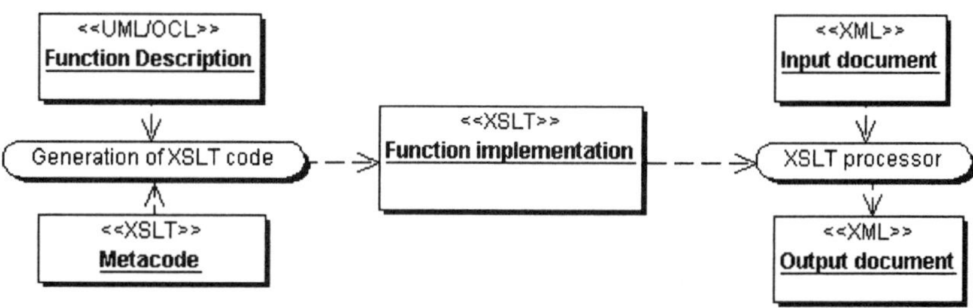

Figure 5. The main idea of the principle of XSLT behavior implementation

In the following we suppose that the function description begins with a use case model (e.g. for the function *DisplaySalaries* see Figure 4). The meaning of the function *DisplaySalaries* is to produce the report of salaries for each employee. Subsequently the more detailed model for functions is developed, usually documented by the sequence diagram. On Figure 6, there is the first decomposition of the function *DisplaySalaries*. It says, that this function can be achieved with the help of another function *GetSalaries*, which is the part of employees' container called *Employee List*. The appropriate class model is displayed on Fig, where the container EMPLIST extends the basic elementary class EMP, and the function *GetSalaries* is a member of this class. The detailed specification of this function in OCL has to be developed.

The function *GetSalaries* goes through employees' list and creates a list of pairs <name,salary> for each member. It means, that in the context of *EMPLIST*, the result of the function *GetSalaries* can be constructed as an object of the type *ItemList*, which is a vector of pairs of the type *Item*. Pairs of the type *Item* are constructed by the constructor *Item*, and can be added to the list of items via function *add* (the standard function of the vector container). The detailed specification in the OCL language can look as follows:

```
context EMPLIST::GetSalaries() post :
 let X : EMPLIST = self.empVector in forall
  (EMP : e in X implies result =
    ItemList.add(Item(e.name, e.salary)))
```

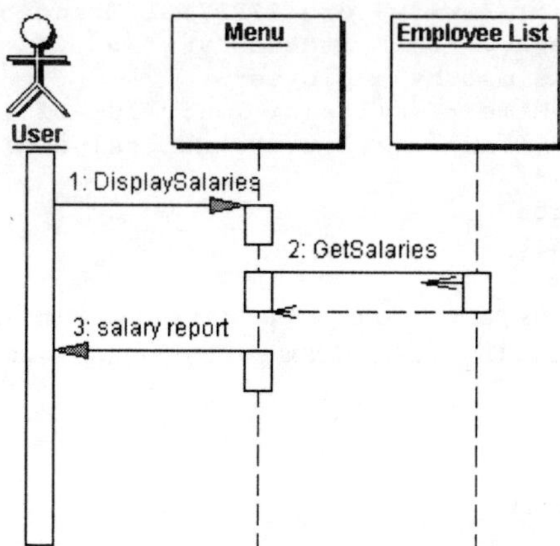

Figure 6. Display salaries sequence diagram

On Fig the description of the function *GetSalaries* is presented in OCL. The classical implementation of this function in Java can look like following:

```
/* @stereotype query
   @semantics
   Operation GetSalaries goes through employee list and creates
   list of pairs <name,salary> for each member.
<<OCL>>
   context EMPLIST::GetSalaries() post :
     let X : EMPLIST = self.empVector in forall (EMP : e in X
        implies result  = ItemList.add(Item(e.name, e.salary)))
*/
public ItemList GetSalaries() {
    ItemList X;
    for (i = 1; i <= emps(); i++)
      X.add(Item(empVector[i].name,Item(empVector[i].salary);
    return X;
 }
```

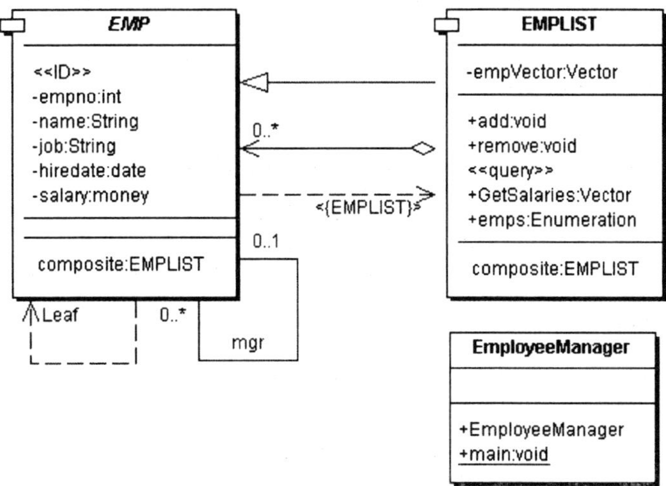

Figure 7. The part of the class diagram for employees

5. TRANSFORMATION META-STRUCTURE

The whole specification of an information system can also be converted into XSLT code. The skeleton for XSLT-stylesheet contains templates generated from business rules. The generated code has to be again XSLT transformation. So XSLT fragment of the skeleton (the part of generated code) can be:

```
<?xml version="1.0"?>
<xsl:stylesheet
xmlns:xsl="http://www.w3.org/1999/XSL/Transform">
<xsl:output method="xml" indent="yes"/>
<xsl:template match="/">
  <!- The resulting stylesheet begins here -->
  <xsl:text >
    <xsl:stylesheet xmlns:xsl=
       "http://www.w3.org/1999/XSL/Transform">
    <xsl:output method="xml" indent="yes"/>
    <!- meta-code for the functions -->
      <xsl:apply-templates select="GetSalaries" />
    <!- The templates for all functions has
       to be included here -->
       . . .
    <!- The resulting stylesheet ends here -->
    </xsl:stylesheet>
  </xsl:text>
</xsl:template>
</xsl:stylesheet>
```

This skeleton should be completed by the derived XSLT code for business functions.

6. DERIVING XSLT CODE FROM THE FUNCTION DESCRIPTION

Any function definition has to be converted into XSLT code, that simulates its behavior. In the case of the *GatSalaries* function, the XSLT code derived from the OCL specification can look as follows:

```
<!– The template for the function GetSalaries -->
<!– <<OCL>> context EMPLIST::GetSalaries() post :
            let X : EMPLIST = self.empVector in
            forall (EMP : e in X implies
              result = ItemList.add(Item(e.name, e.salary)))
                                                         -->
  <xsl:template match="employees">
    <ItemList>
    <xsl:for-each select="employee">
      <Item>
        <xsl:text>Name:</xsl:text>
            <xsl:value-of select="name"/>
        <xsl:text>Salary:
            </xsl:text><xsl:value-of select="salary"/>
      </Item>
    </xsl:for-each>
    </ItemList>
  </xsl:template>
```

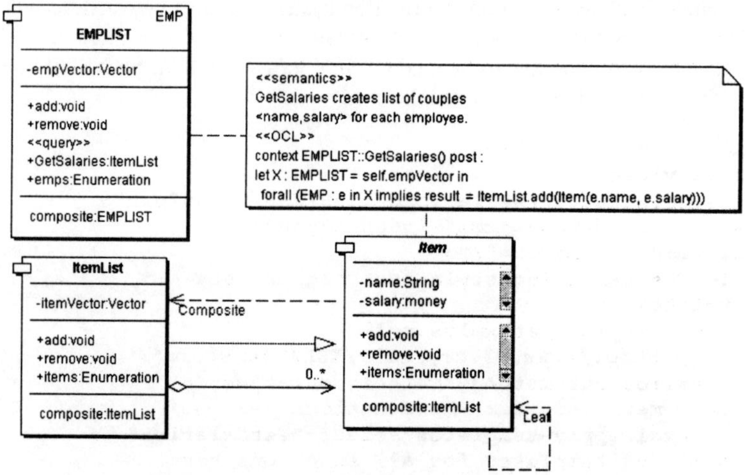

Figure 8. The description of GetSalaries

This XSLT code rewrites the input XML-document that represents the input state of information system into another XML-document, which represents the resulting listing. The output listing is the XML tree rooted by `<ItemList>` element and containing `<Item>` sub-element for each employee in the input document.

In our simple example the transformation is straightforward. Other possibilities for the description of arbitrarily complex rules are out of scope of this paper. Such complex rules suppose more precise specification of syntax and semantics. In (Badawy and Richta, 2002; Bisová and Richta, 2000; Richta, 2001) the function specification in UML is discussed, and we derived XML syntax and system documents from a system specification in UML/OCL.

7. AN EXAMPLE OF REWRITING

Let us suppose the state of the information system as it was presented above:

```
<?xml version="1.0"?>
<!DOCTYPE employees SYSTEM "emp.dtd">
<employees>
  <employee EMPNO="E7344" MGR="E7999">
    <name>John Smythe</name>
    <hiredate>22.2.2000</hiredate>
    <salary>20000.00</salary>
  </employee>
  <employee EMPNO="E7999">
    <name>Peter King</name>
    <hiredate>12.6.2000</hiredate>
    <salary>50000.00</salary>
  </employee>
</employees>
```

The result of the function *GetSalaries* prototype is the document in the XML format as follows:

```
<ItemList>
  <Item>
    Name:John Smythe
    Salary:20000.00
  </Item>
  <Item>
    Name:Peter King
    Salary:50000.00
  </Item>
</ItemList>
```

This is the canonical form of output - the meaning of the function *GetSalaries.*

8. CONCLUSIONS

The paper briefly suggests one new idea how to construct an executable prototype from a specification with the help of transformations in XSLT language. The entire project seeks to develop an environment for business functions prototyping (see also (Badawy and Richta, 2002; Bisová and Richta, 2000; Richta, 2000; Richta, 2001). We already studied more traditional methods for prototype construction:

- direct interpretation of a specification in an environment like OBJ3 or FOOPS,
- the transformation of a specification into a functional language like Lisp,
- the translation of a specification into a logical language like Prolog,
- the translation of a specification into the code of a special rewriting machine.

The main advantage of a solution presented in the paper can be availability of XSLT, which is inbuilt into the majority of Web browsers. The XSLT transformation can be viewed as an abstract rewriting machine, that can assists as a tool for prototyping. There is wide area for optimization of XSLT code. At the present time we deal with the translation of specifications into XSLT code by compiling all rules for given function simultaneously. The anticipated development will be another code construction for selecting rules. In a typical case no reconstruction of terms is needed if matching fails.

The paper only addresses the idea; it suggests a new method utilizing commonly available tools instead of specific intermediate tools. In (Brom, 2003) the simulation of some specifications is ellaborated, e.g. the specification of the quick sort algorithm. The specification written in the algebraic specification language was interpreted by specialized processor BOBJ (Goguen, 2002). Simultaneously we translated the specification into XSLT and interpret it via Saxon interpreter. The results are comparable, and in some cases the XSLT transformation was quicker (see **Table 1**).

Table 1. The comparison of rewriting results

No. of elements	BOBJ 0.9	XSLT Saxon 6.5
5	1 s	11 s
10	18 s	15 s
15	infinite	25 s
20	infinite	40 s

After considerable experience with our method, we can compare results with well-established prototype development methods and techniques, and optionally ascertain its usefulness.

ACKNOWLEDGMENTS

I am pleased to thank to TogetherSoft Corporation, whose kind software enables me to prepare drawings for this paper.

REFERENCES

Badawy, M., Richta, K., 2002, Deriving triggers from UML/OCL specification, in: *ISD 2002: Advances in Methodologies, Components, and Management* (ed. Kirikova, M. et al.), Kluwer Academic/Plenum Publishers, pp. 271–280.

Bisová, V., Richta, K., 2000, Transformation of UML models into XML", in: *Proceedings of Challenges 2000 ADBIS-DASFAA*. Prague: MATFYZPRESS UK, pp. 33–45.

Brom, C., 2003, The translation of OBJ rewriting rules into XSLT, Diploma thesis, Dept. of Software Engineering, Faculty of Mathematics and Physics, Charles University in Prague.

Dershowitz, N., and Jouannaud, J. P., 1989, Rewrite systems, in: *Handbook of Theoretical Computer Science*, North-Holland.

FMP (Formal Methods Pages), 2002, http://www.afm.sbu.ac.uk/.

Goguen, J. A. , 2002, BOBJ Project, http://www.cs.ucsd.edu/groups/tatami/bobj/.

OMG (Object Management Group), 2003, http://www.omg.org/.

Pokorný, J., 2000, XML functionally, in: *Proceedings of IDEAS 2000*, B.C.Desai, Y. Kioki, M. Toyama, eds., IEEE Comp. Society, pp. 266–274.

Pokorný, J., 2001, XML: a challenge for databases?, in: *Contemporary Trends in Systems Development,* Maung K. Sein, ed., Kluwer Academic Publishers, Boston, pp. 147–164.

Richta, K., 2000, Specification-Driven Maintenance of Integrity Constraints, in: *ISD 2000: Evolution and Challenges in System Development*, New York, Kluwer Academic/Plenum Publishers, pp. 271–280.

Richta, K., 2002, Using XSL in IS development, in: *ISD 2001: New Perspectives on Information Systems Development: Theory, Methods, and Practice*. New York, Kluwer Academic / Plenum Publishers, pp. 309–319.

XML (Extensible Markup Language), 2003, http://www.w3.org/TR/REC-xml.

W2C (World Wide Web Consortium), 2003, http://www.w3.org.

OLD TRICK, NEW DOGS:
Learning to use CRUD matrices early in object-oriented information system development

Ilona Box*

1. INTRODUCTION

Developing CRUD matrices to check and aid the creation of analysis and design artefacts is well established. The use of CRUD matrices in object-oriented information system development (OOISD) is typically late in the development cycle, when design is taking place. At this design stage the CRUD process focuses on small portions of the system identifying the collaborations between classes within a use case or the operations within a class. Few have documented the use of CRUD matrices early in OOISD.

This paper places CRUD analysis early in ISD, during analysis, after developing high-level use cases and the initial class diagram. Three types of matrices are developed: class, attribute, and association. The development of these matrices is described in detail. The advantages to students are: 1) reinforcement of object thinking, and 2) increased confidence in the accuracy and completeness of their high-level use cases and class diagram.

An example of the use of the CRUD analysis technique concludes this paper.

2. BACKGROUND

CRUD commonly stands for Create, Read, Update, and Delete. CRUD analysis is a process by which we carefully examine the static characteristics of the system we are developing relative to the four CRUD processes.

CRUD analysis is associated with Martin's Information Engineering (Dennis, Wixom, & Tegarden, 2002). Martin initially referred to the artefact produced from CRUD analysis as the CRUD matrix. In the Martin object-oriented development process the artefact is referred to as an object activity matrix (Gottesdiener, 1998).

CRUD analysis has been used at various stages in structured and OOISD processes. One example of CRUD analysis in structured ISD is the development of a CRUD matrix

* Ilona Box, University of Western Sydney, Penrith, NSW, Australia, 1797.

to represent where the CRUD processes occur within a system. It is suggested (Kendall & Kendall, 2002) that the CRUD analysis take place while developing physical data flow diagrams. This is quite late in the ISD process when commitments to a design are being made.

Another example of CRUD analysis in structured ISD makes use of the tool earlier in the development process (Fertuck, 1992). After identifying activities and data, an Activity-Entity Usage Matrix is built by placing a C, R, U, or D in cells in the matrix as appropriate. The CRUD analysis is of which organisation activity will create, read, update, or delete a record belonging to the entity named.

OOISD processes making use of CRUD matrices tend to use the tool when deciding about the collaboration of objects. This is during the design process when interaction diagrams such as sequence diagrams are being developed. Satzinger et al. (2002), make brief mention of an activity-data matrix and that activities requiring access to objects can be found on the sequence diagrams. Maciaszek (2001) mentions using supplementary methods to discover operations in classes not revealed in the sequence diagrams can be helpful. He mentions CRUD operations but does not provide details on the supplementary methods. Brown (2002) also makes brief mention to check for CRUD during identification of responsibilities and attributes, but does not describe a method to do so. Dennis *et al.* (2002) presents a class vs class matrix to discover collaborations of objects. Again, this is late in the ISD process, while building collaboration diagrams. Though the matrix is for each use case, which is a thorough usage, the interaction between instances is ambiguous if it is not known that the matrix is read row vs column rather than column vs row.

Brandon (2002) reports that a CRUD analysis of use cases vs object types with the letters C, R, U, and D as appropriate in intersecting cells is introduced by Armour (2001). However, Armour's approach is included in a work written for those trained or experienced with use case modelling and who are developing large-scale systems (AMS, 2003).

Another approach, Brandon asserts, has for each use case in turn, all the classes in the system listed row-wise in the first column. Columns two to five are headed C, R, U and D respectively. A check mark, where appropriate, is placed in the intersecting cell to indicate if the class is created, read, updated, or deleted in the use case. This approach is results in a lengthy matrix. For, instance if there were ten use cases and ten classes there would be 111 rows in total in the matrix.

Box and Ferguson (2002) present a CRUD analysis technique for use early in an OOISD process. The technique has been used with students of OOISD. This paper reviews and expands on the technique, including the advantages to students of the technique.

3. CRUD ANALYSIS TECHNIQUE FOR NEW DOGS

Box *et al* (2002) describe a prescriptive, simplified, ISD process. The process is explicitly documented to provide a well-defined, end-to-end ISD process by which students, with very limited computing experience, can learn ISD. CRUD analysis is introduced early in the process compared to most other object-oriented processes that use CRUD. It is introduced toward the end of the system definition phase, the second phase, when a large portion of the requirements have been gathered and documented. At this point in the process, the business processes have been described as high-level use cases. The high-level use cases are short descriptions of the essential, business processes that the information system is to support. The static structure of the system is captured in an initial class diagram that shows classes, attributes and associations. (Class methods are defined later, during use case development cycles.) The initial class diagram is a version of the class diagram considered complete at this early stage of the project. Other requirements are also captured, such as environmental constraints. However, it is the high-level use cases and initial class diagram that are the inputs to the CRUD analysis.

Just after defining high-level, essential use cases and the initial class diagram CRUD analysis is introduced for the first time. CRUD analysis is introduced early in the ISD process to help avoid errors of omission and reinforce the students' object thinking. For industry projects, by this stage of development, the investment in the project is small relative to the entire project. So, the earlier we can detect errors of omission the lower the cost of correcting these errors. For students, anecdotal evidence shows that the earlier they can detect errors of omission the more likely they are to succeed at "good" analysis and design; the more confident they feel about learning and doing ISD and the better their object thinking.

CRUD analysis is a systematic process that the students are directed to apply to inspect each static element of a system to ensure that it is created, used, kept current, and in due course destroyed. If any of these activities are missing then the student has identified a potential error of omission. It must be examined and where relevant, corrected.

The students use the CRUD analysis iteratively to check that their set of high-level use cases and class diagram are complete. For example, let's say there is a class called ClassA. Objects of type ClassA must be created. The student cannot identify the use case that has responsibility for the creation of objects of type ClassA. The student completes as much of the CRUD matrices as they can. Noting that ClassA is not created by a use case, the student writes a high-level use case that will do this. The student corrects the high-level use cases and class diagram as required for the rest of the CRUD matrices. The student then iterates the CRUD analysis.

When undertaking CRUD analysis the students are required to consider the information system in terms of both the business processes, i.e. the use cases, and the information that is stored within the information system, i.e. the classes, the class attributes and the associations. These static characteristics are all represented in the initial class diagram. The students complete CRUD matrices by systematically examining each class, each attribute in each class, and each association between classes, within the information system. There are three types of matrices: a CRUD class matrix; a CRUD association matrix; and a CRUD attribute matrix (for each class).

3.1. CRUD Class Analysis

The CRUD class analysis is done first. Figure 1 shows the format and Figure 8 an example of the CRUD class matrix. One row in the matrix is used for each class in the initial class diagram.

In alphabetical order, the name of each class is entered in the Class column.

In the column headed "Type", a P for a class with persistent objects, a "T" for a class with transient objects, or an "A" for an abstract class is entered. The distinction is needed as the significance of the remaining columns varies between P, T, and A. This is one point at which the students have their object thinking reinforced. They need to understand the concepts of persistent and transient objects and abstract classes to be able to make the right entry in the Type column. The Type column is not used in any other CRUD matrix found in the literature.

Classes with persistent objects are dealt with in the following manner. The Create column must have an entry of a use case name. As well, to encourage good system design, only one use case should have the create responsibility so there should be no more than one possible entry in this column. By explicitly stating this restriction the student is forced to think through what is happening to the objects (analysis) without knowing how it happens (design). If the students know there must only be one use case that is to create the objects in the class, they must be careful about the choice they make. They need to understand the business process captured in the high-level use case description, i.e. be able to "see" the system from a real-world view and also "see" the system as the creation of an object or objects from a class that will exist as software. Students find the use case to enter into the intersecting cell of Class vs. Create, by answering the question:

> "Which use case has responsibility for creating objects of this class?"

Each Class vs. Read cell should have at least one entry of a use case name. The use case is one that utilises objects of this class. It could be the same use case that creates the objects. Often, many use case names can be entered in this cell. Entering all the use case names that utilise the objects makes the students more certain about what each use case is doing. At least one is needed to show that objects of this class are utilised in the system. Students find the use case or use cases to enter into the intersecting cell of Class vs. Read, by answering the question:

> "Which use cases have the responsibility of utilising, that is "reading", objects of this class?"

Each Class vs. Update cell should have an entry of the use case name that keeps objects in this class up-to-date. This should also be a single entry although in some systems multiple use cases may share this responsibility. Very occasionally, a class may have objects that do not require maintenance. When this is the case, "No Maintenance" is entered in the cell. Students find the use case to enter into the intersecting cell of Class vs. Update, by answering the question:

> "Which use cases have the responsibility of keeping up-to-date objects of this class?"

Similar, to Create and Update entries, there should be only one possible entry of a use case name in the Destroy column. Destroy replaces the more common Delete heading as objects are destroyed rather than deleted. Students find the use case to enter into the intersecting cell of Class vs. Destroy, by answering the question:

> "Which use case has responsibility for destroying objects of this class?"

By phrasing the questions as responsibilities the students develop their ideas about the encapsulation of classes and use case behaviour. They begin to show an understanding that behaviour is isolated, in the first instance within a use case.

CRUD Class Matrix

Class	**Type**	**Create**	**Read** (utilise)	**Update** (maintain)	**Destroy**
ClassName	*P/T/A*	*Use case name*	*Use case name*	*Use case name*	*Use case name*

Notes: ____

Figure 1. CRUD class matrix format. One row of the matrix per class is used.

The entries in the CRUD class analysis matrix for each class with transient objects, if any are shown on the initial class diagram, are very similar to those for classes with persistent objects. The questions to which students need to find use case names as answers remain the same.

An abstract class does not have any objects. An "A" in the Type column identifies an abstract class. Thus, Create, Read, Update, and Destroy have no meaning in terms of objects in an abstract class. For each abstract class in the CRUD class matrix, an N/A (not applicable) is entered in each intersecting cell. It is perhaps convenient to leave abstract classes off the matrix. However, matching a count of the classes in the matrix and classes in the initial class diagram is easier if all classes are included in the matrix. Also, the explicit treatment of abstract classes during the CRUD class analysis reinforces this concept with the students.

Each CRUD matrix has a notes section. From time to time entries in the matrix require clarification. Notes are added to the notes section and cross-referenced in the matrix when this is necessary. The students are encouraged to use the notes to suggest the use case name of missing use cases if they can. This makes them aware that their high-level use cases need revisiting.

When all classes in the initial class diagram have been through the CRUD class analysis then the iteration is complete. The matrix is examined for empty cells. All objects must be created, destroyed, and, except for those where we specifically decided otherwise, require updating. An empty cell in one of these three columns identifies an error of omission. The high-level use cases and class diagram are revisited to rectify the error, often by adding a use case. An empty cell in the Read column identifies a class whose objects are never used. Again, the high-level use cases and initial class diagram are revisited and the question, "Why is this class or its objects required in the system?" needs to be answered. The answer to this question will identify which use case utilises the objects, may require corrections to use cases, or may allow the removal of the class.

3.2. CRUD Association Analysis

The CRUD association analysis is conducted in a similar way to the CRUD class analysis. The CRUD association matrix format is shown in Figure 2. An example of a CRUD association matrix is shown in Figure 9. A CRUD association matrix was not found in the literature. It may be appropriate to assume that the associations between classes are "CRUDed" with the classes. However, it is advantageous to encourage students to think through what is happening in a use case in terms of the navigation of the class diagram. The students become aware of the collaboration of objects that is required.

The name of each association, formed by combining the two class names separated by a hyphen, is entered alphabetically in the Association column. The association/s of the first class in the CRUD class matrix is first in the CRUD association matrix. All the associations of each class in the order listed in the CRUD class matrix are dealt with in turn so that not any of the associations are missed. For example, let's say there are three classes, ClassA, ClassB, and ClassC (which would be listed in this order in the CRUD class matrix). Each class is associated with the other two, as shown in Figure 3. The CRUD association matrix would have in the Association column a list of the associations in alphabetical order, i.e. ClassA-ClassB, ClassA-ClassC, and ClassB-ClassC. The order might change if the association is uni-directional, however, this is usually not known at this stage of the project.

CRUD Association Analysis

Association	Create	Read (utilise)	Update (maintain)	Destroy
ClassAName-ClassBName	*Use case name*	*Use case name*	*Use case name*	*Use case name*

Notes: ____

Figure 2. CRUD association analysis matrix format. One row of the matrix for each association.

In the circumstances where the association is named, such as when two or more associations exist between two classes and UML notation is use so that both associations are named, then the association name is used in the Association column entry. For example, in Figure 4, an Employee class is associated as a member to a Department class and Employee class is associated as a manager to a Department class. The Association column entries would be, in order, Department-managed by-Employee and Department-member of-Employee. The association name is a used without alteration to ensure traceability between the class diagram and the CRUD association matrix.

Each association is now examined in turn. A similar process to the CRUD class analysis of classes with persistent objects is followed. The use case with responsibility for establishing links, i.e. instances of the association, is identified and entered in the Association vs Create cell. Students identify the use case by answering the question:

"Which use case is responsible for establishing the links between objects of these classes?"

The name of at least one use case that utilises, "reads", the link/s between objects is identified and entered. Students identify the use case by answering the question:

"Which use case is responsible for utilising the link between objects of these classes?"

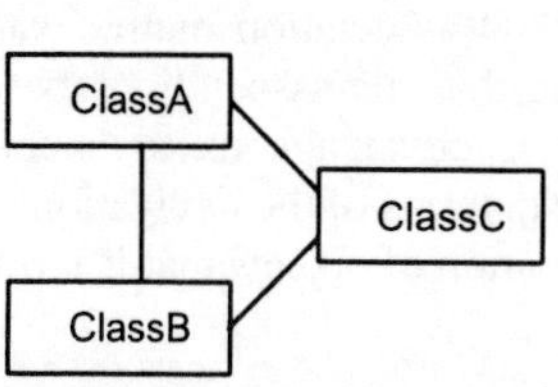

Figure 3. A simple class diagram.

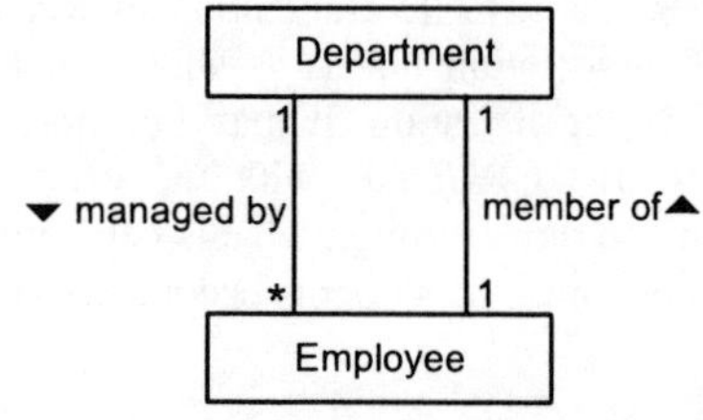

Figure 4. Example of named associations.

If the links between objects of the two classes may change, the use case with this responsibility is identified and entered in the Association vs Update cell. Students identify the use case by answering the question:

> "If it is possible that the link will change, which use case is responsible for changing the link?"

For example, a student may change from one course to another. Initially, studentObject1 is linked to courseObjectA. The student decides to change from courseA to courseB. The link must be changed so that there is a link from studentObject1 to courseObjectB. Even though how this will happen is likely to be in two steps of creating and destroying links, the focus remains on what the use case must do (analysis) not how it will happen (design).

The use case with responsibility for destroying links is entered in the Association vs Destroy cell. Students identify the use case by answering the question:

> "Which use case is responsible for removing the link between objects of these classes?"

When the CRUD association matrix is complete it is examined for empty cells. As with objects, all links must be created and destroyed and, except for those where we specifically decided otherwise, require updating. All associations should be utilised. An empty cell identifies an error and high-level use cases and class diagram are revisited to rectify the matter.

3.3. CRUD Attribute Analysis

A separate CRUD attribute matrix is created for each class in the class diagram, in the order listed in the CRUD class matrix. Figure 5 shows the CRUD attribute matrix format. An example of a CRUD attribute matrix is shown in Figure 10. A CRUD attribute matrix was not found in the literature, though Brown (2002) mentions something like this. As with associations an assumption that the attributes are "CRUDed" with the classes could be made. However, for instance, in the CRUD class matrix two use cases may appear in a Class vs. Read cell, in the CRUD attribute matrix there use cases may appear in different Attribute vs. Read cells.

The class name is recorded in the heading of the matrix and each attribute name is entered in the Attribute column.

When an object is created the attribute value may be a system default value, usually null, empty, zero, or the appropriate value for the data type. This may be satisfactory for some values of attributes in objects of the classes. If the system (programming language) default value is used when an object is created a "Default" is entered in the Attribute vs Initialise at Create cell. For attributes in the class where an initial value is set, i.e. not defaulted, then the name of the use case with this responsibility is entered in the Attribute vs Initialise at Create cell. Students identify the use case by answering the question:

> "Which use case is responsible for assigning the value to this attribute when the object is created?"

In the Attribute vs Read cell the name of at least one use case that utilises the attribute value is entered. Students identify the use case by answering the question:

> "Which use case is responsible for utilising the value stored in this attribute?"

Over time values stored in an attribute of an object may change. In the Attribute vs. Update cell, the name of the use case with responsibility for keeping the attribute up-to-date is entered. Rarely, this column contains "No Maintenance". Students identify the use case by answering the questions:

> "Which use case is responsible for ensuring that the value in this attribute is correct and up-to-date?"

and

> "Which use case is responsible for updating the value in this attribute?"

Attribute values are destroyed, i.e. no longer exist in the system, when the object is destroyed. However, occasionally, a system might require that the data value of an object be changed back to an initial value for the attribute data type, such as null, empty, or zero. If so, the name of the use case responsible is entered in the Attribute vs Reset cell, otherwise "No" is entered. Students identify the use case by answering the question:

> "If it is a requirement of the system that the attribute is set to a null value (blank or zero), which use case has this responsibility?"

Once the CRUD attribute matrices are complete they are examined for empty cells. An empty cell indicates a potential problem. The high-level use cases and class diagram are revisited and the artefacts are corrected as necessary.

This completes the description of the CRUD analysis technique which takes place in the system definition phase. The CRUD matrices are reviewed as part of quality assurance as each use case is taken through a development cycle. The CRUD matrices are checked against the developing use case and system increments to ensure that what was expected to happen is actually happening, or adequate reasoning exists why it is not happening.

4. AN EXAMPLE CRUD ANALYSIS

The following section shows an example CRUD analysis based on a case study. Extracts of the case study, high-level use cases, the initial class diagram, and CRUD matrices from Box et al. (2002) are shown and then discussed.

4.1. Case Study

The Moggan Bay Sailing Club requires an information system to support the management of its sailing regattas. In this information system, known as the Regatta Tracka system, we are concerned only with the racing activities of a sailing club.

CRUD Attribute Analysis – Class: *ClassName*

Attribute	Initialise at Create	Read (utilise)	Update (maintain)	Reset
attributeName	*Use case name*	*Use case name*	*Use case name*	*Use case name*

Notes: ______________________________

Figure 5. CRUD attribute analysis matrix format. One row of the matrix for each attribute.

At the Moggan Bay Sailing Club, all boats are the same class. That is, all boats are the same design, or model. Boats race in regattas held by the club. A regatta is a series of races. A regatta is over a relatively short time such as a day or weekend. When the sailing club committee decides to conduct a regatta, the committee determines the number of races, the course that will be used for each race and the date and time that each race will be held.

A boat owner who wishes to race nominates for the regatta. Each nominated boat races in each race of the regatta. The nomination to race is not taken on a race-by-race basis. It is for all the races in the regatta.

Each boat is sailed by its owner, who is the skipper. When the boats are sailing, each boat has two crewmembers. Thus when racing, there are three on board.

When sailing races take place, the boats compete in a number of races to determine a regatta winner. At the completion of each race, each boat is awarded a place (first, second, third, etc). Points are awarded according to the boat's place in the race. The points awarded for each race in the regatta are added for each boat. The boat with the lowest total for the regatta is the winner.

The club has an existing system called MemberMaster. Management of membership information will be tackled later.

The Regatta Tracka information system is required to manage information regarding: 1) Regattas and races in regattas; 2) Nominations of boats for regattas; 3) Skipper details for each boat; 4) Crew details for each boat in a regatta – the crew for a boat may vary from regatta to regatta; 5) Each boat result for each race in a regatta and the regatta result; 6) A history of race and regatta performance for each boat.

4.2. High-level Use Cases

The high-level use cases in Figure 6 are an extraction of the set for the case study.

4.3. Initial Class Diagram

The initial class diagram in Figure 7 is an excerpt from the complete diagram in the case study.

4.4. CRUD Matrices

Extracts of the CRUD matrices are shown: the CRUD class matrix in Figure 8; the CRUD association matrix in Figure 9; and a CRUD attribute matrix in Figure 10.

4.5. Discussion of the Sample CRUD Matrices

In the CRUD matrices, we discover that there are cells with no entries. The high-level use cases and the initial class diagram are reviewed. In the case of the classes Race and Regatta, it is clear that we have missed defining use cases that maintain the objects in these classes or perhaps they never change. We resolve the query through consultation with the business manager/user. We learn a regatta and/or its races can change. Thus, additional use cases are required. The additional use cases would fill the cells Race vs. Update and Regatta vs. Update in the CRUD class matrix (Figure 8) and all Attribute vs. Update cells in the CRUD attribute matrix (Figure 10) for the Regatta class.

Use case: **Accept nomination** **Category:** Core
Actors: Skipper **Trace:** Business Functions: 2, 2.1, 2.2, 2.3
Description: This use case begins when a skipper submits a nomination to participate in a regatta. The skipper, the crew, and the boat listed in the nomination are checked for eligibility for the regatta. The boat is recorded as a nomination in the regatta. The use case ends when the skipper is advised of the acceptance of the nomination.
Notes: The submission may be online or on a form that is received and entered into the system by the race administrator.

Use case: **Calculate race results** **Category:** Core
Actors: Race administrator **Trace:** Business Functions: 4, 4.1, 4.1.1, 4.1.2, and 4.1.3
Description: This use case begins when a race is finished and the race administrator has entered all boat finish data for the race. Actual finish time is used to determine each boat's result in the race. Race points are allocated to each boat in the race. The use case ends when the successful completion of boat race result calculation is notified.
Notes: Calculation of handicap results (Business Function: 4.1.4) is excluded, as this business function is optional in this system development.

Use case: **Calculate regatta results** **Category:** Core
Actors: Regatta administrator **Trace:** Business Functions: 4, 4.2, 4.2.1, 5.1
Description: This use case begins when all race results for the regatta have been calculated and the administrator chooses to proceed with regatta result calculation. The race points for each boat in each race in the regatta are aggregated to determine the regatta result. The use case ends when regatta result calculation is complete and notification of the result is made.
Notes: Calculation of handicap results (Business Function 4.2.2) is excluded, as this business function is optional in this system development.

Use case: **Define regatta** **Category:** Core
Actors: Regatta administrator **Trace:** Business Functions: 1, 1.1, 1.2
Description: This use case begins when the administrator accepts a completed regatta program. The detail for the regatta and its races are recorded. The use case ends when the race administrator is notified that recording of the regatta details is completed successfully.
Notes: The regatta organising committee provides a completed regatta program.

Use case: **View nominations** **Category:** Adjunct
Actors: Skipper **Trace:** Business Functions: 2, 6
Description: This use case begins when a skipper requests to view particular nominations to participate in regattas. All the particular nominations for the skipper are found and presented to the skipper. The use case ends when the skipper indicates that he/she has finished viewing the nominations.

Use case: **Withdraw nomination** **Category:** Adjunct
Actors: Skipper **Trace:** Business Functions: 6, 6.1
Description: This use case begins when a skipper requests to withdraw a nomination to participate in a regatta. The nomination is checked for existence in the regatta. The boat is recorded as a withdrawn nomination from the regatta. The use case ends when the skipper is advised that the withdrawal of the nomination has been recorded successfully.
Notes: The withdrawal of a nomination only by an authorised person (Business Function: 6.2) is excluded, as this business function is optional in this system and the required details for determining an authorised person will not be available for this generation of the product.

Figure 6. An extract of the high-level use cases for the Moggan Bay Regatta Tracka case study.

There is a single instance of the SailingClub class. No obvious use case utilises the object but, on consideration, it is very likely that the data in this object is required for display on interfaces and in reporting. We feel confident that usage of SailingClub will become apparent as the system development proceeds. The SailingClub vs Read cell may be left empty and a note made why. Later, during use case development cycles, when the CRUD matrices are used for quality assurance and review the SailingClub vs. Read cell would be filled in. However, it is clear that we do not have a use case with the responsibility for maintenance of SailingClub. Once this is rectified, by writing another use case, the SailingClub vs. Update cell will be filled in during the next CRUD class analysis iteration.

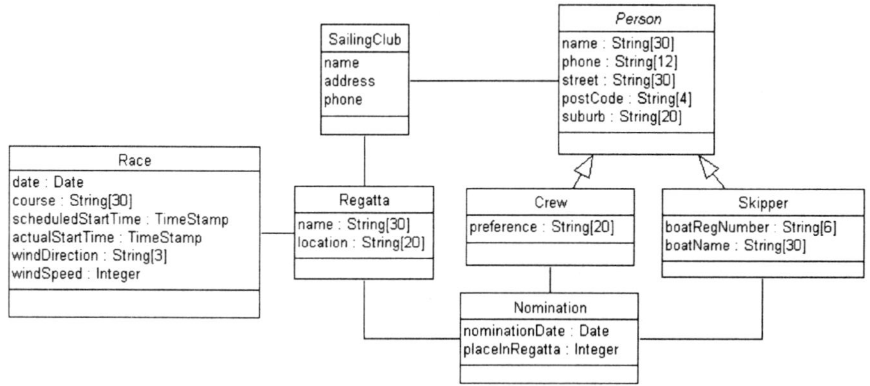

Figure 7. An extract of the initial class diagram for the Moggan Bay Sailing Club Regatta Tracka case study.

CRUD Class Matrix

Class	Type	Create	Read (utilise)	Update (maintain)	Destroy
Nomination	P	Accept nomination	View nomination	Withdraw nomination Accept nomination (Note 1)	Withdraw nomination
Person	A	N/A	N/A	N/A	N/A
Race	P	Define regatta	Calculate race result		Cancel regatta
Regatta	P	Define regatta	Calculate regatta result		Cancel regatta
SailingClub	P	(Note 2)			N/A (Note 3)

Notes:

1. A nomination is changed by first withdrawing a nomination and then re-entering a new nomination.
2. A single sailing club instance must be created when the system is installed. Requirement for system set up, which should have a use case written to do this.
3. Single sailing club instance should never be destroyed.

Figure 8. Sample CRUD class matrix.

CRUD Association Matrix

Association	Create	Read (utilise)	Update (maintain)	Destroy
Crew-Nomination	Accept nomination	View nomination	(Note 1)	Withdraw nomination
Nomination-Regatta	Accept nomination	Calculate regatta result	(Note 1)	Withdraw nomination
Nomination-Skipper	Accept nomination	View nomination	(Note 1)	Withdraw nomination

Notes:
1. Nominations are updated by removing an existing nomination and then entering a new nomination. This will update the link.

Figure 9. Sample CRUD association matrix.

CRUD Attribute Matrix – Class: Regatta

Attribute	Initialise at Create	Read (utilise)	Update (maintain)	Reset
name	Define regatta	View nominations	? (Note 1)	no
location	Define regatta	View nominations	? (Note 1)	no
regattaStartDate	Define regatta	View nominations	? (Note 1)	no
nomClosingDate	Define regatta	Accept nomination	? (Note 1)	no

Notes:
1. Use case omission identified - see CRUD Class Analysis table.

Figure 10. Sample CRUD attribute matrix.

5. SUMMARY

CRUD matrices, also known as object activity matrices, are used during structured and OOISD. Their use in OOISD is typically late in the development cycle, when design is taking place. At this design stage the CRUD analysis focuses on small portions of the system identifying the collaborations between classes within the use case or the operations of a class. This paper put the use of CRUD analysis early in ISD, during analysis, once high-level use cases and the initial class diagram have been developed.

A CRUD analysis technique was described for use in the second phase of an OOISD process. The process is prescriptive, simplified and explicitly written for use by students of OOISD. The CRUD analysis technique is done by the students completing CRUD matrices by systematically examining each class, each attribute in each class and each association within the information system. There are three types of matrices: CRUD class analysis; CRUD association analysis; and CRUD attribute analysis (for each class). The matrices each have a set of questions to help the students find appropriate entries for the cells in the matrices. The CRUD analysis is iterated until the student is confident of the accuracy and completeness of their high-level use cases and class diagram. The CRUD matrices are used during use case development cycles for quality assurance and review.

The CRUD analysis technique is advantageous to students because it reinforces their object thinking and increases their confidence in the accuracy of their ISD artefacts.

An example of the CRUD analysis technique was shown.

REFERENCES

AMS, 2003, *AMS best practices use cases:* Advanced use case modeling. Retrieved 7th May, 2003, from www.ams.com/bestpractices/usecasesbook.asp

Armour, F., and Miller, G., 2001, *Advanced Use Case Modelling: Software Systems*, Addison-Wesley.

Box, I., & Ferguson, J., 2002, *Object Oriented Software Development: Step by Step*. Sydney, Pearson Education.

Brandon, D., Jr., 2002, CRUD matrices for detailed object oriented design. *The Journal of Computing in Small Colleges,* 18(2), 306–322.

Brown, D. W., 2002, *An Introduction to Object-Oriented Analysis, Objects, and UML in Plain English* (2nd ed.): John Wiley & Sons.

Dennis, A., Wixom, B. H., and Tegarden, D., 2002, *Systems Analysis and Design: An Object-oriented Approach with UML*, John Wiley & Sons, Inc.

Fertuck, L., 1992, *Systems Analysis and Design with CASE Tools*, Wm. C. Brown Publishers.

Gottesdiener, E., 1998, OO Methodologies: Process and Product Patterns. *Component Strategies,* 1(5).

Kendall, K. E., and Kendall, J. E., 2002, *Systems Analysis and Design* (5th (International) ed.) Upper Saddle River, NJ, USA: Pearson Education.

Maciaszek, L. A., 2001, *Requirements Analysis and System Design: Developing Information Systems with UML*. Harlow, England: Addison-Wesley.

Satzinger, J., Jackson, R., and Burd, S., 2002, *Systems Analysis and Design in a Changing World* (2nd ed.). Boston, MA, USA: Course Technology.

FROM VERNACULAR TO RATIONAL DESIGN IN SOFTWARE ENGINEERING

Consequences of the designer's changing role

Paul R. Taylor*

1. INTRODUCTION

Convention dictates that an information discipline matures from an informal shared practice to a defined and repeatable process through the externalisation and formal expression of its underlying theory. This progression is sometimes typified by the emergence of disciplined and professional practice from early forms of vernacular or craft-like work—software engineering evidences this kind of progressive definition over three decades. This paper examines the tension between software engineering's professionalisation of the software design role—exemplified by the software architect—and its antithesis, the software craftsperson, a characterisation that continues to emerge despite attempts to suppress the reliance on individual skills and abilities through software engineering process. In non-software design disciplines, the professionalisation of design marks a distinct progression from *ad hoc*, unrepeatable, unselfconscious craft to a self-conscious, demarcated type of design found in most forms of engineering. Software engineering has partially failed its attempts to make this transition and this failure undermines the validity of the engineering metaphor and engineering-based process models as a theoretical and practical model of software design. Software methods must acknowledge and find ways of incorporating vernacularism.

* Department of Computer Science and Software Engineering, Monash University, PO Box 197, Caulfield East, 3145, Australia.

2. DESIGN AND PROGRESS

An historian who took the time examine the chronicles of software engineering could be excused for concluding that 'design' has always had the status of second class object. In software engineering, design finds expression in the techniques of first-class things such as programming languages, architectures, modelling techniques and the mechanical modus operandi of the production of software fabric. We comprehend design and exercise our design knowledge and skills indirectly via the domain-specific filters of common software development techniques—user interface prototyping, pattern-driven architecture evolution, and use case analysis, for example. Unlike other disciplines in which design also plays a central role—architecture and industrial design being the two exemplars—software engineering has not yet elevated design beyond its expression in techniques to professional specialty, to a communication medium for the explicit reflection of local or societal values, or as fulcrum for global social or economic change. Design, as far as it finds expression in software, is both underdeveloped as a sub-discipline of software engineering and as a profession in its own right. Questions about the relationships between individual practice, theory and collective professionalism are at the core of what it is we do as software producers.

Design primarily serves the purpose of development and delivery, or of bringing product to market, and it must be presumed that the discipline, industry and community make this so, promoting and demoting the role of design in software as in other technological and even social movements. Identifying possible reasons for this necessitates both a highly specialised understanding of the nature of software and its design as well as a broad exposure to design beyond any one particular domain. The relative immaturity of software design beyond program-level design is one reason that is repeatedly suggested. Shaw (1996), among others, claims that software architecture is an *ad hoc*, immature craft-like activity, applied only in an idiomatic fashion. *Ad hoc* design activity is generally discredited in software engineering, but not so in design theory outside software (Jencks and Silver, 1973), where an appreciation for the skills of the bricoleur have interesting implications for a perspective of design in general (Louridas, 1999), as well as software design (Taylor, 2000a).

In general, the need to progress from craft to science is taken for granted. This attitude may be seen to have its roots in the human struggle for ascendancy, the basis of science and the scientific method (Weatherall, 1979), and more specifically in the industrial revolution. Those who have questioned the need and appropriateness of this progression in design (such as Christopher Alexander in architecture) have at times been branded brave, stupid or both (Grabow, 1983). In the software discipline, the need to professionalise design has clearly been motivated by economics—software development processes prone to bottlenecks at key design points did not scale and were therefore not feasible in the emerging software application marketplace of the 1970s. Whereas a craftsperson designs and makes a one-off piece of furniture, jewellery or linen in isolation, the software designer's artefact is more the scale of a house, bridge or office tower and the complexity of a thousand such domestic or decorative objects. The analogies are rich but can equally be specious (Baragry and Reed, 2001).

The progression towards ever-increasing levels of design professionalism presents two questions—is it the right progression in the case of software, and what are the implications of this progression for the ways we design software? The first question challenges the canon, even the *status quo*, with all of the attendant risks. An attempt at distilling the design consequences of an alternate metaphor, one that counters this notion of inevitable progress has been started (Taylor, 2001). This paper examines the second question—how has software design been shaped by the force of professionalisation through software engineering?

3. FROM VERNACULAR TO RATIONAL DESIGN

Design, both noun and verb, is so pervasive that it risks losing common meaning from its expression in so many objects and activities. Etymologically, the word 'design' comes from the Italian *disegno*, which since the Renaissance has meant the drafting or drawing of a work, and in general, the idea at the root of a work (Hauffe, 1998). Software design is pervasive, creative, and multi-dimensional (Glass, 1999). It is widely regarded as a foundation of all systems development (Booch, 1994). Design problems of the class that are typically tackled by software development projects have been referred to as 'wicked' problems (Budgen, 1994; Rittel and Weber, 1984), meaning they have non-linear, unpredictable and unmanageable characteristics. To focus on the nature of design in software necessitates understanding the progression from traditional to post-industrial design.

3.1. Self-Conscious and Unselfconscious Design Processes

Some observers align this progression to the designer's self-awareness. Alexander (1964) introduces a broad distinction between two kinds of design processes, one he calls 'unselfconscious', the other 'self-conscious'. Roughly speaking, the unselfconscious process is that which goes on in primitive societies or in the traditional craft or architectural vernacular contexts, while the self-conscious process is that which is typical of present-day, educated, specialised professional designers and architects.

The real distinction between these processes, in Alexander's view, can be observed by looking at the way in which design and the production of useful objects is taught in either case. In the unselfconscious craft situation, the teaching of craft skills is through demonstration, and by having the novice imitate the skilled craftsman until he or she gets the "feel" of the various tools and techniques. Thus the novice learns by practising the actual skill. In the "self-conscious" process, the techniques are taught by being formulated explicitly and explained theoretically. In the unselfconscious culture, the same form is repeated over and over again, and all that the individual craftsperson must learn is how to copy the given prototype. But in self-conscious design there are always new contexts of use arising for which traditional given solutions are inappropriate or inadequate. These necessitate some degree of theoretical understanding in order to be able to devise new forms to meet the new needs.

In software engineering, the unselfconscious designer—working in isolation to merge experience with skill, evolving the function, structure and aesthetics of a complex software architecture or component in piecemeal fashion—is a highly believable and familiar image. It may well be a suppressed image. If current economic, engineering, and business practices collude to force the natural emergent, situated behaviours of the expert designer underground, then we have good reason to question the canon, and even to rethink how we organise, host and foster software creation activity. Vernacularism is a force in software design that we must understand and deal with.

3.2. Vernacularism

The techniques, tricks, mores and means passed from building to building via builders are informal, causal and astute. Design as a communication medium—or the ability of a building or artefact to harbour representations of its designer's intentions beyond basic function—has long been recognised by architectural theorists (Eco, 1997), and vernacular design does this with maximum efficiency. "Vernacular" is a term borrowed from linguists by architectural historians to mean "the language of a region". Vernacular buildings are anything not designed by architects or professional designers. Familiar examples include the Cotswold villages, Cape Cod houses, and any other style that evolved locally under the collective influences of isolation, climate, locally available materials and cultural stability. In architectural terms, vernacular buildings are seen as the opposite of whatever is contemporary, high style, or polite. Dormer (1988) writes that "the craft aesthetic is anti-technology, anti-science and anti-progress" (p. 135). It is little wonder that, in their clamour for business respectability and engineering credibility, software theorists rejected vernacularism outright.

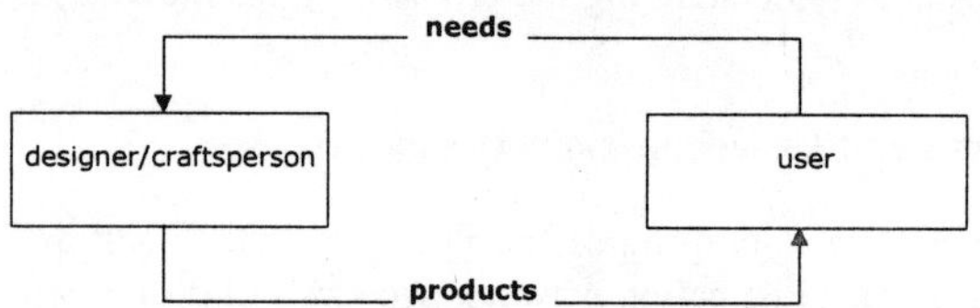

Figure 1. Designer-user interactions for pre-industrial makers (Mayall, 1979).

Vernacularism, however, has much to recommend it. Vernacular buildings evolve extremely well. As each successive generation of design imitates its predecessor, the best buildings, techniques and uses of materials are copied while the less ideal are forgotten. According to Brand's (1994) analysis of how buildings "learn" (that is, how they evolve to embody fit-for-purpose design over time), the heart of vernacular design is about form, not style. The evolutionary development of a vernacular style influences rooms and rooflines rather than colours or stylistic appliqué. The most striking feature of Brand's vernacularism is the effect of human use and habitation over time as the predominant selector of designs—"style is time's fool; form is time's student" (p. 133). Others have written on theoretical aspects of the evolution of designs (Hull, 1988; Steadman, 1979; Stebbins, 1971) and design knowledge (Gero, 1996; Kaplan, 2000). Similar work focuses on software and software design alone (Foote and Opdyke, 1995; Kemerer and Slaughter, 1999; Lieberherr and Xiao, 1993; Taylor, 2000b).

There are those in the software discipline who regard vernacular design as the only kind that has actually been seen to work. Borenstein (1991), for example, thinks that anecdotes (programmer's stories, word of mouth, narratives and case studies) convey more software design knowledge than any theory or method. A primary motivation of the software design patterns movement is to express common software designs that are known to have occurred in at least three different contexts (Coplien, 1996). The emergence of the so-called Agile methods and eXtreme Programming acknowledges less formal approaches to design and knowledge transfer.

Vernacularism exists to a degree in all design contexts. Even as the most prominent and extreme modernists attempted to rid early twentieth century design of its human foibles by seeking a new kind of beauty in the ultimate elevation of function over form and aesthetics, a kind of 'industrial vernacular' was created (Berman, 1988). The semiotic language of modernist design was sparse and minimalist but a distinct, readable language nonetheless, with touches of regional colour and recognisable personal idiosyncrasies (Venturi et al., 1977). If vernacularism cannot be expunged in the relentless pursuit of rationalism, it must exert its influence by degrees. A litmus test for the presence or absence of vernacularism in a design context is the relationships between stakeholders — the designer, the maker and the user. Mayall (1979) illustrates his view of these relationships between the pre-industrial designer or craftsman, and the user (Figure 1). Its vital characteristic for healthy design is unhindered communication and a tightly bound, responsive feedback loop.

This simple closed loop relationship still exists between designers and craftspersons and their patrons today. It also occurs between many architects and their clients, and consultants and their clients. It is so pervasive because it works so well. Its simplicity leads to some obvious problems—it does not scale well, the customer may not know what to request or may interfere too closely with the designer's work causing constant re-direction and thrashing; or the customer may get too involved in the design process or otherwise not comprehend the represented complexity. Walker and Cross (1976) elaborate on the vernacular "mode of design" in Figure 2.

These diagrams are read as follows: the rectangles with rounded corners represent roles, the product is shown as a circle, and dialogue is represented as a triangle. The exertion of pressures and needs (i.e. requirements) is represented by a jagged line superimposed over the thick arrow that represents the normal interactions during design and construction activity. In Walker and Cross' vernacular design (a), user, client, designer and maker are one, and the craftsperson is unimpeded in his or her control of the object. This is a representation of classic craftsmanship, and if you substitute "object" or "component" for "product", it is equally applicable to the software developer's routine work of detailed design, coding, testing, and evolving a software artefact. If the object has no visibility to other developers or to the software system's user, and is a consequence of the software developer's particular design, the illusion is complete, and the cameo of the software craftsperson emerges. When the designer designs a product for someone else (or when the developer iterates the development of a component that provides user interface or services to a system user) the designer is still free to use vernacular solutions and techniques but must select, synthesise and arrange them to meet the negotiated requirements of the patron (b).

In pre-industrial times before mechanised alternatives, all objects were made using craft processes in which the planning and the making of objects were inseparable aspects of the same process. Using hands-on, trial-and-error techniques, craftwork was evolved directly within the context in which it would be used to suit each client's specific requirements. In most forms of vernacular design, the designing and making are indivisible and lead to an intimate knowledge of and familiarity with the fabric—what Schon (1987) has called a "conversation with the materials". However, the emergence of new materials eventually and inevitably broke down this most basic and natural way of designing.

3.3. The Separation of Designing and Making

The craftsman's direct experience of materials, patterns of use and clients is in sharp contrast with the isolation of post-industrial product designers from the manufacture, use and users of their designs. Software methodologists may legitimately blame the inability of vernacular design to scale, or to be managed in contemporary business environments, as the primary reasons for its rejection. But in industrial design it was the emergence of new materials in standard sizes, forms and quantities that motivated the advent of designer as separate from manufacturer.

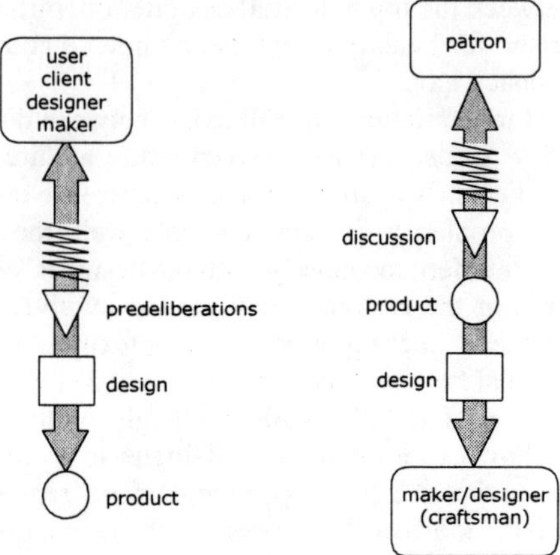

Figure 2. Two representations of vernacular design; (a) vernacular design; (b) the empirical exchange (Walker and Cross, 1976, p. 58)

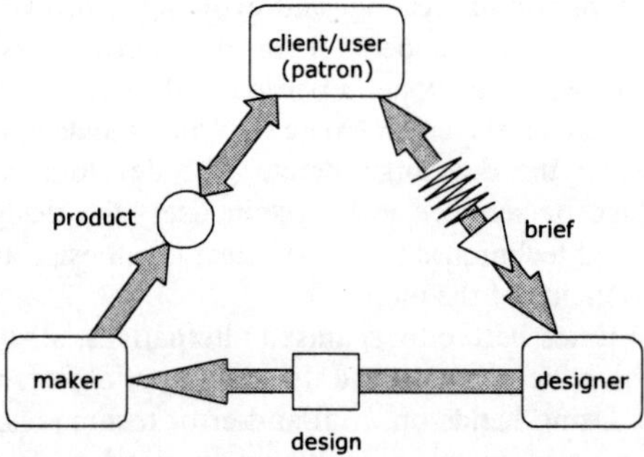

Figure 3. Direct patronage (Walker and Cross, 1976, p. 57).

In Walker and Cross' depiction (Figure 3) a new token appears—a rectangle that represents "the design" in a form that the maker can interpret. The design is the designer's interpretation and transformation of the brief from the client, user and/or patron. The fact that the patron and user interact only with the designer and the product, and never with the maker, reinforces the commodification of making in this (post-industrial) paradigm. The separation of designing and making opened the door for professionalisation, as typified by the architecture profession. Now, one group claimed ownership (and took control) of the conceptual and aesthetic dimensions of design whilst delegating the detailed engineering and structural design to others. This division of responsibilities split concept from detail, image from functionality, and momentary perception from long-term occupation. The emergence of rational design processes sacrificed responsiveness and contextual relevance for uniformity and universality. Each additional identification and separation of roles in time and space brought greater reliance on specification and process. The success of professionalised design in industrial manufacturing appeared as a glimmering chimera to those in other design domains looking for proven models of design and manufacture to adhere to.

3.4. Rationalism

The separation of designing and making is not, however, a universal justification for the elimination of vernacular design in software development—rationalism brings costs and consequences. Mayall's perception of the emergence of rational design emphasises the loss of responsive feedback loops. According to Mayall, machine-based industrialisation caused the break-up of the designer/craftsperson into the four roles (Figure 4).

The management–design–manufacturing split was a direct consequence of the growth of specialisation stimulated by the industrial revolution and larger, international markets that depended upon quantity manufacture. The breakdown of communication between designer and user followed from the introduction of new types of product and manufacturing processes that could not be judged or assessed until they had been tried out for some time. Feedback loops became strikingly elongated. Walker's depiction of rational design completes the picture that we are so familiar with today (Figure 5). Users are depicted as a separate stakeholder group from the designer's clients. Ultimately, users create the forces that motivate the design and construction processes, and users evaluate the results. The three major artefacts of the rational design process are the brief (requirements), the design (drawings and models), and the artefact or product itself. It does not seem too big a claim to generalise that most contemporary software methodologies assume this model of the context and function of design, and these roles and relationships dictate the methodological framework by which software artefacts are produced.

4. FAILURES OF RATIONAL DESIGN

Historically, experience with the rational design paradigm has yielded some consistent themes. These include the disconnection of design from manufacture, the disconnection of design from the context of use, the elongation of critical feedback loops, and the repression of "natural" informal and vernacular design practices. Other characteristics of traditional design clashed with the rational paradigm with varying consequences.

4.1 Stasis

A good place to start is with the claim that rational design actually works on realistic problems—that it delivers workable solutions. Jean Claude Garcias, writing on France's changing cities (Myerson, 1993) observes that the myth underlying the thinking of Le Corbusier and his colleagues was that of zoning—that by carefully re-ordering the city, by separating its functions, it would be possible to solve social ills. But functional decomposition, or master-planning as it is known outside of software, has not worked absolutely, and we now see that the modern design of cities has increased their problems, Garcias claims. The rational master-plan failed to recognise that the most vibrant, stimulating and functionally coherent cities are those in which the city's structure allows for localised control and expression, and that these properties are emergent rather than consequential. This assertion has been made about other design structures, including software structures (Coplien, 2000a; Foote and Yoder, 1999).

The adherent to rational design processes must work hard to avoid an over-reliance on *a priori* master-planning. In designing complex structures embedded in larger, non-deterministic social systems, a solution structure can only designed for the context as it is perceived. This hard reality of rational design-in-a-snapshot contrasts markedly with the fiction of successful rational design for all eventualities within a given planning horizon. Inevitably, in software and in other structured systems, today's solution becomes tomorrow's problem.

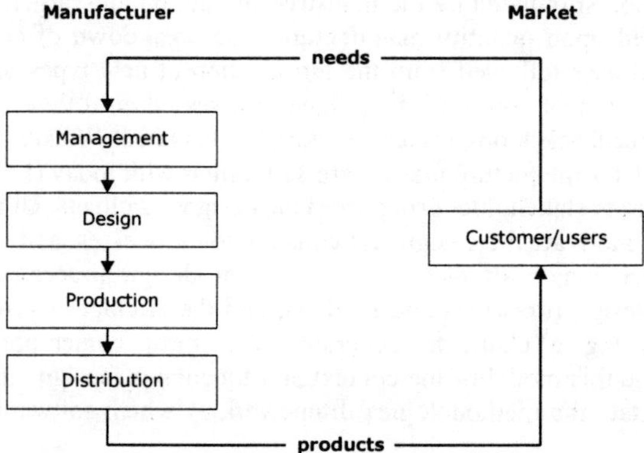

Figure 4. Designer-user interactions for pre-industrial makers (Adapted from Mayall, 1979).

4.2. Continuity

The rational paradigm does not support ongoing or evolutionary design process at all well. During the analysis and design phases of a rational system development process, aspects of social complexity are modelled using a variety of tools, techniques and methods of abstraction. This methodological approach, often sold in the form of packaged product-methodologies and encased within a project culture, is inherited from science, drawing on formalism and notions of optimality. Scientific positivism impels the rational methodologist toward universal approaches to a wide family of problem situations, reducing them to an abstract set of symbols (often diagrammatic), thereby allowing a series of semi-autonomous transformations to deliver a solution. At a philosophical level, this approach aims to assure that we develop credible knowledge about the present and possible future states of the world (Lycett and Paul, 1998)—it is as much about effecting risk management and transfer as it is about predictable, repeatable design.

The methodological approach to systems development (Lycett argues) assumes social structures, mechanisms and processes as 'invariant regularities' that only have to be revealed to be understood. In the long term, methodological systems will—in most important cases—disappoint, as they do not allow internal variety to evolve in line with the environment. They are prone to represent temporal snapshots, ultimately leaving us with static systems that must operate in a dynamic world. Lycett concludes that design should be an inherently ongoing process, not one where the designer is required to predict or control change and articulate every requirement of a design. Continuous design was also recognised by design theorists outside of software, where a transition from a focus on product to process has been advocated in recent decades (Jones, 1988; Mitchell, 1988).

4.3. Memory

Rational design has no convincing answer for one of the strengths of vernacular design—its ability to embody design knowledge in artefacts and local culture. Rational design methods have been consistently criticised for their inability to capture and preserve design justifications, design alternatives, and the motivations or reasons why the chosen solution alternative was selected. This propensity to discount history and individual or local memory manifests most extremely in modernism. Postmodernism responded to this loss by reinstating local references, sometimes in the form of stylised and even tongue-in-cheek appliqué (Venturi et al., 1977). Its message was that design had

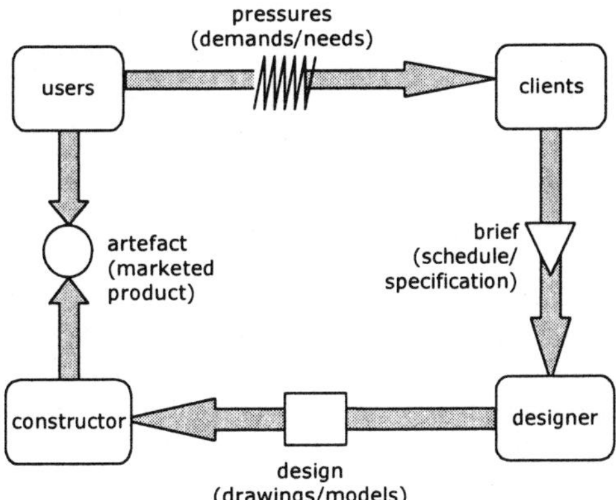

Figure 5. The rational network (Walker and Cross, 1976, p. 56).

to deliver an articulate environment, and that to do this, design needed signification. Thackara (1988) wrote that "postmodernism has one central theme, to correct the disappearance of a sense of history ... the way in which the entire contemporary social system has little by little begun to lose its capacity to retain its own past" (p. 12).

4.4. Reactionism

In recent software engineering history, some authors have begun to question the exclusivity of the rational basis of the predominant underlying software creation metaphors and methods. Blum (1996) systematically deconstructs the current software engineering paradigm using the failures of positivism and universal science, and the situatedness of observed contextual design as evidence, and argues for an adaptive paradigm of software design. Gabriel's Feyerabend project (2001) meets regularly to enact exercises and workshops to similarly deconstruct preconceptions of software construction. Baragry (2001) has claimed that software must abandon its associations with inappropriate metaphors (architecture and engineering) in order to be able to define a more appropriate philosophical basis. Many outside of software (Feyerabend, 1993) have expressed similar views.

Again, history appears to be repeating. Originating in Great Britain and spreading to America, one such reaction against industrialisation's suffocation of design quality and craftsmanship was the Arts and Crafts movement. Artisans who worked in the Arts and Crafts style attempted to revive the medieval guild system, re-establish high quality standards of workmanship, and instil the idea of 'truth to materials' as the basis of design (Naylor, 1990). The recent history of software development has witnessed a similar reaction, although in a considerably reduced timeframe. Coplien (2000b) draws a direct parallel between the Arts and Crafts reaction and the replacement of large-scale industrial software processes (such as the Capability Maturity Model) by developer-centric lightweight methods. Beck's (2000) "eXtreme programming" and SCRUM (Beedle et al., 2000) are methods based on pair programming and time-boxing respectively that attempt to relocate design responsibilities on all levels of abstraction back to the individual developer. These "agile" methods attempt to empower the individual developer within a larger scale project management methodology by separating project management responsibilities from design responsibilities. This difficult balancing act is the essence of the critical challenge facing software methodologists—to find ways of combining rational and vernacular design modes within a post-modern design framework.

5. RELATING THE RATIONAL AND VERNACULAR

Figure 6 illustrates a view of the sources of the competing forces that this discussion has surveyed. Those forces that shape software design practice that do not explicitly fit rational method or vernacular craft performance are represented as 'professionalism'. The diagram of the left summarises current—albeit idealised—attitudes to rationalism, professionalism and vernacularism in software design thinking. This paper has argued that vernacular design is a profoundly natural and in many ways suitable perspective from which to think about design in the software fabric, but that the incumbent rational paradigm of software design has no place for vernacularism. Addressing this oversight creates the intersection that appears on the right of Figure 6, which raises important questions about which characteristics of software design belong in each of the set intersections, and why.

The influence of professionalism is a force not to be underestimated in shaping how the rational and vernacular elements of design might be brought together. A shared sense of professionalism filters practices and legitimates some techniques over others. But the emergence of techniques within the context of a standard body of knowledge is different to the professionalisation of design. Professionalisation selects models and modes of designing over time, and is subject to market pull and economic push. Professionalism draws selectively from rationalism, using rational arguments to support behaviours that suit the individual or the enterprise. It groups a set of largely socially constructed phenomena. The intersection of rationalism and professionalism must be carefully scrutinised in every software design landscape to discern which rational methods and techniques are appropriate and contribute genuine value and which are there for other reasons.

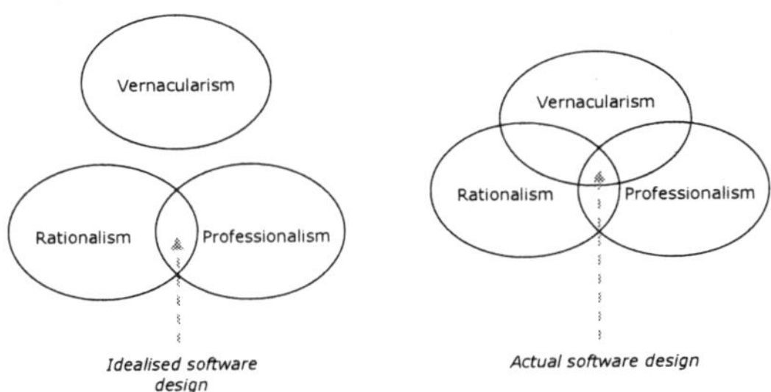

Figure 6. Representation of idealised and actual software design

Professionalism-meets-vernacularism is an under-recognised and under-rated juncture. This intersection is typified by the use of the professional or collegiate network, reflection, altruism, mentoring, and enculturation. Here, designers seek out peers to source and validate potential solutions and experience for personal reasons. Software engineering methodology has not acknowledged the value of this behaviour, and as a result, some informal, *ad hoc* designer behaviours are unnecessarily under-valued.

Rationalism-meets-vernacularism is a non sequitur in design theory and history. This intersection, to the degree that it exists at all, is best enumerated by countless accounts of the domination of rational design over vernacular craft. As noted, reactionary software design methods have begun to address this.

The intersection of professionalism, rationalism and vernacularism represents the greatest challenge to the applied field of software construction. No one would sensibly claim that rationalism in contemporary software design is fatally flawed. However, as has been argued, many observers of industrialisation, both within and outside of software, perceive problems in a unilateral devotion to rational philosophy. As the discipline of software engineering has attempted to transform software craft into a fully-fledged member of the engineering family, the role of software designer (amongst several others) has evolved. Careful observation of its changing features serves to illustrate the ever-present dangers of over-correction. The formalising forces of professionalisation of the craft of software development have had similar effect. Of interest to software engineering professionals and methodologists is the degree to which these problems reflect on treatments of design in contemporary methodology and what, if any action should be taken to mitigate the associated risks.

In summary, a number of objections to rational design have been raised. These include the disconnection of design from manufacture (a distinction that makes little sense in software construction); the disconnection of design from the context of use (a problem that has achieved more prominence in information systems literature than in software engineering); elongation of critical feedback loops, and repression of 'natural' informal and vernacular design practices. The problems that surface as a result of these mismatches stem from the underlying tension between the incumbent rational model of software design and other paradigms of thought and action that influence how practitioners approach software construction. This tension has the potential to retard progressive thought and innovative software design practice. Suggestions for paths forward range from incremental methodological evolution (as much of the current software engineering research would seem to suggest) to full-scale Kuhnian paradigm shift. Either way, the environmental factors that will select the methodological variants that prosper in the next chapter of the history of software design and construction—increasing need for software on a global scale, the need for quality, responsiveness and flexibility to name a few—will significantly test our current notions of rationalism, vernacularism and professionalism.

REFERENCES

Alexander, C., 1964, *Notes on the Synthesis of Form*, New York, Harvard University Press.

Baragry, J. and Reed, K., 2001, Why we need a Different View of Software Architecture, Working IEEE/IFIP Conference on Software Architecture, Amsterdam, The Netherlands,

Beck, K., 2000, *Embracing Change: Extreme Programming Explained*, Cambridge, Cambridge University Press.

Beedle, M., Devos, M., Sharon, Y., Schwaber, K. and Sutherland, J., 2000, SCRUM: A Pattern Language for Hyperproductive Software Development, in: *Pattern Languages of Program Design 4*, Vol. 4, N. Harrison, B. Foote and H. Rohnert, eds., Reading, Massachusetts, Addison-Wesley.

Berman, M., 1988, The Experience of Modernity, in: *Design After Modernism*, J. Thackara, ed., London, Thames and Hudson.

Blum, B., 1996, *Beyond Programming: To a New Era of Design*, Oxford University Press.

Booch, G., 1994, *Object-Oriented Analysis and Design with Applications*, Redwood City, California, Benjamin Cummings.

Borenstein, N.S., 1991, *Programming as if People Mattered: Friendly Programs, Software Engineering and Other Noble Delusions*, Princeton, New Jersey, Princeton University Press.

Brand, S., 1994, *How Buildings Learn: What Happens to Them after they're Built*, New York, Penguin.

Brooks, F. P., 1987, No silver bullet: Essence and accidents of software engineering, *IEEE Computer*, 20(4): 10–19.

Budgen, D., 1994, *Software Design*, Addison-Wesley.

Coplien, J. O., 1996, *Software Patterns*, New York, Lucent Technologies, Bell Labs Innovations.

Coplien, J. O., 2000a, *Architecture as Metaphor*.

Coplien, J. O., 2000b, Patterns and Art, *C++ Report*, 12(1): 41–43.

Dormer, P., 1988, The Ideal World of Vermeer's Little Lacemaker, in: *Design After Modernism*, J. Thackara, ed., London, Thames and Hudson.

Eco, U., 1997, Function and Sign: the Semiotics of Architecture, in: *Rethinking Architecture: A reader in cultural theory*, N. Leach, ed., London, Routledge.

Feyerabend, P., 1993, *Against Method*, London, Verso.

Foote, B. and Opdyke, W. F., 1995, Lifecycle and Refactoring Patterns that Support Evolution and Reuse, in: *Pattern Languages of Program Design*, J. O. Coplien and D. C. Scmidt, eds., Addison-Wesley.

Foote, B. and Yoder, J., 1999, Big Ball of Mud, in: *Pattern Languages of Program Design 4*, Vol. 4, N. Harrison, ed., Addison-Wesley.

Gabriel, R. P., 2001, The Feyerabend Project (http://www.dreamsongs.com/FeyerabendW1.html)

Gero, J. S., 1996, Creativity, emergence and evolution in design: concepts and framework, *Knowledge Based Systems*, 9(7): 435–448.

Glass, R.L., 1999, On Design, *IEEE Software*, Mar/Apr: 104–103.

Grabow, S., 1983, *Christopher Alexander: The Search for a New Paradigm in Architecture*, Chicago, University of Chicago Press.

Hauffe, T., 1998, *Design: A Concise History*, London, Laurence King Publishing.

Hull, D. L., 1988, *Science as a Process: An Evolutionary Account of the Social and Conceptual Development of Science*, Chicago, The University of Chicago Press.

Jencks, C. and Silver, N., 1973, *Adhocism: The Case for Improvisation*, New York, Anchor Books.

Jones, J. C., 1988, Softecnica, in: *Design After Modernism*, J. Thackara, ed., London, Thames and Hudson.

Kaplan, S. M., 2000, Co-Evolution in Socio-Technical Systems, *Computer Supported Cooperative Work 2000*, Philadelphia, ACM.

Kemerer, C.F. and Slaughter, S., 1999, An Empirical Approach to Studying Software Evolution, *IEEE Transactions on Software Engineering*, 25(4): 493–509.

Lieberherr, K.J. and Xiao, C., 1993, Object-Oriented Software Evolution, *IEEE Transactions on Software Engineering*, 19(4): 313–343.

Louridas, P., 1999, Design as bricolage: anthropology meets design thinking, *Design Studies*, 20(6): 517–535.

Lycett, M. and Paul, R.J., 1998, Information Systems Development: The Challenge of Evolutionary Complexity in: *Sixth European Conference on Information Systems*, W.R.J. Baets, ed., Aix-en-Provence, France, Euro-Arab management School, Granada, Spain.

Mayall, W. H., 1979, *Principles in Design*, New York, Van Nostrand Rienhold.

Mitchell, T., 1988, The Product as Illusion, in: *Design After Modernism*, J. Thackara, ed., London, Thames and Hudson.

Myerson, J., 1993, Design renaissance: Selected papers from the International Design Congress in: *International Design Congress* J. Myerson ed., Glasgow, Scotland, Open Eye Publishing.

Naylor, G., 1990, *The Arts and Craft Movement: A Study of its Sources, Ideals and Influence on Design Theory*, London, Trefoil Publications.

Rittel, H. J. & Weber, M. M., 1984, Planning problems are wicked problems, in: *Developments in Design Methodology*, N. Cross , ed., Wiley.

Shaw, M. and Garlan, F., 1996, *Software Architecture: Perspectives on an Emerging Discipline*

Steadman, P., 1979, *The Evolution of Designs: Biological Analogy in Architecture and the Applied Arts*, Cambridge, Cambridge University Press.

Stebbins, G. L., 1971, *Processes of Organic Evolution*, Englewood Cliffs, New Jersey, Prentice-Hall, Inc.

Taylor, P., 2000a, Adhocism in Software Architecture – Perspectives from Design Theory in: *International Conference of Software Methods and Tools (2000)* J.G.a.P. Croll, ed., Wollongong, IEEE Computer Press.

Taylor, P., 2000b, Evolution of Software Design Knowledge in: *Australian Conference on Knowledge Management and Intelligent Decision Support (2000)*, F. Burnstein ed., Melbourne, Monash University.

Taylor, P. R., 2001, Patterns of Software Craft in: *Second Australian Conference of Pattern Languages and Programs (KoalaPLoP 2001)* J. Noble and N. Harrison, eds., Melbourne, University of Wellington.

Thackara, J., 1988, Beyond the Object in Design, in: *Design After Modernism*, J. Thackara, ed., London, Thames and Hudson.

Venturi, R., Scott Brown, D. and Izenour, S., 1977, *Learning from Las Vegas*, Cambridge, Massachusetts, The MIT Press.

Walker, D. and Cross, N., 1976, *Design: The man-made object*, The Open University Press.

Weatherall, M., 1979, *Scientific Method*, London, The English Universities Press Ltd.

PICTURING PROBLEMS

Mike Metcalfe[1]

ABSTRACT

This paper is about designing collaborative problem-picturing; the act of drawing pictures to aid thinking. The author's concern is that a picturing process needs to be designed to ensure a problem domain, such as a system development, is well analysed and well synthesised. Specifically this paper will argue that problem picturing can be improved by explicitly incorporating Dewey's (1910) concept of synthesis. The evidence provided to support this argument includes a summary of the problem picturing literature and a summation of the systems thinking literature on problem solving. The two are then draw together in an example of a picturing process that learns from these two literatures.

1. PICTURING PROBLEMS

Collaborative problem definition in an ever more complex environment needs careful consideration. Picturing methods that allow for easy communication on complex concepts and a range of thinking styles have become even more relevant, especially in the concept forming stages of problem definition. Bronte-Stewart, (1999) and the conceptual mapping literature (Eden and Ackermann, 1998) suggest that the drawing of "cartoon like" pictures may be one solution, but fail to provide any conceptual frame for how and why they might work. On his web site, Lanzing (1997) attempts to classify mapping or picturing so as to distinguish between flow-charts, E-R models, metaphor icons and brainstorming picturing. However, he does not seem to identify the important difference between whether the picturing is to help those present think in a collaborative way or whether its aim is a finished format intended to act like text and be useful to communicate process to strangers. Socio-network analysis graphics are an example of the latter, while an abandoned informal whiteboard collaborative sketch is more typical of the former. Moreover, collaborative problem picturing can use very different iconography, such as cartoons, icons and the box and line charts typical of conceptual mapping in information systems design. The collaborative picturing used here is an

[1] University of South Australia, mike.metcalfe@unisa.edu.au

attempt to combine the node and line iconography of socio-metric networks with thd "cartoon" style many will associate with Checkland's Rich Pictures" (2000).

This paper is divided into three parts. The concepts used to design a process of collaborative problem picturing to aid problem solving is discussed first. Next, the problem solving concepts of inherent in one stream of systems thinking will be introduced as a perspective on how to design a picturing facilitation. Last, an illustration of a problem being pictured will be provided followed by a brief suggestion how tentative solutions might be argued through.

Bronte-Stewart (1999) presents a fairly comprehensive review of the numerous forms of "cartoon" iconography, none of which explicitly suggest socio-metric networks yet most show relationships between entities or nodes. He shows a broad divergence of forms for a wide range of applications and concludes with a reminder of their purpose: "[u]sing such a diagram may… improve communication amongst people in the problem situation and build a deeper, more shared understanding". Picturing as discussed in this paper is designed to be used in an iterative fashion to help those discussing a problem understand each other's thoughts. However, if some broad guidelines are provided as how to set about the picturing process, then it is hoped the picturing can also be used as a device to assist the group to think about the problem driven from some conceptual frame. Williams (2002) argues for these two interactive functions. The first is seen as a representation tool and the other as a creative tool. As a representation tool, the elements of the picture form proxy realities that make an unfamiliar situation more familiar. As a creative tool, picturing can provide for the continuous construction and deconstruction of perspectives so that a bA4ter understanding can be formed about the problems and possible solutions. Uses for problem pictures may therefore be seen as either a representative type tool for communication or a creative application tool design to help understand a problem in an interactive but well conceptualised manner. Both are relevant to the wicked problem of systems design in a virtual or globalised situation. The conceptual frame this paper intends to apply has two related dimensions. The first is to provide an alternative to the waterfall model of problem solving. The second is to use this sort of picturing to improve problem solving by teasing out the dialectic between analysis and synthesis.

The decision to use picturing as a means to apply a conceptual frame means that a choice has to be made about the detail of any directions given. One way is to provide no instructions to those gathered to talk about a problem other than to suggest they use sketching to co-ordinate their thinking. This sketch could then be used at the end of the session to ask the group to identify the range of concepts and relationships more formally so as to draft a table from which a database may be designed. This approach might be thought of as going from synthesis to analysis. The advantage of this approach is that there is a clear outcome from the sketching. However, the act of trying to derive concepts and relationships from a free form sketch is thought to raise more issues than it solves. The approach suggested in this paper is to use a conceptual frame to provide the group with some broad upfront guidelines to collaborate picturing that they can use as a mode of facilitation for the meeting and which encourages synthesis through questioning. This latter approach is thought preferable provided the guidelines are not too rigid partly because, at a pragmatic level, it provides a path into discussion between disputing shareholders. However, the outcome of the picturing process has to go beyond everybody having "a better appreciation" of the problem. To solve this, some options will be suggested which involve identifying a short list of tentative solution statements.

1.1. Guidelines?

Before suggesting a process for collaborative sketching, some thought seem appropriate on the task of turning a conceptual frame into guidelines. Checkland (2000), Hughes (1998) and others point out that doing this through drafting a detailed formal methodology is now considered problematic in systems design. Every problem situation is unique, including the preferences of stakeholders, so will demand mutations on any suggested formal methodology. The more experienced project leaders have their own conceptual frames which they may or may not even appreciated they have, but will invariably clash with the formal methodology. These will act to present the 'obvious' way they should set about any problem solving. The new generation of methodologies will need to either merely provide means of critiquing an implicit methodology (Metcalfe, 2002) or provide what Argyris (1996) calls actionable knowledge and Kogut (1998) "simple rules", or "one liners" to be used as solutions to the small crisis that always 'dog' projects. Put another way, process instructions need to be pitched at the right conceptual level. General Systems Theory, for example is believed to be too conceptual (Philips, 1969) and formal methodologies too prescriptive. Checkland (2000), in his 30 year retrospective, discussed this balancing act as he moved from his overly complex CATWOE methodology to his very conceptual LUMAS action thinking approach. Interestingly, adoptions of his rich pictures tool (disassociated from CATWOE) are proving popular in their own right which suggests these provide actionable knowledge (Bronte-Stewart, 1999; East, 2002). On the other hand, something like Ackoff's application of Dewey's thinking (2000) is thought to lack sufficient process for many managers. Calls for connectivity rather than dissection, and synthesis not analysis are still not understood by a generation of managers brought up solely on goals, visions and statistical analysis. Therefore, the process suggested here for picturing problems will try to steer the middle road between excessive and insufficient detail while driven by a desire to tempt the problem-solving group to seek appreciation and possible solutions by switching between synthesis and analysis.

The process suggested here is intended to apply the concepts developed from one stream of systems thinking that encouraged both analysis and synthesis by encouraging the stakeholders to communicate with each other and appreciate the problem from different perspectives. It could not be said to be a process that somehow produces a mechanical solution like some linear programming algorithm. It also avoids the classic waterfall model of problem solving; gather data, analyse data, formulate solution, and implement solution, which has been heavily criticised by systems thinkers such as Checkland (2000) and Guindon (1990). Rather, it provides an approach that integrates the steps. Apart from Checkland's soft systems LUMAS model, other alternatives to the waterfall model have been documented. Some of these use Popper (1963) and Crosswhite's (1996) evolution theory understanding of how we think. This turns the waterfall model on its head, arguing that we are very quick to jump to possible solutions (conjectures) that need to be confirmed by supporting evidence such as reasoning or empirics. Gelder (2002) goes so far as to suggest designing the picturing process around the process of argument. A tentative solution (conjecture) is called for right at the start and the evidence for and against this conjecture mapped in a box and arrow diagram (assisted by his picturing software). When it becomes clear that the tentative solution is not going to work, another one is called for and attempts shifted to mapping evidence for or against this. The limitation of this theoretically well-founded approach is that the group's imagination may let them down. His approach needs to be supported by some form of idea generation process beyond group discussion. An alternative, but related approach has been incorporated in the IBIS and Questmap (2002) picturing process. It appears to draw on Guindon's (1990) empirics of how lift engineers actually solved their problems. Guindon observes what he calls 'opportunistic thoughts' (tentative solutions) were randomly produced and then talked through in an interactive manner incorporating the technical facts and previous tentative solutions. As tentative solutions were found wanting, they were on occasions used as stepping stones to alternative tentative solutions. The collaborative picturing process that will be outlined here follows this assumption that both tentative solutions, usually presented as perspectives in social problems, and empirical facts are the input for further, hopefully improved, solutions. These alternative solutions need to be argued through.

A little bit unusually, it is intended to suggest in this paper a picturing process that combines systems thinking concepts, cartoon like collaborative picturing and the more formal presentation of the graphical methods used in socio-metric network analysis (Lanzing, 1997). While not normally associated with the collaborative problem picturing or with systems thinking, socio-metric network analysis clearly aligns with the connectivity concept in systems thinking by providing a visual method for the analysis of relationships. One approach (Netmap) involves the visualisation of networks as nodes around the edge of a circle that represent a system where the nodes represent things, organisations or people associated with that system. As a visual mapping tool to help find answers to problems, it encourages the perception of problems as a series of connections independent of physical relationships. This format also allows for relationships between nodes to be shown as diagonal lines across the circle, connecting these nodes. However, it can also be used to mix an analysis of the problem with a synthesis.

2. SYNTHESIS

Most readers will be comfortable with the concept of analysis, which Dewey (1910) calls "picking to pieces", and Phillips (1969) defends encouraging use of a "zooming in" metaphor. Systems thinking as a perspective shifting (also see metaphoric analysis) approach also intends to encourage expansive perceptions or "zooming out" (Weber, 1986; McFadzean, 1988; Nossiter and Biberman, 1988). This aligns with Ackoff's (2000) call for problem solvers to think of the wider system (the context), and Churchman (1979), Linstone (1999) call for a holistic perspective. This "zooming out" aligns with Dewey's definition of the word "synthesis" but may not be sufficient. I am going to try to distinguish synthesis from perspectival thinking (Haynes, 2000) and from seeking worldviews (Checkland, 2000) by defining synthesis as the search for perspectives that assist in seeing a particular problem as a subset of some larger problem. My understanding of perspectival thinking is that it is about separating the object under study from the perspective being taken of that object. Seeking stakeholders' worldviews is about appreciating how they are seeing a problem and possible solutions. Synthesis is constructed here to mean using the things, people and organisations involved in a problem to provide a perspective on the problem. So, in an example provided later, the buildings materials industry's perspective is used to think about a dispute between a local politician and an international aid agency.

> ...so synthesis is thought to be a sort of physical piecing together... [it] takes place wherever we grasp the bearing of facts on a conclusion... [it] is placing... [it] gives what is selected its context, or its connection with what is signified... it is synthetic in so far as it leaves the mind with an inclusive situation within which the selected facts are placed.
>
> (Dewey, 1910, p. 114)

Dewey, whose ideas are used extensively by systems thinkers like Ackoff (2000), also draws on the metaphor of constructing a jig-saw puzzle, where the first piece is laid down and slowly the whole picture emerges as the other pieces are reasoned into place. The literature on designing systems to help define, appreciate and synthesise human activity problems is still rather diverse and has not really been drawn upon by mainstream information systems (IS) practice or education. Even the idea of thinking of information systems design (ISD) as problem solving would sound strange to many developers, maybe because they draw on a green-site construction perspective: no problem, think positive. The systems for thinking literature used here is that advocated by authors such as Ackoff, Argyris, Boulding, Checkland, Churchman, Linestone, Schon, Ulrich and Vickers. These writers draw on a perspective of IS as being the solution to a problem. However, few of these writers mention 'synthesis' explicitly. Some attempt to visualise the relationships between concepts and researchers is presented in Figure 1. By way of introducing the use of socio-network analysis graphics of interest in this paper, the concepts and researchers are presented as nodes around a circle, and their relationship as diagonal lines across the circle. This is a presentation style adopted by Netmap. Notice that the concepts and authors are linked with no timelines and no physical orientation. The diagonal lines in this example represent authors who have discussed the concepts.

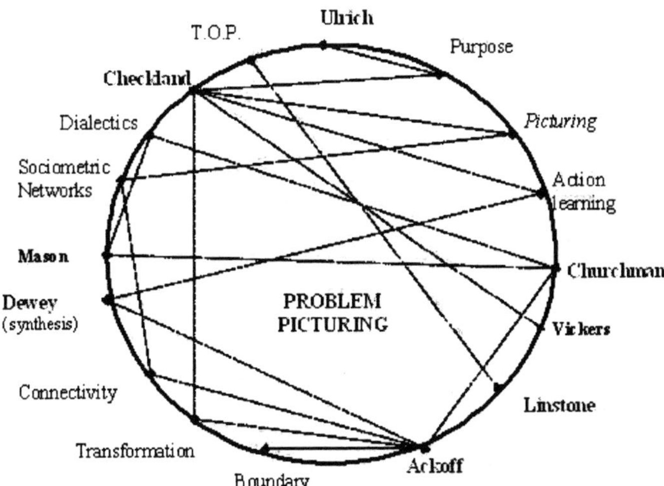

Figure 1. Problem Picturing and Synthesis: A Socio-Network

Dewey's (1910) book, *How We Think*, which has been foundational to the system thinking stream used here, lays the basis for learning by doing, empirics as informing prior thoughts, and the rally cry, "Don't analyse, synthesise". This cry, although still being used by Ackoff (2000), needs a little translation for younger researchers as the word synthesis has changed first to mean "compromise" and now to a chemical process. Its meaning as a thinking style seems faint, while the term analyse has become synonymous with thinking. Dewey sees "analyse" as reductionism, looking inwardly at the problem not outwardly, dividing the problem into elements (variables) and studying these separately. This is the preferred approach of scientific thinking. By synthesis, he appears to mean stand outside the problem - the problem is an example or subset of wider problem. What is the bigger problem of which it is a part? Think of analogies to the problem. He uses the example of the problem of suction water-pumps and why water can be sucked up only to a height of 33 feet. Analysis means looking at the water, pump and vacuum perhaps at a chemical level. Synthesis means asking what a 33 foot tube full of unsupported water is analogous to. Dewey argues that synthesis leads to understanding there must be some force pushing down on the water to force it up so high - thus an appreciation of atmospheric pressure. This synthesis approach therefore suggests that an appropriate problem-solving question is, "What is the problem part of, what is the wider system, and what is analogous to the problem situation?"

2.1. Connections

Ackoff (2000), who seems to use a lot of Dewey's thinking, has been trying to promote innovative human activity problem solving for a long time. It is tempting to think it started when his schoolteacher dismissed his innovative solution to a paper and pencil exercise. He is now over 70. For a 3 hour video summary of his work see "Judgelink" (2000). His famous style is to explain his system for answering problems by recounting problem solving experiences (storytelling?), allowing the student to induce the systems thinking concepts. Coupled with this is his student project approach to teaching problem solving, which aligns with Argysis' double loop learning-by-doing using an intellectual upfront frame. Given this style, the author induces that Ackoff draws on at least the following set of core concepts as mental prompts towards a synthesis approach to problems. These include exploring the connections between entities in the problem, seeing the problem as a sub-set of a larger system and seeking the perspectives of those involved in the problem. Later these will be used to design a problem picturing process.

2.2. Purpose

Ulrich's (1983) system to find answers to human activity problems draws heavily on the concept of purposefulness. He identifies purpose as an emergent property of complex thinking that only humans have achieved. Humans can have "purposeful actions" and problems occur when purpose is frustrated. Purpose is distinguished from other teleology concepts such as vision and goals as being inclusive of a "why" explanation. The purpose explains why an action is being undertaken, so my purpose in writing this paper includes "because" I want feedback on my picturing process. Ulrich calls for synthesis by thinking about the purpose given to a problem solution attempt by all stakeholders; why are they trying to solve the problem and why do they like certain solutions. The designer may see a different purpose than users and operators. Objectifying the problem away from these stakeholders' purpose is discouraged because it provides the intrinsic motivation of the stakeholders. Purpose (stating why) defines the relationships that are important for the system to transform its inputs into its outputs.

Ulrich also makes the point that stakeholders do not know what they don't know, suggesting the need for a process that encourages stakeholders to "systematically appreciate" a problem, and so think about things that might have been forgotten or blind-sighted. For example, the process might encourage questions like, "Why does the problem exist in the first place?" Some Australian Aboriginal peoples have long used this question as a problem appreciation process by suggesting that troubled people go to a place symbolic of their birth and think what their ancestors would advise. The reasoning being that Aboriginal people have successfully existed for over 40,000 years, so the ancestors must have solved this problem. The problem would not exist if the ancestors' ways had been followed. This type of thinking can be listed as a synthesis as it encourages thoughts about whether there is an analogous system that does not have the problem.

2.3. Perspectives

Linestone (1999) has also developed a system for thinking about problems, which is similar to ideas from Popper, Freud and Boulding. His TOP approach uses the idea of introducing explicit perspectives to a problem by way of linguistic hints, which draw on the idea of perceiving problems into how a scientist would see the problem and reasonable solutions (a technical analysis, T), how an organisational head (or sociologist) would see the problem and reasonable solutions (an organisational analysis, O) and how individuals (or psychologist) would see the problem and possible solutions. This can be woven into Boulding's division of the world into things (T), organisations/culture (O) and people (P). These can then be operationalised into three levels of iterations; boundary, analysis and synthesis. The first level, boundary setting, involves broadening the thinking by simply asking what and who are the 1) things (T), 2) organisations (O) and 3) people (P) involved in the problem. At the second or analysis level, TOP can be used to seek details about the problem maybe from the stakeholders by asking them for their personal, technical and (if relevant) organisational concerns. Asking for the stakeholders' technical (T) concerns might prompt questions about possible computations or machine specifications relevant to the problem. The organisational (O) perspective might include inter-organisational tensions (see Nielsen's types of tensions discussed below) due to say power issues, different work ethics, self interest and so on. The P or personal perspective might include questioning how the problem affects the self-esteem (mana) of those involved and what individuals could do in response. At the third or synthesis level, the TOP can be used to turn the things (T), inter-organisational tensions (O) and people (P) into broadening perspectives, not *their* perspective but *as a perspective*. For example, at the first or boundary level, a thing (T) involving the stock exchange may include a ticketing machine. At the second or analysis level, its rate of producing tickets per second may be its technical (T) analysis. At the third or synthesis level, ticketing machines can be used as a perspective on the problem, for example, how the ticketing machine industry would perceive the stock exchange problem. This folding back of TOP into three phases of boundary, analysis and synthesis is a core concept in the picturing illustration provided below.

2.4. Perspective Knowledge

Churchman's (1971, 1979) system for finding answers to problems is outlined in books like Systems Thinking and Its Enemies, and The Design of Inquiry Systems. He focuses on taking a synthesis approach to the inquiry process. He points out that all evidence will be flawed to some extent and the point of acquiring knowledge is to increase the number of choices. Knowledge, as supported by Kuhn's (1970) idea of paradigms, involves both seeking detail about objects but also seeking new perspectives. A new perspective provides new knowledge. He points to five epistemologies, saying utilising all of them overcomes the perspective limitations of each. For example, each has a different way to guarantee quality of knowledge. Churchman's approach to synthesis comes out as his putting heavy emphasis on asking questions about the context, including history, of problems. Context includes appreciating that the values of a stakeholder will alter his or her perspective of the problem and what the satisfactory answer is for him or her.

Nearly all the systems designs for answering problems mentioned here, especially Churchman's, advocate the importance of appreciating and questioning the perspective of all stakeholders. This is based on an interpretive epistemology where human problems occur because people have different perceptions of events treated as real. Synthesis often includes "mixing' these stakeholders" perspectives (metaphors). That is, innovation is seen as bringing new combinations of perspectives to an old object. These perspectives seem to come in two forms. The first, which might be called people's primary lens, value driven perspective or "concerns", result from a person's background, experience and worries, and affect how they see a problem and possible solutions. Monk and Howard (1998) agree that the design of human activity needs to take into account these divergent *concern perspectives* of stakeholders. The second type of perspective, which Haynes (2000) calls "Perspectival Thinking", is more externally imposed such as when Morgan (1986) calls for a metaphoric perspective on organisational activity, and Linstone (1999) calls considering a problem in terms of the things, organisations and people (TOP). Argyris's theory in use versus espoused theories (Argyris and Schon, 1996) may be another way of making this distinction, as Argyris is concerned that people will espouse imposed rational perspectives for believing a problem exists or resisting a solution (such as efficiency) rather than the personal perspective (such as loss of face). Synthesis is seen to include making both these perspectives explicit, but it is believed that the more personal ones will dominate reasoning. This can be used to design problem picturing.

2.5. Underlying Tensions

Karl Marx is not well known as a system thinker but Sowell (1985), argues that Marx and Engle's inquiry approach encourages synthesis by suggesting that physical events need to be thought of in terms of the "underlying dialectic forces" that created them. Appreciating these forces was believed to help solve problems, such as the plight of the working class. Analysing their situation in terms of their numbers, location, income, health or hours worked per week was not enough. Marx used the classic example of saying that careful analysis of caterpillars will provide a poor sort of knowing if you do not know about the butterfly. The underlying tensions they were mainly concerned with were the political and social forces associated with the class struggle. Their method, however, can be extrapolated to all human activity problem solving by questioning the underlying tensions that created the problem. Mason and Mitroff (1981) and Mason (1969) have, over a number of years, elaborated on the concept of dialectics following on from Churchman's (1971) work. They are mainly interested, however, in the use of competitive tension to improve synthesis. Nielsen (1996) provides a classification of possible tensions in organisational change problems, pointing out that these can differ in terms of resulting emotionality; they do not have to be quarrelsome, aggressive or conflictive but they can be. They include tensions caused by differing ideas, in a gap between practice and policy, in a failure to use established bureaucratic procedures, having different visions of the future and in vying for resources. Understanding these tensions provides a synthesis for a problem but the tensions may also be used to improve synthesis of a situation by encouraging stakeholders to be competitive in their thinking.

2.6. Reflection

Checkland (2000) summarises his work in a thirty-year retrospective on the evolution of his system for finding answers to problems (soft systems methodology) drawing heavily on his 1983 book *Systems Thinking, Systems Practice*. He seems to integrate the idea of purpose with "root definition" and "transformation", saying they define each other. Interestingly for those who claim to be "outcomes" focused, he wades into this as being too prescriptive in dynamic situations, using Vickers as his reference. He sees purpose as defining the set of acceptable outcomes. Thereby focusing on purpose gives problem solutions more flexibility. Checkland's "LUMAS" model seems to be the essence of his system for problem appreciation, which, while he rarely makes the connections between his and other "system for thinking" researchers' work, does look like a useful operationalisation of Argyris and Schon's double loop learning. The essence being that problems need to be treated as dynamic – they change through thinking about them and a think, trial an idea, and reflect, re trial etc… is a preferable way to answer problems. As mentioned earlier, he advocates using a process of picturing as a learning-by-doing act, which doubles as a way of building of common understanding of a problem. Argyris and Schon (1996) suggest that the action of picturing is reflected upon against a pre-conceived explicit perspective or intellectual framework. The intellectual frame presented here is synthesis, which, when coupled with picturing, can act as an aid to systematically thinking about human activity problem.

3. SYNTHESISING SYSTEMS-THINKING FOR PROBLEM PICTURING

Some attempt will now be made to combine this mainly systems thinking literature to suggest a facilitation process that involves drawing a picture as part of a collaborative thinking process. Put more formally, the literature above will provide the theory, (perspective, intellectual frame) to design a problem picturing process. To escape the label of rich picturing and to emphasise it as an interactive process rather than a finished object, the term "problem picturing" will be used. To ease the explanation of the application of the frame to the process, an illustration is provided. The aim is to use the synthesis concepts from systems thinking but to keep the process rules to a minimum. What follows is merely one possible approach so readers are, of course, encouraged to develop alternatives. No attempt will be made to "prove" that the approach is useful, or collect the impressions of users, as the main aim of this short paper is to develop one possible frame for problem picturing.

The illustration used is that of wishing to "systematically appreciate" the problem of aids monies not being used effectively in some countries due to political corruption.[2] This picturing process is best undertaken using a stakeholder group, but can be used to think about the problem privately. In both cases, the stages suggested below should be thought of as discussion prompts aimed at encouraging thought so as to avoid "blind-sighting". The ritual for problem picturing involves defining the boundary of the problem and its analysis by identifying the relevant elements that exist inside this boundary. Once drawn, the picturing elements can be used to encourage a wide range of creative perspectives on the problem. This, it is hoped, will lead to a creative solution, but, at worse, should provide a systematic appreciation (definition) of the problem domain. As was stated at the outset, the picturing process is intended to provide a systematic means of thinking about a problem. It is not intended to produce a chart that can be used like text to communicate with those who were not present. East (2002) reports that such picturing was useful in reminding those who were present of some of the issues that were raised at the meeting.

3.1. Set The Problem Boundary

1. Using Ackoff's and Ulrich's ideas, first state in a short sentence what the problem is – using Ackoff's definition of a problem as the gap between what is happening and what is sought. This problem statement can make up the picturing title. In this example, it is that international aid monies are not being spent effectively on the assigned projects. East (2002) reports, as argumentative inquiry supports (Crosswhite, 1996) that getting this upfront statement of the problem is important as, without knowing the exact problem, some confusion about the purpose of the whole picturing exercise can become unclear.
2. Using ideas from the socio-metric network research, draw a large circle to denote what you identify as the system that bounds the problem; e.g. monitoring aid projects in Africa. Using Checkland's and Ulrich's ideas on purpose, state why the system exists; eg. to ensure the $$$ are well spent (see Figure 2)

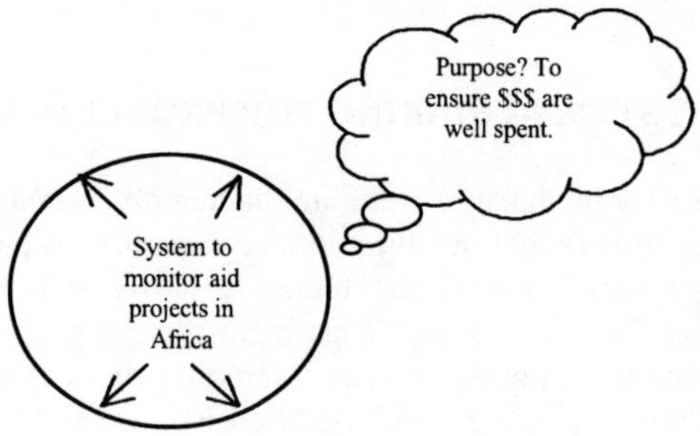

Figure 2. System and purpose

[2] With acknowledgements to David King, University of South Australia.

3.2. Analysis

1. The next step is to seek more details of the system, ie. to analyse. Linstone's TOP can be used here as prompts to include as much as the group feels is relevant. Draw as nodes around the circle the P(eople) (stakeholders) in this system a) the analysts or scientists observing the system and reporting to decision makers; b) those who represent organisations that have an interest in the system eg. bank managers and; c) those who represent the general public or users. It is up to those present to identify and classify these as they think most relevant to the problem domain.

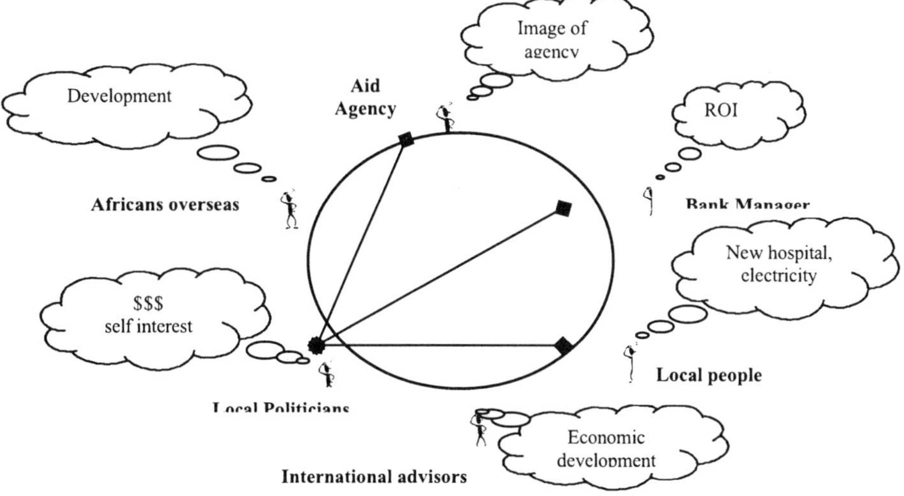

Figure 3. Stakeholders' concerns

2. The next part of the analysis is to seek the stakeholders' main concerns over this system. This may be drafted as text in thought bubbles (see Figure 3). To keep things simple, assume the concerns of the stakeholders are aligned with their perspective as presented in step 1. The analyst or scientist (Ts) will be concerned about technical issues such as quantities and specifications. The people representing organisations (Os) will be concerned about organisational issues such as their organisations exposure to risk. The general public or users (Ps) will have personal concerns like safety, face and food. If these stakeholders' concerns are seen to be in conflict, then draw a tension line across the circle between the two in conflict. This is intended to reveal underlying tensions as suggested by Neilsen (1996) and Sowell (1985).
3. Next draw as nodes the objects or (T)hings involved in the problem, eg. building materials, communications (telephone, Internet ...), the project itself, other infrastructure and so on. Note that under the socio-metric analysis perspective, all the nodes placed on the circle edge are "interconnected" as parts of the system. The advantage of the circle representation, rather than some physical or

process mapping, is that all preconceptions of physical or process "association" have been removed.

4. Last, add the nodes for the (O)rganisations involved. As many of these will already have been included as persons, an alternative is to add "concepts". For example, concepts like democracy, open government, and community collaboration might be added (see Figure 4).

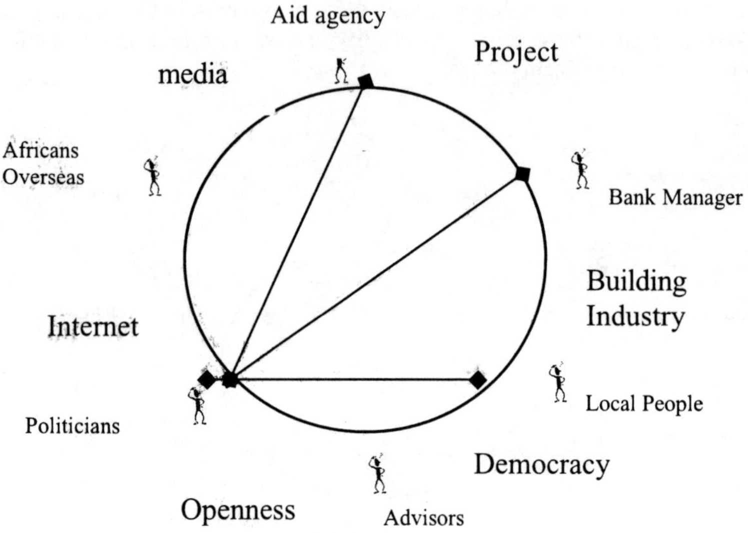

Figure 4. Organisations and concepts

3.3. Synthesis

The intention here is to broaden thinking about the details in the picture by encouraging a standing back and seeing the problem as a sub part of wider system or "zooming out". The people, things and organisational tensions presented around the circle and through the circle can be used to generate perspectives (not *their* perspective). For example, using the building materials node the problem can be thought about from the building industry's perspective. How would the building supplies companies see this problem of aid monies not being used effectively? Are they losing sales opportunities, is it just an extreme form of the security problems they deal with all over the world? Another perspective may be that of the media node. How does the international media see the problem? Maybe they see it as a free speech issue, where the role of the media as whistleblower has been oppressed. The tension between local politicians and the bank financial controls due to corruption may be used to seek another perspective. How does the corruption industry see this problem? Syphoning public expenditure corruption may be seen as one style of decision-making or costs in dealing with Governments which has its advantages and disadvantages. Honest but conflicted politicians and democratic process can be expensive in its own way.

It may well be worth recording the attempts made here to see the problem from the different perspectives provided by the picturing. Possible solutions to the problem often lie in these perspectives as they do in appreciating that these perspectives exist.

3.4. Analysis Revisited

Of course, a solution may not automatically fall out from the picturing process just suggested. The purpose was to apply some sort of systematic approach that first analysed the problem domain and then synthesised the perspectives. As mentioned in the introduction, it is very important to get the waterfall model of problem solving out of our minds (Guindon, 1990). Rather, the intention here is to provide a process that integrates the problem appreciation and solution processes. If a metaphor is sought to replace the waterfall one for what is imagined here, it might be the children's board game "snakes and ladders" where good ideas provide "up-ladders" and "formal evaluation" possible "down-snakes". This aligns with Guindon's and other's observation that while going through a problem appreciation exercise like the above, those present will automatically form what might be called "tentative conjecture solutions" which are ill thought out solutions that, if discussed within the group, might lead to a useful solution or at least some learning.

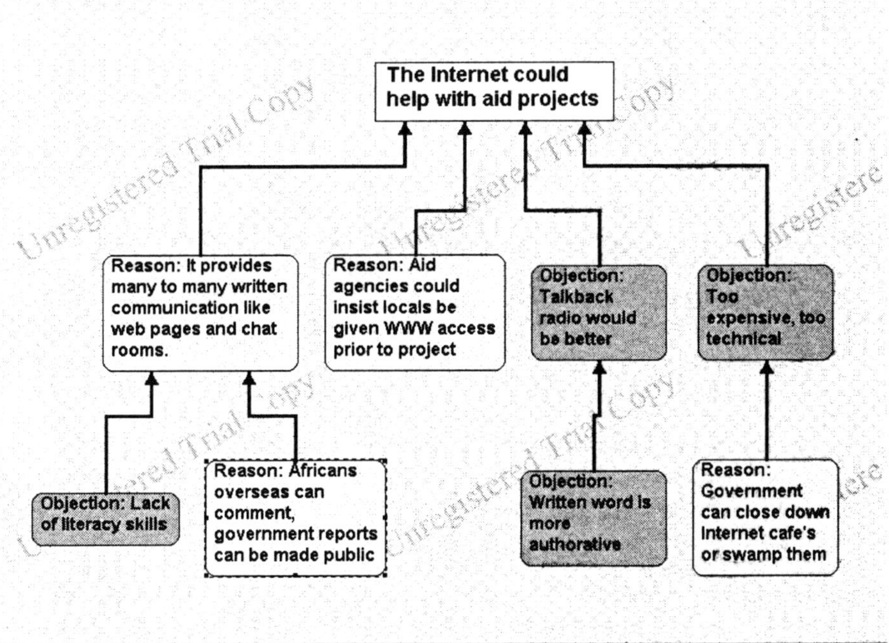

Figure 5. An Example of an Argument Map

Therefore, if a solution has not been found after the analysis and synthesis picturing suggested above, a closure analysis stage may be undertaken. The intent is to bring some explicit closure by having something concrete to take away from the process. What is suggested is at least the recording of some of the tentative conjecture solutions as recorded statements.

Drawing on the Miller's Magic Number 5 research,[3] either during or immediately after the discussion generated by the picturing, those present should be asked (independently if possible) to suggest 5 to 7 tentative conjecture solution statements that they feel the majority present may agree with, i.e. tentative common-ground solutions. An example maybe that, "the internet could be used to provide project details and stakeholder feedback on aid projects if it were insisted upon and supported by the aid agencies". Those present could be asked to edit these statements (and the others) until the majority present agree (List, 2001). Alternatively, these tentative solution statements could be prioritised and then used as input to a further mapping process such as Gelder's (2002) argument mapping which he uses to assist group think through the supporting and counter evidence for the tentative conjectures. An example of a finished map is provided in Figure 5 with a sample tentative statement at the top and the supporting and counter evidence below. The tentative conjecture is being analysed for supporting evidence.

4. CONCLUSION

This paper has argued that part of system design, problem definition and appreciation, may be improved by developing picturing techniques that assist collaborative thinking. System development as a wicked problem is expected to get more complicated, a wider range of worldviews will need to be appreciated, while cross cultural and function communications can be expected to add to the problem. There are a few tools available to help the developer think but these do not appear to have been developed from the Dewey inspired systems thinking literature so a possible picturing approach using his synthesis ideas was discussed. The method also drew from a mixture of perspectival thinking and socio-network analysis. It was presented as being useful as a stand-alone tool to aid problem appreciation or for problem solving when used with tentative conjecture statements and argumapping. The central idea was to use the picturing first to ensure all the elements of the problem domain were present (analysis), and then to use each of these elements to produce a synthesis of perspectives on the problem. An example was provided.

Pictures that are created as part of and to assist collaborative thinking need to be distinguished from using 'finished' pictures such as flow charts that only act to aid asynchronous communication. This paper was concerned about the former. As an aid to thinking, problem picturing can be used to stimulate thought while overcoming the problems of inter-cultural communications and text-based brainstorming which with globalisation is becoming an important issue. Problem picturing, as a process, is also believed to interactively normalise diverse stakeholders' mental images of the problem domain and, with the particular approach suggested in this paper encourage a dialectic between analysis thinking and synthesis thinking. However, this sort of picturing is of

[3] Which is a good example of Argyris' one-liner actionable knowledge.

little use to those not present at the picturing session, so care must be taken to avoid using the finished map in the same way as flow or entity-relationship maps are used to communicate with strangers asynchronously.

Picturing to assist thinking about problem solving is an interesting methodology. As presented here, it also serves to provide an alternative to the waterfall approach to problem solving. Problem appreciation and evolution of tentative conjecture solutions into new solutions presents a much more "snakes and ladders" approach to socially constructing solutions to wicked human activity problems. It was hoped that this paper will prompt further thought and research in providing a conceptual basis for the use of picturing to aid collaborative thinking.

REFERENCES

Ackoff, 2000, www.judgelink.org

Argyris C., 1996, Actionable Knowledge, *Journal of Applied Behavioural Science*, Vol 32(4), 390–406.

Argyris, C. and Schon, D. A., 1996, *Organisational Learning II*, Massachusetts: Addison Wesley.

Bronte-Stewart, M, 1999, Regarding Rich Pictures as Tools for Communication in Information Systems Development, *Computing and Information Systems,* Vol 6, 83–102

Checkland, P., 2000, Soft Systems Methodology: A Thirty Year Retrospective, *Systems Research and Behavioural Science,* Vol 17 Number 1, S11–S58.

Churchman, C. W., 1979, *Systems Thinking and Its Enemies,* NY: Basic Books.

Churchman, C. W., 1971, *The Design of Inquiring Systems*, Wiley, New York.

Crosswhite, J., 1996, *The Rhetoric of Reason,* University of Wisconsin Press.

Dewey J., 1910, *How We Think,* Lexington Mass: DC Heath.

East, C., 2002, Structuring Rich Picturing: A Case Study, *IFIP 8.6*, Sydney, August.

Eden, C. and Ackermann, F., 1998, *The Journey of Strategic Change*, Chichester: Sage.

Gelder, van T., 2002, *Argument Mapping*, http://www.austhink.org/

Guindon, R., 1990, Designing the Design Process, *Human Computer Interaction*, Vol 5, 305–344.

Haynes, J., 2000, *Perspectival Thinking*, NZ: OneIdea Company.

Hughes, J., 1998, Selection and Evaluation of IS, *IEE Proceedings Software*, Vol 145 (4), 100.

Kogut, B., 1998, The Network as Knowledge, University of Pennsylvania, Wharton School Working Paper.

Kuhn, T. S., 1970, *The structure of scientific revolutions*, 2nd Ed., University of Chicago Press.

Lanzing, 1997, Conceptual Mapping, http://users.edte.utwente.nl/lanzing/cm_home.htm also see Analytic Technology, 2002, Socio-metric networks http://analytictech.com/

Linstone, H. A., 1999, *Decision Making for Technology Executives: Using Multiple Perspectives*, Artech House Publishing: Boston.

List, D., 2001, The Consensus Group Method, Working paper: University of South Australia, 2001.

McFadzean E., 1988, Developing and Supporting Creative Problem Solving Teams, Management Decision, Vol 40(5), 463–475.

Mason, R. O. and Mitroff, I. I., 1981,*Challenging Strategic Planning Assumption,* John Wiley and Sons, New York, NY.

Mason, R. O., 1969, *A Dialectical Approach to Strategic Planning*, Management Science, Vol 15, B-403–B-414.

Metcalfe, M., 2002, The Argumentative Systems For IS Design, *IT and People* Vol 15(1), 60–73.

Monk, A. and Howard, S., 1998, The Rich Picture: A tool for reasoning about work context, *Interactions*, March/April.

Morgan, G., 1986, *Images of Organisations,* Calif.: Sage Publications.

Nielsen, R. P., 1996, Varieties of Dialectic Change Processes, *Journal of Management Enquiry*, vol 5, issue 3.

Nossiter, V. and Biberm'n, G., 1988, Projective Drawings and Metaphor, *Journal of Managerial Psychology* Vol 5(3), 13.

Phillips, D. C., 1969, Systems Theory, a Discredited Philosophy, 5th Canberra Seminar on Administrative Studies, ANU May.

Popper, K., 1963, *Conjectures and Refutations*, London: Paul Routledge.

Questmap, 2002, http://www.touchstone.com/tr/wp/IBIS.html

Sowell, T., 1985, *Marxism*, London: Unwin.

Ulrich, W., 1983, *Critical Heuristics of Social Planning,* Wiley, New York.
Williams, M. C., 2002, Application of Soft Systems To Reveal Management Problems in a Computing Company, *Journal of Applied Systems Studies*. (forthcoming)
Weber, S., 1986, Systems To Think With, *Journal of Management Information Systems*, Vol II(4), 85–97.

USING COGNITIVE MAPPING FOR PROBLEM ANALYSIS IN INFORMATION REQUIREMENTS DETERMINATION

Judy McKay and Peter Marshall*

1. INTRODUCTION

This research grew out of concerns that information systems projects (defined here to include both in-house development, and the acquisition, modification and implementation of externally-produced package software) often result in less than satisfactory outcomes, with stories of failure and disappointments with respect to information systems (IS) being relatively common in both professional and academic literature (Montealegre and Keil, 2000; Keil and Robey, 2001). An analysis of the literature considering these failures suggests that there are repeated concerns that the analysis conducted at the early stages fails to pay sufficient attention to human and organisational issues, and that the subsequent requirements specification developed fails to accurately reflect the real needs of users and organisations (Martinsons and Chong, 1999). Failure to adequately determining requirements almost certainly indicates that the implemented system will disappoint or fail in use (Korac-Boisvert and Kouzmin, 1995; Ewusi-Mensah, 1997).

Similar issues in Management Science/Operations Research (MS/OR) resulted in the emergence of "soft" MS/OR approaches, designed specifically to take account of the range of human and organisational issues encountered in organisational problem solving (Jackson, 2000). Thus, it was decided to conduct research to see whether one such approach, cognitive mapping (Eden and Ackermann, 1998), could effectively be applied to the early stages of requirements analysis to help ameliorate some of the problems currently occurring in IS projects.

---

* Judy McKay, Monash University, Melbourne, Victoria, 3145. Peter Marshall, Mt Eliza Business School, Melbourne, Victoria, 3004.

2. CAUSES OF FAILURE IN IS PROJECTS

Following an analysis of the literature concerning IS failures, a number of recurrent themes emerge of direct interest to this research. Amongst those factors often cited as contributing to failure and difficulty with systems development projects are the following:

- The IS basically addressed the 'wrong' problem (Ewusi-Mensah 1997, Keil et al. 1998)
- Errors were made in identifying user information requirements (Ewusi-Mensah and Przasynski 1994, Keil et al. 1998).
- Communication difficulties existed between and amongst groups of users and analysts (Ewusi-Mensah 1997).
- The information and systems requirements changed during the process of ISD, rendering the delivered product inappropriate to meet current needs (Korac-Boisvert and Kouzmin 1995, Siddiqi and Shekaran 1996, Ewusi-Mensah 1997, Flynn 1998).
- Broader organisational issues, such as the culture and political climate tended to be ignored or overlooked (Flynn 1998, Martinsons and Chong 1999).
- User expectations of the system were unrealistic (Keil et al. 1998).

These common threads of ISD failure, all associated with the IRD phase, namely inaccurately assessing the scope and nature of the problem, ignoring broader organisational issues, communication difficulties, and the challenge of accurately defining information requirements were all seen as interrelated, and hence were the subject of this research. If IS are to consistently contribute to enhancing organisational performance along a number of dimensions, then our understanding and practice of IRD needs to improve if the problem of systems failures and disappointments is to be redressed.

3. SOFT MS/OR AND COGNITIVE MAPPING

Soft MS/OR approaches generally acknowledge the primacy of human actors in any problem solving activity (Jackson, 2000). The main concern of these approaches is to explore the perceptions, values, beliefs and interests of stakeholders in the problem solving activity, and hence they need to articulate a procedure for exploring or structuring debate about differing, often conflicting viewpoints (Checkland, 1981). Thus, learning about and understanding the mental models by which individuals make sense of their environment and construct their social reality is an important function (Jackson, 2000).

Cognitive mapping is an approach designed to support decision makers in dealing with the complexity and interdependency inherent in many organisational problem situations (Eden, 1989). It is based upon an interpretivist and subjectivist view of the individual and organisations (Jackson, 2000). Thus, in an organisational problem solving context, individual members are each regarded as possessing their own almost unassailable view of what constitutes the problem, and of what would constitute an improvement in that problem context (Eden, 1989), expressed via a cognitive map. Problems, thus, are not believed to "exist" in the real-world, but arise from differences in perspective and interpretation of situations in the real-world. Problem solving activity thus involves the airing of individual perspectives and interpretations, the surfacing and discussion of different individual constructs by which a situation is deemed to be problematic, and negotiation on ways of moving forward (Eden and Ackermann, 1998). Cognitive maps have been described as "graphic representations that locate people in relation to their information environments" (Fiol and Huff, 1992). Thus, a cognitive map is typically a representation of beliefs about a particular situation, based on the knowledge, experience and value system of that individual. Cognitive mapping is used as a modelling device, providing a representation of a situation (or perceptions and interpretations of a situation), thus aiding description, analysis and understanding. Cognitive maps serve an important function for a number of reasons. Firstly, they serve to help each individual clarify and structure their thinking, and to gain a deeper appreciation of their own understanding of the problem context (Eden, 1992). Thus, they are helpful in providing structure to individual perceptions and interpretations. Secondly, the maps act as negotiative devices between and amongst analyst and participants, with the aim of gaining shared understanding, increased creative thinking, and moving the group towards a consensus (Eden, 1989).

Given the problems associated with IRD, and the specific orientation of cognitive mapping, a research project was designed to establish its effectiveness for IRD.

4. RESEARCH OBJECTIVES AND QUESTIONS

The research was conducted with one overarching aim, that of establishing whether cognitive mapping is effective for problem analysis in the information requirements determination. Given the arguments leading to this research, and yet still within this broad aim, a number of subordinate questions can be identified.

1. *Are key participants in the IRD process (users and analysts) satisfied that cognitive mapping is helpful in defining the nature and scope of the problem at hand?*

Adequately defining the scope of the problem, and indeed, having a good understanding of the 'real' problem that the proposed system is supposed to ameliorate, was previously argued to be a major contributing factor to problems with IRD. However, it is not necessarily a simple task for users to articulate the nature of their problem situation. Thus, it is imperative that approaches to IRD support the articulation and understanding of the problem(s) of concern.

2. *Does cognitive mapping seem to be helpful in supporting the articulation and validation of information requirements?*

The modelling technique of cognitive mapping is viewed as an important device in helping the articulation and validation of information requirements.

3. *Does cognitive mapping support the emergence of different perspectives and the management of the human and other organisational issues inherent in IRD?*

A variety of human, social, cultural and political issues have been found to emerge and cause difficulty during the IRD process. If an approach is to improve the IRD process, then it would need to offer some means of managing interpersonal, political and other issues that may negatively impact on both the process itself and output of the IRD process.

4. *Does cognitive mapping facilitate communication, negotiation and dialogue during the IRD process, thus contributing to an improved shared understanding amongst the key participants?*

Poor communication and a lack of shared understanding amongst and between analysts and users was shown previously to have consistently caused problems during IRD (Ewusi-Mensah and Przasynski, 1994). In addition, failure to reach agreement on requirements to improve the problem situation can also result in less than satisfactory outcomes (Siddiqi and Shekaran, 1996). Proponents of cognitive mapping, have consistently argued that the maps act as powerful negotiative devices, facilitating dialogue out of which grows an increased shared understanding. These would seem key features of an approach if it were to be helpful in improving the practice of IRD.

5. RESEARCH METHOD AND DESIGN

The nature of the research objectives dictate that the research be conducted in a real-life organisational setting without contrivance. The research does not seek to impose some external objective scheme to measure the effectiveness of outcomes, but instead relies on the subjective perceptions and evaluations of those directly affected by the organisational intervention. All these factors indicate that an interpretivist philosophy is underpinning the research.

There is no way of trying out a new methodology for IRD without intervening in the problem context (Baskerville and Wood-Harper, 1996). Thus a major strength of action research, and a key factor for selecting it for this research, was its acceptance of researcher involvement and collaboration with participants in the research context.

An organisation willing to participate in the research with an appropriate IRD-type problem was identified, and negotiations to establish who would participate, their respective roles, responsibilities and accountabilities, resource requirements, the boundaries and scope of the intervention, and the goals and objectives for the project were held. The actual organisational intervention was planned to involve the use of cognitive maps with the participants to support problem analysis and articulation of requirements, all guided by the SODA methodology. In an iterative process, cognitive maps were drawn based on workshop-type discussions with the participants, and were subsequently verified by the participants, with additions and modifications made. Thus process continued until reasonable stability was achieved and significant insights emerged. Some time after the end of the workshops, participants were interviewed as to their thoughts and feelings on the process that had been followed and the outcomes that had been achieved. Participants were also asked to complete a short questionnaire to ensure there was some consistency in their responses. Thus, the main data items collected and analysed were a series of cognitive maps, showing evolution and development over time, individual interviews, taped and transcribed, and individual questionnaire responses (based on an instrument developed by Limayem and Wanninger (1993) to assess participants' perceptions of the IRD process).

6. ACTION RESEARCH INTERVENTION

The research reported in this paper was undertaken in a semi-autonomous government agency (PA) established to manage a large port in Australia, where a review of the existing Workers' Compensation System (WCS) was deemed necessary and desirable.

6.1 Phase 1: Reconnaissance, Fact Finding, and Planning

The existing WCS had been built in 1989, and had been designed to provide support for and to automate parts of the previously existing manual system developed to administer the workers' compensation claims process at PA. However, it was somewhat limited in its functionality. The actual computerised component of the system required the same data to be entered more than once, inevitably resulting in inaccuracies and redundancies, and there were a number of known faults with the system. There were two main users of the system (referred to as P1 and P2), and they were supportive of the idea of revisiting the perceived problem(s) and their information requirements prior to redeveloping the system. The scope of our involvement (to support problem analysis and IRD for their new WCS), the process that was to be followed (SODA and cognitive mapping), our research interests and requirements, and accountabilities and responsibilities were identified, clarified and agreed upon by all parties prior to the commencement of the project.

6.2 Phase 2: Taking Action, Monitoring, Initial Evaluation and Reflection

At our initial meeting, we ranged over a variety of issues concerning the WCS, with Figure 1 capturing some of the reasons for their need for an efficient and effective WCS.

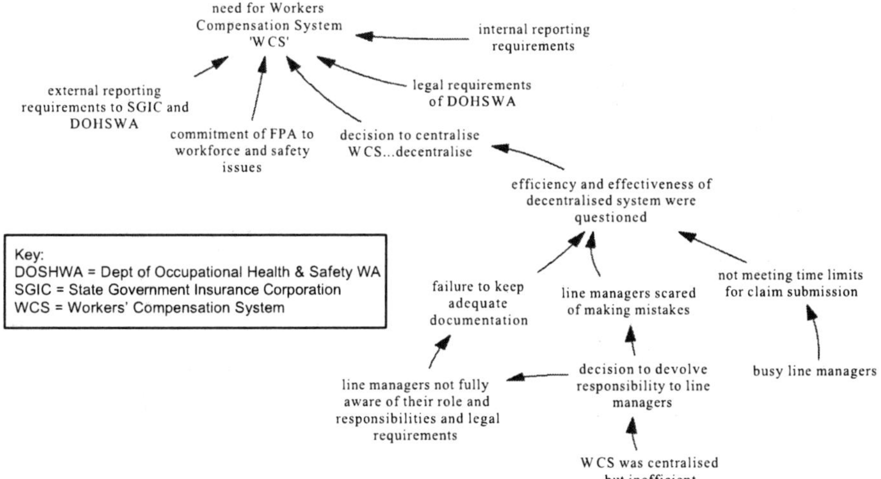

Figure 1. Mapping Early Conversations

Over time, some others issues emerged (see Figure 2). A discussion and analysis of the cognitive maps revealed that the real problem that they were experiencing with the existing WCS was not so much the cumbersome paperwork involved or the fact that there were a few known errors in the system, but had much more to do with safety issues.

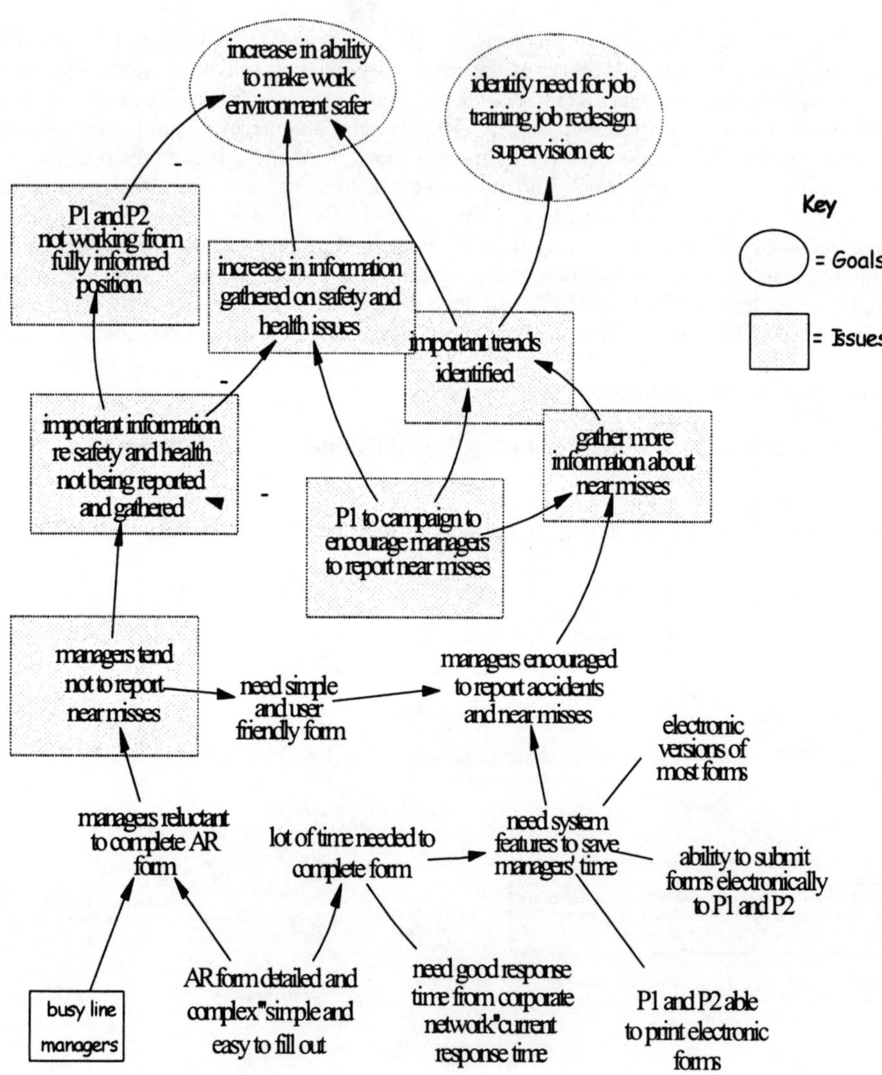

Figure 2. Emergent Needs for the WCS

With changes in the structure and management focus at PA, there was sudden interest and emphasis on occupational health and safety issues. P1 was frustrated at not being easily able to identify problems and trends in this regard. He had no way of knowing, for example, whether particular sections or occupations at PA were more prone to accidents and injuries than others, whether training and/or improved work procedures were effective in reducing accidents, whether seasonality could be a factor in accidents, whether particular employees were more prone to accidents than others, and so on. His frustration at not being easily able to access the information was being manifested in complaints about the WCS. But what the cognitive maps seemed to be indicating was that a clear set of goals and issues to do with port safety were emerging, and that existing systems provided no help with these matters.

Thus, an important function of the cognitive maps emerged. It seemed that the "goals" identified by the cognitive map (see Figure 2) were somewhat of a surprise to them, but were in fact in harmony with the way they thought. They just had not articulated those thoughts previously. So, for example, the map indicated that "improving safety" and "protect FPA from future claims" were goals of the system development effort, which P1 and P2 totally supported, but clearly from their reactions, they had not explicitly articulated nor thought of these as goals previously. They always spoke as though their needs were entirely based around rectifying problems with the old WCS.

By focusing on the expressed problem (that there were problems with the existing WCS which needed to be remedied), we had all tended, not unnaturally, to focus on the existing system, and had thus not "looked outside the box". Our investigations, conversations and analyses had thus apparently tacitly assumed that we were looking for and at the problems with the existing WCS, rather than perhaps posing the more challenging question of "What is/are the perceived problem(s)/issue(s) here? What is causing/contributing to this sense of unease that makes us believe that a new WCS is required?" By turning our focus to the goals emerging in the cognitive maps, it become very obvious that concerns about safety at FPA, about identifying trends, training needs and so on, and indeed in creating a work environment that was as safe as possible were emerging as being more important than the problems with the old WCS.

7. CONSIDERATION OF THE RESEARCH QUESTIONS

7.1 Research Question 1

Of interest here is to consider the participants' perceptions of the contribution of cognitive mapping in determining the nature and scope of the problem. Analysis of the interview transcripts reveal strong support for the role of cognitive mapping in helping to scope to problem area. Consider some of these responses:

P1: Very helpful in...in exploring the nature of a problem, and recording the...not only the logical flow of the argument. In a sense, it's ...it's everyone's ideas is captured in the...in the maps. So, it's not just a logical flow of argument, it's... it's several person's flow of argument, and...and their views of the issues.

P1: (responding to a question about the problem focus) Yes, it's as if, er, because we were not clear on the nature of the problem, and the previous technical analyst assumed that our problem was purely workers compensation because we'd somehow named the system that way...that he...that it was missed that the ..the real problem involved a lot of safety issues, because I think he was absolutely fixated on taking the workers compensation system as he saw it, and getting it down into computer and played up on screens.

In response to questions on what contributed to us uncovering a much broader scope to the problem, or in fact, two problems, these are indicative of their responses:

P1: *It was a ...a um, more informed and well rounded, er problem solving session, where the views of the participants were placed down on cognitive maps, maps which had a visual um... where you could see groups of ideas and their relationships, ...*

R: *But, so...in other words, this visual, the ability to visualise on the maps was very important for you, was it?*

P1: *Made an incredible difference. Made a huge difference to the way in which we approached the problem, the way we discussed issues, our focus on the issues, learning about the problem situation was um...helped very much by the cognitive mapping pictures of ideas, of relationships of concepts, of pictures of the sub-concepts within concepts,...*

P2: *Yes, it er...the cognitive maps have allowed us to chart our process...our progress in finding our requirements, and finding the nature of this problem. Actually I should say...um...what has appeared is that our worries we thought our worries were with the WC issue...system I should say...but the real issues were really in a separate but related area...that is the area of safety...*

On the post project questionnaire, the only question dealing directly with scoping the problem was Q18, for which both participants expressed strong agreement. Q19, Q20, and Q22, which are all rated as "greatly agree" or "strongly agree", also imply that the process of cognitive mapping was considered very effective in helping participants better understand the nature of scope of problem.

Table 1. Questionnaire Responses for Research Question 1

		P1's rating	P2's rating	Overall Assessment
18.	The process followed helped me to refine my understanding of the nature and scope of the problem.	7	7	Very strong agreement
19.	The process followed uncovered valid considerations that I did not think of individually.	7	7	Very strong agreement
20.	The process made me critically re-evaluate the validity of considerations that I had thought of individually.	6	7	Strong agreement
22.	The group meeting and the group maps enabled me to better understand the opinions of other members of the group.	6	7	Strong agreement

Considering the analyses of all the data collected, we believe we are justified in concluding that there is very strong support for research question 1.

7.2 Research Question 2

Analysis of the interview transcripts reveals quite strong support for the notion that SODA and cognitive mapping were helpful in supporting the articulation of the requirements for the system. Some comments made regarding this issue are as follows:

P1: Yes, they helped in...they helped us have a real...a graphic diagram of our understanding of the problem and to have that validated by other managers was ...was quite, er, help...was quite important in giving us confidence that we really understood the situation and that others understood the situation in...in the same way. That they ...they in fact validated our ...our...analysis of the situation.
R: So, would you say it's been an effective process?
P1: The most effective, um requirements determination process I've been involved in. Yes, very effective.

In terms of the questionnaire responses, Q21 deals directly with requirements, with both responses offering agreement or strong agreement on this score. Their support of this point was not quite as effusive as that for the first research question, but this may reflect the nature of this project as it evolved. We spent less time worrying about requirements per se, and devoted more time to concerns about what the problem "really" was.

Table 2. Questionnaire Responses for Research Question 2

		P1's rating	P2's rating	Overall assessment
21.	The process followed was helpful in enabling me to understand and articulate my requirements for this system.	7	5	Fairly strong agreement

When considering the data gathered, we feel quite justified in claiming that there is good support for research question 2.

7.3 Research Question 3

Perspectives emerged as an important issue for our participants. One of the notions that both P1 and P2 kept on bringing up during the interview was how useful cognitive maps were in being able to 'see' other people's views. Some of their comments on this were as follows:

P1: I was also helped by the...maps, and in particular, I was helped by being able to see the others' ideas, to see issues that I hadn't thought about and how they connected with what I thought was important.

P2: Yes, it...it enabled me to see that the reasoning in my um...in my own, er, views of the problem and my own arguments, but it also helped me really greatly in seeing what P1 and some of the others also thought...

Thus we see that an important feature for P1 and P2 was in being able to understand where others were coming from. Note how they always talk about another person's ideas, or views, and not about person themselves directly. This feature of problem solving approaches of various types has been found to reduce and manage conflict and political manoeuvring. This being the case, it might suggest that the cognitive maps are vital in getting ideas, not personalities, "out there" for discussion, and subsequently help to focus the debate on the issues, not the personalities.

Looking at the questionnaire data seems to reveal more support for this research question. Questions 6, 7, 8, 9, 16, 22 and 23 all tend to look at issues to do with the management of the process and understanding of other's perspectives. Thus we can conclude that according to our participants, the process was carefully developed, typically efficient, co-ordinated, fair, understandable and satisfying, that they were in agreement with the outcomes, that they had received reached a better understanding of other's ideas, that participants had been constructive examining issues, and had made fairly significant progress in reaching a consensus.

Table 3. Questionnaire Responses for Research Question 3

		P1's rating	P2's rating	)verall ssessment
6.*	The process followed through the project was: (1=carefully developed, 7=carelessly developed)	2	2	Strong agreement
7.	The manner in which the participants examined the issue was: (1=non-constructive, 7=constructive)	7	7	Very strong agreement
8.	The group's movement towards reaching a consensus on the project question was: (1=insignificant, 7=significant)	6	6	Strong agreement
9.*	How would you describe the process? a) (1=efficient, 7=inefficient)	1	2	Very strong agreement
	b) (1=coordinated, 7=uncoordinated)	2	2	Strong agreement
	c) (1=fair, 7=unfair)	1	1	Very strong agreement
	d) (1=understandable, 7=confusing)	1	2	Very strong agreement
	e) (1=satisfying, 7=dissatisfying)	2	2	Strong agreement
16.	I am satisfied with the group's conclusions and assumptions	6	6	Strong agreement
22.	The group meeting and the group maps enabled me to better understand the opinions of other members of the group.	6	7	Strong agreement
23.	Compared to before the process started, I have a much better understanding of how other members of the group view this issue.	6	7	Strong agreement

** indicates that a low rating is desirable*

Thus, consideration of all the data gives us confidence to assert that this suggests quite strong support for research question 3.

7.4 Research Question 4

The interview transcripts reveal some important views on the ability of SODA and cognitive mapping to aid communication and facilitate a shared understanding. Let's consider some of these comments:

P1: Yes I did...I, um, possibly to me the greatest advantage was to...well, there were two advantages as P2 said. To clarify my own thinking, and to get a detailed view of the other offices and managers that are involved...
P1: Yes, I think the...it becomes, you become much more aware of when you're digressing, than if you didn't have that map of idea.
P2: No, for me the greatest thing was being able to understand other people's viewpoints from the maps.
P1: thought the cognitive maps were a lot easier to understand than other diagramming techniques he had been exposed to.
P1: (talking about previous experience in communicating with an analyst) It was as if many of the things that I would mention that...problems with workers' compensation, with safety issues, with accidents, and so on, would go straight over his head, and we'd purely be discussing storage issues, the numbers of characters in things, some technical difficulties with the computers and screens and so on...screen layouts, and that sort of thing. We never...I could never get across to him that ...that there was some real business problems in this.

Further support for the research question is drawn from a consideration of the questionnaire data. Q8, 15, 16, 17, 19, 22, and 23 all seem indicative of high levels of satisfaction when it comes to issues of communication and movement towards a shared understanding.

Table 4. Questionnaire Responses for Research Question 4

		P1's rating	P2's rating	Overall assessment
8.	The group's movement towards reaching a consensus on the project question was: (1=insignificant, 7=significant)	6	6	Strong agreement
15.	I feel committed to the group's conclusions and assumptions.	7	7	Very strong agreement
16.	I am satisfied with the group's conclusions and assumptions	6	6	Strong agreement
17.	I am in complete agreement with the group's conclusions and assumptions	6	6	Strong agreement
19.	The process followed uncovered valid considerations that I did not think of individually.	7	7	Very strong agreement
22.	The group meeting and the group maps enabled me to better understand the opinions of other members of the group.	6	7	Strong agreement
23.	Compared to before the process started, I have a much better understanding of how other members of the group view this issue.	6	7	Strong agreement

Thus we would consider there to be strong, persuasive evidence to support research question 4.

8. CONCLUSION

Our study using cognitive mapping resulted in a recognition that a decision made (fix the WCS) was inadequate to address the concerns of affected parties, and that an alternative decision (specify the requirements for a safety management system) would result in better outcomes for the organisation. As researchers, we were able to test the effectiveness of cognitive mapping for problem analysis in IRD. Our beliefs about the efficacy of cognitive mapping for IRD, based on an extensive review of the literature on IS failure, IRD and soft MS/OR, were essentially upheld: the study confirmed that in the context of PA, cognitive mapping was helpful to support understanding the nature and scope of the problem, articulating requirements, managing perceptions, and for communicating and developing a shared understanding. Moreover, the participants showed strong satisfaction with both the process followed and the outcomes achieved.

REFERENCES

Checkland, P. B., *Systems thinking, systems practice*, Wiley, Chichester, 1981.

Eden, C., Using Cognitive Mapping for Strategic Options Development And Analysis (SODA), in: *Rational Analysis for a Problematic World*, J. Rosenhead, ed., Wiley, Chichester, 1989, pp. 21–42.

Eden, C., On the Nature of Cognitive Maps, *Journal of Management Studies*, 29:3, May 1992, 261–265.

Eden, C. and Ackermann, F., *Making Strategy: the Journey of Strategic Management*, Sage, London, 1998.

Ewusi-Mensah, K, Critical Issues in Abandoned Information Systems Development Projects, *Communications of the ACM*, 40:9, September 1997, 74–80.

Ewusi-Mensah, K. and Przasnyski, Z. H., Factors Contributing to the Abandonment of Information Systems Development Projects, *Journal of Information Technology*, 9:3, March 1994, 185–201.

Fiol, C. M. and Huff, A. S., Maps for Managers: Where are We? Where do We Go from Here?, *Journal of Management Studies*, 29:3, March 1992, 267–285.

Flowers, S., Information Systems Failure: Identifying the Critical Failure Factors, *Failure & Lessons Learned in Information Technology Management*, 1:1, 1997, 19–29.

Flynn, D. J., *Information Systems Requirements: Determination and Analysis*, 2nd ed., McGraw-Hill, London, 1998.

Flynn, D. J. and Arce, E. A., A CASE tool to support critical success factors in IT planning and requirements determination, *Information and Software Technology*, 39(5): 311–321.

Goldkuhl, G. and Rostlinger, A., Joint Elicitation of Problems: Important Aspects of Change Analysis, in: *Human, Organizational and Social Dimensions of Information Systems Development* (A-24), D. Avison, J.E. Kendall, and J. I. DeGross, eds., Elsevier Science, North Holland, 1993, pp. 107–125.

Hepworth, J. B., Vidgen, G. A., Griffin, E. and Woodward, A. M., The Enhancement of Information Systems through User Involvement in Systems Design, *International Journal of Information Management*, 12:2, June 1992, 120–129.

Jackson, M. C., *Systems Approaches to Management*, Kluwer Academic/Plenum Publishers, New York, 2000.

Keil, M. and Robey, D., Blowing the Whistle on Troubled Software Projects, *Communications of the ACM*, 44:4, April 2001, 87–93.

Keil, M., Cule, P. E., Lyytinen, K. and Schmidt, R. C., A Framework for Identifying Software Project Risks, *Communications of the ACM*, 41:11, November 1998, 76–83.

Korac-Boisvert, N. and Kouzmin, A., IT Development: Methodology Overload or Crisis?, *Science Communication*, 17:1, September 1995, 57–89.

Limayem, M. and Wanninger, L. A., The Use of a Group CASE Tool to Improve Information Requirements Determination, *Document de Travail*, 93-33, Université Laval, Quebec, Canada, 1993.

Martinsons, M. G. and Chong, P. K. C., The Influence of Human Factors and Specialist Involvement on Information Systems Success, *Human Relations*, 52:1, January 1999, 123–152.

Montealegre, R. and Keil, M. De-escalating Information Technology Projects: Lessons from Denver International Airport, *MIS Quarterly*, 24:3, June 2000, 417–447.

Siddiqi, J. and Shekaran, M. C., Requirements Engineering: the Emerging Wisdom, *IEEE Software*, 13:2, March 1996, 15–19.

A QUALITY MODEL FOR THE EVALUATION OF SOFTWARE REQUIREMENTS SPECIFICATIONS

Jennifer L. Gasston*

1. INTRODUCTION

A number of models for software *product* quality have been defined in the literature. *Hierarchical models* (for example McCall et al., 1977; Boehm et al., 1978) *Quantitative models* (for example Gilb, 1985, 1987) and *Product/process-based models* (for example Kitchenham, 1987). However, criticisms have been aimed at the product quality models in terms of the difficulties involved in their practical application.

Evaluations of product quality are largely limited to the identification of the presence of specific high-level intangible quality attributes such as functionality or reliability. The difficulties in identifying appropriate quality-carrying characteristics which relate to the high level attributes, and the lack of appropriate methods and tools to carry out product quality evaluations are the reasons that primarily product quality evaluations have been limited to the work products from the implementation phase.

In this paper we look at the development of models to evaluate the work products from other phases of the system development lifecycle (for example, the requirements specification, the system design and the final software). It has been argued that Requirements Engineering (RE) is one of the most important processes in systems development (Curtis et al., 1988; Lubas et al., 1993; Sommerville and Sawyer, 1997; Nuseibeh and Easterbrook, 2000). Therefore this is an appropriate starting point.

The work product from the Requirements Engineering process is the System Requirements Specification (SRS) document. Nuseibeh and Easterbrook (2000) give an excellent overview of Requirements Engineering, suggesting that the process draws upon cognitive psychology, anthropology, sociology, and linguistics, to "provide both theoretical grounding and practical techniques for eliciting and modelling requirements". The authors' discussion has contributed to the identification of the characteristics of a "quality" Software System Requirements Specification used to define a set of quality-carrying properties for each higher-level quality attribute in the model developed in this study.

* Jennifer L Gasston, Software Quality Institute, School of Computing and Information Technology, Griffith University, Nathan Qld, Australia.

The work of Dromey (1995, 1996) in the development of product quality models provides a practical framework for the development of a model since it provides us with a set of high-level quality attributes applicable to the work products from each software development phase. A feature of the framework is the need for the identification of, and a process for identification of, a set of *quality-carrying properties* for each product quality attribute, which provides a means of achieving a more detailed level of evaluation. Dromey's framework has been used in this study to explore the research question: *How can we evaluate the quality of Software Requirements Specifications?*

In order to address the research question, two sub-questions have been developed:

- *What are desirable quality attributes of the products produced from the Software Requirements Analysis and Specification process? and*
- *What are their corresponding quality-carrying properties?*

An evaluation instrument, in the form of a questionnaire, which relates to the achievement of the quality-carrying properties, has been developed from the quality model described in this paper. A set of questions relating to the achievement of each characteristic has been used during the evaluation process. The questions incorporate a multiple-point ordinal scale, suggested by Kitchenham and Pfleeger (1996) as important to the assessment of documentation quality. The validity of the approach has been tested through the examination of the work products of the Software Requirements Analysis and Specification processes used in two large projects within a case study organisation. An additional evaluation of the specifications was carried out using the ARM tool (Wilson et al., 1996) for evaluating software products.

The rest of the paper is organised as follows. In section 2, the framework used to develop the quality model is described. In section 3 the findings from the application of the model are presented and the paper concludes with some ideas for future research.

2. THE QUALITY MODEL TO EVALUATE SOFTWARE REQUIREMENTS SPECIFICATIONS

In 1991 an International Standard for Software Quality Measurement was developed: ISO/IEC 9126 (1991), which reflects the user-view of quality. The standard defines a general purpose quality model which identifies six *quality characteristics*: *functionality, reliability, usability, efficiency, maintainability* and *portability*. A set of *quality sub-characteristics*, which relate to quality aspects visible to the user, are presented to refine each quality characteristic. Developed for use with ISO/IEC 9126 (1991) is the ISO/IEC 14598 (1999) series which provides an overview of software product evaluation processes, providing guidance to developers, acquirers and independent evaluators on the evaluation of the quality of software products. The characteristics identified in ISO/IEC 9126 provide a basis upon which to build a model for software quality, as shown in the discussion of Dromey's (1995, 1996) framework for developing a software quality model.

Dromey's framework for software quality is aligned to the ISO/IEC 9126 set of six quality attributes but also includes the high-level attributes ***reusability*** and ***process mature***. Dromey's framework attempts to link **tangible internal** product properties of software components to high-level **intangible external** quality attributes. As Dromey points out, most studies of software product quality attributes focus on the identification and measurement of high-level quality attributes and little study has been made of tangible (measurable and/or assessable) internal product properties and their influence on high-level quality attributes. "A product's tangible internal characteristics or properties determine its external quality attributes" (Dromey, 1996). An appropriate basis upon which to classify the tangible quality-carrying properties of components, suggests Dromey, are: *correctness*, *internal, contextual* and *descriptive*.

If *correctness* properties were violated the software product would not perform as intended. The properties may be associated with individual components (internal) or associated with the way components are used in context (contextual). For example when looking at software system requirements:

- An individual software requirement, as a component of the Software System Requirements Specification must be complete and precise to assure accuracy and understandability of the specification – an internal correctness property.
- Software requirements must be consistent to assure that the requirements are accurate and able to be implemented – a contextual correctness property.

A component's *normal form* is its *internal* property. For example, two requirements' internal properties are that the requirements are explicit and non-redundant. *Contextual* properties deal with how components are composed and their possible relationships, for example modifiable. *Descriptive* properties relate to the understandability of the software product and apply to requirements, designs, implementations and user interfaces.

Dromey's process for the construction of a testable, assessable and refinable quality model for the key products of software development entails the following steps:

1. Identify a set of high-level *quality attributes* appropriate to the software product;
2. Identify the product *components;*
3. Identify and classify the most significant tangible quality-carrying properties that belong to each component;
4. Propose a set of axioms for linking high-level product properties to qualityattributes, and
5. Evaluate the model, identify its weaknesses and either make appropriate improvements or discard it and start again.

Dromey (1996) identified an appropriate set of high-level quality attributes and sub-attributes (quality-carrying properties) of requirements. Table 1 identifies the high-level quality attributes as: *accurate, understandable, implementable*, *adaptable* and *process mature* (Dromey, 1996). In defining a set of measurable quality-carrying properties a number of changes have been made to Dromey's (1996) list.

The product quality model for Software Requirements Specifications, Figure 1, shows the links between the software product component, *Individual Requirement,* the quality-carrying properties, the product properties' classification, and their effect on quality, *High Level Quality Attributes.* The product properties have been classified according to Dromey's property classification: correctness, contextual, internal and descriptive, discussed earlier. An instrument, in the form of a questionnaire has been developed to assess each of the quality-carrying properties.

Table 1. Software Requirements Specification product attributes and characteristics

High-level Attribute	Quality Characteristics	Definitions
Accurate Freedom from error	Precise	Adequate accuracy preserved in computations.
	Correct	Degree to which the specification satisfies the customer's mission objectives and is free from defects (Wilson et al, 1996).
	Complete	All identified requirements are defined in the specification. Structural form has all necessary elements to define and implement the structural form so that it may fulfil its intended role in a way that will not impact reliability or functionality (Dromey, 1995).
	Consistent	No improper use or side-effects. No conflict between individual requirements Capability functions and performance level must be compatible and the required quality features (for example, reliability) must not negate the capability's utility (Wilson et al, 1996).
	Traceable	Each requirement must be uniquely identified. A consistent and logical scheme for assigning identification to each specification statement within the requirements document must be used (Wilson et al, 1996).
Understandable All stakeholders can easily comprehend the meaning of each requirement.	unambiguous	Each requirement statement can be interpreted in only one way.
	self-descriptive	Purpose, strategy, intent and properties clearly evident from the choice of names for modules and various identifiers are meaningful and congruent with the context of the specification (Dromey, 1995).
Implementable It is possible to put into operation each requirement	testable	A set of test cases can be developed which will test for the presence of each function of the software.
	achievable	Each requirement is able to be put into operation.
Adaptable Effort required to accommodate changes, expansions, enhancements to the System Specification document.	modifiable	Related concerns must be grouped together and unrelated concerns must be separated (two refs 6 and 10 from Wilson et al, 1996).
	reusable	Requirements may be adapted to help solve another problem.
Process-mature	Performed, managed, well-defined	In accordance with Levels 1 to 3 of ISO/IEC TR 15504 (1998).

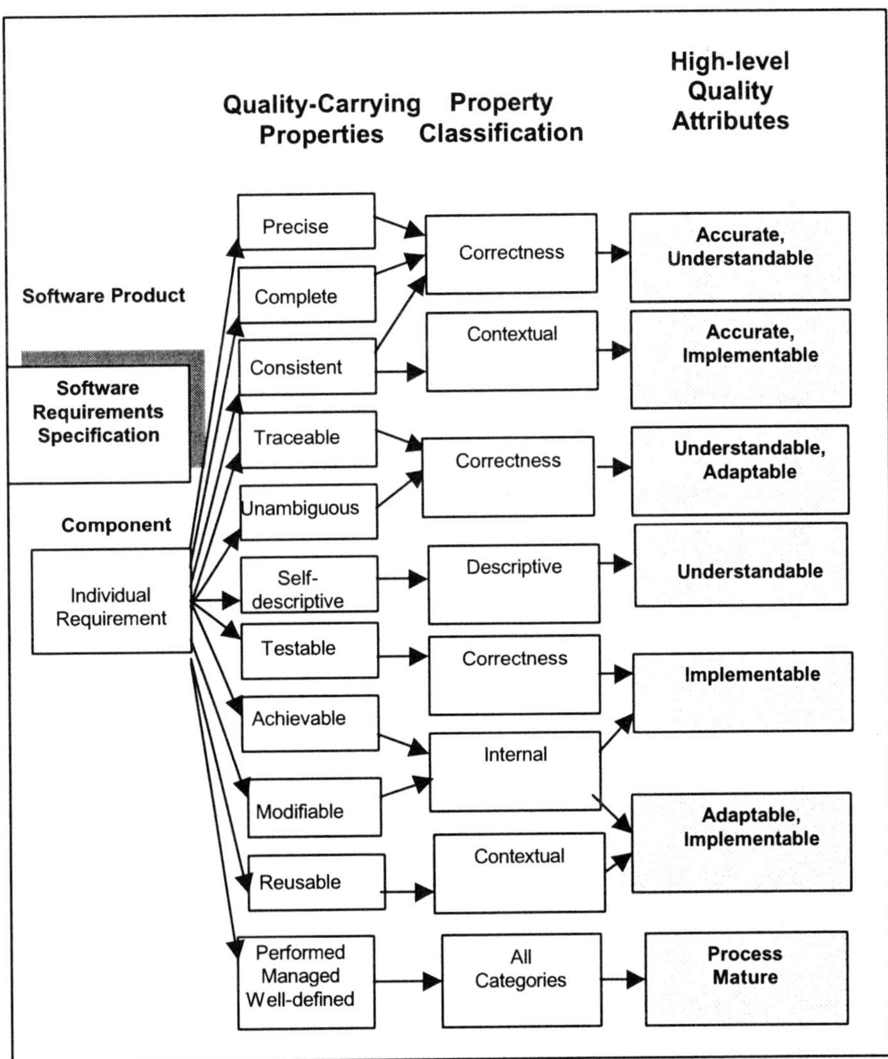

Figure 1. Software Product Quality Model for Software Requirements Specifications

Fundamentally the quality-carrying properties of a Software System Requirement should demonstrate that:

- adequate accuracy has been preserved in the specification of each individual requirement;
- all inputs and outputs have been described;
- any constraints on the system inputs and outputs have been clearly identified;
- any relationships between the inputs and outputs have been described.
- the specification of the requirement has all necessary elements to define and implement the requirement so that it may fulfil its intended role in a way that will not impact reliability or functionality;
- pre-conditions and post-conditions should be provided for all functions and other significant computations.

INDICATORS OF QUALITY ATTRIBUTES

Categories of Quality Indicators	Quality Attributes										
	complete	consistent	correct	modifiable	ranked	testable	traceable	unambiguous	understandable	validatable	verifiable
Imperatives	X			X			X	X	X	X	X
Continuances	X			X	X	X	X	X	X	X	X
Directives	X		X			X		X	X	X	X
Options	X					X		X	X		
Weak Phrases	X		X			X		X	X	X	X
Size	X					X		X	X	X	X
Text Structure	X	X		X	X		X		X		X
Spec. Depth	X	X		X			X		X		X
Readability				X		X	X	X	X	X	X

Figure 2. Quality Indicator/Attribute Relationships ARM Tool (Wilson et al., 1996)

The ARM tool (Wilson et al., 1996), developed by the Software Assurance Technology Centre (SATC) of the Goddard Space Flight Center has been used to carry out a comparative assessment of the work product characteristics. The ARM tool searches software requirements documents for terms which have been identified as quality indicators of requirements specification quality attributes (some of which are included in Figure 1). Figure 2 shows the relationships between requirements specifications' quality attributes and the categories of indicators measured by the ARM tool.

The categories of quality indicators which relate to the entire requirements document are: size, specification depth, readability and text structure. The categories, which relate to individual specification statements, are: imperatives, directives, weak phrases, continuances and options. An explanation of the manner in which the categories of indicators are applied to a specification document is given in Wilson et al. (1996).

3 APPLICATION OF THE MODEL

The quality model (Figure 1) has been applied to the evaluation of the Software Requirements Specification documents produced for two large projects developed for the same client by the case study organisation, a software development organisation which employed 570 people at the time of this study. In accordance with the confidentiality agreement between the researcher and the case organisation, synonyms have been given to the projects: FUNCTION and ACCOUNTS.

The initial project deliverables for the FUNCTION project were a functional specification for the implementation of the FUNCTION and ACCOUNTS systems for the client organisation and a fixed price estimate. Risk was assessed to be medium. The final project deliverable was the system implementation to replace the client's existing Sales Invoicing and Credit Systems which included: invoicing, credit notes, cash receipts/payments, debtors status, and to return relevant data and reports to the client's systems, to allow existing procedures and reports to continue functioning without change. The total function points for Release 1 of the system was 4089.

The functionality of the ACCOUNTS system included:

- extraction of production information from existing systems stored on enterprise databases at the end of each accounting period;
- summarising and reporting on data passed to RS6000 and into a SAP system.

Table 2 shows the results from using the "Automated Requirement Measurement" (ARM) tool (Wilson et al, 1996). The similar results found from the use of the evaluation instrument developed from the Software Product Quality Model are discussed later in this section.

The results indicate the following about the respective project System Requirement Specification documents:

- The ACCOUNT specification has multiple, complex requirements.
- The imperative counts for the FUNCTION project are at "the lower end of forcefulness" which suggests that the specification is not explicit. The ACCOUNTS specification, although all 95 imperatives are "will", is also not explicit.

- Both specifications contain very few examples or diagrams to aid understandability.
- The FUNCTION specification contains five options which "loosens" the specification.
- The low score of zero for "incomplete" on both specifications only indicates the extent to which the statements within the document are complete. This rating gives us no indication as to whether or not all the system requirements have been captured within the document.
- The low scores for "weak phrases" is an indication that documented requirements are not ambiguous and less likely to be incomplete.
- The FUNCTION numbering structure suggests that the specification has not maintained a reasonably consistent level of detail. The numbering structure for the ACCOUNTS specification indicates that the document is reasonably well organised below level 1. Far too much detail is at level 1 of the specification.
- The low ratio of Specification Structure to Total Lines of Text for the FUNCTION specification is an indication that the document is inconcise in specifying requirements. The ratio of Unique Subjects to Specification Structure for the same specification shows that the specification has sufficient detail.
- The ratio scores for the ACCOUNTS specification indicate that the document is reasonably concise and detailed.
- The number of continuances in the ACCOUNTS specification indicates complex and detailed requirements suggesting that the requirements may not be easily modified nor tested. This in turn suggests potential implementation problems.

Table 2. Product Quality Evaluation Results – ARM Tool

INDICATOR	FUNCTION PROJECT	ACCOUNTS PROJECT
Imperatives	19, the majority of which are within the lower end of "forcefulness"	95, all of which are "will"
Continuance	13	42
Directives	1	1
Option Phrases	5	1
Weak Phrases	0	2
Incomplete	0	0
Numbering Structure	Depth 1 = 1 Depth 2 = 13	Depth 1 = 14 Depth 2 = 1 Depth 3 = 10 Depth 4 = 19
Specification Structure	Depth 1 = 0 Depth 2 = 17	Depth 1 = 0 Depth 2 = 0 Depth 3 = 18 Depth 4 = 29 Depth 5 = 78
Total Lines of Text	129	281
Unique Subjects	17	60
Ratio Specification Structure to Total Lines of Text	0.1317829	0.4448398
Ratio Unique Subjects to Total Specification Structure	1	0.48

When the Product Quality Evaluation Questionnaire, developed from the product quality model, was used to assess the specifications similar results were found to those above, as shown in Table 3 below.

Table 3. Results using the Product Quality Model

ATTRIBUTE		RATING
FUNCTION		
Accuracy	Not explicit, inconcise, sufficient detail Imprecise, incomplete	Low
Understandability	Few examples, no diagrams, Achievable	Low
Implementability	Major change	Medium
Adaptability		Low
ACCOUNTS		
Accuracy	Not explicit, reasonably concise and detailed. Incomplete	Low
Understandability	Few examples, diagrams	Low
Implementability	Complex requirements not easily tested	Low
Adaptability	Some complex requirements not easily modified	Medium

The high-level quality attribute *process mature*, and the quality-carrying properties performed, managed and well-defined, were examined through performance of a software process assessment, using the embedded assessment model in ISO/IEC TR15504-5 (1998).

Four process were evaluated during the process assessment. All processes for both projects exhibited low levels of maturity (Level 1) as shown in the process maturity profiles in Table 4 below.

Table 4. Process Maturity Profiles

PROCESS	FUNCTION Maturity Levels	ACCOUNTS Maturity Levels
Identify Customer Needs	1	1
Perform Joint Audits and Reviews	1	1
Develop Software Requirements	1	1
Develop Software Design	1	1

Level 1 rating indicates that the process is "Performed". The implemented process achieves its defined purpose. The processes were found not to managed nor well-defined. The key findings from conducting the software process assessment are:

- Key users were not consulted in the elicitation of requirements;
- Failure of communication between the project team and the users, inadequate communication mechanisms were extablished;
- Most if not all reviews were carried out by individual document review rather than by intensive group review processes;
- Requirements and Functional Specifications were not baselined.
- The effectiveness of reviews, in terms of defect detection was poor, judged by the number of recorded issues on review reports;
- Problem areas identified when assessing higher levels of maturity were:
- Inadequate provision of tools to support the processes;
- Insufficient provision of appropriate training , particularly in domain knowledge
- Plans, standards and procedures were not always used.
- Lack of traceability from requirements was the main contributing factor to the weakness in the process: Develop software design.

4. CONCLUSIONS AND FUTURE WORK

The processes were assessed in the case study projects in one case historically, after the design phase and in the other after acceptance testing had taken place in order to evaluate the product quality attribute *process mature*. Inclusion of this attribute in the product quality model and the subsequent evaluations provided valuable insight into the potential links between process and product quality. Many of the problems incurred during the later stages of the FUNCTION project were a result of an *incomplete*, often *ambiguous* set of user requirements produced by the client organisation. Considerable problems in specifying user requirements were encountered by both project managers.

Although the data collection method for the evaluation of product quality was the use of the ARM Tool (Wilson et al., 1996) and the Product Quality Evaluation Questionnaire developed from the quality model, interview data, collected during the software process assessment provided an essential additional means of evaluating the product. Traceability problems, implementation issues, difficulties in identifying the right requirements, incomplete and ambiguous requirements, which were highlighted during the latter phases of the development of the systems, may not have been evident had the specifications been evaluated earlier in the projects. However these are clearly indications of an immature software development process.

The aim of product quality models is to alert systems developers to potential problems so that they "can *engineer-in* tangible quality-carrying properties that eliminate, anticipate, or avoid problems that could otherwise subsequently show up as product defects" (Dromey, 2003). As Dromey suggests, in software quality we should be aiming for developers of software systems to use a preventative approach to quality.

In this paper, the difficulties in operationalising a product quality model have been discussed. Dromey's framework was presented as the most appropriate means of developing a model for this study. The key here is that Dromey's framework is component-based suggesting that tangible properties must be engineered-in to all components at all levels of a software system (Dromey, 2003).

This study is limited to the evaluation of Software Requirements Specifications. The usefulness of Dromey's (1995, 1996) framework in developing quality models to assess the products from other phases in the development process should be tested. The ARM tool (Wilson et al, 1996) is only applicable to the evaluation of requirements specifications. An area useful to pursue might be the development of an appropriate profile for products of the design phase, for example, and the development of an automated tool to support the evaluation process.

REFERENCES

Basili, V. R. and Musa, J. D., 1991, The future engineering of software: A management perspective, *Computer*, September 1991, 90–96.

Boehm, B. W., Brown, J. R., Kaspar, H., Lipow, M., MacLead, G. J. and Merrit, M. J., 1978, Characteristics of software quality, Volume 1 of *TRW Series of Software Technology* North-Holland, Amsterdam.

Curtis, B., Krasner, H. and Iscoe, N., 1988, A Field of Study of the Software Design Process for Large Systems, *Communications of the ACM*, 31(11), 1268–1287.

Dromey, R. G., 2003, Software Quality-Prevention versus Cure?, *Softare Quality Journal*, 11, 197–210.

Dromey, R. G., 1995, "A Model for Software Product Quality", *IEEE SoftwareEngineering*, Vol 21, No 1, 1–18.

Dromey, R. G., 1996, Cornering the Chimera, 1996, *IEEE Software*,Vol 13, No. 1, Jan. 1996, 33–43.

Gilb, T., 1985, Tools for design by objectives, in: *Software requirements specification and testing*, Anderson, T., ed., Blackwell Scientific, UK, pp. 50–63.

Gilb, T., 1987, *Principles of Software Engineering Management*, Addison-Wesley, Reading, Mas. USA.

ISO/IEC TR 15504-5, 1998, Information Technology – Software process assessment – Part 5:An assessment model and indicator guidance, Technical Report type 2, International Organization for Standardization, Geneva.

ISO/IEC 14598- 1-6, 1999, *Information technology - Software product evaluation,* International Organization for Standardization, Geneva.

ISO/IEC 9126, 1991, *Information Technology - Software Product Evaluation – Quality Characteristics and Guidelines for Their Use*, International Organization for Standardization, Geneva.

Kitchenham, B., 1987, Towards a constructive quality model, Part 1: Software quality modelling, measurement and prediction, *Software Engineering Journal*, Vol 2, No 4, 105–113.

Kitchenham, B. and Pfleeger, S. L., 1996, Software Quality: The Elusive Target, *IEEE Software*, January, Vol 13, No 1, 12–21.

Lubas, M., Potts, C. and Richter, C., 1993, A Review of the State of the Practice in Requirement Modelling, *IEEE International Symposium on Requirements Engineering,* San Diego, CA, USA, IEEE Computer Society Press.

McCall, J. A., Richards, P. K. and Walters, G. F., 1977, *Factors in Software Quality*, Vol. 1, 2, 3, AD/A-049-014/015/055, National Tech. Information Service, Springfield, VA.

Nuseibeh, B. and Easterbrook, S., 2000, Requirements Engineering: A Roadmap, in: *The Future of Software Engineereing 2000, 22nd International Conference on Software Engineering,* Finkelstein, A., ed., ACM, pp. 37–46.

Sommerville, I. and Sawyer, S., 1997l, *Requirements Engineering: A Good Practice Guide,* John Wiley and Sons, NY.

Wilson, W .M., Rosenberg, L. H. and Hyatt, L. E., 1996, Automated Quality Analysis of Natural Language Requirements Specifications ARM Tool, in Proceedings of 14th Annual Pacific Conference NW SW QC. October 1996.

A QUALITATIVE METHOD FOR IDENTIFYING FACTORS THAT INFLUENCE USER SATISFACTION

Bernard J. Terrill and Andrew Flitman*

1. INTRODUCTION

Understanding what influences users' satisfaction, or otherwise, with computer systems is a topic of importance to many within the field of information systems. Research into this question has typically relied on quantitative methods; in the course of a formal research project, a new method was developed which investigates the question using qualitative techniques. The method, along with the practical and theoretical context that gives it relevance, is described in this paper. For clarity, the method will be referred to herein as MIFIUS-Ql (a Method for the Identification of Factors Influencing User Satisfaction – Qualitative).

2. THE IMPORTANCE OF USER SATISFACTION

For information systems practitioners, an issue of obvious importance is the degree to which end users are satisfied with the delivered system. If the users are not satisfied with a system – if there is a constant stream of complaints, "urgent" change requests, and even instances of users not using the system when they should – then overall evaluations of the system as such, and the responsible implementation project, will be affected. In extreme case, the project may be regarded as a complete failure and the system completely removed from productive operation. In other cases, the project may still be regarded as an overall success (the project may have delivered large cost savings for example), but the lack of user satisfaction would likely mean the project is not evaluated as highly as it otherwise might have been.

This importance of user satisfaction, and the relationship of user satisfaction to the overall success of a system, is reflected in information systems theory. In (1980), Peter Keen identified five issues which he felt had to be resolved by the field of management information systems (MIS). One of these issues was to identify, or agree upon, **the** dependant variable for MIS: what is it that we, practitioners and academics alike, are all

* Bernard J. Terrill, School of Business Systems, Monash University, Melbourne, Australia 3800. Andrew Flitman, School of Business Systems, Monash University, Melbourne, Australia 3800.

Constructing the Infrastructure for the Knowledge Economy
Edited by H. Linger *et al.*, Kluwer Academic/Plenum Publishers , 2004

striving to achieve. In (1992), DeLone and McLean published a foundational paper which addressed this issue. They stated that IS success, the success or otherwise of a system, is the dependent variable of the field and provided a comprehensive review of methods by which researchers had attempted to measure this variable. One method they identified, commonly used by researchers, is to measure user satisfaction and use this as an indication for the success, or otherwise, of the system.

This is not to argue that, in evaluating the success of a system, the opinions of end users are the only opinions that matter; nor is it to argue that the only way to measure the success of a system is to measure user satisfaction. A general perception of ERP projects, for example, is that they do not deliver a high degree of user satisfaction yet are regarded as successful because they deliver other important benefits (such as cost reductions flowing from retiring a large number of legacy, heterogenous legacy systems). Delone and McLean (1992) themselves identify five other relevant variables: system quality, information quality, use, individual impact and organizational impact. It seems reasonable though to regard user satisfaction as a factor that at least influences the success or otherwise of most information systems; in some cases it may be a sufficient condition, in most cases it would be at least a necessary condition.

3. THE VALUE AND MEANING OF "INFLUENCING FACTORS"

A desire to achieve high levels of user satisfaction implies a desire to know what factors influence user satisfaction. If practitioners know what factors influence user satisfaction, they can use this knowledge in improving existing systems or building new systems.

The use of the term "influencing factors" is deliberate and is drawn from Ballantine (1998). The term is used as MIFIUS-Ql does not provide evidence sufficient to say that the identified factors will be applicable in **every** systems development effort. Influencing factors must be understood as factors that, **in at least some cases but not necessarily all cases**, act to increase or decrease the satisfaction users have with a system. For some systems, the factors may be sufficient conditions; for other systems, the factors may be necessary conditions but not sufficient; in still other systems the factors may not be relevant at all. MIFIUS-Ql provides evidence sufficient to term something an "influencing factor", according to the above definition, but it does provide evidence sufficient to support a wider generalization.

This limitation does not mean the method yields valueless results. Practitioners would approach a list of such influencing factors with an attitude of: "Here is a list of things that I should take into account in order to increase user satisfaction with the system; not all of them are necessarily applicable but some of them may be.", and would then use their judgement to decide which factors are important in the context of their particular project. This is the type of reasoning that explains the common and valuable use of "Tips and Tricks" and "Lessons Learned" type documents. These documents do not contain scientifically validated generalisations, nor do they contain statements of research methodology; the documents contain mid level generalisations – inductions usually based upon the experience of one project only – that are **potentially** applicable to other projects. It is up to the readers to determine if, and how, the items apply to their particular context. So to with influencing factors identified by using MIFIUS-Ql.

4. RESEARCH SETTING

MIFIUS-Ql was developed during a research project investigating the factors that influence user satisfaction with integrative knowledge management systems. Knowledge Management Systems (KMS) are a relatively recent class of IS that have emerged to support the increasing interest in knowledge management. They may be defined as "...a class of information systems applied to managing organizational knowledge. That is, they are IT-based systems developed to support and enhance the organizational processes of knowledge creation, storage/retrieval, transfer, and application." (Alavi & Leidner, 2001)

Within this general category, there is a wide array of different systems. Integrative KMS are a subset characterised by the storage of documents in a large repository of some type. Employees share relevant knowledge by contributing documents (Word, Excel, Powerpoint, Acrobat etc) to the repository. Other employees can utilise this knowledge by accessing the repository and retrieving the relevant documents. For example, Ernst & Young International, a global accountancy and consulting firm, utilise an internally developed KMS referred to as the "Knowledge Web" (Kweb). Amongst other things, this Lotus Notes based repository contains deliverables from previously executed projects. A consultant interested in say, SAP engagements, can quickly retrieve sample project plans, deliverable templates, functional and technical designs and more (Rollo & Clarke, 2001). This type of KMS is very common; indeed, it is often what many practitioners are referring to when they discuss KMS. It may be distinguished from another class of KMS, "interactive KMS", which focuses on sharing knowledge amongst employees using real time collaboration (rather than explicit documents of some type).

The primary aim of the project was **not** to develop and test MIFIUS-Ql; the primary aim was to identify influencing factors; the method emerged as the research progressed. At each stage of the research, considerable time was spent reviewing alternative research methods, choosing the most appropriate one, and then tailoring the method as required by the specifics of the research project. For example, a number of interviewing methods were reviewed with Repertory Grid being chosen as the preferred method. The general strictures of Repertory Grid interviews were then applied to the specific problem of investigating factors that influence user satisfaction. MIFIUS-Ql, therefore, should not be viewed as an entirely new research method; rather, it represents existing methods, chosen from other alternatives, arranged in logical order, and specifically tailored to the research objective of identifying factors, which influence user satisfaction.

Space does not permit extensive discussion of the rejected alternatives and why they were rejected; a full discussion will be included in the thesis resulting from the integrative KMS research project.

5. METHOD DESCRIPTION

MIFIUS-Ql consists of four main phases: 1. Preparation, 2. Repertory Grid interviews, 3. Qualitative analysis, and 4. Secondary analysis.

5.1. Preparation

The preparation phase involves gaining access to one or more organisations and thereby gaining access to suitable interview candidates. One is interested in factors influencing user satisfaction so the interview candidates must be end users of a system of the type being researched. In the integrative KMS research project (described above), the system type being researched was integrative knowledge management systems; the end users required were therefore end users of this type of system. As is common in qualitative research (Kvale, 1996), MIFIUS-Ql does not require random sampling methods. The sampling methods used in the above research were Snowball (or Chain Referral) sampling (Kumar, 1996; Neuman, 1999) to identify an initial population of potential candidates; and then Theoretical sampling (Burgess, 1984; Minichiello, Aroni, Timewell, and Alexander, 1995) to reduce this initial population to the required sample size.

Sample size is determined using a "saturation point" approach described by Strauss (1987) and Kvale (1996) whereby the number of subjects is arrived at by considering the time and resources required for each additional interview and the law of diminishing returns, whereby the addition of each interview yields incrementally less knowledge. In the integrative KMS research project, the researcher chose an initial sample size of four subjects. The four subjects were interviewed twice each; one interview focusing on retrieving knowledge from the KMS, the other interview focusing on contributing knowledge to the KMS. After these eight interviews, the data was analysed in random order and a calculation performed to see if the saturation point had been reached; the calculation is shown in Table 1.

As the percentage increases were so small, it was decided that the saturation point had been reached; it was expected that an additional interview would yield no, or very few, additional factors. If the saturation point had not been reached, more interviews would have been conducted.

The preparation phase should also include designing the specifics of the Repertory Grid interviews (see below) and creating a detailed interview schedule. If the researcher is not familiar with Repertory Grid interviews, one or two trial interviews are recommended (Stewart and Stewart, 1981); the interview schedule may be amended as a result of these trials. Stewart and Stewart also contains a number of exercises which may be used to familiarise oneself with the interviewing technique.

Table 1. Additional factors identified in fourth interview

Interview Type	Factors after 3rd interview	Factors after 4th interview	Increase	Increase (%)
Retrieving	77	79	2	2.53
Contributing	65	67	2	2.99

5.2. Repertory Grid Interviews

Repertory Grid interviews are one part of the larger "Repertory Grid Technique" which is an operationalisation of George Kelly's "Personal Construct Theory (PCT)" (Fransella and Bannister, 1977; Kelly, 1955). The method provides a systematic approach to eliciting people's opinions about certain aspects of reality. The interview subject is presented with successive sets of "elements" which are specific instances of the aspect of reality being researched. Typically, each set consists of two elements (referred to as a "dyad") or three elements (a "triad"). The user is asked to consider each set and to identify similarities or differences between them, from a certain perspective. The identified similarities and differences are referred to as "constructs".

In the case of MIFIUS-Ql, the aspect of reality being researched is a particular system type. The elements used are therefore specific experiences the user had with the system. After standard opening remarks, these elements are "elicited" by asking the following four questions:

1. Your most recent use of <system name>
2. Your next most recent use of <system name>
3. A positive experience with <system name>
4. A negative experience with <system name>

The subject is asked to briefly describe each experience and provide a short name by which the experience may be identified; each element name is written on a separate memo card.

Following Hunter (1997), two additional elements are added: "The best possible experience" and "The worst possible experience". These are hypothetical elements designed to generate the highest possible degree of contrast. This corresponds to the "IDEAL" element(s) recommended by Stewart and Stewart (1981).

After element elicitation comes the "construct elicitation" phase of the interviews. A dyad (two elements) is presented to the user who is asked to identify similarities and differences "in terms of what satisfied them or did not satisfy them" or "in terms of what they liked/did not like". For each response by a subject (each construct), the researcher must obtain the "likeness pole" and the opposite of the likeness pole, the "contrast pole". So, to use a simple example, a user considering a dyad may state, "a difference between them was response time, in this experience (pointing to one memo card) there was good response time, in this experience (pointing to the other memo card) there was poor response time". In this case, the likeness pole is "good response time", and the contrast pole is "poor response time". The construct is thus denoted, "good response time – poor response time". Obtaining the two poles in this manner helps clarify exactly what the construct means to the subject.

For each elicited construct, the technique of "laddering", originated by Hinkle (1965), is also used. Laddering allows the researcher to explore more deeply what the construct means to the subject, and allows the researcher to obtain the construct at the desired level of abstraction. If the user provides a highly specific construct, the researcher "ladders upwards" to obtain a more generally applicable answer; if the provided construct is very vague and abstract, the researcher "ladders downwards" to obtain more detail. For more information about laddering, Consult Terrill and Flitman (2002), Hunter (1997), and Stewart and Stewart (1981).

When no more constructs are forthcoming for a given dyad, the next dyad is presented. How the elements are combined into dyads, and the order in which dyads are presented to the subject, is referred to as the "sort order". The sort order is predetermined prior to the interview and detailed in the interview schedule.

The interview ends when no new constructs are forthcoming, all possible dyads are exhausted or the allocated time expires.

In the integrative KMS research project, the interviews were recorded and full transcripts made. If this was considered too time consuming, extensive notes should be taken; at a minimum, these notes should detail the likeness and contrast pole of each construct and the key points made during laddering.

The above description is relatively brief and some important details are omitted. For general descriptions of Repertory Grid interviews, consult Hunter (1997), Stewart and Stewart (1981), and Fransella and Bannister (1977); for specific information about how MIFIUS-Ql utilises Repertory Grid interviews, consult Terrill and Flitman (2002).

5.3. Qualitative Analysis

MIFIUS-Ql primarily relies on the qualitative analysis techniques detailed in Dey (1993). Dey is a relatively recent work and draws upon the well known texts of Miles and Huberman (1994), Strauss (1987), and Strauss and Corbin (1990), in addition to some lesser known works by Patton (1980), Becker and Geer (1982), and Bliss, Monk and Ogborn (1983). The reference to Strauss and Corbin should not be taken to mean Dey's techniques are the techniques of grounded theory; as Dey himself states, "...I have made no effort to remain within the restrictive confines of grounded theory." (1993). The overall goal of Dey's techniques, a goal he shares with the previously mentioned authors, is a focus on categorizing textual data and then making connections between these categories.

The qualitative analysis begins with an initial "reading and annotation" of the data. This initial reading is necessary to become familiar with the data and to gain an initial understanding of what it communicates. As the data is read, ideas and connections that occur to the researcher should be noted in annotations to the data itself; Dey refers to such annotations as "memos".

Expressing a theme common throughout his methodology, Dey stresses the importance of having a particular purpose in mind when conducting this initial reading. He suggests constructing a "checklist" of questions, "the substantive issues with which the researcher is concerned" (1993), to keep in mind when reading; these questions help direct focus towards the more relevant data.

For MIFIUS-Ql, the substantive question is, "What factors influence user satisfaction with <system type>". This question is borne in mind whilst conducting the initial reading; statements by participants that bear upon this particular question are regarded as more relevant than statements related to other issues.

Dey warns against reading, and later analysing, the transcripts in the same order as which the interviews were conducted; doing so can introduce a bias as, "...almost inevitably attention may focus on those interviews...which happen to come first." (1993). The transcripts are therefore read, and later analysed, in random order.

A major part of Dey's methodology involves the creation of a categorization scheme by which the raw data is organised. In essence, creating the categorization scheme involves: assigning sections of the data to one or more categories; defining definitions for each category that explain why data has been assigned to the category and why other data was not assigned; and arranging the categories themselves into a hierarchy.

The key process guiding the categorization is the identification of similarities and differences. Data that is similar, according to defined criteria, is assigned to the same category; data that is different, data that does not meet the criteria, is not so assigned. Each category is assigned a "definition" which specifies the criteria by which statements were selected for inclusion and other statements were excluded. Consider an example from the integrative KMS research project: a number of participants made statements indicating, "the quality of the retrieved knowledge" is a factor that influences their satisfaction when retrieving from a KMS. Even though the specific wording may have been different, all such statements were similar in that they all referred to the quality of knowledge; so they were all assigned to the same category: "Knowledge Quality". Statements that did not refer to the quality of knowledge were not assigned to the "Knowledge Quality" category; they were assigned to some other category. "Grouping data in this way therefore involves developing a set of criteria in terms of which to distinguish observations as similar or related. Typically, this is done through the development of a set of categories, with each category expressing a criterion (or a set of criteria) for distinguishing some observations from others, as similar or related in some particular respect(s)." (1993).

Not all statements have to be categorized. The research objective is to identify factors which influence user satisfaction; so it is therefore only necessary to categorize statements that bear upon this objective, i.e. statements that indicate items which influenced the user's satisfaction, or otherwise, with the system.

The categories themselves are organized into a two level hierarchy: the "parent" categories being a general category, such as "Knowledge Quality", and the "child" categories being either specific types of the parent category or components of the parent category. Primarily, the child categories are obtained through downward laddering in the Repertory Grid interviews; for example, laddering down to obtain more detail about the parent category, "Knowledge Quality" revealed components such as "currency of the knowledge", "professional presentation" and "accuracy".

An initial categorization is created by the first pass through the data and then refined through subsequent iterations. Each iteration can involve reassigning text from one category to another, refining the category definitions, renaming categories, deleting categories, creating new categories, and altering the two-level hierarchy.

In the integrative KMS research project, Nvivo, qualitative analysis software by QSR International, was used to facilitate the above analysis tasks.

The result is a list of influencing factors (the parent categories), and child categories providing more detail about the parent categories. Attached to each category, parent and child, is a definition describing why statements were assigned to the category and why others were excluded from it; this clarifies the meaning of the category. Attached to each category is text, statements by the participants, which acts as supporting evidence for the category; if someone asks, for example, "On what basis do you claim the quality of knowledge influences user satisfaction with integrative KMS?", the assigned text, subject to some qualifications, may be shown as the answer.

5.4. Secondary Analysis

In industry settings, the evidence provided by the qualitative analysis phase may be regarded as sufficient. In academic research, however, it is necessary to integrate one's findings with other research in the field by way of a secondary analysis of relevant literature. This analysis strengthens the validity of the findings in two ways. Firstly, it can provide references supporting influencing factors identified in the qualitative analysis and, secondly, it can reveal significant influencing factors not identified in the qualitative analysis.

The secondary analysis may also contribute towards a cumulative tradition in MIS. Instead of every influencing factor being regarded as a new phenomenon, it may be that the findings provide further evidence supporting influencing factors identified in previous research, or it may be that the findings demonstrate the relevance of the factor in different settings (with a different system type for example).

Two broad types of literature may be examined: peer reviewed research, and case studies involving the particular system type being researched. The secondary analysis involves examining the selected literature for evidence of influencing factors. For each factor found, the researcher decides if the factor corresponds to one identified in the qualitative analysis, in which case the reference is noted down as further supporting evidence, or is in fact a new influencing factor, in which case the factor is added to the existing list. Negative findings, research that indicates a particular factor may not be relevant, must also be incorporated

Typically, it will not be feasible to guarantee that every relevant piece of literature has been found and examined. Rather, MIFIUS-Ql involves the use of the "saturation point" approach described in the above discussion on interview sample size: when new references consistently repeat already identified factors then the review is stopped.

The result is a list of influencing factors, possible expanded, with each factor supported by evidence from the interviews or evidence from the literature, or evidence from both.

6. SAMPLE RESULTS

In the integrative KMS research project, MIFIUS-Ql was used to identify seventeen influencing factors, nine related to user satisfaction when retrieving knowledge from the KMS, eight related to user satisfaction when contributing knowledge to the KMS. These factors are shown in Table 2.

Table 2. Influencing factors

Retrieving	Contributing
• Search and Navigation Quality	• Effort and Time to Contribute
• Knowledge Quality	• Conviction Item will be Found
• Abstract Quality	• Feedback and Recognition
• Support Services	• Effort and Time to Cleanse
• Able to Contact Contributor	• Support Services
• Able to Locate Knowledge	• Conviction of Value Add
• Training and Documentation	• Technical System Quality
• Expectations	• Training and Documentation
• Technical System Quality	

Associated with each factor are a definition and a number of child categories that, as explained above, represent specific types or components of the parent category. Each child category, in turn, has an associated definition. Expanded detail for one influencing factor is shown in Table 3.

Of the factors listed above, one (Retrieving – Support Services) was identified only in the secondary analysis. Other factors identified in the secondary analysis relate to either a parent category or a child category identified during the interviews.

Empirical evidence supporting each category, parent and child, is provided by the relevant excerpts from the interviews and references identified in the secondary analysis. More detailed results are available in Terrill and Flitman (2003); the thesis resulting from the research will also contain full results, including results of the secondary analysis.

7. VALIDITY AND RELIABILITY OF THE METHOD

Validity and reliability are two fundamental principles that guided the methodological decisions underlying MIFIUS-Ql. Many items in the method are there for the sole purpose of improving validity and/or reliability. Space does not permit a full discussion, but some key points follow.

Validity refers to the "degree to which the researcher has measured what he set out to measure" (Smith, 1991). In general, qualitative researchers accept the principle of validity but in practice tend to apply it differently than do quantitative researchers. Qualitative researchers interpret validity more as "authenticity" (Neuman, 1999): ensuring the account they give, and the conclusions they reach, match as closely as possible the facts being investigated. It would be a violation of the principle of validity, for example, for a qualitative researcher to omit certain statements simply because they were inconvenient or contradicted the "desired" conclusions.

Table 3. Detail for one influencing factor

Influencing Factor	Description	Child Categories
Feedback and Recognition.	User satisfaction is influenced by receiving some type of feedback or recognition from other parties in regards to a contributed item.	• Feedback from actual users of the knowledge. • Feedback from manager. • Feedback via a formal review process. • Feedback via notification of "hits" (retrievals) of the contributed item. • Feedback from acknowledged experts in the field.

Fransella and Bannister (1977) support the validity of the Repertory Grid Method as such. The method does provide information about what it purports to measure: people's constructs and the relationships between them. They warn however, that specific incarnations of the method can be invalid. To be valid, the interviews must be designed so that they do provide information relevant to the research objectives. The design decisions outlined in the "Repertory Grid Interviews" section above , and detailed further in Terrill and Flitman (2002), were made to ensure this aspect of validity.

The validity of MIFIUS-Ql is also enhanced by maintaining the relationship between the raw data (the interview transcripts) and the findings. By viewing the findings in light of the relevant excerpts, others can decide for themselves how authentic the findings are. The use of Nvivo, or another qualitative software package, also enhances this aspect of validity. Armed with the same software, and the research database, others can, with one or two mouse clicks, retrieve and review all excerpts related to a given category.

The secondary analysis stage also enhances validity by possibly supplying further evidence in support of a category or supplying categories not identified in the interviews (Dey, 1993).

Reliability is a measure of the extent to which a given test will produce the same results under constant conditions (Kumar, 1996). To some extent, studies have demonstrated the reliability of Repertory Grid interviews by showing that the method, used on the same people but on different occasions, elicits almost the same elements and constructs (Fransella and Bannister, 1977).

In qualitative research, it can be difficult to establish reliability due to difficulties in keeping conditions constant and difficulties in exactly specifying the detailed procedural steps involved. As Dey states however, "If we cannot expect others to replicate our account, the best we can do is explain how we arrived at our results. This gives our audience the chance to scrutinise our procedures and to decide whether, at least in principle, the results ought to be reliable." (1993). MIFIUS-Ql helps establish reliability in this manner as it provides a detailed account of the procedural steps followed to produce results; something that is sometimes missing in qualitative research (Dey, 1993).

To further enhance reliability, Dey recommends deliberately searching for possible causes of error. It was for this reason that MIFIUS-Ql recommends multiple iterations when analysing the data. In the integrative KMS research project, three iterations were performed.

The secondary analysis also acts to enhance reliability by integrating the results with previous research.

8. VALUE OF THE METHOD

MIFIUS-Ql, a combination and application of existing research methods that has not previously been discussed in the qualitative literature, may be of value to both practitioners and researchers. Practitioners may use the method to identify influencing factors specific to particular applications. The method could be used instead of, or as an adjunct to, the more traditional "feedback survey" which is normally sent by email. A disadvantage of such surveys is that they already contain factors predetermined as important by the researcher; MIFIUS-Ql, in comparison, allows users to express factors that are important to them, using terminology of their own choosing. The Repertory Grid interviews also carry the advantage of "drawing out" factors which a survey, even one with open ended questions, might not reveal; see Terrill and Flitman (2002) for more on this point. Practitioners may choose to omit the secondary analysis phase.

The method may also be of value to academic researchers investigating user satisfaction. It provides a combination of deliberately chosen existing research methods; other researchers would be saved the time involved in considering and choosing amongst possible alternatives (different interviewing methods and qualitative analysis methods for example).

Perhaps the greatest benefit of the method however could be in contributing towards a qualitative cumulative tradition in this particular research area. Each research project, during the secondary analysis phase, would integrate the findings to previously established results. The body of knowledge in the area would gradually grow: identifying influencing factors with new system types, identifying new influencing factors for already researched system types, and adding additional evidence to support already established influencing factors. Further, as additional system types are researched, rather than regarding certain influencing factors as applicable only to a certain system type, the cumulative body of evidence may warrant generalising some influencing factors to information systems as such.

9. FUTURE RESEARCH

The most obvious shortcoming of MIFIUS-Ql is that it has only been used and tested in one research project. Whilst the method proved useful, it would obviously benefit from further applications.

A common way to establish the reliability of a method is to investigate the same question using alternate techniques. If a comparison of results reveals similarities then this reflects positively on the method's reliability. In the integrative KMS research project, the results from the use of MIFIUS-Ql have been formulated into a preliminary model of factors influencing user satisfaction with integrative KMS. This model is to be subjected to validation via a detailed single case study within a large organisation that uses integrative KMS. Different research methods will be used and the results compared with the preliminary model. Apart from casting light upon the accuracy of the preliminary model, the case study results will, in the manner described above, also provide information about the reliability of MIFIUS-Ql.

REFERENCES

Alavi, M., and Leidner, D. E., 2001, Knowledge management and knowledge management systems: Conceptual foundations and research issues, *MIS Quarterly,* **25**:107–136.

Ballantine, J., Bonner, M., Levy, M., Martin, A., Munro, I., and Powell, P. L., 1998, Developing a 3-D model of information systems success, in: *Information Systems Success Measurement,* E. J. Garrity and G. L. Sanders, eds., Idea Group Publishing, Hershey, pp. 46–59.

Becker, H., and Geer, B., 1982, Participant observation: The analysis of qualitative field data, in: *Field Research: A Sourcebook and Field Manual,* R. Burgess, ed., Allen & Unwin, London.

Bliss, J., Monk, M., and Ogborn, J., 1983, *Qualitative Data Analysis for Educational Research: A Guide to Uses of Systemic Networks*, Croom Helm, London.

Burgess, R. G., 1984, *In the Field: An Introduction to Field Research*, Allen & Unwin, London.

DeLone, W. H., and McLean, E. R., 1992, Information Systems success: The quest for the dependent variable, *Information Systems Research,* **3**:60–95.

Dey, I., 1993, *Qualitative Data Analysis: A User-friendly Guide for Social Scientists*, Routtedge, London.

Fransella, F., and Bannister, D., 1977, *A Manual for Repertory Grid Technique*, Academic Press, London.

Hinkle, D., 1965, *The Change of Personal Constructs from the View Point of a Theory of Construct Implications*, Unpublished PhD Thesis, Ohio State University, Ohio.

Hunter, M. G., 1997, The use of RepGrids to gather interview data about information systems analysts, *Information Systems Journal,* **7**:67–81.

Keen, P. G., 1980, Reference disciplines and a cumulative tradition, Proceedings of the First International Conference on Information Systems, pp. 9–18.

Kelly, G. A., 1955, *The Psychology of Personal Constructs*, W. W. Norton & Company Inc., New York.

Kumar, R., 1996, *Research Methodology. A Step-by-step Guide for Beginners*, Addison Wesley Longman, Melbourne, Victoria.

Kvale, S., 1996, *Interviews : An Introduction to Qualitative Research Interviewing*, Sage Publications, Thousand Oaks, Calif.

Miles, M. B., and Huberman, A. M., 1994, *Qualitative Data Analysis: An Expanded Sourcebook*, Sage Publications, Thousand Oaks, Calif.

Minichiello, V., Aroni, R., Timewell, E., and Alexander, L., 1995, *In-Depth Interviewing: Principles, Techniques, Analysis.*, (2nd ed.), Longman Cheshire, Melbourne.

Neuman, L. W., 1999, *Social Research Methods: Qualitative and Quantitative Approaches*, (4th ed.), Allyn and Bacon, Boston.

Patton, M., 1980, *Qualitative Evaluation Methods*, Sage, London.

Rollo, C., and Clarke, T., 2001, *International Best Practice – Case studies in Knowledge Management. HB 275 Supplement 1-2001*, Standards Australia, Sydney.

Smith, H. W., 1991, *Strategies of Social Research*, (3rd ed.), Holt, Rinehart and Winston, Orlando.

Stewart, V., and Stewart, A., 1981, *Business Applications of Repertory Grid*, McGraw-Hill, London.

Strauss, A., 1987, *Qualitative Analysis for Social Scientists*, Cambridge University Press, Cambridge.

Strauss, A., and Corbin, J., 1990, *Basics of Qualitative Research: Grounded Theory Procedures and Techniques*, Sage Publications, Newbury Park, Calif.

Terrill, B. J., and Flitman, A., 2002, Using Repertory Grid Analysis to gather qualitative data for information systems research, Proceedings of the Thirteenth Australasian Conference on Information Systems (ACIS), Melbourne, Australia, December 4-6, 2002, pp. 745–756.

Terrill, B. J., and Flitman, A., 2003, Factors influencing users' satisfaction with integrative knowledge management systems: A preliminary investigation, Proceedings of the 11th European Conference on Information Systems (ECIS), Naples, Italy, June 19–21, 2003.

DOMAIN MODEL DRIVEN APPROACH TO CHANGE IMPACT ASSESSMENT

Darijus Strašunskas and Sari Hakkarainen*

1. INTRODUCTION

Information system development is a highly iterative process in which developers seek to capture the needs and desires of all stakeholders. The goal is to transform the requirements into a complete system consisting of both manual and computerized parts. The product of such a development project undergoes changes because of its iterative nature. Extensive attention is given to traceability as a means to relate different different system descriptions and to allow changes in one of the system descriptions – requirements specification, design, code, documentation, or test scenarios – to be predicted and traced to the corresponding fragments of the other descriptions.[1] Such correspondence relationships should be maintained throughout the lifetime of a system in order to manage the artifact.

Change impact management and change propagation have received much attention in the requirements engineering literature,[2, 3] as changes during requirements elicitation process are continual. However, there is a lack of tools to support the full lifecycle, starting from artifact inception to its use. Different representation formats that are used throughout the development process make it complicated to cover the whole lifecycle of an artifact. Given, that a single requirement maps to multiple architectural and design concerns, which are used to derive it, it is difficult to maintain the consistency and traceability between the fragments. Moreover, an architectural or a design component has a number of other relations to various requirements. The task becomes even more difficult in the face of a large system that is being build to satisfy thousands of requirements.

In a geographically distributed project, developers may use different tools to create and modify product fragments, which can be refined iteratively and processed further by colleagues. After the system descriptions are produced, they are interchanged and shared among members of the project, which places elaborate requirements on that colleagues interpret artifact correctly. The main challenges are to relate all artifacts in different

---

* Dept. of Computer and Information Science, Norwegian Univ. of Science and Technology, NO-7491 Trondheim, Norway; dstrasun@idi.ntnu.no and sari@idi.ntnu.no

representation formats that are produced in a distributed manner using different tools and to cover the whole product lifecycle.

The objective of this work is to present an approach to product fragments[†] management and change impact assessment in distributed collaborative development process. The assumptions are that there are related concepts in the problem domain and that the fragments can be associated with them. Given that, the semantics of an artifact is increased by the artifact mapping to the corresponding concepts, which enables predicting and assessing fragment change impact on other fragments.

The overall structure of the reminder of this paper is as follows. In section two, related work is analyzed. In section three, the domain model driven approach to enable change impact assessment by relating fragments in different representation formats is presented. In section four, a case study is applied and illustrated by using Bayesian Belief Networks as a candidate technique for quantitative analysis. Finally, in section five, the work is concluded and its possible shortcomings with some insight on how to solve them are discussed.

2. RELATED WORK

Over the recent years, a number of techniques have been proposed for providing traceability and facilitating change management. Some examples[2] are cross referencing schemes, based on some form of tagging, numbering, or indexing and some are requirements traceability matrices. Studies in the field of traceability have mainly focused on specific parts of the development process[4] – mostly in the areas of pre-requirements traceability,[5,6] and linking requirements to architectural components.[7, 8]

Some of the approaches are based on a specific modeling language and /or a tool. A much cited tool is TOOR (Traceability of Object-Oriented Requirements),[5] which is based on FOOPS, a formal object-oriented language. Integrating textual specifications and UML (Unified Modeling Language) model elements is used by Letelier,[9] as a framework for configuring requirements traceability. Both approaches are restricted to FOOPS and UML respectively and can subsequently only be applied to software processes based on the same language.

Some approaches establish links among dependent fragments after most of the system is developed, i.e., after producing requirements specification, code, etc., and, per se, contribute mainly for product maintenance. Frezza et al.[10] base their approach on simulation where both the requirements and the implemented system are simulated in order to obtain a set of result data. The data from the requirements and the implementation phase are then compared, which results in a quantitative measure of how accurate the running system implements the requirements. Egyed[11] uses a scenario driven approach to acquire runtime information about a system and relates the information – the footprints – to the requirements and a model of the running system. The footprints are analyzed in a tool, which shows how the components of the system interact when performing specified scenarios. Thus, it provides additional trace information on how the running system actually fulfills its requirements and which parts of the design are affected.

[†] We will use notions of "fragment" and "artifact" interchangeably in this paper.

In summary, existing approaches fall into two categories: (a) specific notation dependent and (b) post-analytical. The usage of the former enforces developers to learn a new language, which is expensive and error-prone. Usually, these approaches are created with a special purpose and cover only part of system development lifecycle. The latter group of the approaches contributes mainly to system maintenance. So, there is a lack of support for the whole product lifecycle. There is also an apparent lack of support for distributed teams that use different tools, representation techniques and notations. Below, an attempt to fill in these gaps is presented.

3. PROPOSED APPROACH – MAPPING TO THE DOMAIN CONCEPT

It is essential to enable change notification and impact prediction through all phases of development in the distributed projects as mentioned above. To cover the whole lifecycle means that different tools and, most likely, different notations are used during the development project. A list of requirements for product development environments in order to enable collaboration in geographically distributed software products development[12] is described by Farshchian. Here we adopt the requirements (**Req_n**) as follows.

Req_1 Unrestricted product object types – a product development environment should allow the developers to share any type of objects that they might find useful for supporting their cooperation.

Req_2 Unrestricted relation types – a product development environment should allow the developers to create any type of relation between any two objects of product.

Req_3 Incremental product refinement – a product development environment should provide the developers with flexible mechanisms for incrementally refining the product. Hence, the developers should be allowed to start with vague products and to refine them into more complete and formal ones.

The above three requirements were selected in order to cover support for collaboration in distributed projects. Here, the method should meet the requirements **Req_1** to **Req_3**. As this approach is based on the fragments mapping to domain concepts, we say a `fragment` is a well-defined piece of specification and has semantics, machine readable representation and identity, and a `concept` is a well-defined unit of terms found in a specific domain description. Further, there are two basic assumptions (**$Assmp_n$**) underlying the approach as follows.

$Assmp_1$ CASE-tools (Computer Aided Software Engineering) that are used during the product development support an XML (eXtensible Markup Language) or an XML-dialect format output for the developed fragments.

$Assmp_2$ There is a problem domain and it can be characterized by well-defined, interrelated concepts. Furthermore, these concepts are represented as nodes having weighted relationships, which show the strength of the relationship between the concepts, i.e., a relatedness value between the concepts.

The former assumption is reasonable since most CASE-tools maintain model interchange formats derived from XML and the latter is more restrictive since not all the relationships can easily be expressed by weights and the domain model should be shared and agreed by all participants. Based on these assumptions, the overall process (figure 1) applied in this approach consists of three basic steps (**$Step_n$**):

$Step_1$ **Building a conceptual domain specific model.** This step consists of two main sub-steps: ***$Step_{1a}$*** - extraction of domain specific concepts and ***$Step_{1b}$*** - weighing of relationships between concepts.

$Step_{1a}$ Syntactical analysis of textual documents has been investigated severely in the last few decades. Natural language processing is the main technique used to extract more structural information out of documents. Efforts are directed to build models from requirements specification in natural language. The naïve approach is to use nouns as candidates for entities and verbs for relations between entities. However, there is necessity for more sophisticated techniques to handle linguistic variation when proposing model elements and constructing domain models from a large set of documents. The approach[13] of natural language analysis for semantic documents modeling is reused in our approach.

$Step_{1b}$ Quantification of the relationship between concepts is done using linguistics and natural language processing techniques for analyzing the documents from a domain. Correlation analysis, collocation techniques, similarity thesaurus[14] are used to evaluate the strength of relationships between concepts. Computation is expensive. However, these weights have to be computed only once before starting the project. The values should be refined by the domain expert – this reflects the domain expert's belief in how much the concepts are related in a particular domain. So, these numbers come from either objective data or the experiences of the domain expert accumulated from the development of similar projects. These ranges are used to represent the high (0.7 to1.0), medium (0.4 to 0.6) and low (0.0 to 0.3) degree of relation.

$Step_2$ **Fragmentation of artifacts into semantic fragments**. The produced artifact is translated to XML format and is logically fragmented according to its semantics. Fragmentation is done by a traceability module, which gets the XML file as input and where the fragment boundaries are defined by the developer. As an output, an XML file with added tags to identify start and end positions of a fragment is produced.

$Step_3$ **Fragments mapping to the concepts.** Candidate concepts to build a domain model are suggested automatically by the processing of the fragments. Techniques from **$Step_1$** are adapted to extract the concepts, if possible, from the fragments and to propose the closest related concept from the domain model to map to it. Fragments can be linked directly to other fragments if developer finds them related or if one fragment is a part of another. Further, a fragment can be linked to a domain concept, see the meta-model description below for more detailed explanation. The weighting scheme is similar to the one described in ***$Step_{1b}$***. The mapping rate is revised and confirmed by the developer, who created new or a version of the fragment and checked-in to the repository. The relationship information is encoded using XML tags. Finally, the fragments are stored in a central repository.

The domain model is constructed and the concepts are related with weighted links according the strength of the concept relations. The weights are then used to evaluate relations between fragments when mapped to the domain concepts and to estimate the likelihood of impact of one fragment on another.

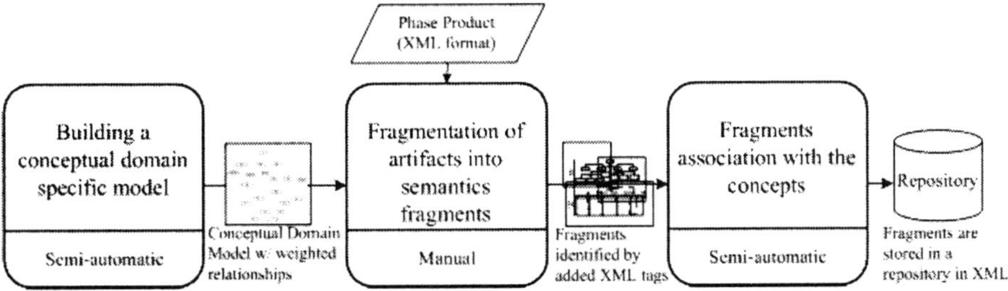

Figure 1. Main steps to enable change impact assessment

Thus, dependency relations are based on the semantics of the artifacts. Fragments are linked to the concepts from the domain model; all selected fragments are mapped and linked through the conceptual domain model as follows.

There exists a set of concepts $\{C_1, C_2, \ldots, C_n\}$ and a set of fragments $\{F_1, F_2, \ldots, F_m\}$, then consequently:

– If fragment F_i is mapped to a concept C_i and fragment F_j is mapped to C_i, then transitively F_i also relates to F_j (Eq.1).

$$(F_i \rightarrow C_i) \wedge (C_i \rightarrow F_j) \Rightarrow F_i \rightarrow F_j \tag{1}$$

– Given, the related concepts C_i and C_j, and if fragment F_i is linked to a concept C_i and a fragment F_j is linked to C_j, then dependency to certain degree exists between F_i and F_j (Eq.2).

$$(C_i \rightarrow C_j) \wedge (F_i \rightarrow C_i) \wedge (C_j \rightarrow F_j) \Rightarrow F_i \rightarrow F_j \tag{2}$$

The meta-model for the proposed approach, based on the settings above, is depicted in Figure 2 using RML (Referent Model Language).[15] RML is an EER-like (Extended Entity Relationship) language with strong abstraction mechanism and sound formal basis.

Meta-model describes the scope of the approach. We deal with product development, using system development tools (Syst.Dev.Tool), system development tool can be also seen as product, when it is under development. Every product development has specific lifecycle consisting of different phase type (e.g., business analysis, requirements engineering, design, implementation, testing, etc.). Each phase type has a distinct phase product type (e.g. requirements specification, design, code, user manual, and software itself), which is result of particular lifecycle phase. A product is final result of the development project, and it consists of the interrelated phase product type.

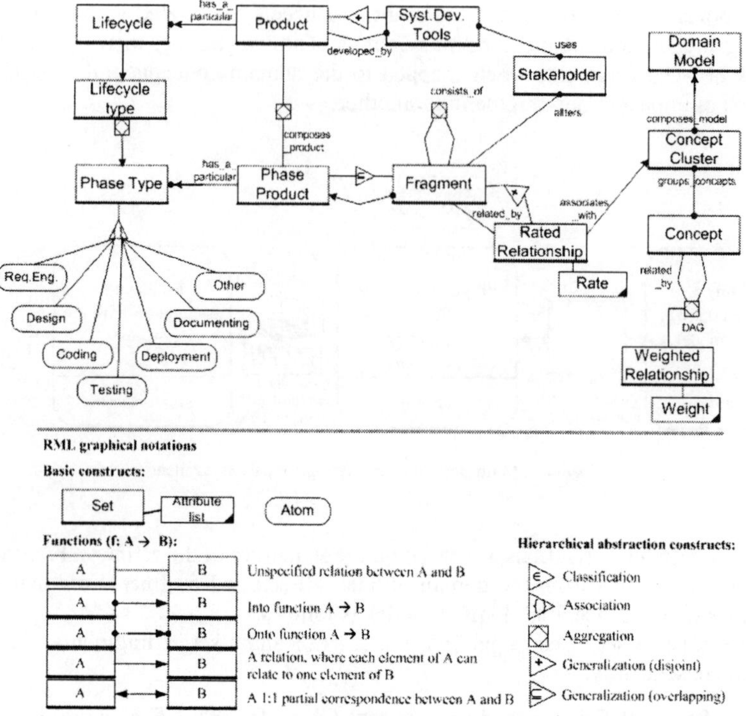

Figure 2. Meta-model to relate product fragments through the conceptual domain model

A fragment is a semantic piece of phase product type in a certain granularity level, e.g., it can be a document, a model, a diagram, a section in a document, a text specifying a non-functional requirement, an use case, a class, an attribute, etc. Fragment can consist of fragments. It should be noted that fragment is inreflexive, asymmetric, and non-transitive. Fragment can have a direct dependence link to another fragment. Every fragment has semantics, which relate the fragment to one or more concept cluster. Rated mapping relationship is used to distinguish fragment coherency to a particular concept. Concept cluster groups related concepts and composes domain model. Concept is connected to other concept by direct acyclic graph with weights (weighted relationship). Weights of those relations are calculated based on degree of the concept relatedness.

4. APPLICATION OF THE APPROACH

In this section we present a case example to test practical applicability and illustrate the proposed approach in empirical settings. Description of the application of the approach consists of a realistic case of and a candidate technique for quantitative analysis – Bayesian Belief Network.

4.1. A Case Study

A case study is based on MEIS (Model Evaluation Information System) system, used for the basic course of information systems SIF8035.[16] MEIS system is used for exercise delivery and evaluation. There are two groups of users: students that are also reviewers of others' solutions, and student assistants, who check all deliveries including both solutions to an exercise and evaluation of those solutions and either accept or reject them. The domain concepts in exercise delivery and evaluation and the relationships among them are depicted in Figure 3. Here, the quantification of the relationships between concepts has been performed manually based on our knowledge of the domain. For example, the weight of relationship between "Student" and "Reviewer" is equal to 1.0 only in this domain, where students are also reviewers of others' solutions.

Next, during the development of the MEIS system every requirement was treated as a separate fragment. Some of them are listed below and additional examples of the product fragments are presented in Figure 4. Requirements for the MEIS system are[16]:

Req.1. It should be possible to create users' profiles from a textual file.
Req.2. A student should be able to upload a solution:
- **Req.2.1.** A solution should be stored in the student's folder.
- **Req.2.2.** A reference (link) to a solution1/2 should be kept in the MEIS database.

Req.3. StudAssist should accept/reject a solution1/2.
- **Req.3.1.** The system should provide the possibility to reject a solution1/2.

Req.4. StudAssist should form a reviewer groups for a solution1/2.
- **Req.4.1.** The system should provide StudAssist a list of students, whose solution has been accepted.
- **Req.4.2.** StudAssist should form a reviewer group based on the student list in Req.4.1.

Req.5. Reviewer should deliver evaluations of both the solution1 and solution2.
- **Req.5.1.** Reviewer should evaluate the DFD/APM model of the solution1/2.
- **Req.5.2.** Reviewer should upload Word documents with evaluation for the DFD/APM model of the solution1/2.
- **Req.5.3.** File with evaluation for the DFD/APM model of the solution1/2 should be stored in the database.

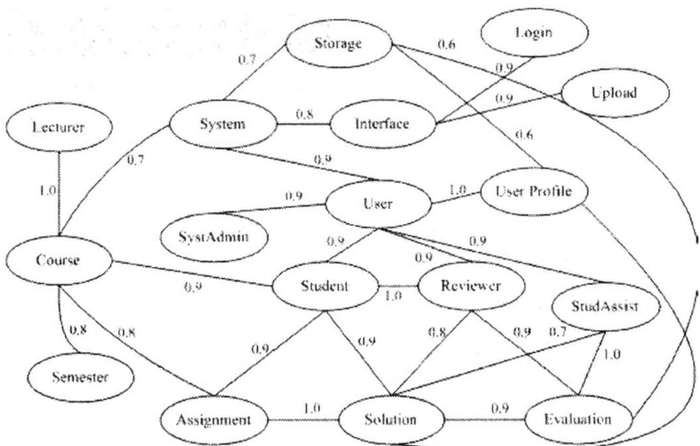

Figure 3. Domain model for MEIS

As described in the previous section, developers will be provided with the tool for semi-automatic fragments mapping to domain concepts. Additional XML tags are entered to keep information about the related concepts and the weight of their relationships, as a fragment could have one or more related concepts. For example, requirement "Req.5.2: Reviewer" should upload Word documents with evaluation for the DFD/APM model of the solution1/2" provides hints about the relation to the concepts "Reviewer", "Upload", "Evaluation" and "Solution". Nevertheless, the requirement is mainly about "evaluation upload". Therefore, it is mapped to the concepts "Upload" and "Evaluation" with the assigned weights 0.9 and 0.7, respectively. A partial graphical representation of the fragments as mapped to the domain model is depicted in Figure 5. The concepts and fragments from the example above are gray shaded. It should be noted that Figure 5 is not intended normative for fragments mapping, but is used here only for illustrational purposes.

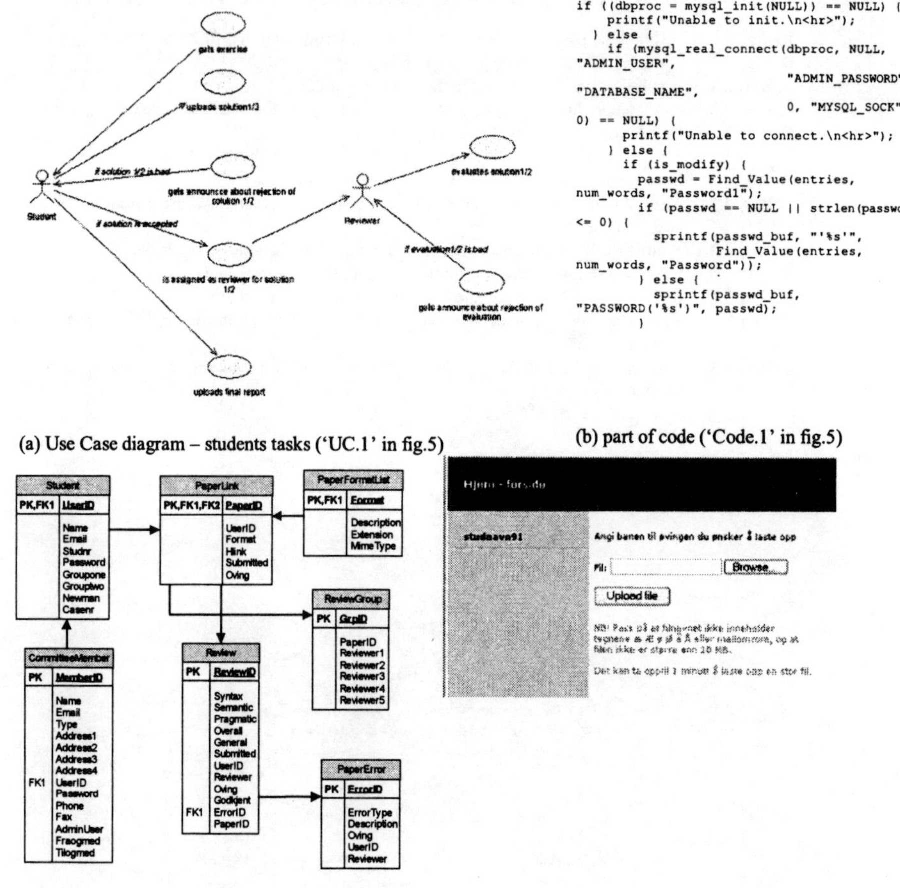

(a) Use Case diagram – students tasks ('UC.1' in fig.5)

(b) part of code ('Code.1' in fig.5)

(c) ER diagram of MEIS database ('Dsgn.1' in fig.5)

(d) Interface screenshot ('Doc.1' in fig.5)

Figure 4. Examples of fragments[16]

4.2. Bayesian Belief Network

One candidate for implementing the approach for product traceability is Bayesian Belief Network (BBN, also called Bayesian Network or Probabilistic Networks). BBN is a powerful technique for reasoning under uncertainty[17, 18] and representing knowledge. It provides a graphical model that resembles human reasoning. In the recent decades, Bayesian Belief Network has attracted attention from both the research and industrial communities. BBN provides a natural way to structure information about a domain. One advantage of the BBN is that it not only captures the qualitative relationships among variables (denoted by nodes) but also quantifies the conceptual relationships. This is achieved by assigning a conditional probability to each node in the BBN[‡].

In a BBN, for each variable x with parent Parent(x), there is a corresponding conditional probability distribution P(x|Parent(x)). For example, in the MEIS domain, the probability of having an impact on requirement "Req.5.1" is directly conditioned by the relation of the two concepts "Reviewer" and "Solution" – "Req.5.1" is mapped directly to them, with the concept which has mapped the changed fragment. Thus, the conditional probability is given as P(Impact.Req.5.1 | Reviewer, Solution).

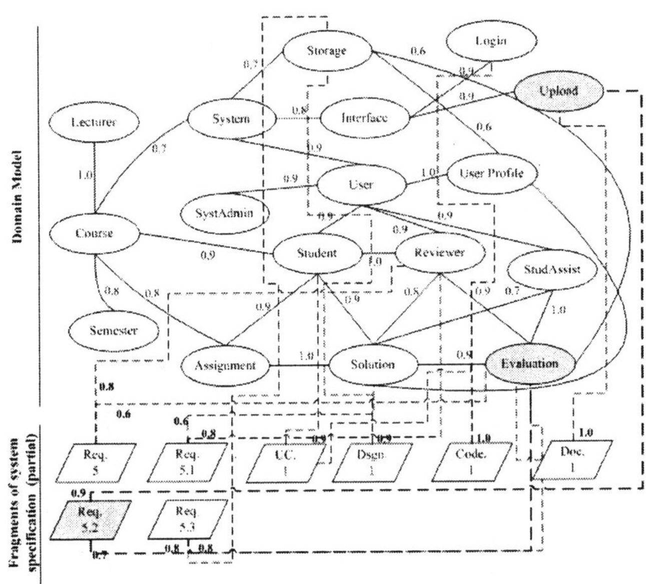

Figure 5. Graphical representation of MEIS fragments mapping to domain concepts (partial)

The applicability of BBN is demonstrated by continuing the example in the sub-section above and using tool MSBNx (Microsoft Bayesian Network Editor and Tool

‡ This has also been the main disadvantage of the BBN – human labor intensity and domain expert dependency.

Kit).[19] MSBNx tool was chosen as it offers an extensive COM-based API for editing and evaluating Bayesian Networks.

So, during the system development, the stakeholder decided to create a standard web form for evaluation instead of delivering an evaluation in a Word file. As a consequence, requirement ("Req.5") has been changed to:

Req.5. Reviewer should be provided 2 (two) web evaluation forms for each solution1/2.

Assessments of the impact probabilities on the other artifacts caused by this change are shown in Figure 6. As all mapped fragments are assessed, only the ones with the highest probability of impact should be checked. Of course, a probability threshold should be defined for notification posting. Further, in large development projects, the threshold value depends on specific project settings and requires attentive empirical study. The definition of the impact relations between phase products facilitates the management of the calculated change impact probability values. In this case, when altering the requirement, only possible changes in the requirements specification and the related phase (e.g., design) should be notified and checked first. Change notification should proceed only if the related design fragment is found impacted, where the developer will need to check the next phases in the impact chain.

The values in Figure 6 show for example, that most likely the fragments "UC.1", "Req.5.1" and "Req.5.2" are impacted. The changed requirement "Req.5" is mapped to the two concepts "Reviewer" and "Evaluation". As "UC.1" is mapped to the concepts "Student", which is strongly (1.0) related to "Reviewer" in this domain, and "Evaluation", the probability to be impacted is relatively high.

Node Name	State 0	State 1
Code.1	Impacted 0.5824	Not Impacted 0.4176
Doc.1	Impacted 0.7361	Not Impacted 0.2639
Dsgn.1	Impacted 0.6958	Not Impacted 0.3042
Req.1	Impacted 0.5396	Not Impacted 0.4604
Req.2	Impacted 0.7600	Not Impacted 0.2400
Req.2.1	Impacted 0.6318	Not Impacted 0.3682
Req.2.2	Impacted 0.6386	Not Impacted 0.3614
Req.3	Impacted 0.5838	Not Impacted 0.4162
Req.4	Impacted 0.5660	Not Impacted 0.4340
Req.4.1	Impacted 0.5890	Not Impacted 0.4111
Req.4.2	Impacted 0.5198	Not Impacted 0.4802
Req.5.1	Impacted 0.8049	Not Impacted 0.1951
Req.5.2	Impacted 0.7932	Not Impacted 0.2068
Req.5.3	Impacted 0.7034	Not Impacted 0.2966
UC.1	Impacted 0.8133	Not Impacted 0.1867

Figure 6. Impact probability evaluated by using MSBNx

5. DISCUSSION AND CONCLUDING REMARKS

In this paper, a methodological approach to facilitate product change management in the distributed development projects has been described. The proposal is based on semantic enrichment of produced fragments by mapping them to related concepts from a specific domain model. This information is used to abstract away from heterogeneous representation details and to capture information content. In this way, domain specific conceptual model is used to interoperate across different representation formats used in the system development. Further, the relations between the fragments and concept as well as the relations among the concepts in the domain model are weighted. Weights assigned to relationships are used as the basis for impact prediction and assessment.

The contribution of this work is threefold. First, unlike other approaches, the proposed approach (a) covers whole lifecycle. Second, as the nature of collaborative development is usually highly iterative, the approach (b) supports the relating and interchanging fragments of a product at different stages of its incremental refinement (e.g., from abstract sketches to a formal representation, see **Req$_3$**). Third, it (c) does not bind the developer to some specific tool and/or modeling language (see **Req$_1$** and **Req$_2$**) provided the preferred tool supports XML format. The use of XML enables use of this approach in settings where the involved artifacts are created and managed by heterogeneous tools, such as text processors and CASE-tools.

The approach can be beneficial for companies working in specific domains where typically the domain model is stable and commonly agreed, and an expert's knowledge is available. In the case of entering a new domain, the company should work out a specific domain model, which needs to be comprehensible and agreed by all developers.

An evolving domain model is a challenge, which should be resolved in future work. The adding or removal of some concepts from a conceptual domain model in the middle of a project raises the question of what to do with the fragments which have been mapped to the concepts. If a new concept is added, the relatedness between the concept and closest fragments could be automatically calculated and the most related fragments could be re-mapped. A concept deletion should not remove the concept from the domain model, but should lock it order to prevent mapping to any new fragments. This would preserve existing links between the concepts and fragments.

Further, large domain model with thousands of concepts could be a challenge for developers in finding the relevant concepts and to link the fragment in question. A candidate solution here is concepts clustering, which could facilitate the selection of the right concept. Developments in the area of ontology mapping could also provide useful methods and techniques which could be used both to find the most relevant concept for the fragment and to develop a stable and a commonly agreed domain specific model for new domain, where several interpretations of the domain and the model exist.

However, where the main contribution of this paper is in change impact assessment as being vital for large development projects, simultaneously, it is perhaps the most risky and error-prone task. The proposed approach enables to calculate the probability objectively from subjective materials – how likely some product fragments are to be impacted by a change of a 'semantically related' fragment. The probability value is calculated based on the weighted relations between domain concepts, where the weights depend on experts' knowledge of the domain. As the calculation operating on those weights is the backbone of this approach, the process of weight assignment should be well reasoned and methodologically described as well as empirically tested – big challenges for future work lie here.

ACKNOWLEDGMENTS

Special thanks go to Sobah Abbas Petersen and the anonymous reviewers for proof reading. This work has been partially supported by the Simula foundation in Norway.

REFERENCES

1. S. Greenspan and C. McGowan, Structuring Software Development for Reliability, *Microelectronics and Reliability*, 17, 75–84 (1978).
2. O. C. Z. Gotel, A. C. W. Finkelstein, An Analysis of the Requirements Traceability Problem, in: *Proceedings of the 1st International Conference on Requirements Engineering* (ICRE'94), (IEEE Computer Society Press, Colorado Springs, Colorado, USA, April 1994), pp. 94–102.
3. R. Watkins, M. Neal, Why and How of Requirements Tracing, *IEEE Software,* 11(4), 104-106 (1994).
4. D. Strašunskas, Traceability in a Collaborative Systems Development from Lifecycle Perspective, Proceedings of the 1st International Workshop on Traceability, co-located with ASE 2002, Edinburgh, Scotland, UK, September 2002, 54–60
5. F. Pinheiro and J. Goguen, An Object-Oriented Tool for Tracing Requirements, *IEEE Software*, 13(2), 52–64 (1996).
6. K. Pohl, PRO-ART: Enabling Requirements Pre-Traceability, Proceedings of the Second International Conference on Requirements Engineering (ICSE '96), Colorado, USA, 1996, 76–85.
7. P. Grünbacher, A. Egyed, and N. Medvidovic, Reconciling Software Requirements and Architectures – The CBSP Approach, in: *Proceedings of the 5th IEEE International Symposium on Requirements Engineering* (RE'01) (Springer-Verlag, Toronto, Canada, 2001), pp. 202–211.
8. K. Pohl, M. Brandenburg, and A. Gülich, Integrating Requirement and Architecture Information: A Scenario and Meta-Model Based Approach, Proceedings of the Seventh International Workshop on Requirements Engineering: Foundation for Software Quality (REFSQ'01), Interlaken, Switzerland, 2001.
9. P. Letelier, A framework for Requirements Traceability in UML based projects, in Proceedings of the 1st International Workshop on Traceability, co-located with ASE 2002, Edinburgh, Scotland, UK, September 2002, 32–41.
10. S. T. Frezza, S. P. Levitan, P. K. Chrysanthis, Linking requirements and design data for automated functional evaluation, *Computers in Industry*, Volume 30, Issue 1, Elsevier Science Publishers B. V., 13–25 (1996).
11. A. Egyed, Reasonings about Trace dependencies in a Multi-Dimensional Space, Proceedings of the 1st International Workshop on Traceability, co-located with ASE 2002, Edinburgh, Scotland, UK, September 2002, 42–45
12. B. A. Farshchian, A Framework for Supporting Shared Interaction in Distributed Product Development Projects, PhD thesis, NTNU, Trondheim, Norway, 2001.
13. T. Brasethvik and J. A. Gulla, Natural Language Analysis for Semantic Document Modeling, Proceedings of the 5th International Conference on the Application of Natural Language for Information Systems (NLDB '2000) in Versailles, France, June 2000.
14. R. Baeza-Yates and B. Ribeiro, *Modern Information Retrieval.* (Addison-Wesley, 1999).
15. A. Sølvberg and T. Brasethvik, The Referent Model Language, Technical Report, NTNU, Trondheim, Norway; http://www.idi.ntnu.no/~ppp/referent/
16. R. Matulevičius, MEIS requirements specification, Technical report, NTNU, Trondheim, NTNU, June 2003.
17. F.V. Jensen, *An Introduction to Bayesian Networks*, (UCL Press, London, 1996).
18. J. Pearl, *Probabilistic Reasoning in Intelligent Systems: Networks of Plausible Inference*, (Morgan Kaufmann. 1988).
19. Microsoft Bayesian Network Editor and Tool Kit; http://research.microsoft.com/adapt/MSBNx/

TRACKING BUSINESS RULES FROM THEIR SOURCE TO THEIR IMPLEMENTATION TO SUPPORT IS MAINTENANCE

Marko Bajec, Damjan Vavpotič, and Marjan Krisper*

ABSTRACT

Business rules describe how organisations are doing business. Their value has also been recognised within the information system (IS) domain, mostly because of their ability to make applications flexible and amenable to change. In this paper we argue that business rules can be used as a link between organisations and their ISs. We show that business rules originate in organisations and that many business rules are explicitly or implicitly captured in enterprise models. We advocate, based on research work, that if business rules are managed in an appropriate manner they can help keeping IS aligned and consistent with the business environment. In the paper we propose a business rule management scenario for managing business rules from an organisational perspective. The scenario recognises business rule management as an interface between enterprise modelling and IS development and maintenance.

1. INTRODUCTION

In the last decades business rules have become popular in the IS community. Researchers and practitioners suggest business rules should be used as an instrument for developing flexible applications and databases that are amenable to change (Layzell and Loucopoulos, 1988; Youdeowei, 1997; Date, 2000; Widom and Ceri, 1996; Morgenstern, 1983). Various kinds of tools and systems have been developed to help IS developers to manage business rules during the IS development life cycle (Herbst, 1996; Struck, 1999; Assche et al., 1988). However, business rules do not pertain to the IS or to its application software, but are set and owned by the business. This means that there should be no rule in an application that the business would not know about. Each rule that is formalised and

* Marko Bajec, Damjan Vavpotič, Marjan Krisper, University of Ljubljana, Faculty of Computer and Information Science, Tržaška 25, 1000 Ljubljana, Slovenia.

automated in some application software has or should have a motivation that comes from the business world and explains its existence.

In this paper,† we argue that business rules can be used to implement the link between business and supporting IS. To this end we suggest that business rules are captured and refined already during enterprise modelling and that in IS development the early set of business rules, derived directly from the enterprise models is used as an important source of requirements determination.

The paper is organised as follows. Section 2 discusses business rules from the organisational perspective, focusing on the relationship between tacit and explicit knowledge rules. The section explains why the link between business rules and the organisational knowledge, from which business rules are derived, is significant. This is used as basic motivation for modelling business rules within the enterprise models. Section 2 also introduces the basics of the enterprise modelling, providing additional motivation for business rule manipulation at the enterprise level. In section 3, a scenario for business rules management is depicted and described. A short conclusion and a review are given in the last section.

2. RULES IN ENTERPRISES

From an enterprise perspective, rules can be defined as assertions that constrain patterns of the enterprise behaviour (Morabito et al., 2001). They exist in all kinds of forms, ranging from simple to very complex and dynamic. Depending on their information contents, they can be based on either explicit or tacit knowledge. Explicit knowledge is formalised knowledge that is easy to express in form of principles, procedures, facts, figures, rules, formulas, etc. Contrariwise, tacit knowledge is not easily expressed and visible (see Nonaka and Takeuchi, 1995). When information contents of a business rule correspond to sufficiently routinized behaviour, the rule takes the form of explicit knowledge. Such are, for example, rules that govern important operations, for instance customer credit approval in a bank, damage declaration in an insurance company, or billing, payroll, and other similar operations that can be found in almost every company. In the IS development, transformation of rules that apply to such operations (into requirements) is almost straightforward, since specifications of the rules are already present in documents, procedures, policies, regulations, user manuals etc. However, in a typical organisation there are many other rules that are not explicitly stated but are more or less a result of subjective knowledge of specific business workers. Such rules are often based on tacit knowledge and are dynamic in nature and hard to express. They are highly personal and subjective, based on experiences, ideals, emotions and intuition. They can be formed and destroyed dynamically as a consequence of a process execution and feedback. In the IS development such rules need to be elicited from business people and if possible, refined and transformed into unambiguous declarations.

---

† The paper is based on a research work that has been partially supported by the Slovenian Ministry for information society and the Ministry for education science and sport.

The relationship between explicit knowledge rules and tacit knowledge rules is very important. An explicit rule that expresses a specific assertion is very different from the knowledge contents on which it is based. Explicit rules are only a manifestation of a richer tacit knowledge. For example, in every organisation we can find operation procedures that are standardised as a result of experience and feedback from their use. Business rules that are derived from the routinized operations can be documented and translated into an IS. In this way, they become available to those who lack the knowledge of the operation. In other words, tacit knowledge that was once required to develop the operation heuristics is now being available in form of explicit rules. However, in order to understand why a certain explicit rule exists, and what kind of motivation is behind it, one must first comprehend the knowledge on which the explicit rule is developed. This argument tells us that we should always know the sources and motivation behind the rules that are supported within the organisations IS.

A commonly known approach that deals with enterprise knowledge and that can be used to describe the knowledge content underlying business rules is enterprise modelling. The modelling of business rules within the development of enterprise models is discussed in the next section.

2.1. Modelling business rules in enterprise models

Enterprise modelling (EM) is an activity that is used to create abstractions (models) of different aspects of an enterprise (government department, academic institution, private company, or other organisation) (Persson and Stirna, 2002) typically with a purpose to understand and share the knowledge of how the enterprise is structured and how it operates. EM is applicable in a variety of contexts, e.g. business process reengineering, strategy planning, enterprise integration and IS development (Fraser, 1994).

There is a number of different ways for an adequate representation of enterprise aspects (cf. Eriksson and Penker, 2000; Nilsson, 1999; Bubenko et al., 2001). For the purpose of our research we have studied the following views: business vision view, business concepts view, business process view and business structure view. Each of the views is represented through a sub-model that belongs to the overall enterprise model.

- The business vision model describes a goal structure for the company and illustrates problems that must be solved in order to achieve those goals. It presents one of the most important aspects of the business as it sets up the overall strategy for the business, defines the goals of the business, and serves as a guide for modelling the other views (Eriksson and Penker, 2000). When developing a business vision model, several business related concepts have to be considered, including Vision, Mission, Goals, Objectives, Strengths, Threats, Weaknesses, Opportunities, Critical factors, etc.
- The business concepts model establishes a common vocabulary for all the concepts that comprise the business environment (e.g. products, services,

information resources, etc.). It helps us to avoid misunderstandings and different interpretations of terms used in the business.

- The business process model represents the key business processes that create value in the business and illustrates the interactions between the processes and resources in order to achieve the purpose of each goal. It is based on the business vision model as it describes the activities that must be undertaken to achieve an explicit goal.
- The business structure model describes structures among the resources in the business, such as organization structure or structure of business products and services.

As mentioned in the introduction we propose that business rules are addressed within EM and that in requirements analysis of a particular system the first set of rules is derived directly from the enterprise models. To ensure business rules are fully traceable, we propose that when new rules are discovered or refined in the system analysis they are traced back to the elements from the enterprise model. Our position is based on the following facts/assumptions:

- The enterprise model captures knowledge which explains the motivation for the existence of rules.
- The enterprise model is an abstraction of the overall enterprise and not just of a particular part of the business to which an IS applies. If the rules are addressed from the organisational perspective we can assume that they are consistent across the overall enterprise. In IS development, on the other hand, consistency problems are much harder to avoid, since the focus is typically limited only to selected departments or organisational units.
- In enterprises, several different systems are typically developed to provide all the necessary information that is essential for establishing a productive and efficient working environment. In practice, these systems are never developed all at once but it usually takes more than a few projects to develop them. Instead of discovering business rules for each particular system individually, the enterprise model can serve as a useful starting point.
- The enterprise model has to reflect the real business environment otherwise it can not serve to its purpose. Enterprise models are therefore continuously adopted and maintained. Thus, focusing on business rules as a part of enterprise modelling assures the rules are up-to-date.
- Enterprise modelling also addresses strategic elements, such as vision, mission, critical success factors and goals of the enterprise. These elements very often present direct or indirect motivations for business rules. In IS development, on the other hand, the enterprise strategic perspective is very often neglected.
- There are many business rules that are already inherent in the enterprise models.

2.2. The business rule model

The idea of addressing business rules within EM is not new. According to the method for EM known as EKD – "Enterprise Knowledge Development" the business rule sub-model (BRM) is a compulsory part of enterprise models (Bubenko et al, 2001). But the focus in EKD in respect to the business rules is essentially on the relationships between business goals and the rules that either support or constrain the achievement of those goals. In our opinion, there is much more information that can be deduced from an enterprise model. We think that BRM comprises not just rules that are acquired explicitly when developing the BRM, but also rules that are captured implicitly through the modelling of the other perspectives. For example, the business process model consists of a number of rules that trigger processes or their activities. Similarly, the concepts model comprises several rules that present constraints or definitions of the concepts included in the model. And finally, the business structure model defines structures e.g. organisational units that define the jurisdiction of the business rules.

In our study we carried out extensive research on relationships that bind business rules to a number of concepts modelled in the other business views. Due to the limitations of space we can only provide a list of the most common relationships. Details can be found in (Bajec, 2001).

- A business rule supports achievement of a business goal.
- A business rule hinders achievement of a business goal.
- A business rule triggers a process or activity.
- A business rule restricts execution of a process or activity.
- A business rule defines an ECA structure (event, condition, activity) with the following meaning: if the event happens and the conditions are met then execute the activity. Each business process can be described as a composition of ECA structures (Herbst, 1996).
- A business process executes (or uses) a business rule.
- A business rule description consists of business terms. Each business rule is written in some syntax and is based on some vocabulary.
- A business rule defines a business concept. For example, "A customer can be a company or a person" is a rule that defines an association between the two concepts of some business environment.
- A business rule is executed in an organisation unit.
- A business rule is a part of a business function.
- A business role is responsible for execution of a business rule.

The main components of BRM are depicted in Figure 1. The Business rule concept is in the centre of the meta-model and represents an atomic piece of information that either defines or constrains the structure or behaviour of the business. Among business rules there are many relationships, for example a business rule supports another business rule, a business rule is in conflict with another, etc. (Rule Impact). As shown in the meta-model, business rules relate to several components of an enterprise model and to several components of an IS.

According to their source, business rules can be either internally or externally driven. Internal rules are defined within the organisation, whereas external rules come from the outside world. External rules include government regulations and laws that govern behaviour in a given industry, or rules that derive from professional practice, e.g. rules that result from standards within the profession itself.

In general, business rules fall into three categories: derivations, constraints and actions triggers. *Constraints* represent rules that specify policies or conditions which restrict business structure and behaviour. They can be further divided into static constraints and conditional constraints. Static constraints are time-independent and must hold at every state. Conditional constraints are different in this respect. They are time-dependent, as they must hold only if certain conditions are satisfied. *Derivations* are expressions that are used to compute or infer derived facts. While a base fact is something that we know about the business domain, a derived fact is created from other facts, either by an inference or through a mathematical calculation. *Actions rules* define circumstances under which specific actions have to be invoked. Typically, these rules define conditions that must be satisfied in order to invoke actions when specific events occur.

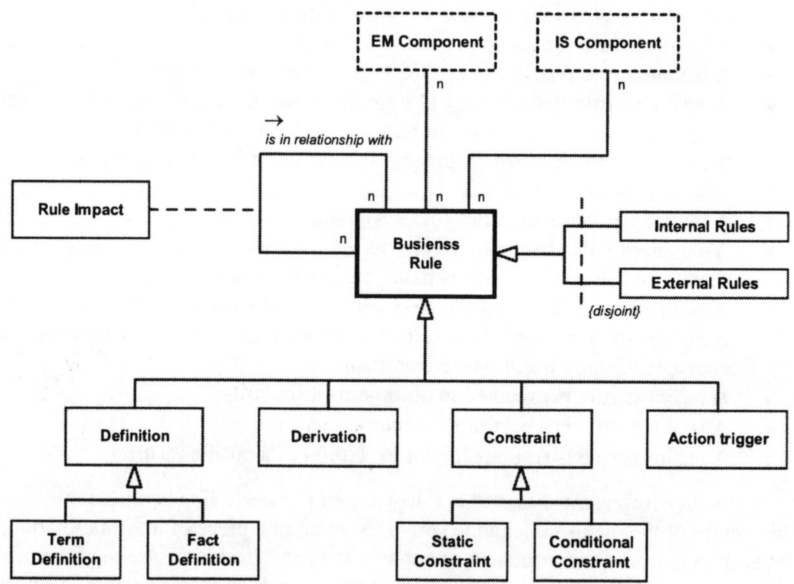

Figure 1. The business rule meta-model

An additional type of a business rule is Definition. Definitions have been introduced and elaborated in the GUIDE project (Hay and Healy, 1997) but have never been widely accepted. Their role is to define concepts and relationships between concepts of the business domain. Definitions can be further divided into terms and facts. Terms are specifications which define business terms that have a specific meaning for the business. Facts, on the other hand, define associations between two or more terms.

When developing the BRM, rules can be specified at different levels of formality (Bubenko et al., 2001):

- Informally by using normal language,
- Formally by using a semi formal language, such as structured English, or
- Formally by using specially designed rule languages, such as External rule language (McBrien, 1991), Object Constrain Language (Warmer and Anneke, 1999), RossMethod (Ross, 1997), etc.

In our approach we suggest that rules are specified by using natural language, in a simple, consistent prose, with a precise use of terms which are defined in a common glossary of the problem domain. To ensure higher clarity and consistency we recommend using rule templates, which can be seen as sentence patterns for descriptions of business rules of the same category. For example, all rules of action trigger type can be specified by using the following template "*when [Event] if [Conditions] then [Action]*"

3. THE BUSINESS RULE MANAGEMENT SCENARIO

In the previous section we described the business rule model as a reasonable constituent of an enterprise model. We will now show how the business rule model can be populated and how can than serve in IS maintenance and development. The activities that we propose in this regard are embraced in the business rule management scenario. The scenario comprises activities performed within EM, activities performed within IS development and additional rule management activities (see Figure 2).

3.1 Activities performed within EM

Activities performed within EM include: Identification of high-level business rules, Identification of externally imposed rules, Refinement of high-level business rules, Identification of the business rule resources and actors, and Business rule consistency and conflict validation.

3.1.1. Identification of high-level business rules

In this activity the high-level business rules are identified typically with respect to the goals that define the enterprise's vision. The high-level business rules are seen as statements that describe how the business has chosen to achieve its goals and how the most important business policies will be implemented. Since business rules are often abstract at this stage, and contain more then just one rule, it is difficult to express them in a formal way. Therefore we suggest that they are specified in natural language using simple sentences and terms consistent with the vocabulary of the problem domain.

3.1.2. Identification of externally imposed rules

Besides the rules that specify how an enterprise has decided to implement its business tactics, there would usually be many other rules, coming from outside of the company. Such rules may include government laws, regulations, industry- or profession-specific rules, etc. These rules should be carefully studied as they can set important business restrictions, affecting the enterprise from several aspects. The most common way of determining externally exposed rules is to examine the Business vision model and to identify constraints that come from the outside world. Externally exposed rules present supplementary information to the group of high-level rules.

3.1.3. Refinement of the high-level business rules

Once the high-level business rules are captured, it is often necessary to refine them and decompose into more clear and unambiguous specifications. We recommend that this is done through close examination of the business process model, which describes the processes that are set to achieve the business goals. Business rules that are accepted as a way of achieving a certain goal are executed in business processes that support that goal. Such rules may decompose into more detailed rules, governing specific business process activities or even further into rules that control operations inside these activities. It must be pointed out, however, that it is not the job of this activity to detail business rules to the maximum extent. The business rules should be only detailed to an extent that allows a clear and unambiguous interpretation (at this stage, most of the rules should be clear enough to be arranged into one of the available rule categories (see section 2.2) In addition to the examination of the business process model, several business rules may also derive from the Business concepts model. In particular rules that define relationships and constraints can contribute to more complete set of business rules. We recommend that all non-trivial rules specifying relationships and constraints are captured and included in the BRM. Even if this seems redundant to information which is already included in the BCM, it is not that dispensable. For example, specifications of relationships and constraints in form of business rules can provide useful information, especially for business users who are very often unable to understand formal modelling techniques. Another advantage of having rules separated and written in the BRM instead of just presenting them in a BCM, is that in this way all the rules are specified in one place and in the same language.

3.1.4. Identification of the business rule resources and actors

This is the last activity performed within EM. Its responsibility is to re-examine business rules and update the BRM with additional information about the resources the rules are using, and in particular about the actors that play any role in regard to the business rules. For example, an actor defined the business rule, is responsible for the rule execution, etc. Most of the information can be derived directly from the Business process model and the Business structure model.

3.1.5. Business rule consistency and conflict validation

Once we have captured all the rules that are essential for the enterprise, we must recheck the rule consistency and see if there are any conflicts. This can happen quickly as there are often differences in how organisation units interpret and perform the enterprise's business policy.

3.2. Activities performed within IS development

Additional activities for managing information about the business rule evolution are performed during IS development.

3.2.1 Determination of the initial set of business rules for the problem domain

The purpose of this activity is to determine the early set of business rules that apply to the system's problem domain. The initial set is derived directly from the Business rule model which is developed during the EM. The rules can be filtered using different criteria, such as rules that apply to a specific business process, rules that belong to a jurisdiction of a particular organisational unit, rules that are of a particular type, etc.

3.2.2. Business rule analysis and classification

Even though business rule refinement is done already during EM some of the rules will still need to be decomposed and refined further. In addition, new rules will be discovered during systems requirements determination. The purpose of this activity is to provide a complete set of rules and to make sure that each rule is atomic, belongs to exactly one category and is specified using predefined rule language.

3.2.3. Business rule consistency and conflict validation

For the overall organisation this activity is done already during EM. Here it is performed again for the systems problem domain to ensure that the complete set of business rules includes only the rules that are consistent and do not conflict among themselves. Basically, the activity needs to be repeated here because of the rules that are additionally discovered in the systems requirements determination.

3.2.4. Business rule modelling

In this activity each business rule is modelled by using some modelling technique. This technique depends on the type of the system being developed, the development approach, the rule category, etc. and can vary from simple graphical representation to a complex mathematical language. In our approach we do not suggest what technique to use, because as said before this depends on many factors. The business rule repository only captures information about the business rule implementation components, while the information about the business rule evolution through the system analysis and design is managed within the system that is used to develop the IS. It is highly recommended however that rules are treated as distinct concepts across the entire development process and that the path of their evolution is not lost after the systems analysis and design is finished.

3.2.5. Business rule implementation

The last business rule management activity performed during the system design is the business rule implementation. Today, many different technologies and supporting tools are available to support business rules implementation and maintenance within a particular system (Struck, 1999). They range from the database oriented tools, that enforce rules using database mechanisms, such as triggers and stored procedures, to the rule oriented systems that offer declarative rule specification languages and special mechanisms to take care of the rule execution. Which technology will be or should be used depends again on several factors, but particularly on the type of the system being developed. For example, in an expert system, rules will be captured and stored in a rule base and executed by a rule engine. In a typical workflow system, business rules will be integrated in the workflow definition, which will be used by a workflow engine to run the workflow (WMFC, 1999). And in a typically database oriented system, business rules will be probably spread across the entire application. It is definitely desirable that rules are physically stored in one place and that they are executed centrally, but this is not always possible. In our approach we do not prescribe what technology should be used. We only advise that information is kept about where (in which system component) the rules are implemented.

3.3. Business rules maintenance

Apart from the activities that are performed during EM and IS development, the business rule management scenario prescribes additional tasks that take care of the business rule changes through their lifecycle. These activities include:

3.3.1. Change control

The purpose of this activity is to coordinate business rule changes. In general, the motive for business rule changes always arises from the enterprise business environment and consequently from modifications of the enterprise model. If it seems that a business rule has changed because of some technical issue or because of some new IS requirement, and that from the business perspective there is no need for the change, then this is not really a business rule. Business rules are owned by the business and are always tightly connected with the business environment. Accordingly, for each change in the Business rule model there must be an explanation at the business level describing why the change is necessary. Moreover, to be able to control changes, information has to be managed about who has requested changes, who has approved them, when they will be implemented, etc.

3.3.2. Version control

Due to their dynamic nature, business rules can have several versions in time. In some cases it may even happen that there will be several versions of the same business rule in use in an enterprise's IS. For example, one rule version will be used in one subsystem, while other subsystems will be using a different version. In order to know which version is in use in which system as to be able to perform assessments for different rule versions, the business rules history has to be tracked.

3.3.3. Impact control

Business rules are rarely independent, which means that a change to a particular rule may cause several other rules to change. To manage changes, all dependencies between rules and other components have to be tracked. Before a business rule is changed, the impact analysis must be done to find out if there are any obstacles in changing the rule.

All information about the business rules captured within EM, IS development or later in the business rules lifecycle, is stored in the repository which implements the Business rule model. The repository is essential for the business rule management scenario as it serves as a global store for business rules of an overall organisation. The repository manages information about:

- The business rules (specifications in a selected business rule language)
- The references to other components of the enterprise model (actors, resources, goals, processes, activities, etc)
- The business rule implementation components (the systems in which the rule is implemented and the system components that implement the rule)
- The business rule history (the rule versions, the rule changes, the reasons for changes, etc).

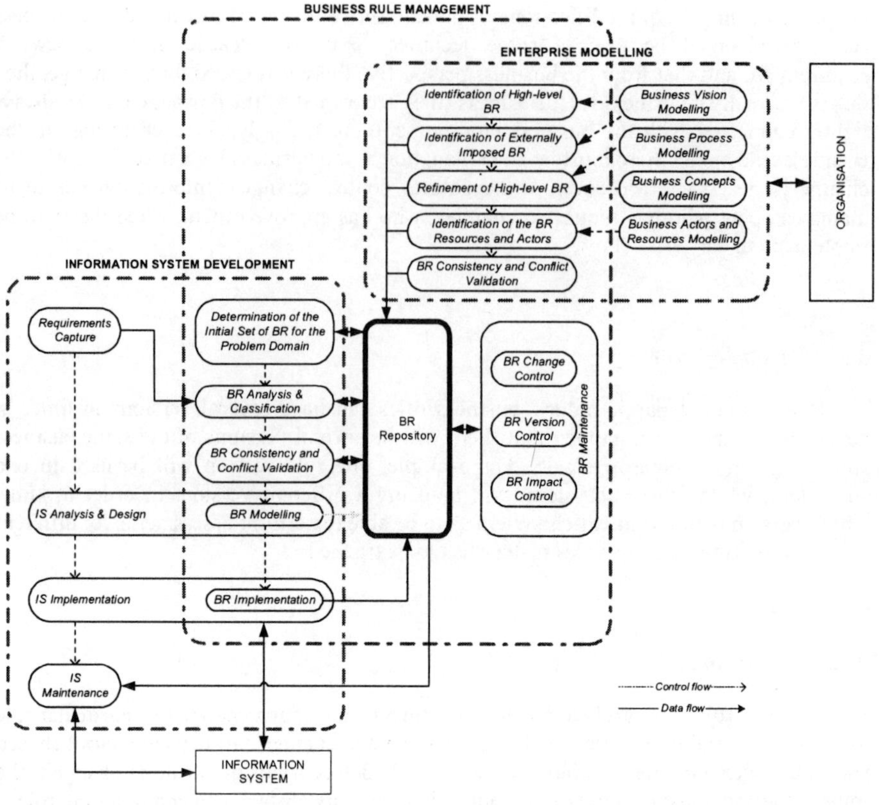

Figure 2. The business rule management scenario

4. PRACTICAL IMPLICATIONS

In practice, business rule management as described in this article has not been yet accepted as vital or even important activity. Even though in the business community everybody would agree business rules are important, they are very often neglected as stand-alone elements, since they represent rather atomic piece of business information, which is at the most captured through other elements, such as goals, threats, opportunities, problems, etc. In this way, business rules remain invisible at the business level. In fact, it is very difficult to motivate companies to capture and formalize their business rules, as there seems to be no direct benefit. The idea, which we try to push through, is to capture business rules within enterprise modelling or IT/IS strategy planning and than to set up some kind of business knowledge repository which can be used as a polygon to simulate business changes and observing the consequences at the information system's level.

In our opinion, business rules present the hardest link between business and information systems. To this end we have developed a prototype that provides facilities to capture business rules from business' and system's perspective. The tool can be used either as a support for managers that work with business knowledge at the business level or for developers that are interested primarily in system development. Using the tool they can easily determine the business rules that are important for the area for which the system is being developed. In addition, if a particular business rule has been already implemented in some other system, the information that was captured during analysis, design and implementation is already stored in the repository.

5. CONCLUSIONS

We have presented an approach for business rule management in organisations, supporting it with a scenario. Instead of working with business rules at a system level, which is a common way in systems development, we proposed that business rules are acquired, analysed and maintained at the organisational level. Business rules are first identified within EM through examination of various aspects of the enterprise. A first step involves examination of business goals, which represent the most abstract motivation for existence of business rules. Since the rules that support or constrain business goals (high-level rules) are often vague, ambiguous and complex they need to be refined into more detailed and concise business rules. The refinement and decomposition is done through the examination of other aspects of the enterprise. There additional information on business rule components and resources can be discovered. All the information about business rules is modelled in the business rule sub-model. When the enterprise decides to develop a system in support of its business the business rule sub-model is used to develop the set of business rules that apply to the system's application domain. The rules that are derived from the business rule sub-model only represent a preliminary set of business rules and are further detailed through the system analysis, design and implementation. As a feedback the business rule sub-model is updated with supplemental information about where and how the business rules are implemented in the enterprises' IS and its components.

With respect to the literature, the contribution of this paper is in synthesis of traditional and special activities that deal with business rules explicitly within an enterprise modelling, information system development and further through an entire business rule evolution. The scenario and tool support described in the paper support business rule management for an entire organisation, providing a means to keep the organisation's IS aligned with the business environment. While it has been recognised before that it is important to establish explicit links between business objectives and strategies and IS development, it has not been shown how business rules can be used in this regard, or any scenario that would explain how this could be achieved.

REFERENCES

Assche Van, F., Layzell P. J. and Anderson M., 1988, RUBRIC – A Rule-Based Approach to Information Systems Requirements, Proceedings of the 1st European Conference on Information Technology for Organisational Systems, Athens.

Bajec, M., 2001, Definition of the Conceptual Framework for Business Rule Management in Organisations, PhD Thesis, Laboratory of Information Systems, UL - Faculty of Computer & Information Science, Ljubljana, Slovenia.

Bubenko, J. A., Persson, A. and Stirna, J., 2001, D3 Appendix B: EKD User Guide, Royal Institute of Technology (KTH) and Stockholm University, Stockholm, Sweden.

Bubenko, J. A. and Wangler, B., 1993, Objectives driven capture of business rules and of information systems requirements, Proceedings of International Conference on Systems, Man and Cybernetics, Systems Engineering in the Service of Humans, vol.1., 670–677.

Date, C. J., 2000. *What Not How: The Business Rules Approach to Application Development.* Addison Wesley Longman, Inc.

Eriksson, H. E. and Penker, M., 2000, *Business Modelling with UML, Business Patterns at Work.* John Wiley & Sons, Inc.

Fraser, J., ed, 1994, Enterprise State of the Art Survey, Part 5, Technologies Supporting Enterprise Modelling, DTI ISIP Project Number 8032, AIAI, The University of Edinburgh.

Hay, D. and Healy, K. A., 1997, GUIDE Business Rules Project, Final Report – revision 1.2. GUIDE International Corporation, Chicago.

Herbst, H., 1996, Business Rules in Systems Analysis: A Meta-Model and Repository System. *Information Systems*, 21 (2), 147–166.

Layzell, P. J. and Loucopoulos, P., 1988, A Rule-Based Approach to the Construction and Evolution of Business Information Systems, Proceedings of the 4th IEEE International Conference on Software Maintenance, Phoenix, Arizona, USA, 258–264.

McBrien, P. J., Niézette, M., Pantazis, D., Seltveit, A. H., Sundin, U., Theodoulidis, B., Tziallas, G. and Wohed, R., 1991, A Rule Language to Capture and Model Business Policy Specifications, in *Proceedings of CAiSE 1991*, Spinger-Verlag LNCS 498, 307–318.

Morgenstern, M., 1983, Active Databases as a Paradigm for Enhanced Computing Environments, Proceeding of the 9th International conference on Very Large Databases, Florence, Italy, 34–42.

Persson, A. and Stirna, J., 2002. An explorative study into the influence of business goals on the practical use of Enterprise Modelling methods and tools, in: *New Perspectives on Information Systems Development: Theory, Methods and Practice,* G. Harindranath et. al., eds., Kluwer Academic, New York, USA.

Struck, D. L., 1999, Business Rule Continuous Requirements Environment, PhD Thesis, Colorado Technical University, Colorado Springs, Colorado.

Warmer, J. B. and Anneke, G. K., 1999, *The Object Constraint Language: Precise Modelling With UML,* Addison-Wesley Object Technology Series, Addison-Wesley.

WMFC. Workflow Management Coalition, *Terminology & Glossary*, Document Number WFMC-TC-1011, February 1999.

Widom, J. and Ceri, S., 1996, *Active Database Systems – Triggers and Rules For Advanced Database Processing*, Morgan Kaufmann, San Francisco.

Youdeowei, A., 1997, The B-Rule Methodology: A Business Rule Approach to Information Systems Development, PhD Thesis, Department of Computation UMIST, Manchester, United Kingdom.

PROCESS OF REQUIREMENTS EVOLUTION IN WEB-ENABLED EMPLOYEE SERVICE SYSTEMS

Pradip K. Sarkar and Jacob L. Cybulski*

1. INTRODUCTION

In recent times, according to the Association for Payroll Specialists, the adoption rate of web-enabled employee service systems (ESS) in Australia has accelerated to a point where one in 10 Australian firms now have such systems in place for employees to view and update their details online (Nixon, 2003). The main objective of web-based support for HR solutions was to replace paper-based documents and the multiple steps of the HR process with online data entry and interaction by employees and managers themselves. Furthermore, the adoption of such services was greatly influenced by the organizational strategic plans that basically translate into operational goals of improved productivity, data accuracy, and the reduction of paperwork and administrative overheads. Despite the optimism and success stories, these systems have their share of obstacles. One of these obstacles is the plain fact that only a fraction of employees have access to the web and computers (Lapointe, 1997). Such systems necessitate infrastructure support in the forms of increased security features, workflow and transaction management, and web administration. Moreover, these systems have been designed keeping in mind that the users will be casual and untrained. Also, the stakeholder base will be far wider than that of conventional non-web HR systems, which are traditionally used by HR staff alone (Lapointe, 1998). The broad, diverse, and expanding stakeholder base, characteristic of web-enabled information systems (WBIS) in general (Nazareth, 1998; Carter, 2002; Standing, 2002; Stevens and Timbrell, 2002), raises the issue of multiple and possibly conflicting viewpoints regarding the various facets of the web system (Easterbrook, 1994; Sommerville et al., 1997).

So, in light of these complexities, how are the requirements for WBIS established? Gordijn and associates (Gordijn et al., 2000) criticize the currently practiced process of requirements gathering as largely inadequate for web development. In particular, they claim that requirements for web-based information systems are commonly "created from

* Pradip K. Sarkar & Jacob L. Cybulski, School of Information Systems, Faculty of Business and Law, Deakin University, 221 Burwood Highway, Victoria 3125, Australia,
Email: pks1@deakin.edu.au, jlcybuls@deakin.edu.au

scratch" by developers themselves rather than being discovered through the normal process of identifying system stakeholders and gathering their requirements. This is indeed true in light of the fact that most WBIS are built for a specific business purpose by developers and then offered and sold as a product to clients with an avid plan to disseminate services via the web. This is why the requirements analysts associated with web development often fail to identify and characterize the potential users of their future web systems (Russo, 2000). Review of relevant literature on the development of web-based information systems reveal that such systems are commonly "configured" using an evolutionary approach, whereby the version of the application, acquired from the vendor, is first deployed as a *pilot*, in order to gather user feedback before the evolutionary cycles commence (Fraternali, 1999). Subsequently, the web system typically undergoes continuous evolution until it eventually becomes a system capable of providing fully-fledged web services (Ginige, 1998; Siau, 1998; Standing, 2001).

However, the purpose of this paper is to understand and elucidate the experience of project initiators in pursuing the evolution of web services, a process that undoubtedly involves dealing with stakeholder issues. In this regard, existing literature fails to adequately capture and discuss the experience of stakeholders associated with the diffusion, usage, and evolution of web services. The Internet Commerce Development Methodology (ICDM), proposed by Standing (2000), deals with great many problems of web development. Web IS Development Methodology (WISDM) (Vidgen, 2002b) is yet another web-specific methodology. Having emerged from Multiview2 (Avison, et al., 1998), WISDM is inherently associated with the overall development of web-based information systems. These approaches are essentially methodological prescriptions for web development, but do not shed any light on the experiences of project initiators in fine-tuning the various features of the solutions and their subsequent rollover throughout the realm of end-users. Initiators are organizations or organizational units that propose the web services to their clients (Riggins and Mukhopadhyay, 1999).

The concept of the *stakeholder* originates from literature in strategic management (Freeman, 1984). Accordingly, a stakeholder could be defined as any individual, groups, or organizations whose actions can influence or be influenced by the development and use of the system whether directly or indirectly (Pouloudi, 1999). Sharp and colleagues (1999) have used the term "baseline" stakeholders to imply individuals or groups who are *directly* involved or interact with the information system, and have included users, developers, and decision-makers or initiators as belonging to this category. In this paper, the concept of stakeholders has been adopted to refer to "baseline" stakeholders.

2. RESEARCH METHODS

As the experience of project initiators in promoting the further evolution of web-based services is inadequately substantiated in the professional literature, an exploratory study was designed with the aim of gaining some understanding of the phenomena of interest. This understanding can be induced using an *interpretivist* approach which we adopted in our study (Strauss and Corbin, 1990; Walsham, 1993; Klein and Myers 1999).

The conducted study aimed at uncovering and examining the experience of project managers who had initiated and overseen the introduction and evolution of web services in their organizations. Hence our study had to probe deep into the complex stakeholder interactions and institutional settings for the projects, which pointed us to adopting qualitative methods of analyzing the collected data (Kaplan and Maxwell, 1994). Furthermore, to understand the emerging practice in ESS diffusion, we undertook investigation of several projects in their natural settings, which in turn justified the use of multiple case studies (Yin, 1994; Darke et al., 1998). Phenomenology is the underlying philosophy behind the analysis of the empirical findings of the study, as it examines the "lived experience" of project leaders in dealing with stakeholder concerns (Moustakas, 1994; Moreno Jr., 1999; Hancock, 2002). Therefore, the analysis considers the meaning of "dealing" with stakeholder concerns in the context of the evolution of ESS within organizations, the various types of stakeholder concerns experienced, and the consequences of the actions – positive or negative - of projects teams in dealing with those concerns. Boland (1979; 1985) employed phenomenology and hermeneutics in his research on information systems. According to him, the interactions between system developers and users are investigated in order to interpret the significance and potential meaning they hold. Thus, phenomenological studies and hermeneutics can be employed to gain an understanding of the phenomena examined in the study (Galliers, 1985). We proceeded to conduct our case studies in the context of five organizations responsible for initiating and operating web-enabled employee support and payroll services.

At the time the empirical studies begun, the adoption of web technology by outsourced payroll providers and HR departments was relatively new, though it had gained some popularity in the US a few years earlier (Lapointe, 1997). The investigated organizations focused on providing ESS services in quite diverse business settings. Three of the WBIS used in our study were operating in tertiary educational institutions, while the remaining two were deployed as a medium through which outsourced payroll companies provided services to their clients. In all our case studies, we focused on the collection of data reflecting the experience of project leaders in dealing with concerns of the most significant stakeholders in the ESS environment (Marshall and Rossman, 1989; Creswell, 1994). This was supplemented by the investigation of audiovisual materials, such as demonstration software, user manuals, project notes and presentations of "awareness" programs.

3. DISCUSSION OF FINDINGS

The empirical data was analyzed in accordance with the steps of the modified *Van Kaam Method of Analysis of Phenomenological Data* discussed by Moustakas (1994) and based on the principle of the *hermeneutic cycle,* which is essentially an iterative analysis of textual data (until it was determined that no more new issues could be uncovered) undertaken to produce meanings and interpretations (Gadamer, 1976; Lee, 1994). Owing to the aim of the paper and space limitation, the textural-structural description of each case will not be discussed. Instead, we focus of the *synthesis* of the composite descriptions that represent all the five cases.

3.1. The model of the evolution process

The model, illustrated in Figure 1, was derived from a composite structural description of the processes of evolution in the five cases. Most often organizational projects are given the impetus by the strategic plans of the organization (Irani, 2002), indicated by the arrow from Strategy to Business Needs. In the case of ESS, the

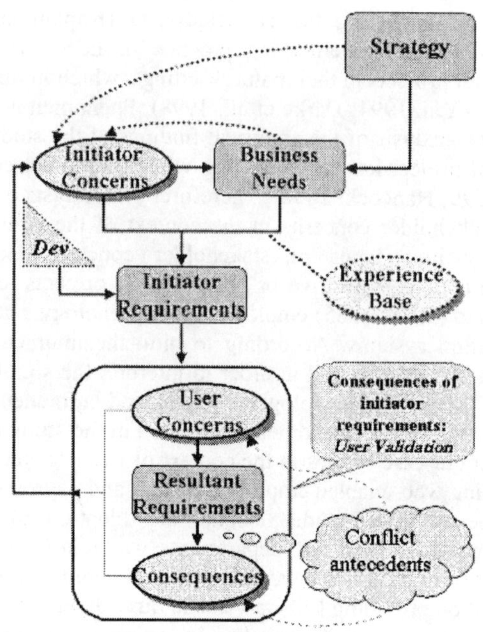

Figure 1. ESS Evolution: An Iterative Model

significance of the translation of strategic objectives into business needs is quite apparent (Lapointe, 1997; Lapointe, 1998). The strategies brought about some of the initiator concerns (indicated by the dotted arrow from Strategy to Initiator Concerns in Figure 1), thus necessitating the elaboration of the business needs. Business needs are also driven by the concerns of the project initiators, indicated by the arrow in the figure. Some of these include concerns surrounding issues of productivity, cost reduction, and improvement of the quality of its services. This direct link between initiator concerns and business needs was found to be more explicit and direct. On the other hand, the impact of business needs on concerns was much less apparent and indirect, which is shown by the dotted arrow.

The process of ESS evolution in the iterative progression of web-enabled applications began at the stage of formulating the initiator's requirements, thereby confirming the notion proposed by Boehm (1986). All the organizations, except one, purchased the WBIS from a vendor, which included features that were more or less a direct reflection of the HR and payroll requirements. In one case, the system was developed in-house by the IT division, shown by the dotted triangle labeled as *Dev* in the figure, and it played a part in setting the initial requirements for the WBIS.

Initiator requirements had their consequences (as shown by the callout in Figure 1). The initiator consequences encompass a sub-process, which includes user concerns, resultant requirements, and consequences. What this indicates is a causal relationship between the initiator requirements, and the concerns of the users. In other words, each initiator requirement may trigger some concerns among users, which need to be looked into in order to motivate them to use the web system or to minimize their resistance toward it. This is shown by the thin arrow from User Concerns and leads into the thick arrow to Initiator Concerns as shown in the figure. This relationship also represents the validation of the system features, initiator-driven, by the users. Resultant requirements represented the actions taken by the initiators to address the user concerns, which in turn, had their share of consequences that raised concerns, thereby leading to another cycle of refinements and validation. Thus, the model was perceived to iterative and evolutionary.

3.2. Experiencing Stakeholder Concerns and the Manifestation of Conflict

Despite the differences in the organizational setting of the two groups of enterprises, we discovered remarkable similarities in the manner in the perceptions of project managers with issues they considered to be stakeholder concerns. As illustrated in Figure 1, the ESS was launched for beta testing equipped with the standard requirements, which were either put forth by the initiators or reflected their viewpoints (Initiator Requirements in the rectangle). During the various cycles of validation of the initiator requirements, users provided feedback, which varied from suggestions for minor modifications, such as a more soothing colour for the GUIs, to more serious issues related to the fact that some of the target users had no ready access to the Internet or even a PC. It was essentially the feedback of the latter type that the initiators perceived as "concerns". In this regards, the definition of a concern that we induced from our interviews with the project leaders is:

> A concern is an issue voiced by a particular stakeholder with regards to some aspect of the proposed information system, which impacts the stakeholder's involvement in this system and which when addressed will determine the need for further evolution of the system.

Thus, there was no doubt that this evolution was greatly dependent on the various cycles of concern consideration and subsequent setting of requirements solutions. At any point, if a concern was ignored or could not be dealt with, *tension between the stakeholders surfaced!* This is illustrated by the "clouds" of conflict antecedents looming over the process of evolution and linked (by broken arrows) to the user concerns and consequences. Furthermore, owing to the fact that the clouds loom over concerns and consequences, they have both been represented as ellipses. On the other hand, strategies, business needs, and requirements are actions undertaken by the project teams, and are thus shown as rounded rectangles. It should be noted that concerns also varied in their degree of criticality. In other words, though antecedents were apparent in all concerns, only in some situations did the failure to address the concerns appropriately result in full-blown conflict. The less critical concerns, on the other hand, exposed points of disagreement that could be sorted out without "drawing swords".

What was interesting was the fact that we discovered variations in the criticality of these concerns between the universities and the outsourced payroll companies. Project leaders in universities experienced a significantly greater number of highly critical concerns than did their payroll counterparts. Thus, the former had to be a lot more careful and tactful in how the concerns were dealt with. This was much more straightforward in payroll companies. The matter could be attributed to the different business settings and nature of stakeholders prevailing in the two types of cases. The power structures and relationships, and vested interests in universities were inherently complex and politically charged. Though they had gained support from the higher echelons of university administrations, the project teams had to convince the stakeholders that the ESS was to going to generate a broader range of benefits for everyone than just productivity gains for the Human Resource (HR) divisions. Added to this complexity was the even within a particular stakeholder group, there was a lack of uniformity in traits. Thus, no two academics or departmental administrators shared the same set of characteristics. Some of them were IT proficient and willing to become avid users of the web system, while others, already overburdened with their regular tasks and having no PC on their desks, viewed the project as an imposition on their work lives.

To cite an example to discuss this complexity prevailing in universities, in one of the case studies, the HR and IT divisions were two separate units within the organization, each with its own viewpoints and aspirations. Since both units were part of the same enterprise, they were driven by the same set of strategic objectives, but their association with different cliques resulted in conflicting viewpoints over the requirements for the WBIS. To generate an in-depth understanding of the aspects of contention, thorough interviews were conducted with both the project leader (who was basically an HR manager with computer skills and proven track record) and the head of the IT division. One of the main points of dispute was the security requirement involving the use of digital signatures, a facet proposed and enforced upon the system, with the approval of the top management, by the developers (IT) in line with their culture of technological innovativeness. The HR members of the project team were against this, as they perceived the requirement necessitating the dedication of vast resources, thereby rendering it somewhat infeasible proposition. The end-users of the system, the supervisors and departmental administrators, were likewise, not keen on digital signatures either. From the feedback obtained as part of the incremental approach to the evolution of the web system, it was revealed that they considered the implementation of this technology as a burden because it was time consuming to install and required additional training for effective usage of the technology. However, the concerns of both the HR unit and the users were not taken into account. In the words of the HR manager:

> This digital signature initiative was railroaded by the developers, it was not an HR requirement... since, the IT division (developers) knew how to use the technology (in line with their culture of going for cutting-edge stuff)...everyone else should use this...this was their justification. This impeded our progress in the roll-over and further evolution of the web system.

Thus, the conflict between the two stakeholders manifested as a roadblock to the further diffusion of the ESS, owing to which the feature had to be ultimately dropped.

With outsourced payroll companies, the situation was definitely less volatile. They were basically offering the same set of services to their clients but through a web medium, in line with their web or e-business strategy of enhancing the value of services to existing clients, attracting new clients from their websites, and streamlining certain internal operations, such as data entry. In accordance with this new strategy, they embarked upon promotional programs aimed at dispersing the web services to their existing and potential clients. One of the main motivators for clients to become recipients of web-based payroll services, as perceived by the project managers, was the delivery of premium services. Realizing that not all their clients were IT proficient, the payroll companies also kept the option of service delivery through conventional modes, such as fax and courier services. Some of the concerns raised by clients, who had adopted to become web-based service recipients, were significant enough for the initiators to consider, but the level of criticality did not pose the threat of conflict with the clients.

This is apparent in light of the fact that the payroll companies were in no way involved with the power structures existing within the client firms. They were customers and thus, needed to be served optimally in order to ensure their satisfaction with the web services. This did not imply that conflict antecedents did not exist in these projects. If the adoption rate of the web services among clients failed to reach the established target, tensions among the power groups within the payroll companies themselves could soar to a point where the structure and composition of the project teams were under threat. Therefore, gaining and retaining customers for the web services were paramount to the success of the projects, thereby necessitating devotion of resources toward the effective management of the WBIS and appointment of competent Helpdesk personnel.

3.3. The Implicit Experience Base

As illustrated as a dotted ellipse in Figure 1, most of the projects studied had made use of some sort of a experience base, though this was not an apparently an institutional practice. In some of the enterprises, the knowledge base represented previous developmental experience, which promoted reuse, as stated by a web developer:

> We adapted the web interface for the Student Information System to the web-enabled employee services application and added the middleware. In terms of reusability, we have definitely tried to write our web application in such a way that the code is reusable not only in the student information system but also in this system...

In another organization, the project team had conducted observations of a similar WBIS that was running "live" in other institutions. According to the project manager:

> ... we started exploring a couple of sites (set up by our vendor) that were up and running. These systems we observed live as they were being used by some universities. Some of these sites were in the beta testing stages... plus it's a fact that organizations are increasingly adopting these kinds of systems and we followed suit.

Therefore, this project team claimed to have "learnt" and reused their experience from observing the same kind of web applications being used in similar organizations. This undoubtedly uncovered the existence and use of an implicit experience base in the projects studied.

In one of the projects studied, the members constituted the experience base. Owing to this, the level of organizational knowledge dropped when a manager quit the team, which reflected the *exceptional designer* syndrome discovered by (Curtis et al., 1988) According to the former team leader:

> ...the next most experienced person to me left (after me), and we went down from a cumulative experience of 14 years to 6 years, and basically lost a lot of that organization knowledge.

4. SUMMARY AND CONCLUSIONS

Our case studies of the projects enabled us to induce a number of facts about the social process inherent in the diffusion of ESS. We observed that the majority of web projects begin with dissemination of promotional information to create "awareness" about the proposed services among the user community. Such dissemination is commonly carried through seminars, newsletters, "Updates" on websites, to name just a few. However, no broad base requirements gathering process usually takes place. Instead the web applications are rapidly launched as "requirements prototypes" for pilot testing (Leffingwell and Widrig 2000). This is designed to assist the initiators in obtaining feedback from users in order to validate the requirements placed on the ESS. However, while analysts frequently have difficulties in gathering explicit user requirements, they manage to collect the abundance of feedback from the users regarding the proposed system features. Some of this feedback merely reinforced the notion that the web services will yield benefits for all the parties involved. However, the predominant feedback received by the project teams studied were a cause for "alertness" and possibly "alarm" and termed as *concerns*. Thus, concerns called for attention from the initiators, which typically lead to the further evolution of the WBIS as additional requirements were generated to alleviate these concerns. Some of these resultant requirements also had their own consequences, which caused concerns for the project initiators, and needed to be tackled on their own merit.

Of course, the concerns varied in their levels of criticality. Some were just "alert" concerns that needed consideration to ensure user adoption and satisfaction of services. On the other hand, concerns that caused "alarm" posed the imminent threat of organizational conflict if not seriously taken on-board and negotiated. The latter type of stakeholder concerns, perceived by the project leaders, exposed the power play between the prime interest groups prevailing in most enterprises. It also indicated the fact that if a project team directly involved groups with incompatible viewpoints, it created a fertile breeding ground for disputes over what should or should not be incorporated in the WBIS, thereby jeopardizing the projects (Sommerville and Sawyer 1997). Hence, stakeholder concerns were perceived to be highly significant in light of their predictive capacity to provide hints and clues to social issues that could "make or break" ESS projects.

Another profound discovery from the studies were the existence of implicit experience bases in the projects. According to Ginige (1998) and Standing (2001), the implementation of web projects can be improved by "learning through experience". Indeed, the projects in which some form of experiential learning took place reported gains such as relatively faster pace of iterations and less drastic modifications. Yet, the experience bases and their use (or reuse) were commonly not institutional, which is why the benefits of knowledge sharing and reuse were not always apparent in the end, i.e. saved development time in some areas but offset by hurdles in others

The findings of the studies challenge the functionalist perspective held by most web development methodologies. The complexity surrounding web projects is such that the application of objective measures to predict their outcomes and correlate the various facets inherent is largely difficult. The results of the studies on ESS projects bear similarities to the social implications of BPR projects discussed by (Moreno Jr., 1999). Thus, this paper presents a novel viewpoint to the field of web technology dispersion by revealing the underlying social process that inevitably needs to be considered in any organizational undertaking. Indeed, (Vidgen, 2002a), the points to the importance of drawing from social theories to understand and explain web projects. Moreover, the studies can contribute an answer to the "web crisis" forewarned by Murugesan (1999).

It should be noted that absolute knowledge about a phenomenon is impossible to achieve, as there will always be room for further learning and re-learning (Boland, 1985). Thus, future research can be directed at analyzing the experience of the users of ESS and the vendors who provide such solutions. In this way, the viewpoints of other stakeholders can be examined, thereby enabling a more comprehensive understanding of the phenomenon of the spread of web-based services.

ACKNOWLEDGEMENTS

The authors would like to thank all the co-researchers (participants of the phenomenological case studies) for sharing their experiences with us, and the reviewers for invaluable comments to the paper.

REFERENCES

Avison, D. E., Wood-Harper, A. T., et al., 1998, A Further Exploration into Information Systems Development: The Evolution of Multiview 2, *Information Technology & People,* **11**(2): 124–139.

Boehm, B., 1986, A Spiral Model of Software Development and Enhancement, *Software Engineering Notes,* **11**(4): 22–32.

Boland, R., 1979, Control, Causality and Information System Requirements. *Accounting, Organizations and Society,* **4**(4).

Boland, R., 1985, Phenomenology: A Preferred Approach to Research in Information Systems, in: *Research Methods in Information Systems*, A. T. Wood-Harper, ed., Amsterdam, NorthHolland.

Carter, J., 2002, *Developing E-Commerce Systems*, Prentice-Hall.

Creswell, J. W., 1994, A Framework for the Study, in: *Research Design: Qualitative & Quantative Approaches*, SAGE Publications.

Curtis, B., Krasner, H. et al., 1988, A Field Study of the Software Design Process for Large Systems, *Communications of the ACM,* **31**(11): 1268–1287.

Darke, P., Shanks, G. et al., 1998, Successfully Completing Case Study Research: Combining Rigour, Relevance and Pragmatism, *Information Systems Journal,* **8**: 273–289.

Easterbrook, S., 1994, Resolving Requirements Conflicts with Computer-Supported Negotiation, in: *Requirements Engineering: Social and Technical Issues.* J. Goguen. London, Academic Press: 41–65.

Fraternali, P., 1999, Tools and Approaches for Developing Data-Intensive Web Applications: A Survey, *ACM Computing Surveys,* **31**(3): 227–263.

Freeman, R. E., 1984, *Strategic Management: A Stakeholder Approach.* Boston, Pitman.

Gadamer, H.-G., 1976, *Philosophical Hermeneutics*. California, University of California Press.

Galliers, R. D., 1985, In Search of a Paradigm for Information Systems Research, in: *Research Methods in Information Systems*, A. T. Wood-Harper, ed., North-Holland, UK: 3–9.

Ginige, A., 1998, Web Engineering: Methodologies for Developing Large and Maintainable Web-Based Information Systems, IEEE International Conference on Networking India and the World, Ahmedabad, India.

Gordijn, J., Akkermans, H., et al., 2000, Value Based Requirements Creation for Electronic Commerce Applications, The 33rd Hawaii International Conference on Systems Sciences, Hawaii: 1915–1924.

Hancock, B., 2002, *An Introduction to the Research Process*, Trent Focus Group.

Irani, Z., 2002, Information systems evaluation: navigating through the problem domain, *Information and Management,* **40**(1): 11–24.

Kaplan, B. and Maxwell, J. A., 1994, Qualitative Research Methods for Evaluating Computer Information Systems, *Evaluating Health Care Information Systems: Methods and Applications*, S. J. Jay, ed., Thousand Oaks, CA, SAGE: 45–68.

Klein, H. K. and M. D. Myers, 1999, A Set of Principles for Conducting and Evaluating Interpretive Field Studies in Information Systems, *MIS Quarterly,* **23**(1): 67–94.

Lapointe, J. R., 1997, Trends in Employee Self-Service, *Benefits and Compensation Solutions Magazine*, Accessed 2003.

Lapointe, J. R., 1998, Several Steps to Successful ESS (Employee Self-Service). *HR Focus*, (Special Report on HR Technology, **75:** 13–16.

Lee, A. S., 1994, Electronic Mail as a Medium for Rich Communication: An Empirical Investigation Using Hermeneutic Interpretation, *MIS Quarterly*: 143–157.

Leffingwell, D. and Widrig, D, 2000, *Managing Software Requirements: A Unified Approach*, Addison Wedley.

Marshall, C. and Rossman,G. B. (1989). *Designing Qualitative Research*, SAGE Publications Inc.

Moreno Jr., V., 1999, On the Social Implications of Organizational Reengineering: A Phenomenological Study of Individual Experiences of BPR Processes, *Information Technology & People,* **12**(4): 359–388.

Moustakas, C., 1994, *Phenomenological Research Methods*, SAGE Publications.

Murugesan, S., Y., Deshpande, et al., 1999, Web Engineering: A New Discipline for Development of Web-Based Systems, Proc First ICSE Workshop on Web Engineering, Los Angeles: 1–9.

Nazareth, D., L, 1998, Designing Effective Websites: Lending Structure to a Chaotic Process, Fourth Americas Conference on Information Systems, Baltimore, Maryland: 1011–1013.

Nixon, S., 2003, Net pay is all the wage, with its future now on the line, *The Age*, Melbourne.

Pouloudi, A., 1999, Aspects of the Stakeholder Concept and their Implications for Information Systems Development, 32nd Hawaii Conference on System Sciences, Hawaii.

Riggins, F. J. and T. Mukhopadhyay, 1999, Overcoming Adoption and Implementation Risks of EDI, *International Journal of Electronic Commerce.*

Russo, N. L., 2000, Developing Applications for the Web: Exploring Differences Between Traditional and World Wide Web Application Development, in: *Managing Web-Enabled technologies in Organizations: A Global Perspective*, M. Khosrowpour, ed., Idea Group Publishing, 23–35.

Sharp, H., Finkelstein A., et al., 1999, Stakeholder identification in the Requirements Engineering Process, in: *Proc. Database and Expert Systems Applications (DEXA 99)*, Florence, Italy, IEEE Computer Society Press, pp. 387–391.

Siau, K., 1998, Method Engineering for Web Information Systems Development: Challenges and Issues, Fourth Americas Conference on Information Systems, Baltimore, Maryland: 1017–1019.

Sommerville, I. and Sawyer P., 1997, Viewpoints: Principles, Problems, and a Practical Approach to Requirements Engineering, *Annals of Software Engineering,* **3**: 101–130.

Sommerville, I., Sawyer, P. et al., 1997, Viewpoints for Requirements Elicitation: a Practical Approach, The 3rd IEEE International Conference on Requirements Engineering, CO, USA: 74–81.

Standing, C., 2000, *Internet Commerce Development*, Artech House Inc.

Standing, C., 2001, The Requirements of Methodologies for Developing Web Applications, *ECIS*, Bled, Slovenia: 548–556.

Standing, C., 2002, Methodologies for developing Web applications, *Information and SoftwareTechnology* **44**(3): 151–159.

Stevens, K. J. and Timbrell, G. T., 2002, The Implications of E-Commerce for Software Project Risk: A preliminary investigation, *IFIP*, Copenhagen.

Strauss, A. and J. Corbin, 1990, *Basics of Qualitative Research: Grounded Theory Procedures and Techniques*, Newbury Park, CA, SAGE Publications.

Vidgen, R., 2002a, Constructing a Web Information System development Methodology, *Information Systems Journal*, **12**: 247–261.

Vidgen, R., 2002b, What's so different about Developing Web-based Information Systems?, European Conference in Information Systems, Gdansk, Poland: 262–271.

Walsham, G., 1993, *Interpreting Information Systems in Organizations*. London, Wiley & Sons.

Yin, R. K., 1994, *Case Study Research: Design and Methodology*. Thousand Oakes, Sage Publications.

DISTRIBUTING USABILITY
The implications for usability testing

Lejla Vrazalic*

1. INTRODUCTION

In his article, "Trouble in Paradise: Problems Facing the Usability Community", Rhodes (2000) begins with a gloomy prospect for usability by stating "usability as we know it is dying". He argues that usability is outdated, misunderstood and faces serious challenges in the face of emerging web technologies because new usability ideas, techniques and methods are not being developed. Rhodes' (2000) language is strong, but his observations are not new. The Human Computer Interaction (HCI) and usability communities are being faced with mounting and pressing concerns for which an instantaneous remedy is not readily available. It is the premise of this paper that in order to begin resolving these concerns, it is necessary to reflect on the very fundamental concept that the discipline is based on – the concept of usability, and then examine the implications of this on our methods, techniques and tools.

This paper will begin by arguing that there are intrinsic problems with our current definition of usability and that it is necessary to redefine usability to encompass more than just the computer system in isolation. Spinuzzi's (1999) notion of distributed usability will be proposed as a means of achieving this. The implications of doing this are significant to our existing usability evaluation methods, and usability testing in particular owing to its role in user-centred design. A case will be made that the problems associated with current usability testing are symptomatic of the traditional view of usability and can be overcome by developing a testing method based on distributed usability. Activity Theory, and its associated principles, will be proposed as the underlying framework for developing this method. A brief description of the method will be provided with two examples to demonstrate its benefits. An operational model of the method is currently under development. For the purposes of this paper, the terms "computer system" and "system" will be used interchangeably.

* Lejla Vrazalic, Information Systems, University of Wollongong, Wollongong 2522, Australia.

2. TRADITIONAL USABILITY

HCI as a discipline bases itself on the need to design, evaluate and implement computer systems for human use (ACM SIGCHI, 1992). The notion of usability is therefore fundamental to HCI. Usability is an abstract concept intended to encase and encompass both the design and evaluation of computer systems. It is the glue that binds the entire systems design and development process together. To some, usability is a science. To others, it is an art form. As such, usability is a concept that does not lend itself to a precise and clear-cut definition. Generally, usability refers to the ease of operating a system interface. The simplicity of this statement may appear to be misleading due to the plethora of other, seemingly more comprehensive, definitions of usability that exist. However, most of these definitions are based on this central notion of "ease of use" (Miller, 1971 cited in Shackel, 1986). Since the notion of ease of use is somewhat vague, researchers have defined usability in terms of multiple high-level criteria or attributes.

Shackel (1986) proposes that usability can be specified and measured numerically in terms of four operational criteria: effectiveness (a required level of performance by a percentage of specific users within a range of usage environments), learnability (a pre-defined time period from the start of user training and based on a specified amount of training), flexibility (the levels of adaptation and variability in possible tasks) and attitude (user satisfaction levels after continued use). Nielsen (1993) views usability as a narrow concern when compared to the issue of system acceptability, and models usability as an attribute of system acceptability. However, similarly to Shackel (1986), Nielsen argues, usability itself can be further broken down into five attributes: learnability (the system should be easy to learn), efficiency (the system should be efficient so that high levels of productivity are possible), memorability (the system should be easy to remember and not require re-learning), errors (the system should have low error rate and enable quick recovery after errors) and satisfaction (the system should be pleasant to use).

In contrast to these high-level criteria and attributes, Norman (1988) conceptualises usability in terms of design principles based on a combination of psychological theory and everyday user experiences. The aim of these principles is to help designers make improvements to the system and explain different aspects of their design to the various stakeholders (Thimbleby, 1990). While numerous principles have been operationalised in HCI, the most well-known have been proposed by Norman (1988) and include: visibility (system functions are visible so that each function corresponds with a control), mapping (direct relationship between controls and their functions), affordance (perceived and actual properties of an object that determine how it can be used), constraints (limiting the behaviours and possible operations on an object) and feedback (sending back information to the user about what action has been done).

It is clear that a single universal definition for usability does not exist, which makes it a confusing concept to explain and, more importantly, justify to the business community (Rhodes, 2000). However, the general implication in most definitions of usability is that usability is located within the system itself and can be thought of purely as an attribute of the entire package that makes up a system (Dumas and Redish, 1993). This attribute can be ease of use, learnability, memorability, visibility, mapping or any other of the attributes and principles discussed above. Shackel (1986) was one of the first researchers to alert the HCI community to need for an extended view of usability, embracing four principal components (the user, the task, the system and the environment). Usability, Shackel argued, was about achieving harmony in the interaction between these four components. Since then, a number of other researchers have increasingly become critical of the "traditional" localised view of usability (Thomas and Macredie, 2002; Spinuzzi, 1999; Nardi and O'Day, 1999; Beyer and Holtzblatt, 1998; Nardi, 1996; Engeström and Middleton, 1996; Hutchins, 1995; Kling & Iacono, 1989) because it does not take into consideration those attributes which extend beyond the computer system, including the social context, the work practices and the historical development of the activities that the computer system supports. Thomas and Macredie (2002) went so far in their criticism of traditional usability as to argue that the current conceptions of usability are ill-suited, unwieldy, meaningless and unable to handle the "digital consumer" (p 70). As a result, an alternative notion of distributed usability has emerged.

3. DISTRIBUTED USABILITY

Spinuzzi (1999) argues that the traditional view of usability is inadequate because it localizes usability as an attribute or quality of a single artifact (a specific system) and disregards the influences and consequences of contextual factors such as the interaction between humans, the use of artifacts other than the system and the actual work practices of users. Karat (1997) supports this view by describing usability as an attribute of the interaction with a system in a context of use. In Spinuzzi's (1999) opinion, usability is distributed across an activity network which is comprised of assorted genres, practices, uses and goals of a given activity. An activity network represents a unit of analysis that takes into account individual users working with others as part of a larger activity. Thinking about usability in this way provides us with a more encompassing view of the system (and its interface), the users, as well as the users' goals, and, Spinuzzi argues, leads us to consider solutions that we may not have if we had studied individuals alone. For example, in his study, Spinuzzi found that breakdowns in the users interaction with the system (as defined by Bødker, 1991) were not caused simply by the size of the mouse pointer or even the levels of user training, but could be attributed to deeper discoordinations between the interface and other genres relating to the context of use. This interpretation of usability would not have been possible if only localized attributes of the interface, such as ease of use, learnability and memorability, were examined.

Spinuzzi advocates the study of on-screen and off-screen genres, or typified forms, and their mediatory relationships in the context of an ecology of interrelated tools and activities. Nardi and O'Day (1999) also view this arrangement of tools, which jointly mediate activities, as belonging to an information ecology. They define an ecology as a "system of people, practices, values, and technologies in a particular local environment" (p.49) which focuses on human activities served by technology, rather than technology itself. Indeed, where traditional views of usability relate only to a system consisting of hardware and its associated software, distributed usability proposes to extend the system to include an ecological context consisting of people, their work practices and activities (supported by the hardware and software system as well as other *tools*) and the social context of these activities. This idea echoes Shackel's (1986) four principal components of usability (the user, the task, the system and the environment), however Spinuzzi (1999) and Nardi and O'Day (1999) view these components as being interrelated. The components cannot be fully understood individually because together they make up an extended system that is more than just a sum of its parts.

The distribution of usability across this extended system or ecology has significant implications for both the design and evaluation of systems. Clearly, the design process could not proceed without taking into account and devoting substantial resources to understanding the larger context of user activities, and incorporating this context into the design process. The implications for system evaluation, however, are even more considerable in light of existing evaluation methods, which rely on the traditional view of usability and therefore primarily focus on the system as an artifact in isolation and on assessing the localised attributes of that isolated system. If the HCI community is to adopt a distributed view of usability, it will be necessary to revisit our existing evaluation methods to determine their usefulness, reliability and validity, and develop new methods that are based on a fundamentally different notion of usability. To this end, a distributed usability testing method is currently being developed and tested.

4. USABILITY TESTING

Usability testing is "the gathering of information about the use of prototypes of software products from users who are not involved in the design of the products themselves" (Holleran, 1991). In the 1980s, laboratory based usability testing, as described by Rubin (1994) and Dumas and Redish (1993) emerged as the golden standard for usability evaluation (Lewis, 2001). Since then, other usability evaluation methods have been developed, including heuristic evaluation (Nielsen & Molich, 1990) and cognitive walkthroughs (Polson et al., 1992). Unlike, usability testing, which involves observing users directly interact with a system, these methods are predictive and conducted by teams of experts. Bailey (1993) and Tullis (1993) have questioned experts' ability to predict usability problems following empirical studies, which indicated that experts experienced problems when trying to predict human performance. The results of these studies should come as no surprise to anyone who has been involved in usability testing with users. Gould and Lewis (1985) laid down the basic principles of user-centred design as being early focus on users and tasks, empirical measurement and iterative design. Usability testing is fundamental to the achievement of all three principles because it involves users, it enables empirical measurement to be undertaken, and it supports the notion of iterative design following testing of early system prototypes. Due to this central role of usability testing in user-centred design approaches, it was decided that usability testing, rather than predictive evaluation methods, would form the basis for developing a method to demonstrate the use of distributed usability. However, usability testing in its current form is plagued by practical and methodological problems.

4.1. Problems Associated with Usability Testing

Evolving from formal experiments, usability testing methods have traditionally been situated in a laboratory setting. This artificially created space carries with it a series of negative connotations, with users known as *subjects*, *controlled* by the evaluators measuring specific *variables*. The laboratory has also constrained the usability testing process by the lack of contextual factors that are inherent to real user activities, such as the ones identified by Whiteside et al. (1988). In fact, testing carried out in a laboratory is radically different to the natural, everyday practices that humans engage in through interaction with other humans, systems and tools. Furthermore, a laboratory necessitates the use of cameras and video-recording equipment for observation. One of the main disadvantages associated with this technique is the user involved in the testing feeling self-conscious and altering his/her behaviour and performance as a result. This introduces a significant bias into the testing process and, thus, a contamination of the data collected.

Holleran (1991) argues that usability testing is also plagued by sampling problems due to the difficulty of selecting the sample size to ensure generalizability of the results. In fact, the number of users required for a usability test has been the subject of some debate recently (Spool and Schroeder, 2000) following Nielsen's (2000) rule of "5 users: 85% of usability problems". Another sampling problem raised by Holleran (1991) is choosing the subjects for the testing to be representative of the group for which the system has been designed. Defining a "representative" group of users has become even more challenging in the World Wide Web era. Even if a sample of representative users is found, usability test tends to focus on how one individual interacts directly with a computer in an isolated setting. The cognitive processes and abilities of the individual, including memory, perception and motor skills, are scrutinised and measured using performance based metrics such as time taken to complete a task, number of errors made and perceived ease of use. This "micro-level" analysis of the lone user has serious implications for the motivation and perseverance of users (Holleran, 1991) who persist in their attempts to complete the task even though they may not ordinarily do so. The tasks selected for the usability test are another controversial issue due to the fact that they may not be representative of typical or real user activities both in terms of content and duration. This poses the question of how valid and reliable the results of a usability test are if the representativeness of the users or the tasks is dubious? Finally, the end result of a usability test is a series of, presumably, usability problems that need to be fixed. Just as there is no clear definition of usability, the usability problem remains elusive.

The characterization of a usability problem can perhaps be seen as one of the "holy grails" of HCI. The term usability problem is commonly used to refer to any difficulties or trouble a user may have while using the system, or any faults in the system which cause a break down in the interaction. However, there is no explicit criteria defining when such a difficulty or fault constitutes a usability problem (Hertzum and Jacobsen, 2001) and so any problem reported is deemed to be a usability problem. Different evaluation methods identify different usability problems and no one single method can be relied on to uncover every usability problem with a system. In fact, it is quite possible for the same method to produce different outcomes. Molich et al. (1998, 1999) conducted the Comparative Usability Evaluation (CUE) studies to determine whether usability testing laboratories worldwide would detect the same usability problems in two commercial systems. The differences in the rate of problem detection were substantial with two or more laboratories identifying less than 10% of the problems causing an astonishingly trivial overlap between the results. More than 90% of the problems were reported by a single usability testing laboratory, inferring that other laboratories did not detect the problem or did not perceive it to be a usability problem.

The problems with usability testing identified above are symptomatic of the narrow, traditional view of usability as a localised attribute or quality of a single system. Sweeney et al (1993) support this view by arguing that usability testing in a laboratory tends to be driven by the system. The use of a laboratory for the testing process enables evaluators to focus only on the system and eliminate any external or contextual variables that would interfere with the assessment of the system performance, thus making it easier to isolate and identify problems. The system and its functions drive the selection of users for the test sample because representative users are usually chosen *after* the functions of the system are known. The tasks developed for the usability test are also based on the system functions, rather than user needs. Instead of assessing whether the system does what the users want it to do, usability testing usually tests how well the system does what it can do.

By adopting the notion of distributed usability as the starting point for the development of a usability testing method, it may be possible to eliminate the problems discussed above. However, a notion in itself is insufficient for this purpose. It is necessary to support the notion with a theoretical framework on which to base the new method. Cultural Historical Activity Theory (CHAT) offers such a framework.

5. CULTURAL HISTORICAL ACTIVITY THEORY

Cultural Historical Activity Theory, or simply Activity Theory (AT) as it is widely known, provides a broad conceptual framework that can be applied to the human-computer interface in such a way as to empower the computer user with the necessary tools to work though the interface in order to achieve desired outcomes. Historically, AT draws on the Vygotskian (1978) theory of tool mediation or the mediation of human activities by the use of tools. This approach deviates from the cognitive approach in that the computer system is seen as distinctly different in both character and composition to its human user. From an AT perspective, people are embedded in a socio-cultural context and their behaviour cannot be understood independently of it. Furthermore, they are not just surrounded by the context but actively interact with it and change it by creating new tools. This complex interaction of individuals with their surroundings has been called an activity and is regarded theoretically as the fundamental unit of analysis, a system that has structure, its own internal transitions, transformations and development (Leont'ev, 1981).

AT is becoming more widely known by HCI researchers in the West (Kuttii, 1996; Engeström, 1995; Kaptelinin, 1994; Bødker, 1991; Nardi, 1996) since it was introduced in Russia in the eighties and early nineties. It's most current and widely-adopted form is Engeström's (1987) systemic model shown in Figure 1 below. In this model, the subject refers to the individual or group engaged in the activity, while the object refers to that (either "raw material" or "problem space") at which the activity is aimed. The object defines the activity and is transformed into an outcome using physical and symbolic mediating tools. The community consists of individuals who share the same object of the activity, while the division of labour refers to both the horizontal division of tasks between the members of this community and to the vertical division of power and status. The rules refer to the explicit and implicit regulations, norms and conventions constraining the interactions within the activity system (Engeström, 1987).

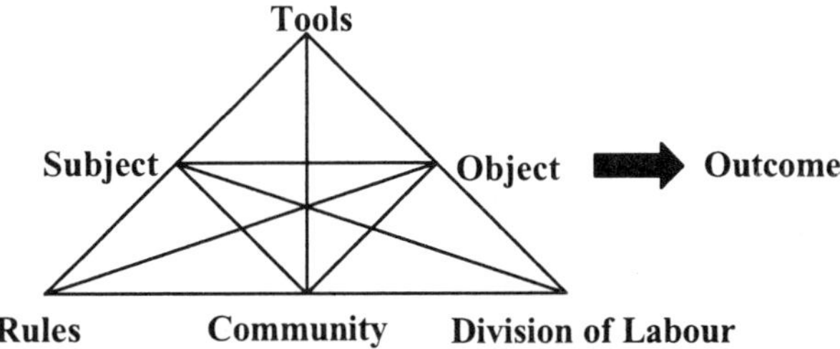

Figure 1. The Human Activity System (Engeström, 1987)

Kuutti (1996) describes the key principles of AT as follows:

5.1. Activity as the basic unit of analysis

Instead of analysing only human actions, AT proposes to analyse the minimal meaningful context for these actions - an activity.

5.2. History and development

Activities are in a constant state of evolution and therefore, it is necessary to historically analyse them in order to gain an understanding of the current situation. A hierarchical system of contradictions is inherent to activity systems and it is these contradictions that cause an activity to develop over time. Engeström (1987) states that four levels of contradictions emerge as a result of conflicts within and between activity systems:

- Primary contradictions *within* the elements of the central activity, usually between the value and exchange value of an element;
- Secondary contradictions arise *between* the elements of the central activity;
- Tertiary contradictions take place between the object of the activity and the object of a more culturally advanced activity, and
- Quaternary contradictions occur between the activity and its 'neighbouring' activities, such as the tool-producing activity, subject-producing activity, etc.

5.3. Artifacts and mediation

Activities are mediated by artifacts and artifacts themselves are created during the development of an activity. This dual relationship further implies the developmental nature of activities.

5.4. Structure of an activity

An activity is directed towards an object and the object is what distinguishes one activity from another. The transformation of the object into the outcome motivates the existence of the activity. Furthermore, the object and motive could undergo changes during the development of an activity.

5.5. Levels of an activity

An activity, which is driven by motives, is realised through conscious actions which are directed towards specific goals. Those actions, in turn, are implemented through operations dependent on the available conditions. The relationship between the elements of this hierarchy, depicted in Figure 2, is dynamic. For example, when working with a computer for the first time, using a mouse is a conscious action requiring the deliberate attention of the user. Through practice, this action will collapse to the level of operations where it becomes habitual and subconscious. However, if the conditions change such that the mouse stops working, the user will be forced to focus his/her actions towards the mouse once again, returning the operation to the level of a conscious action. This type of interruption in the internal structure of an activity is termed a breakdown (Bødker, 1991). Breakdowns occur for various reasons, but they are evident in system use when the system itself becomes the object of the user's actions, rather than having a mediating role.

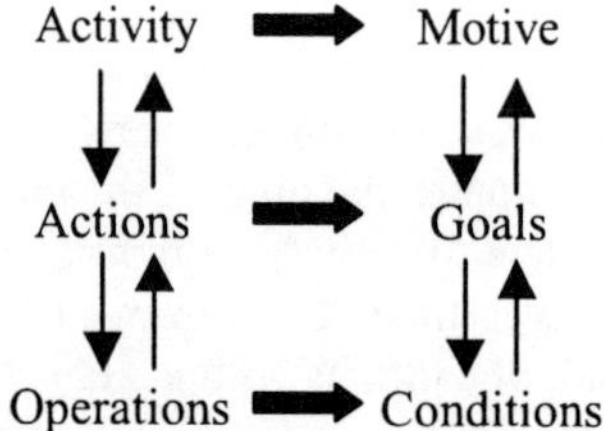

Figure 2. Structure of an Activity (Leont'ev, 1981)

The notion of distributed usability implies the distribution of usability across an activity network comprised of assorted genres, practices, uses and goals of a given activity. Activity Theory provides a unifying framework for these elements because the given activity is the basic unit of analysis consisting of the users (the subjects), their task (the object), the system and other objects utilised to complete the task (the mediating tools) and the social context (the community, the division of labour and the rules). Furthermore, the structure of an activity is concerned with the users' motives, their goals and the conditions in which these are made possible. A distributed usability testing method based on Activity Theory is currently being developed and validated. The following section will briefly outline the operationalisation of this method.

6. DISTRIBUTED USABILITY TESTING METHOD

The Distributed Usability Testing Method (DUTM) reduces the computer system to a support role as one of the many mediating tools in user activities. The focus, instead, is on identifying problems across the entire activity network. Specific usability attributes, such as ease of use, learnability and memorability are not examined or measured. The main concern is to identify usability problems which are caused by breakdowns in the interaction and contradictions in the activity network. A working model diagram of the method is shown in Figure 3.

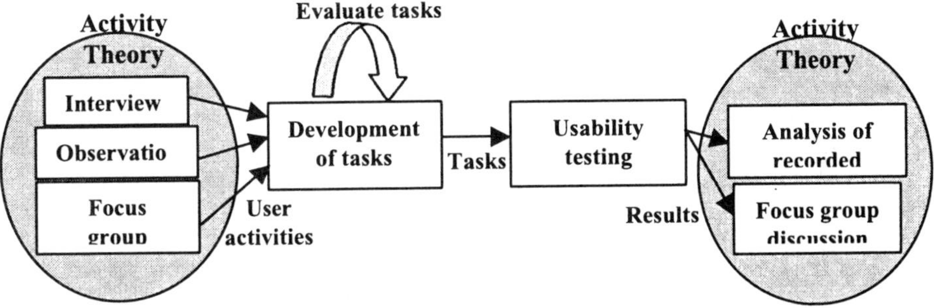

Figure 3. A model of the Distributed Usability Testing Method

6.1. Defining user activities and scenarios

The initial phase involves defining real user activities by observing and interviewing users who actually use the system being tested in their everyday activities. However, the system itself is not the central focus of this phase. It is only important to the extent to which it supports the users' activities. Where appropriate, field interviews and observations can be carried out in order to understand users' needs, desires and their approach to the work they do (Beyer and Holtzblatt, 1999). The interviews can be carried out on a one-to-one basis or in focus groups involving teams that carry out the same activity. This provides a forum for discussing the social interactions between users, and developing an understanding of the social context by gathering information, stories and anecdotes. Due to the problematic nature of gathering this type of ad hoc information, the AT principles described previously can be used to make sense of the information gathered and also provide evaluators with a common vocabulary (Nardi, 1996) as AT terminology is a close reflection of users' activities and, as such, easily understood by users.

The information collected from the interviews or focus groups would provide an integrated, holistic view of the main activity and other intersecting activities and a description of the various mediating tools used in performing the activity, as well as an explanation of how they are used. It is also important to note carefully all the different types of interruptions and disruptions which occur in the users' environment, such as phone calls, queries from colleagues, etc. The key objective of this phase is to explore the users' work practice (Borgholm and Madsen, 1999) and gain an understanding of real user activities. It is important to allow the evaluators to immerse themselves in the users' practice and, by applying AT principles, gain a shared understanding and interpretation of what transpires during a typical activity which is supported by the system being evaluated. Once a common interpretation has been developed, the evaluators can proceed with phase two, which involves developing tasks to be used during the usability testing process. The tasks should be developed iteratively in collaboration with the users and reflect the users' activities. This is in contrast to traditional usability testing which uses the system as the starting point for developing tasks.

6.2. Usability Testing and Analysis

Due to the sterility and artificiality of usability laboratories, the DUTM proposes that testing be carried out in the user's natural environment. This setting enables evaluators to study the impact of the activity context and is made possible by the use of mobile computing technologies and screen capture software. Since the DUTM does not focus on attributes of the system, the use of cameras is not required and interaction is captured using recording software so that the system can be analysed in terms of the breakdowns that occur. A facilitator is present during the usability testing so that notes can be made about the use of other tools (such as pen and paper), the interruptions that occur in the environment, as well as the interaction with other individuals in the community. The recording and the notes are then used to analyse breakdowns (as defined by Bødker (1991)) in the interaction with the system and co-relate the breakdowns to the contradictions (as defined by Engeström (1987)). This is done during the analysis phase, in a team. Essentially, the breakdowns are observed and documented when reviewing the screen recording. The breakdowns are then mapped to the contradictions that are identified within and between activities. The mapping of breakdowns and contradictions defines the usability problems in the activity network. This process will be demonstrated with two examples. In both examples, it is assumed that the data collection and usability testing phases have been completed.

In the first example, let's assume that a breakdown in the interaction was observed when a user, using word processing software, tried to insert a footer into a report. The user selected what she thought was the appropriate menu, however, the menu did not contain the option for inserting a footer into the document. This caused the user to divert her focus to the tool (the word processing software) and away from the object (writing a report). What was up to this point a subconscious operation, became a consciously directed action, resulting in the temporary abandonment of the original activity. The breakdown was caused by a secondary contradiction between the tool and the object of the user's activity because the tool did not enable the user to effectively and effortlessly accomplish her object. Instead, this object was neglected and superseded by the object of finding how to insert a footer. This constitutes a usability problem because the misplacement of the footer option has led to a breakdown in the interaction and can be directly attributed to a secondary contradiction between the tool and the object.

The second example is based on a system described by Nielsen (1990). The LYRE system, a French hypertext system used for teaching poetry, allows students to analyse poetry by adding new annotations to poems using hypertext anchors. The system was based on the French tradition of students working within a framework set up by the teacher, so it did not allow students to add new viewpoints, a facility reserved only for the teachers. In Scandinavian countries, the focus of teaching is on increasing students' potential to explore and learn independently. Had the LYRE system been implemented in Scandinavia, its use would have resulted in a series of breakdowns caused by primary contradictions within the tool (LYRE), secondary contradictions between the tool (LYRE), the subjects (the students and their expectations), the object (to explore and learn independently) and the division of labour (between the teacher and the students). Tertiary contradictions would also have occurred between the object of the French teaching activity (to analyse poetry) and the object of the Scandinavian activity (independent student exploration and learning). By identifying usability problems with the system as breakdowns caused by these contradictions, it would have been possible to determine whether the system supports the students' activities, instead of focusing on the ease of use, learnability or memorability of the system. It would have been possible to establish that the system is intrinsically flawed.

The DUTM will offer several advantages to both researchers and practitioners once it has been fully operationalised and validated. Primarily, the method will overcome most of the problems associated with traditional usability testing described previously, by focusing on users and their activities, avoiding the use of a laboratory for the testing process, and having a clear understanding of what constitutes a usability problem. The most important of these benefits, however, is that system will no longer be examined in isolation from other elements in the activity network. This will only be possible by starting off with a view to distributed usability in the first place.

7. CONCLUSION

This paper has argued that fundamental problems with our current understanding of usability have emerged and that it is necessary to redefine usability to encompass more than just the computer system in isolation. The notion of distributed usability has been proposed as a means of achieving this. However, the implications of redefining this basic concept are significant to our existing usability evaluation methods, and usability testing in particular owing to its role in user-centred design. It has been argued that the problems associated with the current usability testing method are symptomatic of the traditional view of usability and can be overcome by developing a testing method based on distributed usability. Activity Theory, and its associated principles, has been proposed as the underlying framework for this method. A brief description of the method has been provided with two examples to demonstrate its benefits. Further work is currently under way and it is anticipated that a preliminary operational model of the method will be validated in the near future.

REFERENCES

ACM SIGCHI, 1992, *Curricula for Human-Computer Interaction*, ACM Press.

Bailey, R. W., 1993, Performance vs preference, Proceedings of the Human Factors and Ergonomics Society 37th Annual Meeting, 282–286.

Beyer, H. and Holtzblatt, K., 1998, *Contextual Design: Defining Customer-Oriented Systems*, Morgan Kaufmann Publishers.

Beyer, H. and Holtzblatt, K., 1999, Contextual Design, *interactions*, **6**, 32–42.

Bødker, S., 1991,*Through the Interface: A Human Activity Approach to User Interface Design*, Erlbaum.

Borgholm, T. and Madsen, K. H., 1999, Cooperative Usability Practices, *Communications of the ACM*, **42**, 91–97.

Dumas, J. S. and Redish, J. C., 1993, *A Practical Guide to Usability Testing*, Ablex Publishing.

Engeström, Y. and Middleton, D., 1996, *Cognition and Communication at Work*, Cambridge University Press.

Engeström, Y., 1987, *Learning by Expanding: An activity-theoretical approach to developmental research*, Orienta-Konsultit.

Engeström, Y., 1995, Polycontextuality and Boundary Crossing in Expert Cognition: Learning and Problem Solving in Complex Work Activities, *Learning and Instruction*. **5**, 319–336.

Gould, J. D. and Lewis, C., 1985, Designing for Usability: Key Principles and What Designers Think, *Communications of the ACM*, **28**:3, 300–311.

Hertzum, M. and Jacobsen, N.E., 2001, The Evaluator Effect : A Chilling Fact About Usability Evaluation Methods, *International Journal of Human-Computer Interaction*, **13**:4, 421–444.

Holleran, P.A., 1991, A methodological note on pitfalls in usability testing, *Behaviour & Information Technology*, **10**:5, 345–357.

Hutchins, E., 1995, *Cognition in the Wild*, MIT Press.

Kaptelinin, V., 1994, Activity Theory: Implications For Human Computer Interaction, in: *Human-Machine Communication For Educational SystemsDesign*, M.D. Brouwer-Janse and T.L. Harrington, eds., Springer-Verlag.

Karat, J., 1997, User-centred software evaluation methodologies, in: *Handbook of Human-Computer Interaction*, Helander, M. G., Landauer, T. K. and Prabhu, P. V., eds., Elsevier Science, pp. 689–704.

Kling, R. and Iacono, S., 1989, The Institutional Character of Computerized Information Systems, *Office: Technology & People*, **5**:1, 7–28.

Kuutti, K., 1996, Activity Theory as a Potential Framework for Human-Computer Interaction, in: *Context and Consciousness: Activity Theory and Human Computer Interaction*, B. Nardi, ed., MIT Press.

Leontiev, A. N., 1981, *Problems of The Development of The Mind*, Progress Publishers.

Lewis, J. R., 2001, Current Issues in Usability Evaluation, *International Journal of Human-Computer Interaction*, **13**:4, 343–350.

Molich, R., Thomsen, A. D., Karyukina, B., Schmidt, L., Ede, M., van Oel, W. and Arcuri, M., 1999, Comparative Evaluation of Usability Tests, in: *Proceedings of CHI'99*, ACM Press.

Molich, R., Bevan, N., Curson, I., Butler, S., Kindlund, E., Miller, D. And Kirakowski, J., 1998, Comparative Evaluation of Usability Tests, Proceedings of the UPA Conference, 189–200.

Nardi, B., 1996, Activity Theory and Human-Computer Interaction, in: *Context and Consciousness: Activity Theory and Human Computer Interaction*, B. Nardi, ed., MIT Press.

Nardi, B. A. and O'Day, V. L., 1999, *Information Ecologies: Using Technology with Heart*, MIT Press.

Nielsen, J., 2000, Why you only need to test with 5 users, *Alertbox*, March 19.

Nielsen, J., 1993, *Usability Engineering*, Academic Press.

Nielsen, J., 1990, Designing for International Use, in: *Human Factors in Computing Systems, Proceedings of CHI'90*, ACM Press, pp. 291–294.

Nielsen, J. and Molich, R., 1990, Heuristic Evaluation of User Interfaces, in: *Proceedings of CHI'90*, ACM Press, pp. 249–256.

Norman, D. A., 1988, *The Psychology of Everyday Things*, Basic Books.

Polson, P. G., Lewis, C., Rieman, J. and Wharton, C., 1992, Cognitive Walkthroughs: A method for theory based evaluation of user interfaces, *International Journal of Man-Machine Studies*. **36**, 741–773.

Rubin, J., 1994, *Handbook of usability testing: How to plan, design, and conduct effective tests*, Wiley.

Rhodes, J. S., 2000, *Trouble in Paradise: Problems Facing the Usability Community*, (April 17, 2003); http://webword.com/moving/death/ html.

Shackel, B., 1986, Ergonomics in Design for Usability, in: *People and Computers: Designing for Usability, Proceedings of the 2nd Conference of the British Computer Society Human Computer Interaction Specialist Group*, Harrison, M. D. and Monk, A. F., eds., Cambridge University Press, pp. 45–64.

SINTEF Group, 2002, The Foundation for Scientific and Industrial Research at the Norwegian Institute of Technology, (March 15, 2003); http://www.oslo.sintef.no/avd/ 32/3270/brosjyrer/ engelsk/6.html.

Spinuzzi, C., 1999, Grappling with distributed usability: A cultural-historical examination of documentation genres over four decades, Proceedings of the 17th annual international conference on Computer documentation, New Orleans, 16–21.

Spool, J. and Schroeder, W., 2001, Testing Websites: Five Users is Nowhere Near Enough, in: *Proceedings of CHI'2001*, ACM Press, pp. 285-286.

Sweeney, M., Maguire, M. and Shackel, B., 1993, Evaluating user-computer interaction: A framework, *International Journal of Man-Machine Studies*. **38**, 689–711.

Thimbleby, H., 1990, *User Interface Design*, Addison Wesley, Harlow, UK.

Thomas, P. and Macredie, R. D., 2002, Introduction to The New Usability, *ACM Transactions on Computer-Human Interaction*, **9**:2, 69–73.

Tullis, T. S., 1993, Is user interface design just common sense?, Proceedings of the 5th International Conference on Human- Computer Interaction, 9–14.

Vygotsky, L. S., 1978, *Mind in Society*, Harvard University Press.

Whiteside, J., Bennett, J. and Holtzblatt, K., 1988, Usability engineering: our experience and evolution, in: *Handbook of Human-Computer Interaction*, M. Helander, ed., North-Holland.

INTEGRATING SECURITY DESIGN INTO INFORMATION SYSTEMS DEVELOPMENT

Murray E. Jennex and Margaret Lowe[1]

1. INTRODUCTION

There are numerous methods for designing information systems (IS) and for designing security into an IS, including rapid application development, checklists, threat analysis and security development methods. However, these methods are not integrated into an overall design methodology that can be used to ensure security requirements are identified and then implemented. Siponen and Baskerville (2001) attempted to resolve this by proposing a security design paradigm that relied on meta-notation to abstract and document integrated security requirements into IS development methods. However, this paradigm has not been widely adopted.

This paper proposes using barrier analysis and the concept of defense in depth to modify Siponen and Baskerville's (2001) integrated design paradigm into a more graphical and easier to understand and use methodology. In addition to the meta-notation proposed by Siponen and Baskerville (2001), this paper proposes the use of barrier diagrams in conjunction with barrier analysis to provide an integrative approach to adding security into systems design, and to ensure that adequate levels or layers of security are in place at all stages of the software development life cycle. Barrier Analysis is a concept developed by William Haddon, Jr., M.D. in 1973 (Haddon, 1973). Barrier Analysis is most widely known in the Nuclear Energy arena, and has been improved upon by the System Safety Development Center, a training division of the Department of Energy, Clemens (2002). Barrier Analysis is a method of identifying hazards or threats, and determining the effectiveness of the preventative/mitigating factors that are constructed to prevent the occurrence of the hazard/threat. Barrier Analysis can also be used after an event has occurred to determine the root cause and to help develop barriers to prevent repeat occurrences, Crowe (1990).

To document the validity and usefulness of the proposed methodology, barrier analysis and defense in depth was tested by a group of graduate students as part of their systems design project. The goal was to determine if the concept of barrier analysis and

[1] Murray E. Jennex, Ph.D., P.E., and Margaret Lowe, MSBA, San Diego State University.

barrier diagrams could be effectively used in information systems design, and whether or not this methodology is useful in discovering and implementing security requirements. The pilot study was done to determine if further studies and research should be performed to demonstrate that this is a useful methodology that should be adopted as an industry standard practice for ensuring that security requirements are thoroughly discovered, documented, followed and tracked throughout the systems development life cycle.

2. BACKGROUND

Information and systems security is a growing problem. According to a survey performed by the Computer Security Institute (CSI) and the FBI, 90 percent of respondents of large corporations and U.S. Government agencies reported security breaches during 2001, and 80 percent reported financial losses due to these violations, equating to billions of dollars worldwide, (Computer Security Institute, 2002). The losses included not only lost revenue, but also costs relating to cleanup, data loss, liability issues and most importantly, loss of customer trust, Allen, et al. (2002). These figures, coupled with the research finding that current hacking tools require decreased intruder technical knowledge (Jennex and Walters, 2003), suggests that there are greater numbers of potential hackers (Allen, et al., 2002) and suggests that despite the overwhelming efforts made on the part of organizations by means of security policies, practices, risk management, technology, security architecture and design, security for information and systems is still a serious concern.

2.1. IS Security Design Paradigms

There are two main paradigms for designing security solutions in Information Systems as defined by Baskerville (1993). The mainstream paradigm is based on the use of checklists while the integrative paradigm uses engineering processes or logical abstractions and transformational models to combine viewpoints and functions into a single security model. These paradigms are discussed further below.

2.1.1. Mainstream Paradigm

The mainstream paradigm is focused on risk identification, analysis, and assessment to identify security needs and then uses checklists, best practices, and/or cookbook approaches to select known solutions to mitigate the identified risks. According to Siponen and Baskerville (2001) there are three underlying flaws with these approaches:

1. By design, the checklist approach is template in nature, and does not address the unique and individual security needs of an organization. Furthermore, when developers encounter a situation that requires a decision on the part of management, the checklist approach cannot offer a solution.
2. Developmental duality, the conflict created by the disparate requirements of creating security and IS development, is a problem with the use of checklists, risk management and formal development.
3. The social nature of the organization is ignored with the "mechanistic and functionalistic" characteristics of checklists and formal method development.

2.1.2. Integrative Paradigm:

Given the limitations of mainstream approaches for security design, the need for more integrative approaches has produced integrative paradigms such as information and database modeling approaches, responsibility approaches, business process approaches and the security-modified IS development approach. According to Siponen and Baskerville (2001) there are four basic weaknesses with the existing integrative approaches, pushing the need for further development in the integrative approach arena:

1. The current integrative approaches lack a comprehensive modeling support for security for the three levels of modeling, which are organizational, conceptual and technical.
2. Most of the existing approaches are difficult or sometimes impossible to integrate into the IS development process, leading to the problem of developmental duality.
3. These approaches stifle the creativity and autonomy of the developer, sometimes limiting the developmental approach the developer normally would choose to use.
4. Emerging IS methods create an ongoing gap between IS development and the implementation of the necessary security, since the methodology is not always implemented the same way in practice.

Siponen and Baskerville's (2001) approach adds meta-notation to the development process. Meta-methodology seeks to provide a means for rapidly developing computer-aided systems analysis and software engineering. Meta-notation is considered to be a key feature of most methods and meta-methods. The meta-notation includes five areas: security subjects, security objects, security constraints, security classifications and security policy. By addressing each of these five dimensions in the development process, Siponen and Baskerville (2001) suggest that security is addressed in IS development in an integrative approach. As an applied example, Siponen and Baskerville (2001) demonstrate meta-notation as applied in a typical use case. The actor becomes the security object, and the security classification is added to the use case. Additionally, the security policy and preconditions are included in the use case to show the application of security in the use case model. This insures that security is addressed for each actor, that the appropriate policy is in place, and addressed appropriately as part of the IS design.

Lee, Lee, and Lee (2000) also have proposed an integrative approach. Their approach integrates mainstream security approaches with standard software engineering approaches and the software development lifecycle. This approach provides a roadmap between lifecycle processes, security engineering, and lifecycle data for the supply, development, and operations and maintenance processes. However, this is still using standard, checklist and is only successful in limiting the development duality issue discussed above with the other issues still being valid concerns.

2.2 Threat Analysis

A threat is defined as a set of circumstances that has the potential to cause loss or harm, Pfleeger and Pfleeger (2003). These circumstances may be caused intentionally, unintentionally, or even by natural events. Another perspective comes from Jennex

(2003) where threats are the capabilities and intentions of adversaries to exploit an information system; or any natural or unintentional event with the potential to cause harm to an information system, resulting in a degradation of an organization's ability to fully perform its mission. Risk analysis is the identification, categorization, and assessment of threats.

There are many methods for identifying threats including the use of Courtney's (1977) exposure groups, Fisher's (1984) Exposure-Identification Structure, and Hutter's (2002) tree diagramming process. The most classical of these are Courtney's (1977) exposure groups where six groups of threats are identified: accidental disclosure, accidental modification, accidental destruction, intentional disclosure, intentional modification, and intentional destruction. Jennex (2003) identifies risks based on location and intention and offers five basic threat groups that are somewhat consistent with Courtney (1977): external accidental, external intentional, internal accidental, internal intentional, and acts of God (natural events such as equipment failures, fires, earthquakes, etc.). Each of these five threat groups has three classes of risk: destruction of data, unplanned modification of data, and unapproved disclosure of data. This paper uses the Jennex (2003) threat groups. These threat groups are complete for penetration type attacks, however they do not account for attacks designed to prevent legitimate external users from accessing the system. Denial of Service attacks is a class of attacks that are external to the system and which need to be protected against with the Internet Service Provider. Additionally, it is recommended that risk analysis be used to determine which threats and risks need to be protected against.

2.3 Barrier Analysis

Barrier Analysis is a method of identifying hazards or threats and, determining the effectiveness of the mitigating factors that are currently in place. Barrier Analysis can also be used after an event has occurred to determine the cause and to help develop barriers to prevent repeat occurrences.

Barrier systems can be classified as material or physical, functional, symbolic and immaterial, Hollnagel (1999). For example, material or physical could be containment, such as walls, doors, or restriction of physical access. By functional, we mean preventing or hindering, such as with passwords, pre-conditions or delays. Symbolic refers to countering, regulating, indicating, permission or communication, such as coding of functions, procedures, signs, work permit or clearance. Finally, by immaterial, we mean monitoring or prescribing, such as with visual inspection, checklists, rules or restrictions, Hollnagel (1999).

When we think of barrier analysis, it is the analysis of the placement or design of these types of barriers against possible risks or threats. Obviously, with higher risk, there will require more barriers between the object being protected, and the possible threat (Jennex, 2003). Barrier analysis seeks to demonstrate what is being protected and how. Furthermore, barrier analysis is used in the event of barrier failure to determine the cause, and to correct the problem by determining future preventive action, Crowe (1990).

The advantage of using barrier analysis is that it helps to identify the causal factors and the actions needed to correct the problems, Crowe (1990). The disadvantage of barrier analysis is that the method does not insure that all failed barrier will be recognized, and the effects of the risks or threats that are applied in barrier analysis may not be properly identified, Crowe (1990).

3. BARRIER ANALYSIS AND DEFENSE IN DEPTH AS A DESIGN PARADIGM

3.1. Barrier Diagrams

In terms of the original design or purpose of barrier analysis and barrier design, barrier diagrams show the necessary ingredients for an accident, which per Trost and Nertney (1995), include the environmental condition that causes the harm, vulnerable people or objects that can be hurt by the condition, failure/lack of controls that are designed to keep them apart, and events that lead into the final accident. Crowe (1990) uses a simpler approach that utilizes the threat, the chain of barriers designed to prevent the threat, and the asset being protected. Barrier analysis is then used to assess the overall effectiveness of the barrier system, and of each individual barrier in preventing the event. Figure 1 illustrates a Crowe (1990) barrier diagram. This is the format chosen for use as a proposed method for modeling IS security.

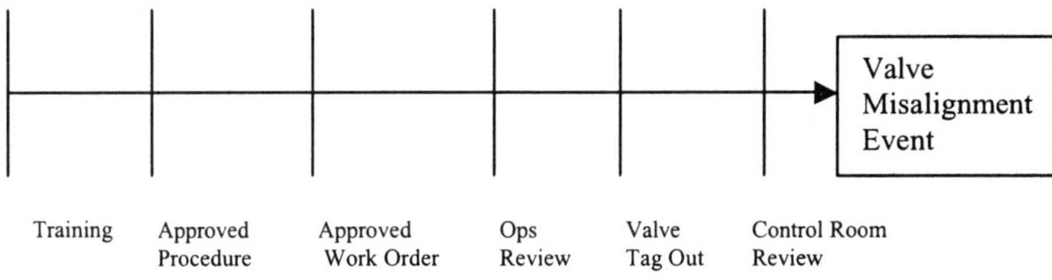

Figure 1. Crowe (1990) Sample Barrier Diagram

3.2. Defense in Depth

Hartman (2001), suggests that any IS security design that relies on a single point of protection will probably be defeated. To counter this, it is suggested that defense in depth be used. Defense in depth is a concept that utilizes multiple compensating control mechanisms to prevent or reduce a threat (Bass and Robichaux, 2002). Defense in depth uses a layered approach to increase the level of effort that would be required to damage the integrity of the system and or the data, Hartman (2001). These threats could be intentional or unintentional, internal or external, or any combination of these options. The number of layers and the intensity of each defense layer are contingent on the level of the threat, and the importance of the data and the system. There must be a balance between the risk/threat, and the cost or overhead in protecting the system, (Jennex (2003) and Allen, et al. (2002)).

4. PROPOSED METHODOLOGY

This paper proposes the use of barrier analysis and defense in depth as a design methodology and paradigm. We propose a modification of Siponen and Baskerville's (2001) integrated approach. Siponen and Baskerville (2001) used meta-notation to add security detail to existing system development diagrams such as Use Cases. This paper proposes using barrier analysis diagrams as a graphical method of identifying and documenting security requirements and adding meta-notation to those diagrams. Barrier diagrams will be used to identify the necessary barriers to prevent events caused by credible threats that are identified through risk analysis. The defense in depth paradigm will be used to ensure that there are multiple security barriers between threats and events. Additionally, it is intended that the process follow Lee, Lee, and Lee's (2000) approach of integrating security design into the software development lifecycle.

Security requirements are identified in the requirements phase of system development, through the use of vulnerability assessments and the generation of barrier diagrams. Vulnerability assessments are used to determine credible threats and key assets. Barrier diagrams are used to document those threats that need to be guarded against, those assets needing to be protected, key processes where threats could intervene, and key actors involved in those processes. Barriers will be identified based on stakeholder input, existing security policies, existing barriers in support and infrastructure systems, and using the defense in depth philosophy. Stakeholders for this phase include system analysts, users, management, and any existing security team or group. Data Flow Diagrams (DFDs), Entity Relation Diagrams (ERDs), and Use Cases should be used to assist in asset, critical process, and key actor identification. The final use of the barrier diagrams will be to gain concurrence from the users and other stakeholders that all threats and assets have been identified, and that adequate security requirements have been identified. The systems requirements document should include security requirements identified by the barrier diagrams and the actual barrier diagrams as a security model. Additionally, the organization should initiate any needed security policies to support the identified security requirements.

Security design specifications are identified in the design phase of system development. Analysts, developers, and security experts identify technologies and methods for implementing the security requirements of the identified barriers from the barrier diagrams. Design specifications are determined using the security plan, policies and procedures; the existing security and technical infrastructure; and standard data integrity and fault tolerant design practices. Specifications can be added to the diagram as meta-notation and these diagrams are included in the system design specification.

Security is built into the system during the system development phase. Developers and security experts use the barrier diagrams and security design specifications to build security into the system. Barrier construction should be determined using security policies, processes, and procedures; existing security infrastructure; checklists/best practices of security tools/practices; and data integrity and fault tolerant construction practices. Implementation details can be added to the diagrams as meta-notation.

Testing of the security barriers occurs during the system testing and implementation phases. The barrier diagrams should be used to generate test scripts and success criteria, user training requirements, and the implementation plan. Details of these plans and scripts should be linked by document reference to the barrier diagram meta-notation.

Integrity of the defense in depth security barriers is maintained during the maintenance phase. The barrier diagrams are used to track continued implementation of security requirements and to verify that enhancements and fixes do not reduce the effectiveness of security barriers either individually or within the context of defense in depth.

Finally, barrier diagrams and analysis can be used in all phases to analyze security events. In these cases, the analysis would use the diagrams to determine which barriers failed to perform as expected and to determine what corrective actions or design implementations need to be taken to prevent recurrence of the event.

5. BARRIER DIAGRAM EXAMPLE

The case of a knowledge management system (KMS) will be used to illustrate how barrier diagrams and the defense in depth paradigm can be used. For this example it is assumed the KMS is Internet based to allow both internal and external access by employees, and the knowledge base is located in a single database on a single server.

The requirements phase would involve the systems analyst, key knowledge users, management, and the security group. There is consensus that all knowledge in the knowledge base needs to be protected and that project experience related to the core business area is critical. There is also consensus that all five threat groups; external accidental, external intentional, internal accidental, internal intentional, and acts of God for all three degrees (except Acts of God which only has inappropriate destruction), inappropriate disclosure, modification, and destruction, need to be protected against. Table 1 summarizes the threat analysis. Identification of key knowledge base assets is accomplished through meta-notation in the form of comments added to the Entity Relation Diagram or Data Dictionary. The basic barrier diagram for the external intentional and accidental threats with inappropriate disclosure, modification or destruction is shown in Figure 2. The diagram for the internal intentional and accidental threats with inappropriate disclosure, modification, and destruction is shown in Figure 3. The diagram for the Acts of God threats with inappropriate destruction is shown in Figure 4. Requirements identified from the diagrams are added to the system requirements specification (SRS) with the threat table and barrier diagrams added as supporting documentation. Finally, the current security plan and policies are reviewed to ensure policies exist for the identified security requirements.

Table 1. Sample Threat Analysis

Threat	Modification	Destruction	Disclosure
External Intentional	Hacker (all types), Criminal, Disgruntled or Terminated Remote User	Hacker (all types), Criminal, Disgruntled or Terminated Remote User	Hacker (all types), Criminal, Disgruntled or Terminated Remote User
External Accidental	Remote User training, carelessness, inattention	Remote User training, carelessness, inattention	Remote User training, carelessness, inattention, Improper disposal of equipment
Internal Intentional	Disgruntled or Terminated Employee	Disgruntled Employee or Terminated	Disgruntled Employee or Terminated
Internal Accidental	Employee training, carelessness, inattention	Employee training, carelessness, inattention	Employee training, carelessness, inattention, Improper disposal of equipment
Acts of God	None	Fire, Earthquake, Flood, Loss of Power	None

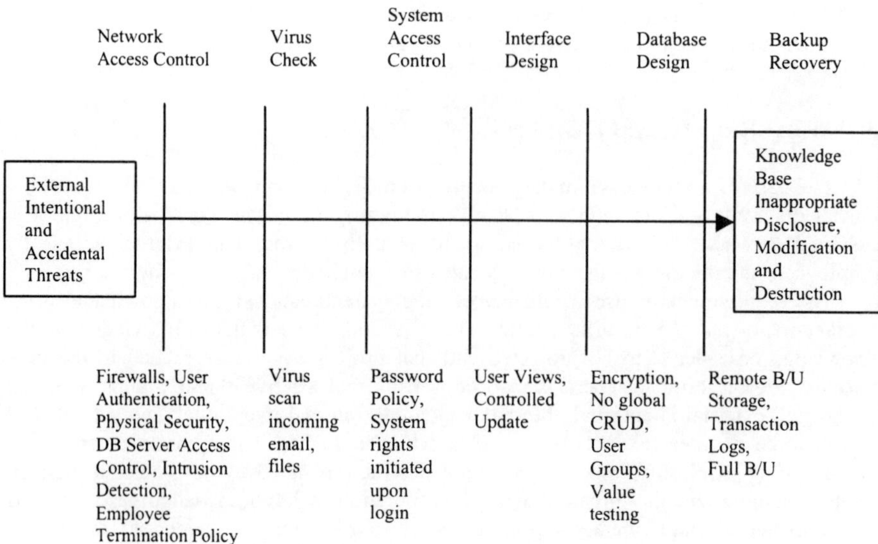

Figure 2. External Intentional and Accidental Threats Requirements phase barrier diagram

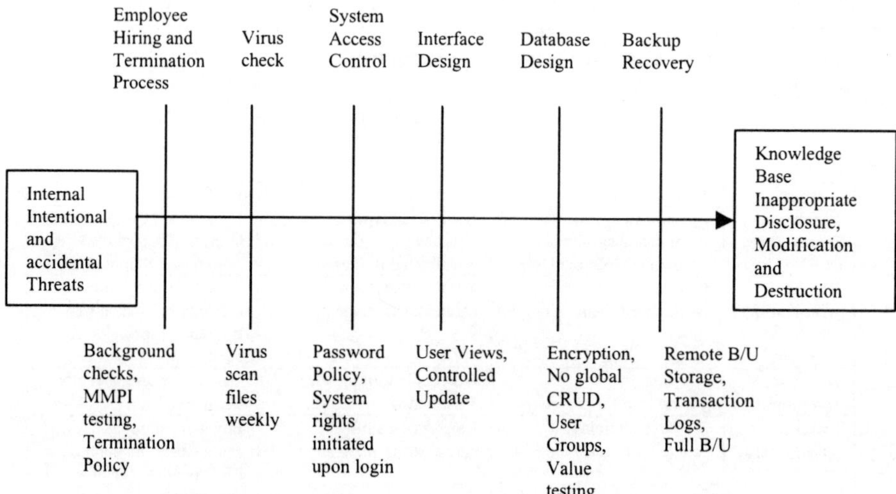

Figure 3. Internal Intentional and Accidental Threats Requirements phase barrier diagram

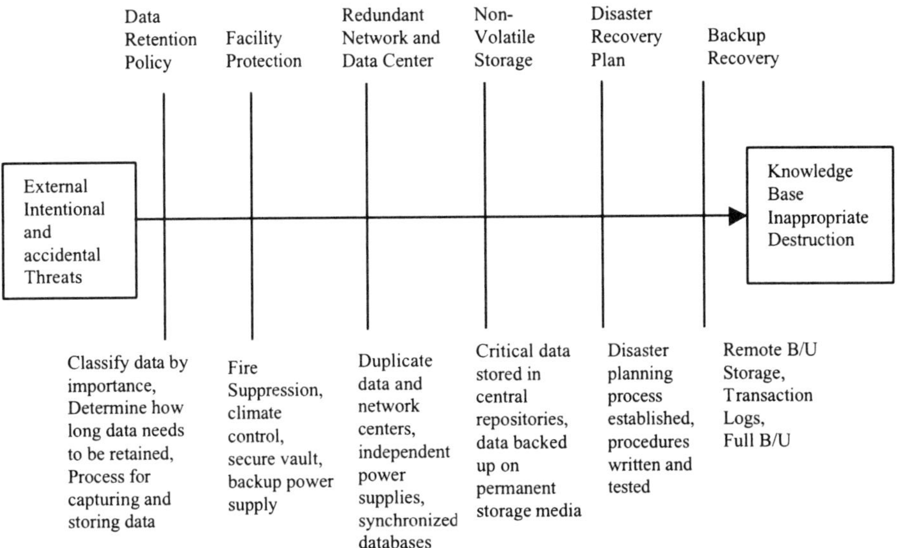

Figure 4. Acts of God Threats Requirements phase barrier diagram

The boxes at the ends of the barrier diagrams represent the threat entity (left end) and the asset to be protected (right end). The line connecting the boxes represents the path the threat takes to get to the protected asset. The lines perpendicular to the threat path are the barriers erected by the system designers to prevent the threat from reaching the protected asset. Top text lists the barrier type while lower text lists the requirements for each barrier. Barriers and requirements vary based on the threat group but that there is some overlap, this is expected since security strategies may be applied to multiple threats.

The above barrier diagrams also illustrate the philosophy of defense in depth by showing that there are six barriers that integrate multiple, different, security technologies and approaches with existing security policies and infrastructure for each set of threats. Figure 2 illustrates the application of the authorized user access, virus protection, authenticated user, user groups, data validation, data encryption, and backup and restore security philosophies to erecting an integrated security system. Firewalls are used to screen for authorized users, passwords are used to authenticate user identities, user rights groups and user views are used to limit user access to what is needed, data entry testing is used to validate data before it is stored to prevent potentially incorrect data from being stored, encryption is used to prevent unauthorized data disclosure, and backup and recovery is used in case all the barriers fail and the threat entity destroys or modifies the data.

Analysts can use Figures 2, 3, and 4 as is or can combine the diagrams into a single master diagram. Either way, the security requirements from each of the barrier diagrams are combined to generate the final requirements specification. Additionally, the barrier diagrams are useful for communicating these requirements to the stakeholders and security specialists and in gaining their concurrence and approval.

Once the security requirements are generated and approved, the analyst can use them to generate the security design specifications. The analyst can continue to develop the meta-notation on the barrier diagram to include more layers of detail, specifically design specifications. Alternately, this detail can be added by supplementing the barrier diagram with tables of design specifications tied to requirements. Table 1 illustrates the table approach to documenting design specifications for the database design barrier in Figures 2 and 3 (no further tables are provided due to paper space limitations). The table approach is recommended to keep the barrier diagrams readable. This detail is generated during the design phase of system development and could be extracted or generated using the logical data model and physical table design chart. Design detail is expressed as design specifications for each of the functional requirement specifications.

Table 2. Sample Barrier Diagram Requirements

Functional Requirement	Design Requirement
Encrypt Critical Knowledge	Encrypt Project_Report.Lessons_Learned attribute
No Global CRUD rights	Instantiate database rights upon login to system
Establish CRUD rights via user groups	Establish Admin user group with administrative rights
	Establish Mgmt user group with partial RU rights
	Establish Update user group with full CRUD rights
	Establish Project Manager user group with partial CRUD rights
	Establish Knowledge user group with partial CRU rights
Check data input before writing to DB	Use choice lists for attributes with finite selections
	Range check numeric and currency attributes
	Format attribute input for those with set formats

During the coding and testing phase, unit and functional test scripts are generated using the design specifications. The barrier diagrams are used to generate integrated system test plans that establish initial conditions, expected system responses, and allow for a series of monitored attacks by a variety of attacker profiles. Attacker profiles are designed to fit the expected attacker profiles of the analyzed vulnerabilities. The barrier diagrams show how the security system is supposed to work and provides a basis for analyzing failures in individual barriers. Testers need to develop scenarios that test the ability of total security system, i.e. of all the barriers working together, to protect the assets. Testing is completed when scenarios cannot be generated that successfully penetrate the asset. If scenarios are found that result in penetration, then designers need to revise the security system to counter it. Scenarios that result in some barriers being defeated need to be reviewed to determine if there are vulnerabilities in the barrier design. Testing can be performed by using "white-hat" hackers to attempt penetration. These testers would use their skills to attempt penetration and to identify vulnerabilities in the overall security plan should they penetrate the outer network security. Additionally, automated network security scans can be used to identify vulnerabilities in network security. Ultimately, it should be assumed that network security will be penetrated and the other barriers need to be tested to determine their effectiveness in protecting or minimizing damage to the assets.

The barrier diagrams and vulnerability assessment are used during the maintenance phase to assess system changes for impact to the security design. As new knowledge bases are added, they are assessed for criticality and the need for encryption. As the organization expands to new locations the diagrams provide a blueprint for designing local facility and network security. As employees change jobs, are hired, or quit, the diagrams provide guidance to what user groups need to be modified. Finally, as new threats are identified, the diagrams are used to assess any needed changes to the security system.

The final use of the diagrams is in assessing the impact of attempted penetrations, events, or internal acts that defeat some or all of the barriers designed to prevent the penetration, event, or internal act. Security specialists can use the diagrams to identify security implementations that failed and what caused the failure. The goal is to identify user behaviors, policy issues, or weak technologies that need changing or improving.

6. EXPERIENCE USING BARRIER DIAGRAMS AND DEFENSE IN DEPTH

Barrier diagrams and defense in depth was pilot tested by a team of graduate students designing a web site for the International Student Center for San Diego State University. The web application is for potential students to contact the university as well as for existing international students to participate in the International Students Association. Functions of the web application include databases of members and committees, web forms for joining the association, a schedule of events and meetings, forms for scheduling events and meetings, and supports the use of online chat for members and potential students to discuss issues relative to international students. Security requirements were determined through a threat analysis and the generation of barrier diagrams. The diagrams were generated based on discussions with the chair of the university's IS security committee and were validated as correct. Design specifications were generated, documented in tables, and discussed with the chair of the university's IS security committee for approval. The specifications were approved and the final design documented in a system design specification. Interviews with the project team found that the diagrams were very effective and useful in identifying the full set of security requirements needed for the system and in generating the system security design specifications. The diagrams were also found to be effective in conveying security requirements. The team also stated that the diagrams helped them discover weaknesses in their security design that they would have otherwise not have thought of.

7. CONCLUSIONS

Barrier diagrams provide a graphical tool for identifying and determining security requirements. Graphical tools enhance understanding and communications between stakeholders. This tool is expected to enhance understanding of, and compliance with security requirements.

The Defense in Depth paradigm enhances security by providing multiple barriers to prevent threats from causing damaging events. When coupled with barrier diagrams it provides a tool for all stakeholders to integrate security needs and efforts and provides a process for ensuring security measures work together and not against each other.

Combining these tools provides a means for integrating security design and implementation across the full software lifecycle. While the traditional lifecycle was discussed, these tools can be applied to any lifecycle approach. Integrating security design and implementation into the lifecycle should improve overall system quality.

Finally, barrier diagrams and analysis can be used much as it is used in the United States nuclear industry, as a tool for determining root cause. This tool provides an analysis tool for determining what failed and how preventative actions can be taken to prevent future security breaches.

7.1. Areas for Future Research

This is a proposed process. It needs to be used in a real world environment to determine its true worth. Further research can be conducted in an academic setting to test and fine-tune the process. Following this, some target organizations need to be found to test the process in a real world environment. Additionally, research needs to be conducted on how to apply the process to threats such as denial of service.

REFERENCES

Allen, J. H., Mikoski Jr., E. F., Nixon, K. M., and Skillman, D. L., 2002, Common sense guide for senior managers: top ten recommended information security practices, in: *Internet Security Alliance*, 1st Edition.

Baskerville, R., 1993, Information systems security design methods: implications for information systems development, *ACM Computing Surveys*, 25(4), 375–414.

Bass, T. and Robichaux, R., 2002, Defense in depth revisited: qualitative risk analysis methodology for complex network-centric operations, http://www.silkroad.com/papers/pdf/archives/defense-in-depth-revisited-original.pdf.

Clemens, P.L., 2002, Energy Flow/Barrier Analysis, 3rd Edition, http://www.sverdrup.com/safety/energy.pdf.

Computer Security Institute, 2002 CSI/FBI computer crime and security survey, *Computer Security Issues and Trends*, 8(1).

Courtney, R., 1997, Security Risk Assessment in Electronic Data Processing, AFIPS Proceedings of the National Computer Conference 46, 97–104.

Crowe, D., 1990, Root Cause Training Course for Catawba Nuclear Station, General Physics Corporation.

Fisher, R., 1984, *Information Systems Security*, Prentice-Hall, Englewood Cliffs, NJ.

Haddon Jr., W., 1973, Energy damage and the ten countermeasure strategies, *Human Factors Journal*, 15.

Hartman, S., 2001, Securing E-Commerce: an overview of defense in-depth, http://www.sans.org/rr/start/sec_ecom.php.

Hollnagel, E., 1999, Accident analysis and barrier functions, http://www.hai.uu.se/projects/train/papers/accidentanalysis.pdf.

Hutter, D., 2002, Security Engineering, http://www.dfki.de/~hutter/lehre/sicherheit/securityengineering.ppt.

Jennex, M.E., "Security Design", System Design Lecture, IDS 697, San Diego State University, 4/21/03.

Jennex, M.E. and Walters, A., 2003, A comparison of knowledge requirements for operating hacker and security tools, The Security Conference, Information Institute.

Lee, Y., Lee, Z., and Lee, C. K., 2002, A study of integrating the security engineering process into the software lifecycle process standard (IEEE/EIA 12207), 6th Americas Conference on Information Systems, AMCIS, 451–457.

Pfleeger, C. P. and Pfleeger, S. L., 2003. *Security in Computing*, 3rd Edition, Prentice-Hall, Upper Saddle River, NJ.

Siponen, M. and Baskerville, R., 2001, A new paradigm for adding security into IS development methods, 8th Annual Working Conference on Information Security Management and Small Systems Security.

Trost, W.A. and Nertney, R.J., 1995, Barrier Analysis, http://ryker.eh.doe.gov/analysis/trac/29/trac29.html.

INTEGRATING SECURITY PROPERTIES WITH SYSTEMS DESIGN ARTEFACTS

Khaled Md. Khan*

ABSTRACT

This paper makes an attempt to propose a framework that enables systems developers to express and integrate security properties with the system functionality from the beginning of the information systems (IS) development process. We propose a UML based security integration framework that will enable IS developer to specify and incorporate underlying security properties with the corresponding functional properties in the design artefacts. In current practices, a system is analysed and designed around business objects and operations. IS developers only consider objects and functionality during the system analysis and design process, whereas security designers define the security of the system. We use UML to show how the security properties defined by the security experts can be incorporated with the use case, class diagram, and interaction diagrams along with the systems functionality designed by systems analysts and designers.

1 . INTRODUCTION

This distributive characteristic of information systems presents tremendous challenges for information security and systems architecture as well. Security is a system-wide property referring to a non-functional system requirement of information systems. Security architecture alone cannot protect a system unless security properties are well mapped with the corresponding systems functionality at the early development process. Information systems developers need to define the systems functionalities with their supporting security properties much earlier than they do in the current practice, and these need to be incorporated and reflected in the design artefacts.

* Khaled Md. Khan, School of Computing and Information Technology, University of Western Sydney, Locked bag 1797 South Penrith DC, NSW 1797 Australia. Khaled is also affiliated with Monash University.

In this paper, we do not propose any new security architecture; rather we explore how security as a non-functional property could be incorporated in the systems design artefacts. The requirements for the systems security are typically done either at the end of the system design, or assigned this task to the security experts who are not usually involved in the entire IS development process.[1] In most cases, security properties are bolted-in to the system at the end of the development process. In 2001 the US President's special advisor for cyberspace security Richard Clarke said that members of the IT industry must build information security into their products at the point of development and not treat it as an afterthought.[2]

System architecture is commonly described from multiple views. Each view addresses a specific set of concerns, and captures some particular aspects of the system. In the current practice, system architecture only reveals the systems functionality, business objects and their collaborations. The current state of practice and theory ignore the non-functional aspect of the system to be addressed at the architectural level[3]. Systems level non-functional properties such as maintainability, usability, security, portability, reusability are not integrated with the design artefacts due to lack of proper supporting framework or methodology. Getting the non-functional properties correct with the system functionality and operations would definitely set the stage for everything to come in the system's life. Ignoring these issues during the analysis and design phase means that the quality of the entire system may go dangerously wrong, which may cause the entire fabric to unravel.[6] In this endeavour we address only security as one of the important non-functional properties of information systems.

Today's trust on information systems is based on consent, that is, the end-user is explicitly asked to consent or decline to use an information system[5]. At the user level such a consent based trust perhaps works fine for end-users, but for systems analysts and designers, a universal shallow commitment on security of a system such as "the system is secure" is dangerously illusive. Stating that a system is "secure" can only lull some stakeholders into a false sense of trust, which may not have any qualified basis. Trust requirements for analysts and designers in a development environment are quite different from those for end-users of application systems.[8]

Without incorporating the security properties of information systems along with the systems functionality at an earlier development stage, information systems developers consequently may end up with wrong architectural designs by unknowingly contradicting the security features of the system.[1] Even a modification or alternation of a design feature may unknowingly undermine the already employed security features of the systems. Any modification in the system functionality, source code, or design artefacts can introduce vulnerabilities to that system. It may lead to a change to the security features of the system as well. A security feature is sensitive to any software modification irrespective of the size of the modification. The question is how a system designer knows whether a design decision or a modification plan would not contradict the underlying security policies of the system. Unfortunately, no modelling tools or techniques are available to make the security policy incorporated with the systems design decisions in a single artefact. To address this, we need to find a fresh approach to address this pressing issue.

In a development environment, security must be incorporated into the system architecture. These will certainly help all stakeholders of the system such as users, and developers to understand how the security functions are employed to specific systems functionality in the system architecture. Systems analysts and designers need to know more on how various security properties would eventually work in tandem with systems functionality from the beginning. The intention "to know" is primarily based not on the speculation made about the quality of the security functions employed, rather largely on the fear of unknown security properties employed to systems functionality they have designed. This knowledge would certainly help IS developers to identify any conflicting design issues between the security features and application design.

The issue of tagging security properties with analysis and design artefacts of the system remains unexplored. A quick browse of the current published work suggests that this issue has received less attention from security and information systems research communities. Most notable work on security specification with the design artefacts have recently been reported in work by Ghosh et al,[2] Jurjens,[7] and Ribeiro-Justo et al.[9] Most security research currently focuses on fixing security problems after the system is installed or in operation. In our approach we define a framework with which systems developers could tag the elicited security properties with the early design models of the system.

The paper proceeds as follows. In the next section, we outline the main concepts of security properties and our framework. The example described in section 4 is used to illustrate the applicability of the framework. The paper finally concludes in section 5.

3. INTEGRATION FRAMEWORK

Our framework is based on security properties and the UML generated analysis and design artefacts of information systems. We integrate the security properties with functional properties at various abstraction levels.

3.1 Security Properties

An information system may offer one or more functionalities to its environment. A functionality may have its own *security properties* to protect its computational assets or business objects. Security properties are based on the actual *security functions* that a system employs to accomplish one or more *security policies*. Generally speaking, security functions are the implementation of *security policies* defined to withstand certain security threats and risks. Security policies define the rules by which the system governs access to and protect its resources. Security policies have certain *security objectives* which are essentially defined to withstand identified security threats and risks. A security function enforces the security policy and provides required capabilities.[10] Security properties are typically derived from security functions. Security properties reflecting the security functions are used for various reasons such as to authenticate components, and to authorise their operation, to ensure confidentiality and integrity, and so on. Examples of security properties can be passwords, private keys, secret keys, public keys, shared keys, digital signatures among others.

The classes of security properties discussed in this paper are based on ISO/IEC-15408 Common Criteria (CC).[10] Security properties of information systems are categorised into eleven classes in the common criteria such as security audit, communication, cryptographic support, user data protection, identification and authentication, security management, privacy, protection of system security functions, resource utilisation, system access, and trusted path and channels. In this paper we only discuss a subset of security classes defined in CC just to give a snapshot of our framework.

Table 1. Some security properties, their descriptions and objectives.

Security properties	*Descriptions*	*Security objectives*
encrypted(X, K^+) (PKI encryption)	Object **X** is encrypted with the public key $\mathbf{K^+}$	Authenticity of **X**
signed(X, K^{-1}) (digital signature)	Object **X** is digitally signed with the private key $\mathbf{K^{-1}}$.	Authenticity, integrity and non-repudiation of **X**
acl(P, R, X, O, C) (access control list)	**P** with the role **R** can perform operation **O** on the object **X** with condition **C**	Availability and authorisation of the action **O** on object **X**.
password(Q,L,P) (password–based)	**Q** should have valid login **L** and corresponding password **P**.	Authorisation of **Q**

In the current practice, security experts analyse the security threats and vulnerabilities for the system. Based on their analysis, they define security policies for the system. In Table 1 we cite some of the security properties defined in CC. The '*Descriptions*' column in Table 1 explains the corresponding security properties cited in column 1.

3.2 UML-based Approach

In object oriented analysis and design, the modelling language UML is widely used. UML provides a ready-to-use, expressive visual modelling language, so IS developers can develop and exchange meaningful models without loosing information or imposing excessive work to map their models.[4] It consolidates a set of core modelling concepts that are generally accepted across many current methods and modelling tools. We base our framework on UML generated use cases, class definition, and interaction diagrams –each of these is briefly described here.

Use case in UML is an essential tool in understanding the functional requirements of an information system, and the communication of those functional requirements with the system environment.[4] We develop use cases to express systems functionalities and their interactions with their environments in terms of actors and functions. Description of the functionality is expressed from a business or system point of view. Each use case describes a complete business function – the things that the system will do. A business function is a functionality serviced to the end-users of the system.

Use cases do not model the system characteristics of things, people and concepts that are within the systems functionality. It is the class diagram which models the things, people and concepts in the system functionality. A class diagram captures structure and properties of business objects. A class defines its associated methods in the class. Methods contribute to achieving one or more systems functionality in collaboration with objects and other methods. In interaction diagrams, systems events are identified corresponding to the methods defined in the class diagram. An event is a noteworthy occurrence that triggers an action or transition in the system.[4]

3.3 Security Integration Process

Our framework proposes that the security objectives defined by the security experts need to be mapped, integrated and expressed with the analyst's defined functionality that a use case represents. The proposed security integration approach with the traditional systems and security analysis and design practices are shown in column 3, Figure 1.

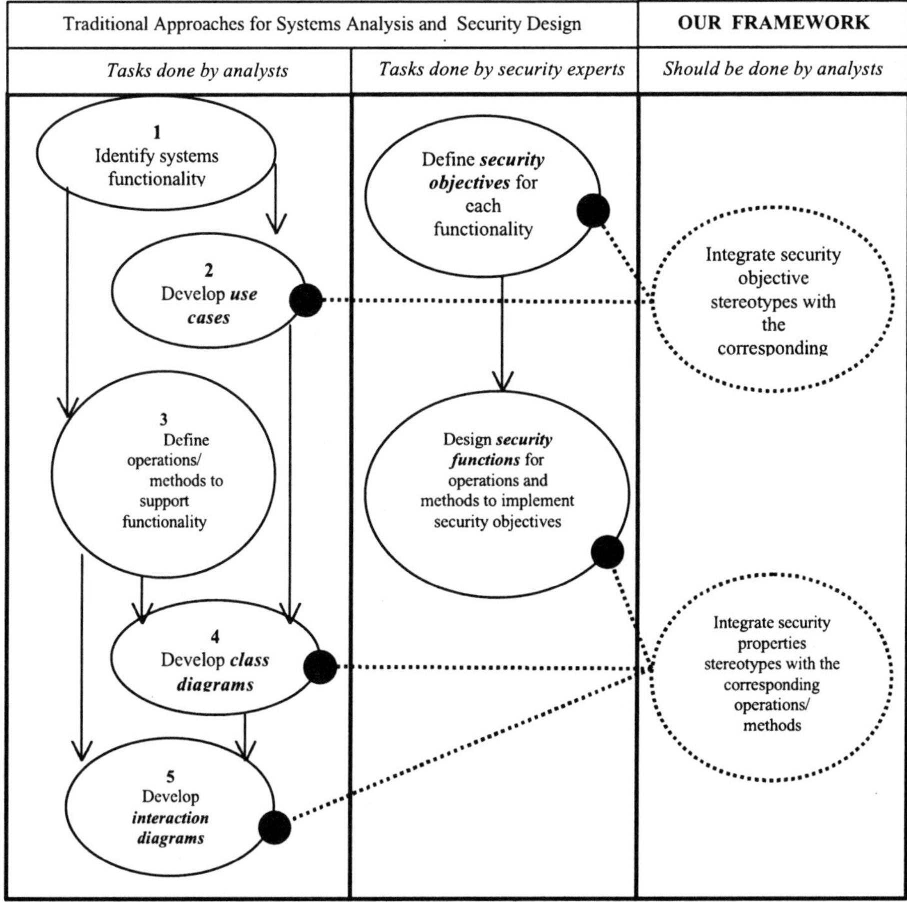

Figure 1. Traditional systems analysis and design, security design, and our approach.

In Figure 1, three columns are shown with their properties. The first column represents the current practice of object oriented systems analysis and design in brief. The number in each oval denotes the sequence of the tasks typically done in a development environment. The arrows represent relationships between two tasks. The relationship could be dependency between two tasks, or associations between tasks. For instance, task 1 depends on task 3. It signifies that defining a functionality is meaningless without defining the corresponding operations and methods in task 3 at a later stage. Column 2 represents the tasks typically carried out by security experts. Security professionals design the required security policies and functions for the system's critical functionalities and business objects. Security experts implement the corresponding security functions of the security objectives. These are not usually done concurrently with the systems analysis and design process. A task depends on the later task as depicted with the arrow. In column 3, we propose that the efforts traditionally done by the analysts and security experts separately should be brought together at the systems artefact level. Security integration processes are shown with the dotted ovals and round-headed filled arrows with dotted lines.

The security integration mapping scheme presented later in this section requires a structure for specifying the security properties of individual function. The security properties of functions can be visualised with a predicate-like structure such as

security_properties(security_functions, security_attributes)

where, *security_functions* are a set of security related operations such as encryption, decryption, and digital signature; whereas *security attributes* are the operands such as passwords, private keys, public keys, shared keys and so on. In the structure we can also include other properties such as identities of the entities, classes of entities, object names etc. The security properties as stereotypes are used in UML with double brackets such as << >>.

The functionality defined in the use case depends on one or more corresponding systems operations. Systems operations are defined as methods in the classes. Hence the *security objectives* of each use case are implemented with *security functions* which are defined with methods.. Each of the use cases defined by the systems analysts may have its own *security objectives. Security objectives* are related to the use cases, whereas *security functions* are related to systems operations. In our framework, the defined *security functions* are mapped, integrated and expressed with the definition of the method in the class.

In interaction diagrams a system event causes the system to execute and perform one or more corresponding operation(s) or method(s). Interaction diagrams illustrate how objects interact via messages to achieve certain system functionality. In our framework, we map, integrate and express the defined security functions with the events specified in the interaction diagrams.

To make an effective integration between various systems components we need a mapping schema. Defined security properties for various systems components need to be mapped and integrated with the corresponding systems artefacts at different levels of the IS development process. Such an integration mapping schema is depicted in Figure 2.

3.4 Integration Mapping Schema

The schema cited in Figure 2 represents the relationship between various objects generated from the processes shown Figure 1.

The rounded rectangles represent systems analysis and design artefacts typically produced during object-oriented analysis and design using UML as shown in column 1, Figure 1. The double-framed rectangles denote the security properties and objectives produced by the security professionals as cited in column 2, Figure 1. In Figure 2, the arrows show the direction of the relationship we should read. The text with the arrow depicts the name of the relationship between various systems and security properties. This mapping schema can be used to integrate all functional and security properties related to one use case. Such a schema would definitely reveal the security features related to a particular design issue of the information system. In the following section we illustrate our framework with a small example.

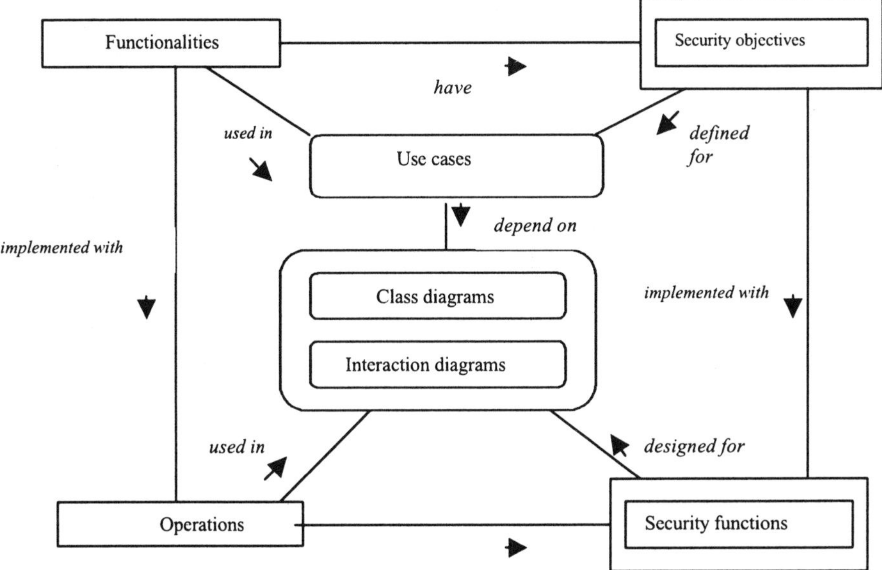

Figure 2. Correlation between security properties and systems design artefacts in an integration mapping schema.

The instances of the mapping schema store design information about the systems functionality and security; and encompassing which functionality is incorporated with which security properties. Such an artefact can preserve the correlations between two different classes of design decisions. In systems maintenance or new development, these instances of mappings would be available for ready reference.

4. APPLICABILITY OF THE FRAMEWORK

A college requires an automated system to allocate students to tutorial sessions of a course. Students themselves enrol to the tutorial sessions of the course. The lecturers of the course know which students belong to which tutorial sessions. Only administrative assistants can change the tutorial sessions for the students. To enrol for a tutorial session, students must enter their login and passwords. To move a student from one session to another, administrative assistant must be authorised to do so. The authorisation is granted based on the encryption key of the admin assistant. To get an access to the student list, the lecturer needs to supply his/her password and login details to the system.

Systems analysts define three use cases for this system as shown in Figure 3. Based on the security requirements of the use cases of the system, security experts define the security objectives such as authenticity of the student for the enrolment to the session, authorisation of the actor, and availability of the functionality to the authorised actors and so on. Figure 3 shows the security objectives stereotypes with the use cases.

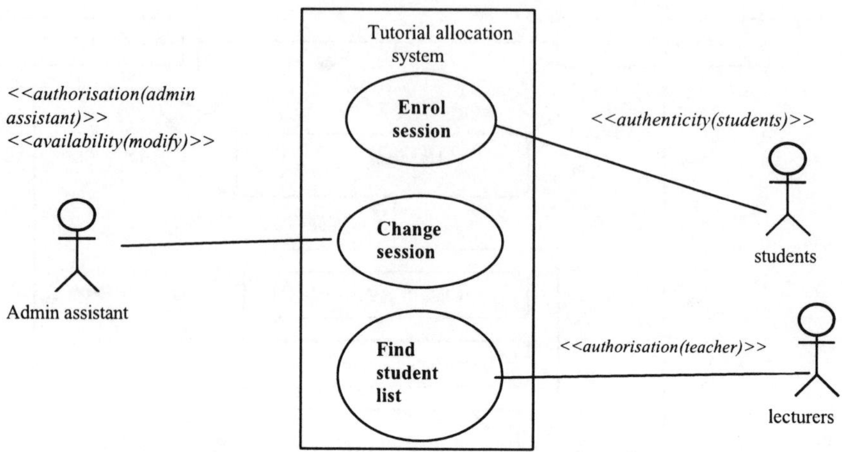

Figure 3. Use cases with some security functions.

The use case *'enrol session'* may have two operations such as find the session, and enter student name. The security objective of this use case is <<authenticity(students)>>. The security function for this objective <<password(login, password)>> is defined along with the method enter(ID) in the class *Tutorial* in Figure 4. Since the student needs to enter his/her password and login name, the security objective in this case would be the authentication of the student identity.

Figure 4 also shows that the method *find(session, course)* does not have any security properties. The security property <<password(login, password)>> of the method *enter(ID)* is the realisation of the security objective *<<authenticity(students)>>* defined related to use case 'E*nrol session*'. The methods edit(ID, session) and getList(session) accomplish the functionalities for use cases 'Change session' and 'Find student list' respectively. Two security properties defined along with these two methods are the implementation of the corresponding security objectives for two use cases 'Change session' and 'Find student list'. The method search(ID, session) does not have any security properties. The argument L in the security property <<acl(L, admin_asst, session, modify, NULL)>> denotes the login name of the actor. Other arguments used in the security functions are self-explanatory.

The interaction diagrams of the use cases along with their security properties are shown in Figure 5. Three interaction diagrams in Figure 5(a), (b), (c) show how the security property stereotypes are reflected with their corresponding system events.

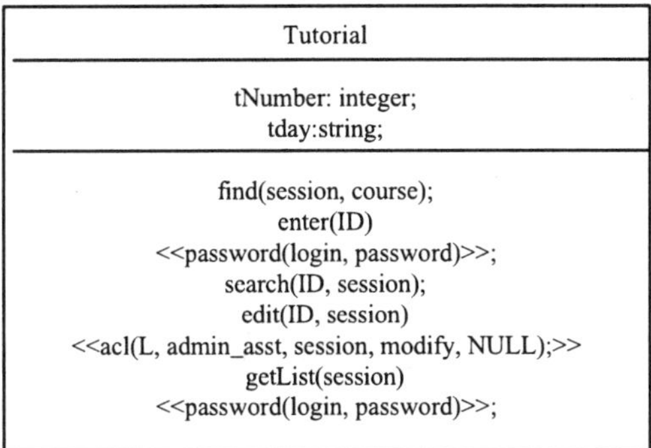

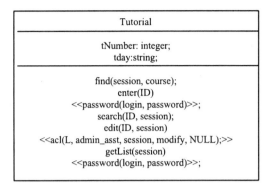

Figure 4. The class definition of the class Tutorial.

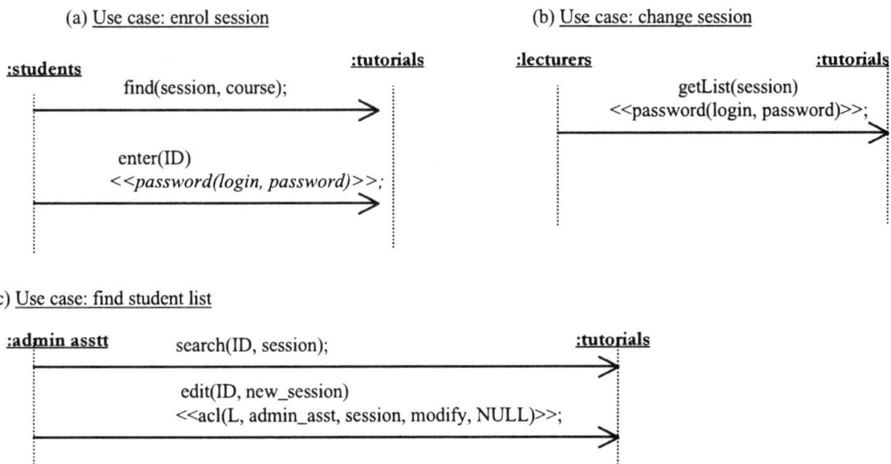

Figure 5. Interaction diagrams for three use cases.

We now relate all these security properties with the functional properties using our integration mapping schema in Figure 6. The integration schema instance for the use case 'change session' in Figure 6 illustrates not only the correlations between various systems functional properties and the security properties, the relationships among the same kind of properties are also established in one artefact. That means, it captures which class is related to which use case and interaction diagrams, for instance. Regarding security, it also maps particular security property with the corresponding security objective. We could develop similar two more schema mapping instances for each of the remaining use cases.

In Figure 6, the schema will clearly indicate the inconsistency between properties. For example, if we replace the security functions acl() with another function, the class definition, interaction diagram, and the security objectives need to be changed accordingly. If we modify the functionality, all other properties may require change. We find this framework is very useful in accommodating any design changes. The schema reflects the changes and inconsistency between classes of properties. We can design mapping schema for other non-functional properties such as maintainability, reusability, usability and portability for information systems.

The mapping schema could possibly be transformed into well-defined relations to preserve the design knowledge about the systems functionalities and their corresponding security properties. Further research can be initiated to see the possibility for an automatic support of this framework.

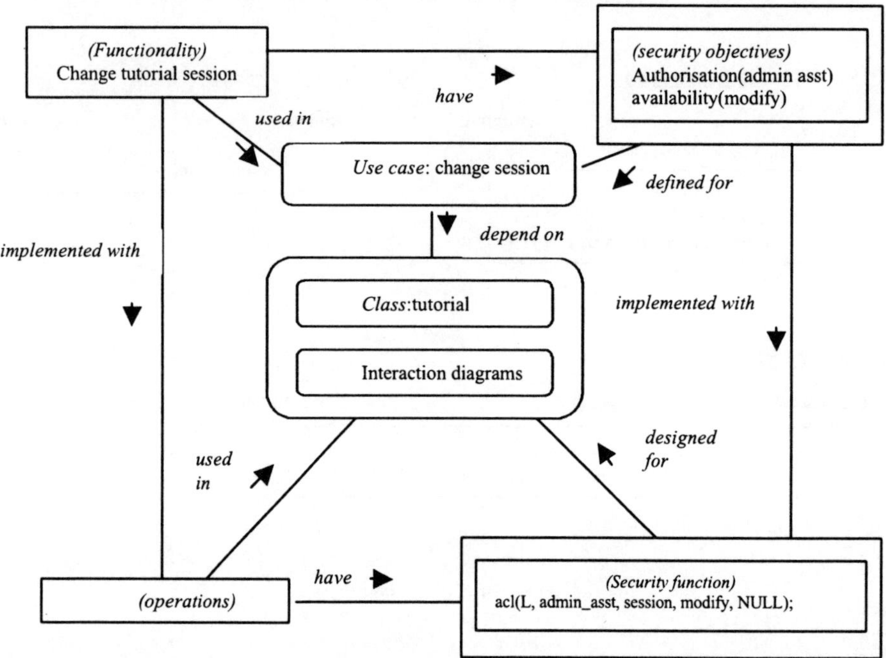

Figure 6. Mapping between the functional properties of the use case "Change session" and its security properties

5. CONCLUSION

Our proposed framework for integrating the security profile of systems functionality in design artefacts could be a part of systems analysis and design process. The existing analysis and design tools and methods can be extended with this framework such a way that the mapping schema instances can be used by all stakeholders to retrieve the security-related information of the systems design properties. When the security properties are spelled out in simple comprehensible terms, systems developers or security experts are better positioned in advance to evaluate the strengths, weakness and conflicts of any of the design and security features of the system. They are also well informed what to expect from the system functionality in terms of security of the system. We understand that more work need to be done for the integration of security properties with other functional properties such as collaboration diagrams. We believe that quality-based systems analysis and design paradigm which integrates non-functional properties into the systems functional design artefacts would be increasingly popular, and challenging too. This paper only gives a snapshot on how security properties can possibly be integrated with the analysis and design process and artefacts during the early systems development process. Repeated experience suggests that security design and systems analysis processes could better serve if the integration of these processes and their artefacts are some how coordinated and incorporated in a unified way. From a system development process point of view, there is a huge gap between the security experts and systems analysts. We must explore further on how to bridge this gap, and this has to be done urgently.

ACKNOWLEDGEMENTS

The research work reported in this paper has been fully funded by a seed grant project No. 80375, the University of Western Sydney, Australia.

REFERENCES

1. J. Viega, G. McGraw, Building Secure Software: How to Avoid Security Problems the Right Way. (Addison-Wesley, Reading, Mass., 2001).
2. A. Ghosh, C. Howell, J. Whittaker, Building Software Securely from the Ground Up, *IEEE Software*, Vol. 19, no. 1, 14–16 (IEEE CS press, Los Alamitos, Calif., 2002).
3. G. Abowd, R. Allen, and D. Garlan, Formalizing Style to Understand Descriptions of Software Architecture, *ACM Trans. on Software Engineering and Methodology*, 4(4), 319–365 (1995).
4. C. Larman, *Applying UML and Patterns* (Prentice Hall, 1997).
5. B. Friedman, P. Kahn Jr., and D. Howe, Trust Online, *Communications of the ACM*, Vol. 43, No. 12, 34-44 (ACM press, December 2000).
6. L. Bass, P. Clements, R. Kazman, *Software Architecture in Practice* (Addison-Wesley, 1998).
7. J. Jurjens, UMLsec: Extending UML for Secure Systems Development, Proc. 5th International Conference on UML, 412–425 (Springer-verlag, 2002).
8. K. Khan, J. Han, Composing Security-Aware Composition, *IEEE Software*, Vol. 19-1, January-February 34–41 (IEEE CS press, Los Alamitos, Calif., 2002).
9. G. Ribeiro-Justo, A. Saleh, Non-functional Integration and Coordination of Distributed Component Services, Proc. 6th European Conference on Software Maintenance and Reengineering, (IEEE CS press, Los Alamitos, Calif. 2002).
10. Common Criteria ISO/IEC-15408. Common Criteria for Information Technology Security Evaluation, version 2.0, (NIST, USA, 1999), http://csrc.nist.gov/cc/

KNOWLEDGE CREATION THROUGH SYSTEMS DEVELOPMENT

Helen Hasan[1]

1. INTRODUCTION

There is a distinction between the descriptive and design sciences where, according to Simon (1981), "design sciences do not tell how things are but how they ought to be to attain some ends". Design sciences aim not only to develop knowledge for the design and realisation of artefacts but also to improve the understanding of how to solve the social and organisational problems for which the artefact is designed. IS research draws its significance from the uniqueness of computer-based information and communication tools and their place in shaping recent human, social and organisational history. Advances in the field result from a better understanding of how to develop and use these tools and what impact they have on the way we work, and live. The question posed by Gregor (2002, p. 12) is: what constitutes a contribution to knowledge when research is of this type? Papers describing such research typically contain "no hypotheses, no experimental design and no data analysis" (ibid, p. 13) and so often pose a dilemma for reviewers. This does not necessarily invalidate this type of research and the challenge is to conduct and report it in ways that identify the rigour and contribution of the research making it acceptable to journal editors and reviewers.

This paper will address the concept of *systems development* as a knowledge creating activity, and thus as a legitimate research *method*. In the process of systems development not only is knowledge created about the development process itself but also a deeper understanding emerges about the organisational problem that the system is designed to solve. The paper will begin with a brief overview of research in the design sciences and a comparison of a range of research methods that are concerned with the design, and use, of information systems. This will be followed by an assessment of the way systems development as a research method deals with the scientific research processes of data collection, analysis, synthesis and display. A case study, where the systems development research method was adopted, will be described and used to gain a better understanding of this approach. The paper then suggests a pragmatic way by which systems development research can be designed, with the results presented and justified.

---

[1] Department of Information Systems, University of Wollongong, Wollongong, Australia.

2 THEORETICAL BACKGROUND

Information Systems (IS) is a developing and applied field, and members of the IS community are questioning some of the more traditional ideas of what constitutes research and in what ways legitimate research can be conducted in the field. The characteristic of IS that distinguishes it from other management fields in the social sciences is that it concerns the use of "artifacts in human-machine systems" (Gregor 2002). Conversely the characteristic that distinguishes IS from more technical fields, such as Computer Science and Information Technology, is its concern for the human elements in organisational and social systems.

Research can be defined as "diligent and systematic enquiry or investigation into a subject in order to discover facts or principles", which are "accepted or professed rules of action" (*The Macquarie Dictionary*, 1981). The same source defines knowledge as "acquaintance with facts, truths or principles as from study or investigation" and the outcome of research adds to the body of knowledge of a discipline and it is appropriate to emphasise the strong conceptual link between research and the processes of knowledge discovery and creation. In IS the quality of research is usually determined by the applicability of the knowledge that has been created.

An important determinant of the quality of research is through its relationship to sound theory. IS researchers have frequently borrowed and adapted theories and methodologies from older, more established disciplines. New theories and methodologies are also evolving appropriate to the unique socio-technical nature of the IS field. Kaptelinin (1996) describes the computer as a social and psychological tool unlike any other in the history of human endeavour because of its capacity to mediate human learning and communication. The objects of study in IS research, information systems, are therefore a complex interaction of human, social and technical components that mediate organisational processes. While IS researchers continue to rely on a wide variety of existing and new theories for the range of topics covered by the field, the identification of a single unifying or at least prominent, theory for IS is proving to be difficult.

In a classification of types of theories, among those for analysing, describing, understanding, explaining and predicting, Gregor (2002, p. 12) proposes that a "theory for design and action" is most relevant for IS research. This design and action theory is about the construction and use of artefacts, and about methodologies and tools for "how to do something" (*ibid*). This type of theory is dynamic so that it can be informed by other theories and can, in turn, provide feedback to augment traditional theories.

To be able to identify what is, and what is not, research in information systems development, it is useful to distinguish between systems that *automate* and those that *informate*, using the term introduced by Zuboff (1988). Where the former are conceptually simpler than the latter, taking an existing manual process and replacing it with a computer-based system. Many *informate* type systems are conceptually complex and the high failure rate of systems such as decision support systems, executive information systems, groupware and knowledge management systems is indicative that they are not well understood. Markus et al. (2002) have used the description "systems that support emergent knowledge processes (EKP)" for these complex *informate* type applications and have shown that they require a new IS design theory. Examples of EKPs are basic research, new product development and strategic business planning. These have the characteristics that there is no best structure or sequence to the process, and have an actor-set that is unpredictable and requires knowledge that is complex, evolving dynamically and distributed across a community of people. EKP involve innovation by sense-making, building knowledge through a recursive, participatory and evolutionary manner (Boland and Tenkasi 1995). Most knowledge intensive emergent processes involve high-level professional and technical personnel with have a high degree of autonomy and so have challenging information requirements, needing knowledge and expertise to apply this information.

Much of the early research in Information Systems has resulted in improved understanding of methods and techniques for the construction and use of *automate* or low-level *informate* systems. Markus et al (2002) have developed a design theory for *informate* systems to support EKPs however these are generally not standard and tend to be dependent on the specific context. What works in one organisation department or group may not work in another so that much knowledge about such systems is not transferable.

This paper investigates the proposition that many IS projects concerned with EKP could be considered a piece of original research where the requirements, design and even implementation is original and contains new knowledge towards a general understanding of how to productively manage data and information in complex situations. Many of these systems evolve through a series of prototypes, which are constantly evaluated with the results fed back into the systems requirements and design. Through the activities of systems analysis and design and the programming of computers to be tools for complex social activities such as EKP, people are engaged in higher mental activities from which new insights and knowledge emerge. This is not a design theory but rather a grounded method of generating theory from a participatory action research process mediated by the unique characteristics of information and communications technology.

3. SYSTEMS DEVELOPMENT AND RELATED RESEARCH METHODS

Following the lead of Nunamaker et al. (1991) this paper will adopt the term *systems development method* (SDM) for the design science research approach in IS. However there are other related approaches, mostly in the realm of qualitative and interpretive research, some of which are action research, grounded theory, engineering, constructivism, pragmatism, tool-mediation of activity and developmental research. These are now presented in order to clarify and enlighten the discussion.

A *systems development method* (SDM) for data collection, analysis and theory building has the reflective and iterative attributes often associated with participatory action research, combining research and practice in such a way that action brings about some situational improvement and research increases a broader understanding. However there are two particular characteristics that distinguish SDM from the general action research approach. Firstly, in SDM there are always three inter-related domains where this research method can generate knowledge, those of: (a) the techniques of systems development, (b) the properties of system itself, and (c) the situation where the system is to be used. Secondly, the research project is both constrained by the limits that current information technology places on the development of systems and is enabled by the uniqueness of this technology, which can, as a tool, mediate human learning and communication.

SDM also has qualities found in grounded approaches to research. As explained in the award winning paper of Orwlikowski (1995), a grounded approach enables IS research to incorporate the criticality of organisational context in shaping technology use in organisations. Grounded theory is an inductive, discovery methodology with the aims of generating a descriptive and explanatory theory while iteratively gathering rich data from one or more sites. Concepts are suggested by the data rather than imposed from outside and are organised through the identification of recurring themes into theory. SDM however differs from traditional grounded theory research in the way data is coded and categorised.

The term *engineering-type research* is mentioned by Burstein and Gregor (1999) who claim that this type of IS research method is not always recognised as such and is comparatively poorly understood. Engineering is a traditional discipline concerning issues mainly related to the construction of artefacts and is relevant to IS research that studies the design, delivery, use and impact of information and communications technology (ICT) in organisations and society. However, ICT can be considered more than physical artefacts or tools but rather ones that incorporate logic, in the form of software, and interact with people in a way no previous artefact has done. Information systems are both physical and mental tools so that in IS construction can be considered a form of constructivism that relates closely to SDM. In the context of learning and development, constructivism is a theory, which came out of the work of Piaget and is a philosophy of learning founded on the premise that, by reflecting on our experiences, we construct our own understanding of the world we live in. Each of us generates our own *rules* and *mental models*, which we use to make sense of our experiences, much in the same way as models are constructed though the processes of systems analysis and design.

A precursor of construction is design, so that, related to the discipline of engineering, is the field of design. Niiniluoto (2001) and March and Smith (1995) distinguish design science from the natural or descriptive sciences in research. March and Smith (1995) recognise knowledge in design, and see the design process as one of creating knowledge, which is evident though the building and evaluation of the thing designed. The aim of design research is to explain how and why the constructs, models, methods and instantiations work. Architecture, for example, can be viewed as a design science and one of the concepts emanating from architecture is the concept of patterns (Alexander et al. 1977), to explain how good designers conceptualise and reuse their ideas. The concept of pattern has more recently been applied to IT development (Lyon 2000).

Research methods, involving activities of design and construction, are akin to grounded approaches to research such as pragmatism, the philosophy that truth is what works in practice. In IS activities of interest are found in the development of socio-technical systems involving computer-based tools. Typical methods used in IS research, where the design and construction of a system is involved, are observation, action or participant research often with various forms of prototyping (Baskerville and Wood-Harper 1998). The evidence for validity of this type of research, in terms of knowledge creation, is usually referred to as *proof of concept.*

It could be stated that there is a parallel between pragmatic, constructive research methodologies and the developmental methodologies used in practice for systems analysis, design and production. When using the term *methodology* in IS it is often hard to determine where practice stops and research begins. Rather than separate research and practice it may be more beneficial to investigate ways of combining and reconciling the two. A way to do this is by relating research to the concept of tool-mediate activity emanating from the original concepts of Vygotsky (1978). Vygotsky's approach may be called social constructivism because he emphasized the critical importance of culture and the importance of the social context for development.

Vygotsky, and subsequent scholars in Activity Theory such as Leoniev (1981) and Engestrom (1987), saw learning, development and work as holistic human activity, which both mediates, and is mediated by, the tools used and the social context of the activity. This two-way concept of mediation implies that the capability and availability of tools mediates what can be done and the tool, in turn, evolves to hold the historical knowledge of how the community works and is organised. It is through the dynamic process of mediation that learning and development occurs, both in the individual and in the society as a whole (Hasan and Crawford 2002).

The type and quality of the tools used for human work determines, to a much greater extent than they have in the past, the pattern and rate of development. New technology is driving changes to organisational structures and activities and this in turn is placing increasing demands on the capability and capacity of the technology. The changes that ICT, and in particular the Internet, has made to the way information is perceived and used in society today, is illustrative of this concept. It is proposed that research in this area is so closely related to an evolving practice that it must be embedded in, and immediately applicable to, that practice.

An approach that incorporates this concept is development research, which is disciplined investigation conducted in the context of the development of a product or program for the purpose of improving either the thing being developed or the developer. It is therefore ideal for this investigation as it is both contextual and evolutionary, where a prototype model is constructed, used with the target group, which is observed and questioned before the prototype revised.

4. THE STAGES OF SYSTEMS DEVELOPMENT RESEARCH

SDM research incorporates many of the concepts mentioned above, design, construction, dynamic tool mediation and developmental aspects. These are found in the five stages of systems development research proposed by Nunamaker et al. (1991) namely, concept design, constructing the architecture of the system, prototyping, product development and technology transfer. These stages will be adopted in this paper, although in contrast to Nunamaker et al., it is proposed here that the stages do not follow a linear progression but rather one that is interactive and dynamic as determined by the concept of tool mediation mentioned above. This suggests that what is being done, the research activity, is continually influencing, and being influenced by, the tools used in these five stages. Therefore the distinction between the stages is blurred, they may be continually revisited and not all systems development research involves all stages: The five stages are as follows:

Concept design: In this first stage there needs to be an adaptation and amalgamation of current technical and theoretical advances in the area of interest. The researcher must find, synthesis, use, apply existing knowledge to identify gaps or limitations of existing systems and develop a meaningful research objective. This stage may involve a substantial literature review although the time taken to get research published probably means that the current state of the art is better gleaned from direct communication with practitioners and other researchers in the field. While this stage is more one of locating and synthesising existing knowledge, rather than discovering or creating new knowledge, it could result in the publication of a review paper on the topic.

Constructing the architecture of the system The second stage is overtly one of new knowledge creation that should be accepted as genuine research. The researcher engages in the creative and innovative design activity of architecture development, defining components, models, algorithms and data structures.

Prototyping This is the stage where proof of concept is often used to demonstrate that a system can be built based on the results of the previous stage. This may be done with a single working prototype or involve the iterative analysis, design and implementation of an evolving prototype. Learning occurs through the evolutionary system building process where insight is gained about the problem and the complexity of the system. The evolutionary prototyping development process includes regular expert/user evaluation feeding back into the systems development process. In many cases of systems development the research stops at this stage because it fails to meet expectation or is not feasible be further developed for commercial use. (Koskivaara 2002)

Product development At the conclusion of the prototyping stage it is possible to freeze and formalise the systems specifications to build, test and evaluate a robust system. In some cases of systems development research there is a particular client sponsoring the research is interested in adopting the systems produced. If commercialisation occurs the new knowledge emerging from the project is often confidential and there is no public release of knowledge.

Technology transfer If the production stage is successful the product may interest a general audience. At this stage it may be possible to evaluate the use of the system with case and field studies or laboratory experiments, consolidating experiences learnt and even developing new theories of use. This may feed back into a new research cycle.

5. A CASE STUDY IN SYSTEMS DEVELOPMENT

This case study, an example of systems development research undertaken by the author, concerns the development of a knowledge management system (KMS) to support the work of professional groups such as a research team. This project aims to add to the understanding of how information and communication technologies can contribute to the practice of knowledge management (KM) of such teams.

Recent advances in ICT have heightened organisational interest in knowledge as a critical, strategic resource (McLure-Wasko and Faraj 2000) and many organisations are looking to information technologies for solutions to knowledge management efforts (Schultze and Boland 2000). However, despite the increasing sophistication and complexity of current ICT, there remains incongruence between their prescriptive requirements and the intangible and volatile nature of knowledge. The need for structure in ICT, has meant that most computer-based KMS attempt either to measure and codify knowledge, including intangibles such as intellectual capital, intellectual property and intellectual potential, or to enable the sharing of knowledge, which essentially resides in people. This presents quite a challenge and Schultze and Boland (*ibid*) report low success rates of around 30% for KM type systems, attributable to technologists' lack of understanding of the situated work practices of user communities. They believe that systems designers do not have accepted models for the large invisible and complex nature of work that KMS are expected to support.

This project aimed to explore ways to use the capacity of ICT to create KMS with the capacity to enhance knowledge creation and learning in groups. The project began over two years ago investigating the KM needs of professional groups and the potential for ICT to provide support for this need.

5.1. Concept Design and Research Questions

The KM literature and practical management forums espouse diverse views on KMS. Many organisations have systems they refer to as KMS while others would call by different titles such as document management systems, data warehouses and so on. There is much talk of the need to capture the tacit knowledge of employees in *knowledge repositories*, particularly text from exit interviews as organisations are loosing large numbers of staff through downsizing or imminent retirement of the extensive baby-boomer population bubble.

In the KM literature there are two conflicting views of organisational knowledge. One view sees knowledge as an object that can be codified and then stored in a computerized system to be made available on demand and so "the fundamental purpose of all knowledge management activity is to acquire, capture, access and reuse knowledge throughout the organisation" (Fowler 2000). The implication is that knowledge can be separated from its source and context. The other view says that knowledge can only reside in people and a KMS enables individual knowledge seekers to identify and communicate with knowledge sources, i.e. experts. The implication here is that group knowledge is simply the sum of the knowledge of its members and "the goal for KMS is to create a connected environment for knowledge exchange - a technical embodiment of corporate memory." (Mentzas et al 2001)

Assuming both views of organisational knowledge have some truth and merit, the project described here decided to follow the pragmatic view of Alavi and Leidner (1999) who describe KMS as an evolution of information systems into computer-based systems designed specifically to facilitate the sharing and integration of knowledge. This bypasses the argument as to whether knowledge can be stored by concentrating on the development of a KMS tools that mediates the activity of the group whether or not it is actually knowledge that is in the system.

Researchers and practitioners in information systems have, over several decades, developed and refined techniques for modelling the real world and these techniques are routinely used to design a large range of computer-based business systems. The resulting systems invariably have an *architecture* determined by some practical *unit of analysis*, such as a *record* in a relational database, an *object* in an OO program or a *rule* in an expert system. For a KMS there is a dilemma in choosing a unit of analysis as it must cope with the complexity and richness of real-world knowledge but have sufficient structure for processing in the computer-based environment. In other words there is a need for something more structured than text with keywords and tags, but more flexible than a database or expert system shell.

Given the close relationship of organisational knowledge to work practices, it was proposed in the project that a promising *unit of analysis* for the architecture of KMS is that of *activity*, as determined by the Cultural-Historical Activity Theory proposed by Leontiev (1981). As mentioned above, this is based on the social constructivist approach of Vygotsky (1978) and has through subsequent work determined its own structure: the hierarchical breakdown of an activity into actions and operations (Leontiev 1981), the relationship between the components of activities (Engestrom 1987) and the relationships between activities (Engestrom 2002). The main research questions therefore became:

- was it possible to create a knowledge architecture where the building block was *activity*?
- Could a KMS based on the activity knowledge architecture be successfully implemented so that information on group activities could be stored in a meaningful way?
- Could such a system be so integrated into work-practices that the knowledge repository will continue to be maintained? Would group members be motivated to keep the knowledge in the system up-to-date?
- Could members of the group extract useful knowledge of their historical and current activities in a meaningful way?

5.2. Constructing the Architecture of the System

A knowledge architecture with activity as the unit of analysis has been developed and constructed from the structures of Tables 1 and 2.

Table 1. Elements of the activity-model for KMS

Activities: who is doing what, for what purpose
Components of each activity as listed in Table 2
Relationships between those activities.
Actions and Operations by which Activities are carried out
An historical record of the above elements

Table 2. Components of activities according to Engeström

Component:	Definition and Clarification
object	the purpose and motives that define the activity.
subjects:	the person or people who carry out the activity
outcomes:	both intended and unintended results of carrying out the activity
tools/instruments:	both physical and non-physical instruments that are used in the conduct of the activity
community:	the community in which the subjects carry out that activity
rules	the formal and informal rules that the community imposes on the subject
division of labour	relationships in the community that determine the roles that subject have in carrying out the activity

The meaningfulness of this representation of work has been tested with three typical workgroups where members were asked to identify their activities, their components and relationships. A paper describing this work has been recently accepted for publication (Hasan, 2003) and the reader is referred to this article for further explanation of the research beyond the scope of this paper.

5.3. PROTOTYPING

An evolutionary prototyping process, with regular usability testing, has been used to produce an implementation of the architecture created in the previous stage as *proof of concept*. The prototype was first implemented in Microsoft Access and Visual Basic and then using a Web interface was developed with a database in MySQL. It was found useful to have a team of two developers, one with an in depth knowledge of the architecture and Activity Theory and the other with some appreciation of the theory but excellent technical skills. In this way the understanding of what was required grew quickly and seemed to be an activity where process knowledge was being created.

It is clear that much has been learnt in this process. This has been a challenging and evolutionary process where the architecture itself has been refined to enable a rich history of the group's knowledge to be retained and be easily accessible. The applications used for prototyping have been extended to their limits and there are aspects of the original specifications that have been too difficult to implement. The development of an innovative and complex system is time consuming and new development tools are continually becoming available. These are worth evaluating but a decision to change tools is fraught with the danger that it may consume more time.

The question for this paper is whether this prototyping stage of systems development is a separate piece of research or simply the proof of concept of the architecture designed in the previous stage. The experience from this project suggest that new knowledge is constructed through the prototyping process and that this is separate from the knowledge of the system architecture and so be publishable in its own right. This is an aspect of systems development research that needs to be better understood as a knowledge creating activity.

5.4. Product development and technology transfer

Although there is a customer interested in using this product, the difference between a successful research prototype and a fully operational system is apparent. It has taken four months of intensive work to bridge this gap and produce a system that would be acceptable to the customer. Even so, use of the product will be closely monitored by the researcher as it is used.

A process of continued development and evaluation of the system in use will focus on two critical issues:

- the motivation of people to continue to enter content throughout the life of the system and
- the meaningfulness of information and knowledge that can be extracted from the contents of the system

While it is believed that the successful implementation of the system is a significant research outcome, it is felt that the next publication of this work will come when these two issues have been resolved.

As this particular research project is in the field of knowledge management, the author is particularly conscious of the knowledge creation process both in relation to the production of a specific working knowledge management product for an organisation and in the creation of general knowledge as the output of the research process for academic publication.

6. DESIGNING, PRESENTING AND JUSTIFYING SYSTEMS DEVELOPMENT RESEARCH

6.1. Using SDM Research

A definition of research as "diligent and systematic enquiry performed to discover rules of action", is paraphrased from the Introduction to this paper A cursory overview of the development of *informate* systems that support EKP shows that the following can be considered research using an SDM:

- Creating group decision support systems added to the understanding of group planning and administration processes
- The growth of applications in the field of Artificial Intelligence led to the creation of the field of cognitive science and our understanding of both machine and human information processing.
- The development of executive information systems using online analytic processing systems led to a better understanding of the executive management processes and their information needs.
- The use of expert systems shells to set up knowledge bases has clarified the knowledge of many specific domains such as medical diagnosis.

In the same vein it is claimed that the case described above uses SDM and conforms to the definition of research. IS research aims to increase the understanding of organisational individual and social processes and how information and communications technology tools can support those processes. The output of Stages 1 to 3 can be considered as contributions to new knowledge as follows:

- From Stage 1 an analysis of KM literature in the light the Cultural-Historical Activity Theory led to an original concept, that of *activity* as a unit of analysis for a KMS. This provided the research questions and plan for the project as a whole.
- In Stage 2 it was shown that *activity* as a unit of analysis was understandable by people working in a EKP team and so that a KMS based on that unit could be flexible enough to support knowledge rather than information of the historical record of the team.
- In Stage 3 a prototyping process demonstrated that a KMS could be built based on the activity concept. Each iteration of the prototype modified and clarified the representation and structure of complex human activity in the system to be a workable repository of the historical knowledge of a team of people engaged in an EKP. This is a continuing process that is adding to the knowledge of how communities can use technological systems for their knowledge management.

6.2. Research Design

Although the progress of a systems development project is usually determined by the systems requirements, the fact that it is also research means that there must be a research agenda.

In order to present systems development research as research, the researcher must state at some stage the research problem, the objective and the questions to be addressed in terms of what are the gaps in, or the limitations of, existing knowledge in the area. The researcher must then be able to interpret the findings from the research in terms of its contribution to knowledge. The contribution may be in the innovative nature of the product, its ability to improve performance in the workplace or in the illustration of a new method of product development. There must also be some way that this contribution can be verified, and in systems development research this can be done through the success of the system as proof of concept. This may be supplemented by evaluations of the systems concept or the usability of the system itself, as in the KMS project described above.

6.3. Dealing with Data

In general any research project involves the collection of data by measurement, observation or other form of investigation. The research then consists of processes of data collection, analysis, presentation and either verification of hypotheses or the drawing of some conclusions that add to the accumulated knowledge of the field of study (Miles and Huberman, 1994). To be accepted as valid research, the systems development approach must have either some methodical data collection and analysis or an alternative rigorous procedure appropriate for systems development research. Data collected in research using SDM can be empirical, such as that from systems testing, qualitative, such as descriptions of the development process, or even implicit, in that the *data* of interest are embedded in a system's design or implementation. The latter is somewhat unusual but must be considered if the systems development method is to be widely used in IS.

It should be noted that many of the techniques for the design of research and analysis of research data are similar to, and overlap, the IS skills of analysis and design applied to systems including modelling the situation, documentation of the process, justification of choices, planning and conducting systems testing.

Presenting the results of data analysis may take different forms in SDM research. At stage two this may be the architecture itself or its justification. At stage three this may be the system itself as proof of concept. At stage four it may be the impact of the system on an organisation. From a research perspective a valid outcome may be lessons learnt from a failure with knowledge of what doesn't work. The test by which a systems development project can be considered valid research is by a demonstrable contribution to knowledge and a verifiable statement of what has been learnt.

7. CONCLUSION AND OBSERVATIONS

IS research has contributed significantly to the knowledge of how ICT systems can be created and used effectively but this is often not recognised as research. Even though the process of data collection, analysis and display are not as easily recognised and the distinctions between them blurred, these three processes can be said to be present in the systems development approach to research. Certainly the *display* is evident in the system itself but findings of the research are also evident in innovations to the way that the organisation conducts those activities for which the system was designed, with consequent improvements to organisational performance.

Researchers with ICT skills often use this approach but may not have an appreciation of how it constitutes research. We have observed that people with a purely technical focus place more emphasis in getting the product to work than in learning from the process. However it is probably not difficult to insist that systems development research papers contain an explicit statement of the research problem, objective and questions and conclude with a description of the outcomes in terms of the contribution to knowledge. There may often be no clear boundary between aspects of the systems development method and the research method, in many cases of this type of research. This is especially so with complex *informate*-type systems used to support EKP, but that should not mean that the research is any less valid if a contribution to knowledge can be demonstrated.

It is hoped that a tradition in the use of the systems development research method can be established as legitimate research so that worthy papers can be readily approved for publication.

REFERENCES

Alexander, C., Ishikawa, S., and Silverstein, M., 1977, *A Pattern Language: Towns, Buildings, Constructions*, Oxford University Press, NY.

Alvai, M. and Leidner, D., 1999, Knowledge Management Systems: Issues, Challenges and Benefits, *Communications of the Association for Information Systems*, 1/7.

Baskerville, R., and Wood-Harper, A. T., 1998, Diversity in information systems action research methods, *European Journal of Information Systems*, 7, 90–107.

Blackler, F., 1993, Knowledge and the Theory of Organisations: Organisations as Activity Systems and the Reframing of Management, *Journal of Management Studies*, 30/6, 863–884.

Boland, R. and Tenkasi, R., 1995, Perspective Making and Perspective Taking in Communities of Knowing, *Org Science*, 6/4, 350–372

Burstein, F., and Gregor, S., 1999, The systems development or engineering approach to research in Information Systems: an action research perspective, Proceedings of ACIS99, Wellington, NZ, 122–134.

Engeström, Y., 1987, *Learning by expanding: An activity-theoretical approach to developmental research*, Orienta-Konsultit, Helsinki.

Engeström, Y., 2002, Cultural-Historical Activity Theory, notes available at: http://www.helsinki.fi/~jengestr/activity

Fowler, A., 2000, The role of AI-based technology in support of the knowledge management value activity cycle, *Journal of Strategic Information Systems*, 9, 107–128.

Gregor, S., 2002, A theory of Theories in Information Systems, in: *Information Systems Foundations: Building the Theoretical Basis*, S. Gregor and D. Hart, ANU Canberra, pp. 1–20

Hasan, H., 2003, An Activity-based Model of Collective Knowledge, accepted for Proceedings of HICSS36.

Hasan, H. and Crawford K., 2002, Codifying or Enabling: the Challenge of Knowledge Management Systems, *Journal of Operation Research*.

Kaptelinin, 1996, Computer-Mediated Activity: Functional Organs in Social and Developmental Context, in: *Context and Consciousness: Activity Theory and Human-Computer Interactions*, Nardy, B., ed., Cambridge, Mass: The MIT Press.

Kasanen, E., Lukka, K. and Siitonen, A., 1993, The Constructive Approach in Management Accounting Research, *Journal of Management Accounting Research*, (Fall), 243–264.

Koskivaara, E., 2002, Design Science Approaches to Information Systems Research, in: *Information Systems Foundations: Building the Theoretical Basis*, S. Gregor and D. Hart, ANU Canberra, pp. 205–216.

Lyon, K. L., 2000, Using Patterns to Capture Tacit Knowledge and Enhance Knowledge Transfer in Virtual Teams, in: *Knowledge Management and Virtual Organisations*, Y. Malhotra ed., Idea Group Publishing, Hershey PA.

March, S. T., Smith, G. F., 1995, Design and natural science research on information technology, *Decision Support Systems*, 15, 251–266.

Markus, L. Majchrzak, A. Gasser, L, 2002, A Design Theory for Systems that Support Emergent Knowledge Processes, *MIS Quartery*, 26/3, 179–212.

McAdam, R. and McCreedy, S., 1999, A Critical Review of Knowledge Management Models, *The Learning Organisation*, 6/3, 91–100.

McLure-Wasko, M. and Faraj, S., 2000, "It is what one does": why people participate and help other in electronic communities of practice, *Journal of Strategic Information Systems*, 9, 155–173.

Mentzas, G., Apostolou, D., Young, R. and Abecker, A., 2001, Knowledge networking: a holistic solution for leveraging corporate knowledge, *Journal of Knowledge Management*, 5/1, 94–106.

Miles, M. B. and Huberman, A. M., 1994, *Qualitative Data Analysis*, Sage Publications, Thousand Oaks, CA.

Niiniluoto, I., 2001, Futures studies: science or art?, *Futures,* 33, 371–377.

Nunamaker, J. F., Chen, M., Purdin, T., 1991, Systems Development in Information Systems Research, *Journal of Management Information Systems,* 7/3, 89–106.

Orlikowski, W., 1993, CASE Tools as Organisational Change: Investigating Incremental and Radical Changes in Systems Development, *MIS Quarterly*, 17/3.

Schultze, U. and Boland, R, 2000, Knowledge management technology and the reproduction of knowledge work practices, *Journal of Strategic Information Systems*, 9, 193–212.

Simon, H., 1981, *The sciences of the artificial,* The MIT Press, Cambridge MA.

The Macquarie Dictionary, 1981, Macquarie University Press, North Ryde, Australia.

Virkkunen, J. and Kuutti, K., 2000, Understanding organisational learning by focusing on "activity systems", *Accounting, Management and Information Technology,* 10, 291–319.

Vygotsky, L.S., 1978, *Mind and Society*, Harvard University Press, Cambridge, MA.

Zuboff, S., 1988, *In the Age of the Smart Machine*, Heinemann Professional, Oxford.

FROM PHILOSOPHY TO KNOWLEDGE MANAGEMENT AND BACK AGAIN

Jeremy Aarons[1]

1. FROM PHILOSOPHY TO KNOWLEDGE MANAGEMENT

It is almost impossible to read an introduction to Knowledge Management (KM) without some mention of philosophy. Indeed, the KM literature is literally riddled with references to philosophers and philosophies. Yet surprisingly, despite the consistent mention of philosophical theory, it is rare to seen any detailed connections made between the theory of knowledge *qua* philosophy and the practice of knowledge management.

In this paper I explore the relationship between philosophy and Knowledge Management. I look at how philosophical theory has contributed to the development of KM, and also at how additional philosophical insights can be applied to help further the enterprise of KM. In doing so, I point out some areas of philosophy that are of little relevance to KM, despite the attention paid to them in the KM literature. In particular, traditional philosophical discussions about epistemology are quite limited in their application to KM, since they focus on the *production* of individual or personal knowledge, rather than *sharing* and *use* of knowledge in a collaborative context. I then identify some ways in which philosophy can be relevant to KM, highlighting the areas of philosophical theory seem most promising in their practical application to KM. My suggestion is that the most promising theoretical insights for KM come from recent work in both the *philosophy of science* and *social epistemology*.

Before continuing, I must mention an important caveat to much of what I say in this paper. My background is primarily in philosophy, and I am a relative newcomer to the field Knowledge Management. Thus I approach the KM literature primarily from the perspective of a philosopher, aiming to interpret what KM is and to assess how KM appeals to various philosophical insights. Because of this much of my discussion is focused on introductory texts in knowledge management, and not on more detailed and more specific publications. Thus my focus is mainly on student textbooks as well as some of the expository works that first presented the theoretical foundations of KM. This

[1] Dr. Jeremy Aarons, School of Information Management and Systems, Monash University, 26 Sir John Monash Drive, Caulfield East, Victoria 3145, Australia. Email: jeremy.aarons@sims.monash.edu.au

source material should be more than sufficient for my purposes, since these works purport to present the foundational basis for KM, outlining the essential tenets of KM.

Approaching the KM literature in this way has some clear advantages, as well as some obvious disadvantages. The main advantage is that I am approaching the KM literature with a fresh mind and a critical attitude, unburdened by preconceptions that others with more experience in this field may possess. In particular, coming to this work as a philosopher means I am particularly well placed to make assessments about the *soundness* of definitions and approaches in KM, and the accuracy and applicability of the various philosophical theories that are discussed. The disadvantages are that my own understanding of the scope and detail of work done under the label "knowledge management" is rather limited, and that certain subtleties and implications in the literature may pass me by. Thus I try to remain fairly cautious in what I say, and focus more on the use of philosophical theory in the KM literature rather than knowledge management per se.

My understanding of KM has been derived mainly from two sets of sources. The first sources are the various textbooks, websites and discussion papers that present the foundational concepts of KM to a relatively general audience. The second sources are the particular KM projects being undertaken within the KM Research Program at Monash University, School of Information Management & Systems. In particular, I have been most influenced by the Meteorological Forecasting project (Linger and Burstein, 2000). These two sets of sources portray KM in a fairly different way. The textbooks and expository literature tend to emphasise KM as being a business oriented discourse, and it is portrayed and discussed in such a way in the bulk of KM literature. Thus KM is defined as "the process in which a company both values its knowledge resources and seeks to manage it effectively within the main stream of company activities" (Gordon and Smith, 1998). Similarly "KM is the process through which organizations generate value from their intellectual and knowledge-based assets."[2] Given that the KM discourse is developed within organisational environments, and that much of the work done under the label of KM is largely driven by management concerns in a business context, this approach isn't too surprising. It also isn't surprising that more theoretical questions about the nature of KM work have tended to be seen as peripheral. The clear purpose of KM is not to deal with any deep conceptual questions, but to basically drive company growth. This point is stated clearly in many introductory discussions on KM. For example, the website for CIO magazine CIO.com states that "A creative approach to KM can result in improved efficiency, higher productivity and increased revenues in practically any business function."[3]

In contrast to this, the KM projects within the KM Research Program place less emphasis on the purely business oriented aims of company growth and increased revenues. Instead there is a clear emphasis on broader organisational goals. For example, in the case of the Meteorological Forecasting KM project the aim of the project is to develop a KM system that will assist with the task of generating weather forecasts. It achieves this by effectively integrating the skills and knowledge resources of the human forecasters with a technological system that stores, shares and assists with the product generation tasks of the forecasters. Here effective KM is primarily concerned with the relationship between the different participants in the forecasting process – the multitude

[2] http://www.cio.com/summaries/enterprise/knowledge/

[3] *ibid*

of human forecasters, the technologies that assist their forecasting, the systems they use to store and distribute the forecasts, the products they generate, and the customers that receive and use the forecasts. All of these are knowledge-based components of the broader system, and cannot be understood or managed without an intimate understanding of the relationship between all the parts of the system.

What this shows is that KM is primarily concerned with knowledge as it is generated, shared, stored and used within a collaborative environment. KM is also concerned with *all* aspects of knowledge within an organisational framework: the *factual* knowledge of the individuals within the organisation, as well as their *practical* knowledge, *tacit* knowledge, and *technological* knowledge. Thus if we are to look to philosophical theory to provide a foundation for the tasks of KM, we must look for those areas that can deal with these practical issues, as well as provide insights into these differing forms of knowledge and the relationships between them. The philosophical theory must also help our understanding of the underlying *processes* that are relevant for KM. Towards the end of this paper I shall explore some areas of recent philosophy that do offer insights into these processes. However before then I wish to spend a bit of time exploring the relationship between philosophy and KM, especially as regards the uses of philosophy in the KM literature.

2. KM AND THE APPEALS TO PHILOSOPHY

The relationship between the foundations of knowledge management and philosophical theory is a fairly intimate one. Some of the most significant and influential works in KM explicitly appeal to a number of philosophers and philosophical theories. From a perusal of the seminal works some of the groundbreaking theorists in KM, in particular Sveiby, Nonaka and Takeuchi, it is clear that the application of philosophical insights has laid the groundwork for much of their pioneering work in knowledge management.

K. E. Sveiby (1994, 1997, 2001) mentions the works of many philosophers in his discussions on the nature of KM. Most particularly, Sveivy appeals directly to the works of both Polanyi and Wittgenstein in his explanation and investigation into the grounding of knowledge management. Polanyi's idea of *tacit knowledge* is also central to Svieby's understanding of KM – for Sveiby the business of managing our tacit knowledge resources is the main aim of KM. Sveiby also mentions Wittgenstein's approach to meaning and knowledge, which he sees as being closely related to Polanyi's, although he doesn't go into the details of how these ideas relate to his views on KM.

Nonaka (1994), Nonaka and Takeuchi (1995) mention a wide array of philosophers, and a range of different philosophical perspectives in their influential works on KM. Chapter 2 of Nonaka and Takeuchi (1995) includes an extended discussion on the history of philosophy from Plato and Aristotle, through Descartes and Locke; Kant, Hegel and Marx; Husserl, Heidigger, Sartre, Merleau-Ponty, Wittgenstein, James and Dewey. They also mention Herbert Simon, Gregory Bateson, and also pay particular attention to the Polayni's ideas about tacit knowledge. They also briefly mention a number of other philosophical works, such as Johnson-Laird's (1983) *Mental Models,* Fred Dretske's (1981) *Knowledge and the Flow of Information,* as well as Shannon's information theory. Interestingly Nonaka and Takeuchi recognise some of the limitations of these philosophical theories. For example, they make the point that these approaches are inherently limited when it comes to explaining organizational knowledge creation – they claim it leaves out *innovation.*

A number of other important philosophical figures are mentioned in the KM literature. Adding these names to those already mentioned give a long and distinguished list of thinkers who have contributed, albeit indirectly, to the present understanding of Knowledge Management:

- Gilbert Ryle (1940-50s): the distinction between *knowing that* and *knowing how.*
- Michael Polanyi (1966): *tacit knowledge*
- Ludwig Wittgenstein (1920s): *meaning is use*
- Michel Foucault (1970s): *knowledge is power*
- Thomas Kuhn (1970s): paradigms
- Karl Popper (1960s): *three worlds.*
- Jean-François Lyotard (1984): *The Postmodern Condition* – data, information, knowledge.
- Jurgen Habermas (1984): *The Theory of Communicate Action, Volume One: Reason and the Rationalization of Society*
- Charles Saunders Peirce (1839-1914) and other American the pragmatists (James, Dewey, Rorty)

Clearly the field of KM is deeply indebted to the ideas of many philosophers: definitions, categorisations, and distinctions to do with the term "knowledge" are derived directly from the work of many philosophers. Such philosophical theories certainly seems central to the foundations of KM – but in what way are they significant, and why?

Despite this widespread appeal to philosophers and philosophy I feel that the actual connection between philosophical theory and the practical details of KM is rather weak. The problem is that it isn't clear how the philosophical ideas actually contribute to the theoretical understanding of how to go about doing KM. For example, in Nonaka and Takeuchi (1995) although there is quite a lot of discussion of philosophers and philosophy in the early chapters, when they move on to discussing the practical details of KM there is little or no connection made back to the philosophical ideas they previously mention. In particular, there is little explicit appeal to philosophical ideas made in their practical discussion on how one goes about the business of knowledge management. It is almost as thought the philosophical discussion is presented more for peripheral interest, rather than as providing deep insight into the discussion of KM. Thus it isn't clear how the philosophical ideas provide more than just the introductory context for their discussions on KM. In particular, it isn't clear how any of their appeals to philosophy relate to their practical suggestions, and thus it isn't clear what sort of philosophical basis exists for their KM framework. Thus it is worth looking in more detail at the actual connection between philosophy and KM – looking at how each discipline defines knowledge, why the concept is significant for each discipline, and what each discipline says about the concept.

Here it is worth emphasising that my discussion will focus primarily on the relationship between KM and philosophy as it is practiced within the Western Analytic tradition. Thus the "philosophers" I refer to here are those working within the Western Analytic tradition of philosophy, and when I use the term "philosophy" I am generally referring to this tradition. This tradition traces back to the ancient Greek philosophers, and has been deeply influenced by philosophers such as Descartes; the British Empiricists

Hume and Locke and the German Idealist Kant; early twentieth century philosophers such as Frege, Russell, and Wittgenstein; and modern American philosopher such as Quine, Davidson, Kripke, and Rawls. This tradition contrasts with what is often called the "Continental" tradition in philosophy, which flows through the work of thinkers such as Neitzche, Hegel, Heidigger, Husserl, Derrida and Levinas. This has similar roots to the analytic tradition, but diverges sharply in terms of both methodology and the sorts of questions it tackles. Some have characterised the difference as follows: the analytic tradition is narrow but deep, aiming for argumentative clarity and precision, while the continental tradition is broad but shallow, being more concerned with actual political and cultural issues and the human situation more generally.

My reasons for focusing on the Western Analytic tradition rather than the Continental tradition are twofold. Firstly, much of the KM literature does actually appeal to this tradition, in particular to the Cartesian account of knowledge and its successors. Thus the relationship between these disciplines clearly is worthy of analysis. The second and more important reason is that I believe the Analytic tradition can provide important insights for KM, which may conflict with some of the approaches endorsed in the Continental tradition. Interestingly, some of the most useful philosophical insights for KM have come from the continental tradition, since that approach tends to look more broadly at the social, political and pragmatic concerns surrounding a concept, which can tend to get overlooked in the fine-grained, logically precise approach of the analytic tradition. However I feel that the Continental approach tends to deal with questions that are too broad even for the concerns of KM, and in doing so loses the important connection between knowledge and truth. In this regard, at the end of this section I shall argue that the analytic approach to these questions can provide KM with some important guidance.

One thing that immediately strikes an analytic philosopher when they first encounter the KM literature is the way the term "knowledge" is used. When philosophers talk about "knowledge" they tend to mean something quite different to what KM authors refer to as knowledge. Philosophers have typically defined knowledge as an essentially *personal* item that concerns true facts about the world: knowledge is an individual's *true, justified belief.*[4] Knowledge involves more than someone *believing* a certain fact about the world: to genuinely know something you must believe it, you must have good justification for believing it is true, and it must actually be true. Thus traditional approaches to epistemology – the theory of knowledge – are concerned primarily with *what* knowledge is and how it can be identified, rather than *how* knowledge is created or used.

This approach to defining knowledge contrasts markedly with the definitions typically proposed in the KM literature. For example, in an introductory text on Knowledge Management Rumizen defines knowledge as "Information in context to produce actionable understanding." (2002: 6, 288) Similarly, Davenport and Prusak define knowledge thus:

> Knowledge is a fluid mix of framed experience, values, contextual information, and expert insight that provides a framework for evaluating and incorporating new experiences and information. It originates and is applied in the minds of knowers. In

---

[4] This formal definition of knowledge is quite controversial, and is the subject of ongoing vigorous debate. However philosophers tend to agree that this definition is *roughly* correct, and the controversy is mainly over the fine details of this approach.

> organizations, it often becomes embedded not only in the documents or repositories but also in organizational routines, processes, practices, and norms. (1998: 5)

These definitions do not view knowledge as essentially personal true, justified belief, but instead have a notion of knowledge as a practical tool for framing experiences, sharing insights and assisting with practical tasks. For KM, knowledge is something other than just an individuals understanding of the true facts of the world – it is a *pragmatic* tool for manipulating and controlling the world. It is in this sense that Iivari proposes the following four theses about knowledge:

- Knowledge is communal.
- Knowledge is activity-specific.
- Knowledge is distributed.
- Knowledge is cultural-historical. (Iivari 2000: 261)

From the perspective of traditional epistemology, this approach to defining knowledge sounds decidedly odd. Approaching these theses as an analytic philosopher it is difficult to understand the connection between this conception of knowledge and the concept of knowledge as philosophers have typically defined it. If knowledge is essentially personal, how can it then be communal or distributed?

The differences can be best explained by understanding the different ways the two disciplines have approached the problem of defining knowledge, and understanding why the disciplines are interested in the concept of knowledge in the first place. Philosophers have generally focussed on the problem of identifying and justifying our knowledge. In contrast, KM has focused not so much on the justification knowledge, but instead on understanding the uses of knowledge in order to effectively deal with the practical tasks that involve knowledge-based activity. In turn, the disciplines of philosophy and KM have approached the question of defining knowledge in a fundamentally different way. The main difference lies in the fact that philosophers have been concerned primarily with the problem of *scepticism,* whereas KM has looked at knowledge in terms of *pragmatics.* This is a fundamental difference, and it leads to quite different conceptions of the definition and importance of knowledge.

The personal aspect of knowledge is something that arises from the way philosophers have approached the question of what constitutes genuine knowledge. Contemporary debates in epistemology essentially trace back to the work of René Descartes and his method of doubt. In his *Meditations on First Philosophy* (1640) Descartes undertakes an inquiry into the nature of knowledge. Here Descartes attempts to find the foundational principles upon which our knowledge rests, by trying to identify some sort of fact that we can be entirely certain of. Thus he advocates that we need "to demolish everything completely and start again right from the foundations" (Descartes 1996:12). For Descartes the real challenge here is scepticism – if there is any possibility of doubt about so-called knowledge being true then it cannot be genuine knowledge. Descartes' inquiry tries to ascertain just what facts about the external world are beyond scepticism, in order to discover the basis of all our knowledge. Following this methodology Descartes famously arrives at the proposition "*cogito ergo sum*" – I think therefore I exist – which he claims puts the proposition "I exist" beyond doubt. Contemporary epistemology has followed strongly in this Cartesian tradition, focusing of the question of the justification of knowledge in the face of scepticism. Because of this, questions about the actual generation of knowledge, and of the uses and contexts of knowledge, have been of peripheral concern for the majority of theorists in epistemology.

In clear contrast to this, KM is concerned precisely with these sorts of pragmatic questions. For KM knowledge must be far more than just personal certainty about the world – it must involve practical ability as well as conceptual understanding. More importantly, KM is concerned with far more than just the justification of knowledge – it is concerned with the production, storage and processing of knowledge in a group or shared sense. Thus the relevance of the concept of knowledge for KM is quite different to its relevance for philosophers.

The point I wish to emphasise here is that, as far as KM is concerned, there are significant limitations in traditional approaches to epistemology. Traditional epistemology focuses on questions of *individual* or *personal* knowledge, with the main issue being how we come to know something as an individual – reliance on sense-data, experience, testimony, etc. As such, philosophers have done an excellent job of defining knowledge in this sense. However traditional epistemology is not concerned with the production and processing of knowledge in a group or shared sense – it is not really concerned with the *pragmatics* of knowledge production and use. The main issue in epistemology is the status of the final product rather than the process of getting there and what happens after knowledge is acquired. Yet these are precisely the factors that are of interest for KM.

The upshot of this is that, beyond an initial analysis of what knowledge is, this traditional approach to epistemology can actually offer very little in the way of useful insights for KM. Thus we must look elsewhere to find useful contributions from philosophy. We must also be sensitive to the different senses of the word "knowledge" as it is used by philosophers, and understand that KM applies a very particular conception of knowledge. This really shouldn't be surprising news for people working in KM, for I think this is a point most KM theorists are actually quite aware of. Yet, despite this awareness, it is a point that is often overlooked, especially in the introductory literature, and this could generate some serious confusion for someone coming to KM for the first time.

There is however one very important lesson for KM that should be drawn from this discussion: KM should not dismiss the importance of the philosophical insights into the nature of knowledge. Although the different disciplines have fundamentally different interests in the concept of knowledge, the concepts in each discipline are still very closely related. The standard approach in epistemology may be too limited and too narrow for KM, but it also isn't totally irrelevant. At its foundation the KM conception of knowledge should at least be *compatible* with the epistemological definition, since even thought the disciplines have different interests in the concept at its base it is still essentially the same idea.

This point harks back to my emphasis on the Western Analytic tradition rather than the Continental tradition. Here my feeling is that the KM conception of knowledge has diverged too far from the epistemological roots of the concept of knowledge and needs to be reigned back in. It is on this point that lessons should be taken from the Analytic philosophical tradition: traditional epistemology emphasises that genuine knowledge must be true. Although the philosophical definition of knowledge as being *true, justified belief* is not without controversy, it is fairly clear that something cannot be knowledge without it having some strong connection with the real facts of the world. How can you genuinely know something without that knowledge being true and accurate? You can't *know* that aliens live amongst us if there are in fact no aliens. However the way "knowledge" is defined in the KM literature it appears to have lost the specific connection with the idea of *truth.* The problem is that according to the KM definition it is more like the concept of *belief* – these definitions seem to have lost sight of the importance of justification and truth also being necessary for knowledge.

Take for example Rumizen's definition of knowledge: "Information in context to produce actionable understanding." (2002: 6, 288) Now if something cannot be called "information" without it being true then this definition seems fairly acceptable, at least from the viewpoint that knowledge must have some connection with truth. But we often use the word "information" in a far looser way than this, which admits the possibility that information may be false. Thus it makes sense to say that someone can base a (false) belief on *false information.* However we tend to think that someone cannot have false knowledge – in this case we would just say that someone doesn't know anything since what they thought they knew was false. More importantly, it seems possible for something to meet this definition without being genuine knowledge, since it may be possible for false information to "produce actionable understanding" – what you do may work, but that may just be a matter of sheer luck.

Similar sorts of worries apply to Davenport and Prusak's definition of knowledge: "Knowledge is a fluid mix of framed experience, values, contextual information, and expert insight that provides a framework for evaluating and incorporating new experiences and information." (1998: 5) This definition seems even more problematic than Rumizen's, since defining knowledge as "framed experience" allows almost any human belief to be a form of knowledge, whether or not it is an accurate or true belief. Following this definition I could "know" that aliens live amongst us, that Elvis is still alive, that AIDS was sent by God to punish infidels, or that human DNA was created by aliens by cloning.

Now maybe KM is actually interested in a conception of "knowledge" that allows spurious or unjustified claims such as these to be genuine knowledge. Perhaps KM should be concerned with managing all forms of belief in all belief systems, and not just with true beliefs. In other words, maybe Knowledge Management should really be called *Belief* Management? To do so, however, I believe would be a mistake. The important point here is that KM should be concerned with *relevant* and *applicable* knowledge, and I claim that any thorough conception of knowledge as such must maintain a connection with truth. This is because, at its base, knowledge must be grounded in real world properties and processes, even though our conceptions of these may be socially constructed in some sense.

To some, especially those grounded in the Continental or hermeneutic approach to knowledge, these ideas will seem extremely contentious. In particular, my emphasis on truth may seem misplaced, especially if one wishes to emphasise the idea of knowledge as a social practice. To those with these intuitions my response is that the social conception of knowledge is not only compatible with the idea of knowledge as truth, but is required for a thorough analysis of the production of knowledge in science. This is a point emphasised by a number of recent philosophers such as Hacking (1999) and Kitcher (1993, 2001), who have explored these ideas, showing how one can reconcile the idea of knowledge as a social practice with the conception of knowledge as true, justified belief. Hacking in particular, argues that social constructivism does not conflict with appeals to truth, and that we can have a rich social understanding of many concepts, both scientific and social, without losing the important connection with real world properties and processes.

The reason that an appeal to realism and truth is compatible with a social conception of knowledge is that it does not deny the fact that social factors are real. An excellent example that illustrates this point perfectly is the way we talk about economics and finance. There is a sense in which *money* is purely a social construct – the concept only acquires its significance through social convention and agreement. There is no money in nature. Yet money is also quite real, and all our talk of interest rates, budgets, financial markets, etc. is clearly about real entities as opposed to purely fictional entities. For example, when I say that the $AUS to $US exchange rate is 0.67 I am making a real factual claim about the world, even though this is a socially constructed fact. Importantly, this claim can be true or false, and the truth value of this claim can make a significant practical difference – if, for example, I was a bank teller. It is the importance of truth in this sense that I wish to emphasise for a philosophical understanding of knowledge for KM. An appeal to truth does not deny the importance of culture or interpretation or understanding. All it involves is an ultimate appeal to some real facts about the world.

The overall point here is that there need not be any conflict between social constructivism and knowledge as truth – indeed, a connection to the truth seems an essential part of even a social account of knowledge. Thus I plead the KM maintains a connection with genuine knowledge, and not just belief.

3. RELEVANT PHILOSOPHY – PHILOSOPHY OF SCIENCE AND SOCIAL EPISTEMOLOGY

I have said that traditional epistemology can only be of limited use to KM since it focuses on the origins and justification of personal knowledge, rather than the pragmatics of knowledge use, sharing and dissemination. Since KM is primarily concerned with knowledge as it is generated, shared, stored and used within a collaborative environment, if we are to look to philosophical theory to provide a foundation for the tasks of KM, we must look for those areas that can deal with these practical issues, as well as provide insights into these differing forms of knowledge and the relationships between them. The philosophical theory must also help our understanding of the underlying *processes* that are relevant for KM.

Here my suggestion is that the most fruitful places to look for relevant philosophical insights for KM is in recent work in both the *philosophy of science* and the emerging field of *social epistemology*. Although there are still limitations associated with these philosophical theories, these areas are engaged with fairly similar questions to those that interest knowledge management, and can thus provide insights into these issues. Thus they should be able to provide some useful theoretical tools that can be applied to building a theoretical account of knowledge work.

There is already a strong tradition within KM of applying insights from the philosophy of science. In particular the works of Kuhn (1970) and Popper (1959, 1972) have been of great interest to a number of KM theorists. Kuhn's notion of a *paradigm,* a particular world view, has played a pivotal role in understanding how a community of thinkers – or *knowledge workers* – need to share certain base beliefs in order to work together effectively. Kuhn's ideas on incommensurability have also been extremely important for many KM theorists. Popper's insights into the basis of scientific knowledge have also helped enrich the understanding of KM. However KM has paid very little attention to more recent developments in the philosophy of science, which take a quite different approach in their investigations. The trend in the philosophy of science over recent years has been to shift from trying to develop a general account of what science is (as evident in the work of Popper and Kuhn), to looking more closely at the fine detail of science. These fine details concern the complex methods by which scientific theories are developed, in terms of how scientists work, reason, *experiment, collaborate, etc.* Thus Cartwright (1989a, 1989b) emphasises the importance of *causal capacities* in science, and Dupré (1993) explores the metaphysical implications of the disunity of perspectives that coexist across the ranges of sciences. The detailed work of Galison (1996, 1997) looks at the role of social dynamics and politics in the theoretical life of nuclear physicists. Hacking (1999) also explores these issues in some detail, showing how the social construction of the world does not entail losing contact with traditional epistemological ideals such as accuracy and truth. Finally, Kitcher (1993) develops a complex model of scientific reasoning in a collaborative environment, that factors in the interactions between different researchers in building up a detailed picture of knowledge production in group context.

This approach is in sharp contrast to current approaches in knowledge management. At present, much of the work in KM has been informed and influenced by studies in the philosophy and sociology of science, such as those by Latour and Woolgar (1986) and Charlesworth *et al.* (1989). However, while these are excellent sociological accounts of collaborative knowledge work environments, they are based in a problematic metaphysics of social constructivism that fails to maintain the link between knowledge and truth. In particular, my concern is that these approaches provide a weak metaphysical foundation for such research, and do not provide a clear enough account of the underlying processes at work in knowledge production and knowledge-using environments. Here the approaches of experimentally focuses of philosophers of science such as Galison and Kitcher can be of assistance, as they emphasise taking into account *all* the relevant cognitive factors, including social dynamics and collaborative factors, in a complete analysis of knowledge production.

The other promising area of philosophical inquiry is the emerging field of social epistemology. This is actually fairly closely related to the approaches in philosophy of science just discussed, and many of the same people are working in this field. Some of the most significant works in this field include Kitcher (2001), Longino (2001), Solomon (2001), Goldman (1999) and Turner (1994, 2002). Social epistemology is an extension of traditional epistemology, which adds in the relationship between the social and rational factors in its analysis of the knowledge production process.

While there is still much debate within social epistemology about the importance of truth and the significance of relativism (especially between Longino and Kitcher) it is clear that these approaches could support a theory of collaborative knowledge work within a *realist* and *pluralist* metaphysical framework (as outlined in Cartwright, 1999). This would acknowledge the significant social dimension in knowledge production, while retaining the idea of knowledge being deeply connected to real properties and processes. Thus applying insights from the social epistemology will make it possible to build a theory of knowledge work that is grounded in reality, but also incorporates the relevant social, practical, and pragmatic concerns that are central to the tasks of knowledge management. The starting point of such an analysis would be to determine precisely what aspects of knowledge are relevant to the enterprise of knowledge management, and to give an account of the factors that underlie these knowledge components. This will involve assessing the relevant cognitive, social and pragmatic factors involved in KM projects. This will develop into a theoretical foundation for the practical work done in KM that maintains a connection with real-world processes and properties. Such a foundation will avoid the problematic conclusion that knowledge is purely socially constructed, and thus will present a powerful analysis of knowledge work.

However, in terms of the aims of knowledge management, current approaches in the philosophy of science and social epistemology are still somewhat lacking. As they stand they provide a detailed account of knowledge *production*, but little or no account of knowledge *use*. Thus, at present, they have little to say about the pragmatics of knowledge storage, knowledge sharing, and knowledge dispersal, all essential aspects of knowledge management projects.

Part of the problem here is that philosophers just don't seem to be interested in the sorts of questions that are essential for KM. Philosophers are still largely stuck in the Cartesian paradigm, obsessed with understanding the origins and justification of knowledge rather than the dynamics of knowledge as a process. Here we can actually turn things around and look to KM to provide some inspiration for philosophy. The challenges posed by KM projects can be used to show how these issues are indeed significant ones, which need to be investigated in detail. The insights gained from current KM projects can also be fed back into the philosophical theory. This will involve extending the accounts of collaborative knowledge production, as provided by philosophy, to broader accounts of collaborative knowledge use. This is where the practical dimension of KM can actually help to enrich our philosophical understanding of the nature of knowledge, and thereby lead to stronger approaches to KM grounded in coherent and sound philosophical theory.

REFERENCES

Cartwright, N., 1989a, *Nature's Capacities and their Measurement*, Oxford: Clarendon Press.

Cartwright, N., 1989b, Capacities and Abstractions, in: *Scientific Explanation,* Minnesota Studies in the Philosophy of Science, Volume 13, Kitcher, P. and W. C. Salmon, eds., Minnesota: University of Minnesota Press, pp. 349–356

Cartwright, N. 1999, *The Dappled World,* Chicago: University of Chicago Press.

Charlesworth, M., Lyndsay Farrall, Terry Stokes, David Turnbull, 1989, *Life among the scientists: an anthropological study of an Australian scientific community*. Melbourne: Oxford University Press

CIO.com, 2002, Knowledge Management, (May 2003) http://www.cio.com/summaries/enterprise/knowledge/

Davenport, T. and Prusak, L., 1998, *Working Knowledge: How organisations manage what they know*, Boston, Mass.: Harvard Business School Press.

Descartes, René, 1996, *Meditations on First Philosophy*, translated by John Cottingham. (originally published 1640) Cambridge: Cambridge University Press.

Dretske, F., 1981, *Knowledge & the Flow of Information,* Cambridge, Mass.: MIT Press.

Dupré, J., 1993, *The Disorder of Things: Metaphysical Foundations of the Disunity of Science*, Cambridge, Mass.: Harvard University Press.

Friedman, M., 2001, *Dynamics Of Reason,* Stanford, Calif.: CSLI Publications.

Galison, P., 1996, Computer Simulations and the Trading Zone, in: *The Disunity of Science: Boundaries, Contexts, and Power*, Galison, P. and D. Stump, eds., Stanford: Stanford University Press, pp. 118–157.

Galison, P., 1997, *Image and Logic*, Chicago: University of Chicago Press.

Goldman, A. I., 1999, *Knowledge in a Social World,* Oxford: Clarendon Press.

Gordon, J. L. and Smith, C., 1998, Research: Knowledge Management Guidelines, (May 2003) http://www.akri.org/research/km.htm

Hacking, I., 1983, *Representing and Intervening*, Cambridge: Cambridge University Press.

Hacking, I., 1999, *The Social Construction of What?*, Cambridge, Mass.: Harvard University Press.

Hume, D., 1888, *A Treatise of Human Nature.* (1960 facsimile reprint, edited by L. A. Selby-Bigge.) Oxford: Oxford University Press.

Iivari, J., 2000, Reflections on the Role of Knowledge Management in information Economy, in: *Knowledge Management for Information Communities,* Burnstein and Linger (eds.), Australian Scholarly Publishing, Melbourne, Australia, 2000.

Kitcher, P., 1993, *The Advancement of Science,* Oxford: Oxford University Press.

Kitcher, P., 2001, *Science, Truth, and Democracy*, Oxford: Oxford University Press.

Kuhn, T., 1970, *The Structure of Scientific Revolutions*, Chicago: University of Chicago Press.

Kuhn, T., 1977, *The Essential Tension: Selected Studies in Scientific Tradition and Change*, Chicago: University of Chicago Press.

Latour, B. and Woolgar, S., 1986, *Laboratory Life; The Construction of Scientific Facts*, Princeton, N.J.: Princeton University Press.

Linger and Burstein, 2000, Implementing a knowledge Management System: The Case of Meteorological Forecasting, in: *Knowledge Management for Information Communities,* Burnstein and Linger (eds.), Australian Scholarly Publishing, Melbourne, Australia, 2000.

Longino, H., 2001, *The Fate of Knowledge*, Princeton, N.J.: Princeton Uni Press.

Lyotard, Jean-François, 1984, *The Postmodern Condition: A Report on Knowledge*, Minneapolis: University of Minnesota Press.

Nonaka, 1994, A Dynamical Theory of Organizational Knowledge Creation, *Organization Science,* Vol. 5, No. 1.

Nonaka and Nishiguchi (eds.), 2001, *Knowledge emergence: Social, technical, and evolutionary dimension of knowledge creation*, Oxford: Oxford University Press.

Nonaka and Takeuchi, 1995, *The knowledge creating company*, Oxford: Oxford University Press.

Polanyi, M., 1966, *The Tacit Dimension,* Gloucester, Mass.: Peter Smith (Reprinted 1983).

Popper, K., 1959, *The Logic of Scientific Discovery,* London: Hutchinson.

Popper, K., 1972, *Objective Knowledge*, Oxford: Oxford University Press.

Ruggles, R. L. (ed.), 1997, *Knowledge Management Tools,* Boston: Butterworth-Heinmann.

Rumizen, M., 2002, *The Complete Idiot's Guide to Knowledge Management*, Hemel Hempstead: Prentice Hall, 2001.

Ryle, G., 1949, *The Concept of Mind*, Chicago: University of Chicago Press.

Solomon, M., 2001, *Social Empiricism*, Cambridge, Mass.: MIT Press.

Sveiby, K-E., 1994, Towards a Knowledge Perspective on Organisation, Doctoral Dissertation 1994 University of Stockholm S-106 91 Stockholm. http://www.sveiby.com/articles/Towards.htm

Sveiby, K. E., 1997, *The New Organizational Wealth - Managing & Measuring Knowledge Based Assets*, San Francisco. Berrett Koehler

Sveiby, K. E., 2001, What is Knowledge Management, (accessed in May 2003) http://www.sveiby.com http://www.sveiby.com/articles/KnowledgeManagement.html

Turner, S., 1994, *The Social Theory of Practices: Tradition, Tacit Knowledge and Presuppositions*, Chicago: University of Chicago Press.

Turner, S., 2002, *Brains/Practices/Relativism*, Chicago: University of Chicago Press.

KNOWLEDGE MANAGEMENT STRATEGIES

Leaders and leadership

Suzanne M. Zyngier and Frada Burstein*

1. INTRODUCTION

Organisational knowledge is that knowledge which is required at a specific instance to meet a specific organisational need. The need may be ongoing or a single occurrence. Meeting that need requires the aggregation of knowledge available at that specific instance. That is, "knowing what you need when you need to know it" (Snowden, 2002). The aim often is to achieve just in time delivery of a product or service to the relevant client base. This strategy to manage organisational knowledge can enhance innovation and creativity within and through the value chain of organisational activity potentially affecting revenue, the quality of staff output, and staff satisfaction.

This paper derives from the findings of research into current knowledge management practices in the Australian financial services sector (Burstein and Zyngier, 2002). We look at the role of the knowledge management task and how the strategies to manage organisational knowledge are initiated, championed and supported by an individual. We address the question of the implications for knowledge management strategies when that individual moves on to another position or to another organisation.

The paper is structured in three sections. In the first section current literature is surveyed to canvass knowledge management strategies and techniques and the research methodology is described. In the following section we examine research findings on the nature of the knowledge management task and the importance of leadership in a knowledge management strategy. The final section draws conclusions on the importance of the leadership role and the implication for the centralisation of strategies to manage knowledge. This final section also draws out areas for further research.

* Suzanne M. Zyngier and Frada Burstein, School of Information Management and Systems, Monash University, Melbourne, Australia, PO Box 197, Caulfield East 3145, Vic. AUSTRALIA

Constructing the Infrastructure for the Knowledge Economy
Edited by H. Linger *et al.*, Kluwer Academic/Plenum Publishers, 2004

2. STRATEGIES TO MANAGE KNOWLEDGE

Knowledge management literature over the last decade has shown that the field has developed and matured from the initial phases that identified knowledge as an organisational resource that could be harnessed to enhance productivity and employee satisfaction thereby capturing and retaining knowledge for use and reuse. The later phase is characterised by the knowledge management technology boom where the capture of explicit knowledge dominated the vendor interest in the knowledge management movement. Currently we find ourselves reading materials on the need to transfer knowledge between individuals using communities of practice and storytelling techniques (Wenger et. al., 2002; Denning, 2001; Snowden, 2002). Knowledge transfer has become a personalised strategy that seeks to transfer knowledge beyond that which can be captured and stored in digital form.

A review of knowledge management literature reveals a number of differing types of strategies that have been identified, all of which are intended to harness explicit and tacit knowledge, to capture it, to store it, organise it and make it available for reuse. These are represented in both the theoretical and the "how to" literature and can be largely divided into several streams being organisational learning, best practice, leadership, "communities of practice" and storytelling. Each contributing to the body of knowledge however, our research reveals a gap in the analysis of the role of knowledge workers.

Senge (1990) defined organisational learning as a strategy to manage knowledge. He applied systems thinking onto studying organisational learning framework. This resulted in a contemplation of the organisation as a whole rather than looking at the learning of individuals as components of a learning system. The emphasis was transferred to the learning needs of the organisation rather than the learning needs of the individual. Learning for the common aim of the organisation required the evaluation of the overall knowledge needs of that organisation. Thus, knowledge acquisition is managed via the management of learning.

O'Dell, Grayson and Essaides (1998) demonstrated that the study results of the Emerging Practices in knowledge management Consortium Benchmarking Study (APCQ, 1996) corroborate hitherto anecdotal evidence that systematic Best Practice transfer is the one strategy pursued by 100 percent of the organisations pursuing value-through-knowledge. Therefore knowledge transfer as the transfer of best practices becomes a measurable function.

Communities of practice are groups of people who share a common interest or problem and who enhance their knowledge about that domain through regular interactions (Wenger et. al., 2002). These interactions may be personal or virtual, however it is the mutual development and accretion of knowledge and interest that binds the group. Communities of practice can be developed from a group of professional peers or from a group of individuals with differing practice backgrounds but who share a common interest. Strategies to develop and support these communities of practice aim at developing organisational knowledge. Informal strategies to manage knowledge have included teams and interest groups gathered together for a project. What differentiates them from Communities of Practice is that the development of knowledge is not the main focus. As one respondent commented "The problem is that with most projects, we seem to be calling on the same people time and time again so, as well as doing their regular jobs, they may be involved in several projects as well". Thus a sense of frustration can develop.

Storytelling has developed recently as a technique to transfer tacit knowledge and some knowledge that would otherwise be made explicit. Narrative helps the listener to understand complexity through the context and characterisation of the story as told by the storyteller (Denning 2000). Organisational story telling is when an incident or concept is told as part of a connected sequence of events or concepts relevant to the work at hand. This story has additional meaning provided by the context in which it is being told. The story presents all listeners with a common perspective and thus enables a group to share this embedded knowledge thread (Snowden, 2002).

These latter techniques focus on human capital rather than infrastructure and technologies alone. All these strategies require significant leadership effort at the time of development and implementation of a strategy. The following discussion of the role of leadership and of organisational culture in KM implementation reveals omission of the analysis of the mechanisms for the organic transfer of knowledge and of its relevance to the process.

3. LEADERSHIP AND CULTURE

3.1. The Role Of Leadership

The main focus of our paper is the concept of leadership that is so often used in the context of the development and implementation of a knowledge management strategy. To lead is to direct, to conduct or to guide (*Oxford English Dictionary*, 1973). Therefore a knowledge management leader has these functions in the implementation of such a strategy. A leader will investigate the need, align it with the organisational strategy, plan, and execute the plan to manage knowledge to support the value proposition and mission of the organisation.

Leadership is acknowledged widely as being instrumental in the effective deployment of a knowledge management strategy in an organisation. (Davenport and Prusak 1998; Nonaka and Takaeuchi, 1995; O'Dell et. al., 1998; Probst et. al., 2000) Hackett comments, "CEO commitment is essential in the absence of that commitment, even well executed and conceived practices may remain locked within a single organisational unit for the duration of the project" (Hackett, 2000, p. 36). Accordingly for there to be an overall change in organisational attitude there needs to be explicit management commitment to follow through and the example of "follow me" leadership.

A knowledge leader may not actually create the vision of the future but has the responsibility to create the framework within which the knowledge stakeholders will be able and be enabled to create that vision. It is the process of vision creation that is managed by the leader. It is also the responsibility of the leader to see the articulation of that vision both within and outside the organisation.

3.2. Organisational Culture

Executive management leads and establishes the culture and consequent ability of an organisation to capture, share, and to manage its knowledge. The culture of an organisation is developed by the structure and by the attitude of management; it is developed by the example of management. Krogh et. al. (2000) describe how effective management and support of knowledge creation depends on the physical, virtual and emotional context in which it is manifest. The task of management in the creation of a knowledge management strategy is to create a culture that sees the creation, dissemination and utilisation of knowledge as being a normative function within the organisation. Where there is a strong commitment at the level of executive management to change organisational culture an organisation is able to begin to create the values that lead to knowledge sharing across boundaries (O'Dell, et al., 1998; Hackett, 2000).

Organisational culture is the prime influence on and organisation's capacity to implement a knowledge management strategy. It determines how individuals react in the workplace and how they perform on a daily basis. The culture creates a set of spoken and unspoken rules and values – i.e. explicit and implicit rules that are the organisation's cultural framework. Trust and ability to communicate are a part of this framework. That is the capacity of the organisation to produce an environment of trust and open communication on which knowledge sharing is so dependent. These in turn lead to the encouragement or support of risk-taking on which innovation relies.

4. METHODOLOGY

The aim of the original research was to derive an indicative understanding of the status of knowledge management in the Australian financial services sector. To achieve this end two types of data were required. Quantitative data was required for a measurable indication of trends in knowledge management. Qualitative data was required to gather a rich picture of individual companies for comparative and confirmatory purposes. The quantitative data for the Australian financial institutions was derived from the study of knowledge management strategies in Australia conducted by researchers from the School of Information Management and Systems, Monash University (Zyngier, 2001). That research represented the status of views and activities relating to knowledge management and of its uptake trends in the Australian corporate environment between March and July of 2001. The sample included the top 130 banking institutions and insurance companies, 20% of these companies responded to the survey questionnaire (Burstein and Zyngier, 2002).

The following information was sought:

- What is the organisational understanding of knowledge management?
- What systems are in place to convey knowledge management principles and to implement strategy?
- What are the benefits expected from and arising from the management of knowledge?
- What factors contribute to the success and what obstacles have been encountered in the management of knowledge?

Additional to the survey data, qualitative data were gathered from evidence-based analysis (Schwab, 1999) using the interview transcripts as evidence and by the extrapolation of data from the interviews. A series of ten selected one hour interviews were conducted with the Chief Executive Officers or the Managing Directors of a purposive sample of organisations in the financial services sector.

The rich data collected in these interviews canvassed:

- The corporate philosophy or approach behind the way that the organisation manages knowledge
- Whether there is a specific initiative to manage knowledge, and if so what prompted it
- The implementation of any such initiative and the role and distribution of the responsibility for effecting it
- What impact if any the size and distributed nature of this company has had on the effective implementation of the management of knowledge

To avoid bias, the participants were not asked leading questions about knowledge management strategies. Instead knowledge management strategies were deconstructed into components for example: planning to acquire to acquire and exploit knowledge, displaying awareness of internal knowledge sources, awareness of the replication of knowledge creation, tracking the reuse of knowledge or tracking experts. This allowed the research to identify those organisations without formal strategies but with some effective methods for knowledge transfer on a pragmatic level.

5. RESEARCH FINDINGS

5.1. The Field Has Outgrown Information Management

Knowledge management initiatives in respondent organisations (see Figure 1 below) were most strongly shown as ongoing plans to manage knowledge (92%) and an organisational demonstration of the awareness of internal knowledge resources (76%). These two factors are well recognised as core contributors to KM implementation (Davenport and Prusak, 1998). This ranking of knowledge management initiatives demonstrates that organisations are seriously committed to implementing a knowledge related activities. The lesser acknowledgment of tracking of the reuse of knowledge in the organisation (at 44%) indicates that there is consideration of this need in organisations. While sharing of best practice consumes a portion of theoretical knowledge management literature it is not prominent (44%) as an initiative employed in the respondent organisations. Only 8% of respondents claimed existence of the organisational centralised repository for explicit knowledge as a defined strategy or part of a defined strategy to manage knowledge. Thus, the majority of respondents did not consider this factor important enough for managing knowledge probably attributing such repositories as more of a part of the traditional IT infrastructure. This is a confirmation of the disconnection between knowledge management strategies and IT. Where IT is a tool in the strategy but not the strategy itself.

The management of knowledge can be vitally supported by organisational information systems but that this is not the whole picture. Respondents indicated that organisational knowledge needs increasing support in terms of human resources and personnel issues. That is that they are turning their attention to the personalised attributes of knowledge transfer. This indicates that the practice of the management of knowledge in the Australian financial services sector has moved far beyond regarding knowledge needs as being part of an information system or information technology based solution.

By turning their attention to the personalised attributes of knowledge transfer organisations are moving further towards organisational learning, communities of practice and storytelling as strategies to meet their organisational knowledge needs.

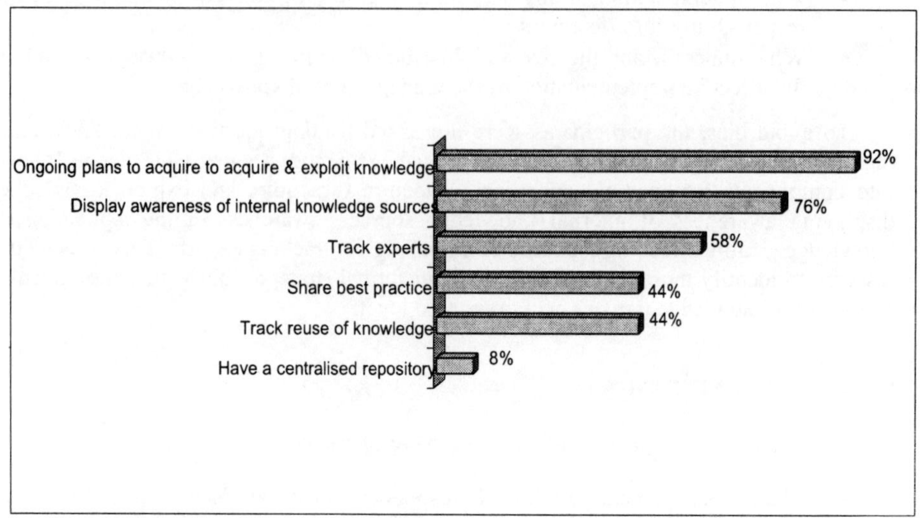

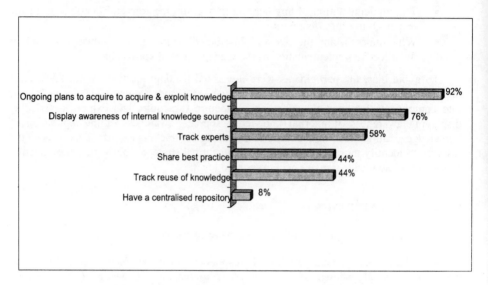

Figure 1. Current status of company programs to manage knowledge

5.2. Knowledge Management Strategies

As indicated that management of knowledge in this sector has moved beyond regarding knowledge needs as being part of an information system or information technology based solution as reflected in the surge in importance of Human Resources as the actor in organisational knowledge needs. We found that it is the Human Resources department who is the player in organisational learning strategies with our interview participants. It is the Human Resources department who is a key participant in change management strategies that are used to encourage knowledge transfer strategies for interview participants. It is the Human resources department who is most keenly aware of the organisational political rivalries that can be the downfall of an organisations strategy to manage their knowledge.

In their detailed study of the failure of a knowledge management strategy, Storey and Barnett (2000) found that the political rivalries between the IT department and the Publications department so severely undermined the development of infrastructure to support the knowledge management strategy as to seriously jeopardise its' success. Further they revealed that where the team driving the initiative fails to address these issues together with failure to address other cultural change issues, then they were open to accusations of lack of organisational sophistication in their approach.

5.3. Relationship Between Knowledge Workers and Leadership roles

We asked the organisations how they perceived the task of those assigned to the role of managing knowledge (see Figure 2 below). Where there is a defined knowledge management task it is most commonly to gather the knowledge (in 33%) of organisations and to disseminate the knowledge (in 34 %) of organisations. Defining a strategy or route map to transfer knowledge is not a main focus for this position in the organisation 23% and learning from the knowledge within the organisation are of lesser prominence at 24%. There is less emphasis on ensuring that knowledge is being used or on the use of knowledge by the knowledge manager.

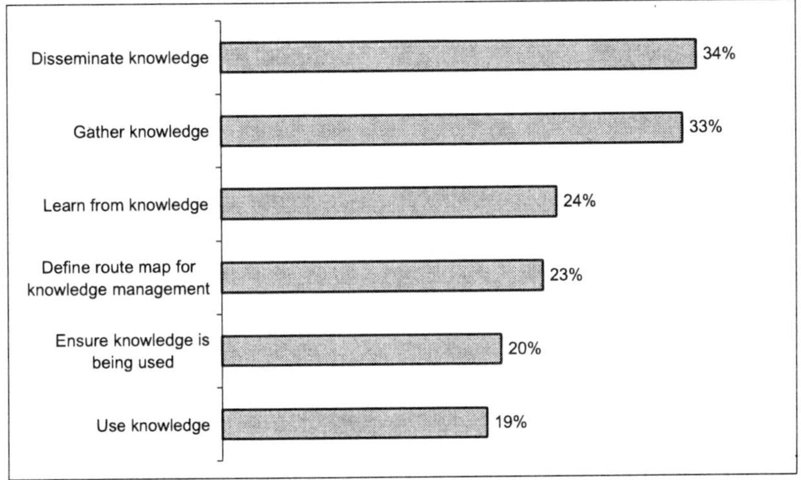

Figure 2. The role of the knowledge management task

Can there be a strategy without analysis or planning? We argue not. The data that was gathered in the interviews of business leaders for this research supports this assertion. One business leader even put this in words: "We have pieces of it and we've been using it for several years, but the biggest issue for us is mapping it in a total business fashion." And another who acknowledged the systematic change management required in the planning of a knowledge management strategy in that "it does take a lot of leadership on my part particularly. I've got to really talk up the need to change and better ways of doing things". Strategic planning and leadership are acknowledged needs.

5.4. Leadership

In relation to the organisational responsibility for knowledge management (see Figure 3) the respondent organisations indicated that it was in a form of leadership from their Chief Executive Officers (12%) and from several directors or managers (18%). Most substantially the responses indicate that the responsibility is either "everyone's job" (24%) or that there is no formal role in place (31%).

It can be implied that where the responsibility belongs to everyone but there is no direct leadership, the ongoing development of a strategy may be severely compromised. How then do we interpret these statistics that it is everyone's job or that no formal role exists? Conversely these same organisations demonstrate awareness of knowledge management and the organic ability to transfer knowledge as reflected by Probst et. al., (2000) in the six core processes of identification, acquisition, development, sharing and distribution, and the utilisation and retention of knowledge.

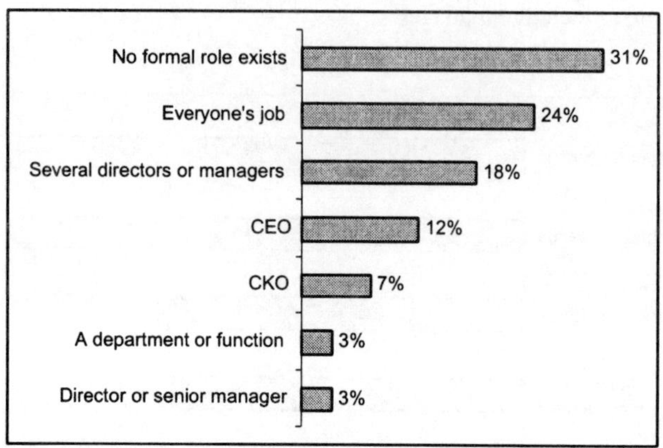

Figure 3. Who has the organisational responsibility for knowledge management?

The same survey identified a range of practices that are recognised by the knowledge management community as being effective. We suggest that when there is no framework or strategy then such endeavours are merely an *ad hoc* or random actions in response to meeting immediate needs. The development of strategy in any management activity implies skill in attaining an end. The required skills in the development of a knowledge management strategy include an audit of the knowledge resources available disclosing sources of and gaps in supply. Audit should be followed by mapping the flow of knowledge within that organisation to gain an understanding of what is current status and what should be in place in order to ensure efficient and effective distribution of information/knowledge flows. Based on the value proposition of the organisation, the strategy can then be developed to meet its knowledge needs. Ideally the strategy would support the whole process of knowledge acquisition, knowledge retention and knowledge utilisation within the organisation.

The current reality for many corporate entities is that often an ongoing implementation of a knowledge management strategy falls too heavily on a single person. It may be the CEO, CKO or a senior director (in our study 22% of organisations - see Figure 3) whose capacity to achieve all the goals of knowledge transfer can be limited.

An apt quote from a Chief Executive Officer sums up the responses of others, he said: "Not only do we have a person nominated as our *networker*, but he is our Knowledge Manager in Australia, and if that sounds good, then it's probably the reality compared to the title, slightly different, so he tends to be a bit of a projects man, but certainly the intention was that he be the knowledge officer, but I think that as I said, the reality falls something short of the goals of knowledge management."

Can this be reconciled with 24% of respondents informing that knowledge management is "Everyone's job"? The reality of those organisations with a formal strategy to manage their knowledge both affirmed the value of such strategies but also raised questions on the real understanding of the complexity of the task and of current knowledge management theory and practice to the workplace.

Leadership of a knowledge management strategy plays a central role as the decision-making authority and provides an executive framework to deliver the expected benefits of that strategy. This must be exercised in a controlled manner, through the establishment of checks and balances in the delivery mode. It must also ensure that evaluation of the strategy feeds back into the model or strategy, and that all stakeholder needs and expectations are being met. If they cannot be met, then the leadership will be able to justify why or alternatively why not.

5.5. If It Doesn't Feel Natural Then It Won't Be Perpetuated

In all organisations there is some form of transfer of knowledge. Traditional forms of transfer have included: the mentoring of new employees by more senior employees, staff meetings, induction programs, the development and use of manuals for procedures and practices. These traditional forms of staff management also act as an organic form of the management of knowledge transfer. It is therefore important is to understand and to include these processes in the detailed mapping of organisational knowledge. We suggest that it is vital to understand the flow of the existing patterns of knowledge transfer. That is what is the current culture, what is successful, where do the problems lie and what causes them within the organisation before attempting to develop a new strategy.

The role of strategy to manage knowledge transfer is to actively enhance knowledge transfer within an organisation thus enabling that organisation to increase its productivity and creativity. The need to manage the changes that this undertaking requires are well documented, however – if it doesn't feel natural then there is a great danger that it won't be perpetuated

In our interviews, we found that there were a number of organisations without a defined strategy to manage their knowledge but at the same time having a clear understanding of the value of their knowledge resources. These organisations display an organic form of knowledge transfer; the transfer mechanisms that are embedded in organisational culture in mentoring, staff meetings, staff conferences, rotation of jobs, induction programs, document management initiatives and those in standardised procedures and practices. One aspect that was pronounced in organisations without a defined strategy to manage their knowledge was the use of the "I" pronoun. By this we mean that the Chief Executive Officer, Director or Manager with whom we were speaking, used "I" in the description of the mode of knowledge transfer within the organisation. For example "I" in discussion rendered: "I know, in my team" and of those who are the lynch pin for knowledge transfer within the organisation there were examples like: "and I said 'Well, you should talk to somebcdy in marketing, because they do market research'".

These existing patterns of knowledge transfer are embedded many current organisational cultures. It is vital to identify them, to identify what is successful, what are current problems and their causes in order to develop a strategy that can be easily and naturally perpetuated. New approaches must embed the strategies within the organisational culture to ensure knowledge management strategies are not initiated, championed or supported by an individual or very small group. Thus removing the threat to those strategies when that individual moves on to another position or to another organisation or the group is broken up or distracted by other organisational priorities.

5.6. Organic Knowledge Transfer

When the interviewees described an organisational matrix that ensured product management accountability and that also acted as a means of knowing who to ask, could this be described as a strategy to manage knowledge? When an organisational leader told us that they "have a strategy of trying to develop our products to keep ahead of the market and to keep up to date with everything that's going on." Could this be described as a strategy to manage knowledge? We suggest that while these are good examples of organic means of knowledge transfer, and indeed indicate good management practices, they do not in themselves constitute a strategy.

These same organisations are truly examples of organisations without a knowledge management strategy and yet they exhibit many of the knowledge management techniques and tools that are suggested in the theoretical literature. For example there are instances of placing a high value on knowledge, of having a clear understanding of the knowledge flows within internal resources and of inflows and outflows to and from external resources. There is clear evidence of organisations making explicit knowledge available using manuals that are tools of continuous improvement through continuous updating and annotation by staff and putting information into databases. There was evidence of the promotion of creativity and innovation through formal means such as product development committees and also of competition in "rewards for clever ideas". Intranet technology is seen as a great tool by management for linking people, for explaining what different sectors of the organisation is doing and particularly for the transfer of ideas and as a platform for the online launch of captured organisational knowledge in the form of manuals and forms. A noteworthy observation is that the smaller the organisation the more personable the interaction and more open the lines of communication that makes knowledge transfer so much more informal. As one company director clearly pointed out: "this quantity of scale [in the size of an organisation], which everyone talks about nowadays – that's an objective of most companies. There's a trade-off and that is that the management becomes a lot less elastic and the voice of the people of the coal face becomes a lot less heard."

These understandings and actions require some consideration. Not because they are of any surprise in the fact that good and perceptive management has many common sense attributes that include an understanding of the importance of organisational knowledge. This is also not because technology is seen more and more as a tool of management and is no longer a holy entity in its own right. As one Managing Director put it "I think the role of technology is huge, but people have to manage the technology. Technology is a tool. I don't see technology as being that great at managing anything. I think it's the people behind the technology, the people who are using the technology, that are the managers of technology."

Therefore we must ask ourselves whether these indicators can be described as an organic form of the management of knowledge transfer. This being the case what is important is to understand in a detailed manner, the existing patterns of knowledge transfer that are successful in an organisation under examination before strategies are put in place to manage knowledge transfer. That is what is the current culture, what is successful, where do the problems lie and what causes them.

The issue of organisational culture as addressed earlier in this paper, mentions the role of executive management and of organisational structure. What is not mentioned in the literature is the problematic issue of organisational politics and of human resources issues that are more and more important as the mobility of the workforce is transformed from a job-for-life mentality to that of changing workplace every five years. Additionally the fluctuating economies of the corporate environment pressure organisations to juggle priorities both to the external environment and within the internal environment.

6. CONCLUSIONS AND FUTURE RESEARCH

The role of leadership in knowledge management needs to be separated conceptually from the solitary efforts of a single knowledge manager within the organisation. A combination between top down and bottom up strategies to manage knowledge is affirmed by this research and that the level of success of any such strategy consideration be strike a balance between he two approaches

This research has raised the following questions for further research:

- Is the complexity of the leadership of a knowledge management strategy adequately supported in an organisation without formal mechanisms to govern that role?
- What relationship does the organic pattern of knowledge transfer in an organisation have to the ultimate success of a formalised strategy to manage knowledge?

Approaches to the management of knowledge transfer need to take into account the complexity of the implementation process beyond consideration of the immediate processes environment to include a plan for successful outcomes based on and embedded in the culture of the organisation. This is particularly important to those organisations that also operate within the framework of a distributed entity locally, or more and more frequently within a global dynamic. Accordingly strategies can be built to address the complexity of combining elements that are connected to perform knowledge management functions, which cannot be performed, by the elements in their singular state. These elements are sourced from human resources, their structural interrelationships and the specific supporting infrastructure within which the practitioner develops knowledge management strategies.

ACKNOWLEDGEMENT

This research is partly supported by Monash University and Fuji/Zerox sponsorship grant.

REFERENCES

Amidon, D. M., and Macnamara, D., 2003, The 7 C's of Knowledge leadership: Innovating Our Future, in: *Handbook on Knowledge Management 1: Knowledge Matters*, Vol. 1, C. W. Holsapple, ed., Berlin: Springer-Verlag, pp. 539–551

Burstein, F. and Zyngier S., 2002, Knowledge Management in Australian financial institutions: Preliminary results of the comparative analysis between European and Australian companies, School of Information Management and Systems and Fuji Xerox Australia, Melbourne, Internal Report.

Davenport, T. H., and Prusak, L., 1998, *Working Knowledge: How Organizations Manage What They Know*, Boston: Harvard Business School Press.

Denning, S., 2000, *The Springboard: How Storytelling Ignites Action in Knowledge-Era Organizations*, Butterworth-Heinemann, Boston, USA.

Hackett, B., 2000, Beyond Knowledge Management: New Ways to Work and Learn, *The Conference Board*, New York, 71.

Korac-Kakabadse, N., and Kakabadse, A., 2001, IS/IT Governance: Need for an Integrated Model, *Corporate Governance*, 1(4), 9–11.

Krogh, G. V., Ichijo, K. and Nonaka, I., 2000, *Enabling knowledge creation: How to unlock the mystery of tacit knowledge and release the power of innovation*, Oxford University Press, Oxford.

Long, D. W. D. and Fahey, L., 2000, Diagnosing cultural barriers to knowledge management, *The Academy of Management Executive*; Ada, 14, 113–127.

Nonaka, I., and Takeuchi, H., 1995, *The Knowledge-Creating Company : How Japanese Companies Create the Dynamics of Innovation*, New York: Oxford University Press.

O'Dell, C., Grayson, C. J. and Essaides, N., 1998, *If Only We Knew What We Know; The Transfer of Internal Knowledge and Best Practice*, The Free Press, New York.

Probst, G., Raub, S., and Romhardt, K., 2000, *Managing Knowledge; Building Blocks for Success*, Chichester: John Wiley and Sons, Ltd.

Roos, J., Roos, G., Dragonetti, N. C. and Edvinson, L., 1997, *Intellectual Capital: Navigating the New Business Landscape*, MacMillan Press, Basingstoke Hampshire.

Schwab, D. P., 1999, *Research Methods for Organizational Studies*, Manwan, N.J.: Lawrence Erlbaum Associates, Publishers.

Senge, P. M., 1990, *The Fifth Discipline*, Doubleday Currency, New York.

Snowden, D., 2002, Complex acts of knowing: paradox and descriptive self-awareness, *Journal of Knowledge Management*, 6, 100–111.

Wenger, E. C., McDermott, R. and Snyder, W. M., 2002, *Cultivating Communities of Practice: a guide to managing knowledge*, Harvard Business School Press, Boston.

Zyngier S., 2001, Knowledge Management Strategies in Australia: Preliminary results of the survey of the knowledge management uptake in Australian companies School of Information Management and Systems Technical Report [1/2001].

TRUST, CONTROL, AND DESIGN
A study of computer scientists

Supriya Singh and Christine Satchell*

ABSTRACT

A qualitative study of computer scientists' use of e-mail in Australian universities shows that computer scientists equate trust with control. They seek information that gives them control to personalise and scrutinise the system. In equating trust solely with control, computer scientists are unlike middle-income residential users or young people. The level of control that is demanded is often so great that computer scientists do not use the technologies they design. For "ordinary users," "comfort" and "caring" – are important dimensions of trust. Computer scientists also differ from young users of new information and communication technologies. Young users see control primarily as physical control, rather than control over information to personalize and scrutinize the system.

This difference in the interpretation of trust means that when computer scientists design new information and communication technologies, they prioritise the design that gives them the control they want, rather than simplicity and ease of use, usefulness, comfort and caring. Computer scientists' preference for this single dimension of trust needs to be consciously recognized and supplemented by more general users' perspectives if they are to design technologies that can be easily and comfortably used by the average user.

This paper draws on three separate qualitative studies conducted by the authors. The first and central study is of computer scientists and their use of technologies with a focus on e-mail. The second and third studies – with which the first is compared – are of middle-income residential consumers' use of money and a continuing study of young people's use of technologies.

---

* Supriya Singh, RMIT University, Melbourne 3000. Christine Satchell, RMIT University, Melbourne 3000.

1. THE CONTEXT

This paper draws on early interaction between the User-Centred Design (UCD) team and computer scientists designing smart personal assistants (SPAs) in the multi-university Smart Internet Technology Cooperative Research Centre (SITCRC) in Australia. In the SPA program, computer scientists saw a smart personal assistant or agent as a computer program that helps users conduct routine repetitive tasks using rule based reasoning and often learning from the users' behaviour.

In the first few workshops between the SPA and UCD researchers, it became clear that the computer scientists were implicitly designing for users like themselves. The users were male, in their 30s or 40s, expert computer users with access to an office, working in an academic environment. This self-construct of the user is a common feature in technological design (Cooper, 1999; Vredenburg, Isensee, and Righi, 2002).

The SPA and UCD researchers agreed it was important to make explicit these assumptions of use. We also wanted to discover how these computer scientists differed from "ordinary" users. Singh and Satchell interviewed 12 computer scientists from universities in Melbourne and Sydney. Eleven were working in areas related to agent technology. The 12th saw himself more in expert systems and artificial intelligence applications. Eleven of the computer scientists worked primarily in universities. Three have some industry experience. All but one of those interviewed are male. Age-wise we have a spread from the 30s to 50s.

The study aimed to generate understandings of the way the designers of SPAs themselves managed e-mail and the Web. There was also an action research agenda in that we, the UCD researchers, hoped that a reflection on use would make the computer scientists more accepting of UCD approaches. The study does not aim to be generalisable but it does lead to insights which we have been testing with other computer scientists in the SITCRC for the year since the study was completed.

In this paper we call this study of computer scientists "the SPA study." It was a "grounded" study in that the data helped influence the analytical framework, emerging questions and theories (Charmaz, 2000; Strauss and Corbin, 1990). As we coded and analysed the interviews using NUD*IST (Non-numerical Unstructured Data Indexing Searching and Theorising), a computer program for the analysis of qualitative data, it became apparent that computer scientists saw trust as control and control as a means of personalising and scrutinising the system. This finding led us to compare trust and the use of new information and communication technologies with two other qualitative studies the authors had conducted.

In 1997 Singh led a study of trust and electronic money in the home (Singh and Slegers, 1997). We will refer to it as the "electronic money study." For this study 47 people from 23 middle and upper-income, mainly Anglo-Celtic, households in urban and rural Victoria Australia were interviewed. As with the SPA study, the electronic money study showed that people were more likely to use a technology they trusted. However, these residential users defined trust differently from the way computer scientists spoke of it.

Satchell is currently studying young people's use of the PC Internet, and mobile phone in Australia. She is also taking a grounded theory approach to examine the way in which 29 young people engage with these technologies. The study consists of 15 open-ended interviews, and two focus groups with 14 people. The data were transcribed and coded using NUD*IST 4. One of the major emerging themes relates to control and privacy.

In section two, we consider the literature on trust and the use of new technologies. This allows us to frame the SPA study within the literature from sociology, anthropology, communication and media, and studies of the diffusion of innovations. Before we began the SPA study in late 2002, we also surveyed the SPA literature for insights into the use of SPAs. In section three we discuss trust and control in the SPA study comparing it with the electronic money and young people study. In section four we draw out the implications for designing with control as the pre-eminent need. In the concluding section we summarise our findings and their implications.

2. TRUST

In Computer Science, the use of technologies is not a central concern. Examining 2391 papers cited in a bibliography covering papers from 1984 to 2001 (Helin, 2001) less then five per cent (107 papers) mention the user in the title or abstract (where available). Where use is the focus, it is most often with the design of user interfaces or user modelling where action and information can be expressed in mathematical language (Agre, 1995; Kling, 1994). The user is most often working alone in an office. He (very rarely she) is technically astute as opposed to the "naïve" or "casual" user.

Increasing attention is being paid in the SPA literature to users' need for trust, control, security and autonomy (Azvine et al., 2000; Dean et al., 1996; Friedman and Nissenbaum, 1996; Goldberg et al., 1996; Kautz, 1994; Van Slyke and Collins, 1995). In their paper *Towards a Sociological View of Trust in Computer Science,* Fahrenholtz and Bartelt (2001) acknowledge that trust should be an important issue for computer scientists. They pose the following questions: "Does our model capture all necessary parts of trust?", 'How do we ensure that user trust is in sync with our model?", "How do we monitor system and user performance in terms of trust?", and above all "Do all of us share a valid and common understanding of the phenomenon trust?" (p.2).

Often security is at the centre of discussions of trust, with increasing attention being paid to scrutability, comprehensibility and transparency in the design of SPAs (Sengers, 1999). In the sociological, economics, media and diffusion of innovation literature, it is trust rather than security which is the necessary condition for use. Trust however is difficult to define because it is nebulous and all pervading. People speak of trust most clearly when they speak of a lack of trust. This is especially so in situations where there is a greater risk and where information is less easily available. Luhmann (1988) and Giddens (1994) state that trust presupposes a situation of risk, a distance in time and space, and a choice between two or more alternatives.

As the information imbalance increases, so does the need for trust. Kollock (1994) illustrates how trusted relationships are important for the buying of rubber in Thailand where the quality of rubber can only be determined after extensive processing many months later. With rice, the quality can be ascertained by rubbing two grains of rice together between blocks of wood. Hence the markets are impersonal auction markets where transactions are immediate and relatively impersonal.

2.1 Trust and Security

Security is important for trust, but trust encompasses issues wider than security. David Bollier (1996), reporting on the discussion of the Aspen Forum on Electronic Commerce, notes:

> It may be conceptually useful to distinguish between issues of "hard trust," which involve authenticity, encryption, and security in transactions, and issues of "soft trust," which involve human psychology, brand loyalty, and user-friendliness ... It is important to see that the problems of engendering trust are not simply technical in nature ... Trust is also a matter of making psychological, sociological, and institutional adjustments (p.21).

A constant thread in the literature on trust is that caring, benevolence, and intimacy is important in the use of technologies. Certification and technical expertise is often not enough to ensure trustworthiness. As Blackston (1992) notes, trust "is crucially dependent on something that can best be termed intimacy. Intimacy is the 'brand's attitude' which locks trust into the relationship" (p.82). Trust is strengthened if the customer feels that the designer and provider of goods and services cares for the user experience. Ganeson (1994), who examines vendor/retailer relations from a marketing perspective, refers to this as 'benevolence', or "the extent to which the retailer believes the vendor has intentions and motives beneficial to the retailer when new conditions arise, conditions for which a commitment was not made" (p.3).

It is also important to note the difference between interpersonal trust and system trust. It is like the difference between trusting your spouse with money in marriage and having trust and confidence in the payments system. With interpersonal trust, there is trust in a person, whereas trust in the system is trust in the reliability and security of the system. System trust needs to be further distinguished as trust in physical systems and trust in online systems. With the use of online services, we are dealing with interactive online systems. However, much of the discussion in the literature around trust deals with building trust in a physical, interpersonal environment. As Samarajiva (1997) notes, "Little is known about how to create a trust-conducive environment based on interactive media systems" (p.285). In both interpersonal and system trust, at some level, trust means an absence of questions and a willingness to accept certain things on faith. This faith gets more easily shaken by public exposures of fraud as consumer trust in the security of a system is often built on ignorance of the potential for fraud or level of actual fraud.

3. TRUST IS CONTROL

In our SPA study, we found that academic computer scientists often used the term trust, but it was a synonym for "control" when they talked of using technologies. Trust consisted wholly of control – control over the code, control over the likelihood of the technology breaking down, control over the interface, and over personal information and space.

The data from the electronic money study, and the literature on trust, on the other hand show the criteria that engender "soft trust" fall into three clusters: control, comfort, and caring. Computer scientists did not speak of comfort and familiarity. This was so noticeable a difference that we went back to the data with the search text function of NUD*IST. We had asked about comfort nine times. Only two people spoke of comfort briefly, in relation to technologies. Fiona in her 40s and working in Human-Computer Interaction, spoke of comfort as related to the use of machines. Jake in his 40s and interested in agent technology, also spoke of comfort saying that computer scientists "tend to be more comfortable using computers, exploring them and finding new ways of doing things." Familiarity was taken for granted and not spoken of except in the context of familiarity with computers and with computing languages. Caring was not mentioned at all.

3.1 Dimensions of Control

Edward, 40+[1] in artificial intelligence (AI), distinguishes between at least three levels of control.

- You can accept what the SPA does;
- You have the ability to change a few rules; and
- You can see how it is constructed and does things.

Edward, like the other computer scientists, would want the third and greatest level of control. He does not want things to happen automatically, only when he wants them to happen. He wants to know the thinking behind a conclusion and action. Hence he says he will not use a travel agent (physical agent) for he thinks the agent pushes particular products. It is for the same reason that he does not trust shop bots, for there is business bias in the information they give.

"Ordinary" users, as represented in the 1997 electronic money study, also want control over personal information, security, reliability, and the ability to see what is happening to their money. They want to see what is happening behind the screen so that they can "tweak" it to adapt it to their needs. For these "ordinary users' the term "control" was used "to check and regulate; to exercise restraint over" money. Those interviewed spoke of controlling money in the sense of having access to money and enough information to track, monitor, and regulate the flow of money in different areas of their lives. The physical aspect of money, that it was something tangible, helped to give people a feeling of control. Authenticating the provider, preferably face-to-face, was important. It is this control that results in a person's comfort in money management, and is central to a customer's satisfaction with his or her relationship with a financial services provider. They want transparency, but they are not interested in seeing how the product or service is constructed. Computer scientists however want to go beyond transparency so that they can personalise and scrutinise their software.

In the young people's study, for 12 participants "control" meant physically controlling who used their mobile phone, and preventing parents from accessing email accounts. Another recurring idea of control in the young people study was having access to caller ID so that incoming calls could be screened. As Bridget, 19, a university student in Melbourne, stated, "I will not answer a call unless I know who it is. I would rather let it go to message bank then call whoever it is back even though it means I have to pay twice, once for the message bank call and then again to call the person back."

"Control" over whom they allowed access via their mobile phones emerged as being of major importance to 23 participants in the study. Three of the participants, all of whom

---

[1] The names have been changed

were female university students, two aged 19 and one aged 20, would never answer their phone if they did not recognise the number or if the number did not come up. Twelve of the participants, a mixture of ages and genders, would regularly ignore an unknown or hidden number depending on the circumstances in which the call was received. Eight of the participants, again an even balance of age and gender, would occasionally ignore an incoming call if they did not recognise the number.

Only six participants said they would answer their phone every time it rang. The six included two female university students aged 18 and 19 and four males, three of whom were university students, two aged 18 and one aged 22, and one who was a high school student aged 16. It is important to note that with the six participants who answered every call, with the exception of Genevieve, a university student aged 18, the other five regularly asserted control over their mobile phones by tuning them off when they did not wish to be contacted. Genevieve stated "I cannot not bear to be out of the loop even for a minute. And I would just die of curiosity if I did not answer a call. I would spend the whole day wondering who it was that called me." It is interesting to note that it is a cross section of participants who exercise levels of control over the boundaries of their virtual space. This indicates that control may not be specific to one group of young people such as females or young users but rather a common concern for young people in general.

3.2 Computers Can Easily Go Wrong

Computer scientists' need for control comes mainly from their knowledge of the limitations of computer technology, and how easily computers and software can go wrong. This is true for all the computer scientists we interviewed. Chris, 50+ with a special interest in formal languages, says, "I don't trust computers. I know how they work." He adds that you need to use agents or something acting on your behalf with great caution for

> ...computers are notoriously stupid. And however clever you are at putting them together, you usually don't think of something, and that's the something that comes back and burns you at some point.

Despite this mistrust of computers and software, computer scientists in our SPA study trusted the electronic record. Even Chris with his articulated mistrust of computers had up to 4,500 e-mails in his in-box. Edward and Burt, 31, also specialising in AI, had all their e-mails in their in-box. Don, 50+ who specialises in ripple-down-rules had 6,800 messages in his in-box. Others had folders for their e-mail, classified according to subject, sender, private or official nature of e-mail or urgency of the task. But only one computer scientist in the SPA study spoke of printing e-mails and filing them for record. In this sense the computer scientists in the SPA study were similar to the computer scientists studied in an Australian university in 2001 as part of a study of the use of e-mail (Singh, 2001). Computer scientists either trust the search function to retrieve relevant documents, or they have an organisational system for keeping a corporate electronic record. This approach differs from staff in departments such as Human Resources, where e-mail is treated like ordinary mail and so routinely printed and filed.

It is not clear as yet whether young people have a different attitude to the use of technology. Callum, 25, working with IT and music, for instance feels that it is inevitable that systems will crash, data will be lost, and the technology will fail him regularly. However, he considers this to be merely a minor inconvenience. He still trusts his PC and feels that it is his responsibility to ensure the back up of crucial documents. This theme was confirmed with both focus groups. However as a theme that is still nascent in the study, it warrants further research.

3.3 Personalising and Scrutinising Software

Computer scientists in the SPA study see text based e-mail programs as more transparent, faster, simpler to use and easier to personalise. Ian in his late 30's, who concentrates on search engines, says, "When you are dealing with a lot of e-mail like I am, the time it takes to go through them all in an icon based format is just not an option."

At least five of the computer scientists have written programs to adapt their e-mail program for their way of communicating. Adam, 34, who specialises in computer networking, has written a program which sorts his e-mails so that they appear in different categories when he opens his e-mail. Fiona, in her 40s, who deals with Human-Computer Interaction (HCI) can search her e-mail, the attachments (other than PDF), and her files at the same time. When Harry, 50+ studying AI, receives an e-mail from a person in his address book, or replies to that message, the e-mail goes into that person's folder. He filters out spam by setting up rules to exclude any e-mail, say with the word "Sex." He is also alerted when an urgent e-mail arrives.

When the computer scientists speak of personalising software they speak of it as a normal activity. Jake, in his 40s and specialising in agent technology, for instance has personalised his PDA so that it buzzes him seven minutes before his train home is due. But he is surprised that other users may not be able to download and modify the program as it is freely available on the Web. He assumes an expertise he has.

The personalisation of software is connected by computer scientists' need to scrutinise the workings of the software. Chris says in practice he would want to run the SPA for a while and just observe its behaviour. He says, "It would also help if I built part of it so that I'd at least know what the system was really doing underneath."

Fiona says that she wants the machine to be understandable. She says, "I use this word 'scrutable' because I don't want it always shoving in my face, 'This is why I'm doing it'. But when I choose to scrutinise, to work out what's going on, I should be able to do that."

Personalisation is equally important for young people. However this personalisation was not for scrutinising the workings of the software. Personalisation was to make the device more physically pleasing, or customised for their needs. Every single participant in the young people study personalised their technology in some way. The physical aspects of personalisation took many forms including simply choosing a ring tone for a mobile phone or downloading an image for the mobile phone screen. It also meant snapping on different mobile phone covers, creating different categories of mobile phone profiles for friends, family and work, or /and creating avatars. Others customised gaming platforms for multi-player networked games.

3.4 Ensuring Privacy

Scrutable software or agents are not a complete answer. Computer scientists in the SPA study are reluctant to have the SPA intrude into their time and space. The emphasis on privacy is great enough to prevent usage of a potentially useful device. This is a common theme that runs through the interviews in the SPA study. Greg, in his early 40's and specialising in AI, mentions that the agent may be able to redirect messages from e-mail to voice mail, but it may be intrusive. That would prevent him from using the agent, for he does not want people to think he can always be contacted.

Harry articulates the concern for privacy most strongly, saying he will not use the SPA, for he does not think the SPA will ensure the "absolute control" he wants. He would only use the SPA if he "can guarantee the information is secure." If he were to use the SPA, he would give as little information as possible to the SPA, for systems are designed so that it is hard to roll them back. So scrutability is not a safeguard for "Once the connection is made you can't retract, because the consequences permeate through the whole system." Harry says,

> The more info you give the greater the chance of personality theft...I'm happy to tell the SPA what I'm interested in, what sort of articles and books I like to read, what sort of food I like to eat. Other than that, no more. I use the SPA as a personal financial advisor. It can certainly know things like my attitude towards risk and my preferences towards business to invest in. It does not have to know a lot more than that. I give it as little info as possible for it to perform the task I want.

Information intrusion was not at the centre of young people's definition of privacy. Physical control was entwined with their notions of privacy. Privacy meant being able to make a phone call without anyone overhearing or sending an email without someone looking over their shoulder. Twenty of the 29 participants in the young people study conceptualised privacy this way. Eddie, 18, a university student in Melbourne, said "Privacy is privacy. It means no one is eavesdropping on me when I'm on the phone. What else could it mean?"

Furthermore, 18 participants in the young people study had no objections to data profiles being complied about them and actually welcomed unsolicited e-mail. Lucie, 17, a University student, said "I get really excited when I see an e-mail from say a cool site, and I don't even have to ask for it."

4. DESIGNING FOR CONTROL

Control is at the centre of the design of software for the computer scientists in the SPA study. They differed as to whether technologies could have sufficient control built into them. Those that felt that a sufficient level of control was possible were more inclined to use the technologies. Even in this group, use would be limited to relatively routine and risk free tasks. If the desired level of control was not guaranteed, then computer scientists would refrain from using even the technologies they had designed. Behind this use or non-use of software is also a broader philosophical question of the human-machine relationship.

Chris is one of the computer scientists who thinks that it is possible to technically ensure control. He says:

> The safeguard is the possibility of using formal methods to prove that the system will only behave in certain ways that are acceptable. That's a pretty hard thing to do. It's very hard to do for conventional software, but for an agent which is all the time changing, it's even more difficult.

Harry is at the other end of the spectrum where issues of control prevent use. Cautious use of new technologies is the path most likely to be taken by this group. The computer scientists interviewed in the SPA study say they want the e-mail agent for drafting, prioritising, personalising e-mail, and as a task reminder and better search tool for searching the web for up-to-date material. Content filtering, when possible, would also be of great help. They are reluctant to use the agent for more than routine tasks where there is a risk of getting it wrong. Hence few of the computer scientists we interviewed are willing to embrace the intelligent aspects of the SPA, which is one of the main characteristics that distinguish a SPA from a tool like e-mail. A SPA has the capacity to observe users' preferences and learn from previous behaviour. Ultimately the greatest savings in time and energy come from the ability to automate, to act without the users' specific direction. However, computer scientists find it difficult to have this degree of trust in the software.

The central question behind the control of software is: Can the human brain be modelled as a computer?" Chris who specialises in machine learning, sees the SPA as

> the replacement for a human who would be doing the same job. So if I had … a real personal assistant …I would have them do certain things and one of them would be monitoring e-mail and chasing up things. You know, 'Find me the home page of some person'. ..It's easier to ask that and get the response back than it is to do it, so all that saves time.

He adds "If you could build a SPA to do it really well, it would be better to have a SPA than a person because much of this can be automated. And if it can be automated, let's have the system do it."

Fiona, whose field is user modelling, says, "The machine is not a human. Be clear as to what the machine can and cannot do." Hence her focus is on having realistic expectations, on having the machine share with the user what it is trying to do. It is a collaborative relationship between the human and the machine, rather than one where the machine is expected to act like a human.

4.1 Not Designing For Ease of Use

Traditionally computer scientists consider the dimension of "use" after they have a device that "works." Use is often seen as a problem of interface and a matter of user testing. The data from the interviews agree with surveys of agent literature which show that "use" is not a central theme in the designing of agents (Agre, 1995; Kling, 1994). Hence ease of use is less important. Given functionality and reliability, computer scientists don't mind a messy interface. As Cooper says, they "trade simplicity for control" (Cooper, 1999, p.93).

As Chris in our SPA study, says, "use" has not been an important dimension of the work of computer scientists. "There was just the technological aim of doing a certain thing, building a system which classified certain kinds of objects into 90 percent accuracy." This emphasis on the technological versus use is noted by Scott Berkun (2000) from Microsoft. He says,

> There is a fundamental difference in how technologists and true designers approach products. Technical people tend to start with technologies. We take teams of developers, build a technology, and then shoehorn a user interface and a user experience onto the

> framework dictated by technology. This guarantees that the user experience will be a poor compromise.

In our study, only two of the 12 computer scientists, Don and Luke, who have dealt with knowledge acquisition through expert systems, have needed detailed knowledge of the users and their specific domains. As Don says,

> The technology, as far as possible, shouldn't be making the user ... learn different(ly). Like if they are already a pathology expert, they shouldn't have to learn a whole lot of other stuff about computer science to capture that expertise in a knowledge base.

Needing to consider use does not necessarily make it important. Luke is blunt in his dismissal of use. He says scientists are interested in "making it work, making it work more efficiently. Nobody cares much, who is going to use it."

A focus on "use" is not highly acclaimed in some parts of computer science. Expert systems and HCI – major themes in computer science which consider use – are seen as lower down in the hierarchy of the discipline. As the story told by Don, below, shows, this is because they are not seen as sufficiently complex and mathematical.

Don, in expert systems, tells a story against himself. He was part of a team that designed expert systems based on ripple-down-rules that have been proven to be efficient and reliable for diagnosis in pathology. The pathologists have control and can change the rules without the need to learn code. He says,

> I go along to knowledge acquisition workshops and conferences and I present this stuff and it always goes down like a lead balloon.... People always say, 'Won't the knowledge base get too big because the order in which it is built is chaotic and so on?' The real reason why computer scientists really like engineering and designing things, they really like figuring out how something should work. The structure of these ripple-down-rules... is... very boring... but it really empowers the users... A lot of these people are into sophisticated designs rather than doing something really simple that actually sort of works well.

Some of the most usable designs by the computer scientists we interviewed have been based on personal need and experience. Fiona, Ian and Kevin belong to this second group. Much of the design work Fiona has done comes from her experience of teaching, and her need to make the teaching more collaborative. In her design, the machine shares what it is doing. It is a collaborative relationship between the human and the machine, rather than one where the machine is expected to act like a human. In sharing what it is doing, the machine can make the human more reflective about his or her actions. Fiona says:

> I've done a lot of work on ...personalised systems....I guess ... my specific interest is user modelling. And I got to that because I was really interested in personalised teaching, using computers. And to personalise teaching, you have to really know the person you are teaching.

Kevin who has worked on search queries also designed it with himself in mind. Ian, in his late 30s and specialising in search engines, designed an e-mail system for himself. He found that many of his colleagues also found it useful for they had the same needs.

4.2 Not Using What They Design

Computer scientists' mistrust technology so that they often do not use what they design. As Cooper (1999) says, "programmers typically don't use the software they design" (p.22).

There are two reasons, other than an inadequate level of control, for not using technologies you have designed – the lack of usefulness and the awareness that SPAs lack social and cultural understandings. Greg, who worked in the industry sector and designed a SPA assisted scheduler, says he would not use the scheduler himself. Part of the reason is that it is not useful, for he does not have the kind of life which requires that kind of monitoring of schedules. It would be more useful for him to have a program which told him when he had to begin the paper if he was to meet the specified deadline. But he says, the main difficulty is cultural.

> ...some people may be more important than others...Managers don't usually move their schedules around to accommodate you. So ... there are all of those power relations you might say, that don't get considered in this sort of system.

Luke has designed expert systems for scheduling, but he himself uses a paper diary. He says the electronic diary takes too long. Burt too says that he would not use a SPA because the SPA would need too much personal information to get the social and cultural understandings right. Burt says,

> A SPA in a cultural sense wouldn't work. It "could not know what rules to apply. It wouldn't know your mood or how busy you were. There are too many things it can't know and could be too intrusive. Potentially it could work, but ... how can it know a social context?"

5. TRUST, CONTROL AND DESIGN

Our study of computer scientists in the SPA study showed they identify trust with control. The lack of sufficient control – which at times means absolute control – is enough to ensure computer scientists will not use the technology. As computer scientists most often design for users like themselves, control becomes the overriding factor in the design of new information and communication technologies. Control primarily means sufficient information to personalise, scrutinise, and secure the system. Other factors, which have come to the fore in the study of the diffusion of innovations, are given less importance.

Less importance is placed on the innovation having greater relative advantage compared with the technologies that preceded it. Compatibility with existing values and past experiences is also not at the centre of design. It is also known that innovations are more rapidly adopted if they are less complex (Rogers, 1995). However the culture of the discipline of computer science, and the sequence of design, privileges the complex over simple and easy to use technology.

Comparing the computer scientists with other groups of users such as middle-income residential consumers and young people shows that the computer scientists' have a particularly specific interpretation of trust. Trust is control. And "control" is control over information to personalise, scrutinise, and secure the system. For other user groups, trust has the dimension of security and authentication. But equally important are the aspects of comfort and caring. For young people, control and privacy are seen as control over access and use, rather than control over information. A greater understanding of computer scientists' distinctive understandings of trust would go some way towards consciously ensuring that the needs of the "average user" – including young users, are at the centre of the design of new information and communication technologies.

REFERENCES

Agre, P., 1995, The soul gained and lost: artificial intelligence as a philosophical project. *Stanford Humanities Review*, 4:2.

Azvine, B., Dijan, D., Kwok, C. T., and Wobcke, W., 2000, The intelligent assistant: an overview, in: *Intelligent Systems and Soft Computing,* Azvine, B., Dijan, D., Kwok, C. T., & Wobcke, W., eds., pp. 215–238.

Berkun, S., 2000, Why great technologies don't make great products. Microsoft Corporation, http://msdn.microsoft.com/library/default.asp?url=/library/en-us/dnhfact/html/hfactor9_5.asp, Accessed 10 September 2002

Blackston, M., 1992, Observations: building brand equity by managing the brand's relationships. *Journal of Advertising Research*, **32**:3.

Bollier, D., 1996, *The future of electronic commerce,* A Report of the Fourth Annual Aspen Institute Roundtable on Information Technology. Aspen, Colorado: The Aspen Institute.

Charmaz, C., 2000, Grounded theory: objectivist and constructivist methods. in: *Handbook of Qualitative Research,* (Second ed.), N. K. Denzin and Y. S. Lincoln, eds., Sage Publications, London, pp. 509–535.

Cooper, A., 1999,. *The Inmates are Running the Asylum*. SAMS, Indianapolis.

Dean, D., Felten, E., and Wallach, D., 1996, Java security: from HotJava to Netscape and beyond, Paper presented at the IEEE Symposium on Security and Privacy, Oakland, California.

Fahrenholtz, D, and Bartelt, A., Towards a sociological view of trust in computer science, Eighth Research Symposium on Emerging Electronic Markets, http://www-i5.informatik.rwth-aachen.de/conf/rseem2001/papers/fahrenholtz.pdf, Accessed 15 July 2003

Friedman, B., and Nissenbaum, H., 1996, Software agents and user autonomy, Paper presented at the First International Conference on Autonomous Agents, New York.

Ganeson, S., 1994, Determinants of long-term orientation in buyer-seller relationships. *Journal of Marketing*, **58**:2.

Giddens, A., 1994, *The Consequences of Modernity,* Polity Press, Cambridge.

Goldberg, I., Wagner, D., Thomas, R., and Brewer, E. A., 1996, A Secure Environment for untrusted helper applications. Paper presented at the Proceedings of the 6th Usenix Security Symposium, San Jose, California.

Helin, H., 2001, *Bibliography on Software Agents* AAAI Press, http://www.cs.Helsinki.FI/u/hhelin/agents/agent-bib.html, Accessed 10 August 2001

Kautz, H. A., Selman, B., Coen, M., and Ketchpel, S., 1994, An experiment in the design of software agents, Paper presented at the 1994 Software Agents Spring Symposium, Palo Alto.

Kling, R., 1994, Organizational analysis in computer science, in: *Social Issues in Computing: Putting Computing in its Place,* C. Huff and T. Finholt, eds., McGraw-Hill Inc., New York, pp.18–46.

Kollock, P., 1994, The emergence of exchange structures: An experimental study of uncertainty, commitment, and trust, *American Journal of Sociology*, **100:**2.

Luhmann, N., 1988, Familiarity, confidence, trust: problems and alternatives, in *Trust: Making and Breaking Cooperative Relations*, D. Gambetta, ed., Basil Blackwell, New York, pp. 94–107.

Rogers, E. M., 1995, *Diffusion of Innovations* (4th edition), The Free Press, New York.

Samarajiva, R., 1997, Interactivity as though privacy mattered, in: *Technology and Privacy: The New Landscape*, P. Agre and M. Rotenberg, eds., Institute of Technology Press, Cambridge, Massachusetts pp..277–309.

Sengers, P., 1999, Designing comprehensible agents, IJCAI-99: Proceedings of the Sixteenth International Joint conference on artificial intelligence, **2**.

Singh, S., 2001, The effective use of corporate e-mail, Paper presented at the Pacific Telecommunications Conference, Honolulu, Hawaii, 14–18 January.

Singh, S., and Slegers, C., 1997, *Trust and electronic money,* Centre for International Research on Communication and Information Technologies, Melbourne Australia.

Strauss, A., and Corbin, J., 1990, *Basics of Qualitative Research: Grounded Theory Procedures and Techniques*, Sage Publications, Newbury Park, California.

Van Slyke, C., and Collins, R. W., 1995, Trust between users and their intelligent agents, Paper presented at the CIKM'95 Workshop on Intelligent Information Agents, Baltimore, Maryland.

Vredenburg, K., Isensee, S., and Righi, C., 2002, *User-Centered Design: An Integrated Approach,* Prentice Hall, Upper Saddle River, NJ.

BUILDING AN OPEN DOCUMENT MANAGEMENT SYSTEM WITH COMPONENTS FOR TRUST

Gábor Knapp, Gábor Magyar, and Gergely Németh*

1. INTRODUCTION

Nowadays the Web can be considered as the largest database or more precisely, the largest document archive ever built. None the less the accessible information resources are in the deepness (principally in structured databases), and cannot be accessed by a simple free text search, the agents of Google index more than three thousand million pages. As technology and networking becomes more and more accessible and affordable, the number of documents increases exponentially.

Web search is based on indexes built by search engines. The words of the search query are compared to the terms of the inverted index, and documents that satisfy the logical function (usually "and" by default) between search terms are selected. Typically the list of results is empty, or contains thousands of hits. In the later case the efficiency can be enhanced by ordering hits by relevance, so, although the number of hits is still large, the useful links are on the top. Heavy research is being performed all over the world to extend searchable area to relational databases and to make the relevance of the hits of search and retrieval better by introducing semantics. The effort is hoped to be effective in a few years.

However, even if we imagine an ideal search engine that results only relevant links according to conventional performance indicators as recall or precision. Can we be assured that the really relevant documents could be reached, or the content of the documents found is reliable? No, not at all! But it is not only a technological problem. The trust of human has to be won, and it is usually much more complex problem than computing.

Let's see the two opposite viewpoints of a author and a reader:

- If a scientist works out something wonderful that may change the world (e.g. the perpetuum mobile itself), he has a great motivation to publish his discovery and

* Gábor Knapp, Metainfo Co., Érd, Hungary 2030. Gábor Magyar, Budapest University of Technology and Economics, Budapest, Hungary 1111. Gergely Németh, Budapest University of Technology and Economics, Budapest, Hungary 1111.

reach as wide audience as possible. How great thing is that publishing on the web is so easy! But his second feeling necessarily will be the doubt. What happens is somebody relieves his idea and publishes it as his own on a more frequently visited site?

- As a reader, a research fellow finds a documentation of a new theory that fits his research area. How can he be convinced of the authenticity of the source? As documents can appear on the web in seconds, they can disappear as well. How can he refer this resource in his publication?

Both situations can be found in the traditional world, but technology limitations and legal control could handle the problem efficiently. However nowadays the simplicity of digital creation and publishing, and conversely, downloading and copying documents, or copy and paste document portions make this problem critical.

The challenges of the digital world have to be overcome by the means of digital technology itself. These solutions already exist, but they have to accepted and applied by users, and this takes much more time then changing technology. For the intermediate period, we have to give an easy-to-use way of document management to give practical proof, and enhance trust in technology.

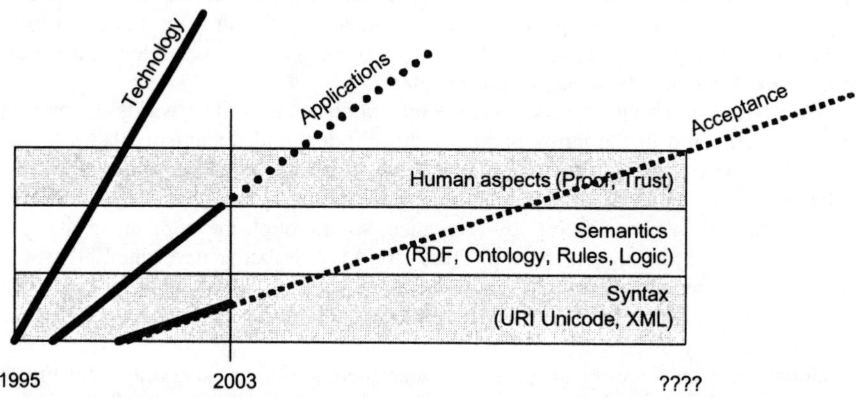

Figure 1. Simplified roadmap of the Semantic Web

The figure illustrates current situation and future trends. While almost all problems can be solved by the means of technology, applications still use syntax level and are just beginning to apply semantics, users are still unfamiliar with even syntax.

Applications should be developed that assemble the existing building blocks, and try to make use of all advantages of the concept of the semantic web. We believe it is worth to do some research in this area even though the technologies are not all clarified, because we hope, that by introducing possibilities, the time scale of the graph can be significantly shortened.

2. PARTIAL SOLUTIONS FOR ENHANCE TRUST

Several techniques are known that provide partial solutions for the described issues. Before introducing them separately, let's summarize some specific problems to be solved and the services that should be provided.

- Provide permanent access: This requirement is twofold: the document has to be accessible at a persistent location, and the document's format has to be "everlasting", generally accepted and used standardized format.
- Inhibit or detect illegal copies: a mechanism is to be implemented that is able to compare documents and select suspicious ore more than suspicious correspondences.
- Enable integration to larger systems: Although the criterion of user friendliness requires customized application, the integration in larger, world wide systems has to be supported. It practically means that a standard set of metadata and standard access protocol has to be the implemented. Future search systems may apply deep web search engines that can reach structured databases, but they need database portals with schema information published.
- Support efficient search: Indexes built during document uploading support free text search, but much more relevant hits can be obtained by adding human metadata according to a standardized, controlled vocabulary.
- Encryption and certification: Public key infrastructure (PKI) algorithms can solve this task suitably. However it is an organisational and regulation problem, much more then technology. In our system an interface to PKI modules is planned, but not implemented yet.

2.1. Reference: PURL – An approach of URN

A great problem for authors that while most scientific publications born digital, but only a portion of them become a real, paper based document. However, even if this metamorphosis occurs, it takes significant time. Publications generally appear first on the web and citations have to be referred by an URL rather than the conventional bibliographic record. Internet hosts can disappear, change their name, URL can be changed, so the reviewer sometimes can hardly follow references.

The idea that every object has to get a – possibly web independent – unique resource identifier (URI) is not new[1], however it hasn't become general yet. The persistent URL (PURL) approach has been suggested as an intermediate solution by Shafer et al.[2] PURL technique applies conventional URL's and use HTTP redirection to point to the real location. Persistency is guaranteed (or at least enhanced) by the centralized database of logical and physical addresses, and traceability of documents is supported further by the protocol so, that if a logical address points to a non existent location, the document history has to be returned on request.

As a side effect of using PURL, the documents can be easily distributed among scalable servers, while the PURL server with much less capacity requirement, needn't change.

2.2. Everlasting documents: Choosing the proper format

The encoding of the stored documents has to meet a number of requirements. In ideal case the document has to be easily displayed according to the intention of the author not depending on the changes in versions of word processors and operating systems. They have to be either machine or human readable, and have to support security tools such as digital signatures or watermarking.

These requirements are contradictory. If a format supports security it can hardly be open and platform independent. Conversely, if a format is open and interoperable, the security features are poor. As we plan a document repository, an archive, the requirement of unconditional reusability has to be sacrificed.

The well known, open standard based portable document format (PDF) satisfies most requirements, and the conflict between security and portability can be tuned. There are free plug-ins for all browsers to display, PDF supports encryption, watermarking and digital signatures. Reusability is restricted, but storing the content also in the original form and as unformatted text, provides a back-stair.

The real problem is not the determination of appropriate format, but conversion. When we upload a textual document made by a word processor, the actual format has to be recognized and the relevant conversion module has to be launched. We believe in the spreading of standardization and in the strength of XML, however the change original formats still supposed for a long period. The identifying and formatting module therefore has to be replaceable and expandable to adapt to novel conditions. Besides automatic detection, the "format" element of the metadata set can help efficiently select the right tool.

2.3. Plagiarism: Copy detection

The primary purpose of copy detection mechanism is the filtering of not allowed usage of citations. The intemperate use of copy-paste technique is especially harmful in education. Students can easily assemble their homework without any real danger of diving. Without technological support, exhaustive knowledge of accessible relevant resources cannot be expected from lecturers or teachers.

One approach to solve this problem is watermarking,[3] using invisible extra spaces, slight line shifts or checksums in documents. However, while watermarking found extremely useful for images, videos or sound, applying it to textual documents is not effective, because word processors can often automatically remove extra formatting elements, and portions of text can't be traced this way. On the other hand, visible graphical or textual watermarking can be used as symbolic sign of intellectual property, making more difficult to extract text and to actuate conscience.

More effective method of copy detection is based on content instead of manipulating layout. There are systems at the Digital Library at Stanford University,[4] valuable studies at Monash University,[5] there are educational organisations[6] and even commercial sites.[7] The algorithms applied based on chunking and hashing, they detect exact duplicates depending on the size of chunks. These methods can hardly recognise copies that made by authors applying small but frequent modifications, using synonyms or changing the order of words.

The copy detection module of the planned system uses a combined approach. As a first step, the documents are converted to a semi-formatted text preserving the paragraph as a unit, but ignoring font types and paragraph layout features. This pure version of the document is stored and serves as bases of further investigation. The processing continues in two separate threads.

On the first branch, the less relevant terms (as "the", "a", "is" etc.) are removed according to the Luhn-Zipf model,[8] and optionally other natural language algorithms are applied to determine the stem (it is especially important in languages that apply often multiple suffixes as Hungarian does). Then a word frequency table is built on each paragraph that is used to characterize it. On the second branch, chunking and hashing is performed for sentences, word groups and paragraphs as studied and described by several previous works.[9] The word frequency tables and the hash tables are both stored in the section of technical metadata attached to the document.

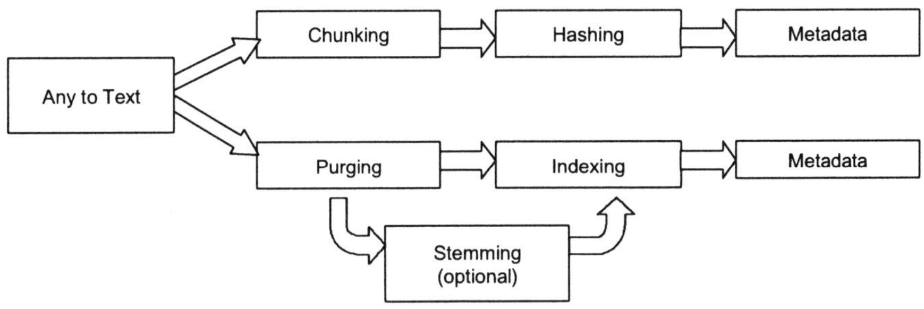

Figure 2. Preparing metadata for supporting search and copy detection

When looking for a duplicate, a free text internet search may be performed applying the most frequent words as search terms using third party search engines. The documents on the top of the hit list are to be downloaded and processed the same way as local documents. The metadata resulted are stored in temporary files (possibly cached for further use but generally deleted). The paragraphs that have very similar word distribution are considered as "suspicious" and the equality of hash values indicate "plagiarism".

It is worth to mention, that in our view copy detection or detection of similar text units is not only a tool against intellectual theft. There are several other circumstances when the mechanism can be useful. Remember, how hopeless is to find a document written by ourselves several years ago, if we can recall only a few words.

2.4. Classification: Metadata with ontology support

Textual content still plays the most important role among documents. Although free text search engines can scan all content, build index to help search, the relevancy and precision of hit list is far from perfect yet. Human added metadata describe much more precisely content. However providing metadata alone is not enough. The metadata schema has to be standardized, and the values of each attribute ought to have a standardized format (e.g. date, character encoding), or, if adequate, have to be originated from a controlled vocabulary.

There is a wide consensus in applying the metadata scheme suggested by Dublin Core Metadata Initiative to describe multimedia content.[10] However, the 15 elements represent a rather draft description of the real world. Specific applications usually need much more detailed characterization of documents. Extension can be made by using qualified DC or any other extra metadata, only the mapping to DC elements is required to assure interoperability.[11] The administrators of an open document system has to built their own, specific metadata scheme, but has to be tactfully enforced to establish the links to Dublin Core elements. It can be done practically, if the metadata structure building module is a part of the document management engine (not the application realizing business logic), and can be accessed and configured by application programming interfaces (API).

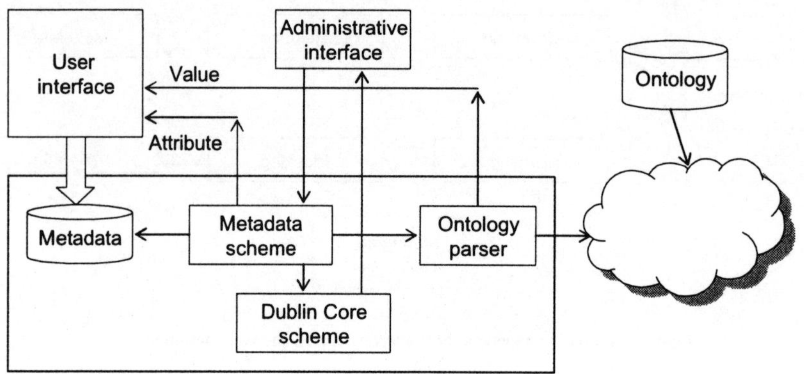

Figure 3. Handling Metadata

Dublin Core does not give any restrictions on the format or range of values. Future search engines can be supported, and the vision of semantic web[12] can be approached by standardizing values. The most appropriate solution to summarize and arrange the concepts and their relations of a selected discipline is to build an ontology. There is no full agreement in the method of implementation. DAML+OIL Ontology Markup has more experience and applications, and OWL (Web Ontology Language) has closer connection to the Semantic Web.[13]

Irrespective of the description method, the ontologies that define the concepts (terms) for a metadata element are assumed to be built outside the system, because interoperability can be obtained only if common concepts are used. In practice each metadata elements may have an ontology parser–ontology URL pair assigned, and the URL usually points to the web.

2.5. Enabling agents: Providing schema information

Documents and associated metainformation are usually stored in structured databases that provide efficient handling. However, conventional web crawlers unable to access the database content, because it cannot be retrieved by simple HTTP protocol. But even if the content could be accessed by a special mechanism, the search cannot be such efficient as it can be expected, because the robots don't know either semantics nor syntax of database.

Research to make databases accessible for search engines is at very early stage, but it seems clear, that some contribution of database owners is needed. Crawler readable information on the resource has to be provided. It seems evident, that the concept of the Resource Description Framework (RDF) has to be used with XML syntax for further extension of applicability. In the future software agents will be able to read and process semantic information, and the new generation of search engines can assemble appropriate structured query (SQL, XML Query or OQL depending on the database platform) to get data.[14]

2.6. Open Access: Metadata Harvesting

Another way of providing information on the document database is to provide a standardized interface for service providers collecting metadata. The Protocol for Metadata Harvesting is a method suggested by the Open Archives Initiative (OAI-PMH).[15]

The protocol spreads intensively due to its simplicity, clear concept. It uses simple HTTP GET method to collect information, and basic Dublin Core metadata set is specified as obligatory service. The planned document management system can serve as a Data provider for the network of OAI compatible Service providers. Since business logic is separated from the document management engine, the OAI interface can be integrated in it without any effect on workflow. Implementing this interface (using free components) provides a short term possibility to integrate the document repository to the world.

2.7. Other issues

There are of course, several other aspects of trust including time stamping, event logging, access control, backup, rights management and version handling that are not emphasized previously, but have to be solved in a system. However strictly observing the concept of openness and modular design and layered structure, additional building blocks can be implemented without changing the basic architecture.

3. SYSTEM CONCEPT: PUT IT ALL TOGETHER

As document management can be considered as one of the most useful and frequent tasks, it is considerable to integrate the techniques described in the previous chapter into a separate subsystem that has its own living, independent of the application on the top level. Adding a new layer into a system always has disadvantages especially in performance and the increasing of complexity. On the other hand, layered structure provides more flexibility, and as a number of components are still under development, we have to be prepared for regular changes.

3.1. System architecture

The document management engine (DME) is not a conventional layer, because it is planned to have an own high level interface for communicating with software agents.

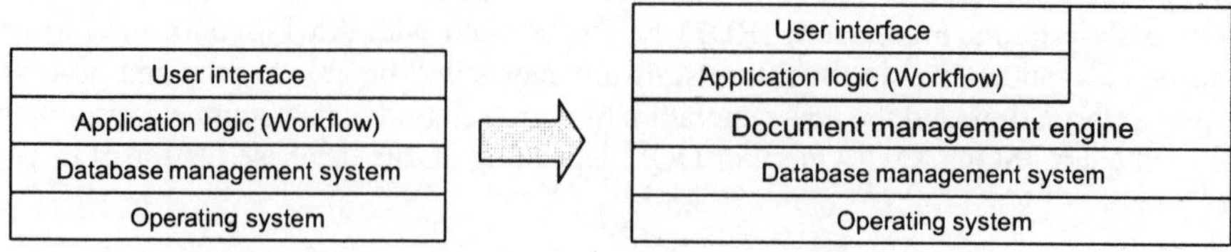

Figure 4. High level system architecture

It is practical to separate the communication of the document management engine from other application issues, because this way the designer of the business application can get rid of the responsibility of keeping interoperability standards. The application communicates with the DME by well defined messages, practically of XML syntax.

On its outer interface, the DME has to accept standard HTTP requests, and has to provide standard responses. If a browser acts as a client, the answer is a HTML form that allows user to search the document repository. If an OAI service provider or a deep web search engine contacts the site, the OAI-PMH protocol, or the schema information has to be sent. Certainly the data to be provided on this interface can be restricted using the appropriate system messages using the DME API. In more complex systems the functions of the application server and the document management have to be separated, so the DME interface has to prepare to handle API calls encapsulated in HTTP packages. Ontologies also linked at the upper interface.

At the low level interface the communication with the database management system is performed by SQL or other database system recognized standardized language (e.g. XML Query).

3.2. Inner structure

The document management engine is assembled from separate modules. Some building blocks used are imported from the result of other projects. Effort is made to use open source components, however for special purposes (e.g. special format conversion) even commercial software blocks also can be integrated. The interfacing and inter-module communication problems have to be solved within the DME, so the three interfaces provided for web agents (machine or human), software developers (implementing the application) and the database engine are fixed, not depending on the origin, number and operation of the building blocks integrated.

As a sample, the simplified structure of the test system is shown on the following figure.

The real system is much more complex. The figure illustrates only the basic information flow. A fundamental element of the system is, that user supplied metadata are provided under tight control of the document management engine. The connection between the metadata set the document itself is performed by an URL, pointing to the document generated by the system and mapped to the persistent URL. Another important feature is, that the conventional web interface is independent from the application, as well as the OAI compatible interface, that serves interoperability with other compatible databases. The metadata schema information is also accessible via the web interface (not included on the figure). The DME-API interface is introduced for expandability, when system dimensions require the separation of the user and administration functionality of the document management system. All user messages can be accepted in HTTP encapsulated form, however administration, configuration can be performed only by standard API for security reasons.

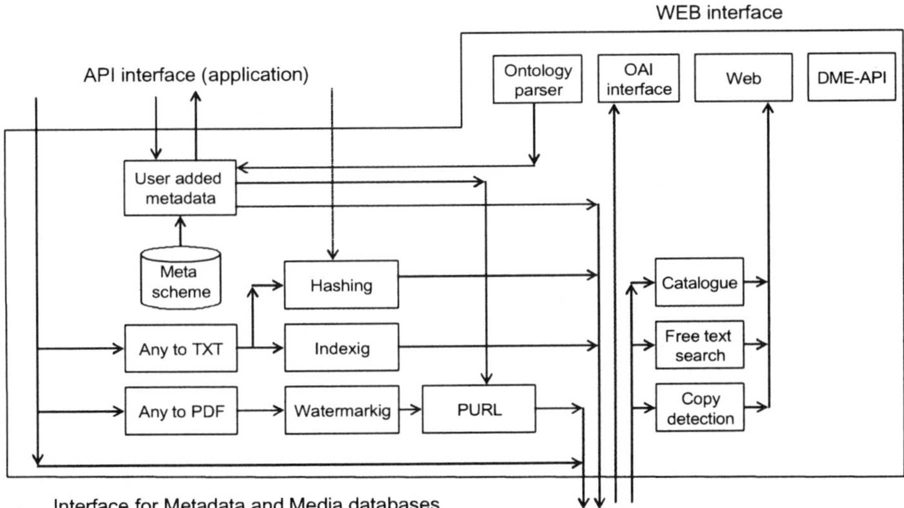

Figure 5. Basic information flow in the DME

As all user interfaces use standard communication forms the system is extremely expandable. All database size sensitive functions can be distributed on several servers. On the document management engine only few data stored, all other databases can be "outsourced" to other servers. Certainly, for small systems – as the test system – all functions can be served by a single hardware.

4. CASE STUDY: THE REPOSITORY OF ACADEMIC WRITINGS

To demonstrate the capabilities of the system a pilot system is built planned to be for a repository of documents authored in higher education. Technical reports, studies, dissertations, scientific publications or any other academic writings are to be published by students, lecturers and research fellows electronically using the application's web interface. The application layer is responsible for authentication, initiates the metadata collection and selects appropriate functions. However, the metadata structure and the rules of filling fields are strictly controlled by document management engine to ensure the standardized data structures.

4.1. Application specific issues

For application developers the basic task seems to be quite simple. Upload documents, provide descriptive metadata and select special functions (e.g. copy detection). Format conversion, cataloguing, indexing is performed by the document management engine itself. And if a document becomes a part of the document repository, additional tasks as search, communication with other data- and service providers are done automatically, independently controlled by messages arriving from the API or the web interface.

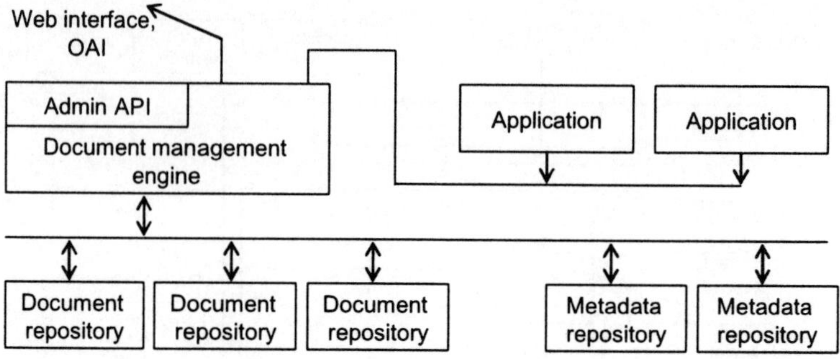

Figure 6. Distributed document management

Due to the wide variety of publications and the organization dependent document handling rules, it is not an easy task to satisfy both organizational and standardization requirements. The workflow is basically realized by the application layer, but the interdependence of documents (e.g. project plan, dissertation, reviews, evaluation and statistics) has to be appeared also in metadata structure in the document management engine. So the freedom of the designers has to be slightly restricted, however efficient support has to be added to meet requirements.

The planning of the metadata structure has to be performed as a "discussion" process between the system administrator and the document management engine. The DME offers basic categories, according to Dublin Core, that can be used unaltered, or can be qualified (using sub-categories) by the administrator, so the mapping to DC scheme is automatically assured. The filling rules for each field, has to be also controlled suggesting standard formats, character sets or vocabularies. According to our experiences in education it is believed that all situations can be handled this way, however it is still a question that cannot been answered at the current stage of research that this restriction (that can slightly alter naming conventions) is acceptable for users and administration or not. The final conception will be worked out taking the results of surveys, interviews and the experiences of the pilot system into account.

4.2. Refining specification

To check organisational readiness, a survey is issued to representatives of the different sectors of higher education including regular universities, postgraduate courses, collages and even primary and secondary schools. The primary purpose of course is to sum up the user needs and application circumstances, willingness of use and collaboration (with us and with other document repositories). The survey is published as a HTML form, the results are summarized by an appropriate application. A part of the survey is as follows:

What components would you use - Microsoft Internet Explorer

http://www.metainfo.hu/docuform.htm

What components would you use?

- ☐ Free text search
- ☐ Uploading documents
- ☐ Cataloguing (using metadata schemes)
- ☐ Knowledge management support (thesauri, ontologies)
- ☐ Copy detection
- ☐ Format conversion
- ☐ Watermarking
- ☐ Log analysis, statistics
- ☐ Persistent accessibility
- ☐ Certification
- ☐ Other (please specify):

What document formats have to be handled (please check)

- ☐ Text
- ☐ Word document
- ☐ HTML/XML
- ☐ PDF
- ☐ Other (please specify):

Figure 7. Survey for refining specification

The survey has a second, also very important highlight also. With the survey we want to focus attention of relevant actors to the possibilities of the planned system, and the overall problem. In conventional educational environment the interpretation of several terms used can be different. The electronic survey has the advantage that context sensitive help, explanation, definition or sample can be added to items.

Besides the survey, the portal gives background information of relevant international efforts, initiatives and specific issues on the legal aspects of copyright protection.

5. CONCLUSION AND FURTHER WORK

It was demonstrated that introducing a modified architecture and a new layer an open, flexible, easy to use document management system can be built that incorporates several modules to establish the technological background of safe document handling, enhancing trust in users.

One of the main purposes was to keep the structure as clear and as open as possible, to present the possibilities, limitations, advantages and disadvantages of each block. The document management engine can be implemented without the significant modification of existing applications, however can enhance their capabilities by new functionalities and tools for standardized interoperability.

The test system is implemented on an open Linux platform using modules written in PHP and C. It is planned in the near future to build a stand-alone version on Windows platform especially for demonstration. Further investigations have to be made on the interoperability of systems using the document management engine (DME) developed and among other independent system using the implemented open interfaces as OAI.

The project is supported by the Hungarian Ministry of Informatics and Telecommunication. It has close relations and co-operations with other projects researching the accessibility of the deep web,[16] concepts and design of the National Digital Archive, Hungary[17] and a project for natural language processing.[18]

The pilot system is planned to be fully operable at spring, 2004, and offered free for test for a number of higher educational institutes, so the dissertations prepared at the end of the next academic year can serve as an excellent test database.

REFERENCES

1. T. Berners-Lee et al., Uniform Resource Identifiers (URI): Generic Syntax, The internet Society, 1998, http://www.ietf.org/rfc/rfc2396.txt
2. K. Shafer, S. Weibel, E.Jul, and J.Fausey, Introduction to Persistent Resource Locators, http://purl.oclc.org/docs/inet96.html
3. J. Brassil, S. Low, N. Maxemchuk, and L. O'Gorman, Document marking and identification using both line and word shifting. Technical report, AT&T Bell Labratories, 1994.
4. N. Shivakumar and H. Garcia-Molina, Building a Scalable and Accurate Copy Detection Mechanism.
5. K. Monostori, A. Zaslavsky, and H. Schmidt, MatchDetectReveal: Finding Overlapping and Similar Digital Documents, Information Resources Management Association International Conference (IRMA2000), 21–24 May, 2000 at Anchorage Hilton Hotel, Anchorage, Alaska, USA.
6. http://www.plagarism.org
7. http://www.turnitin.com
8. Robert M. Losee, Term Dependence: A Basis for Luhn and Zipf Models, in: *Press Journal of the American Society for Information Science and Technology*, 2001.
9. N. Shivakumar and H. Garcia-Molina, The SCAM Approach to Copy Detection in Digital Libraries, D-Lib Program, http://www.dlib.org/dlib
10. The Dublin Core Metadata Element Set, NISO Press, 2000, http://www.dublincore.org
11. G. Magyar and G. Knapp, The Impact of Technological Paradigm Shift on Information System Design, ISD 2002, Rigue.
12. Tim Berners-Lee, James Hendler and Ora Lassila, The Semantic Web, *Scientific American*, 2001.
13. http://www.daml.org
14. G. Magyar et al., SQL Tranparency, Tecnhical report, 2003 (to be published)
15. C. Lagoze et al., The Open Archives Initiative Protocol for Metadata Harvesting, June 2002, http://www.openarchives.org/OAI/openarchivesprotocol.html
16. "In the web of words", Hungarian national project 2002–2005, http://szavak.ik.bme.hu
17. "Feasibility study of the Hungarian National Digital Archive", 2003
18. "Open source Hungarian morphology analyzer", 2003–2004, http://www.szoszablya.hu

KNOWLEDGE REUSE IN PROJECT MANAGEMENT

Jillian Owen, Frada Burstein, and William P. Hall[1]

ABSTRACT

This paper discusses the initial stages of a research in progress addressing knowledge reuse issues in a project management environment and explores how project management companies manage project knowledge. The project tests the statement that the effective transfer of tacit, implicit and explicit knowledge plays a critical role in a project management environment.

The paper presents concepts drawn from the literature covering ways that knowledge is captured and reused in project management context.

We propose a model for knowledge reuse in a project management environment where knowledge is assimilated at the tactical level and flows to the strategic level. This model derives from two prior models: the OODA loop – Observe, Orient, Decide, Act, which focuses on strategic requirements and the Plan Do Study Act (PDSA) cycle, which focuses on the operational or tactical level of projects. Both the OODA Loop and the PDSA Cycle are adaptive learning and decision-making cycles where changes or actions are produced via iterated cycling through that loop.

The initial aim is to use these models as a starting point for analysing and describing how the organization currently captures, manages and reuses knowledge in a project management environment.

1. INTRODUCTION

This paper discusses the initial stages of a research study covering knowledge reuse in a project management environment. The research explores how project management companies manage project knowledge. It is argued that the effective transfer of tacit, implicit and explicit knowledge plays a critical role in a project management

1 Jillian Owen and Frada Burstein School of Information Management and Systems (SIMS), Monash University. William P. Hall, Documentation Systems Analyst, Tenix Defence, Williamstown, Vic. Australia ; Honorary Research Fellow, School of Information Management & Systems, Monash University Caulfield, Vic. Australia

environment. This paper reviews concepts drawn from the literature covering ways that knowledge is captured and reused in project management.

Knowledge is information that has been processed, structured and assimilated for easy understanding and use, to support business objectives or processes.

The initial research will analyse and describe how the organization currently captures, manages and reuses knowledge in a project management environment.

The research questions derived from the literature review and the theoretical model are: "*How do staff in a project management organization primarily convert and reuse knowledge within and between projects?*

Is knowledge converted and reused via social networks (such as communities of practice), technology, or a combination of both?"

2. CONTEXT

To succeed competitively, organizations need to gain knowledge of both the internal and external worlds to achieve their business strategies and goals. An effective knowledge management strategy will help an organization achieve these ends. A knowledge management strategy is a policy developed by the organization for improving the way it develops, stores and uses its corporate knowledge. Both tacit and explicit knowledge are important in the creation and reuse of knowledge at a corporate level. Organizational memory forms the basis of intellectual capital that is held in an organization. Intellectual capital is the knowledge and capability to develop that knowledge in an organization. (Nahapiet and Ghoshal, 1998). Snowden (2002) argues that context is important in knowledge transfer because at one level people exchange knowledge personally based on trust and experience, while at the other level knowledge is coded for an unknown audience whose specific experience is unknown. Snowden (2002) also states knowledge should be managed as a thing and a flow.

Organizational memory comprises the sum of participating individuals knowledge. Once this body of knowledge is created new people can use it and it survives people leaving the organization (Walsh and Ungson, 1991). Nelson and Winter (1982) argued that the sum of an organization's knowledge exceeds the sum of the individuals. They concentrated on the tacit routinization of knowledge and the shaping of other kinds of knowledge at the organizational level. Hall (2003) also argues that organizational memory is much more than the sum of the parts.

Project management organizations are a natural arena for knowledge management as project management staff continually interact with and build on both explicit and tacit knowledge as they move between different projects and phases of the one project. Project Management Institute in the Project Management Body of Knowledge (PMBOK) (2000) defines a project as:

> … a project is a temporary endeavour undertaken to create a unique product or service. Temporary means that every project has a definite beginning and a definite end. Unique means that the product or services is different in some distinguishing way from all other products or services [p.4].

There are different kinds of project management companies: those that focus primarily on short term projects i.e., those where the duration of the project is short compared to the average residence time of an individual in the organisation, versus those that take large, long-lived and complex projects, where many staff will not stay with the organization through a full project cycle. The case study results reported in this paper are from short term projects within a particular project management organization.

As project employees either move onto another project within that organization, or leave an organization after a project has been completed, there is a need for the organisation to assimilate, preserve and manage what they have learned as knowledge.

Developing effective knowledge management strategies is important for project management organizations. Key business objectives for project management companies include:

- Winning more business
- Improving the return on projects won and undertaken
- Better managing and mitigating risks.

If an effective knowledge management strategy is not developed and managed by an organization valuable intellectual capital can be lost, causing rework and lost opportunities. Better identification, transfer and management of knowledge allows intellectual capital to be effectively retained within the organization, allowing it to be reused on other projects, reducing the time staff spend recreating what has already been learned.

Project Management Institute (2000) states that the project lifecycle serves to define the start and finish of a project and in general covers (although this will vary with the type of project):

- Project initiation
- Detailed Design
- Implementation
- Project closeout or Post Implementation review

Knowledge that is created in one phase of a project can be transferred and reused on the next phase of a project (Kotnour, 1999).

3. PROJECT MANAGEMENT KNOWLEDGE REUSE AND TRANSFER

For a project management organisation to be competitive, project managers need to retain and build knowledge and improve project performance (Cooper et al., 2000).

In a project management organisation learning is important as it helps project managers deliver not just one but a succession of successful projects, and to develop the right sorts of capabilities i.e. the project management process, the product development process and the knowledge management process (Kotnour, 1999). Learning within and between projects is required for this. Knowledge needs to be developed within a project, where it is used and tested, before it can be transferred to other projects

Kotnour (2000) (citing Bohn 1994; Fiol and Lyles 1985) defines the process of converting learning to knowledge as: "… learning is the process by which knowledge is created from experience and the path by which improvement takes place" [p.393]. Learning within a project provides an ongoing store of data, information and knowledge (Kotnour, 2000). Knowledge can also be transferred between projects (Kotnour, 2000).

Explicit, implicit and tacit knowledge help to ensure project success. Tacit and implicit (knowledge that is in a person's head that could be coded and stored in databases or documents Nickols, 2000) knowledge held within the corporate structure and contexts (e.g., as described by Nelson and Winter, 1982) and from individuals and explicit knowledge together provide a complete picture of the project. Sharing of knowledge among multiple individuals with different backgrounds is a critical step in project knowledge creation. Tacit knowledge based on previous experiences in a similar context is important to project success, as is the transfer of explicit knowledge (Koskinen, 2000). Knowledge can be captured and transferred tacitly within the organization via social networks, or capture and codify implicit knowledge.

Knowledge that is gained in a project needs to be transferred to an organization's memory for reuse on other projects; the challenge is to capture and index this knowledge for retrieval while it is available, as project teams are temporary (Damm and Schindler, 2002).

4. PROJECT COMPLETION

Project completion is an important phase of the project lifecycle in capturing knowledge and preparing it for transfer to other projects. Post implementation reviews/lessons learned can either occur via the project team members or an independent reviewer. Lessons learned provides a full description of the project with examples that can be used on other projects. In some instances lessons learnt only focus on the success of the project (Disterer, 2002). There is a need to focus on both the good and bad lessons to ensure that successes are identified and publicised and mistakes not repeated. At NASA, to ensure that lessons learned get to the right people, they are "pushed" out to people who have similar profiles and can benefit from the lessons (Liebowitz, 2002). The challenge is to ensure that knowledge is captured without taking project team members away from their day to day tasks.

Kotnour (1999) found that it was useful to review lessons learned at various phases during a project, however this does not always have to be in a form of a formal lessons learned document. Organizational intraproject learning is most likely to occur informally in project discussions or to be recorded in project documentation (such as project meeting minutes, project status reviews, plan versus actual comparison) rather than in formal project reviews. Interproject is most likely to occur in formal situations.

For lessons learned to be effective (both positive and negative) they need to be indexed or searchable for easy retrieval of knowledge for future projects or project phases.

The reason for knowledge reuse failures can be that knowledge capturing processes are too informal, are not incorporated into the organization's processes, or are not supported by the structure of the organization (Komi-Sirvio et al., 2002)

5. KNOWLEDGE REUSE MODELS

In this section a model is proposed in which knowledge is transferred, reused and built on in a project management environment.

5.1. Unit of Analysis

Knowledge management systems within an organisation can typically comprise three different views of knowledge: knowledge as objects, personal knowledge and knowledge embedded in communities of practise. The main challenge for knowledge management systems or knowledge architecture is to find an appropriate unit of analysis (Hasan, 2002). In this case unit of analysis can be defined as the major entity that is being analysed (Trochim, 2002). Hasan (2002) also argues that activity (an overview of what people do) is an appropriate unit of analysis for knowledge management as:

There is difficulty in identifying or documenting a person's formal job description versus what they actually do in reality, as they may perform additional tasks or the job description is out of date. The activity analysis focuses on what people do as opposed to what is in their job description

There is a need to adopt an approach that takes into account the changing business environment

- It supports the different views of knowledge outlined above
- It recognises the importance of the culture and history of an organisation in knowledge creation or learning

Activity as a unit of analysis also takes into account the relationship between people and objects. Two cycles that utilise activity as a unit of analysis are the Observe, Orient, Decide, Act – (OODA) Loop and the Plan-Do-Study-Act (PDSA) Cycle. We follow Nelson and Winter (1982) and von Krogh and Roos (1995) in believing that most large organizations can be considered to be "living" entities (i.e., they are autopoietic). Beyond this, we argue (Hall, 2003) that they possess forms of heredity comprised of objectively persistent forms of knowledge. Autopoiesis implies that they have cognition, memory, and knowledge that transcend the collective cognitive processes of their individual members. It follows from this that they are capable of evolution as this knowledge changes through organizational learning (i.e., adaptive) processes

5.2. Models

In this section we propose a model for how knowledge that is gained from one project can be linked and reused in future projects. The model needs to be flexible enough to change as new knowledge is created and stored. Knowledge that is already captured can be built on/amended from knowledge gained from earlier projects. Project Management Institute (2000) highlights that a project typically delivers a defined piece of work following an organization's strategic plan. Two models are discussed and linked: the OODA loop, which is linked to the strategic level of an organisation and the PDSA cycle, which is linked to projects at an operational level.

5.3. The OODA Loop

The OODA Loop (refer Figure 1) is a learning and decision making cycle where a change or action is produced based on cycling through that loop. The OODA Loop, originally developed in a military framework, can also be applied to the business environment (Hammond, 2002).

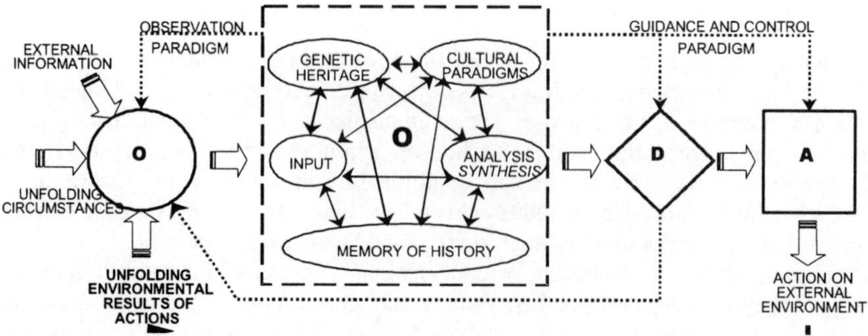

Figure 1. The OODA Loop. John Boyd's OODA Loop Concept, based on Boyd (1996) and cited in Hall (2003)

The OODA Loop comprises 4 steps:

- Observe - the current environment and competitors are observed, data is collected and information is compiled. Information is fed in from outside information, the environment and feedback from previous OODA Loops
- Orient - orientation to the situation occurs based on the culture, previous experience and new information of that business. Analysis and interpretation of the information creates new knowledge, builds on existing knowledge, and allows knowledge to be reused.
- Decide - a course of action is decided upon derived over other options or hypotheses. The information gained at the observe and orient steps allow hypotheses to be developed.
- Act - the decision is acted upon, and unfolding results of the action on the environment and competitors are fed back into orientation for the next OODA Loop (Wilson 1997; Edison, 2002; Thompson, 1995; Hall, 2003).

From a business viewpoint the decisive goal is to operate within the competitor's OODA Loop; that is, for you to be better aware of what they are going to do and operating faster than they can do with their observations of you. A business will gain a competitive advantage or win if they move through the OODA Loop faster than its competitors. This allows a business to find its competitors strengths and weaknesses and to potentially choose an unexpected course of action. This ultimately causes confusion amongst competitors and can bring about their collapse (Edison, 2002). By operating in the OODA Loop information is transformed or processed into knowledge and knowledge is created and reused, saving rework on projects and contributing to a project management's business objectives.

5.4. The Development of the PDSO Cycle

The perception of the PDSA cycle originated from Walter A. Shewhart and has been used by Deming as a process analysis and improvement approach and is also known as the Deming Cycle (Deming, 1992). Kotnour's (2000) version of the plan-do-study-act (PDSA) cycle is used to characterise knowledge creation and learning in a project management environment. The PDSA model explains how knowledge that is gained from one project can be saved and transferred to be reused in future projects. The PDSA cycle is based on the premise that for an organisation to continually improve or learn they need to plan for it, implement the plan, analyse or study the results and act on the analysis (Matthews, 2000). The plan step is where the project team scopes the project and develops a project plan for the project, reusing knowledge gained from earlier projects. The "do" step is where the project team implements the previously defined plan. Results are produced and measured against the project and used to understand and progress the project. In the "study" step the project team reflects and assesses what has occurred in the project (both positive and negative) and produce a lessons learned report. The "act" step is the next step where the cycle is completed and knowledge gained from one project can be input into future projects. A decision to modify or abandon the knowledge is made continuing the ongoing cycle of knowledge production (Kotnour, 2000). This follows the concept that in order for improvement to occur a project manager needs to plan the project, implement the project, produce a lessons learned report and take action for further improvement (Matthews, 2000)

Kotnour's argument suggests that at the Act Step an activity is occurring where knowledge gained from one project can be input into future projects. However in this instance an activity is not occurring rather an orientation to the situation is occurring, similar to the "orient" step of the OODA Loop where knowledge is assimilated based on the changing environment. Following this logic it is suggested that in this instance the PDSA Cycle be renamed so that it becomes the PDSO (plan, do, study, orient) cycle.

The PDSO cycle can be linked to the project management body of methodology defined in the Project Management Institutes' Project Management Body of Knowledge (Kotnour, 1999).

Having a system in place for project knowledge is not sufficient. Business processes, the culture of the organization, the organizational structure and the level and type of technology need to support it. Based on the PDSA cycle (Kotnour, 1999) a model that takes both the PDSO cycle, and the organizational environment (business processes, culture, organizational structure, and technology) is proposed (refer Figure 2).

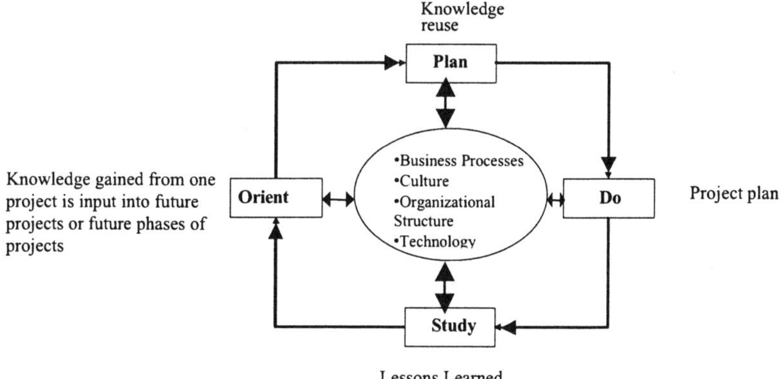

Figure 2. Project Management Knowledge Reuse Model based on Deming (1992) and Kotnour (1999)

The PDSO model provides a structure for knowledge from past projects to be reused, and for knowledge in a current project to be stored and reused in future projects. The model repeats itself continuously allowing for the process to be improved.

The question that needs to be answered is is the model flexible enough to alter during a project, is the cycle flexible enough to allow the knowledge to be stored and reused as required on other projects.

5.5. Comparison of the OODA loop and the PDSO cycle

There are a number of similarities between the PDSA cycle and the OODA loop; both ideas attempt to describe what is happening in the real world—the descriptions are interpretations of the process. Each is based upon continuous improvement and learning reusing knowledge, building on existing knowledge and creating new knowledge. The cycles are a constant loop of innovations and/or improvements

A project management organization's business objectives are to win more business, improve return on projects and to avoid liability and risks i.e. to maintain a competitive advantage. Strategies help an organization achieve their business objectives. The OODA Loop is a process for developing and executing organizational strategies. Projects are often used to deliver an organization's strategies (Project Management Institute, 2000). At a project level the objectives are to continually build on project management capabilities and to successfully deliver projects (Kotnour, 1999). At a tactical or project level the PDSO cycle is a process for planning and implementing projects. While the two models are iterative feedback loops given that projects are used to deliver a specific product or service and have a definite start and end (Project Management Institute, 2000) a model that describes this process and links to an organizational model has been proposed.

When a project is initiated knowledge flows from the Act step of the OODA Loop to the Plan Step of the PDSO Cycle. Project knowledge (relating to a specific project where a Project Manager or project team member may carry specific knowledge) may flow from the Orient Step of the PDSO Cycle to the Plan Step of the PDSO Cycle (refer Figure 3). Once a project (or a particular phase of a project) is completed knowledge flows from the Orient step of the PDSO cycle to the Observe step of the OODA Loop, and as highlighted previously potentially to the Plan Step of the PDSO Cycle.

The linked OODA Loop and PDSO Cycle provide a theoretical framework for analysing what organizations are doing now and what they could be doing better to achieve results. The model is a way of representing some of the things that an organization needs to do. As both cycles are both based on continuous improvement building on data and knowledge assimilated from the external and internal environments, in a project management environment they can both be used to learn and assess/reuse knowledge and the faster that the cycle occurs the greater competitive advantage improving the return on projects won and undertaken, and reducing liability and other risks.

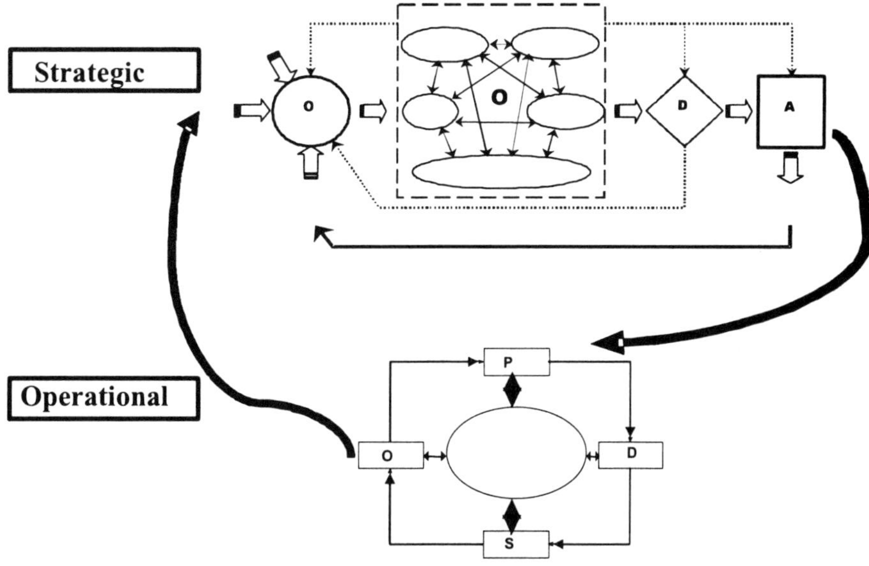

Figure 3. The OODA Loop & The PDSO Cycle Linked

6. METHODOLOGY

To test this broad theoretical framework comprehensively within an organization an exploratory case study methodology will be used as it allows an insight to be gained into a particular issue. Case studies allow a theoretical model to confront reality and to ascertain how the model works in the real world. Data is analysed to look at emerging patterns to the research question. Utilising a number of different methods (content analysis, interviews) will allow patterns to emerge or to view the phenomena in different ways (Stake, 2000).

In this case study various analytical techniques will be used:

- Content or documentation analysis
- Interviews (structured and unstructured).

Content analysis is highly relevant to case study research when appropriate documents (either paperbased or existing in an electronic format) exist. Content analysis will be used in this case study to ascertain what explicit knowledge is available to the project. Relevant documentation will be studied, assessed, and analysed during the case study research. It is envisaged that procedural documentation will be analysed, along with reports, project bulletins, project plans, project documentation, notes, memos and project methodology.

Interviews are an essential component of case study research. Interviews will help to determine where tacit and implicit forms of knowledge exist and are used in the project framework. It is envisaged that interviews will uncover tacit knowledge that the organization is unaware of. An interview can be unstructured where the participant can provide information as well as their own opinion.

7. PRELIMINARY RESEARCH RESULTS

Preliminary results have been obtained from initial research conducted in an engineering, project management organization. Two phases of a project (planning to implementation and closure) have been studied for the purposes of this research. They have been treated as two separate projects by the company with different deliverables and have been analysed as such. Document analysis has been completed and the indepth interviews have commenced, therefore the findings discussed in this section are preliminary findings only.

Preliminary findings;

- Projects are used to execute the organization's strategies. A strategy of the organization is to grow key customers by providing the customer's with additional value. The projects analysed did indeed support the company strategy by executing a customer value proposition (i.e. improved product, price or service etc).
- Knowledge reuse occurs at both the tacit and explicit level of the Plan and Do phases of the PDSO cycle. At the Plan phase of the cycle knowledge is reused from earlier projects. This was observed between the two projects, where knowledge gained from one project was reused or adapted in the next project specifically project documentation, deliverables or lessons learnt (both formal and informal). At the Do phase of the cycle knowledge from previous projects is reused both at the tacit and explicit level. At the Study phase formal lessons learned were only used by the Project Manager, however informal lesson learned occurred during a phase of a project and at the end of a project. Cycling occurs between the Plan, Do and Study phases during each phase, and at the end of a project supporting intra and inter project learning.
- While both tacit and explicit knowledge is used there is a reliance on tacit knowledge via personal knowledge or networks (both formal and informal). The project team manager and senior project team members initially relied on personal knowledge and then their informal networks. Formal networks were only tapped if the relevant knowledge could not be obtained from the other sources, in particular a formal network supported by email. In most cases as well as utilising tacit knowledge people sought out explicit knowledge i.e. People interviewed said it was quicker to ask the person who knew where the relevant documentation was rather than searching for it.
- Explicit, implicit and tacit knowledge are available however in projects studied there is a reliance on tacit knowledge to obtain relevant knowledge. There is much explicit knowledge available in hardcopy or electronically on a server sorted by project job number. However, explicit project knowledge is not held in a knowledge based system, therefore knowledge cannot be searched for at the contextual level.
- During or at the end of project phases or projects cycling does not occur to the Orient phase. All people interviewed agreed that there was no time to orient as

they need to automatically move onto the next project. A question for future research is does Orient occur only at the tacit level? If it only occurs at the tacit level is it implicit knowledge that can be captured and coded?

8. CONCLUSION

This research in progress paper proposes a theoretical model for knowledge reuse based on a review of relevant literature. The literature is mainly concerned with how knowledge is reused in project management environment.

Preliminary results from the fieldwork support the fact that in this particular instance knowledge is reused within and between projects, intra and interproject learning occurs. While explicit knowledge is available and used there is a reliance on tacit knowledge for knowledge transfer and reuse. Social capital plays a major role in knowledge transfer and reuse in project management. While cycling does occur within and between projects in the PDSO cycle the cycling tends to occur between the Plan, Do and Study phases, however cycling does not occur to the Orient phase.

ACKNOWLEDGEMENTS

This research is partly funded by Monash University, we are grateful for the support from the case study site.

The PDSA Cycle (Figure 2 and part Figure 3). Copyright 1982, 1986 by W. Edwards Deming. Reproduced with the permission of Cambridge University Press

The OODA Loop (Figure 1 and part Figure3). Based on an original graphic, John R. Boyd, "The Essence of Winning and Losing".

REFERENCES

Boyd, J. R., 1996, The essence of winning and losing, Retrieved May 5, 2003 from the World Wide Web: http://www.belisarius.com/modern_business_strategy/boyd/essence/eowl_frameset.htm

Cooper, K.G. and Lyneis, J.N., 2002, Learning to learn from past to future, *International Journal of Project Management*, 20 (3) 213–219.

Damm, D. and Schindler, M., 2002, Security issues of a knowledge medium for distributed project work, *International Journal of Project Management*, 20 (1), 37–47.

Deming, W. E., 1992, *Out of the crisis,* Press Syndicate of the University of Cambridge.

Disterer, G., 2002, Management of project knowledge and experiences, *Journal of Knowledge Management*, 6 (5), 512–520.

Edison, T., 2002, Rugby and the ooda loop, Retrieved on January 29, 2003 from the World Wide Web: http://www.belisarius.com/modern_business_strategy/edison/rugby_ooda_loop.htm

Hall, W. P., 2003, Organisational Autopoiesis and Knowledge Management, paper submitted for ISD Twelfth International Conference on Information Systems Development.

Hammond, K. H., 2002, The strategy of the fighter pilot. Fastcompany, June. Retrieved April 15, 2003 from the World Wide Web: http://www.fastcompany.com/online/59/pilot.htm

Hasan, H., 2001, A knowledge architecture using activity as the key unit of analysis, in: Proceedings of Australian Conference for Knowledge Management and Intelligent Decision Support, 184–199.

Komi-Sirvio, S., Mantyniemi, A. and Sepannen, V., 2002, Towards a practical solution for capturing knowledge for software projects, *IEEE Software*, 19 (3), 60–62.

Koskinen, K. U., 2000, Tacit knowledge as a promoter of project success, *European Journal of Purchasing & Supply Management*, 6 (1), 41–47.

Kotnour, T., 1999, A learning framework for project management, *Project Management Journal*, 30 (2), 32–38.

Kotnour, T., 2000, Organizational learning practices in the project management environment, *International Journal of Quality & Reliability Management*, 17 (4/5) 393–406.

Liebowitz, J., 2002, A look at NASA Goddard space flight center's knowledge management initiatives, *IEEE Software*, 19 (3), 40–42.

Matthews, M. M., 2000, *Knowledge-driven profit improvement: implementing assessment feedback using PDKAction theory*, Boca Raton, FL: St. Lucie Press.

Nahapiet, J., and Ghosal, S., 1998, Social capital, intellectual capital, and the organizational advantage, *Academy of Management. The Academy of Management Review,* 23 (2), 242–266.

Nelson, R. R. and Winter, S. G., 1982, *An Evolutionary Theory of Economic Change*, Belknap Press of Harvard University Press, Cambridge, Mass.

Nickols, F., 2000, The knowledge in knowledge management, in: *The Knowledge Management Yearbook 2001-2002*, J. W. Cortada and J.A. Woods, eds., Butterworth-Heinemann.

Project Management Institute, 2000, A guide to the project management body of knowledge, Project Management Institute.

Snowden, D., 2002, Complex acts of knowing: paradox and descriptive self awareness, *Journal of Knowledge Management*, 6 (2), 100–111.

Stake, R. E., 2000, Case Studies, in: *Handbook of qualitative research* (2nd ed.), N.K. Denzin and Y.S. Lincoln, eds., Sage Publications, pp. 435–454.

Thompson, F., 1993, The boyd cycle and business strategy, Proceedings of the Aomori-Atkinson Conference, Aomori Public College, Aomori, Japan. Retrieved October 17, 2002 from the World Wide Web: http://www.belisarius.com/modern_business_strategy/thompson/first_with_most.htm

Trochim, W. M. K., 2002, Research methods knowledge base. Retrieved May 5, 2003 from the World Wide Web: http://trochim.human.cornell.edu/kb/

Von Krogh, G. and Roos, J., 1995, *Organizational Epistemology*, MacMillan Press Ltd.

Walsh, J. P. and Ungson, J. R., 1991, Organizational memory, *Academy of Management Review*, 16 (1), 57–91.

Wilson. G. I., 1997, Business is war. Retrieved on January 29, 2003 from the World Wide Web: http://www.belsiarius.com/modern_business_strategy/wilson/boyd_symposium_1997

DEVELOPING KNOWLEDGE MANAGEMENT SYSTEMS IN BPM CONTEXT

Pin Chen*

ABSTRACT

Unlike Information System (IS) development, Knowledge Management Systems (KMS) development has much less support from methodologies that address specific features and requirements of KMS. This paper discusses a concept, called an information model, which is used to model information and knowledge environments where all processes are performed to produce and use various information and knowledge entities. Such a model is considered as a foundation for KMS to server as an enabler for Business Process Management (BPM) and a knowledge asset for an organisation. Though defining not only classes of entities and relations of information and knowledge but also separates definitions and management of data, information, and knowledge entities from individual descriptions of business processes, it combines knowledge management and BPM, and more importantly, changes the practice of KMS development towards a model-based practice similar to the IS development.

1. INTRODUCTION

In last two decades, information technologies, such as groupware and web-based techniques, have been main enablers and solutions for improvement of knowledge management in large organisations. Successful Knowledge Management Systems (KMS) development is however still a challenging task due to many failures caused by inadequate methodologies used. It is obvious that a sophisticated KMS development approach cannot be simply based on a file/document management solution even supported by modern technologies, such as HTML, XML and web. The key thesis is that enablers of KMS designed for "Knowledge Factory" engineering paradigm often unravel and become constraints in adapting and evolving such systems for business environments characterised by high uncertainty and radical discontinuous change (Malhotra, 2002). It is

* Dr Pin Chen, DSTO C3 Research Centre, Department of Defence, Fernhill Park, ACT 2600, Australia. Email: pin.chen@dsto.defence.gov.au.

believed that envisioning business models and understanding business requirements in KMS development is critical. In order to facilitate ongoing innovation of business and evolution of systems, business modelling and KMS development should be carried out jointly instead of treating them in isolation. An important feature for KM and its development methodologies is thus to develop KMS in a context of the Business Process Management (BPM).

Using the concept of data modelling, this paper studies an information model as an enabling component supporting both KMS and BPM. The information model differs from a conventional data model that supports mainly database-based system development and has a focus of data processing through various application transactions. The information model defines information and knowledge entities or products of the business in a manner like a data model rather than a style of a data dictionary or a document management style. The model enables management of information and knowledge entities in a well-defined knowledge-based context where there are not only class definitions of those entities but also definitions of inter-relations among them and relations or linkages to business processes.

2. KMS AND BPM

Unlike traditional IS development that deals mainly with structured data processing, KSM development traditionally addresses issues like knowledge classification and capturing, information and knowledge sharing and accessibility, collaborative environments and hyper-linkage between knowledge entities. This practice has resulted in that the solutions for KSM are mainly document management-based and difficult for integration with IS and future development. This is because some important aspects of knowledge management are not properly addressed, such as class definitions, attributes, relations, applications, traceability and quality of information and knowledge entities.

BPM is a challenging task related to both IS and KMS facing large organisations in particular in those critical and complicated business areas, such as defence strategic planning and capability development, where business processes and activities deal with complicated data, information and knowledge. The high-level complexity of BPM in these areas is also the result of development and use of various information technology-based tools and environments to support the processes and activities. BPM has become an important part of modern organisation management. In particular it is a key to success of future organisation development, including its information systems development and evolution. Organisation's BPM initiative can ensure its readiness for and success in business design, redesign and re-engineering initiatives like BPR, EAI, CRM and ERP.

BPM defines, manages, monitors, executes and integrates business processes. It uses a comprehensive analytical framework and automated process management tools, streamlining and aligning business processes with their business and system partners. BPM is gradually becoming a critical component of modern information systems development methodologies in particular when the methodologies are used to help develop enterprise-wide systems that need to process various types of information and knowledge artefacts across business areas. BPM presents more sophisticated concepts, methods and techniques to handle business process related concepts and issues than traditional IS development methods such as requirement analysis and system analysis that produce mainly systems design and development products (e.g. requirement specifications and system design documents).

Process modelling methods (e.g. PetriNet, IDEF standards and IPO) and techniques (UML and BPML) are considered as main enablers supporting BPM. BPML is a mate-language for modelling of business processes. It provides an abstracted execution model for collaborative & transactional processes based on a concept of a transactional finite-state machine. While the main purpose of these methods is to model the process, they also to a certain extend capture some aspects of data and information. In particular, IDEF family has three modelling methods related to data and information in a conventional fashion of data modelling, namely, Information Modelling (IDEF 1), Data Modelling (IDEF1X) and Information Artefact Modelling (IDEF10). Figure 1 shows basic components of IPO method. Among the techniques mentioned, what is missing is a method to globally manage information and knowledge entities and resources and an operatable knowledge environment.

It is obvious that KMS development and BPM initiative are related and can be beneficial each other. The realty of practice, however, shows that they are often carried out separately with limited interactions. In order to improve the situation, there is a need to develop adequate concepts and methods to combine these two related activities.

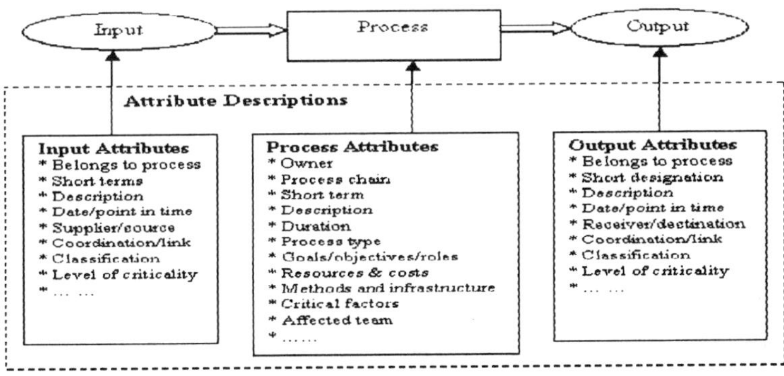

Figure 1. Basic components of IPO method

3. WHAT IS AN INFORMATION MODEL (IM)?

One of the important features of traditional information system development, such as banking systems and library systems, is database-centric. KMS development differs from IS development. A layer structure shown in Figure 2 describes relations between transactions, business processes and decision-making in relations to data, information, and knowledge to wisdom. Unlike traditional transaction-based systems that deal with only data, business processes handle not only data but also more importantly information and knowledge as well. Such a difference implies that a process is carried out in an information/knowledge environment that includes at least three main classes, that is, data, information and knowledge. Business process management, therefore, requires different resolutions for managing data, information and knowledge as a whole. They must address the requirements that cannot be handled by a conventional data model concept that deals with mainly structured data.

An information model is to define an information/knowledge environment for a selected business area where there exist a number of processes in a manner of a data model, which describes all entities of data, information and knowledge and relations among them. This differs from the data aspect description of individual process models, that is, inputs or outputs of a process. It is critical to realise that such a description of the information/knowledge environment is an important part of business process management. Many process modelling methods and techniques (e.g. Petri Net, IDEF standards and UML), however, handle process-related data and information as inputs and outputs of a process. In other words, they consider data/information as part of a process/activity and handle them in individual process/activity models. It mistakenly implies that the existence of data/information as inputs or outputs is because of the existence and requirements of a process. It has been a missing concept in many KMS developments. Developing a KMS without a proper IM just likes developing an IS without using a database.

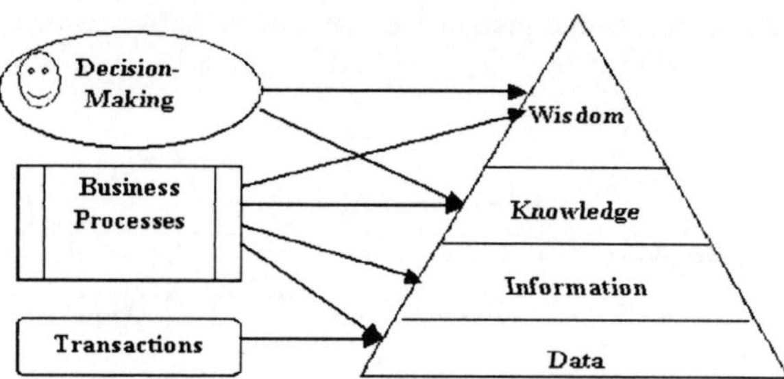

Figure 2. Difference between transaction processes and business processes

Considering the role of the data model and database systems in information system development, we believe that introducing IM can lead to an important improvement of both BPM and KMS since it separates the definition and management of data/information/knowledge entities from individual processes and creates an architecture viewpoint of the information/knowledge environment for all business areas concerned by a BPM initiative. It is expected that a well-developed IM can enhance BPM and other initiatives at least in the following aspects:

- IM can help establish a commonly shared information model that can be viewed as an agreement among all stakeholders on their interests and responsibilities in relations to various data/information/knowledge entities concerned by BPM;
- IM defines data, information and knowledge entities produced and used in processes and relations among them;
- IM can fill the gap between the conventional data-processing information system development and the knowledge management system that focuses mainly on web-based document and information management;
- IM can support business process redesign and BPR;

- IM can provide a basis for an integrated solution of data/information/knowledge management; and
- IM can bridge BPM with other IS development initiatives such EAI, CRM, ERP, enterprise architecture strategies and knowledge management.

IM is a specific "data model" but differs from a conventional data model because of the following features:

- IM supports BPM rather than a transaction-based information system;
- IM covers a broader area than what a conventional data model describes since it includes all aspects of data, information and knowledge of a business area;
- A conventional data model can be part of IM;
- IM defines not only structured data but also non-structured information and knowledge entities;
- In addition to entity definitions, IM also describes context attributes of each entity, including ownership, users, status, ways of access, processes of production and use and relations to other entities;
- IM deals with multiple types and formats of data, information and knowledge;
- Data, information and knowledge entities defined in IM can be generated and managed in different systems or tool environments; and
- IM is a conceptual model that defines entities and relations and requires technical and management solutions for effective production, use and management.

In summary, IM is seen as a concept based on the conventional data model concept with the aim to improve KMS development methods and support BPM as a whole rather than a single system development task. An IM-based KMS differs from a file-based one (e.g. groupware, html or web-based) since it should be more capable in systematically managing the whole information/knowledge environment through effectively handling classifications, relations, business rules and complexity, If the BPM is an enterprise wide initiative, the IM development can lead directly to an enterprise information architecture that is one of key elements of the enterprise architecture and of which the enterprise data model is part. The IM concept reflects not only a need but also possibility to develop a KMS in the context of BPM.

4. INFORMATION MODEL DEVELOPMENT

IM development is to conceptualise the overall schematic of the information environment of the BPM domain. A quality design of IM can reflect the domain information policy that defines the scope, entities and complexity of the information environment rather than ad hoc reporting needs.

Because of the difference between a data model and an information model, IM development requires more strategic thinking on the construction and structure issues and its applications since the model covers broad areas, process environments and systems and handles information complexity at different levels of granularity. Two different approaches to IM development are presented in this section.

4.1 ER Model-based development

Architecture is becoming a critical concept in future development of defence organisations (AWG, 2001) (Chen, 2000). Business processes and development activities involving various issues of architecture are across the whole life cycle of defence capability systems. Architecture practice is now one of most complicated business areas of defence organisations since it involves not only systems development activities and engineering processes but also many relevant business processes, including enterprise architecture initiatives, acquisition reform, strategic planning, capability analysis and planning and information systems configuration and management. Those processes and activities produce, manage and use a variety of architecture products in an extremely complicated data, information and knowledge environment. Complex relations and dependency among these processes and activities are caused by architectural inter-relationship and dependency among various architecture products associated with their correspondent systems in a continuously evolving Systems-of-Systems context.

The architecture practice is a community practice in large organisations that involves many stakeholders who have different interests and responsibilities in organisation business and systems and their future development. Because of its high complexity, a key to the architecture practice success is high-level and effective knowledge management and a well-designed and developed KMS that can effectively interface with various architecture tools. The organisational knowledge related to the architecture practice includes:

- Architecture related processes (production, use and management);
- Systems and their requirements;
- Relations between systems;
- Architecture data resources;
- Relations between architectures.

An architecting process performed by an architect usually requires various architecture information and knowledge, and enablers to generate an architecture solution for a specific system design or evolution.

US DoD realised that various architecture related activities and processes are usually supported by different architecture tools that use their own and different data models to manage a diversity of information resources of architecture data. That made it difficult for architects and systems developers to exchange information and ensure joint interoperability. This kind of architecture development practice became no longer acceptable. Prior to the introduction of the US DoD C4ISR Architecture Framework Version 1.0 in 1998 (recently evolved into US DoD Architecture Framework Version 2.1 in 2000), the C4ISR Core Architecture Data Model (CADM) was designed to provide a common approach for organising and portraying the structure of architecture information. The CADM is a logical information model rather than a physical data model as shown in Figure 3.

The CADM is defined on a basis of 25 entities that, together with their subtypes, other related entities, and their attributes, cover most aspects of the data, information, and knowledge in relation to the applications of the architecture framework and other architecture related initiatives.

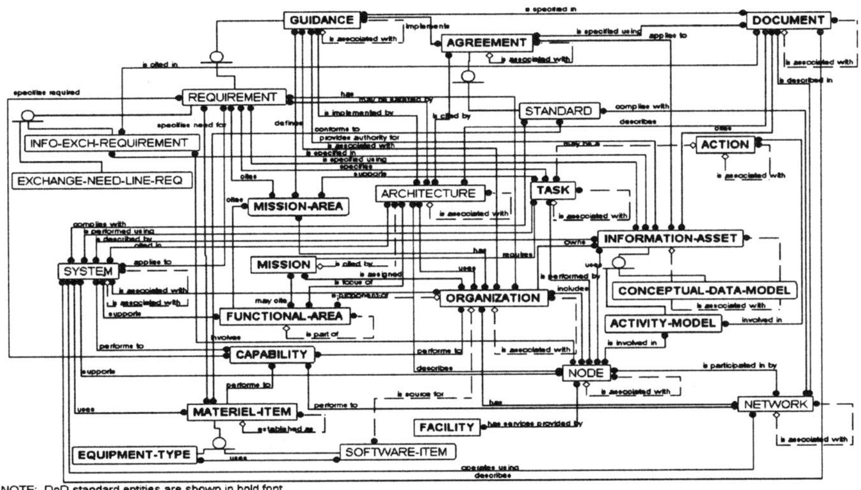

Figure 4. US DoD Core Architecture Data Model (CADM)

CADM development (AWG, 1997) included decomposition of many high-level, composite data structures found in existing architecture databases and data models in order to isolate single-concept entities and attributes. Development also included use, wherever possible, of approved data structures of the DoD Data Model and approved definitions in the DoD Data Dictionary System (DDDS). Some concepts embedded in the architecture data requirements led to new data structures (e.g., for architecture, node, network, and system). The CADM is seen as an information model that can support BPM of the architecture practice of US DoD. Though US DoD didn't have an official initiative of BPM for its architecture practice, the CADM does help various agencies in defining and developing their own architecture related processes, such as the Architecture Development Process Model (ADPM) developed by the Department of the Navy, US DoD.

4.2 Object-oriented model-based IM development

Similar to US DoD, the Australian Defence Organisation (ADO) is also facing a high-level complexity in its architecture practice (Chen, 2000). The Defence Capability Systems Life Cycle Management, including strategic planning, capability development, acquisition and in-services, needs to plan, manage and develop all its capability systems as a whole. In an effort to help the ADO rationalise its architecture practice and effectively integrate it with the business processes involved throughout the defence capability systems life cycle management that is considered here as the business context requiring BPM, a Capability Architecture Information Model is being investigated. The model is designed using a top-down approach starting at the top level that consists of three sub-models: Capability/ Systems model, Architecture model and Scenario model, as shown in Figure 4. These three main concepts are commonly interested by all business areas of the life cycle management. Traditionally, the production, management and use of individual data entities, information or knowledge resources are modelled in process models of individual processes and activities. Through this top-level information model, we explore first the semantic relations among these three concepts and their sup-classes, separate them from individual processes and activities and define them as the common properties or knowledge assets belonging to the whole life cycle management.

Full development of such an information model is not an easy undertaking since it requires a clear understanding of the ADO architecture practice and the capability systems life cycle management, specifically in details about various architecture products and information/knowledge resources and processes and activities related to the products and resources. Although this model has a similar purpose as the CADM, it does have its special requirements from the features of the ADO architecture practice and the life cycle management, in particular with a vision to support BPM. To fully and flexibly explore and define information and knowledge entities and more importantly their relations, an object-oriented model-based approach is used. Through such a model-based approach, we can systematically define information entities in an Object-Oriented fashion: *Classes, Attributes /Relations* and *Methods/Rules*

The initial effort made in CAIM development has defined more than 100 classes of business concepts and information/knowledge entities and over 300 relations associated. We expect the benefits from such a model include:

- Clarifying information/knowledge entities;
- Exploring relations among the entities across areas and tools;
- Coordinating evolutions and improvement of tools or systems; Providing mechanisms and solutions for multi-medium information management (such as tables, graphics, images, video);
- Establishing an environment for advanced use of information.
- Traceability in all aspects of Strategic Planning and Capability Planning
    a. From Strategic Scenarios, Operation Scenarios, capabilities, systems to architectures, and their components;
    b. From configuration, interoperability, scheduling to systems interfaces.
- Visualisation of dependency and relations among scenarios, capabilities, systems and architectures, and interoperability levels;

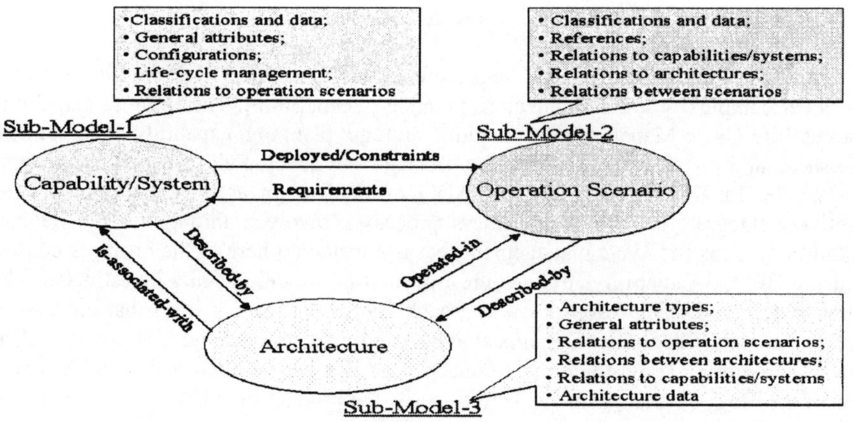

Figure 4. A top-level view of a Capability Architecture Information Model (CAIM)

Different business processes can view the information/knowledge environment described by CAIM from different perspectives. Strategic planning processes look it through the operation scenario sub-model since their responsibility is to define, examine, approve and manage all operation scenarios including both the approved and the newly planned or proposed. Capability development processes (before acquisition) deal with CAIM mainly from the capability/system sub-model to decide what new capabilities should be acquired and how they will jointly operate with others in those scenarios. Acquisition processes use the architecture sub-model as a window to view such an information/knowledge environment. All these areas can have information and knowledge traceability to other areas related.

CAIM initiative generated first a UML-based version of the model, then uses it as a "data model" for developing a CAIM-based architecture data repository that differs from a traditional document-based repository since it uses an object-oriented IM rather than a simple folder structure. It captures more semantics that can help analyse and visualize dependency or establish traceability. In additional to the knowledge and information described in various architecture and document entities, the organisational knowledge captured in CAIM, such as relations between scenarios, capabilities, systems and architectures, provides another critical component of KMS which in past cannot be fully explored in other manners and shared by people.

4.3. Deriving IM from traditional process modelling

Many process modelling methods and techniques, as mentioned earlier, capture certain aspects of data, information and knowledge entities and define them as attributes of the processes or in a conventional data model or a data dictionary. Established process model descriptions provide a basis for deriving IM such that data, information and knowledge entities can be separated from the process descriptions. The approach to derive an IM from the established process descriptions can follow the following steps:

1) Creating lists of data, information and knowledge entities according to data, information and knowledge aspects described in the process descriptions;
2) Based on the lists and obvious relations among those entities, creating ER-model-like data or information models;
3) Merging or decomposing those models to further establish links and relations among entities modelled;
4) Checking if all entities listed have been processed to make sure the IM to be derived can be a complete model for the BPM initiative;
5) Refining and renaming entities defined in those models in order to correct mistakes, improve contents and structures of models and sub-models, and remove inconsistency, redundancy and conflicts in name definitions and attributes specifications;
6) Repeating 2) to 5) whenever it is necessary until a satisfied IM is reached.

A satisfied IM should have the following features:

- All entities of data, information and knowledge described in the process models are defined in the model unless they are purely private to the belonging process;
- All necessary merging and decompositions of models have be considered and done properly;

- All attributes of the entities are defined properly in order to present the context of each entity and to establish links and relations from it to other entities;
- All useful relations and links found among entities are defined in IM;
- All definitions and specifications of entities are modelled through proper notations and presentations; and
- IM is created in a proper supporting environment with functions supporting creation, visualisation, navigation, searching, updating and management.

These features can ensure all process models established can find their input and output information/knowledge entities in the derived IM.

5. IM-ENHANCED KMS AND BPM

Successful KMS development is aimed at deliver a well-developed knowledge environment to support business activities across different areas and processes. As shown in Figure 5, CAIM and its associated capability/systems repository can become a central KMS facility to enable and integrate processes across business areas.

Due to localised definitions of data, information and knowledge entities as inputs and outputs of processes in traditional modelling methods, the impact of the process performance to the whole business domain is not explicitly and clearly modelled and explored. The definition of relations between data, information and knowledge entities defined in IM provides opportunities to describe business requirements and interests in production and use of them. These opportunities lead directly to activities to define business processes. Using the capability architecture information model, we can define a process explicitly with its responsibility in producing a defined sub-set of data, information and knowledge entities and interests in using another sub-set of the model.

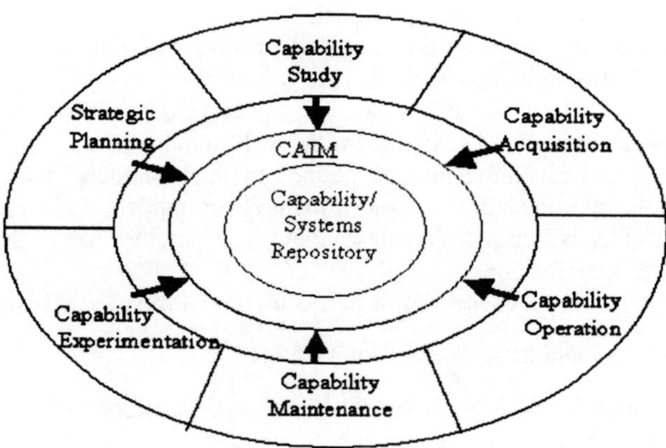

Figure 5. A CAIM-based KMS shared by different processes and areas

In other words, IM can help clarify information concepts in and relations to their different business contexts. For example, the concept of operation architecture (OA) is often used in various areas of the defence capability systems life cycle management. A data dictionary, lexicon or taxonomy can provide a definition of such a term. However, they cannot describe use of the term in various different contexts

Using CAIM, we can define various use cases of OA and their relations not only to other data, information and knowledge entities in all three sub-models and also to processes related. For instance, a particular OA product that is developed for a future capability by either capability development processes or acquisition processes needs also to be examined and managed if possible by strategic planning processes through the operation scenario sub-model. IM can not only help improve or redesign existing processes but also provide opportunities to identify and create new business processes.

Using the information relations between capability/systems and scenarios defined in CAIM shown in Figure 6, we can create a new business process, called the capability-based military operation scenario evaluation. These relations defined in the model can be stated as below:

I. Capabilities/systems are deployed in operation scenarios;
II. Each operation scenario requires an aggregation and a certain configuration of a set of capabilities/systems;
III. Each capability/system must be deployed in a certain manner in terms of its design and function specifications;
IV. Operation scenarios are constrained by the available capabilities/systems and their configurations;
V. Changes to the existing scenarios and new proposed scenarios define the requirements for capability configurations and plans of new capabilities/ systems;
VI. Changes to the existing capabilities/systems have impacts on the performance of the approved operation scenarios.

These relations can lead to definitions of business rules related the new process in order to examine what kinds of military operation scenarios, under the provision of a given set of capabilities/systems, can be performed by a defence force and how at both strategic and operational levels.

6. IM-BASED BUSINESS PROCESS INTEGRATION

The process management across different areas and processes has been the main interests of the workflow management that addresses process integration through mainly two components, process modelling/management and supporting technologies. The evolution of the workflow management technology has experienced several generations from conventional document management, electronic mail, groupware, transaction-based applications, project support software, system design tools to web-based process automation. Such an evolution indicates a trend of increasing complexity of data, information and knowledge processed by processes and changing requirements in methods used by processes. The IM development can provide useful support for business process integration in handling information complexity.

6.1 Process analysis and model integration

Business process analysis is an important activity in organisation change and systems development and carried out on a basis of established process models or descriptions. Business model integration is to conceptually define relations and dependency of both data and functions between or across processes. In other words, it defines the interoperability requirements between processes in terms of what interactions are required.

A common approach for process model integration is to trace both data and function dependency among relevant process models or descriptions through their individual process descriptions, and then to define and rationalise pair-wise connections of dependent processes.

With the support from IM that describes context attributes of each entity, including ownership, users, status, ways of access, processes of production and use and relations to other entities; we can explore interrelationships and dependency among relevant processes in different approaches. The relationships and dependency between processes can be implicitly defined through explicit definitions of relations between information/ knowledge entities.

Based on a conceptual integration of business processes, a physical implementation is achieved through the integration of systems supporting the processes Through using a commonly shared information model, system architects or integrators can first analyse required and concerned data information and knowledge resources without demanding detailed information from individual related systems.

6.2. IM-based repository development

Though IM is introduced as a conceptual and logical model of information and knowledge, it is also likely leading towards a repository solution supporting KMS and BPM if the IM development is carried out with intentions to integrate process supporting tools and environments.

There are different approaches to development of a repository for KMS with different strategies in handling data, information and knowledge resources. A repository solution can be as simple as a file-based one if the resources are stored and managed through using a file directory structure. Web technologies have provided better resolutions for the repository development in three main aspects: 1) hyperlink; 2) web-based publishing; and 3) portal technologies. From a viewpoint of the repository design, however, these technologies can only help improve mainly navigation, access and sharing of the resources.

Through using an IM, the repository development for purposes of both KMS and BRM can be carried out in a style more close to the information systems development with the following features:

- Complete data, information, knowledge analysis;
- Developing a model-based KMS for BPM;
- A shared information model supporting systems integration and enabling work-flow automation; and
- More importantly, provision of a technology-independent design of a repository for managing BPM information and knowledge environment.

7. CONCLUSIONS AND FUTURE WORK

BPM and KMS are related and both require improvement in methods used, in particular, strong binding required between them. This paper discusses the need and importance of more formal approaches to developing KMS in BPM context based on the concept of an information model. It is anticipated that the IM-based BPM and KMS development can help an organisation achieve its information architecture at the enterprise level and provide better support and guidance for future organisation and systems development. In order to make IM become part of KMS and BPM initiatives and potentially be the information architecture of an enterprise, more research and development are required in relation to IM development and applications. Issues to be addressed include modelling, notations, structure, entity granularity, methods and its supporting and implementation environments.

REFERENCES

Al-Mashari, Majed and Zairi, Mohamed, 2000, Revisiting BPR: a holistic review of practice and development, *Business Process Management Journal*, Volume 6 Number 1, 10–42.

Biazzo, Stefano, 2000, Approaches to Business Process Analysis: a Review, *Business Process Management Journal*, Volume 6 Number 2, 99–112.

Browning, Tyson, 2002, Process Integration Using the Design Structure Matrix, *Systems Engineering Journal*, Vol. 5 No. 3, 180–193.

C4ISR Architecture Working Group, 1997, *C4ISR Core Architecture Data Model Version 1.0,* US DoD,.

Chan, Roy and Rosemann, Michael, 2002, A Classification of Knowledge in Enterprise System Roles, Proceedings of the 13th Australasian Conference on Information Systems, Melbourne, Dec. 2002, 421–430.

Chen, Pin and Bulluss, Gary, 2000, A Framework Study for Australian Defence Organisation Architecture Practice, DSTO Report, DSTO-CR-0152.

Hampe, Felix J. and Schonet, Silke, Knowledge Generation and Dissemination in Virtual Communities and Virtual Teams, Proceedings of the 13th Australasian Conference on Information Systems, Melbourne, Dec. 2002, 347–353.

Maire, Ronald, 2002, *Knowledge Management Systems*, Springer-Verlag.

Mahortra Yogesh, 2002, Why Knowledge Management Systems Fails? Enablers and Constrains of Knowledge Management in Human Enterprise, in: *Handbook on Knowledge Management 1: Knowledge Matters*, edited by C.W. Holsapple, Springer-Verlag, pp 577-599.

MODELLING EMERGENT PROCESSES IN KNOWLEDGE-INTENSIVE ENVIRONMENTS

I. T. Hawryszkiewycz*

1. INTRODUCTION

A business process is traditionally made up of a number of tasks carried out by people, who must coordinate their activities to ensure that the process reaches a satisfactory conclusion. Processes can be characterized in the way shown in Figure 1. At one end of the spectrum are predefined processes, where the work in each individual task can be clearly defined and, usually, each task is carried out by one or more specified persons. Predefined processes are currently supported by workflow management systems. Although such predefined processes can support the more traditional organizational functions such as inventory control or financial transactions, they cannot predefine the more emergent processes that take place in knowledge intensive environments such as innovation or the design of specialized products and services.

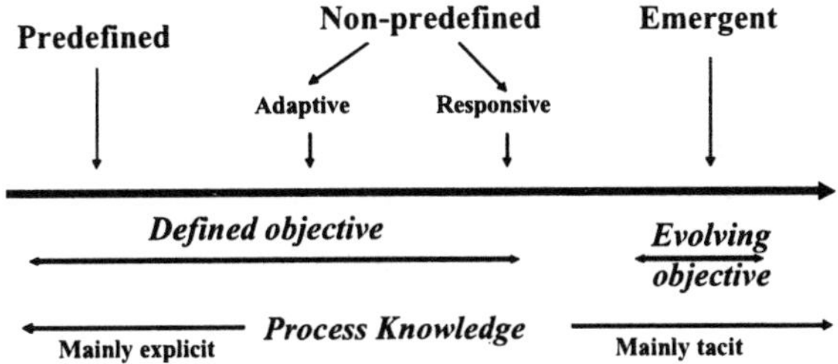

Figure 1. Range of processes

Recently a number of authors have addressed the limitations of predefined systems and suggested alternatives. Jorgensen (2001), for example, distinguishes between rule-based processes and interactive processes. Heinl and others (2001) have a classification that distinguishes between selective and adaptive processes and then identifies ad-hoc

Constructing the Infrastructure for the Knowledge Economy
Edited by H. Linger *et al.*, Kluwer Academic/Plenum Publishers, 2004

processes as also becoming more common. A further classification is whether selection is by type or by instance. Ad-hoc processes in this case are those that are changed by instance but which can also initiate previously unidentified tasks. Such processes are often known as emergent processes.

Different ways have been used to describe emergent processes. Dourish (1998) describes them as the opportunistic creation of new parallel tasks that must be coordinated to a common goal. Hatori and others (1999) describe communities that work towards common goals with personal workspaces connected to community workspaces. Hoffman and others (2000) have described how such communities can evolve and capture knowledge as part of their everyday work. Another characteristic is that the goal of an emergent process itself may gradually change. The different processes also differ in where knowledge process resides. In predefined processes such knowledge is explicit and stored as workflow rules. In emergent processes it is more likely to be tacit as subsequent steps are often chosen by participants in the current step. This change may come from factors external to the process (such as a change in organisational priorities or requirements) or be an internal change in response to information received from users that may result in process improvement. Emergence can also take place at different process levels. There may be a set of high-level process steps, each of which delivers an outcome. These higher level steps may be predefined but the way these steps are carried out may however emerge. Software engineering is one example here. The goal here is to develop a software product. One software engineering task is to define requirements. The way this task is carried out, however, may emerge over time, but it must deliver a set of requirements. Other software engineering steps must deliver further outputs.

There are currently few ways to model emergent processes. This paper proposes a formal approach and defines semantics to describe process emergence and ways to implement these semantics so that processes can be changed dynamically. It defines ways to construct and change processes dynamically as well as ways to maintain awareness across the process. The paper begins with an informal description of emergence and then informally identifies different kinds of emergence.

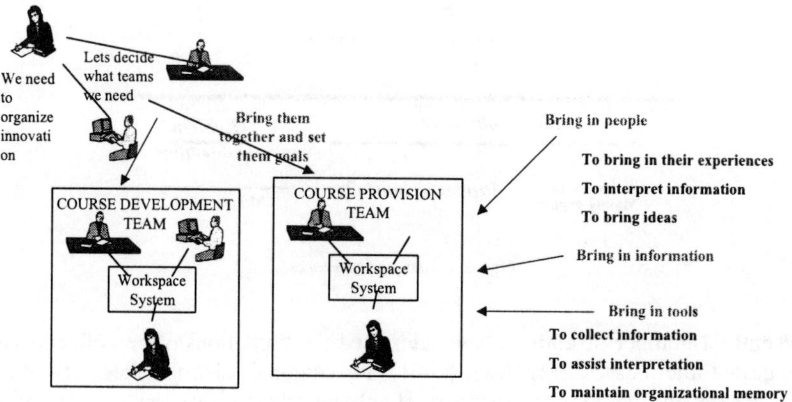

Figure 2. Setting up tasks and teams

2. DESCRIPTION OF PROCESS EMERGENCE

Informally process emergence can follow the steps shown in Figure 2. Here someone may come up with an idea or have a problem to solve. This may be a marketing idea to develop a new service to satisfy a market trend. It can also be developing software requirements and designs or planning a new product. The usual process is to begin with a team and assign responsibilities to different people in the team. The next step is to combine their evaluations and proposals into a common proposal. The work of the teams proceeds through meetings, decisions, and keeping track of changes while working to a fixed schedule. Requires support for ongoing meetings and follow-ups from these meetings. It also requires the work to be integrated in the sense that people in different groups are aware of what is happening and can see their own work in the entire context.

2.1. Classifying Emergence

Emergence goes beyond simple choices of alternate paths. It concerns choosing the best way to do things given a situation. Process emergence can be viewed by some as uncontrolled growth of new activities. For this reason some constraints may be needed on emergence, and support must be given to coordinate newly created processes. One possible classification of emergence is by activity change and by process integration.

In this paper, activity change can be classified as follows:

- *Local emergence* or change to the internal structure of an activity, usually through the addition of new documents to be produced and the creation of new tasks,
- *Extension emergence* of a new but predefined activity simply adding a new prespecified activity when needed. This is usually achieved by creating new activities from templates or from defined object classes. An example here may be to create a new meeting.
- *Specialized emergence* of a variant of a predefined type of activity where the work of an existing activity can be customized to a particular need. An example here may be to create follow-ups to meetings. Each follow-up may be of a different type, and
- *Global emergence* or creation of an activity whose type was not defined earlier.

Process integration can also be classified as follows:

- Activity change is *unconnected* to any existing process and is often part of a global change,
- Activity change is *loosely connected* to existing activities commonly found with global emergence. Such connection is through maintaining awareness by informally notifying related activities and their participants, and
- Activity change is *strongly connected* to existing activities commonly found with extension and specialization emergence. Strong connection is usually achieved through the dynamic creation of new events and workflow rules that are linked to existing activities.

Most groupware systems provide a range of activity changes, which are usually unconnected to existing processes. Any support system must thus provide the ability for emergence to take place in a loose but coordinated way.

2.2 Requirements of Emergent Processes

The requirements of support tools for emergent processes can be summarized as follows:

- An empowered activity participant can at any time initiate some new tasks and define events and milestones which may need follow-up actions. It should also be possible for each participant to personalize their place of work.
- Awareness can be maintained between activities and coordination is usually achieved by maintaining awareness across activities, while allowing users to collaboratively and dynamically define new process steps,
- There is a requirements to both focus on particular tasks within each workspace and provide the governance structures to do so,
- There must be able to support the complete range of awareness change and process integration.
- Activities can be on-going and need not terminate or complete before other activities start.

We now describe a more formal way to model process emergence.

3. MODELLING EMERGENT PROCESSES

Modeling emergent processes is itself an emergent issue. Any modeling technique should be able to create a process instance like that shown in Figure 3. Here the process started with an initial project management activity to achieve some goal. Following meetings and discussions, project management can start a number of tasks, each with their specific objectives. The tasks themselves proceed through their own decision processes, including meetings and follow-ups.

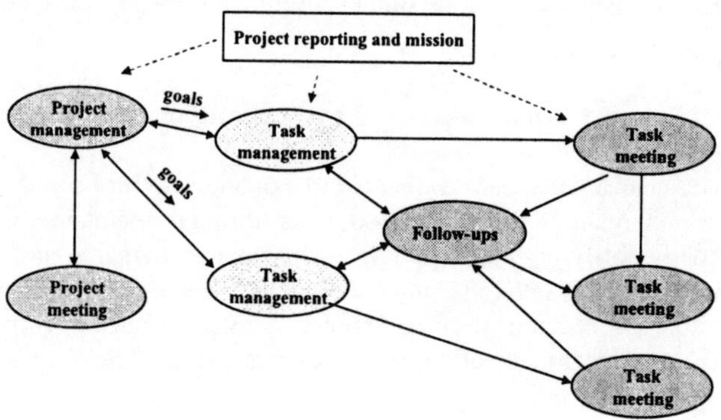

Figure 3. Work Process Dynamics

Most modeling methods center on predefined processes and do not support emergence. There are questions for example, how to model the different kinds of process emergence and the loose coordination between activities. Existing modeling methods do not satisfy these requirements. Figure 4 shows possible models using structured systems analysis and object modelling.

In structured systems methodologies all tasks and processes are strongly connected and predefined. At best they can show alternate paths but creation of new processes is difficult to illustrate. Here the structure of meetings and follow-ups must be predefined as data stores and a particular option can be selected for a given instance. Thus at best there is support for extension emergence. Object modeling can illustrate activity change and the creation of new and specialized activities, which however must be predefined. Again there is support for extension emergence

Perhaps in summary such techniques can be used to model highly constrained form of emergence where there can be a number of similar or alternate activities created from the same activity. They can support extension emergence but are constrained in the kind of specialized emergence. Global emergence however cannot be modelled in either case. To show global emergence would in principle require the creation of new object types during process execution.

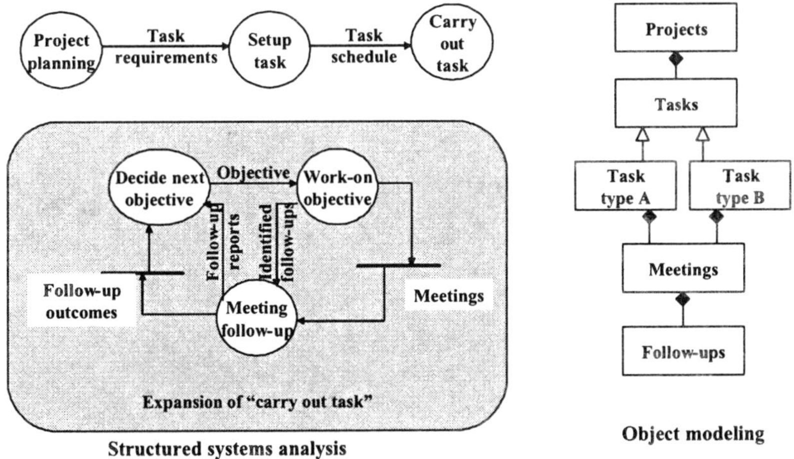

Figure 4. Using existing modeling methods

4. SEMANTICS FOR MODELLING EMERGENT ENVIRONMENTS

We have earlier developed a set of metamodel concepts (Hawryszkiewycz, 2001) to describe such dynamics more directly and developed support tools for such semantics. The metamodel concepts are shown in Figure 5. Each ellipse is a concept and the arrows between indicate relationships between the concepts. The major concepts and semantics are:

- Activities that describe work within a process,

- Groups that describe collections of people that can be assigned to an activity. Groups support scalability as independent groups can exist in the same system but gradually merge or intersect if needed,
- Roles that describe responsibilities within an activity,
- Groups can then be assigned roles in activities,
- An activity 'contains' any number of artifacts, which can be made up of other artifacts or define groups of artifact,
- A person, here called a participant, 'is-in' a group. That person assumes all roles to which the group is assigned. The roles define access abilities to artifacts and 'can-take' the actions,
- Actions 'use or create' artifacts. They can be soloactions, which are taken by individuals, or interactions, such as discussions, which can include more than one participant. Actions 'use' tools. Examples of actions may be setting a milestones, or adding a time record to a task,
- Events that identify completion of tasks. An activity can include a number of event types, which are assigned to roles. Event instances of particular types lead to message being sent to other activities,
- Views can be created to focus roles on particular goals.

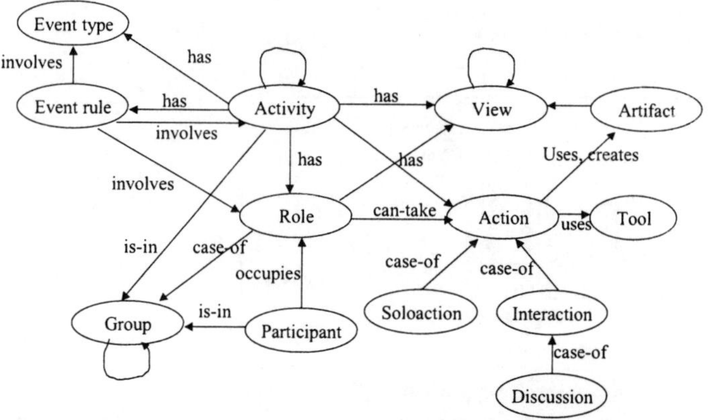

Figure 5. The metamodel for community evolution

4.1. Using open systems techniques

A modified form of rich pictures can model systems using these concepts. A simple example is shown in Figure 6. Here each clouded shape is an activity. The rectangular boxes show the artifacts used in each activity whereas roles are defined through links to the activities. Circles within boxes represent events. For example the event "start-meeting" is included in activity 'task-management' and initiated by the task-leader to start a meeting. Figure 6 only illustrates the basic characteristics of this approach. More detailed diagrams would include the work-items that are part of the activities, as well as roles that respond to events.

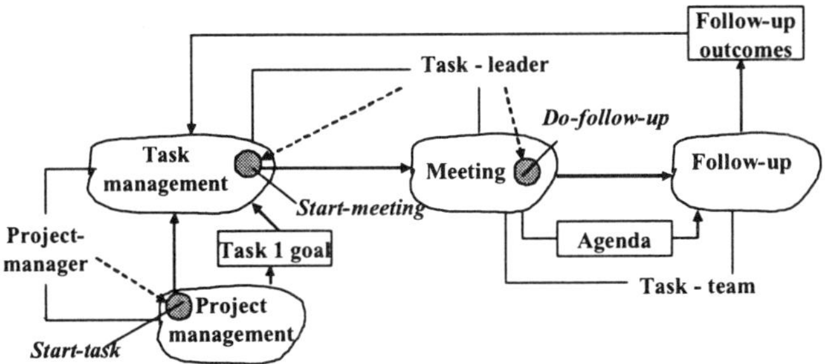

Figure 6. Emergent actions using rich pictures

The semantics here is that activities now need not be strongly process related and they can all be proceeding in parallel. Such loose connections are shown through commonly shared artifacts and roles participating in more than one activity. Artifacts that are used to maintain such awarewness can be shown on the model.

4.2. Support for emergence

The semantics can model any number of different kinds of emergence. Each concept has a number of commands associated with it. Thus an activity has commands to add roles, views, artifacts and to assign people to roles as well as roles to responsibilities. It also has the ability to create new activities this modeling process emergence. The model supports:

- Activities and groups can evolve independently. New roles, groups, artifacts and views can be created whenever needed. This easily supports local emergence.
- New activities can be created at any time thus supporting global emergence.
- Such new activities can evolve independently and thus support both extension and specialized emergence.
- Events can be created dynamically thus supporting all kinds of process integration,
- Notifications of changes can be assigned to roles to maintain awareness.

5. IMPLEMENTATION

We have developed a system, LiveNet, to directly implement these semantics and have used it both in teaching and to develop meeting systems. It allows users to create digital workspaces for their activities. The LiveNet system also provides the flexibility to customize workspaces by adding roles and artifacts, assigning permissions, adding actions as well as defining notifications. The broad architecture of this system is illustrated in Figure 7. Here a system instance is stored as database in the LiveNet foundation. The database structure is based on the semantic model. It is then possible to define interfaces that match the user's intuitive perception to the problem. The foundation is developed using the Java 2JEE platform, which provides the flexibility to both easily add new components as well as developing specialized interfaces. Such interfaces are developed using Java Servlets or using JSP, a process that requires minimal development time.

Development of applications usually requires a mapping between application terms and semantic terms. Often additional presentations that show activities in a wider context require special mapping and procedures to combine information from more than one activity into one presentation.

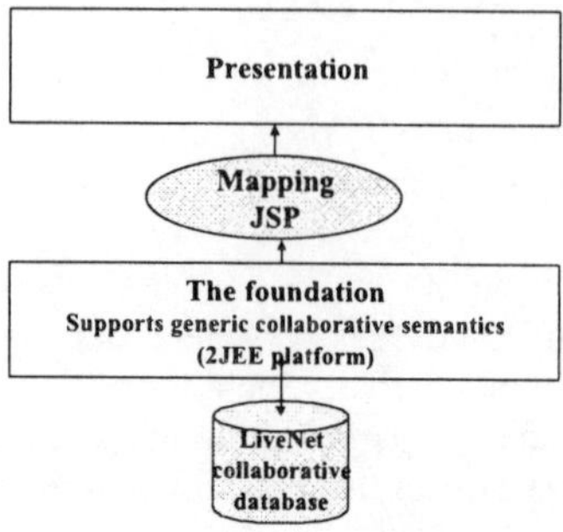

Figure 7. LiveNet architecture

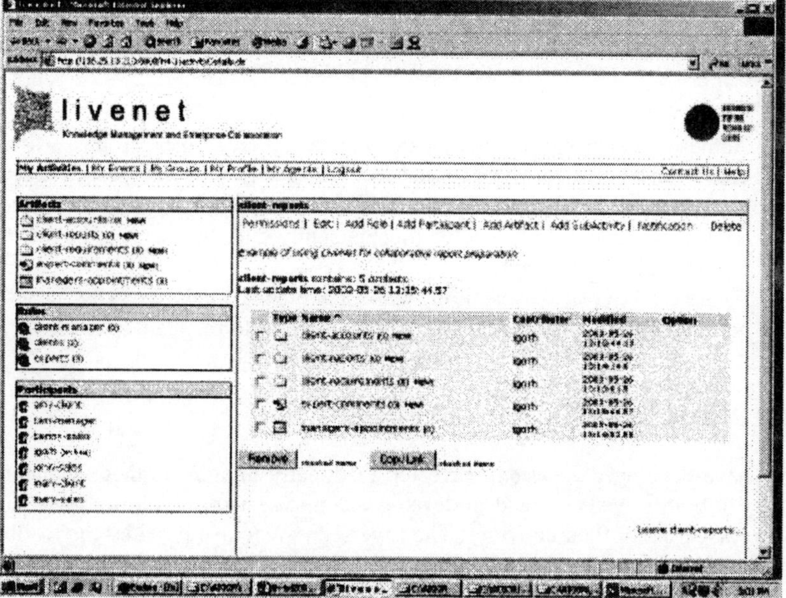

Figure 8. Presentation of metamodel concepts

5.1. Presenting the Semantics

Figure 8 illustrates a general presentation of LiveNet semantics. It shows groups, in this case experts and clients, and activities such as for example, the "technology-diffusion" project.

The system represents activities by a workspace. In the current implementation each workspace has one owner, who is the user, who created the workspace, and any number of participants. The system supports the different kinds of integration.

- Activities for example can be totally unconnected as anyone can create a new independent workspace and their own group,
- Activities can be loosely connected in a number of ways. One is through sharing documents and notifying participants when these are changed.
- Activities can be strongly connected by defining events that result in documents to be transferred for action by other roles in selected workspaces.

Commands provided through this interface can be used to implement the different kinds of emergence. For example:

- Local emergence is permitted through a menu that allows selected users to change the artifacts, add roles and assign groups to the roles in a single workspace,
- Extension emergence can be modeled by creating actions within the activity which can be
- Specialized emergence can be modeled by creating new actions and customizing them to new needs,
- Global emergence can be implemented by creating a new activity.

5.2. Customizing Interfaces

It is easy to generate interfaces that use terms relevant to the problem rather than semantic terms. For example Figure 9 shows an activity called project space. It presents the group concept groups as teams, and the activity concept as my projects. A user can then select a particular project and examine its details. Again process emergence is possible here. It is possible at anytime to create a meeting or new task, invite new people create new teams and assign them to roles within the project. Emergence can now be managed in terms familiar to users. For example instead of creating a new activity we create a new task. Instead of a group we create a new. Instead of an artifact we create a document. Specialized activities include meeting and follow ups thus directly modeling the problem domain.

5.3. Processes integration

Different kinds of process integration can be supported. Strong process connection is supported through the ability to dynamically create events. As an example Figure 10 shows a workflow created for an application process. There is a separate instance for each application. This allows each application to follow a different process, depending on the outcomes at each stage of the process. There are a number of events defined for this process instance. At any time it is possible to delete or edit an event, or to add a new event within the workflow.

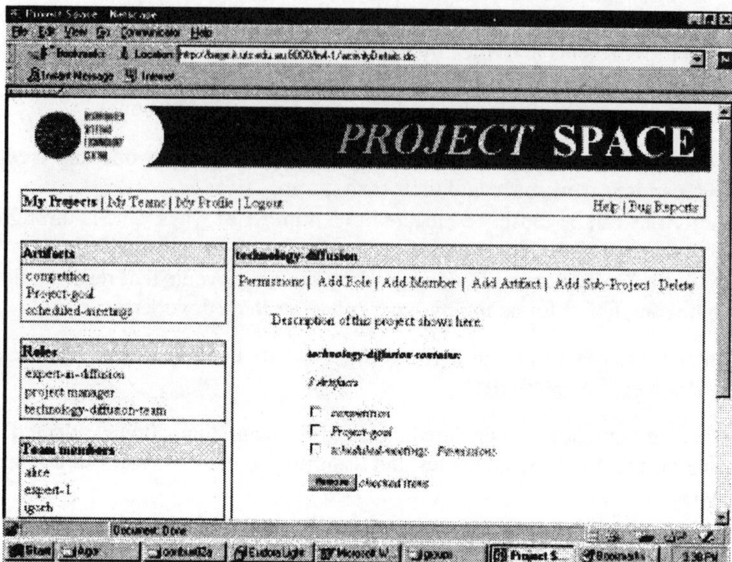

Figure 9. Project Space

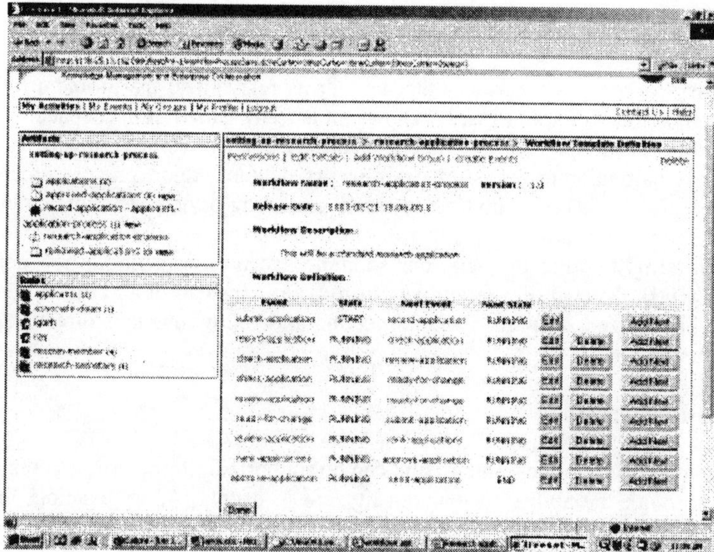

Figure 10. Events for strongly connected processes

Awareness for loosely connected emergence can be maintained in a number of ways. Interfaces that show connections between activities can also be created. One such interface is shown in Figure 11.

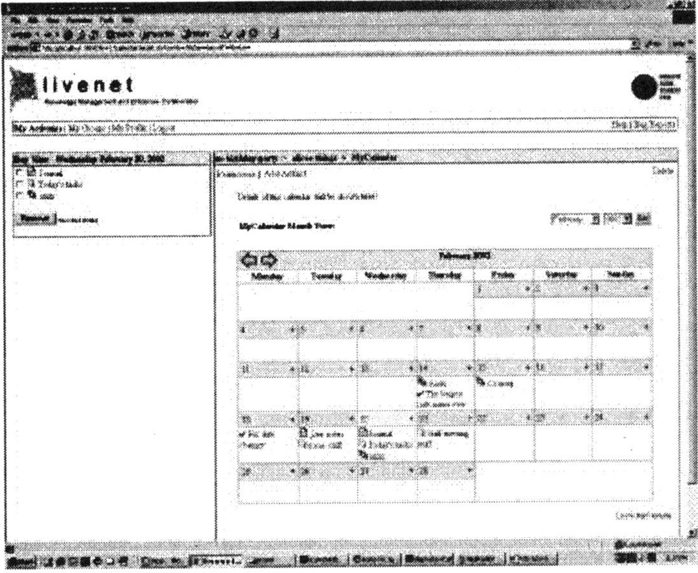

Figure 11. Maintaining Awareness for Loose Process Connection

It is based on a calendar and shows all the activities currently in the system and their important events on each date. Thus there may be a meeting started or a follow-up initiated or some important notification from an on-going activity. The user can decide whether to look at their activities or their teams. If an activity is selected then commands and objects in the activity are presented. As shown in Figure 8 this shows the artifacts, roles and members in the workspace. Commands in the workspace include assignment of permissions, adding roles and artifacts, creating new sub-activities among others.

6. SUMMARY

The paper first described emergent processes and problems in modeling and implementing them. The paper then defined the semantics for modeling emergent processes in terms of generalized semantics and described how they can be used to describe different kinds of process emergence. It then described a general way of implementing them. It suggested that implementations include ways to create domain interfaces to remove cognitive barriers found when using generalized semantics. It suggested that technologies provide ways to customize interfaces that map user's cognitive perceptions in terms of higher level enterprise semantics and described an implementation for project management.

ACKNOWLEDGEMENTS

A number of people contributed to the work described in this paper especially Lei Hu, Luke Cole and Dongbai Xue for assistance in the development of the LiveNet system.

REFERENCES

Dourish, P., 1998, Using Metalevel Techniques in a Flexible Toolkit for CSCW Applications, *ACM Transactions on Computer-Human Interaction*, Vol. 8, No.2, June 1998, 109–155.

Grant, R. M., 1996, Prospering in Dynamically-competitive Environments: Organizational Capability as Knowledge Integration, *Organization Science*, Vol. 7, No. 4, July, 1996, 375–387.

Greiner, C., Hawryszkiewycz, I., Rose, T. and Fliender, T. M., 1996, Supporting Health Research Strategy Planning Processes of WHO with Information Technology, Proc. GI-Workshop on Telecooperation Systems in Decentralized Organizations, Berlin.

Hattori, F., Ohguro, T., Yokoo, M., Matsubara, S. and Yoshida, S., 1999, Socialware: Multiagent Systems for Supporting Network Communities, *Communications of the ACM*, March, 1999, 55–59.

Hawryszkiewycz, I. T., 1997, *Designing the Networked Enterprise*, Artech House.

Heinl, P., Horn, S., Jablonski, S., Neeb, J., Stein, K. and Teschke, M., 2001, A Comprehensive Approach to Flexibility in Workflow Management System, WACC'99, San Francisco.

Hoffman, M., Loser, K-U, Walter, T. and Herrmann, T., 1999, A Design Process for Embedding Knowledge Management in Everyday Work, Group 99, Phoenix, Arizona, 296–305.

Jones, C. T., Hesterly, W. S., and S. P. Borgatti, 1997, A General Theory of Network Governance: Exchange Conditions and Social Mechanisms, *Academy of Management Review*, Vol. 22, No. 4, October, 1997, 911–945.

Jorgensen, H. D., 2001, Interaction as a Framework for Flexible Workflow Modelling, Proceedings of the Group2001 Conference, Sept.30–Oct.3, Bioulder, Colorado, 32–41.

LiveNet: http://livenet4.it.uts.edu.au.

ENABLING PROBLEM DOMAIN KNOWLEDGE TRANSFORMATION DURING OBJECT ORIENTED SOFTWARE DEVELOPMENT

Oksana Nikiforova and Marite Kirikova*

1. INTRODUCTION

Nowadays one the most desirable characteristics of software development process is a high speed of development. However, in many cases the speed of software development is hindered by problems of knowledge acquisition and transformation. Sometimes software developers focus on their tacit knowledge and do not use proper knowledge acquisition and representation techniques for problem domain and requirements description. In that case developers take a known risk to fail with a final product, yet they hasten the process of software development. However, such a risk shall be avoided in large, complex, and expensive software projects.

This paper discusses how speed of object oriented (OO) software development may be increased by automatic or semi-automatic transformation of sufficiently complete and consistent knowledge from problem domain through analysis and design into implementation.

Section 2 examines software development process and a minimal set of UML diagrams to be built according to OO approach. Section 3 introduces a hypothesis that consistent and complete problem domain knowledge enables automatic and semi-automatic transformation of knowledge. This section also comprises an overview and analysis of several existing approaches to knowledge transformation. These approaches are analysed from the point of view of a possibility to prove consistency and completeness of initial knowledge, and a possibility to define formal procedures of knowledge transfer. In Section 4 a two-hemisphere model based knowledge transformation strategy is proposed. This strategy may be used for formal and semi-formal knowledge transformation from the problem domain via analysis and design into an implementation. Conclusions are given is Section 5.

* Oksana Nikiforova, Division of Applied Computer Science, Riga Technical University, Latvia, ivasiuta@cs.rtu.lv. Marite Kirikova, Division of Systems Theory, Riga Technical University, marite@cs.rtu.lv

2. AN OVERVIEW OF AN OO SOFTWARE DEVELOPMENT PROCESS

Considering such approaches to software development as Rational Unified Process,[1] Microsoft Solution Framework[2] and OPEN – Mentor Methodology,[3] etc., a common meta-model of a software development process emerges that consists of three main stages, namely, Analysis, Design, and Implementation (Figure 1).[4] The analysis stage includes acquisition, examination, and understanding of software requirements, exploring their implications, and removing inconsistencies and omissions. Different analytical models are developed in this stage. During the design stage the target software system is organised into components, based on knowledge gained in the analysis stage. The developed design model may be automatically translated into a particular programming language, and thus serve as a basis for software system implementation.

Modelling is one of the most important activities during system development that may facilitate exchange of stakeholders' tacit knowledge as well as acquisition and utilisation of explicit knowledge. Explicit knowledge usually is reflected in a particular framework of diagrams. One of such frameworks, UML, is declared as a standard for representation of software system model and provides a robust notation, which grows from analysis through design into implementation.[5] Figure 1 shows the minimal set of the UML diagrams to be built during object-oriented software development.[4] These diagrams are interrelated, they overlap semantically and, taken together, represent different systems development aspects as a whole. The diagrams themselves and transformations of knowledge between them must be well defined because inaccuracy in model building can lead to wrong functionality of implemented software.[6]

Modelling efforts in OO software development usually start with the identification of *use-cases* for the software to be developed. A use-case reflects interactions between the system to be built and the actor (an outside object in a particular role) that has a particular purpose of using the system. Each interaction starts with an event directed from the actor to the system and proceeds through a series of events between the actor, the system, and possibly other actors, until the interaction initiated by the original event reaches its logical conclusion.

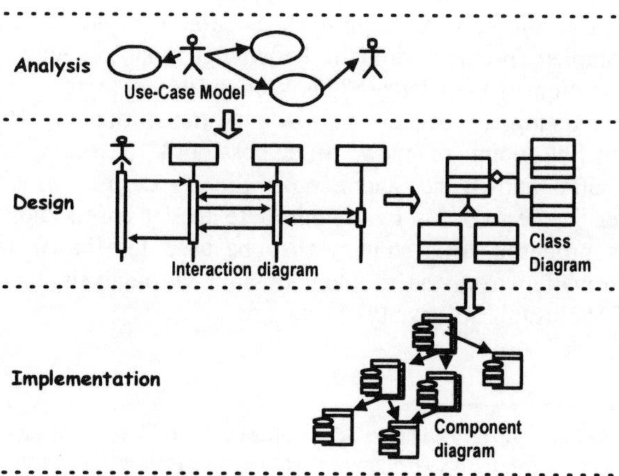

Figure 1. A minimal set of UML diagrams to be built during OO software development

The sequence of interactions can be specified in words or by one or more prototypical scenarios, which then are to be transformed into the elements of an *interaction diagram*. The interaction diagrams are created for each use-case and show the sequence of message passing during certain use-case realization. *Class diagram* shows an overall structure of the software system and encapsulates the responsibility of each class. *Component diagram* represents the realization of classes into particular programming language.[4]

As stated above, program code development for software components may be accomplished by automatic translation of well-defined classes into a particular programming language.[4] This can be achieved by using appropriate CASE-tools, e.g., Rational Rose.[7] Therefore the most important problem is how to define reliable classes that could be translated into the programming language. One of the ways how to achieve it is to use well-defined (even formal) knowledge acquisition and transformation strategy for construction of use-case diagram as well as definition of scenarios for interacting in message passing between class objects and preliminary identification of classes. The main purpose of such strategy is consistency, transparency and clearness of initial knowledge and corresponding transformations of knowledge from problem domain via analysis towards design and implementation.

3. KNOWLEDGE TRANSFORMATION DURING OO SOFTWARE DEVELOPMENT

Block arrows in Figure 1 show main steps of knowledge transformation in OO software development. Knowledge transformation steps have the same sequence as modelling activities described in Section 2. We can distinguish between the following three types of knowledge transformation: informal transformation, semi-formal transformation, formal transformation.

Translation from well-designed implementation model to software code is an example of formal knowledge transformation. Formal transformation of knowledge may be done automatically by software development tools that follow the given transformation algorithm. Automatic transformation may considerably increase the speed of software development. The same refers to semi-formal transformations where human expert employs particular transformation heuristics and part of transformation activities may be supported by a software tool performing in accordance with the built-in transformation rules. Therefore it is essential to utilise all possibilities of semi-formal and formal knowledge transformations in OO software development.

The result of any transformation depends (1) on the quality of knowledge to be transformed and (2) on the method of transformation. Initial knowledge that is gradually transformed into the software code is the knowledge about problem domain and systems requirements. In OO software development this knowledge is usually reflected in use-case diagrams and use-case descriptions. Our hypothesis is that successful semi-formal and formal transformation of knowledge during OO software development is possible on condition that:

- completeness of knowledge reflected in use-case diagram is agreed upon and proven[8]
- consistency of knowledge reflected in use-case diagram is proven[9]

This means that initial knowledge must be organised (or modelled) in a way that enables to check completeness and consistency of that knowledge.

Further in this section several OO systems development approaches are analysed from the point of view of the quality of knowledge to be transformed, and the methods of knowledge transformation utilised. Each approach is illustrated by a set of interrelated diagrams (Fig. 2–5) where block arrows show paths of knowledge transformation. Solid-line block arrows stand for direct transformations and doted-line block arrows represent in-direct transformations.

3.1. Informal Approach for OO Software Development

Informal approach for OO software development[10] does not contain any pre-defined strategy for problem domain knowledge transformation. The software development process is based on a problem statement and conversations with customers and domain experts. The meta-model for this strategy is shown in Figure 2.

Use-case modelling starts with the identification of actors and principal use-cases for the system. It is assumed that actors may be identified in the problem statement and during conversations with customers and domain experts. The method suggests particular questions for identification of actors and identification of use-cases.[10] Each use-case is documented together with a flow of events. The flow of events for a use-case is a description of the events needed for accomplishing the required behaviour of the use-case. The flow of events is described in terms of what the system should do, not how the system does it.

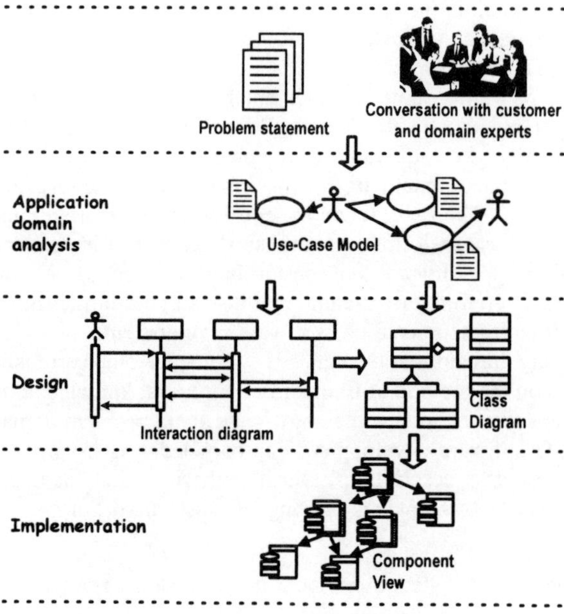

Figure 2. Informal strategy for application domain analysis

Informal approach for OO software development uses particular questions as a basis for transformation of tacit human knowledge into semi-structured use-cases. This may be regarded as semi-formal transformation. All other transformations of this approach (except the last one) reflected in Figure 2 are also semi-formal. There are no formal means for checking completeness and consistency of knowledge reflected in use-cases. Therefore completeness and consistency of initial knowledge here is rather a matter of trying one's luck than a reliable result of knowledge acquisition.

3.2. Problem Domain Model and Application Domain Model Based OO Software Development

In informal approach (see Section 3.1) knowledge externalised by customers and experts is recorded only in application use-case model. In this sub-section, we discuss an approach where knowledge transformation is additionally supported by the domain object/classes model.[11]

Problem domain knowledge transformation starts with an identification of application boundary (see Figur 3). For acquisition of requirements a two prong analysis approach is used, i.e., first, a domain model by capturing domain knowledge is built and then an application model is developed by examining use-cases of the particular application.[12]

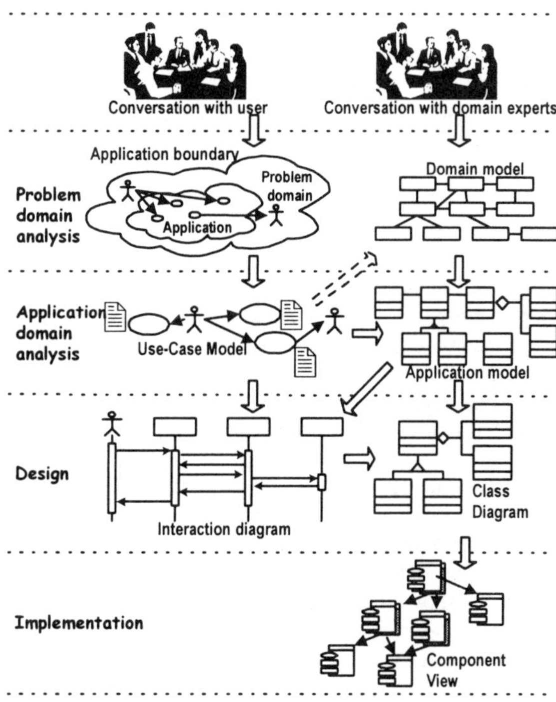

Figure 3. Problem domain model and application domain model based strategy

The following strategies may be used for domain model construction in the problem domain model and application domain model based approach[11]:

1. Domain model is based on the list of important real-world concepts, terminology and jargon in the problem domain. The list is organised into a class model showing their relationships and useful real-world operations on these classes.
2. Using the core semantics of the particular problem statement, which is prepared by domain experts, class model is developed. The semantic computations in the statement become the operations on the domain classes.
3. Domain classes also may be extracted indirectly from use-cases. This is the most indirect approach because the domain objects may not appear in the use-cases directly and may have to be inferred from their views, which do appear.

Application model building starts with listing and examining use-cases to identify application objects and determine how underlying domain information will be formatted and presented to the user. Also devices and interface objects mentioned in the use-case have to be identified. By examining use-cases, the access required of each domain class can be identified.

Similar to the approach discussed above is a method of OO software development[12] based on a detailed knowledge about problem domain and application domain. Detailed knowledge is obtained by exploiting different sources of knowledge including patterns. The strategy of knowledge acquisition and transformation utilised in this method also uses objects as its key concepts in problem domain modelling, and use-cases – as a modelling tool for application domain analysis.

In problem domain model and application domain model based approach application boundary identification inside problem domain is based on the conversation with users and domain experts, which is the main source of knowledge for problem domain analysis. On the basis of this information domain model and application model are also developed. There is no formal strategy how to identify the boundary, however several semi-formal strategies are given for domain class identification. This approach is richer in explicit knowledge than the informal approach for OO software development. Two types of class models, and use-case model are used in problem and application domain analysis. This opens a possibility to use some semi-formal consistency and completeness checks with respect to the initial knowledge to be transformed into the implementation model. On the other hand, there are no means to prove consistency of this knowledge. It is worthwhile to note here that declarative explicit knowledge, i.e., object/class model is provided for both, problem domain and application domain analysis while explicit procedural knowledge (use-case model) is given only for the application domain.

3.3. Requirements Specification Based OO Software Development

Several approaches[13–16] in search of use-cases rely on initial (not final) requirements specification document usually called user requirements documentation. General meta-model of these approaches is shown in Figure 4.

This approach assumes that conceptual model has to be built as a basis for class identification. The identification of concepts, in turn, is part of an investigation of the problem domain.[14, 15] Conceptual model creation is based on the use-cases identified for the software system and depends on use-case descriptions and other documents in which the relevant concepts may be found. Usually preliminary user requirements specification is a document used for this purpose.

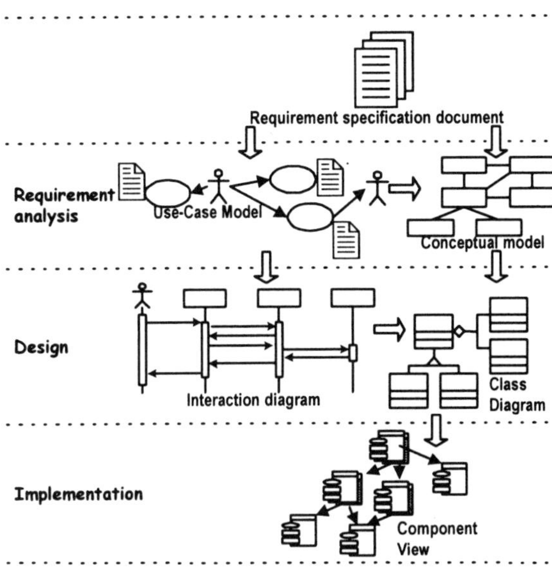

Figure 4. Requirement specification document based strategy

OO software development approach based on requirements specification document uses a semi-formal source of knowledge for construction of initial body of knowledge to be transformed during the software development process. Such approach, on the one hand, provides opportunities for semi-formal completeness check of initial knowledge, but on the other hand heavily depends on the quality of knowledge in the requirements specification provided in the form of the document. Based on requirements specification explicit procedural and declarative knowledge is provided in the form of use-cases and conceptual model. Use-cases reflect application domain knowledge. Conceptual model comprises both problem domain and application domain knowledge elements. Semi-formal methods of knowledge transformation from conceptual model into design class diagram can be applied. However, representation of initial knowledge in a form of use-case does not support any formal methods for consistency and completeness checks of knowledge.

3.4. Business Use-Cases and Business Object Model Based OO Software Development

One more strategy for problem domain knowledge representation and further knowledge transformation during systems analysis and design is based on utilisation of a business modelling approach.[1, 18] A meta-model of the strategy is shown in Figure 5.

In this approach the business modelling is suggested for use in analysis of complex and multidimensional application environments.[18] It has to be noted here that *Business Modelling* is a term that may be interpreted in various ways. In this sub-section it means building business use-cases and business object models.[18]

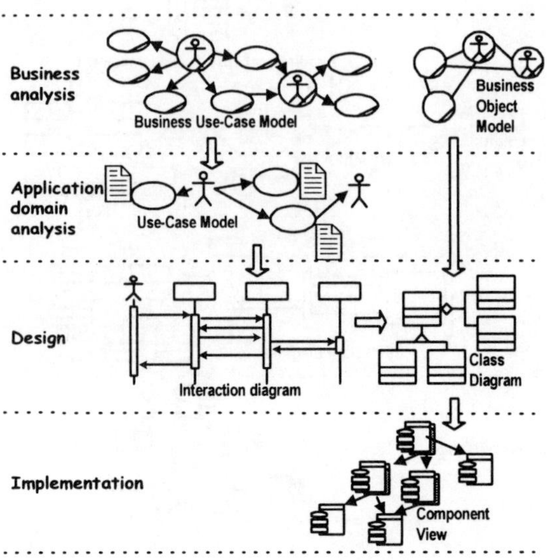

Figure 5. Business use-cases and business object model based strategy

Business level models may be translated into the systems level models in the following way:

- Business workers become actors to the systems to be developed. It is possible because the business object model contains business workers as one type of its objects.
- Behaviours described for business workers are things to be automated, so they help to find system use-cases and define needed functionality.
- Business entities may become things maintained by the help of the system, so they may be used to find entity classes in the analysis model of the system.

Business use-cases and business object model based OO software development approach shows dependencies between business models and system rather clearly and directly. However the knowledge transformation strategy utilised in this approach does not give explicit answers to such questions as: "Should all business systems workers become actors in use-case diagrams?", "Does all potential system's classes (concepts) are identified in the business object model?", etc. Therefore only semi-formal knowledge transformations are possible. The representation of domain knowledge in the form of use-case diagram is a step forward towards completeness of initial knowledge, but it still does not enable the use of formal means for consistency and completeness checking of knowledge amalgamated in the diagrams.

All approaches for OO software development overviewed in this section show that currently only semi-formal knowledge transformation strategies are utilised. The reason why formal strategies are not feasible may be described by a considerable impact of tacit dimension of initial knowledge from which formal transformation could start. If completeness and consistency of this knowledge is not proven, then semi-formal strategy may give better results than the formal one, because, it gives space for improving initial knowledge during transformations. On the other hand, from the point of view of speed of software development, formal strategies are much more desirable than semi-formal ones.

4. TWO-HEMISPHERE MODEL BASED KNOWLEDGE TRANSFORMATION STRATEGY

As it was shown in the previous section, no one of currently available OO software development approaches use models that are suitable for proving consistency and completeness of initial knowledge. However, in process modelling area the approaches that can utilise completeness and consistency checks of knowledge have been proposed.[19] Possibility of integration of such approaches in OO software development process is discussed here by introducing two-hemisphere model based knowledge transformation strategy the meta-model of which is presented in Figure 6.

Initial version of the strategy was proposed in,[4] where the general framework for OO software development was discussed and its application for driving school's software development demonstrated. The strategy supports gradual model transformation from problem domain models into program components, where problem domain models reflect two fundamental things: system functioning (processes) and structure (concepts and their relations).

The title of the proposed strategy is derived from cognitive psychology.[20] Human brain consists of two hemispheres one of which is responsible for logic and the other for concepts. Harmonic interrelated functioning of both hemispheres is a precondition of adequate human behaviour.

Similarly, we propose to start OO software development process on the basis of two-hemisphere problem domain models where one model reflects functional (procedural) aspects of the business and software system, and the other model reflects corresponding conceptual structures. The process of model construction may start from a conceptual model as well as from a functional one. The co-existence and inter-relatedness of models enable the use of formal and semi-formal knowledge transfer strategies from one model to another, as well as utilisation of particular knowledge completeness and consistency checks.

Functional model is reflected in the form of business process model. Although the notation of the business process model may be optional, it must reflect the following components of business processes[21]:

- external entities (processes)
- sub-processes (the number of levels of decomposition is not restricted)
- performers
- information flows
- information (data) stores
- triggering conditions

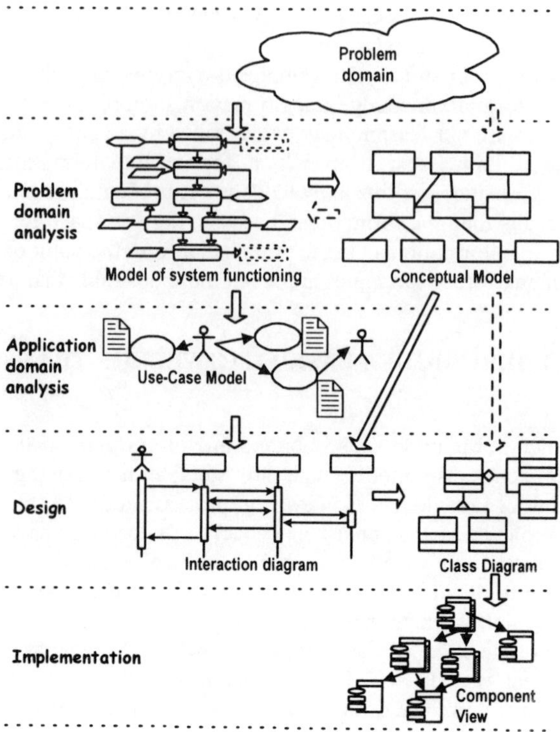

Figure 6. Two-hemisphere model based knowledge transformation strategy

Knowledge reflected by the business process model has both the semantic and the syntactic completeness and consistency. Semantic completeness depends on richness of knowledge behind the model and cannot be formally proven. However, existence of conceptual model gives some semi-formal means for checking completeness and consistency of the business process model. Semantic completeness of business process model can be achieved a wide spectrum of business aspects are taken into consideration, e.g., mission, system of values, goals and constraints, general functions, physical functions, technical infrastructure, etc.[8] *Syntactic completeness of a business process model can be proven* formally (or automatically) by checking particular presence of all components mentioned above for each business process (sub-process) reflected in the model. This possibility enables formal knowledge transformation during OO software development process. It also contributes to the semiformal semantic consistency checking, because syntactically incomplete model cannot be semantically complete.

Real-world classes relevant to the problem domain and their relationships are presented in concepts model (or system conceptual model). Conceptual model shows the things that exist in the problem domain and their relations to other things. The notational conventions of the business process diagram give the possibility to identify concepts by analysing all the data stores in the diagram.[4] Data stores from functional model can be transformed into the concepts of the conceptual model.

Both functional and conceptual models serve as an initial source for further knowledge transformations under system modelling using UML diagrams during OO software development.[4] Formal transformation from functional (business process) model into use-cases is possible, if processes to be performed by software system are identified in the business process model.[22] Processes to be performed by software system become use-cases in use-case model, performers of related processes become actors in use-case model, and scenarios for realisation of use-cases may be defined by decompositions of business processes (sub-processes) corresponding to use-cases.[4]

Interaction diagram is developed for each use-case and is based on its realisation scenario (or sequence of sub-processes). Appropriate interacting objects are extracted from conceptual model. The class diagram is based on conceptual model and is formed according to information in interaction diagram. The class diagram here is already a structure of a software application and contains only those classes whose objects interact during the use-case realisation[4].

The strategy reflected in Figure 6 starts with developing a business process model or a conceptual model. However, a similar result may be achieved if the software development process starts with use-case identification in problem and/or application domain. Identified use-cases and corresponding scenarios may be transformed into the business process model for completeness and consistency checks, and improvement, and then transformed back to use-cases automatically. Thus the knowledge in use-cases becomes more reliable for further transformations.

An attempt to consistently model a problem domain before knowledge transformation to application domain and design has already been made in OO software development approaches discussed in Sections, 3.2, 3.3, and 3.4. In problem domain model and application domain model based,[11–12] and requirements specification based[13-16] approaches the main emphasis in problem domain analysis is on the conceptual model which represents a wholistic class view on the domain. We can say that in those approaches only one modelling hemisphere is utilised. Business use-cases and business object model based OO software development approach[1, 19] uses semi-formal representation of functional perspective in terms of use-case diagram. Here the second hemisphere emerges in domain modelling, but it is in an underdeveloped state because there are no formal means for proving completeness and consistency of knowledge amalgamated in use-cases.

A business process model used in two-hemisphere model based approach reflects knowledge in a more organised way than use-cases, and, as mentioned above, enables formal and semi-formal checking of knowledge consistency and completeness.[22] It also provides an integrated wholistic functional view of the problem domain. Therefore two-hemisphere model based strategy can provide higher quality initial knowledge (from the point of view of its completeness and consistency) than other approaches. High level of organisation and quality of initial knowledge, in turn, promotes formal and semi-formal knowledge transformations during software development process and thus contributes to the efficiency of the development process that, in turn, helps to develop software in a shorter time.

5. CONCLUSION

Analysis of several approaches for OO software development shows that use of formal and semi-formal transformations of knowledge in development process is hindered by impossibility to achieve and assure completeness and consistency of initial body of knowledge that serves as a basis for transformations. Taking into consideration the fact that utilisation of formal and semi-formal transformations may improve efficiency of the development process and shorten development time, the solution to the problem is worth finding.

Two-hemisphere model based strategy for knowledge transformation is proposed as a step forward towards enhancing more formal transformations in OO software development. The strategy prescribes to put emphasis on functional aspects of problem domain to greater extent than common in conventional OO software development approaches. This may be achieved by incorporating the business process modelling experience into OO software development approaches.

More detailed issues regarding methodology and tool support for two-hemisphere model based strategy are left outside the scope of this paper.

REFERENCES

1. I. Jacobson, G. Booch, J. Rumbaugh, *The Unified Software Development Process*, Addison-Wesley, 1999.
2. "Microsoft Solution Framework". Available at Http://www.erigami.com/development.html.
3. B. Henderson-Sellers, The OPEN – Mentor Methodology, *Object Magazine*, 1998.
4. O. Nikiforova, General Framework for Object-Oriented Software Development Process, Scientific Proceedings of Riga Technical University, Series – Computer Science, *Applied Computer Systems*, 13 vol., 2002.
5. OMG Unified Modelling Language Specification, Version 1.3, June 1999.
6. O. Ivasiuta (since 2001 – O. Nikiforova), Comparison Methodology of Software Development Means, PhD Thesis, Riga Technical University, Latvia, 2001.
7. Rational Rose, Rational Corporation web-site – http://www.rational.com.
8. M. Kirikova, Towards completeness of business models, in: *Information Modelling and Knowledge Bases X*, H. Jaakola et al., eds., IOS Press, 1999, pp. 42–54.
9. M. Kirikova, Consistency of Information in Requirements Engineering, in: *Information Modelling and Knowledge bases IX*, P-J. Charrel, H.Jaakola, Hkangassalo, E Kawaguchi, eds., IOS Press, Amsterdam, Berlin, Tokyo,Washigton, DC, 1998, pp. 192–205.
10. T. Quatrany, *Visual Modeling with Rational Rose 2000 and UML*, Second Edition, Addison-Wesley, 2000.
11. J. Rumbaugh, Getting started: Using Use-cases to Capture Requirements, *Journal of Object Oriented Programming*, Sept., 1994, 8–11.
12. L. Mathiassen et al., *Object Oriented Analysis & Design*, Forlaget, 2000.
13. Cr. Larman, *Applying UML and Patterns: An Introduction to Object Oriented Analysis and Design*, Prentice Hall PTR, 1998.
14. M. Fawler, *Analysis Patterns: Reusable Software Models*, Addison-Wesley, 1996.
15. J. Martin and J. Odell, *Object Oriented Methods: A Foundation*, Prentice Hall, 1995.
16. J. Rumbaugh, Models Through the Development Process, *Journal of Object Oriented Programming*, May 1997.
17. R. Abbot, Program Design by Informal English Descriptions, *Communications of the ACM*, Vol. 26 (11), 1983.
18. D. Leffingwell and D. Widrig, *Managing Software Requirements: A Unified approach*, Addison-Wesley, 2000.
19. J. Bubenk jr. and M. Kirikova, Improving the quality of Requirements Specification by Enterprise Modelling, in: *Perspectives on Business Modelling: Understanding and Changing Organistions*, A.G. Nilsson et al., eds., Springer-Verlag, 1999, pp. 243–268.
20. J. R. Anderson, *Cognitive Psychology and Its Implications*, W.H. Freeman and Company, New York, 1995.

21. M. Kirikova, Modelling the boundaries of workspace: A business process perspective, in: *Information Modelling and Knowledge Bases XIII*, H. Kangassalo, H. Jaakkola, E. Kawaguchi, T. Welzer, eds., IOS Press, Ohmsha, Amsterdam, Berlin, Oxford, Tokyo, Washington, DC, 2002, pp. 266–278.
22. M. Kirikova, Business Modelling and Use Cases in Requirements Engineering, in: *Information Modelling and Knowledge Bases XII*, H. Jaakkola, H. Kangassalo E. Kawaguchi, eds., IOS Press, Ohmsha, Amsterdam, Berlin, Oxford, Tokyo, Washington, DC, 2001, pp. 410–420.

WEB DEVELOPMENT

The differences, similarities and in-betweens

Karlheinz Kautz and Sabine Madsen*

1. INTRODUCTION

The IS literature reveals considerable effort concerning the development of web-based systems. Particularly the differences and similarities between traditional systems development and web development and the applicability of traditional development methods are widely and controversially discussed. However, the discussions are still primarily based on normative arguments and lack support of empirical evidence (Eriksen, 2000).

This paper reports on an empirical investigation of how web-based systems are developed in practice and what the differences and similarities between traditional systems development and web development are, as perceived by practitioners working in the industry. The purpose is 1) to understand the interplay of elements that influence and structure the development of web-based systems in practice and 2) to understand the diverse and often conflicting opinions about web development in a broader context.

The paper is structured as follows: section 2 introduces the background and related work of the study. Section 3 introduces the research framework and method, which is used for data collection and analysis. The empirical findings are presented in section 4 and discussed in section 5. The last section provides a summary of the main conclusions.

2. BACKGROUND

Based on an empirical investigation of three companies working on "internet time", Baskerville and Pries-Heje (2001) identified ten characteristics of web development. They report that the two defining characteristics of web development, time pressure and requirements ambiguity, have lead to a shift away from methodology in its traditional

* Karlheinz Kautz and Sabine Madsen, Copenhagen Business School, Department of Informatics, Howitzvej 60, DK-2000 Frederiksberg, Denmark.

form toward a more pragmatic application of prototyping, frequent releases, parallel development, systems architecture, early coding and an increased focus on negotiable quality, good people and new work structures. However, these have been identified as characteristics of systems development long before web-based information systems became a topic of concern (see for example DeMarco and Lister, 1987; Greenbaum and Stuedahl, 2000; on the issues of time and Ross and Schoman, 1977; Pape and Thoresen, 1987; Curtis et al., 1988; and Grudin, 1991, on the problem with complex and ambiguous requirements) and they have been part of the general discussion of the appropriateness and applicability of existing methods for systems development (see for example Bansler and Bødker, 1993; Fitzgerald, 1998). For instance, prototyping has been discussed as a means to solve the problems inherent in development of all kinds of applications since the mid 1980's (see for example Floyd, 1984; Budde et al., 1992).

In line with this, Vidgen (2002) argues that the ten concepts proposed by Baskerville and Pries-Heje (2001) have a more general relevance for systems development. Instead he suggests that the concrete differences between traditional systems development and web development are that in web development the application is more directly related to strategic business goals, the development focus is on the graphical user interface and the typical user is a customer rather than an employee.

Vidgen et al. (2002) state that the similarities between traditional development and web development are due mainly to increased reliance on databases and integration with enterprise applications and they speculate that as the scope of web projects grows larger, the similarities will outnumber the differences. We have also previously argued that large-scale, technically complex web projects do not differ significantly from traditional systems development projects (Kautz and Madsen, 2002).

Besides the ongoing discussion of the appropriateness of systems development methods in general (Kautz and Pries-Heje, 2000; Truex et al., 2000), one stream of literature argues that the traditional methods are applicable for web development (Chen et al., 1999; Murugesan and Deshpande, 2001), while another stream claim that development of web-based systems is fundamentally different and therefore entirely new methods and approaches are required (Braa et al., 2000; Baskerville and Pries-Heje, 2001; Carstensen and Vogelsang, 2001). Between these extremes it has been suggested that front-end oriented web development (of the user interface) requires new methods and approaches, but back-end oriented and technically complex web development (of the functionality) should still rely on traditional methods (Pressman, 1998). This is in line with Howcroft and Carroll (2000), Eriksen (2000) and Vidgen (2002).

Howcroft and Carroll (2000) state that many new web site development methodologies have focused almost exclusively on the user interface, without addressing the wider issues of web-based systems development. Furthermore, based on an empirical study Eriksen (2001) concludes that traditional development methods are useful for development of back-end functionality, but provide little guidance with regard to the web-based front-end and Vidgen (2002) argues that web-based systems development requires a mix of web site development techniques aimed at the front-end together with traditional systems development methods for database modelling and systems design.

3. RESEARCH FRAMEWORK AND METHOD

As shown above, there are a number of opposing views regarding the differences and similarities between traditional systems development and web development and the extent to which traditional development methods are applicable in web-based systems development. However, these diverse opinions are primarily based on arguments rooted in a technical perspective, as for example the distinction between front-end and back-end development. In this paper, the argument goes beyond the technology-centered propositions. To understand web development and to explain the multitude of view-points, we have to gain an understanding of the interplay of elements that influence and structure web development in practice.

We therefore draw on Walsham (1993), who suggests a framework, which is concerned with the interplay between the context, the process and the content of IT-related organisational change. Walsham argues that the literature on information systems and their development has concentrated mainly on the content of change, i.e. the technology, and has paid insufficient attention to the process of change and its links with the intraorganisational and broader contexts. He emphasises that useful research involves both the context, process and content of change as well as their interaction and relationship to each other.

We will apply the framework for analysing the use of systems development methods by looking at 1) the context, in which web development takes place 2) the web development process and 3) the content of that process, i.e. the web-based applications. A number of different elements can constitute and subsequently be included in such a study. From the empirical data we have identified characteristics of the individual developers, such as education and level of experience, and structural elements of the organisation, such as type, size, project organisation and the general use of plans, process models and methods, as useful analytical concepts and we will draw on them for analysis and discussion.

The research presented in this paper is based on an interpretative research strategy and method triangulation, where we use empirical data from multiple sources, as recommended by Järvinen (2001). The primary source of data is eleven qualitative interviews, supported by findings from a questionnaire. A total of 51 questionnaire responses were received, resulting in an overall response rate of 17%. The findings reported below are based on the 28 questionnaires, where the respondents were directly involved in web-based systems development.

4. EMPIRICAL FINDINGS

The subsequent presentation of the empirical findings is structured as follows: the first section includes findings from interviews, which were conducted in web agencies and the second section presents interviews conducted in a consultancy firm. The findings from the interviews will be supported with results from the questionnaire survey. The third section contains the interview participants' and the questionnaire respondents' opinions about the differences and similarities between traditional systems development and web development.

4.1. Web agencies

Four interviews were performed in Danish web agencies. One of the interviews was conducted with a project manager in a small web enterprise with 18 employees. The company's area of expertise is development of sales campaign and advertising oriented web sites for large Danish companies. When the interview was conducted in August 2001, the company had existed for one year. The interviewed project manager had a multimedia education and around 2 years of experience with web development.

The project manager explained that the average project lasts one month and involves a project manager, a web designer, a text writer and a HTML programmer. The main focus is on conveying the right message to the right target group, coming up with an idea for a campaign site and ensuring that the web design is appealing and innovative. The collaboration with the customer and internally in the project team is mediated via a semi executable powerpoint prototype illustrating the screen layout and user interaction. A typical project is divided into two phases, a concept and a design phase. The customer normally determines the deadline in advance, and therefore no formal project plan is outlined. In the concept phase the project team comes up with the idea for the site using group meetings and brainstorming techniques. Based on these meetings the web designer and text writer quickly develop the powerpoint prototype containing just 'enough' web pages, text and graphics to communicate the concept to the customer. This powerpoint mock-up is continuously refined, enhanced and discussed with the customer until all the web pages are complete and fully designed. Subsequently, the powerpoint mock-up is handed over to the HTML programmer, who carries out the actual coding.

In our interpretation the development process described above is best characterised as unstructured and highly iterative. However, the project manager explicated that due to the small team and low technical complexity there is no need for more advanced techniques or tools to mediate the development process.

A further three interviews were conducted with one project manager and one systems developer working in a medium sized agency with around 100 employees and one project manager from a web agency with around 50 employees. The three interviewed individuals in the medium sized web agencies held master degrees in engineering, computer science and information systems respectively and they all had more than 3 years of experience with web development.

Both agencies specialise in business and web strategy as well as the development of information publishing and transaction oriented web-based systems. Project and team size was reported to vary greatly. Some projects last no more than 14 days involving 1 systems developer only, while other projects last 4–6 months involving 6–8 people full time. Both companies had developed their own in-house method. The two methods were divided into distinct phases, but the development process was primarily driven by iterative prototyping. Both agencies use documents such as project plans, requirement specifications, use case and database model descriptions to facilitate the development process, but no formalised methods were used for designing the overall systems architecture and identifying suitable components.

The above findings are well supported by the questionnaire results. The questionnaire respondents were primarily employed in small to medium sized web agencies/

software houses as project managers, system analysts and system developers. In general they had 2–5 years of experience with web development, mainly from information publishing and transaction oriented systems. The average web project was reported to last 3–4 months, with very few reports on projects exceeding 6 months, and on average the project teams consist of 3–4 people.

With regard to application of process models 9 respondents reported to be using incremental development; 2 were using a traditional waterfall model, while 3 were using a combination of incremental development and the waterfall model. Furthermore, 3 respondents reported that they did not use any process model at all. The most widely applied methods and techniques were prototyping, use cases and database modelling. One respondent stated that: "It [web development] has to happen so fast that it is almost impossible to do any kind of analysis. Therefore, we have found that user interface design, ER diagrams and prototyping are the best suited tools for this kind of development".

4.2. Consultancy firm

Seven interviews were conducted in a large consultancy firm with more than 500 employees and considerable experience with systems development. The interview participants all had a master degree in computer science and between 4–10 years of experience with systems development projects.

The study concerned the experiences, which the interviewed consultants had gained while using Rational's Unified Process (RUP) on two large-scale web projects, projects A and B. Project A lasted 12 months and involved 18 people. When these interviews were conducted, the first phase of project B, which lasted five months, had just been completed. Twelve people had been involved, six of these working full time. The second phase is expected to last up to another 15 months and will involve around ten people full time.

RUP is an object-oriented methodology, characterised by a use case driven, architecture centred, iterative and incremental process model. In both project A and B RUP's development case document was used for project planning, while use cases and architecture documents such as class diagrams and domain models were applied for analysis and design purposes.

Both projects were divided into two main phases, a specification phase and an implementation phase, i.e. engineering and production phase according to RUP's terminology. The outcomes of the specification phase were in both cases a requirement specification consisting of around 100 pages of use cases and detailed recommendations regarding choice of systems architecture. In project A, a prototype was developed for visualising the web-based front-end and the users' interaction with the system, but in both projects the development process and the communication with the customer was primarily document driven. Thus, the two project teams did not use RUP as a framework for structuring and managing an iterative and incremental process – as intended in the methodology. Instead the two projects followed a traditional development process, i.e. a waterfall model, supplemented with tools and techniques from RUP.

Our findings from the interviews in the consultancy differ somewhat from the survey results. Similar tools and techniques, such as use cases and prototypes, are applied, but in the consultancy the projects lasted longer, the project teams were larger and the applications under development were more business critical and technically complex than generally reported in the questionnaire results. Furthermore, the consultancy placed much more emphasis on formal analysis and design. Whereas the survey results suggest that web development processes are highly iterative and prototype driven, the findings from the consultancy reveal a more traditional, formal and document driven development process.

4.3. Differences and similarities

When asked about the difference between web development and traditional systems development the three interviewed project managers and the systems developer in the web agencies mentioned time pressure, project size, team size and the relatively lower technical complexity as the most significant characteristics. In contrast, the interviewed consultants all stated that they do not think that web development is significantly different from traditional systems development. The consultants explained that there are some differences, because it is less clear who the users are and because there are technical constraints for the user interface, for instance regarding browser versions. But these are perceived as minor differences. One consultant stated that it is appropriate to distinguish between web applications, which are front-end oriented and mainly concern information publishing and web applications, which are back-end oriented and have to be integrated with components such as enterprise applications etc. The later is fundamentally the same as traditional systems development. The two projects in this case study were both large-scale, back-end oriented and technically complex projects with many people involved, and the interviewed consultants did not experience these projects to be any different from traditional systems development projects.

However, the consultants state that the customer might experience web development as being different, mainly due to the publicity, which dominated the market in the late 1990's. The customers' perception might be reinforced by the fact that they are primarily thinking in terms of the front-end of a web application and do not understand its technically complex features, i.e. the back-end.

The results from the questionnaire survey confirm our interview findings from the web agencies and are well in line with other empirical studies (see for example Baskerville and Pries-Heje, 2001; Vidgen, 2002). Bearing in mind that the respondents' experience with web development stem mainly from information publishing and transaction oriented systems, when asked about the significant characteristics of web development as opposed to traditional systems development, the most widely stated characteristics concerned: web technology has introduced new challenges, front-end related issues such as graphical web design, aesthetics, content and usability are very important, business related issues are important and more directly associated with the overall business strategy, a web project requires a diversity of skills and is in general reported to be shorter in calendar time and conducted under time pressure.

With regard to the appropriateness of traditional system development methods, one respondent stated that the traditional methods and methodologies are not designed to deal with "the particular nature of web development". However, several other respondents report that they do not perceive web development to be any different from traditional systems development and they consider traditional tools and techniques suitable for web development as well. But they too address that development of the web-based front-end requires a focus on design, aesthetics and usability, which the traditional system development methods do not support. Yet again two respondents express a more general skepticism towards methods and report that they have never seen a widespread and structured use of systems development methods in web-based systems development - or in traditional systems development.

The description of differences and similarities as perceived by practitioners working in the industry reveals a diversity of opinions, which resemble the on-going discussions and conflicting views in the literature. In the next section we will try to explain this diversity based on an understanding of the different contexts, in which web development takes place and the interplay of elements that influence and structure web development in practice.

Table 1. Summary of empirical findings

Context			
Organisation			
Type	Web agency	Web agency	Consultancy
Size	Small	Medium	Large
Individual			
Education	Multimedia	Master degrees	Computer Science
Experience	2 years	+3 years	+4 years
Project			
Duration	1 month	1-6 months	12-20 months
Team size	4 people	1-8 people	9-18 people
Process			
Project plans	No	Yes	Yes
Process models	Iterative/Ad hoc	In-house model/Iterative	Waterfall model
Methods	PowerPoint Prototype	PowerPoint Prototypes HTML Prototypes DB models	RUP, a comprehensive systems development methodology
Content			
Application type	Information publishing and advertising sites	Information publishing and transaction oriented web-based systems	Transaction oriented web-based systems, ERP integration
Development focus	Front-end	Front-end and Back-end	Back-end

5. DISCUSSION

Vidgen (2002) puts forward a number of stereotypical differences between traditional systems development and web development. For instance, he suggests that in a traditional project the development focus is primarily oriented toward development of back-end functionality and the user interface is almost an afterthought. In contrast, the development focus for Internet projects is on the web site as a visual artefact, the development often starts with a mock-up of the user interface and graphic design skills are essential (Vidgen, 2002). Though stereotypical and rather simplistic, our findings do lend some support to these generalisations, suggesting that they might be a useful point of reference for conceptualising, not only the differences between traditional systems development and web development, but different types of web development (Table 1).

In the following we will use the companies from the interview study as examples. When we compare the findings in Table 1, it seems reasonable to think of development, as it is carried out in the consultancy, as rather similar to traditional systems development, while the development in the small web agency is quite different. For the medium sized web agencies the development can be characterised as somewhere in-between. We propose that the development focus and how web development is actually conducted in a particular context can be understood as a complex interplay of context, process and application type characteristics.

In the consultancy the development processes for the two web projects followed a traditional waterfall model supplemented with tools and techniques from RUP. The development focus was primarily directed toward back-end functionality and there was considerable less emphasis on design and development of the user interface. This can be explained as caused by the type of applications under development, i.e. technically complex transaction oriented web-based systems reliant on integration with enterprise applications. Due to the technical complexity of the projects, the project duration was longer and the project teams were larger, than one would normally expect of web projects. Thus, not only was there a high degree of technical complexity, but also a high degree of social complexity in that more people were involved over a long period of time and close collaboration with suppliers was needed. The development process and the application of more traditional development methods can therefore be understood as due to the complexity of the task. However, the history and structural elements of the organisation as well as characteristics of the individual developers also explain the development process. The consultancy is a large company with years of experience from traditional development. Furthermore, all the consultants involved in development projects share a similar educational background in computer science and have considerable experience from previous projects. Thus, there is a general knowledge about how to conduct systems development both at the organisational and the individual level. This is also evident from the general use of formal project plans, a well-known development process and traditional systems development methods. In effect, web development is perceived of and conducted in much the same way as traditional systems development in an organisational context, where there is relatively established work practices rooted in a systems development culture.

In the small web agency there is no use of formal project plans, the development process is highly iterative and only mediated via a powerpoint prototype. The development focus is directed almost entirely toward design of the web-based user interface with a focus on creativity in concept development and graphic design. Again, the development process can be understood as caused by the type of applications under development, i.e. information publishing and advertising web sites with very simple or no underlying back-end functionality. Furthermore, the project team is small and the developers are located in the same room facilitating close interaction between team members. Thus, due to the relatively low technical and social complexity, formalisation of the development process and application of sophisticated tools and techniques is, and can be, kept to a minimum. When analysing the findings from an organisational and individual perspective, the agency is a small, new company and the employees have varied educational backgrounds, but with a focus on web development as a multimedia discipline. In effect, web development is perceived of and conducted differently as compared to traditional systems development, there are few established work practices and the professional culture is perhaps more comparable to that of an advertising or media enterprise (See for example Lyytinen et al., 1998; Greenbaum and Stuedahl, 2000; Barry and Lang, 2001, for comparison of this kind of development to advertising, media, multimedia and film production).

The two medium sized agencies had developed their own in-house process models, which in both cases were based on step-wise development according to distinct phases, but the development processes are in practice primarily prototype driven. The development focus is aimed both at development of the web-based user interface and at development of back-end functionality. This can be explained as caused by the type of applications under development, i.e. information publishing and transaction oriented web-based systems typically with database integration. One possible explanation for the development of in-house process models could be that these agencies, to a larger extent than in the consultancy and the small agency, are struggling to accommodate both front-end oriented and back-end oriented development issues into their work practices. Furthermore, the development situations in these agencies are characterised by diversity: diversity in project scale, scope, technical complexity and development focus and there is great diversity in project duration, team size as well as in educational background and level of experience of the individuals involved. In effect, web development is perceived of and conducted in a way, which incorporates elements of both *traditional system development* and *web site development* in an organisational context, where there are few established work practices and where the organisational culture is not rooted in any one professional paradigm, but draws on a range of disciplines.

The findings from the consultancy and the small web agency can be viewed as two stereotypical, though real-world, examples of how web development is conceptualised and conducted in different ways. Between these extremes our findings from the medium sized agencies and the questionnaire suggest that much web development is characterised by diversity and thus lend itself less easy to obvious and clear-cut classification. This is further supported by the diversity of opinions and conflicting views to be found in the literature. We argue that the different opinions about web development, and systems development in general, can be explained by the type of development setting, type of systems development process and type of application, which the practitioner and/or researcher is confronted with. This is in line with Holck (2003). He suggests that whether development of web-based systems seems different from traditional systems development depends on the developer's (or researcher's) background and the people and projects, one is confronted with. In keeping with this, we have argued that there are different types of web development. Whether development of web-based systems seem different from traditional development might depend on, if one is exposed to web development, which is primarily rooted in a traditional systems development paradigm, in a advertising/media paradigm or somewhere in-between drawing on a complex interplay of elements from both worlds.

6. SUMMARY

Our empirical findings show that there are different types of web development. In one case, web development is perceived of and conducted in much the same way as traditional systems development, while in another it is conceptualised and carried out quite differently. Between these extremes our findings suggest that much web development is characterised by diversity, incorporating elements from both traditional systems development and advertising/media production.

How web development is actually conducted in practice can be explained by somewhat technical arguments such as application type and development focus, but also by development process characteristics and history and culture of the particular company. We therefore argue that to understand these different types of web development, we have to understand the complex interplay of context, development process and application type characteristics - their interaction and relationship to each other, in general and in the particular case.

This research further indicates that the different work practices and opinions about web development, which we found in practice, are already to some degree reflected in the literature. It might therefore be more accurately in line with the diversity of practice to view the research results in the literature as, not opposing views, but supplementary perspectives suitable for different types of applications and consequently different development settings and development processes.

REFERENCES

Bansler J. and K. Bødker, 1993, A Reappraisal of Structured Analysis: Design in an Organizational Context, *ACM Transactions on Information Systems*, 11(2), 165–193.

Barry C. and M. Lang, 2001, A Survey of Multimedia and Web Development Techniques and Methodology Usage, *IEEE MultiMedia*, 8(2), 52–60.

Baskerville R. and J. Pries-Heje, 2001, Racing the E-Bomb: how the Internet is redefining Information Systems Development, Proceedings of the IFIP TC8/WG8.2 Working Conference, July, Idaho, USA.

Braa K., Sørensen C. and B. Dahlbom, 2000, Changes – From Big Calculator to Global Network, in: *Planet Internet*, Studenterlitteratur, pp. 13–39.

Budde R., Kautz K., Kuhlenkamp K. and H. Züllighoven, 1992, What is Prototyping?, *Information, Technology and People*, vol. 6, no. 2+3, Northwind, Oregon, USA.

Carstensen P. and L. Vogelsang, 2001, Design of Web-Based Information Systems – New Challenges for Systems Development?, Proceedings of the European Conference on Information Systems (ECIS).

Chen L., Sherrell L.B. and C. Hsu, 1999, A Development Methodology for Corporate Web Sites, First ICSE Workshop on Web Engineering (WebE-99), Los Angeles, USA.

Curtis, B., H. Krasner and N. Iscoe, 1998, A Field Study of the Software Design Process for Large Systems, *Communications of the ACVM*, vol 31, no. 11, 1268–1287.

DeMarco T. and T. Lister, 1987, Peopleware – Productive Projects and Teams, Dorset House Publishing, New York, NY, USA.

Eriksen L. B., 2000, Limitations and Opportunities of System Development Methods in Web Information System Design, Proceedings of the IFIP TC8/WG 8.2 Working Conference, Boston, USA, 473–486.

Floyd C., 1984, A Systematic Look at Prototyping, in: *Approaches to Prototyping*, Budde R. et al. eds., Springer Verlag, Berlin, Germany.

Greenbaum J. and D. Stuedahl, 2000, Deadlines and work practices in New Media Development, Proceedings of the 23rd IRIS conference, University of Trollhättan Uddevalla, 537–546.

Grudin J., 1991, Interactive Systems: Bridging the Gap between developers and users, *IEEE Computer*, April, pp. 59–69.

Holck J., 2003, 4 Perspectives on Web Information Systems, Proceedings of the 36th HICSS conference.

Howcroft D. and J. Carroll, 2000, A Proposed Methodology for Web Development, Proceedings of the 8th European Conference on Information Systems (ECIS), Vienna, July.

Järvinen P., 2001, On Research Methods, Opinpajan Kirja.

Kautz K. and S. Madsen, 2002, Applying System Development Methods in Practice – The RUP example, in:, *Information Systems Development: Advances in Methodologies, Components and Management*, Grundspenkis J. et al., eds., Kluwer Press, pp. 267–278.

Kautz K. and J. Pries-Heje, 2000, Systems Development Education and Methodology Adoption, *Journal of Computer Personnel*, Vol. 20, No. 3.

Lyytinen K., Gregory R. and R. Welke, 1998, The Brave New World of Development in the Internetwork Computing Architecture (InterNCA): or how distributed Computing Platforms will change Systems Development, *Information Systems Journal*, Vol. 8, 241–253.

Murugesan S. and Y. Deshpande, 2001, Web Engineering: A new Discipline for Development of web-based systems, in: *Web Engineering - Managing Diversity and Complexity of Web Application Development*, Springer-Verlag.

Pape T. and K. Thoresen, 1987, Development of Common Systems by Prototyping, in: *Computers and Democracy – A Scandinavian Challenge*, Bjerknes et al., eds., Aldershot, Brookfield, USA, pp.297–311.

Pressman R. S., 1998, Can Internet-Based Applications be Engineered?, *IEEE Software*, September/October, 104–110.

Roos D. T. and K. E. Schoman, 1977, Structured Analysis for Requirements Definition, *IEEE Transactions on Software Engineering*, SE-3, pp. 6–15.

Truex D., Baskerville R. and J. Travis, 2000, A methodical systems development: the deferred meaning of systems development methods, *Accounting Management & Information Technologies*, 10(1), 53–79.

Vidgen R., 2002, WISDM: Constructing a Web Information System Development Methodology, *Information Systems Journal*, 12(3), 247–261.

Vidgen R., Avison D., Wood J. and A. Wood-Harper, 2002, *Developing Web Information Systems*, Butterworth Heinemann.

Walsham G., 1993, *Interpreting Information Systems in Organizations*, John Wiley & Sons.

SEARCHING FOR A METHODOLOGY FOR SMART INTERNET TECHNOLOGY DEVELOPMENT

Jenine Beekhuyzen, Liisa von Hellens,
Michelle Morley, and Sue Nielsen*

ABSTRACT

Participatory Design is an approach to the design of computer-based systems and software that involves the users to a much greater extent than traditional design approaches and draws on diverse fields such as "user-centred design, graphic design, software engineering, architecture, public policy, psychology, anthropology, sociology, labor studies, communication studies, and political science" (Kuhn and Muller, 1993).

This paper explores the use of a particular PD approach, User-Centred Design (UCD), which has been adopted by the Smart Internet Technology Cooperative Research Centre (SITCRC) in Australia. Early experiences of applying this methodology to a multidisciplinary project team developing Smart Internet Technologies (SIT) are discussed.

This research is of interest to those new to Participatory Design, and to those familiar with one or some of the methods but who wish to understand the context of those methods or consider alternative methods. The review aims to stimulate the interest of researchers and practitioners, to encourage the reader to think about the range of Participatory Design methods available and to pursue further reading on those that sound interesting, useful, or relevant to the reader's project.

1. INTRODUCTION

Participatory Design methods have a common concern for the "knowledge, voices, and/or rights of end-users" (Muller, 1993) and this is particularly applicable within the context of diverse Participatory Design (PD) teams consisting of a mixture of researchers and practitioners. This paper discusses the field of participatory design, including the

* Jenine Beekhuyzen, Liisa von Hellens, Michelle Morley, Sue Nielsen, School of CIT, Griffith University, Brisbane, Queensland, Australia 4111

methods, tools, and techniques for PD, and the relationship between participatory design and usability practices. Other names for Participatory Design include Contextual Enquiry, Situated Activity, Work-oriented Design, Design for Learnability, Situated Design (Greenbaum and Kyng, 1991).

User-Centred Design (UCD) as a field of study provides the context for this research and is discussed in this paper as a participatory design method (refer section 3.2). UCD is being used in a longitudinal research project based at the Smart Internet Technology Cooperative Research Centre (SITCRC) in Australia. The main objective of this centre is to develop product innovations that utilise Internet technologies for commercialisation.

This paper discusses the use of the User-Centred Design approach in the early stages of Smart Internet Technology development. More specifically, this paper first attempts to provide an understanding of the usefulness of Participatory Design (PD). Secondly, this paper introduces a particular approach to User Centred Design, which is being developed within the User Needs and UCD subprojects of the SITCRC. The authors are contributing members of these projects. Finally, this paper describes early experiences of applying this method to the product development within the SITCRC.

2. PARTICIPATORY DESIGN (PD)

While Participatory Design can be broadly described as an approach, descriptions such as a movement, a field of study, an area of practice, and a collection of methods and techniques are also appropriate. As an approach, Participatory Design differs from conventional design in terms increased user involvement from the beginning of the design project. Participatory design does not prescribe the use of a particular method, instead there is a "rich diversity of theories, practices, analyses, and actions" (Kuhn and Muller, 1993) within the field of Participatory Design. The common goal of these is to work directly with users (Kuhn and Muller, 1993) in design of systems.

Key features of participatory design are that:

- Responsibility for "quality of the design proposal and the implemented system" is shared between users and system experts (Bjerknes, 1993);
- Methods involve users from the beginning of the design, encouraging users to create the design themselves rather than only to evaluate the designs of experts. Users (or workers) are viewed as "intelligent, creative, and productive contributors" (Miller, 1993).

2.1. Why Participatory Design?

A fundamental principle of Participatory Design is that "active collaboration of the users in the design process of a computer systems development should contribute to successful design and high quality products" (Vimarlund and Timpka 1998). Ellis and Kurniawan (2000) identify three premises that they consider to characterise the "most common interpretation of the PD philosophy". These are:

(i) "The goal of PD is to improve the quality of life, rather than demonstrate the capability of technology;
(ii) "The orientation of PD is collaborative and cooperative…and

(iii) "PD values interactive evaluation to gather and integrate feedback from intended users, thereby promoting design knowledge".

These quotations emphasise that while producing a design is a key goal of Participatory Design methods, there are other goals that can be achieved. Greenbaum (1993), for instance, suggests three different perspectives on PD; a pragmatic perspective, a theoretical perspective and a political perspective.

Much of the literature on Participatory Design discusses a single case study or a single method or technique, while some of the literature discusses the origins of Participatory Designs and examines political issues. A smaller set of literature reviews Participatory Design methods. In 1993, Clement and Van den Besselaar reported that since the 1970's there have been many reports on PD projects, and prescriptive articles drawing on just a few projects, but no "systematic surveys of these experiences as a whole". Their article provides such a survey of Participatory Design projects. Just as a survey of projects was considered to be a valuable contribution to an understanding of PD, a survey of methods, tools, and techniques can be valuable to the practitioner and the researcher.

2.2. Methods of Participatory Design

In the *Communications of the ACM* special issue on Participatory Design, Muller, Wildman, and White (1993b) present a taxonomy of Participatory Design practices in an attempt to resolve two problems arising from the rapid growth in the field of Participatory Design. The first is that "practitioners may need some guidance in finding techniques that are appropriate to their circumstance" and the second that "some practitioners may believe that PD is not appropriate outside Scandinavia's specific legal environment" (Muller et al., 1993b). Muller et al.'s taxonomy addresses these problems by providing the taxonomy of practices and references to projects having used Participatory Design, including many in Scandinavia.

Participatory Design has the goal of placing the users and their needs as the key focus in design. For this paper, the methods of participatory design, specifically user-centred design (Vredenburg, 2002) and storytelling incorporating the use of personas and scenarios (Grudin and Pruitt, 2002) are of particular interest. A number of other PD methods can be used alongside or within the context of user-centred design such as workshops (Muller et al., 1993b; Carmel, Whitaker and George, 1993; Boy, 1996), ETHICS (Mumford, 1993), STEPS (Floyd, 1993), MUST (Kensin, Simonsen and Bodker, 1996) Contextual Design (Beyer and Holzblatt in Bossen, 2002), Ethnography (Crabtree, 1998), Participatory Stakeholder Evaluation (Giordano and Bell, 2000), MINDTAPE tool (Nielsen and Christiansen, 2000), ezSIS Team Method (Ellis and Kurniawan, 2000; Good 1992), PICTIVE (Muller, Wildman and White, 1993a).

User-Centred Design (UCD) is a well established design approach that has been widely adopted by many organisations to deliver products that meet users' expectations. UCD places the user at the centre of the design from the beginning of the design process. To date, UCD has been adopted mostly within the corporate context. For instance, IBM has been a strong adopter of UCD methods to enhance their product development process. They have now consolidated this process with their broader framework of User Engineering. Formal UCD methods have proven successful in the development of effective software across a number of industries such as aerospace and technology. These same methods have also proved successful in the development of a powerful securities trading system currently operating in the world economy (Mauro, 2000).

2.3. A Context for Participatory Design Methods

Participatory Design methods can be applied to the development of products, such as software and electronic devices, for both the home consumer and industrial markets. The focus of participatory design for the home consumer differs from within the workplace (i.e. industrial) for two key reasons. Firstly, "consumer electronics are intended for leisure activities. Users are thus typically inherently motivated to use the equipment, and their activities are directly related to the gratification of their own personal needs" and secondly "skilled operation of equipment in the workplace is presumed to require the acquisition of special knowledge, which is not presumed to be attainable by everyone. In contrast, home electronics are for non-professionals without special training or previously acquired knowledge" (Baerentsen and Slavensky, 1999). A good approach to participatory design outside the workplace is a focus "on multidisciplinary design of the user experience with particular attention being paid to the affective aspects, not only the cognitive and behaviour" (Vredenburg, 1999), which is a "perspective often missing in current practice".

A principle of the political perspective on Participatory Design is the "empowerment of the workers so they can codetermine the development of the information system and of their workplace" (Clement and Van den Besselaar, 1993). While this review does not focus on the political aspects of Participatory Design, it is important to highlight that just as PD is intended to empower workers, it can empower the home user to codetermine the development of the technologies they will use in everyday life.

Ellis and Kurniawan (2000) highlight a "critical aspect" of PD from Ehn's (1988) writings: that "designers gain a knowledge of the work context, so that the new technology explicitly incorporates the values, history, and context of the work system". The Participatory Design approach "generalizes easily to the work of managing one's daily life" (Ellis and Kurniawan 2000).

From a business perspective for the manufacturers, such user involvement could be expected to lead to greater sales. The challenge is achieving the right balance of potential users (as representatives of the entire market) in the design process. The methods, tools, and techniques of Participatory Design, described in this section, are just as applicable to the home consumer as the workplace, even if the philosophies behind their use differs.

3. WHY USER-CENTRED DESIGN (UCD)?

User-Centred Design focuses on the active involvement of the user in the design process, trying to obtain a clear understanding of the exact task requirements, involving an iterative design and evaluation process, and utilising a multi-disciplinary approach. (Vredenburg, 2002) The key focus of UCD, like other participatory design approaches, is that users play a critical role in the design of easy-to-use products throughout the entire development process.

In the corporate context, the core goal of the User-Centred Design principles are to involve the users. This is done by undertaking the following steps during development:

- Set business goals
- Understand users
- Assess competitiveness
- Design the total user experience
- Evaluate designs
- Manage by continual user observation (Vredenburg, 2002)

Interaction throughout the design process is necessary between users and developers in order to understand and define the context of use, the tasks, and how users are likely to work with the future product or system (ETSI, 2002).

In order to make UCD common practice among designers, models for UCD have been proposed based on international standards. ISO 13407 (Human-Centred Design Processes for Interactive Systems) and ISO 18529 (Human-Centred Lifestyle Process Descriptions) are two examples (Jokela, 2002)

4. PRACTICAL APPLICATIONS OF USER-CENTRED DESIGN AT THE SITCRC

The Smart Internet Technology Cooperative Research Centre (SITCRC) is a consortium of Australian universities and industry partners integrating expertise in information systems, artificial intelligence, networking, security, software engineering and social science to develop Internet applications to enhance business and lifestyles in a user-friendly manner.

The SITCRC is comprised of four Technology teams and a User Environment team. The authors of this paper contribute to the User-Centred Design (UCD) team, part of the User Environment team. The UCD team has adopted a User-Centred Design approach to support the development of the SITCRC's commercialisable products. The UCD team's particular approach to User Centred Design is being developed within the team (refer Figure 1, section 4.2). The UCD team is made up of three main research teams in three universities and this discussion is from the perspective of one of the teams, the Griffith University (GU) team. In this context, UCD is used in a collaborative academic and industrial research environment to scope broad project directions leading into specific product development and demonstrators.

4.1. SITCRC: A Case Study

The Mission of the SITCRC is to capitalise the outcomes of world class Internet research and development for Australia. The objectives supporting the mission are:

- To ensure efficient and effective world class research with significant technological and commercial outcomes
- To provide integration between technological innovation and social and behavioural research
- To provide high-value Internet-based technologies, solutions and services that are competitive in the international marketplace
- To provide actual and future benefits 5 times the value of the resources used

- To produce knowledgeable, skilled and enterprising Information and Communication Technology (ICT) professionals required for Australia
- To develop enabling technologies, solutions and services to increase productivity and deliver efficiency gains for Australia through pervasive use of the Internet
- To assist, through technology transfer, the commercial advancement of Australian Industry, including Small to Medium Enterprises (SMEs)

4.2. Experiences of User-Centred Design in Innovation Development

The key question of the User Needs project is **"How can the intended outcomes of the technology programs best meet user needs?"** and it aims to support and encourage 'a culture of user-centred design' throughout the SITCRC.

The steps of the process from the discovery stage to products for commercial commercialization include: formulating the design concept of the products, participating actively in the detailed product design providing an evaluation framework to assess the usability/usefulness of the artifact/products (action research/co-design), and performing the usability testing (iterative design) (Burke, Castro, Singh and Turner, 2002).

UCD has been adopted by the User Needs Project and continues to address this key question. This project assists with the design and implementation of research in the technology programs, and focuses on demonstrators and products with commercial opportunities (UCD, 2002). The UCD project also contributes to the theory on PD through it's three subsidiary objectives:

To explore and record ways of communicating, first within the multi-disciplinary User Needs (UN) group, and secondly between the UN group and the researchers in the technology programs.

To continue to conduct User Research as an input into the technology programs and future demonstrators. The initial segments are SMEs (including professionals and e-lancers), young people, and people with disabilities and other special needs. Key activity areas include: learning, tourism, electronic commerce, collaborative work, emergency services, financial services, health, leisure/entertainment, and personal communications.

User studies will help identify areas where Smart Internet Technologies may be constrained, or have particular opportunity, due to likely responses of potential users. Examples of key areas include boundaries of acceptable natural language interaction, trust, security, universal (also called inclusive) design, cross-cultural variations, organisational characteristics, and particular activity applications requirements.

To continue developing the UCD methodology, extending it from the discovery phase of design to product development. This will be done through interaction with the technology programs and demonstrator projects. This methodology will be communicated and tested in internal and external training programs.

In order to achieve these objectives, a framework for establishing a meeting place was developed by the UCD team. The meeting place provides a tool for effective communication within the group (Figure 1).

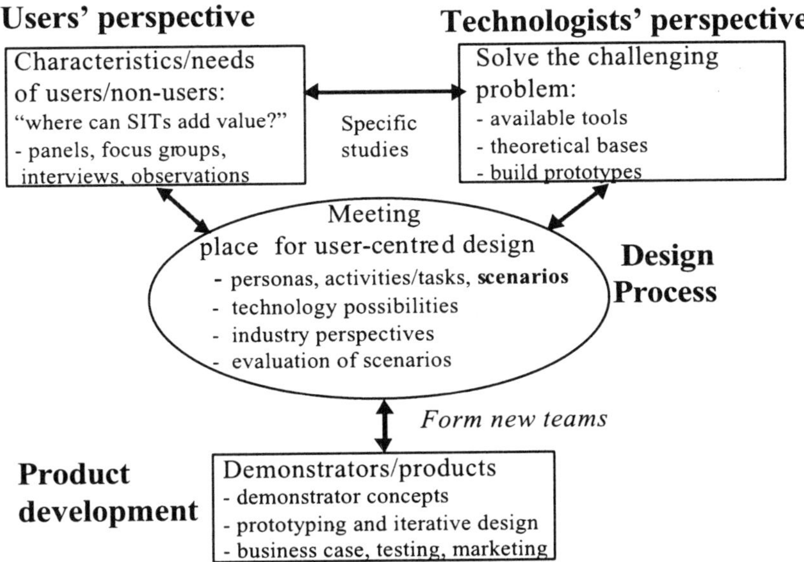

Figure 1. Framework: Establishing the meeting place (Burke et al., 2002)

User-Centred Design has a strong focus on the involvement of the user during the conceptualisation and development stage. It offers both a conceptual approach (through the use of a design model and process based on UCD principles) as well as a practical approach (through workshopping personas and scenarios, for example, and the actual involvement of user groups).

4.3. Use of Scenarios

The use of personas and scenarios helps design future technologies by giving a deeper understanding of how a user will interact with particular technologies.

The GU team is using scenarios in the context of the study of SMEs. Figure 2 represents the process of how scenarios in this context are being used for group communication. For example, based on the literature and informal discussions with users, scenarios are developed by the researchers and proposed to the expert panel. Feedback is incorporated into revisions of the scenarios. Once developed, the scenarios and personas are discussed amongst a sector-based focus group and again, feedback is incorporated in the reworked scenarios. Once complete, the technologies discussed in the scenarios are transformed into demonstrator proposals for development. It is at this point that the UCD team would adjust their role in the technology development, and assist in Human Computer Interface and social issues (refer Figure 1).

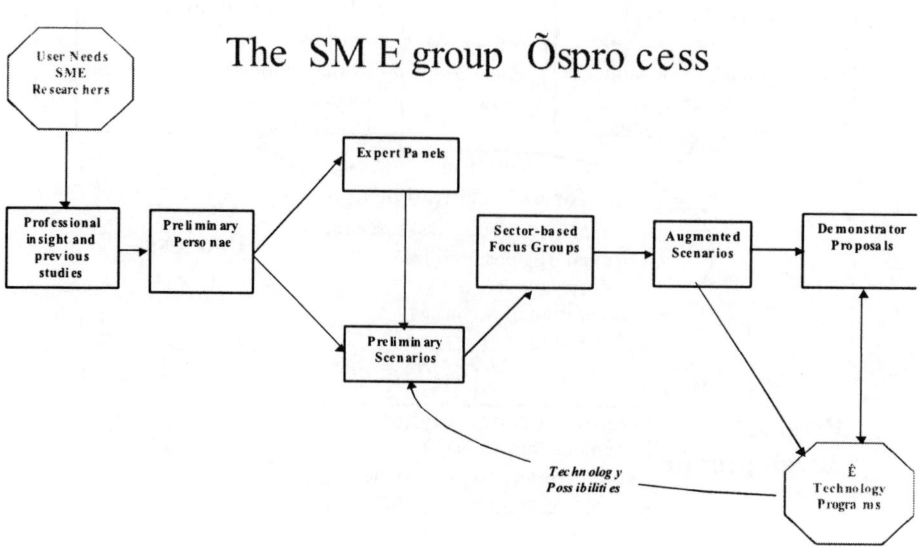

Figure 2. The SME group's process (Burke et al., 2002)

4.4. The GU Team

4.4.1. Phase 1

The initial phase of the SME UCD project aimed to directly influence the design and implementation of the outputs from the technology programs by way of providing SME scenarios highlighting user needs in particular activity areas that could be related to one or more of the technology programs. A particular goal at this stage was to leverage scenarios to engage specific high value sectors to participate in the development and evolution of demonstrators/products.

At this stage, the GU UCD project focused on the development of four initial SME usage scenarios. Initial links with the newly identified expert panel were made and calls for the participation of software developers in the project were made. Sector-specific focus groups were also carried out. These different groups of industry experts are an essential part of the process, as they are involved in the testing and validating the scenarios. During the formation of the participatory team, it was essential for the GU team to continually interact with members of the rest of the UCD team, the technology programs and the SME community.

General Interviews: The GU team interviewed eight people in a range of system and software developers in a mix of roles. The interviewees were asked questions ranging from very general information on software development and future technologies to very specific information about particular known applications. These interviewees also stem from a variety of industries, including, betting/racing/casino, airline, ICT Consulting, education and entertainment.

The information gathered from these interviews was incorporated into the development of the scenarios. Ongoing interviews with software developers have taken place alongside the process of scenario development. This regular interaction with industry professionals aided in the formulation and continual development of new scenarios, and helped to expand the knowledge base in terms of industry sectors.

Focus Groups: The GU team conducted one focus group of six Bachelor of IT student software developers currently studying their final year in IT at University. Their project requires them to undertake a year-long IT project that requires them to develop a system for an existing organisation. The group provided a different perspective to the software development process and opportunities for future technologies than is provided by those now working in industry, such as those who provided information in the general interviews and also those on the expert panel.

Expert Panel: The expert panel comprises software developers. The four people included in the panel come from a range of industries including retail, on-line information services, ICT consulting and development and library management.

The initial SME scenarios developed have been distributed to the various experts on the panel for comments. Their comments will focus on:

- The relevance of scenarios to current situation in industry
- The degree to which scenarios incorporate future directions of the technology
- The degree to which all potential scenarios are accounted for (this is probably one of the main things we are looking for which we have limited knowledge)
- Key features of the system illustrated by the scenarios
- Other equally essential requirements not explicitly mentioned
- Desirable features – not essential features

Experts were asked to comment on a number of cross-cutting issues that were identified by the UCD team. The organisations where the experts are employed are possibly to be included as developers of the demonstrator products in future phases of this project.

This first phase of the GU team project identified that SMEs were very willing to participate with the CRC, and that these organisations were very interested in the applicability of Smart Internet Technologies to their working environment.

4.4.2. Phase 2

The primary aim of the second phase of the SME User Needs project is to develop the meeting place for user centred design and in collaboration with the technology projects move from demonstrator proposals through to prototyping concepts that have value for each of the key stakeholders (refer Figure 1).

To achieve this, the SME User Needs Project has been and will continue to focus on several activity streams. Firstly, to continue engagement with SMEs for validation and further development of scenarios and secondly, to continue engagement with Technology Programs to assist design and testing of program outputs

In June 2002, the GU team initiated fortnightly meetings with the one of the technology groups (SPA) located at the same institution. The meetings did begin weekly, but after initial communication issues, the GU team realised that the SPA group was not at the same point with their schedule, which made the weekly meetings fairly unproductive for both teams.

One of the GU team members began regular communication with one of the technology team (SPA) members, The SPA researcher was very helpful in the UCD process as he provided some excellent feedback on the scenarios presented by the GU team. He particularly discussed breaking down the scenarios so that they would be more useful to the technology group as a whole. He provided a scenario breakdown method, which provided some valuable input to the UCD methodology discussion.

Discussions with the technology team also resulted in identifying the importance for the scenarios to retain their context to qualify as "scenarios". It was suggested that there could be two formats of the same scenario; one that has the full context of the situation, and another that has the scenario broken down into much smaller details. It was also suggested that an executive summary with the some of the task breakdown information could be included with the contextual scenarios to make them more useful to all teams involved.

Continuing activities of Phase 2

Engaging with industry: The GU team will continue to actively engage with members of the SME community in order to assess activities undertaken and outputs delivered. This interaction will lead to the further refinement of scenarios, but will also lead to the development of new scenarios that may lead to potential demonstrator concepts.

Engaging with the UCD Team: The User Needs group (the UCD group) will continue to collaborate over the next six months through a variety of formats including face-to-face meetings, teleconferencing, email/discussion groups, and document and resource sharing. The collaboration is vital for the analysis of the relevance of SITs to user needs.

Engaging with the Technology Programs: The GU team, in conjunction with other UCD researchers, will continue to engage with members of other projects and program areas. This engagement will be based on the development and evaluation of scenarios for use by technology researchers, and the development of concepts and design implications for SME-focused technology demonstrators. Based on expected input and feedback from members of the technology programs, the GU team will identify a number of existing scenarios, which will be further explored and developed into demonstrator projects. The GU team is currently attempting to formulate a project that will be contributed to by all participants to the GU teams institution.

Development of Demonstrator proposals: Based on the four scenarios, which have been developed and refined in the first phase of the GU team project, a number of potential concepts for technology demonstrators were to be developed throughout the second phase of this project. These demonstrators will be developed in conjunction with both members of the UCD project, the technology programs and our commercial partners. Members of the SME community will also provide valuable contributions to this process in terms of identifying business cases and potential usage areas for demonstrator proposals.

Co-design and testing of Demonstrators: Once demonstrator concepts have been initiated, the GU team will work at testing and refining a co-design methodology for these demonstrators. Members of the SME user needs program have begun to form new teams with members from both existing technology programs and industry partners to facilitate the co-design and testing of demonstrator concepts.

The GU team are of the belief that the interactions with the technology team and the teleconferences with the rest of the UCD team have been very beneficial in gaining a wider perspective of the project and what is happening across other teams. The meetings have enabled discussions and the facility for feedback on a fortnightly basis, which has been very helpful to the GU team, helping to bridge the geographical gap. This has been within the context of nurturing the broader linkage between the UCD group and the technology teams.

5. CONCLUSION

This paper has explored the use of a particular Participatory Design (PD) approach, User-Centred Design (UCD). The adoption of UCD is discussed within the context of the Smart Internet Technology Cooperative Research Centre (SITCRC) in Australia. Early experiences of applying this methodology to a multidisciplinary project team were discussed.

The SITCRC attempts to follow Greenbaum and Kyng's (1991) advice in encouraging interdisciplinary teams. They suggest four important issues of which to be aware when using Participatory Design methods: "The need for designers to take work practices seriously, the fact that we are dealing with human actors (rather than factors), work tasks are situated actions, work is fundamentally social".

These issues presented by Greenbaum and Kyng (1991) are high level principles to follow whereas Bjerknes (1993) provides advice on how to conduct a successful PD project. Bjerknes suggests that during establishment, it is important to have management support, specify in a contract how much time users can/shall spend on the project, have a steering group in which conflicts can be discussed, be sure the required equipment is available for system experts and users and most of all, listen to the users and take them seriously!

The UCD team has SITCRC management support and is gaining support from the technology teams. Program leaders have been assigned to projects and deal with any conflicts are constantly required to present the group's research. Also, the users have a very clear role in the project are recognised for their importance. They are always at the centre of any design.

The GU User Needs team has found the UCD Participatory Design approach to most useful as a communication tool, and for a semi-structural approach to the design of their scenarios. The team will continually use the UCD approach and it is envisaged that it will help to strengthen the links between the User Needs and the Technology teams.

Participatory design methods can be employed independent of underlying methodology (assumptions about the nature of methods), however it can be worthwhile to consider these underlying assumptions. The successes of the PD methods presented in this paper do depend on remembering the reason why PD is being used – it's all about creating products with the user!

REFERENCES

Baerentsen, K. B., and Slavensky, H., 1999, A Contribution to the Design Process, *Communications of the ACM* 42(5),73–77.

Bjerknes, G., 1993, Some PD Advice, *Communications of the ACM,* 36(4), 39.

Bossen, C., 2002, Ethnography in Design: Tool-kit or Analytic science? *Proceedings of the Participatory Design Conference: Inquiring into the politics, contexts and practices of collaborative design work*, Malmo, Sweden, 338–343.

Boy, G. A., 1996, The Group Elicitation Method for Participatory Design and Usability Testing, *Proceedings of the CHI'96*, ACM.

Burke, J., Castro, M., Singh, S., and Turner P., 2002, SITCRC User Needs Project * Phase 1 Overview, User Needs Project, User Environment Program, *SITCRC*; http://www.ucd.smartinternet.com.au/papers.html

Carmel, E., Whitaker, R. and George, J., 1993, PD and Joint Application Design: A Transatlantic Comparison, *Communications of the ACM,* 36(4).

Clement, A. and Van den Besselaar, P., 1993, A Retrospective Look at PD Projects, *Communications of the ACM,* 36(4), 29–37.

Crabtree, A., 1998, Ethnography in Participatory Design, *Proceedings of the Participatory Design Conference: Broadening Participation*, Seattle, USA, 93–106.

Ehn, P., 1988, *Work-oriented Design of Computer Artifacts*, Lawrence Erlbaum Associates, Inc., Hillsdale, NJ.

Ellis, R. D. and Kurniawan, S. H., 2000, Increasing the Usability of Online Information for Older Users: A Case Study in Participatory Design, *International Journal of Human-Computer Interaction*, 12(2), 263–276.

Floyd, C., 1993, STEPS – A Methodical Approach to PD, *Communications of the ACM,* 36(4).

Gershon, N. and Page, W., 2001, What Storytelling Can Do for Information Visualization, *Communications of the ACM,* 44(8), 31–37.

Giordano, R. and Bell, D., 2000, Participant Stakeholder Evaluation as a Design Method: A Report on Work In Progress, *Proceedings of the Participatory Design Conference: Designing Digital Environments*, CSPR, New York, USA, 268–272.

Good, M., 1992, Participatory Design of a Portable Torque-feedback Device, *Proceedings of the CHI'92: Human Factors in computer systems*, ACM, New York, 439–446.

Greenbaum, J., 1993, PD: A Personal Statement, *Communications of the ACM,* 36(4), 47.

Greenbaum, J. and Kyng, M., 1991, *Design at Work: Cooperative Design of Computer Systems*, Lawrence Erlbaum Associates, Hillsdale, NJ.

Grudin, J. and Pruitt, J., 2002, Personas, Participatory Design and Product Development An Infrastructure for Engagement, *Proceedings of the Participatory Design Conference: Inquiring into the politics, contexts and practices of collaborative design work*, Malmo, Sweden, 144–152.

Hemmings, T., Crabtree, A., Rodden, T., Clarke, K. and Rouncefield, M., 2002, Probing the Probes, Proceedings of the Participatory Design Conference, CPSR, Malmo, Sweden, 42–50.

Jokela, T., 2002, Making User-centred Design Common Sense: Striving for an Unambiguous and Communicative UCD Process Model. NordiCHI 2002, Finland. 19–23 October

Kensin, F., Simonsen, J. and Bodker, K., 1996, MUST - a Method for Participatory Design, Proceedings of the Participatory Design Conference, CPSR. Massachusetts, USA, 163–172.

Kuhn, S. and Muller, M., 1993, Participatory Design Introduction, *Communications of the ACM,* 36(4), 24–28.

Mattelmaki, T. and Battarbee, K., 2002, Empathy Probes, Proceedings of the Participatory Design Conference, 266–271.

Mauro, C. L., 2002, Formal, User-Centred Design (UCD) process development: benefits, liabilities and return on investment modelling. Taskz; Seminar 2; Executive Summary Series.

Muller, M. J., 1993, Participatory Design: The Third Space in HCI, IBM [Online] Available: Accessed: 16/5/03

Muller, M. J., Wildman, D. M. and White, E. A., 1993a, "Equal Opportunity" PD Using PICTIVE, *Communications of the ACM,* 36(4), 64–64.

Muller, M. J., Wildman, D. M. and White, E. A., 1993b, Taxonomy of PD Practices: A Brief Practitioner's Guide, *Communications of the ACM,* 36(4), 26–27.

Mumford, E., 1993, The ETHICS Approach, *Communications of the ACM*, 36(4), 82.

Vredenburg, K., Isensee, S. and Righi. C., 2002, *User-Centred Design: An integrated approach*, New Jersey, Prentice Hall.

Vrendenburg, K., 1999, Response to Baerensten and Slavensky, *Communications of the ACM*, 42(5), 77.

A PROPOSED TAXONOMY OF MEDIA COLLECTIONS AND ITS IMPLICATIONS FOR DESIGN AND MANAGEMENT OF MULTIMEDIA DATABASES

Valerie J. Hobbs and Diarmuid J. Pigott*

1. INTRODUCTION

The extension of the principles of database management to encompass collections of media artefacts has led to a new range of solutions, and a matching extensive literature covering both research (including content-based retrieval, metadata standards and cataloguing, best practices for media acquisition, and digital preservation) and implementation (from web page content management to online museums, digital libraries, media archives and satellite and medical imaging). To make use of, and contribute to, this literature (whether by further research, design or new implementations) there must first be an overview of the domain. There are two ways in which this overview can be attained: one is to have a continual survey of what exists, and the other is to establish a comprehensive system of classification.

Surveys are found either as enumerative assessments of problem domains, or as justification for comprehensive general solutions. The former (such as Martinez and Mouaddib, 1999; Ozden et al., 1997; Vogel et al., 1995; Yoshitaka and Ichikawa, 1999), while invaluable when published, cannot hope to be exhaustive, and rapidly become obsolete; and we are still left with the (recursive) problem of referencing the surveys themselves. Moreover, we can have no reason to expect that a set of general principles will emerge from these efforts (Quicke, 1993). Even where such surveys begin with a checklist in the form of a taxonomy (such as Martinez and Mouaddib, 1999) the result is still an enumeration with regularised attributes rather than a classification proper. On the other hand, surveys that are made for the purposes of justifying general solutions (e.g. Del Bimbo, 1996; Grosky, 1997) cannot necessarily be treated as comprehensive coverage of the domain, nor will a collection of such surveys ever amount to a complete coverage.

Classifications of multimedia collections should begin with an a priori taxonomy informed by surveys of the literature, but with the intent to comprehensively map out the

* Murdoch University, Murdoch, Western Australia 6150.

entire multimedia domain. Such approaches have proved successful in the fields of visual programming (Burnett and Baker, 1994), data visualisation (Schneiderman, 1996) and media immersion interfaces (Gabbard and Hix, 2003). Taxonomies have the advantage that while the systems that are classified may become obsolete, the framework can deal with new examples and still serve its purpose. This paper proposes such a taxonomy, and describes its implications for design and management of multimedia databases.

1.1. Taxonomic Criteria for Media Collections

Taxonomy enables us to make generalisations about the nature of a domain of investigation by selection of salient features and to establish a set of ordering principles that map out the domain (Knight, 1981). In order to create a taxonomy for media collections, we need to look at the principles of taxonomy and how they apply in this domain, and what can be gained from their application.

The first stage in developing a taxonomy is to establish an appropriate key set for the taxonomy (Table 1). It is important to note that we have chosen these keys in order that our taxonomy may be of use for the field of multimedia database research. We have chosen these keys after an extensive survey of both the literature and of conferences presentations of systems. Constraints of space preclude their presentation here, but exemplars are given below in the exposition of the taxonomy, and a comprehensive treatment is in preparation. For the rest, we have stopped at the node of the dichotomous key that is not of immediate interest for this paper. For those media artefact collections not covered here, further research is warranted before a satisfactory key set can be established. For our purposes, it is important to note (after Quicke, 1993) that the fact of differently levelled branches of a taxonomic system is an acceptable by-product of describing the world using the principles of taxonomy.

Table 1. Criteria for establishment of taxonomic key set

Principle for key	Definition
Discovery (1)	Whether or not the portion of the media artefact universe has been traversed
Mapping (2)	Whether or not the portion of the media artefact universe has been mapped with a secondary organising principle
Indexicality (3)	Whether the management of the media artefacts relies on the artefacts' self-organisation only, or makes use of indexical structures
Telos (4)	Whether the media artefacts are assembled for their intrinsic qualities or as adjuncts
Locus of interest (5)	Whether the media artefacts are of interests as artefacts per se, or as sources of information
Reflexivity (6)	Whether the artefacts have a role as surrogates for real world objects or are illustrative of conceptually defined domains
Origin of collection (7)	Whether the artefact assemblage is of a physical or a logical collection
Usage (8)	Whether the artefacts are gathered for immediate specific use or for general use
Literalness (9)	Whether the artefacts purport to be representative or diagrammatic
Scope of meaning (10)	Whether the artefacts are assembled to have single or multiple meanings

Figure 1 shows the taxonomy after Dallwitz (1980) and Quicke (1993): the items in small capitals are the taxa.

1(0)	A	Media already discovered, traversed and enumerated	*Collections* (2)
	B	Media not discovered	NOT FINDABLE
2(1)	A	Collections with a secondary organising structure	*Organised* (3)
	B	Collection that do not have a secondary organising structure	NOT ORGANISED
3(2)	A	Organised collections with indexicality	*Regularised* (4)
	B	Organised collection that are self-organising	NOT REGULARISED
4(3)	A	Media that comprise a significant collection in themselves	*Media-centric* (5)
	B	Media that have been assembled adjunctively	*Illustrative* (6)
5(4)	A	Media-centric collections that are of intrinsic interest	ARTEFACTUAL
	B	Media-centric collections that are a source of information	INFORMATIC
6(4)	A	Collections of artefacts that map to items in the world	*Surrogate* (7)
	B	Collections where artefacts illustrate logically-defined domains	*Polysemic* (8)
7(6)	A	Surrogate, reflexive of a physical collection	REPRESENTATIVE
	B	Surrogate, reflexive of a logical collection	ICONOLOGICAL
8(6)	A	Polysemic artefacts gathered for a specific purpose	*Explanatory* (9)
	B	Polysemic artefacts gathered for an unspecified future purpose	*Aggregative* (10)
9(8)	A	Explanatory artefacts that are illustrative of something physical	LITERAL
	B	Explanatory artefacts illustrative of something conceptual	FIGURATIVE
10(8)	A	Aggregative artefact collections that suit a single emblematic purpose	CATEGORICAL
	B	Aggregative artefacts collected for multiple concurrent semantic use	GENERIC

Figure 1. The multimedia collections taxonomy

2. A TAXONOMY OF MEDIA COLLECTIONS

We now move to an exposition of our taxonomy. As our aim is to be exhaustive, we take as our starting point the media artefact universe **(0)**: the set of all media artefacts in existence. The first division is when we consider identity. If media artefacts have some means of identification, such as a filename, we can find them again, if not they are lost and we can make no statements about them **(1B)**.

Of those media artefacts that are findable **(1A)**, and thus can be considered *collections*, we can divide into those that have some secondary organising structure (*organised*) and those which do not (*not organised*). The latter category **(2B)** includes media artefacts that are not in any single purposive organised structure, but which can be located by sequential search. Some examples are the image search system on Google, in which media artefacts are only locatable by filename and co-located text (which may be irrelevant; e.g. Lew et al., 2002), and the adult-content blocking on the web where filtering is at best haphazard, and where the alternative of content-based discernment is in its infancy (Chan et al., 1999).

An organised media artefact collection **(2A)** can take its organisation from one of two ways: it can have a consistent mapping between an artefact and its subject (i.e.

between two sets in two domains), or it can be self-organising from its content, but not in a regular way that makes for ready universalisation. In the former collection type, we are adding the principle of indexicality when we make for that mapping. We term the former *regularised*, and the latter *not regularised.*

For the purpose of multimedia databases, this distinction is very significant indeed: with regularised media collections **(3A)**, we have a mapping function between artefact and subject (Fauconnier, 1997), and in this we have the potential for validation, in the definition of the placeholder and the assessment of how well the media artefact fulfils it. It is this category that defines databases proper, and which we describe in the next section.

Non-regularised structures **(3B)** on the other hand have no such separation and validation can only be of the document in isolation. We may certainly ask "Is this web page/document correct?", or "Is this a good web page/document?", but the implications of the answers we get would not generalise beyond the document in question to those of contingent similarity.

This part of the taxonomy is summarised in Figure 2.

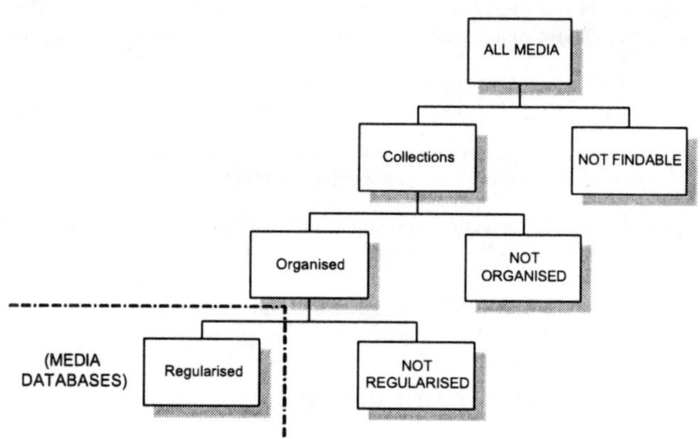

Figure 2. Upper part of taxonomy

2.1. Media Artefact Collections that are Databases

We now consider the multimedia databases proper. We can say that multimedia databases are findable, organised, regularised collections of media artefacts. We now consider the continuation of our taxonomy to discover what forms these multimedia databases may take.

The first consideration we make is whether the primary reason for the database is a significant collection of media artefacts, or whether the artefacts have been assembled for a reason that is data driven. We term the former *media-centric*, and the latter *illustrative*.

Media-centric databases **(4A)** are used to create database systems which are concerned with artefacts whose digital origin is significant. In an age where significant art and music are met with in the digital domain, and where documents of record (such as emails, original recordings or websites) are created, live and retire within the digital domain, the importance of their documentation and archiving requires a stringent set of procedures be established with a regard to ensuring their accurate preservation, and their accessibility to research.

The media-centric databases themselves fall naturally into two categories, those where the original media artefacts are of interest per se **(5A)**, and those where the artefacts are of interest for the information that they convey **(5B)**. We term these the *artefactual* and *informatic* media-centric databases respectively. Artefactual collections include archives of websites, repositories of medical x-rays and online curated digital media exhibitions; informatic collections are where we find digital libraries.

In contrast to the media-centric databases, the illustrative databases **(4B)** derive their purpose from a need to systematically illustrate something in the real world. What exactly the subject of the illustrative intent is may vary quite widely, but the significance of the media artefact in the database will always lie in its need to be faithful to an aspect of the world external to the digital process. Thus, it is with the illustrative databases that we find the potential for validation and reverification of the "truth value" (Roskill and Carrier, 1983) of the media artefacts.

The illustrative databases cover a range of multimedia database systems of different functionalities, from those where the purpose of the media artefact is highly symbolic or multi-purposed to those where it conveys a literal representation of a real-world object. The next categorisation, therefore, concerns the relationship between the media artefact and its real-world equivalent. We can distinguish between databases where the truth value of the media artefact lies in its ongoing mapping against a real world object, and those where this direct mapping has been lost and the artefact may take on additional meaning to illustrate logically-defined domains. We call the former *surrogate* and the latter group *polysemic*. Surrogate collections include representations of historical collections and art museums; polysemic collections include encyclopaedias and bulk image repositories.

The surrogate databases **(6A)** are chiefly concerned with creating a set of media artefacts to a set of non-digital items. Here we have the justification of mapping from the digital domain to a non-digital collection justified at the level of the collection itself. The consequence of this is that the typology of surrogate artefact collections is reflexive, established by the purpose for which the non-digital items have been assembled. Here we see the two types of collections arise: those exhaustive for a physical set (e.g. paintings by Cézanne, contents of the Ashmolean) and those that are enumerative for a set that are conceptually derived (e.g. Warburg's atlas of symbolic images). Thus we have two corresponding media artefact collections – the former we call *representative* **(7A)** and the latter (after Panofsky, 1982; Straten, 1994) *iconological* **(7B)**. Examples of the representative type would be a CD-ROM of the works of Cezanne (Corbis, 2003), or the Ashmolean online Bates Museum of musical instruments (Ashmolean, 2003), while examples of the iconological type are the Warburg Electronic Library at Hamburg ([WEL], 2003).

The polysemic group of databases **(6B)** are divided according to whether the media artefacts are collected for an immediate single purpose, or whether they are gathered for an unspecified future purpose or purposes. Those in the first division are seen to have an *explanatory* purpose: artefacts may be acquired to assist in the explanation of something in the world (physical or conceptual). Those in the latter we term *aggregative*, a term we have chosen to indicate that the collection has no other purpose besides being a collection designed with digital artefact repurposing in mind.

The explanatory databases **(8A)** encompass those that are typically associated with a text component that may provide a large part of the explanatory power of the database, possibly with a complex data model to provide interrelationships among concepts. The media artefacts are selected for their ability to provide additional illustration or explanation to this text component. Typically here we have such things as online encyclopaedias or biological specimen databases.

We can divide the explanatory databases into two broad types according to the purpose of the media: the *literal* group **(9A)** use media artefacts in a representational way to provide the best illustration of something physical, while the *figurative* group **(9B)** use media artefacts to provide information that may be conceptual or metaphorical. A single database may include aspects of both: we can envisage an encyclopaedia of chemistry providing both literal depictions of minerals and figurative explanations of chemical processes.

In the aggregative group of databases **(8B)** we find the typical media repository of 'stock' artefacts collected to be used in publishing or education. These collections have no purpose of their own, but are organised to facilitate location and reuse of artefacts for other purposes (such as the explanatory databases just described). We can divide the aggregative databases broadly into those that fall into predefined categories of an emblematic nature, which we call *categorical*, and those that are selected to be as multiply-purposed as possible, which we call *generic*.

In a categorical archive **(10A)** we might expect media artefacts to be selected for their symbolic ability to convey abstract concepts, such as "war" or "poverty" or "technology". In a generic media archive **(10B)**, we would find artefacts that were suggestive of many different concepts, though possibly of a less abstract nature, and none that might be contradictory (this is the principle behind generic collections of clip-art).

The complete taxonomy for multimedia databases is shown in Figure 3.

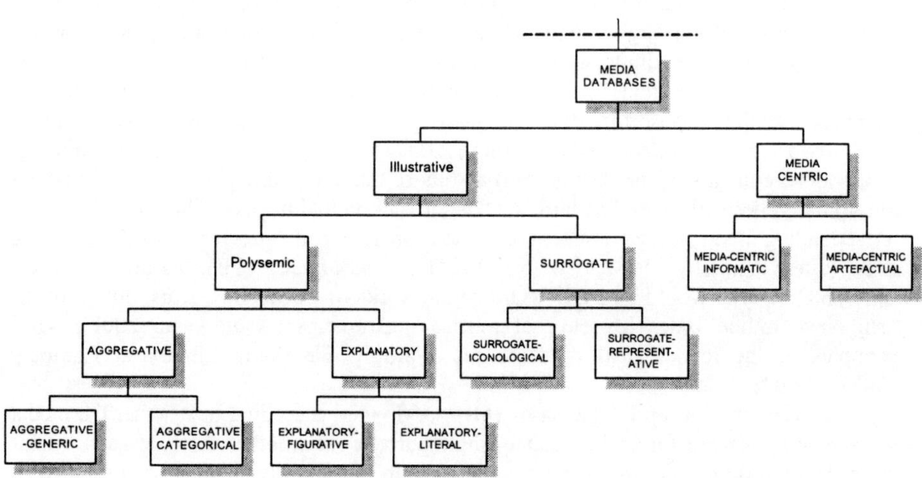

Figure 3. Lower part of taxonomy: all media databases.

3. IMPLICATIONS OF THE TAXONOMY FOR DESIGN AND MANAGEMENT

We shall now investigate the way in which the taxonomy helps us establish our multimedia database rules. The tools at our disposal in a multimedia database are the checking of media quality and appropriateness of subject at the moment of acquisition, correct preparation of the restricted vocabulary, and the judicious preparation of the metadata components, and we must now call on the taxonomy to provide ways in which these tools can be used to ensure correct, consistent and verifiable multimedia databases.

Consider the life cycle of a media artefact: it passes through the stages of acquisition, selection, preparation, annotation with metadata, storage, retrieval, display, and final retirement. The purpose that the media artefact has in the database influences the nature of decisions that must be made at each of these points. The implications for design and management at each life cycle stage (listed in Table 2) will have direct consequences for procedures for both design and deployment of the database, and we discuss these next for each of the different database types.

Table 2. Design implications for lifecycle stages of multimedia databases

Lifecycle stage	Implication
Source of media artefacts	Artefacts may be created expressly for the database, collected from secondary sources, or converted from an intermediate source, according to purpose.
Format and quality of media artefacts	A particular format and quality of media artefact may be required in order for it to fulfil its intended purpose in the database.
Metadata	The extent, nature and balance of metadata between technical and descriptive may vary according to purpose of media artefact.
Search strategy	Search may be keyword based, content-based, or retrieval via the text component of the database.
Validation criteria	Media artefacts must be assessed for suitability and correctness on first accession to database, based on criteria for both semantic content and technical quality.
Review and reverification	Periodic review of media artefact for continuing suitability is essential to maintain correctness and currency of the database. Such reviews may be time based, or triggered by external criteria.
Retirement	The circumstances under which the media artefact would be removed from the database may vary according to media purpose.
Data management	Standards and data models relevant to the database will depend in part on media purpose.

3.1. Media-centric Databases

Media artefacts in media-centric databases are subject to checking at the moment of creation, but thereafter can never become 'false' in terms of content, although they are subject to technological obsolescence. Design and management decisions must therefore consider the policy and process for collection, to ensure the best possible artefact is captured, and thereafter a process of review for technological currency.

Because in a media-centric database it is the media artefact itself that is providing the information content directly, and not its relationship with a designer-determined concept, it is here we find that automatic retrieval on content can be appropriate as a primary means of retrieval, such as content-based retrieval on images or sounds, or information mining in large text documents.

Table 3. Summary of design implications for media-centric databases

Lifecycle stage	Media-centric	
	Media-centric - Artefactual	Media-centric - Informatic
Source of media artefacts	Media artefacts will all be 'born digital'. Collection policy will determine source of artefacts.	
Format and quality of media artefacts	Determined by origin.	Different versions may be required: e.g. for universality of format, ease of access, or preservation.
Technical metadata	Very important, particularly creation circumstances (tools, creator, date, etc).	Not very important.
Descriptive metadata	Less important than technical metadata; often minimal.	Very important.
Search strategy	Content-based retrieval possible, or search via text component in database.	Content-based retrieval, descriptive metadata; browse via conventional data.
Validation criteria	Once established through collection policy, there is no need to consider at the level of the individual artefact beyond checking technical criteria and context with conventional data.	Must be good enough to enable access to information (legible/sharp/clear).
Review and reverification	Unlikely to be updated, since the artefact represents a particular moment in time.	Would be reviewed for technological currency, and possibly migrated to new formats: triggered by time or the appearance of new technology.
Retirement	Unlikely to be retired.	May be replaced by artefact of identical content but technologically superior format
Data management	Catalogue-based, such as MARC or MPEG-7.	Open Text Encoding Initiative/ CIMI/ Open Publishing Standard.

3.2. Surrogate Databases

The media truth for surrogate databases lies in the transparency of the artefact with regard to the item in the original collection for which it serves as surrogate. When a surrogate artefact collection has been established then there must be a surrogate artefact for every item in the real world collection. Similarly, the set of appropriate keywords for an artefact must be equally applicable to the original item, and will continue to apply to the media artefact for as long as they are current for the original.

Table 4. Summary of design implications for surrogate databases

Lifecycle stage	Surrogate	
	Surrogate-Representative	Surrogate-Iconological
Source of media artefacts	Media artefacts are created to match real world objects in a collection. Artefacts are derived from a fixed set, so acquisition involves creating digitised versions of these, preferably directly from the original source to have as much control as possible over the process.	The potential source of media artefacts is all semantic objects in the world. Media artefacts are created to represent real world objects in a virtual collection, assembled according to a symbolic purpose defined by the curator.
Format and quality of media artefacts	High quality is required, since the ideal is to be as close as possible to the real-world object. Possible enhancements to make some points better. Normally scanned with high regard to accuracy of colour from original or slide, preferably to a standard.	Ideally as for Surrogate-Representative, though may not be possible if the artefacts are not directly accessible and the collection is to be assembled from secondary sources.
Technical metadata	Very important; must indicate standards adherence of hardware and software used and details of process and operators.	
Descriptive metadata	As these artefacts are referential to external objects, the metadata content will refer to the artefact and less so to the original object. However there is likely to be extensive descriptive metadata referring to the original object.	
Search strategy	Through associated text data, or through metadata of the original item, rather than metadata of the media artefact, since the original item/collection is what is of interest.	Through associated text data, which will include extensive semantic content about the original.
Validation criteria	Individual artefact assessed as being as true a likeness to the original as possible.	
Review and reverification	Formats would be reviewed for technological currency and possibly migrated for longevity. Otherwise the media artefact would be unlikely to be updated or replaced, unless the collection it was based on changed. Reverification would be based on same criteria as original validation.	
Retirement	Would automatically follow on from removal of mapped item in original collection.	
Data management	Museum standards such as CIMI; vocabularies such as ICONCLASS.	

3.3. Explanatory Databases

Explanatory multimedia databases have media truth of their artefacts according to the extent of their verisimilitude. However this does not imply a high degree of accuracy in acquisition: we are free to get the artefact from anywhere, as it is not necessary to maintain contact with the original resource, and in some circumstances reduced quality images will make better explanatory artefacts altogether (e.g. cropped, enlarged or hue-enhanced shots). Figurative explanatory images, in particular, may be a typifying image, or a technical figure (a vector image or a solid colour bitmap) that lacks all fine detail, as long as it demonstrates a proportion or relation in an unambiguous fashion.

Metadata for media artefacts in an explanatory database is of the utmost importance. Reuse and repurposing of artefacts are often central, and this is done through keywords. A nice benefit of this is that the media artefacts themselves become a true data element in the scheme, with their keywords and content descriptions permitting a path through the database that is completely separate to that in the textual components.

Table 5. Summary of design implications for explanatory databases

Lifecycle stage	Explanatory	
	Explanatory-Literal	Explanatory-Figurative
Source of media artefacts	Can be acquired from any source.	
Format and quality of media artefacts	Normally best possible quality of original artefact is desired. Editing or modification of original may be done to improve the representational or symbolic nature of the artefact.	
Technical metadata	Not important, as the depiction is all that matters – there is no need for a trail of provenance to be maintained with the artefact. Copyright is important as permission may need to be sought from original source.	
Descriptive metadata	Keywords and descriptions are very important.	
Search strategy	Search via text component to locate artefact as illustration of text; or on keywords or descriptions of the artefacts themselves.	
Validation criteria	Verisimilitude – is the artefact a true or useful representation of the type in the real world?	Rhetorical – does the artefact convey the idea or concept intended, and in the most effective way?
Review and reverification	Review for continuing resemblance to type. Review is periodic in time, or triggered by arrival of artefact with potentially better representation.	Review for correctness of explanation, or fashion in symbolism. Review would be time triggered.
Retirement	Retired or replaced when no longer current, or if better representation or symbolism becomes available.	
Data management	Conventional data modelling.	Conventional data modelling combined with keyword thesauri.

3.4. Aggregative Databases

The aggregative databases derive their truth-value from their ability to evoke certain conceptual associations with multiple uses. This leaves them far more open that the other types to a dramatic and sudden obsolescence, such as when certain acceptable symbolisms are revisited after changes in fashion and found to be patronising, or when a sudden turn of events makes media artefacts that previously stood for (e.g.) "trust" or "valour" seem exactly the opposite of what they once were. For an aggregative-derived truth value, there must be regular checks of the framework of assumptions under which the original keywords were assigned – at the level of the restricted vocabulary, and then flowing on to their use in the annotation of the media artefacts. For the individual artefact, the same process would be present in reverse, with a regular review of suitability causing an instantiated review of some of the keywords employed.

Table 6. Summary of design implications for aggregative databases

Lifecycle stage	Aggregative	
	Aggregative-Categorical	Aggregative-Generic
Source of media artefacts	Can be acquired from any source, on a proactive basis.	
Format and quality of media artefacts	Format and quality not important as long as emblematic quality is clear.	Format and quality not important as long as multi-purpose nature is obvious.
Technical metadata	Not important as the depiction is all that matters – there is no need for a trail of provenance to be maintained with the artefact. Copyright is significant and media may be digitally watermarked.	
Descriptive metadata	Extremely important.	
Search strategy	Search will be by keywords. Content-based retrieval inappropriate.	
Validation criteria	Emblematic nature must be obvious.	Multiple emblematic nature must be obvious.
Review and reverification	Review for currency, fashion; triggered by time passing. Artefacts that have lost their emblematic nature would have their keywords updated.	
Retirement	Unlikely to occur unless media artefact becomes unacceptable.	
Data management	Keyword thesauri.	

4. CONCLUSION

The taxonomy we have presented provides useful guidelines for the management of media artefacts across the lifecycle of a multimedia database system, from artefact selection, acquisition and preparation, through to review and retirement or replacement. These guidelines may be customised and criteria defined for particular situations as part of the database development process. While we may expect that the overall "flavour" of a media database is provided by the sum of its parts, its is important that we model at the level of the parts themselves, so that the use and validation of media across the database application is not done collectively, but with reference to the individual points of use within it.

Although we have defined media purpose within a particular type of database in our taxonomy, it is important to note that there is nothing inherent in the media artefact that makes it one type or another. Indeed we may expect significant repurposing across the range of database types: for example, media originally collected for a surrogate purpose could be used to populate an aggregative collection, and an explanatory database could later make use of those artefacts.

We have already discussed the need for controlling such repurposing (Pigott et al., 2001) and have developed a methodology for defining the requirements of media artefacts at a high level, so that they can be modelled as abstractions in a similar manner to entities modelling the abstraction of data (Hobbs and Pigott, 2002). Our methodology proposed a precise requirements analysis that includes identification of candidate formats and description of the purpose of the media at each point. The guidelines for validation and reverification expounded here may be incorporated into that modelling and design process in a straightforward way, and we return to this later.

REFERENCES

Ashmolean, 2003, *The Bate Collection of Musical Instruments*. Ashmolean Museum. Retrieved 9 May, 2003, from the World Wide Web: http://www.ashmol.ox.ac.uk/BCMIPage.html

Burnett, M. and Baker, M., 1994, A Classification System for Visual Programming Languages. *Journal of Visual Languages and Computing,* 5, 287–300.

Chan, Y., Harvey, R. and Smith, D., 1999, Building systems to block pornography, Paper presented at the Electronic Workshops in Computing, Newcastle, Australia.

Corbis, 2003, *Paul Cezanne: Portrait of My World* [CD-ROM]. Corbis Publishing. Retrieved 9 May, 2003, from the World Wide Web: http://www.cdaccess.com/html/shared/cezanne.htm

Dallwitz, M. J., Paine, T. A., and Zurcher, E. J., 1980, *User's guide to the DELTA system: a general system for processing taxonomic descriptions*. Melbourne: CSIRO Information Services.

Del Bimbo, A., 1996, Image and Video Databases: Visual Browsing, Querying and Retrieval. *Journal of Visual Languages and Computing,* 7, 353–359.

Fauconnier, G., 1997, *Mappings in thought and language*. Cambridge, U.K. ; New York, NY: Cambridge University Press.

Gabbard, J. L., and Hix, D., 2003, A Taxonomy of Usability Characteristics in Virtual Environments, retrieved 15 July 2003, from the World Wide Web: http://csgrad.cs.vt.edu/jgabbard/ve/taxonomy/

Grosky, W. I., 1997, Managing multimedia information in database systems, *Communications of the ACM,* 40(12), 73–80.

Hobbs, V. J., and Pigott, D. J., 2002, A methodology for multimedia database design, in: *New Perspectives on Information Systems Development: Theory, Methods and Practice*, D. R. G. Harindranath, John A.A. Sillince, Wita Wojtkowski, W. Gregory Wojtkowski, Stanislaw Wrycza and Joze Zupancic, eds., Kluwer Academic, New York, USA, pp. 473–488.

Knight, D. M., 1981, *Ordering the world : a history of classifying man*. London: Burnett Books.

Lew, M. S., Sebe, N., and Eakins, J. P, 2002, July 18-19, 2002, *Image and Video Retrieval,* paper presented at the International Conference, CIVR 2002, London, UK.

Martinez, J. and Mouaddib, N., 1999, Multimedia and Databases: A Survey. *Networking and Information Systems Journal (NISJ),* 2(1), 89–123.

Ozden, B., Rastogi, R., and Silberschatz, A., 1997, Multimedia Support for Databases, PODS'97, 11.

Panofsky, E., 1982, *Meaning in the visual arts* (Phoenix ed.) Chicago: University of Chicago Press.

Pigott, D. J., Hobbs, V. J., and Gammack, J. G., 2001, An approach to managing repurposing of digitised knowledge assets, *Australian Journal of Information Systems* (Special Issue on Knowledge Management)

Quicke, D. L. J., 1993, *Principles and Techniques of Contemporary Taxonomy*, London: Blackie Academic & Professional, an imprint of Chapman and Hall.

Roskill, M. W., and Carrier, D., 1983, *Truth and falsehood in visual images*, Amherst: University of Massachusetts Press.

Schneiderman, B., 1996, The Eyes have it - a task by data taxonomy for data visualization, paper presented at the Proceedings of the IEEE Symposium on Visual Languages VL96.

Straten, R. v., 1994, *An introduction to iconography* (Rev. English ed.) Yverdon, Switzerland ; Langhorne, Pa.: Gordon and Breach.

Vogel, A., Kerhervé, B., Bochman, G. v., and Gecsei, J., 1995, Distributed Multimedia and QOS: A Survey. *Multimedia,* 2(2), 10–19.

[WEL], 2003, Warburg Electronic Library, University of Hamburg; Technical University of Hamburg-Harburg. Retrieved 9 May, 2003, from the World Wide Web: http://www.welib.de/

Yoshitaka, A., and Ichikawa, T., 1999, A Survey on Content-Based Retrieval for Multimedia Databases. *IEEE Transactions on Knowledge and Data Engineering,* 11(1), 81–93.

XML DATA WAREHOUSE POSSIBILITIES AND SOLUTIONS

Jaroslav Pokorny*

1. INTRODUCTION

A large amount of heterogeneous information is now available in enterprises. Such data stores may be classical formatted databases but also data collections arising from e-mail communication, e-business, or from digital documents produced by enterprise applications. As an increasing amount of such data is becoming available in the form of XML, data warehouses with special capabilities that can deal with this type of semistructured data need to be designed and developed.

A *data warehouse* (DW) is an integrated repository of data generated from many sources and used by the entire enterprise for the specific purpose of data analysis. Typically, this data is modelled as being (multi)dimensional, as this best supports data analysis. The dimensional model (DM) views data structured according to several dimensions that give a possibility to summarize, consolidate, view, and synthesize the user-analyst view of information. As the viable technique in DW environment, DM is widely accepted.[1,2]

Usually, the DW approach dictates a physical integration of data, mapping data from different information sources into a common dimensional database schema. Often, a standard RDBMS is a very popular choice for physically hosting the data within the DW. This enables fast evaluation of complex queries, but demands great effort in keeping the DW up to date, e.g. when data passes from the sources of the application-oriented operational environment to the DW, inconsistencies, redundancies, and missing data have to be resolved. So the DW provides an integrated and reconciled view of the data of the organization.

On the other hand, e.g. in a Web environment, it is not effective to maintain one physical DW. There are several reasons for it. Either data collections are naturally distributed and/or their structures are heterogeneous. This situation occurs now with common existence of relational databases and XML collections in the enterprise. For example, the data stored by a dealer is an XML document describing sales, other XML document describes the component numbering systems used by the suppliers, and a

* Jaroslav Pokorny, Dept. of Software Engineering, Faculty of Mathematics and Physics, Charles University, Malostranske nam. 25, Praha 1, Czech Republic, email: pokorny@ksi.ms.mff.cuni.cz

relational database contains information about customers. However, enabling integrated use of such data requires a logical rather than physical integration. Similar to integration of classical databases, integrating data accessible via Web is done on the logical level of the data model, creating a need for techniques that are usable at the conceptual level, which is more suitable for use by system designers and end users. Views and transformation mechanisms can be used for this purpose.

Recently, XML[3] is increasingly used for data exchange on the Web and as a new data model supporting what is more commonly referred to as *native XML databases.*[4] An alternative is to store XML in *XML-enabled databases*, i.e. via data structures of relational or object-relational databases. With the mainstream availability of XML, XML collections, and new XML query languages (e.g. Xquery[5]), new technologies for enterprise application integration open up a vast range of previously inaccessible data sources to DWs. We do not prefer, a priori, storing XML data in any XML enabled database. We consider rather the databases designed from the ground up to store XML data or native XML databases. However, real situations provide even a mix of classical databases and XML collections, whether centralized or decentralized. We use the term *XML data warehouse* (XML-DW) to capture the aspect that a repository stores XML data and this data are arranged according to a star schema similarly to classical DWs. An XML-DW can also contain external data, for example collected from the Web (as in the case of Xyleme[6]). Such system is often called a *Web warehouse*.

We show how the notion of DM in an XML environment has to be modified and develop a star schema structure with simple hierarchies based on XML data. Since XML data is semistructured and for XML-DWs usually integrated from heterogeneous sources, we have to consider, in contrast with relational databases, redundancies and inconsistencies in XML collections. In a Web environment any cleansing XML data is mostly not supposed. Thus, only approximate querying DW can be required. This approach offers a new XML-DW architecture comparing to the recent commercial solutions.

The paper is organized as follows. Section 2 briefly introduces the main concepts of DW modelling. In Section 3 we give a brief overview over XML. In Section 4 we will distinguish two referential XML-DW architectures. The second one, a native XML-DW, is the described in detail in the rest of the paper. Section 5 defines notions needed for characterization of XML collections, for specifying XML-referential integrity, and for establishing dimensions over XML data. XML views and an approximate matching of XML trees are used to this purpose. In Section 6 we define XML-star schemes with simple dimension hierarchies and dimensional XML-databases. In Section 7 we discuss briefly querying XML-DW. Finally, we summarize the approach and identify further research issues.

2. DW DESIGN

As with other databases, a design of any DW requires certain modelling stages. Contrasting to DM needed to modelling DWs, data sources that serve as input into DW are usually described by E-R schemes on the conceptual level. This does not hold for XML collections that evenly need not own any schema. We will follow the common approach in which the DM makes a separate design stage. It is placed between the conceptual (or business) modelling and the database (or representation) modelling.

It is important to remind that the first two stages are often not distinguished and E-R modelling is mixed with DM in one stage.[7]

2.1 DM Modelling

Informally, a DM-schema is a description of dimension and fact tables. The representation of facts and dimensions involves their database description. An associated diagram is called DM-diagram. A variant of this approach is called a *star schema*, i.e. the case with one fact table surrounded by dimension tables. Each dimension table has a single-part primary key that corresponds exactly to one of the components of the multi-part key in the fact table. We say that the fact table is specified w.r.t. a set of dimension tables. A fact is a focus of interest for the enterprise. It is modelled by values of non-key attributes in the fact table that functionally depend on the set of key attributes. Attributes of dimension tables (dimension attributes) are used as a source of constraints usable in DW queries.

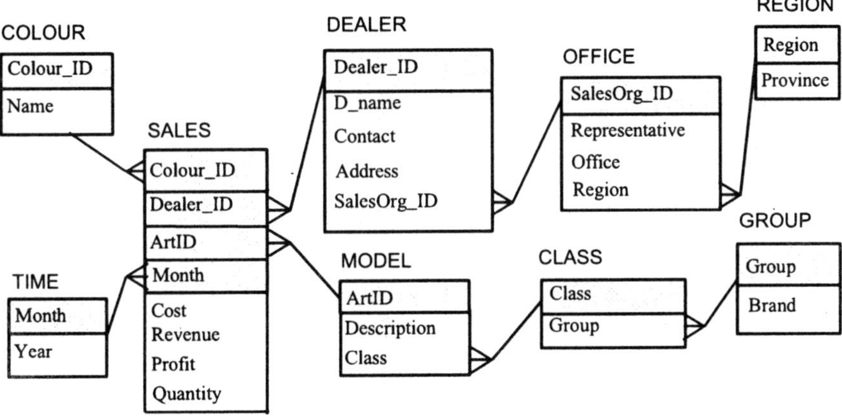

Figure 1. DM-diagram for a fragment of a star schema with simple dimension hierarchies

Although more complex hierarchies are distinguished in literature, we keep to *simple dimension hierarchies*, whose members compose a path in a directed graph. Consequently, we can model such hierarchies by a chain of tables connected by logical references (foreign keys). A fragment of a DM-diagram is depicted in Figure 1. We write usually N: $D_1 \rightarrow \ldots \rightarrow D_k$, where D_i are *dimension members* and D_1 is the *root* of N. This approach, known also as *snowflakes*, simplifies for querying the DW equipped by such a schema.

Formally, a *star schema with simple dimension hierarchies* is a pair $<N, F>$, where N is a non-empty set of simple dimension hierarchies and F a fact table schema specified w.r.t. a set $\boldsymbol{D}_N$ of their roots. A *dimensional database* S^* *over a star schema with simple hierarchies* S is a set of dimension tables and a fact table. A referential integrity between F and each N root as well as between two adjacent members of N is supposed.

2.2 Conceptual Modelling

The most widespread techniques used for describing the conceptual schema for a DM schema are variants of the E-R model[7] or the Unified Modelling Language (UML).[8]

On the conceptual level, particular members of each dimension hierarchy are sets of entities that can be described as entity types. As an example of an E-R diagram consider Figure 12 associated with the DM-diagram in Figure 1. We deal with a binary variant of E-R model with unnamed relationships. Observe that all non-key attributes in the dimension members are mandatory (∗) or optional (º). Weak entities of type SALES are identified via their owner entity types, i.e. by entities of respective hierarchy roots. UML class diagrams look similarly. In both cases referential integrity constraints are inherent in the diagrams. This fact influences positively querying on the conceptual level. Visualizing the conceptual diagrams in a graphical way, any DW becomes an easy accessible and comprehensible database for end users.

3. BASICS OF XML

The data in XML is grouped into *elements* by *tags*. The *content* of an element is information between its opening and closing tag. Typically, the content is a sequence of other elements and/or string data. Notice that the order of the sequence members is essential in XML. XML elements may contain attributes. An unordered set of attributes can be placed in the opening tag of the element. A *DTD* (Document Type Definition) specifies how elements can be nested. Subelement nesting is specified by regular expressions. An XML document *valid* w.r.t a DTD can be the root in any element specified in the DTD.

```
<salesDB>
<sale saleID="s48372">
    <date> 2003-03-02 </date>
    <dealerID> 2347 </dealerID>
    <item>
        <description>The new audio ...
        </description>
        <artID> r12200 </artID>
    </item>
    ...
</sale>
...
</salesDB>
```

Figure 2. XML sales data

```
<?xml version="1.0"?>
<!ELEMENT salesDB (sale*)>
<!ELEMENT sale (date, dealerID, item+)>
<!ATTLIST sale saleID ID #REQUIRED>
<!ELEMENT date (#PCDATA)>
<!ELEMENT dealerID (#PCDATA)>
<!ELEMENT item (description, artID)>
<!ELEMENT description (#PCDATA)>
<!ELEMENT artID (#PCDATA)>
```

Figure 3. DTD salesDB

The sales data in Figure 2 describes each sale made by the dealer 2347 on March 2, 2003. The XML document is valid w.r.t. the DTD in Figure 3.

Applications of XML require appropriate data models both for XML data and DTDs. A tree-oriented model is sufficient in the context of our XML DW. It can be used both for XML data and DTDs. XML trees can be considered as ordered or unordered. In practice, the latter is more useful. He we support rather unordered trees.

A key feature of our approach to XML-DW is use of XML views of XML data. XML views help us to see different XML data in the same way and simulate data cleansing on the logical level. Views can be evaluated by standard view mechanisms, and used for integrity checking and query processing in XML-DWs. For purposes of this paper, an *XML view V over a collection C* is given by a *view query* in a query language for XML data. By the *materialization* of *V in C* we mean a set of XML data, denoted *V*(*C*), which is obtainable by evaluating *V* on *C*. In particular, *V*(*C*) may be empty.

4. ARCHITECTURES OF XML-DW

We will distinguish two architectures of XML-DW. The first one (Figure 4) is based on a logical integration of XML and non-XML data. Particularly, non-XML data can be missing. Obviously, the sources can be both transaction databases and stand-alone DWs. The goal is to see the data as one DW. In general, a middleware is necessary in this case. A significant feature of this approach in practice is the exact matching XML data during the querying process. The second architecture (Figure 5) is new and seems to be a logical consequence of XML-oriented data processing. It supports variability of XML data structures implied by regular expressions in its DTD and relies rather on an approximate matching XML data. In both cases, a form of conceptual querying is considered.

4.1 XM-DW - a shared approach

In the first, more traditional, solution, the source data consists of XML collections and collections containing relational data. Based on DTDs and relational schemes, a common conceptual schema in an appropriate conceptual language is generated by the Design Integrator. For example, UML class diagrams are used for this purpose.[7] Obviously, the approach with E-R schemes[9] can be used as well. The Data Integrator transforms such schema into relational data structures, i.e. a star schema with simple dimension hierarchies in our case. Associated data are usually generated as materialized views.

On the DM or database level the DW can be accessed via SQL through a standard interface ODBC. Another possibility is to use a special query tool built on the top of such (relational) DW. A more advanced possibility would be to query DW directly on the conceptual level. Consequently, querying through a graphical user interface (GUI) would be appropriate. A simple example of such an approach is shown in Figure 12.

Another possibility[7] is offered by the ODMG data model,[10] enabling to use the OQL query language. Unfortunately, its role is rather at the database level than at the conceptual level. Data integrator can also transform DTDs and relational schemes into a higher type system[11] and approach associated data by a functional language.

Commercial solutions of major database vendors (including Oracle, IBM, and Microsoft) are usually a variation of this architecture. Their primary use is for application of so-called *data-centric*[4] XML. Such data is usually converted by the sending application from its original format to XML merely for the process of transmission.

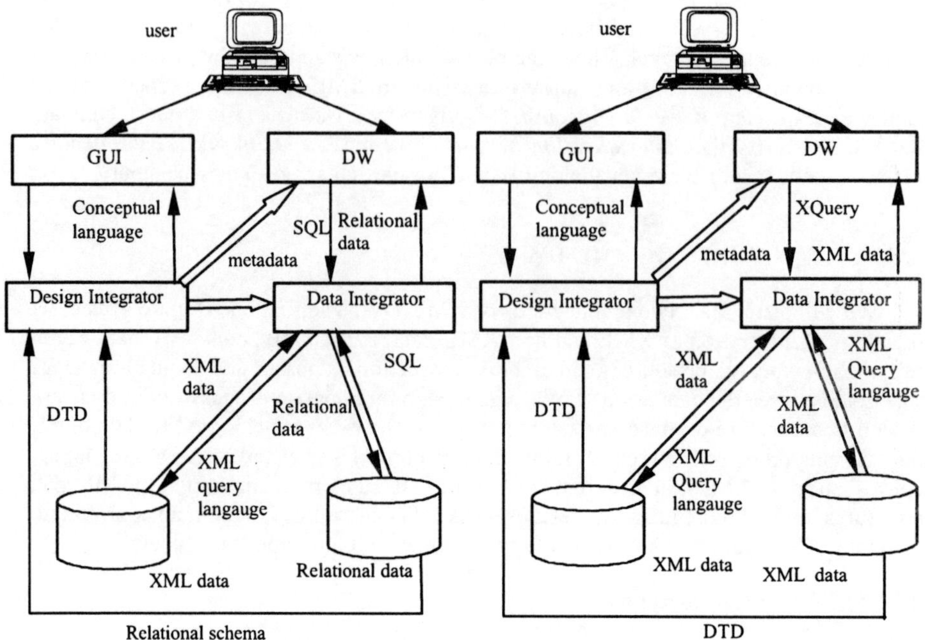

Figure 4. Architecture: a shared approach

Figure 5. Architecture: native XML-DW

4.2. Native XML-DW

We consider *n* XML collections and their respective DTDs. DTD_C denotes the DTD of *C*. The collections may be independent in some sense, i.e. the same information can be represented in two documents with different DTDs in multiple ways, similarly as in distributed databases. Each collection can be a source for one or more dimension members of one or more dimensions. The overall architecture of XML-star schema is drawn in Figure 6. The grey and white rectangles denote source collections and dimension members, respectively.

Since the data of a dimension member is XML data, each two adjacent dimension members should be logically linked by a referential integrity similarly as it is done with dimension tables. Due to the features of considered XML collections specified in Section 1, both integrity constraint checking and query evaluation should be based on an approximate matching XML data. Consequently the XML query language on the database level in Figure 5 should also fulfil this property. For example, an algebraic language with an approximate join or semijoin operation would be suitable for this purpose. The XQuery language can serve as a realistic variant on the DM level due to its extensibility (User Defined Functions).

In the context of native XML-DW we can consider so-called *document-centric*[4] XML documents. They are characterised by less regular or irregular structure.

In this architecture, XML data can be both data- and document-centric. Particularly, in the latter case the contribution to XML-DW processing becomes most significant.

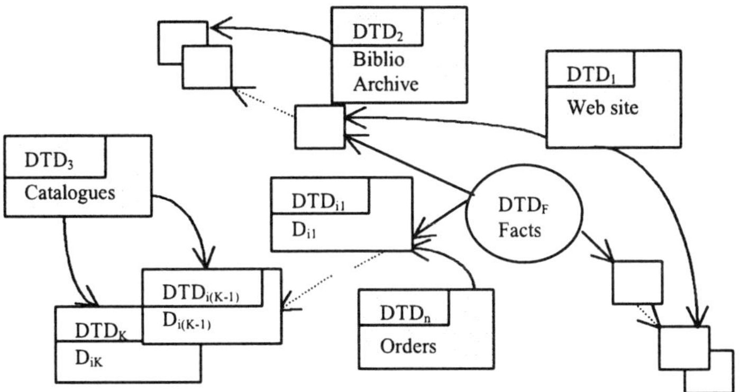

Figure 6. XML-star schema

5. DIMENSION HIERARCHIES IN A NATIVE XML-DW

The design of a dimension hierarchy means to explore dimension members and logical associations among them. The principle *foreign key-key* is not applicable here in a straightforward way. Namely, keys are not a part of XML data model. There are at least the following possibilities how to resolve this issue by:

- natural keys from the real world (like SSN, InvoiceNo, etc.),
- ID-IDREF associations,
- key-keyref associations from the XML Schema,
- key-keyref associations based on keys according to Buneman[12, 13]
- application of XLink,
- application of XML views.

A detailed analysis of these possibilities has been done.[14] The main problem of all approaches except the last two is that they rely on the consistency of the XML data collections. Moreover, it seems that the rigidity of keys inherited from the notion of primary key in relational databases is rather lost in XML environment. For some key expression, though it is not satisfied in a small part of the XML collection, it is satisfied in most of the data, and we could consider it as a valid characterisation. Consequently, our characterizations will meet weaker requirements that those for keys in relational databases. We will speak only about a *weak identifiability* of a dimension member D and introduce techniques enabling to capture it in a reasonable way. The notion of XML view is sufficiently general for this purpose.

5.1. How to Describe a Dimension Member

First, we restrict the source DTD_C to a DTD_D that is more feasible for manipulation. Here we use so-called *subDTD* of the given DTD. Informally, the subDTD is DTD and describes XML data sufficient for the dimension member D specification. An extension of D, D^*, on C contains XML data valid w.r.t. DTD_D and having the same root element tag given in DOCTYPE clause of DTD_D. For example, we can conceive the DTD dealer in Figure 7 as a subDTD of a DTD catalogues.

```
<!DOCTYPE dealer[
<!ELEMENT dealer(d_name, contact?, address+)>
<!ELEMENT d_name PCDATA>
<!ELEMENT address(locality, ZIP?)>
<!ELEMENT locality PCDATA >
<!ELEMENT ZIP PCDATA>
<!ELEMENT contact(fax |phone)
<!ELEMENT fax PCDATA >
<!ELEMENT phone PCDATA >]
```

Figure 7. DTD dealer

A characterization of *D* should

- distinguish any two XML documents in *N* as best as possible,
- be suitably simple,
- be XML data,
- be valid w.r.t. a DTD.

The characterization of *D* on the schema level is called *core* of *D*, shortly *D-core*. On the data level we speak about *core elements*. Each document from *D* generates one core element at most. It is on the designer responsibility to specify this integrity constraint. In the previous work[15] we showed how to define the *D*-core data as a view $V_{D\text{-core}}$ over *D*, and how to find its $DTD_{D\text{-core}}$. XML data, a set $T(DTD_{D\text{-core}})$, extracted from D^* and valid w.r.t. $DTD_{D\text{-core}}$ is called *D-core data*. For example, let us assume only one fax or one phone number is sufficient to identify a dealer. Then the associated view can be expressed in XQuery is shown in Figure 8, a DTD describing its data is in Figure 9. It provides "heterogeneous" core elements, with a fax or a phone for each dealer, who has the contact element non-empty.

```
LET $e := /dealer/contact/*
RETURN <dealer_core> $e </dealer_core>
```

Figure 8. $V_{\text{Dealer-core}}$

```
<!DOCTYPE dealer_core[
<!ELEMENT dealer_core (fax |phone)>
<!ELEMENT fax PCDATA >
<!ELEMENT phone PCDATA >]
```

Figure 9. $DTD_{\text{Dealer-core}}$

5.2. XML-referential integrity

First, we solve a general problem how to specify the constraint XML-referential integrity for collections C_1 and C_2. We need to connect logically those documents $d_1 \in C_1$ and $d_2 \in C_2$ that match on the core data described by $DTD_{C2\text{-core}}$. In other words, d_1 contains data, which is the same (or similar to), as the core data of d_2. C_2-core plays for DTD_{C1} a similar role as a foreign key in a relational database.

We specify a view $V_{(C1\rightarrow C2)\text{-core}}$ that generates XML data from C_1 of the same structure as the data valid w.r.t DTD$_{C2\text{-Core}}$. In other words we map C_2-cores into C_1 documents. We could also specify DTD$_{(C1\rightarrow C2)\text{-core}}$. Observe that DTD$_{(C1\rightarrow C2)\text{-core}}$ is not explicitly needed for checking XML-referential integrity. Any such checking is based on data from $V_{(C1\rightarrow C2)\text{-core}}(C_1)$. It plays a role a pattern. The reason for exploring DTD$_{(C1\rightarrow C2)\text{-core}}$ is that it contributes to a consolidation of semantical and structural differences between C_1 and C_2. In fact, the choice of tags on the view level makes it possible to consider trees both on DTD and XML data level that are comparable.

The problem of checking XML-referential integrity can be mapped to the problem of approximate embedding a pattern tree in the tree determined by $V_{C2\text{-core}}(d_2)$. We denote the relation by symbol $\leq:$.

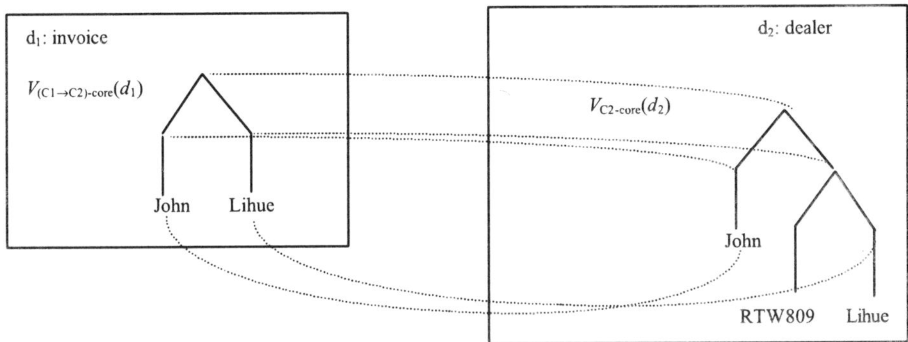

Figure 10. XML-referential integrity

A justification for this choice in our DW environment follows from the intuition that the dimension member D_i^* contains more information about an entity *e* than the linkage data of *e* in elements of D_{i-1}^*. For example, let the dealer_core consist of couples (name, address), where the address is structured as in DTD dealer. Figure 10 shows a partial matching of cores in XML documents d_1 (invoice) and d_2 (dealer). The ZIP RTW809 is missing in d_1. Thus, $V_{(C1\rightarrow C2)\text{-core}}(d_1) \leq: V_{C2\text{-core}}(d_2)$.

Definition 1 (XML-Referential Integrity): Let C_1 and C_2 be collections with DTD$_{C1}$ and DTD$_{C2}$ respectively. Let $V_{C1\text{-core}}$ and $V_{C2\text{-core}}$ be views defining C_1- and C_2-core data, respectively. Then *XML-referential integrity based on C-cores* is satisfied by C_1 and C_2 iff

$$\forall d_1 \in C_1 \exists d_2 \in C_2 (V_{(C1\rightarrow C2)\text{-core}}(d_1) \leq: V_{C2\text{-core}}(d_2)) \qquad (+)$$

The definition behaves according to the notion of referential integrity given for relational databases in the SQL language.

For collections C_1 and C_2, satisfying XML-referential integrity based on C-cores we write $C_1 \subseteq: C_2$. Having DTD$_{C1\text{-core}}$ and DTD$_{C2\text{-core}}$ we can define the statement XML-referential integrity on the schema level. It is a relation between two DTDs. We write DTD$_{C1} \subseteq:$ DTD$_{C2}$. Observe that comparing XML-referential integrity to the relational referential integrity, there may be more d_2 documents satisfying the condition (+).

The principle of XML-referential integrity and its checking is shown in Figure 11. The partial (unordered) tree embedding problem has an effective solution[16] in practice.

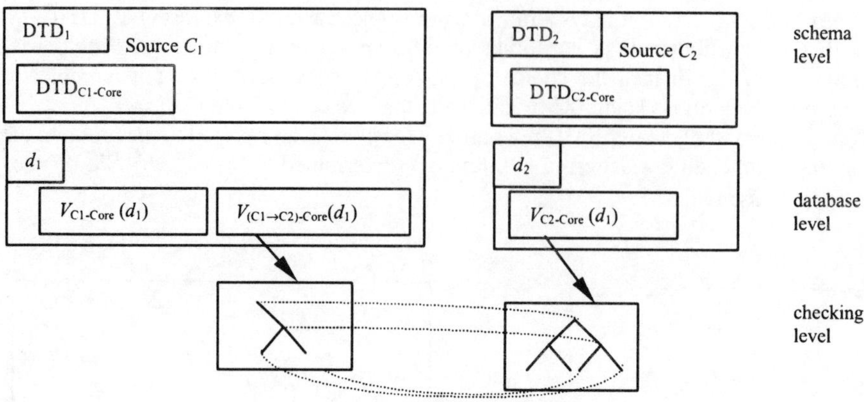

Figure 11. XML-referential integrity

6. XML-STAR SCHEMA WITH SIMPLE DIMENSION HIERARCHIES

Definition 2: Let $\boldsymbol{DC}$ be a set of DTDs. Let $\boldsymbol{D}$ be a set of DTDs whose each member D is a subDTD of a DTD $\in \boldsymbol{DC}$, a $DTD_{D\text{-core}}$ describes its D-core. Then a *(simple) XML-dimension hierarchy* N: $D_1 \rightarrow \ldots \rightarrow D_K$ is an acyclic path, whose nodes are from $\boldsymbol{D}$, and if $(D_i, D_{i+1}) \in N$, then $D_j \subseteq: D_{i+1}$. *Dimensional data for* N is given by a set of D^*_i, $i = 1,\ldots,K$, where for each (D_i^*, D_{i+1}^*) the statement $D_j^* \subseteq: D_{i+1}^*$ is satisfied.

For the sake of simplicity, we represent fact data similar to rows of a fact table in the table model, only its representation is in XML. We say that DTD_F of such fact data *is specified* w.r.t. a set of hierarchy roots.

Definition 3: Let $\boldsymbol{N}$ be a non-empty set of XML-dimension hierarchies, $\boldsymbol{D}_N$ the set of their hierarchy roots, and F a DTD_F specified w.r.t. $\boldsymbol{D}_N$. Then an *XML-star schema with simple dimension hierarchies* is a pair $<\boldsymbol{N}, F>$. A *dimensional XML-database* S^* over an XML-star schema with simple dimension hierarchies S is given by a set of dimensional data for N, for all $N \in \boldsymbol{N}$, and XML fact data F^* valid w.r.t. DTD_F satisfying the constraint $F \subseteq: D$ for each $D \in \boldsymbol{D}_N$.

There are different possibilities how to query an XML-DW. An attractive possibility is to use its conceptual level. We have mentioned the approach with UML in Section 4.1. A mapping between the subset of UML diagrams and the ODMG data model enables the user to use OQL language. Obviously, OQL is a query language rather on the logical level, similar to the relational SQL language. Another example of the querying on the conceptual level is shown in Figure 12. It expresses the query “Find the total profits concerning audio models of each dealer from the Kaunai region in 1998”. Such queries are typical in DW environment. They enable express different granularities in a simple way.

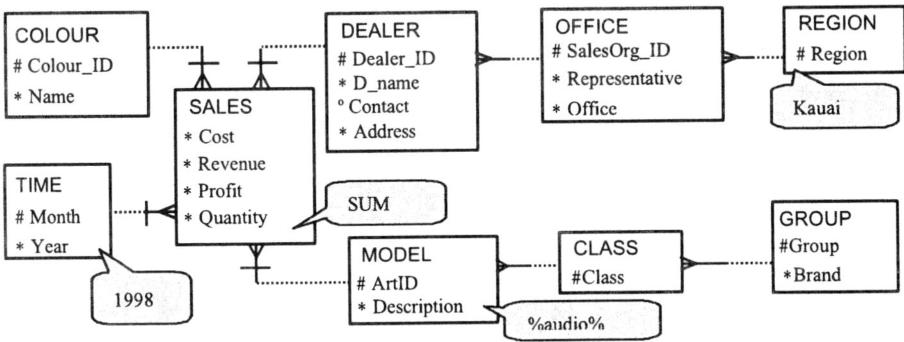

Figure 12. Querying DW on the conceptual level

At the DM level it is possible to use any XML query language, e.g. XQuery. We proposed a simple query language[17] whose queries are expressed by restrictions φ on members D of dimension hierarchies. We can restrict the domain of a member (e.g. by path expressions) and use semijoins for two adjacent members of a dimension hierarchy. For example, the expression dealer[contact/phone = '221914265'] restricts dealer elements to that ones that contain the subelement <phone> 21914265</phone>. Similar to the relational algebra, the semijoin applied to two collections of XML data C_1 and C_2 extracts XML data from C_1, which successfully matches data from C_2. The matching condition is given by the predicate ≤:. This fact distinguishes significantly our approach from the approach.[7] The basic idea how to evaluate a query over a dimensional XML-database is to navigate each dimension hierarchy N from its last member with non-empty φ to the root of N. A transformation of a query from conceptual into DM level is straightforward.

Due to the weak identifiability and an XML-referential integrity based on an approximate matching, we can obtain less information than in classical DW. To measure such impreciseness the notion of support and confidence could be used in XML context.[18]

7. CONCLUSIONS

XML-DWs are the future trend.[19] We have shown two basic architectures for DW based on XML data based on a star schema with simple dimension hierarchies, both at the conceptual and the logical level. The former uses classical means based on exact matching like as it is common in the languages XQuery and SQL. We have focused here rather on the latter architecture. Due to the inherent characteristics of XML data, such as incompleteness, non-uniqueness, and redundancy, it is necessary to release some requirements on the referential integrity known from traditional models based on tables. We have introduced a weak identifiability and used an approximate matching. Except experiments with XML-referential integrity there are empirical studies of this approach. On the other hand, the vision of XML-DW based on above assumptions seems to be a natural solution for future XML data processing.

A conceptual view on XML data is useful both for querying XML-DW and for specifying referential integrities in XML collections. Unfortunately, common conceptual models offer only restricted possibilities to model those features of XML data expressible by complex regular expressions. Moreover, any conceptual data is missing for many XML collections. Another important direction is the use of the approach in the context of digital media warehouses.[21] We would like to investigate these possibilities in our future work.

ACKNOWLEDGEMENT

This research was supported in part by GACR grant 201/03/0912.

REFERENCES

1. R. Kimball, L. Reeves, M., Ross, and W. Thorthwaite, *The Data Warehouse Lifecycle Toolkit* (John Wiley & Sons, Inc., New York, 1998).
2. P. Marcel, Modeling and querying multidimensional databases: an overview, *Networking and Information Systems Journal*, 2(5-6), 515-548 (1999).
3. Extensible Markup Language (XML) 1.0 (1998); http://www.w3.org/TR/REC-xml.
4. R. Bourret, XML and Databases (January 2003); http://www.rpbourret.com/xml/XMLAndDatabases.htm.
5. XQuery 1.0: An XML Query Language, W3C Working Draft 15 (November 2002); http://www.w3.org/TR/xquery/.
6. Xyleme. http://www-rocq.inria.fr/verso/research/xyleme/.
7. M. Golfarelli, D. Maio, and S. Rizzi, Conceptual Design of Data Warehouses from E/R Schemes, in: Proc. of the Hawaii Int. Conference on System Sciences, Kona, Hawaii, 1998.
8. M. R. Jensen, T. H. Møller, and T. B. Pedersen, Specifying OLAP Cubes On XML Data, Technical Report 01-5003, Aalborg University, Department of Computer Science, 2001.
9. M. Golfarelli, S. Rizzi, B. and Vrdoljak, Data warehouse design from XML sources, in: *Proceedings of ACM Fourth International Workshop on Data Warehousing and OLAP* (DOLAP 2001), J. Hammer Ed., (ACM Press, 2001, Atlanta), pp. 40–47.
10. R. G. G. Cattel and D. K. Barry, eds., *The Object Database Standard: ODMG 3.0* (Morgan Kaufman Publishers, 2000).
11. J. Pokorny, XML Functionally, in: *Proceedings of IDEAS2000*, edited by B. C. Desai, Y. Kioki, and M. Toyama (IEEE Comp. Society, 2000) pp. 266–274.
12. P. Buneman, S. Davidson, W. Fan, C. Hara, and W.-Ch. Tan, Keys for XML, in: *Proceedings of WWW10*, May 1–5, Hong-Kong (ACM Press, 2001).
13. W. Fan and L. Libkin, On XML Integrity Constraints in the Presence of DTDs, in: Proc. ACM SIGACT-SIGMOD-SIGART Symp. on Principles of Database Systems, (2001), pp. 114–125.
14. J. Pokorny, Approximate Treatment of XML Collections, in: Proc. of 6th Int. Conf. Business Information Systems, edited by W. Abramowicz and G. Klein, Colorado Springs, USA, (2003), pp. 13–22.
15. J. Pokorny, Modelling Stars Using XML, in: *Proceedings of ACM Fourth International Workshop on Data Warehousing and OLAP* (DOLAP 2001), edited by J. Hammer (ACM Press, 2001, Atlanta), pp. 24–31.
16. T. Schlieder and F. Naumann, Approximate Tree Embedding for Querying XML Data, in: Proc. of ACM SIGIR Workshop on XML and IR, Athens, 2000.
17. J. Pokorný, XML Data Warehouse: Modelling and Querying. Databases and Information Systems II, *Selected Papers from the Fifth International Baltic Conference*, BalticDB&IS'2002, edited by H-M. Haav and A. Kalja (Kluwer Academic Publishers, 2002), pp 67–80.
18. G. Grahne, J. Zhu, Discovering Approximate Keys in XML Data, in: Proceedings of ACM Conf. CIKM'02, November 4–9, McLean, Virginia, USA, 2002, pp. 453–460.
19. XML: Strategic Analysis of XML for Web Application Development, Computer Technology Research Corp. Report, 2000.
20. J. Váòa, Reference Integrity of XML Data. Diploma Thesis, Department of Software Engineering, Charles University, 2002 (in Czech).
21. M. A. Windhouwer, A. R. Schmidt, R. van Zwol, M. Petkovic, and H. E. Blok, Flexible and scalable digital library search, in: Proceedings of the VLDB, edited by P. Atzeni et al, Roma, 2001, pp.705–706.

"WEB PRESENCE"

Formulating a "wicked" research problem

Sherre Roy and Dr Paul Ledington*

ABSTRACT

Businesses want a "Web Presence" but what is such a thing? Can it be designed? What if we see web site developers as the purposeful shapers of "Web Presence", does this affect their design processes? Indeed can "Presence" be defined?

As much as "Web Presence" may open a Pandora's box of questions and issues, this paper does not focus on "Web Presence". It concentrates on the related concept of seeing web site developers as purposeful shapers of a "Web Presence". The research study described in this paper goes "back to basics" to begin to formulate the research problem and demonstrate the feasibility of progress through analysing three research sites of developers creating business "Presence" web sites.

1. INTRODUCTION

Lombard and Ditton convey that an "An enhanced sense of presence is central to the use, and therefore the usefulness and profitability, of the new technologies" (1997) these technologies include the WWW (World Wide Web). Businesses have identified that having a website on the WWW could provide them with increased income. As the popularity of this trend increases, the term website now appears not to convey the correct message with some businesses using the term "Web Presence" to indicate that they have a website on the WWW. As much as "Web Presence" may open a Pandora's box of questions and issues that in research terms defines it as a "Wicked" problem that needs work, this paper does not focus on defining "Web Presence". It concentrates on the related concept of seeing website developers as purposeful shapers of a "Web Presence".

To begin to develop this concept it was identified that by going 'back to basics' so to speak was the best way to move forward in what may be a considered a complex

* Sherre Roy, University of the Sunshine Coast, Maroochydore DC, Queensland, 4558, Australia, sroy2@usc.edu.au
Dr Paul Ledington, CEO of the Australian Systems Institute and adjunct Associate Professor at Central Queensland University, Ledington@bigpond.com

development situation. We are conscious that software-related projects are usefully seen as complex human activity systems that may be shaped by many factors in addition to "Presence". The basic idea therefore became to compare conventional Information Systems (IS) development projects with Web Site Development (WSD) projects in order to recognise the similarities and differences between the two. The starting point was the use of the Systems Development Lifecycle as a normative organising framework of activities reflecting conventional project issues. A language to describe what the project does. In addition the concept of the human activity system was used as a language through which to describe the social system through which the activity was enacted. A language to describe the social network within which activity is done.

Further, the landscape for this study is Web Site Development, but particularly in Small to Medium sized Enterprises (SME's). In Australia this makes up the majority of businesses seeking to have a "Presence" on the World Wide Web. These sites to some degree are static sites for which little research has been conducted. The IS community has an awareness of this WSD landscape with methods being developed to create the more complex Multimedia and Hypermedia web sites. In the following sections this basic research thinking is extended and applied to three situations as a starting point for extending the concept that website developers are purposeful shapers of a "Web Presence".

2. RESEARCH DESIGN

To help focus the research in the desired direction, Checkland's (1985) FMA Framework was used to manage the pilot research process. The subject area (A) under consideration was WSD, however a suitable Framework (F) and Methodology (M) within which to conduct the research were needed.

In keeping with going "back to basics" it was decided to use a Grounded Theory approach employing interpretive field studies as the Methodology for the research. This approach has the "flexibility and freedom to explore a phenomenon in depth" (Strauss and Corbin, 1990, p. 37) that would enable the discovery of concepts and relationships from within the subject area (Strauss and Corbin, 1990, p. 37–38). The use of this approach encouraged the interplay of Methodology and Area, as well as the freedom to explore WSD, without the restriction of a Framework, to identify concepts and relationships. Figure 1 visually represents the intellectual framework for the Pilot Study. Consistent the principles of Grounded Theory no literature review was completed before the interpretive field studies were conducted.

The field studies themselves were conducted with three WSD businesses. They used open-ended questions to collect a rich dataset for analysis. The analysis focused "on naturally occurring ordinary events in natural settings" (Miles and Huberman, 1994, p. 10) and employed the activities of Data Reduction, Data Display, Conclusion Drawing and Verification (Miles and Huberman, 1994 pp. 10–11). The questions concentrated on identifying information about the business and how they develop web sites to give a starting point for a comparison activity. The next section describes these research sites.

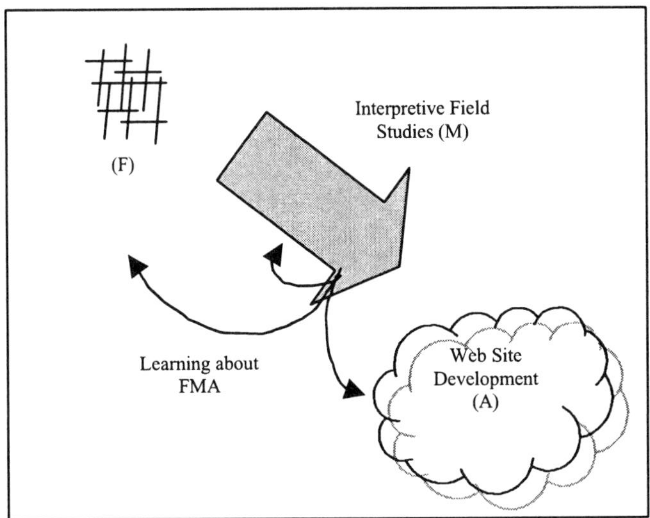

Figure 1. Research approach for FMA

3. INTRODUCING THE RESEARCH SITES

This pilot research was conducted using three sites, all situated in the Sunshine Coast region of Queensland. The first business is a sole operator whose core business is to provide advertising services. He had been introduced to web design by a partner from a previous business venture and worked for large advertising companies before going into business for himself. He is between 30–45 years of age and sees web sites as being another avenue for advertising and marketing. He endeavours to develop and maintain long-term relationships with his clients and provides expertise in developing advertising campaigns and from this the ability for the client to sell their product.

The second business is a company that specialises in WSD as well as website hosting (storing the website on their web servers). It takes a team approach to the development process employing a sales person, two graphic designers, two "coding boys" and a production manager. These employees range in age from 20 to 45. The company has set up a shopping portal on which their clients' websites are placed and also administers a loyalty card program. They see themselves providing a new dimension to the client's business and a way to create more contacts for the business.

The third research site is also a sole operator, with his core service being to provide business applications and web sites, with a definite preference for WSD. He has served ten years in the Defence Forces in an IT management capacity before completing the same job description in private industry. He started his own IT business before following up on a liking for programming and changing the business from an IT focus to a programming one. He was subsequently introduced to website development and Active Server Pages (ASP) by a friend and incorporated website development into his business. He is in the age range of between 30 to 40 years and specialises in providing websites that connect to a database that can be managed and maintained by the owner of the site.

The process used by these developers to create a web site was also identified and this area was the focus of the research. Each business had a slightly different process, but only as far as the information provided to their client; these processes are listed in Table 1. There were enough similarities that an aggregate process could be produced for analysis.

Having identified the processes used to create a web site the research as part if its exploration of the subject area conducted a comparison activity identifying the similarities and differences between ISD and WSD. There are many approach's that could have been chosen to conduct the comparison activity. Keeping with the "back to basics" focus of the research the ISD approach used for the comparison activity was the System Development Life Cycle (SDLC) because it is a well-established approach having structured stages providing allowance for planning, organising and management control. Hirschheim, Klein and Lyytinen (1995, p. 32–33) in tracing the development of ISD approaches place the SDLC in the first generation of ISD approaches, which began in the mid 1960's. The first generation ISD approaches are described as being traditional or classical approaches, with approaches being developed in later generations based on the SDLC. The deciding factor to use the SDLC was that it is the approach upon which most other approaches are based. The SDLC is an approach that has a high technical focus and which divides the complete job into smaller manageable activities, which are sequenced and connected, with the overall aim to provide better project management and control (Avison and Shah 1997, p. 76).

Table 1. Process undertaken by individual business to create a web site

Business 1	Business 2	Business 3
Find Owner requirements	Find Owner requirements	Find Owner requirement and create Flow Chart
Create Flowchart of pages	Create Response	Develop Quote
Get Client Approval	Get Client Approval	Get Client Approval
Approval Obtained	Approval Obtained	Approval Obtained
Create 2-3 pages to ascertain look and feel	Create Home page to ascertain look and feel	Design the site including some rough functionality
Get Client Approval	Get Client Approval	Get Client Approval
Approval obtained	Approval obtained	Approval Obtained
Complete Site	Complete Site and Usability Test	Complete Site
Get Client Approval	Get Client Approval	Get Client Approval
Approval Obtained	Approval Obtained	Approval Obtained
Implement Site	Implement Site	Implement Site

Each activity or stage is required to be completed along with the suitable documentation before the next is started (Fitzgerald et al., 2002, pp. 24–25), providing a structured approach to completing the project. Having introduced the ISD that will be used in the comparison activity the next section will consider the similarities identified.

4. SIMILARITIES

The similarity with traditional development is that the process used to build a web site are very similar to that used in the SDLC. Although not shown in Figure 2 these steps of the process are iterative in nature moving backwards and forwards between the different steps as required. The SDLC does require approval from the client in the early stage of development and at the final implementation to ensure that they are happy with the work done to each strategic stage. The website steps are also iterative in nature but only in as much as that at any stage requiring client approval, non-approval returns to the step before and approval leads to the next step as visually represented in Figure 2.

Having identified that a similarity exists in the steps taken to achieve a final product, does this similarity extend further? To establish this, the research will now consider two things: Who the victims, beneficiaries, actors and owners are in relation to the final product and the nature of each step: what it does and how it is accomplished as well as what measure of performance is used to indicate completion.

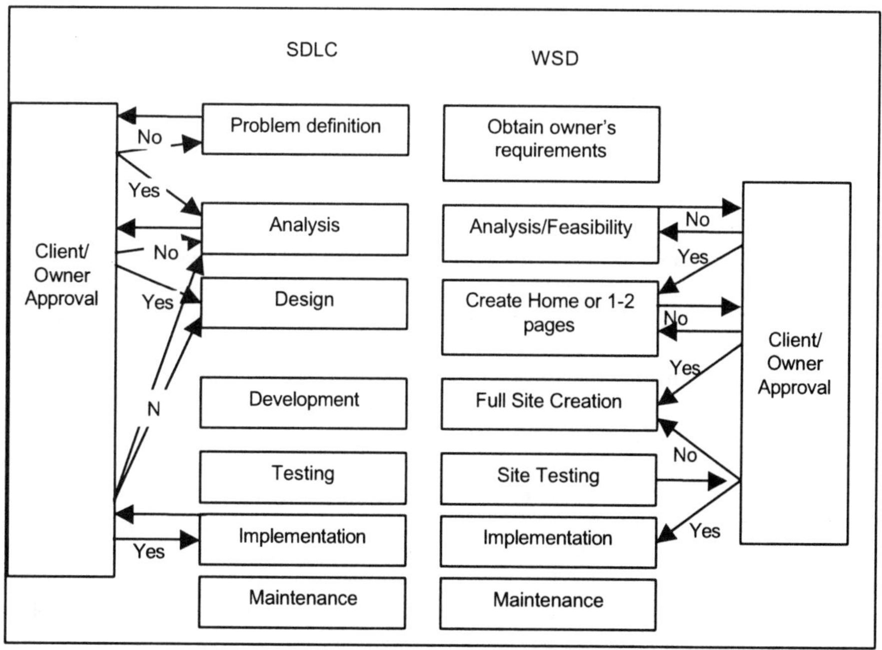

Figure 2. Comparison of the SDLC and WSD

Table 2. Summary of discussion about Owners, Beneficiaries, Victims and Actors

	Software Application	Website
Owner	Business Owner, Manager	Business Owner, Manager
Beneficiaries	Owner, Employees, Clients	Owner, Employees, Clients
Victims	Owner, Employees, Clients	Owner, Employees, Clients
Actors	Developer	Developer

Firstly, an application whether software or website will have owners, beneficiaries and/or victims and actors. These are defined by Checkland and Scholes (1990, p.35) as follows.

Owners	Those who can stop the creation of the final product.
Beneficiaries	Those that benefit from the introduction of the product.
Victims	Those that do not benefit from the introduction of the product.
Actors	Those that would create the final product.

The owners of both a software application and a web site are those that commission and pay for the developer to complete the product, i.e. the business owner or manager.

With any software application there are beneficiaries and/or victims and this will depend on the application. If the employees like the application and use it then there will be beneficiaries, who are the employees, the owner and the clients. If the employees resist using the application then there are victims who are the employees, the owners and the clients. These are the extremes and there could be cases where there are both beneficiaries and victims from the range of options between the extremes.

For a web site the circumstances are similar. It is the end user, being the public as the prospective clients that will make a site successful. If the user does not like the site, they will not deal with the owner of the site. In this extreme the victims are the owner and possibly current employees. These same people along with the end user are the beneficiaries if the site is well liked and used regularly.

The actors for both software and web sites are the developers. Even though there is input from the business as to what is required it is the developer that ultimately creates the end product. Table 2 summaries the above discussion about Owners, Beneficiaries, Victims and Actors.

The research to this point identified that similarities do exist between ISD and WSD and now was ready to move on and conduct a comparison between ISD and WSD at each step of the process. During this comparison activity more similarities were identified with the findings summarised in Tables 3 and 4.

The research has identified that between ISD and WSD the similarity exists not only in name but the types of activity undertaken and the outputs achieved. Having considered the similarities there is one question that needs to be considered; why is there the similarity? Fitzgerald, et al. (2002, p. 25) identify that the basic steps considered in this research are used by many disciplines, including IS, as a common approach to problem solving. The steps are a logical approach to problem solving and can be "seen as a checklist to govern when and how different activities should be performed and what resources would be required" (Fitzgerald et al., 2002, p. 25).

Table 3. Comparison of SDLC (Davies 1994) and Web Site Development

SDLC Name	Description	Web Description	Web Name
Problem Definition	Identify the problem, define the cause, outline a solution strategy and identify requirements	Identify the reasons why the site is wanted, its purpose and what content will be on it	**Obtain Owner Requirements**
Analysis	Determine what must be done to solve the problem	Establish the number of pages and work associated in creating the site	**Analysis/ Feasibility**
Design	Determine how the problem will be solved	Design a couple of pages to establish that the client is happy with the way the pages will look and the functionality	**Create page/s for look and feel**
Developmen t	Create the system, write the program, install hardware, write procedures and manuals and train the User	Design the rest of the pages that will form the full site	**Full Site Creation**
Testing	Test the system to ensure it does what it is designed to do	Test the site for Usability. Ensure the navigation and links all work	**Site Testing**
Implementat ion	Release the system to the user	Upload the site onto the Hosting Computer	**Implementation**
Maintenance	Keep the system functioning.	Ensure the page is updated regularly, testing the broken links and adding new elements	**Update/ Maintenance**

Table 4. Summary of comparison between ISD and WSD development steps

	Step Name	Step Activity	Step Tools	Step Outputs
Step One				
ISD	Problem Definition	Identify the problem, define the cause, outline a solution strategy, identify requirements		Feasibility Study
WSD	Obtain Owner Requirements	Identify the reasons why the client wants the site, the purpose and what they want on it		Hand Drawn Site Map
StepT wo				
ISD	Analysis	Determine what must be done to solve the problem	Data Flow Diagrams, Decision Trees, Decision Tables, Structured English	System Specifications, Solution alternatives and Recommendations
WSD	Analysis/ Feasibility	Establish the number of pages and the work associated in creating the site	Hand Drawn Site Map	Quote/Response for approval by Client

Table 4 (continued). Summary of comparison between ISD and WSD development steps

	Step Name	Step Activity	Step Tools	Step Outputs
Step Three				
ISD	Design	Determine how the problem will be solved	Application to develop GUI	Specification Package for Programmers to use
WSD	Create page/s for look and feel	Design a couple of pages to establish that the client is happy with the way the pages will look and the functionality	Application to create pages eg. Dreamweaver	Between one to three pages
Step Four				
ISD	Development	Create the system, write the program, install hardware, write procedures and manuals and train the User	Coding Application	Manuals, files, Completed System
WSD	Full Site Creation	Design the rest of the pages that will form the full site	Application to create pages eg. Dreamweaver	Completed Site
Step Five				
ISD	Testing	Test the system to ensure it does what it is designed to do		Completed Test Plan and Site
WSD	Site Testing	Test the site for Usability. Ensure the navigation and links all work		Completed Site
Step Six				
ISD	Implementation	Release the system to the user		Signoff by Client accepting system
WSD	Implementation	Upload the site onto the Hosting Computer		Site signed off and uploaded to the Hosting Computer
Step Seven				
ISD	Maintenance	Keep the system functioning		
WSD	Update/ Maintenance	Ensure the page is updated regularly, testing the broken links and adding new elements		

Despite the similarities there are fundamental differences between Software Application Development and Web Site Development; the differences are in relation to the purpose and development techniques.

5. DIFFERENCES

In ISD there are some almost fundamental concepts which are tacit in nature to those within the IS discipline. These concepts need to be made explicit, to be able to appreciate the differences between ISD and WSD. The analysis for this stage identified four concepts where the differences are significant.

The first is the user of the application. In ISD the end user, generally internal to the business, is not only they who commission the application but also their management and employees. For WSD however the end users are those external to the business i.e. the public.

Secondly, the purpose of the application is a concept containing significant differences. The purpose of the ISD application is centred on data with the application being required to capture data entered by the user, store it and then allow the user to change or delete data as well as produce reports relating to the stored data. The purpose of the WSD is entirely different. The site is developed to engage the user in some form, whether to provide information, encourage the purchase of a product or allow contact with the owners of the site.

Thirdly, who is involved in the development process? For ISD, particularly those developed using Structured Systems Analysis and Design Method (SSADM), Effective Technical and Human Implementation of Computer based Systems (ETHICS), Soft Systems Methodology (SSM), etc, a large component of the designing stage involves the inclusion of the end user in the design decisions as well as the developer and those in authority i.e. owner and management. For WSD the inclusion of the end user is virtually impossible (Lane and Koronois, 2000). It is incumbent upon the developer particularly to create an image of who the user is.

Table 5. Differences between Software Development and Web Site Development

	Software Application Development	**Web site application development**
User of application	Internal	External
Purpose of application	Capture data Store data Add data Change data Delete data Produce reports	Engage user Inform user Encourage purchase of product Encourage user to contact business.
Application developed by	Developer in conjunction with owner, staff and users	Developer in conjunction with owner and staff
Why business develops an application	Improve business process by: Streamlining current process Make current more efficient Identify new and better process	Expand current marketing/advertising campaign Increase sales Increase profit Expand client base Expand business – add new dimension

The creation of this image with the assistance of the owner and staff will dictate what elements will be included that will draw the user to the site.

Lastly, why do businesses develop applications? An ISD application is developed to improve business processes either by streamlining the current process or identifying a new and better process. The WSD however is developed to expand the business in some form; this expansion is generally to the current marketing/advertising campaigns, with the intention to increase sales/profits and to expand the client base.

These four concepts, summarised in Table 5, establish that website developers need not only to have the technical skills to create a web site but also an understanding of the business and its culture as well as appreciate the hidden target market and its needs.

The research in having identifying similarities and differences provokes the question; is it desirable for Website Developers to use the SDLC? There is no one right answer. It is desirable in any project to have guidelines available, ensuring that the project remains on track. The steps of the SDLC provide a checklist or a set of guidelines to assist in project management. However the focus of the SDLC is on the technical aspect of a project, concentrating on the data, process, inputs and outputs. It does not focus on the social aspect of the business such as what the culture is and how employees and management interact to achieve the business objectives. This aspect of the SDLC means that it is not a desirable model for gaining understanding of the social aspects of a business. A website as an extension of the business's marketing campaign seeks to convey the culture, structure and image of the business to its target market of users on the dynamic platform of the WWW.

The SDLC then is not desirable as a tool for developing an appreciation of the business, its objectives, culture and target market of users. This yes and no answer identifies that other methods and tools are needed for use by developers to meet the client's requirement.

The results of this analysis lead the researchers to wonder how, given the differences between ISD and WSD, does the WSD developer appreciate the development process. This question was addressed as part of the research, but is a paper in itself.

6. RESEARCH OUTCOMES

Using the "back to basics" focus the SDLC was a necessary starting point for analysis and it is not surprising that it provides many similarities with the subject area. This is to be expected given the dominance of the model within the discourse of Information Systems. There are however indications – and the data is not strong enough for any other interpretation, that the requirement stage of the process is more uncertain and more iterative than in the conventional approach. The evidence also suggests that the SDLC is rather clumsy as an analytical framework and therefore frameworks based upon Rapid Application Development, Decision Support Systems Approaches, and Prototyping should be considered. Approaches could be chosen that emphasise business analysis rather than functional design.

The social system analysis proved more useful. Increasingly it emerged that the nature of the "User" was different between conventional IS and websites. Conventionally the system owner could define the "user" in terms of functionality, data, and processes and to some degree legislate for use of the system. A company defines who uses its accounting system and to some degree that they do use it. The user falls within the control of the system owner. A website by contrast is a "public" entity, in principle at least open to all. Further, to use it is the choice of the user – they could turn to that of another company. The research has identified that the concept of Web Site Developers are purposeful shapers of a "Web Presence" is most likely, with the actual building of the web site being routine. It is in the requirements stage where the context of 'presence' is social, public, and competitive and does not fall under the control of the system owner in the same way as in conventional IS that the Web Site Developer needs to employ the skills that are required to build a "Web Presence", something that is part location, part identifier, part marketing and part cultural insignia, icon and metaphor for the Business commissioning the website.

The project cannot possibly be definitive at this stage but it does suggest that the notion of "Web Presence" cannot be dismissed yet. A basic research approach has been demonstrated as feasible and practical and suggestions for a modified approach have been made. The need to examine "presence" from a social system perspective has emerged and some progress has been made in developing a basic language with which to examine the area.

7. SUMMARY AND CONCLUSIONS

This paper has surfaced the notion of "Web Presence" as an important practical concept but one which has yet been neglected by research. It was also argued that the concept is underdeveloped and therefore represents a "Wicked" research problem. A set of propositions upon which research might be based were proposed and a research design based upon them described. The results of a pilot study of three research sites were discussed leading to suggestions for the next cycle of research activity and particularly highlighting the different nature of "Web Presence" as a design problem.

REFERENCES

Avison, D. and Shah, H., 1997, *The Information systems Development Life Cycle: A First Course in Information Systems*, McGraw Hill International, London.

Checkland, P. B., 1985, From Optimizing to Learning: A Development of Systems Thinking for the 1990s, *The Journal of the Operational Research Society*, Vol. 36, no. 9, 757–767

Checkland, P. B. and Scholes, J., 1990, *Soft Systems Methodology in Action*, Wiley, Chichester.

Fitzgerald, B., Russo, N. L. and Stolterman, E., 2002, *Information Systems Development: Methods in Action*, McGraw-Hill Education, New York.

Hirschheim, R., Klein, H. and Lyytinen, K., 1995, *Information systems development and data modeling: conceptual and philosophical foundations*, Cambridge University Press, Cambridge, New York.

Lane, M. S. and Koronios, A., 2000, A Balanced Approach to Capturing User Requirements in Business-To-Consumer Web Information Systems, Proceedings of 11th Australian Conference on Information Systems, Brisbane, Australia, viewed 15th October 2001, http://www2.fit.qut.edu.au/ACIS2000/full_papers.html.

Lombard, M. and Ditton, T., 1997, At the Heart of It All: The Concept of Presence, *Journal of Computer-Mediated Communication*, Vol. 3, No. 2, viewed 15th July 2003, http://www.presence-research.org

Lyttinen, K., Rose, G. and Welke, R., 1998, The Brave New World of Development in the InterNetwork Computer Architecture (InterNCA): Or How Distributed Computing Platforms Will Change Systems Development, *Information Systems Journal*, vol. 8, no. 3, 241–253.

Miles, M. B. and Huberman, A. M., 1994, *Qualitative Data Analysis: An Expanded Sourcebook*, 2nd Edition, Sage Publications, Thousand Oaks, California.

Powell, T. A., 2000, *Web Design: The Complete Reference*, Osbourne/McGraw-Hill, Berkley, California.

Strauss, A. and Corbin, J., 1990, *Basics of Qualitative Research: grounded theory procedures and techniques*, Sage Publications, California.

AUTOMATIC TOPIC MAP CREATION USING TERM CRAWLING AND CLUSTERING HIERARCHY PROJECTION

Witold Abramowicz, Tomasz Kaczmarek, and Marek Kowalkiewicz*

ABSTRACT

There is an increasing interest in automating creation of semantic structures, especially topic maps, by taking advantage of existing, structured information resources. This paper gives a preview of the most popular method – based on RDF triples, and suggests a way to automate topic map creation from unstructured information sources. The method can be applied in information systems development domain when analyzing vast unstructured data repositories in preparation for system design, or when migrating large amounts of unstructured data from legacy systems. There are two innovative methods presented in the paper – Term Crawling (TC) and Clustering History Projection (CHP), which are used in order to build a topic map based on free text documents downloaded from the Internet. A sample tool, which uses described techniques, has been implemented. The preliminary results that have been achieved on the test collection are presented in concluding sections of the article.

1. INTRODUCTION

Topic maps are becoming more and more popular as a structuring mechanism for repositories. The phenomenon of topic maps can be observed during many conferences, such as XML Europe, in newsgroup discussions (the Oasis society), and in practice – in many applications throughout the world (LMTM, 2002; Forskning.no, 2003; and Liechtenstein, 2003). The basic idea of topic maps has been neatly described in "The TAO of Topic Maps" (Pepper, 2000), a more detailed – and standardized – view has been presented in ISO 13250 (2000), and one of the first attempts to sketch the idea of using topic maps for structuring content has been made in "Topic Maps for repositories" (Ahmed, 2000).

---

* Witold Abramowicz, Tomasz Kaczmarek, Marek Kowalkiewicz, The Poznań University of Economics, Poznań, Poland

Topic maps as semantic structures can be used in information systems development in several areas. They act as a tool supporting system design. The semantics carried by topic map may be used to understand the domain and analyze the requirements for system design. One way to use topic maps would be to identify subjects and patterns that may exist in unstructured data analyzed for system modeling. The tools, supporting topic map visualization, help to analyze domain and design database. The other potential application area is migration from unstructured data or text repository to the structured one. Automatically created topic maps provide insight into unknown data structure thereby imposing partial structure constraints.

At the beginning, the idea, as a descendant of the DocBook (Walsh, 1999) standard, was to create topic maps from scratch. Therefore, the process of creating topic maps would be to identify resources, try to describe them as it was needed, and link subjects with the other ones (a good introduction to that can be found in the mentioned work of Steve Pepper). One of challenging tasks would be to identify all required occurrences of each topic, and then to associate them with this topic. Recently, the topic maps community has focused on automated topic map creation from already existing resources. The automated process is more "occurrence driven", which means that building mechanisms first analyze the source base (for example a set of HTML files), and then create a topic map. In this approach, occurrences finally play a smaller role – their content is treated as a base for creating topics and associations in the map, and afterwards source occurrences can even be omitted. As it is explained later in the text, in order to create such a map, one needs to have access to some structured sources, or mechanisms for Natural Language Processing (NLP). The aim of this article is to suggest a method for automated topic map creation for unstructured sources with no need to use NLP – this makes the process more flexible (e.g. mostly independent from language of source base).

2. AUTOMATED TOPIC MAP CREATION

The issue of automated topic map creation has been widely discussed in many publication in 2002, two years after publishing an ISO standard document for the topic maps. There is currently a number of running projects focusing on creating topic maps from existing data sources, one such example is the Ontopia's MapMaker toolkit. The approach can be described as "identify – describe – create topic map" procedure, whilst specific solutions differ. Here, we will illustrate the topic map creation process by analyzing usable data sources, propose four step procedure for its creation, and show the three approaches to using the procedure.

2.1. Data Sources

In most cases, there is no need to create topic maps from scratch. Existing information resources in organizations can be used as a critical mass which will leverage the process. Topic maps, in its simplest form, can be described as a collection of Topics, Associations and Occurrences, the so called TAO of topic maps. Therefore, the most efficient information resources are those, that can be effortlessly converted into subjects, relations between them, and subjects' instances. Examples of such sources include:

Relational databases – where primary keys describe topics, fields within one record can be occurrences, and relations help to establish associations

Web sites – where URLs identify topics, webpage contents are occurrences, and hyperlinks show associations with other web pages
Directory systems – where directory objects point at topics, directory schema describes topic types, objects themselves are occurrences, and associations are derived from the tree-based structure of directory
Content management systems – which are similar to the websites, but store smaller units of data (paragraphs) and often provide more detailed descriptions
Files in file systems – which can be treated similarly to directory systems, and again, files of specific types can contain metadata, which can afterwards be used in preparing more detailed topic map

Other way to enumerate the data sources – a more general one – would be based on source characteristics. And therefore we can identify:

Structured knowledge – ontologies and classification systems, database schemas, document type definitions (DTDs) and XML schemas, metadata schemas
Structured document content – with emails, newsgroup messages or accounting documents as examples
Unstructured document content – where preparations must involve more sophisticated techniques, such as Natural Language Processing with Named Entity recognition, Concept extraction, and taxonomic classifications. Most NLP based processing tools require only raw text, therefore document transitions are not complicated
Document metadata – analyses include properties stored in a file (such as Microsoft Office's properties, RDF-PDF or HTML Dublin Core) or externally stored properties (RDF, MPEG 21, Document Management System metadata)

2.2. Procedure

The procedure of automated topic map creation can be split into four steps. The procedure bases on a common assumption, that before creating a final map, there is a RDF model prepared, which is used as input data afterwards. The four steps are as follows:

Subject recognition
Information extraction and preparing
RDF modeling
Mapping RDF model into a topic map

Whilst the fourth step can be done using available tools (such as those from Ontopia), the previous three are most interesting, and let us experiment and develop methods for converting source data into a Resource Description Framework model. In this part we analyze current routines, further in the paper we will propose a method based on the two experimental concepts: term crawling and clustering hierarchy projection. Both concepts, aside from abstract considerations, are also undergoing implementation tests – sample results are presented in the text.

2.2.1. Subject Recognition

In order to identify potential topics and say something about subjects, one has to locate data sources – subject occurrences. This is highly dependent on content type. For example, in relational databases this will mean analyzing a database schema and deciding, which tables contain candidate entities (one can also create his own queries based on selected tables); in document repositories the subject recognition will mean selecting a set of documents, which will be processed later on. Once we have identified the subjects and their occurrences, we should prepare unique URIs. The most common method is to use one's own registered domain name to create Universal Resource Identifiers. Example URI would then be http://www.mydomain.org/URI/apps/msword - which would identify the Microsoft's application.

2.2.2. Information Extraction and Preparing

After the subjects are recognized, one has to extract data needed for processing. When analyzing structured sources, such as XML documents, emails etc. this is quite obvious – one has to decide which document properties are important and, optionally, to prepare them. Preparing includes data conversion, value normalizing, splitting single values into multiple values, aggregating multiple values into single values, traversing hyperlinks to collect additional data etc. For semi-structured and unstructured data, this can be trickier, and advanced information processing techniques, such as Shallow Text Processing (Abramowicz and Piskorski, 2002), Natural Language Processing (Named Entity recognition, Concept extraction, and taxonomic classification) have to be used. Further parts of the paper will show that Term Crawling and Clustering History Projection techniques can help here as well.

2.2.3. RDF Modeling

RDF models describe objects, which correspond to topics in a topic map; their properties correspond to occurrences or associations with other topics. A RDF model consists of statements (often called triples), which have three parts: subject, property, and value. Subject describes a resource, the statement is about; Property describes the property type assigned to subject; Value contains a specific value of the property of the subject. Subject, property, and value can contain URIs, value can also contain other data types, such as strings, integers etc.

2.2.4. Mapping RDF Model Into a Topic Map

This step, performed mostly by automatic tools, involves analyzing RDF triples, and deciding whether a triple describes a topic, an association, or an occurrence. Preparing topics, associations and occurrences is the final step in the topic map creation, and further activities focus only on refining the map.

2.3. Processing Approaches

The described procedure of automated topic map creation can be used in a variety of environments, using a wide spectrum of source data. Depending on expected application, one of three approaches can be chosen from: one-time processing, repeated batch processing, and continuous processing.

1.1.1. One-Time Processing

One time move from legacy system to topic map is very effective, because the legacy system is no longer used and full power of topic maps can be used from the beginning. The disadvantages include need to roll out legacy indexes or supporting users who have not rolled out, and therefore do not have access to the latest data.

1.1.2. Repeated Batch Processing

The repeated batch processing can be triggered or scheduled. It allows for using existing, legacy indexes, and topic map at the same time. However this procedure is more resource consuming, less reliable (especially when source data schemas change), and does not guarantee that topic map is up to date.

1.1.3. Continuous Processing

Continuous processing, or wrapper around existing system, is a most complex technique. It lets users use existing tools and indexes and at the same time it updates the topic map, so that it is always up to date. However, if the existing system changes, significant development efforts may be required in order to maintain operability.

The approach proposed in this article can be applied in all the approaches mentioned above. It is also feasible in the last, most complicated, case. When a document collection is changing (new documents are added), the topic map should change in order to resemble new structure. In our approach it is possible to track new vocabulary which may be introduced with new documents, and include it in one of the dictionaries used in the procedure described below (Clustering Hierarchy Projection and Term Crawling).

3. ENHANCING CURRENT METHODS

Methods of automated topic map creation, sketched in the previous part of the text, are very efficient for structured and semi-structured data. However, when we try to apply the described procedure to unstructured data, such as collections of plain text news documents from the Web, a number of questions arises. There is no easy way to point out subjects, and associations. One, previously mentioned, way would be to use Natural Language Processing techniques, however they require significant effort to build rules for different languages (as, obviously, not only English documents may be processed), associations proposed by those techniques base only on documents' contents (and therefore overlook assumedly well known relations – contextual information). Our suggestion is to make use of two other techniques - both basing on methods used in information systems sciences. The first one – Term Crawling – will let us automatically identify relations between concepts, the second one – Clustering Hierarchy Projection – will allow clustering documents into groups basing on our needs. The two methods, jointly used, provide a framework for creating RDF triples from unstructured data, and eventually creating a topic map, which would not be possible when using standard methods.

3.1. Clustering Hierarchy Projection (CHP)

The basic idea behind clustering is that the documents can be grouped according to their content similarity without any prior knowledge or assumptions concerning this content. There are various approaches to clustering as described in Bhatia (1998) or Steinbach (2000). Usually the techniques are divided into K-means clustering and hierarchical clustering. The former is based on the following procedure:

1. Select initial K points among documents (each document is represented by vector of its terms frequencies) – these points are called centroids. The mathematics defines centroid of n point masses m_i located as points x_i as a center of mass with the formula like in Eq. (1)

$$\overline{x} = \frac{\sum_{i=1}^{n} m_i x_i}{\sum_{i=1}^{n} m_i} \tag{1}$$

   In our case the x would be terms frequencies and m – their weights.
2. Assign all remaining points to the closest centroid therefore creating clusters
3. Recompute centroid for each cluster.
4. Repeat 2 and 3 until centroids don't change.

However this approach proved to give worse clusters than the hierarchical clustering, which is usually described as below:

1. Create primary set of clusters where each document is represented by single cluster.
2. Compute similarity between all clusters using selected similarity measure – this creates similarity matrix.
3. Reduce the clusters number by merging the closest clusters.
4. Update the similarity matrix.
5. Repeat steps 3 and 4 until the desired number of clusters is reached.

Hierarchical clustering comes in different flavors depending on the similarity measure taken. Average linking is based on the mean of documents vectors – the centroid (also defined as a centre of a cloud of points – in most approaches it is simply a vector of average term frequencies from all documents in the cluster). Complete linking uses the dissimilarity measure which is the greatest distance among points in compared clusters. Single linking uses dissimilarity in the opaque way – here the dissimilarity is defined as the minimum distance between any points in compared clusters.

Various distance metrics are used to compute similarity or dissimilarity but the most common is the cosine measure which is dot product of the two vectors divided by their lengths product. In the tool described in this article we also use this measure.

Hierarchical clustering is particularly interesting in our approach because the algorithm generates hierarchical tree of clusters as it merges them into bigger clusters. The Figure 1 shows the sample hierarchy generated by hierarchical clustering algorithm. The initial clusters (Cluster 1, Cluster 2 ... or C1, C2 etc.) are merged during the subsequent iterations of the algorithm, based on their similarity. The bottom part of the picture shows inclusion of the primary clusters in their conglomerates.

Clustering proved to be valuable in dividing large document collections into smaller, meaningful parts (i.e. clusters represent certain topics). The rationale behind our approach is to use clustering to assign certain topics, created by the clustering algorithm, to clustered documents. We use the hierarchy of generated clusters to create hierarchy of topics and their occurrences – the documents. Except from using hierarchy of clusters (which is usually discarded in clustering applications) we use several dictionaries in the algorithm. Classical approach to the clustering uses single cleared dictionary. The stoplist is used to eliminate junk-words and in some approaches the words are stemmed (according to the algorithm first described in (Porter, 1980)). In our approach we split this dictionary to obtain smaller dictionaries for specific aspects of a domain that the documents regard. The clustering of the same documents set using different dictionaries produces different hierarchies of clusters. This can be viewed as a projection of n-dimensional term space (where n is the number of terms in the whole dictionary) to a set of m-dimensional spaces (where m<n). One could argue that we loose some information because clustering is done with smaller dictionary. But in exchange we gain a general view on the document collection and we can build the topic map based on several hierarchies and associations between them, which emerge from co-occurrences of the same documents in each hierarchy.

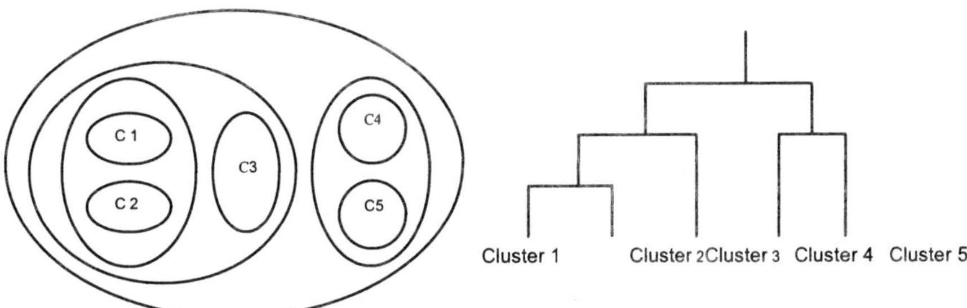

Figure 1. The hierarchy tree generated by a clustering algorithm

3.2. Term Crawling (TC)

The aim of term crawling method is to build a network of associations between terms. The semantic network is built by analysis of concurrent term presence in documents on the World Wide Web. Assuming that there is a tool for gathering information from Internet sources and assessing their relevance, term crawling aims to indicate, that even unstructured data of limited trust can be utilized in information systems.

The network of associations, created by term crawling will then be used in creating associations between clusters created by CHP (Clustering Hierarchy Projection).

1. In order to build a semantic network of associations between terms, we have to specify a starting point – this will be the primary term.

2. The primary term is used as a query, and – through Google API (GoogleAPI, 2002) – submitted to the search engine, which replies with a list of web pages relevant to the query.
3. Web pages are downloaded
4. Value of web pages for the process is assessed – this includes length, format, and language analyses.
5. Downloaded web pages are tokenized, and tokens weights are estimated – this leads to creating n-dimensional matrix, where n is equal to number of aspects of each token (at least its URI and weight).
6. The matrix is then processed. The processing techniques are still in the experimental phase and we are looking for the most efficient technique. Currently we create intersections of term sets from each webpage and as a result, after applying stop-word list, we get a list of terms related to the primary term.
7. In that phase, the network of associations can be updated. If related terms are already contained in a network, then new associations are created, otherwise new nodes and associations are created.
8. Then, according to user's needs, recursive searches can be deployed. Breadth-first search attempt is preferred. Continuous running of term crawling mechanism leads to building large semantic networks of associations between terms. Apparently, such algorithm will result in gigantic maps, if not constrained by depth boundaries. The boundaries should be specified beforehand.

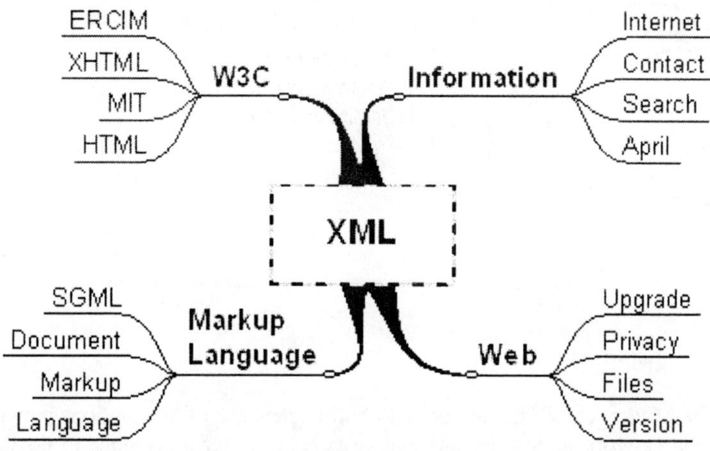

Figure 2. Network created with Term Crawler – "XML" as an initial term

Figure 2 shows a sample map created with Term Crawling algorithm, with crawling depth limited to two levels and stop list applied. As it can be observed, not all results are valuable for further processing (see "April" – a term associated with "Information"), but overall structure looks very promising.

The term crawler is implemented in Visual Basic .Net and uses extensively Google API, based on Web Services. The semantic network, created by term crawler may be stored in XML files or relational database. This is out of the scope of this paper, but it is worth mentioning, that the semantic structure can be successfully used for user query modification (broadening queries and including related terms), which can be of a great value for e-business. Catalog browsers can for example propose products that are in some way related to those specified by customer (moped instead of a motorcycle etc.). The semantic network can be also treated as a preview of present-day associations between subjects, with respect to their evolution (which can also be represented in the network).

4. TOPIC MAP CREATION PROCESS

Topic map creation is a two faceted process – first, there should be created an initial topic map, basing on a document collection. After that, there is a place for a continuous process of updating topic maps (as described in point 3.3 – Processing approaches). The following part of the paper focuses on a first facet – creating an initial topic map from a document collection. We highlight six main steps of the process: preparing document collection, generating base dictionary, performing term crawling and clustering (those two subprocesses can be run in parallel), identifying associations, and preparing RDF triples for further processing.

1.1. Document Collection

The collection that we use for creating topic map is gathered from the CNN.com portal – it is a set of several hundred news stories from main categories (e.g. health, politics, travel, technology). The documents are partially described with metadata (publication date, title and category).

The most interesting results of Clustering History Projection and Term Crawling can be obtained for collections of documents of different subjects – this is also an advantage of topic maps. Still, in order to use thesauri efficiently, the documents should belong to some general domain. Topic maps, CHP, and TC are not necessarily the best solution for document collections of highly specific domains.

4.2. Base Dictionary

The base dictionary, which contains selected words from the document collection, may be divided into domain specific dictionaries. The standard stoplist for English language is used to clear the dictionary, and typos are removed. Then the dictionary is split into smaller dictionaries (this is hand-made). The number of child dictionaries depends on the main topics that we would like to distinguish in our topic map. The most basic approach would be to divide the dictionary according to main categories found in a document collection. More sophisticated approach would be to identify topics based on geographical names or economic entity names. The dictionaries used for subsequent passes of clustering algorithm do not have to be disjoint.

However, the above remarks are only heuristics, and the final decision concerning rules of the dictionary split depends both on the collection (its specialization and range) and the desired result. Sometimes repeated experiments are necessary to obtain satisfying results. In fact, expert's skills are required to asses the aspects of the collection that should be identified and used in the procedure. This is a potential subject of future publications.

4.3. Term Crawling

After the base dictionary has been created, term crawling mechanism is used to identify and store relations between terms. Each term is taken from the dictionary, and related terms are searched. Depth of term crawling should be set manually, but two levels (as in Figure 2) seem to be efficient for most applications. The term crawler filters only stop words – association network may contain non-dictionary terms as well. As an outcome of term crawling, there will be created a network with N vertices (where N is a number of terms in dictionary incremented by other related terms found out by TC) and M edges (term relations, as indicated by TC).

4.4. Clustering

The next step is to cluster documents with all the dictionaries. Every iteration of the algorithm is logged. This information is used to create the hierarchy of clusters. This hierarchy may differ in depth, depending on the technique used to create the tree. The sample tool allows for adjusting that. For example, when merging two clusters of similar size (measured in number of documents in each cluster) they form a new, more general cluster. On the other hand, merging single-document cluster with a cluster containing several documents does not produce a new cluster. The single-document one is joined with the bigger one.

Cluster can be characterized by a set of terms that appear in its documents and in the dictionary used for clustering. These terms can be ranked according to their frequency in the whole cluster or according to their input to the similarity of the documents in the cluster (the smaller is a distance between documents computed using single term frequency, the more similar documents are and therefore the better given term describes the whole cluster). In current stage these terms are used by human author of a topic map to give the topic name. Automatic assignment of a topic name can be achieved using thesaurus which is discussed in section 6 of this paper.

Clustering also provides linking topics to occurrences – the documents in a document collection. Such link has a form of URI pointing at a given document. Although, using our technique this is achieved in an obvious way, this becomes a non-trivial task when creating a topic map without automating tools. Identifying all occurrences of a given topic in an enormous collection may be challenging for a human author, but is easily achieved (with certain degree of accuracy) by a retrieval machine.

The outcomes of the clustering mechanism are several hierarchies of clusters that can be mapped to topics in an arising topic map. The next step is to create or interpret the existing associations.

4.5. Associations

The preceding procedure produces data structures that suggest existence of certain associations between topics. These associations can be divided into:

Generalizing – these associations are derived from hierarchies generated during the execution of clustering algorithm. Merging two clusters into one more

general allows creating association of a type: *generalization*, which connects smaller cluster with the bigger and more general one.
Specifying – these are the opposite of the "generalization" associations, but they are created from more general to more specific clusters, down the hierarchy tree.
Unnamed associations between different hierarchies – these are based on the co-occurrence of the same documents in the clusters belonging to the hierarchies created with different dictionaries. The hierarchy trees are compared and the list of suggested associations is created. The list is created in the following manner: the more common documents appear in compared clusters, the stronger the association is assumed to be, and therefore it appears higher on the list. Of course the bottom clusters (containing single documents) are not taken into account. This list is presented to the human author, who can discard an association, if he considers it unnecessary, or give it a name. For example if one hierarchy was obtained with the dictionary containing corporations' names and the other with the dictionary containing product names, the association name could be "is a product of".
Unnamed associations between clusters as indicated by term crawling – each of clusters is described with a term (or set of terms). Those terms, further converted into topics in a topic map, are compared with a network created by term crawling mechanism. The comparison lets us identify relations between clusters – depth of association network searching can be decided upon each time a topic map is generated. Similarly to unnamed associations between different hierarchies, unnamed associations between clusters produce a list of suggested relations, which can be processed by human authors afterwards.

4.6. RDF Triples

The Resource Description Framework Model and Syntax Specification (RDF 1999) defines the RDF data model, and basic serialization syntax. It became a W3C (World Wide Web Consortium) recommendation in 1999. The data model is basically a directed graph. Its elements include entities and binary relationships. The relationship is represented by RDF statement (also called RDF triple). A statement can be represented by two nodes and a directed arc between them:

Subject – the resource the statement is about (URI)
Property – the property, being assigned to the subject (URI)
Value – value assigned to the property (URI or string literal)

In our case, most popular RDF triples would be for example:

(http://my.org/news/1, #topic, http://my.org/thesauriitems/54) – representing occurrence of a specific term
(http://my.org/thesauriitems/23, #generalizing, http://my.org/thesauriitems/66) – representing generalization of topics (terms)
(http://my.org/thesauriitems/66, #specifying, http://my.org/thesauriitems/23) – representing specification of topics (terms)
(http://my.org/thesauriitems/38, #suggested, http://my.org/thesauriitems/95) – representing suggested association between terms, based on term crawling, and

identifying associations based on coexistence of documents in different clusters (as described above)

After creating RDF triples, the process of creating a topic map becomes obvious, and existing tools can be used for that purpose.

5. FUTURE WORK

The proposed solution, although not fully automating the topic map creation process, has proven to be useful when creating a topic map describing a document collection. The approach could be further enhanced in several areas. There is significant effort towards identifying topics in plain text files. These topics may be both single words or short phrases and whole text parts or chapters devoted to specific subject. Identifying topics is not enough, one have to name them. Thesauri structures can be used to support it at a larger scale. These structures contain information about words synonyms, hierarchies of meaning and phrases, which may be useful when naming topics.

A serious effort in the information retrieval and document understanding is aimed at automatic topic recognition in texts. Here, the word topic stands for a larger part of a given text, devoted to some specific subject. Such techniques may be helpful when identifying topics for topic maps. Attempts have been made to use the described method to support continuous processing of the document collection. As mentioned above it involves modifying the topic map as new documents (potentially significantly different from others in the collection) appear. The approach involves creating new dictionary from the new terms found and adding topic hierarchy generated to the already existing. Some associations can be provided by term crawling, but further research in this field is necessary.

The most troublesome on this level of generality is association creation and interpretation. In the existing solutions associations are created based on examined language structures. In our approach a number of general associations is created, however naming the unnamed ones is currently not solved in our solution.

The applications of topic maps in the domain of information systems development demands further research. The insight into unstructured data or text semantics that may be obtained using automatic topic map generation can be useful for system design, as pointed in the Introduction. However this requires further improvement both concepts and tools.

REFERENCES

Abramowicz, W., Kowalkiewicz, M., and Zawadzki, P., 2002, Tell me what you know or I'll tell you what you know: Skill map ontology for information technology courseware, *Issues and Trends of Information Technology Management in Contemporary Organizations*, Mehdi Khosrow-Pour, ed., Information Resources Management Association International Conference, Seattle, USA, 2002, Information Science Publishing.

Abramowicz, W., Kowalkiewicz, M., and Zawadzki, P., 2003, Ontology Frames for IT Courseware Representation, in: *Knowledge Management: Current Issues and Challenges*, E. Coakes, ed., IRM Press.

Abramowicz, W., and Piskorski, J. 2002, Information Extraction for Free Text Business Documents, *Issues and Trends of Information Technology Management in Contemporary Organizations*, Mehdi Khosrow-Pour, ed., Information Resources Management Association International Conference, Seattle, USA, 2002, Information Science Publishing.

Ahmed, K., 2000, Topic maps for repositories, proc. *XML Europe Conference*, Paris.

Baeza-Yates, R., and Ribeiro-Neto, B., 1999, *Modern Information Retrieval*, ACM Press, Addison Wesley Longman Limited, USA.

Bhatia, S. K., and, Deogun, J. S., 1998, Conceptual clustering in information retrieval, *IEEE Transactions on Systems, Man and Cybernetics*, Part B, 427–436.

The DARPA Agent Markup Language, Retrieved April 26, 2003 from: http://www.daml.org/

Ding, C., and He, X., 2002, Cluster merging and splitting in hierarchical clustering algorithms, 2002 IEEE International Conference on Data Mining, Maebashi, Japan.

forskning.no, Retrieved April 26, 2003 from: http://www.forskning.no/

Dornfest, R., 2002, Google Web API. The O'Reilly Network. Retrieved September 16, 2002, from http://www.oreillynet.com/lpt/wlg/1283

Gómez-Pérez, A., 1999, Evaluation of taxonomic knowledge in ontologies and knowledge bases, Proc. of the Knowledge Acquisition Workshop.

Grønmo, G. O., 2000, Creating semantically valid topic maps, XML Europe Conference, Paris, France.

Grønmo, G. O., Automagic topic maps, Retrieved April 26, 2003 from: http://www.ontopia.net/topicmaps/materials/automagic.html

Gruber, T. R., 1993, Toward principles for the design of ontologies used for knowledge sharing, International Workshop on Formal Ontology, Padova, Italy.

International Organization for Standardization, ISO/IEC 13250, 2000, Information technology – SGML applications – topic maps, Geneva.

Knight, J. R., 1996, Discrete Pattern Matching Over Sequences and Interval Sets, Ph.D. Dissertation, Department of Computer Science, The University of Arizona.

Ksiezyk, R., 2000, Answer is just a question [of matching topic maps], *XML Europe Conference*, Paris, France.

Principality of Liechtenstein, Retrieved April 26, 2003 from: http://llvweb.liechtenstein.li/lisite/html/liechtenstein/index.html.en

Lernen mit Topic Maps, Retrieved April 26, 2003 from: http://www.lmtm.de/

Moore, G., 2001, RDF and Topic Maps – An Exercise in Convergence, Retrieved April 26, 2003 from: http://www.topicmaps.com/topicmapsrdf.pdf

Oommen, B. J., and de St. Croix E. V., 1994, String taxonomy using learning automata, *IEEETSMC: IEEE Transactions on Systems, Man, and Cybernetics*.

Pepper, S., 2000, The TAO of Topic Maps, finding the way in the age of infoglut, XML Europe Conference, Paris, France.

Pepper, S., 2002, Ten Theses on Topic Maps and RDF, Retrieved April 26, 2003 from: http://www.ontopia.net/topicmaps/materials/rdf.html

Pepper. S., 2002, The Ontopia MapMaker, Retrieved April 26, 2003 from: http://www.ontopia.net/topicmaps/materials/MapMaker_files/frame.htm

Porter, M. F., 1980, An algorithm for suffix stripping.

Resource Description Framework (RDF) Model and Syntax Specification, Feb. 1999. W3C Recommendation.

Sowa, J. F., 2000, *Knowledge Representation: Logical, Philosophical, and Computational Foundations*, Brooks Cole Publishing Co., Pacific Grove, CA.

Steinbach, M., and Karypis, G., and Kumar V., 2000, A Comparison of document clustering techniques, retrieved April 2003 from: http://www-users.cs.umn.edu/~karypis/publications/Papers/PDF/doccluster.pdf

Walsh N., and Muellner L., 1999, DocBook: The definitive guide, O'Reilly & Associates, Retrieved April 26, 2003 from: http://www.oasis-open.org/docbook/documentation/reference/html/docbook.html

Wrightson, A., 2001, Topic Maps and knowledge representation, Retrieved April 26, 2003 from: http://www.ontopia.net/topicmaps/materials/kr-tm.html

Zhao, Y., and, Karypis, G., Evaluation of hierarchical clustering algorithms for document datasets", Retrieved April 2003 from: http://citeseer.nj.nec.com/zhao02evaluation.html

DISCOVERING WWW USER INTERFACE PROBLEMS VIA USER SURVEYS AND LOG FILE ANALYSIS

Jason Ceddia, Judy Sheard, and Renee Gedge*

ABSTRACT

A complex multi-user web site was designed to support industrial experience projects for final year computing students at Monash University. The site was accessed by students, clients, supervisors and subject coordinators. A consistent interface was provided to aid site navigation and ease cognitive overhead, with a fixed navigation bar on all pages seen by all user types. Multiple usability surveys, including provision for free comments, indicated only moderately good usability of the site, but gave no indication as to how usability could be improved. A dedicated server log file was created to record user navigation on the site. Analysis of this log file showed a highly inefficient pattern of student navigation, in which almost every second page access was to the home page. The original site design was found to be inadvertently biased towards the set of staff users who were also its developers. This raised two interesting issues - attempts at consistency by the inclusion of a fixed navigation bar for all users had resulted in a highly inefficient design. In addition, questionnaires to large numbers of final year computing students failed to identify this basic design flaw, although subsequent focussed interviews confirmed students experienced navigation as a problem. A new interface has been designed and is being trialled in 2003, along with a changed evaluation method and more sophisticated log file analysis.

1. INTRODUCTION

The World Wide Web (WWW) is becoming an increasingly pervasive medium for commerce, entertainment and education. In the University environment, more and more subject material is available via a web interface, both to provide resources supporting the traditional lecture delivery and as multimedia applications delivering new self paced courses.[1, 2] In this environment, the lecturer often has to convert their subject material to a

* Jason Ceddia, Judy Sheard, Renee Gedge. School of Computer Science and Software Engineering, Monash University, Australia.

web format. The result can be anything from a static web page with links to powerpoint presentations, through to interactive environments that challenge the students to learn new material.[3]

The WWW is increasingly used to implement Computer Supported Collaborative Work (CSCW) tools (See Bentley et al.[4] for a discussion of the WWW as a CSCW enabling technology), and the different geographical locations of all the stakeholders – students, clients and supervisors- in the Industrial Experience (IE) project at Monash University required some form of network communication for which the WWW is ideal.

The degree of success of on-line teaching materials varies according to the design experience of the lecturer concerned. Much has been written about the cognitive overload that poor design can inadvertently inflict on users of these applications.[5, 6] A great deal of literature also deals with both the practice of user centered design[7] and the specific design of web sites.[8, 9] However, mastering the evolving art of web design as well as the subject content to be provided may require more time and effort than most subject lecturers have available. In a student environment, pedagogical concerns must also be addressed. Barker[10] has described four essential components that should be present in any system for online student interaction:(a) web resources for the basic course content (b) online support infrastructure such as technical help (c) communication strategies for course related online dialogue and (d) learning tasks to be undertaken by the students. The IE website, WIER, includes all of these facilities, plus additional features and functionality.

This paper describes the initial design process, including concerns for site useability, later elucidation of usability problems by server log analysis and subsequent changes to design and evaluation processes. In particular, attempts of the authors to evaluate navigation behaviour in a comprehensive web site are addressed. Section 2 describes the IE program, the facilities provided to the four user groups of the system, and the initial design process. Section 3 presents the survey results and the log file analysis, and finally Section 4 outlines the new interface that is being trialled in 2003 and the proposed evaluation method at the end of the year.

2. BACKGROUND TO WIER

2.1 Overview of Industrial Experience Projects at Monash

Many tertiary computing degree programs offer students an opportunity to do some form of Industrial Experience,[11-14] implemented in a variety of ways. Students in their final year of the Bachelor of Computing degree at Monash University undertake an industrial experience or capstone project, in which they design, develop, and deliver a small computer system for an external client. Students are organised into groups of four or five and this provides them with real-life experience in project co-ordination and management. Each project group is allocated a supervisor who provides guidance and advice as needed, monitors the progress of their group, and is responsible for a major part of their assessment. Two coordinators oversee the project groups and supervisors. A complete description of the project process can be found in.[15]

The co-ordination and management aspect of the unit is complicated by having three overlapping intakes of students each year, in semesters one, two and summer. This overlap can cause some confusion when setting deliverable dates and notifying students and supervisors of upcoming events. Supervisors and clients may have multiple groups in the same or overlapping intakes. See Table 1 for a summary of students, clients and supervisor numbers in 2001.

Table 1. Numbers of students, clients and supervisors per IE intake

	Students	Clients	Supervisors
Intake 1 (sem 1+2)	173	33	30
Intake 2 (sem 2 + summer)	60	12	10
Intake 3 (summer +sem 1)	48	10	5
Total	281	55	45

2.2. Facilities provided by WIER

The WIER site provides facilities for project management, document management, and various forms of communication via news groups and a discussion forum. These features are similar to those provided by other support tools like Netpro,[16] FirstClass,[17] Blackboard[18] and WebCT.[19, 20] However, the WIER site also provides additional facilities, many of which reflect its multiple user-type focus. The philosophy is to provide an integrated tool for four separate user groups: students, clients, supervisors and coordinators. When user accounts are created, the user is categorised as one of the four user types and at logon the system checks their user type and displays the appropriate menu. Facilities for these four groups are as follows:

Students: Provides an integrated learning environment for IE project work. WEIR contains a repository of resources including standards documents, document templates and samples of past projects, available to and shared by the whole class. Other facilities apply to individual groups such as recording group member project activity times, group file management and event scheduler.

Supervisors: Supervisors are able to monitor the progress of their students by viewing their time logs as well as accessing files and documents produced by the group. Monitoring group time is also described by Collofello and Hart[21] for their student project management but they do not implement other CSCW features such as discussion forums.

Clients: Prospective clients can register themselves and propose projects online. Once their projects are accepted, clients can use WIER to communicate with the group, their supervisor or coordinators and monitor group progress .

Coordinators. The IE project coordinators who manage the IE project subject have access to extensive assessment, reporting and survey facilities.

2.3. The Initial Design Concept and Early Evaluation

The WIER Web site was designed in 1999 by staff in the School of Computer Science and Software Engineering (SCSSE) in collaboration with staff from the School of Network Computing and the Gippsland School of Computing. The site was developed during 2000 with funding obtained from a Technology Innovation Fund grant from the

Faculty of Information Technology. The WIER Web site is located at: http://wier.cs-se.monash.edu.au.

The web server is Unix based (Solaris) and is managed by the SCSSE. The pages are coded using PHP scripts that connect to a Faculty managed Oracle database server. Access to most facilities on the site is password restricted.

Co-ordinators have access to menus for all user types as they coordinate all groups, supervisors and clients. Supervisors have full access to the student menu to monitor their groups' progress. The original WIER interface (using a coordinator logon) is shown in Figure 1. This interface allows the coordinator access to the other menus for the other user types simply by clicking on the user type link in the LHS menu list eg. **Student.**

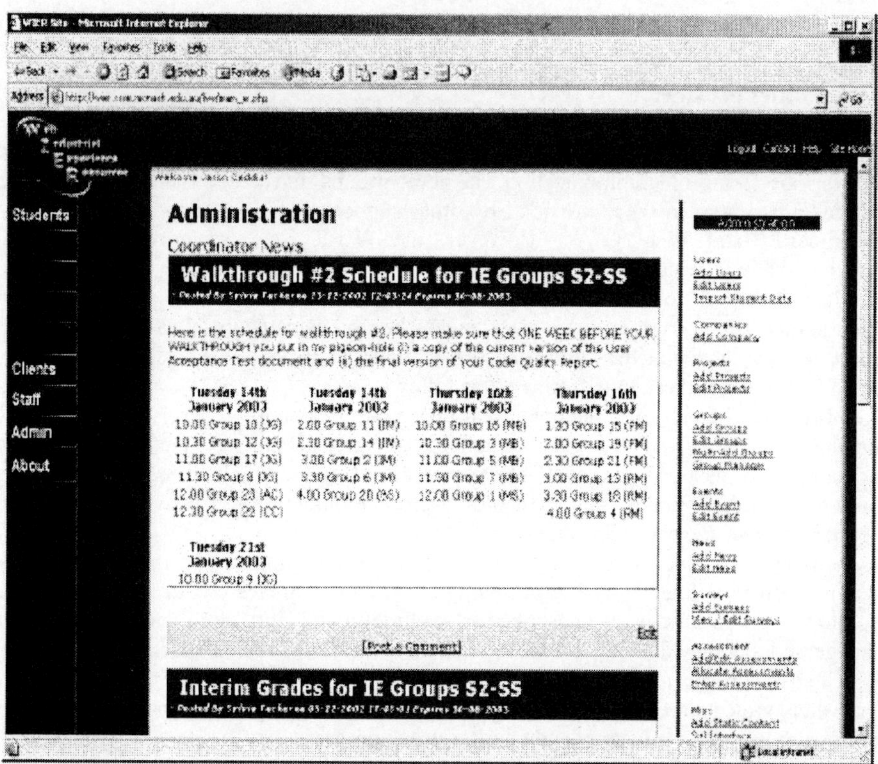

Figure 1. Original WIER screen showing the general navigation bar on the LHS for the different user types and the Administration menu on the RHS.

The WIER design process followed requirements gathering, interface prototyping, implementation, testing, deployment and user training. Most of the content of the site is dynamically produced, navigation features provided by the browser such as back and forward buttons are not used thereby avoiding some of the navigation pitfalls discussed by Cockburn and Jones.[22] Caching of pages is also disabled because of the dynamic nature of page generation. WIER does provide some tool tips and popups to aid in site usage as suggested by Witt & Tyerman.[23] As well as a common navigation bar, consistent fonts, colours and page layout were utilized throughout the site.

Initial informal feedback about the site from students was less enthusiastic than was hoped. This was not suprising though as it was felt that such a complex application may well require considerable training time, and by the end of their year of using the system most students were quite efficient. However, the developers were looking for ways to reduce the initial learning curve, such as reorganization to facilitate easy location of specific functions, and a comprehensive evaluation was undertaken.

3. SURVEY RESULTS AND LOG FILE ANALYSIS

Three separate groups of users were surveyed over two years with similar results – system usability rating fell in the medium range and no specific problems were identified. These evaluation covered site usage, site usability, site usefulness and impact on project management, and results have been reported in Ceddia and Sheard[24] and are reproduced here for convenience in Table 2. It was only after the analysis of navigation patterns from the server logs that deficiencies in the navigation system were pinpointed. This initial analysis was relatively simple, involving visual inspection of coded page data (see Section 3.2 for details). The navigation problems were then confirmed by follow up interviews conducted with a small subset of the last group of students. Once these navigation problems were identified, the designers were surprised they had remained unnoticed for so long. The navigation interface was biased towards the staff user group rather than the student user group, as a direct result of a design process centred around a subset of the four user groups.

3.1 Survey Details

Two on-line surveys were used to determine students' ratings of the usability of WIER. The first survey, which gathered initial reactions to the site, was given to students early in Semester 1 and the second in mid Semester 2. We felt it was essential to determine as early as possible any difficulties students were experiencing with the site and, if possible, make modifications to the site or provide extra instruction in its use. Similar questionnaires were used for both surveys to enable comparisons to be made and establish whether views of the usability of the site changed with familiarity.

Students generally found the site quite usable. The highest rating was for the consistency of the site and there was good agreement amongst the students about this. It is interesting to compare the results of the Semester 2 survey (74 respondents) with that of Semester 1 (22 respondents). It could be expected that with more experience using WIER, students would find it easier to navigate and orient themselves in the site, however t-tests[†] indicated no statistically significant differences between semesters 1 and 2 except for system response time. The students were not particularly happy with the response time on the WIER site in Semester 1, and they were even less happy with this in Semester 2. This could be explained by the additional load on the database server from other subjects in semester 2.

[†] A t-test is a statistical test used to determine the difference in the means between two groups

Table 2. Comparison of Students' Ratings of Usability of WIER in Semester 1 and 2 for 2001

Question (Easy/good=1, difficult/poor=5)	**Semester 1 (n=22)**		**Semester 2 (n=74)**		***t***
	Mean	**SD**	**Mean**	**SD**	
How easy is it navigate the WIER site?	2.9	1.0	2.8	1.0	-0.39(72)
How easy is it know where you are within the WIER site at any time?	2.6	1.0	2.8	1.3	0.55(72)
How easy is it to locate information on the WIER site?	2.9	1.0	3.1	1.0	0.96(72)
How easy is it to view information on the WIER site e.g. is there too much scrolling?	2.9	1.2	3.4	1.0	1.96(72)
How would you rate the consistency of the page layout i.e. does each page have the same look and feel?	2.0	0.9	2.1	1.0	0.40(72)
How would you rate the general layout of the pages in terms of the organisation of the screen elements e.g. menus, text areas?	2.6	1.0	2.7	1.0	0.67(71)
How would you rate the readability of WIER pages in terms of choice of colours, fonts, graphics, etc?	2.3	0.9	2.2	0.8	-0.38(71)
How would you rate the response time of the WIER site?	2.9	1.3	3.5	1.1	2.28(72) *
* $p < 0.05$					

The surveys provided space for comments after each section. Typical comments on useability were:

- *it is not consistent enough sometimes, might need to improve the consistency*
- *no it is fine*
- *mainly redesign time/task tracker*
- *it is very slow when moving between links, at times it doesn't directly go back to a previous page*
- *there were a few bugs, but on the whole it is fine. Sometimes difficult to search results*
- *no, very user friendly and good for us to plan our resources*
- *I think it's weird that you have to click 'student' to get to the student homepage even when we have logged in as a student*
- *it was helpful and made things easier however it could be presented better*

This seemed to be the usual student reaction – some thought it was alright, others thought it needed improvement, but no indication was given of specific problems or improvements required even after extensive use of the site. This is consistent with previous research on questionnaire responses that indicates that respondents rarely proffer additional comments when closed questions are provided.[25] Other research has shown that task oriented users are not able to focus on design issues.[26] It also supports previous findings that there is often a discrepancy between the feedback from surveys and that of actual observation and interview. Further, MacElroy states "Online surveys about Web sites provide context and post-design confirmatory measurements, but cannot assess usability as we have come to understand the mandates of the term."[27]

3.2 Log Analysis

Surveys are intrusive to the user and much work is being done on determining user behaviour through web server log file analysis.[28, 29] The WIER application produces it own server log, which records userid, page URL, date/time stamp and activity. The activity relates to user action on the page. For example when accessing the discussion forum page a user could read a posting, write a new posting, or reply to a posting.

To determine the navigation pattern of users, the log file was sorted by userid and date/time so that the page order access for a particular user on a particular day or session could be determined. The page URL has been given a letter code; for example H for the Home page, T for the Time Tracker page, F for the File Manager page etc. For a particular user session the page access can be represented as a string of letters. A typical string is:

HTHFHTHD

Inspection of the log file immediately showed that the Home page appears as nearly every second page. Why this should be the case is, in hindsight, obvious – the navigation structure forces the students to go back to their homepage to access other resources. For example the students could not access File Manager from Time Tracker; from Time Tracker they had to go back to Home where the File Manager link appeared.

Because of time constraints and the daunting volume of log file information this analysis was not done until September 2002, some 10 months after the first group of students had finished. It was decided to interview students to confirm the navigation behaviour. The results are presented below.

3.3 Interviews

In October 2002, volunteers were requested to take part in an interview study of their use of WIER. Eighteen students eventually took part; each interview session was 30-45 minutes in duration and the students were paid $10 to compensate for their time. Students expressed various reactions to the WIER website in the interviews. There were many positive comments about the site and the resources provided. The following are some examples of these:

- Overall a very good resource for any team project - I would recommend to use it for ITPM (CSE2203) subject as well.
- It's not bad. WIER is an exceptionally, extraordinary which has been provided. My friends did this subject and said it has improved a lot.
- I think the site is quite all right …
- Generally it is friendly … I think it is better than the first time we tried.

However, there were also negative reactions to the site. Some students expressed annoyance and frustration with aspects of the site. The following comments illustrate these views:

- Sometime you need to do something and you can't find it…at that time it is very tedious - it is like "where can I find this information".
- If I can do whatever I need to do I find it useful, and if I can't do it it's annoying.
- I see options which I click and I am not able to read, so it's kind of irritating - things like client, admin - I don't have access to them so why display them.

Although the students did not indicate in the survey that navigation on the WIER website was difficult, when questioned about navigation in the interviews only one student claimed navigation was easy:

- … It's easy to navigate, there is no problem. Everything is close to the Student Home page and we just know that we have to go to the Student Home page.

Most students commented that they found the navigation difficult. One student stated:

- … It can be difficult to navigate through, if you have a specific part of the site you are looking for it can be hard finding out or even remembering what links you have to follow to get there.

The main problems with navigation, which were highlighted by more than half the students, were caused by the menu structure. The following comments summarise these problems:

- You have to keep on navigating back to the home page for most of the tasks because the menu on the right hand side disappears when you go into most of the tasks, so there is no easy way to navigate between the subtasks … It is the thing that causes the most problem for me because I keep having to go back to main, I don't like doing that, I like to navigate because that's how the Web is.
- … after the student has logged in what is the point of keeping the client menu and admin area. … Also, I think the grouping of tasks (in the menu on the left) doesn't make sense to me.
- … The menus here, they are the same before you log in and after you log in. But the menu on the right it only appears on the Home page once you log in it should be on all the pages maybe somewhere at the top.

In summary, there were menu items on the LHS that were not applicable to or accessible by the students and the student subtask menu on the RHS disappeared between tasks. What was most interesting about these responses was that the students when requested specifically in an interview to reflect on how they used the site, did identify a major problem with navigation, but none of them had indicated awareness of it when completing the two questionnaires.

Students expressed a range of opinions on how easy it was to orient themselves within the WIER website. Most indicated this was not a major problem. About a third of the students claimed they always knew where they were on the site or didn't need to remember because they could always find their way back to the Students Home page. These views were expressed in comments such as:

- ... but with WIER it is not possible that we lose the information. If we click on the File Manager, we know File Manager contains all the information of the file for your project - you are in a contained environment.
- Not really, because I just click home and go back. When I am lost I just click student Home page and go back.
- ... because I always open a new window - I never get lost.

The above comments confirm that the fixed LHS menu was useful.

4. CONCLUSIONS AND FUTURE DIRECTIONS

The experience of designing and evaluating WIER has revealed problems with the widely used evaluation method of surveying users. Whilst student motivation is notoriously marks-driven, it is still surprising that large groups of final year computing students failed to identify the navigation problem in questionnaires which included open ended comments. This failure casts considerable doubt over the value of this evaluation method, particularly in this population, and points to the need for other methodologies. Expert walkthroughs were conducted informally, but in retrospect it can be seen that they focused on one user type. More intensive user consultation such as structured interviews did identify the problems but are very time intensive for both user and designer. A simple visual inspection of a coded log file has been seen to be of considerable benefit in analyzing usage patterns and identifying a basic navigation problem.

A new interface design was obviously necessary and had to rectify the two shortcomings identified in the original design. Namely, no option is displayed that is not applicable to the current user type and the menu had to remain fixed and permanently displayed for that user type.

For the Student user, the LHS menu combines functionality from both menus of the original site i.e. the My Group Functions relate to those functions specific to the individual group like Time Tracker and Class Services are those functions available to the whole class such as document templates. This is shown in Figure 2.

The new interface is to be deployed in 2003. The students will be surveyed at the end of the year and these results will be triangulated with log file analysis and student interviews. It is expected that the student rating of the navigation interface will be improved. A new log file protocol will track navigation separately for each user type, and these log files will be analysed to examine the efficiency of the interface for each user group.

The Coordinator user has access to the other user type menus via the horizontal menu bar as shown in Figure 3.

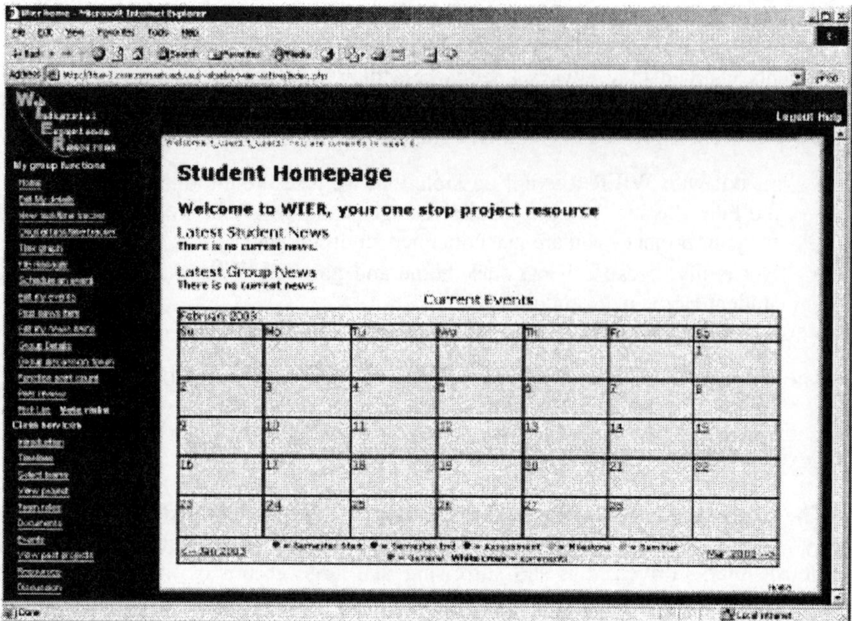

Figure 2. The new student screen

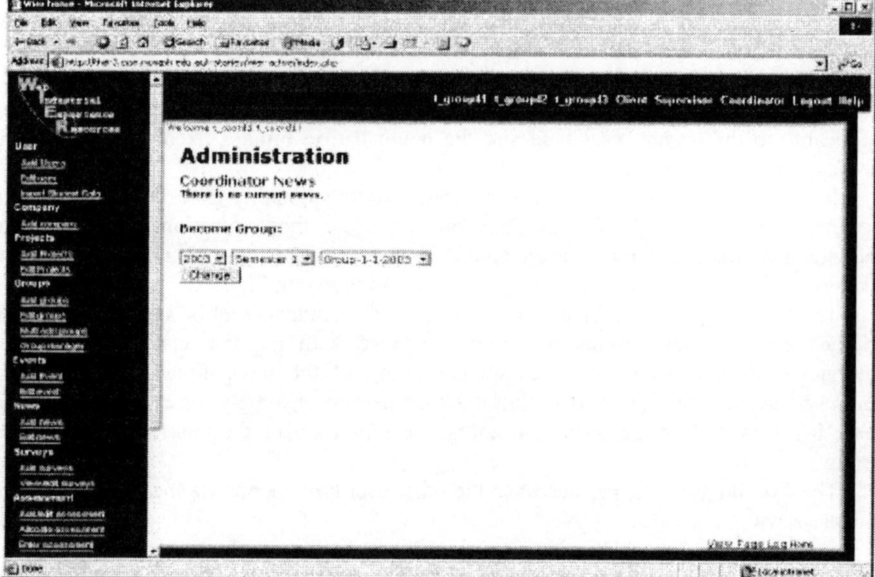

Figure 3. The new coordinator screen

REFERENCES

1. Kandies, J. and M. B. Stern, Weaving the Web into the classroom: An evolution of Web enhanced instruction, in: *SITE '99*, (San Antonio, Texas: AACE, 1999).
2. Wang, L.-C. C. and W. Beasley, Effects of learner control and hypermedia preference on cyber-students performance in a web-based learning environment, *Journal of Educational Multimedia and Hypermedia*, **11**(1), 71–91, (2002).
3. Lie, K. G. and V. Cano, Supporting diverse learners through a website for teaching methods, *Educational Technology and Society*, **4**(3), 50–63, (2001).
4. Bentley, R., Horstmann, T.,and Trevor, J., The World Wide Web as an enabling technology for CSCW: The case of BSCW, *The Journal of Collaborative Computing*, 2–3, (1997).
5. Conklin, J., Hypertext: an introduction and survey, *IEEE Computer*, **20**(9), (1987), 17–41.
6. Beasley, R. E. W., M. L., Cognitive mapping architectures and hypermedia disorientation: An empirical study, *Journal of Educational Multimedia and Hypermedia*, **4(2/3)**, (1995), 239–255.
7. Vredenburg, K., Mao, J. Y., Smith, P. and Carey, T., A survey of User-Centered Design Practice, in Procedings of the SIGCHI Conference on Human Factors in Computing Systems, Minneapolis, Minnesota, USA, (2002).
8. Shneiderman, B., *Designing the User Interface. Strategies for Effective Human-Computer Interaction*, Third ed., (Addison-Wesley, 1998), p. 639.
9. Shneiderman, B., *Designing the User Interface. Strategies for Effective Human-Computer Interaction*, Third ed., (Addison-Wesley, 1998), p. 639.
10. Barker, P. Creating and Supporting Online Learning Communities, in: *EdMedia*, (2001).
11. Grant, D., and Smith, R., Undergraduate software engineering – an innovative degree at Swinburne, *The Australian Computer Journal*, **23**: (1991), p. 106–113.
12. Berztiss, A. T., Failproof team Projects in Software Engineering Courses, in 27th Annual Frontiers in Education Conference, (1997).
13. Biffl, S., Thomas, G., A Course in Software Engineering and Project Management at University Level for Industrial Needs, in: Proceedings of the 8th IEEE International Workshop on (incorporating Computer Aided Software Engineering), (1997).
14. Daniels, M., and Asplund, L., Full Scale Industrial Work in a one semester course, in: 29th Annual Frontiers in Education Conference, (1999).
15. Hagan, D. L., Tucker, S., and Ceddia, J., Industrial Experience Projects: A Balance of Process and Product, *Computer Science Education*, **9**(3), 215–229, (1999).
16. Markkanen, H.a.P., D., Web Tools for Collabrative Project Learning, in: *EdMedia*, (2001).
17. Blanchfield, L.P., and Simpson, O., Computer conferencing for Guidance and Support in OU, *British Journal of Educational Technology*, **31**(4), 295–306, (2000).
18. A'Herran, A., Integrating a Course Delivery Platform with Information, Student Management and Administrative Systems, in: *EdMedia*, (2001).
19. Chan, S. C. F., Ng, V. T. Y. and Wu, A. K. W., Cooperative/Collaberative Learning - Web based Management of Group Projects, in: *International Conference on Computers in Education*, Korea, (2001).
20. *WebCT.* http://www.webct.com, (2001).
21. Collofello, J. S., and Hart, M., Monitoring Team Progress in a Software Engineering Project Class, in: 29th Annual Frontiers in Education Conference, (1999).
22. Cockburn, A. and S. Jones, Which way now? Analyzing and easing inadequacies in WWW navigation, *International Journal of Human-Computer Studies*, **45**: 105–129, (1996).
23. Witt, R. J. and S. P. Tyerman, Reducing cognitive overhead on the World Wide Web, in: Twenty fifth Australasian Computer Science Conference (ACSC2002), Melbourne, Australia (2002).
24. Ceddia, J. and J. Sheard, Evaluation of WIER - A capstone project management tool, in: International Conference on Computers in Education (ICCE 2002), Auckland, New Zealand (2002).
25. Krosnick, J. A., Survey research, *Annual Review of Psychology*, (Annual Reviews, US, 1999), **Vol 50**: p. 537–67.
26. Gomes, P. V., Usability feedback in education software prototypes: A contrast of users and experts, in: *Department of Counseling, Educational Psychology, and Special Education*, (Michigan State University: Michigan, 1996).
27. MacElroy, W., The Role of Online Surveys in the Usability Assessment Process, in *Usability Special Interest Group Newsletter - vol9, no 3.* (2003).
28. Claypool, M., et al., Inferring user interest, *IEEE Internet Computing*, **Nov/Dec**: p. 32–39, (2001).
29. Sullivan, T. Reading reader reaction: A proposal for inferential analysis of Web server log files, in: *Designing for the Web*, (1997).

E-GOVERNMENT SERVICES

One local government's approach

Peter Shackleton, Julie Fisher, and Linda Dawson*

1. INTRODUCTION

While electronic service delivery is the main thrust of e-Government policies at all levels, greater community contact is often seen as more practical and achievable at a local level (Musso et al., 2000; Steyaert, 2000). In recent times, greater focus has been given to local e-Government where significant citizen to government interaction takes place (SOCITM and I&DeA, 2002). Community participation at this level is often much higher than at a national level, however, local governments are often poorly resourced and resistant to change. In the 1980s and 1990s many local government, particularly in countries such as Australia and the United Kingdom, under went massive change and are now faced with a new form of local government (Cochrane, 1993; Gerritsen and Osborn, 1997; Kloot, 1999; Sanderson, 2001; Steyaert, 2000). Local governments today are under pressure to provide efficient and effective e-Government information and services as a result of increased accountability and performance management. The aim has been to increased consumer choice, often by the decrease in direct service provision as the result of outsourcing and competitive tendering, while at the same time reducing costs.

Local government importance is increasing as an administrative arm of state and federal governments with greater emphasis on policy interpretation and implementation locally. In Australia, this has become more evident as local government's role expands to include both traditional areas of infrastructure and town planning and social welfare.

Moves towards electronic government have been more than just a move from a physical delivery environment to a virtual or online delivery environment. Early iterations of electronic government often emphasized service delivery with over-the-counter services replaced by electronic transactions and this continues to be the case (Lenk and Traunmüller (2002). By outlining situations where citizens suffer inconvenience and high compliance costs via over-the-counter service delivery, e-Government policies and performance evaluations are often used as a quantifiable metric

* Peter Shackleton, Victoria University, Melbourne, Australia. Julie Fisher, Monash University, Melbourne, Australia. Linda Dawson, Monash University, Melbourne, Australia.

to claim better service provision using electronic technologies (Multimedia Victoria, 1998; NOIE, 2001).

The current literature suggests that the direction and implementation of e-Government strategies at different levels of government emphasize different elements of service delivery and governance reflecting the different types of contacts citizens have with each level of government. This paper reports on the progress local governments in the state of Victòria, Australia have made utilising the Internet to deliver traditional services and enhance community contact. Through a major case study, it identifies the factors impacting on local government that determine the level, type and support for different forms of information and services.

2. AUSTRALIAN LOCAL GOVERNMENT

It is difficult to find a definition for local government that can be applied universally to countries across the world. It is generally accepted that local government is the lowest level of government with federal and possibly state tiers above it. As a result of the hierarchical position local governments are often subject to control from higher levels of government, but they usually have the benefit of a greater empathy with their communities. The role and responsibilities of a local council, municipality or county as they are sometimes called varies greatly from country to country. Surprisingly, Australian local governments (often known as municipal councils), have no constitutional legitimacy, but have responsibility for the implementation of a large range of services such as roads, waste collection and local town planning. Victorian municipal councils are elected by residents who pay municipal council rates to supplement the provision of local services.

The last decade in Australia has witnessed significant change in provision of services by local governments. Victorian local government has seen the most significant changes of any Australian state. In 1994, 220 were abolished by the State government and replaced with 78. Changes were also made to service provision with the introduction of Compulsory Competitive Tendering and greater emphasis on customer service and quality through enhanced performance measures. (DTLR, 2001; Jones, 1993; Kloot, 1999; OECD, 1996).

Australian State and Federal Governments have endeavoured to benchmark local government practices and now expect them to implement reforms to achieve higher levels of efficiency, effectiveness and accountability (Department of Transport and Regional Services, 1999; MAV, 1993; Mulitmedia Victoria, 2002). Municipal councils have therefore been forced to consider the Internet as an alternative method of delivering information and services to reduce costs. However, despite state and federal government policy, funding for e-Government initiatives has been modest and the implementation and uptake of e-Commerce amongst local government has been mixed.

Australia is ranked second to the USA amongst United Nation member states in e-Government capacity despite the comparatively low level of funding from state and federal governments for these types of initiatives (United Nations, 2002). Australian local governments are not well funded and this often impedes the implementation of innovative reforms. Although the Australian Federal government in 1997, provided $A250 in funding to support a range of e-Government initiatives, only $A5.77 million was allocated to the Victorian Local Government Online Service Delivery Project (VLGOSD project). The project identified nine areas of importance (Figure 1) but funds were restricted to regional councils who typically received fifteen to twenty thousand dollars. Despite these limitations, by the end of 2002 nearly a half of all Victorian councils had implemented some form of web content management system while a lesser number had installed on line payment systems.

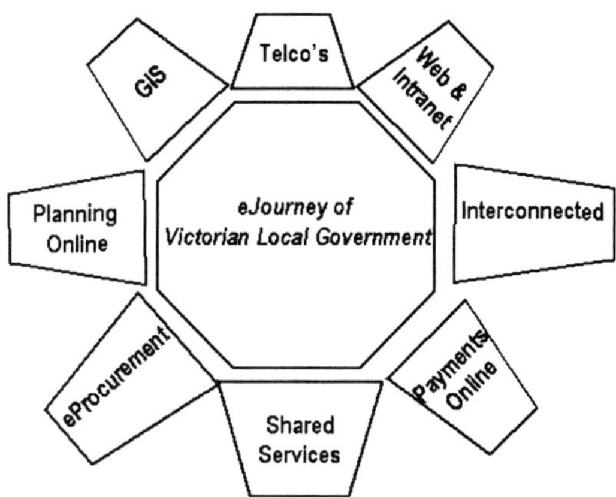

Figure 1. Local Government Online Service Projects (Adapted from Whitehorse Strategic Group, 2002)

Recent research (SOCITM and I&DeA, 2002) comparing local government across the world indicated that local e-Government policy may emphasize different *flavours*; e-services (emphasis on service provision, e-governance (including e-democracy) or e-knowledge (an emphasis on skills and infrastructure to support entrepreneurial endeavours). Australian local governments were seen as opportunistic with an emphasis on e-service provision as a way of driving down operating costs (SOCITM and I&DeA, 2002).

3. LOCAL GOVERNMENT SERVICES

The Municipal Association of Victoria identified twenty two main functions undertaken by Victorian councils (MAV, 1993) although individual municipal councils often see their role as providing more than just services. Some writers suggest that municipal governments across the world are faced with a range of different types of *residents* each demanding different types of services (OECD, 1996; Steyaert, 2000). Residents have a wide variety of contacts with the government sector and in each case the agency may respond differently and play a different role. Shand and Arnberg (1996) outline different *resident roles* that require local governments to provide different types of services. Steyaert (2000) divides the role of the resident into two political categories (*voter and citizen*) and a third category of *client* of a service. Moreover, he establishes five *dimensions* or categories of government services that can be matched to each resident type. These are government information, community information, interaction, service and democracy. Steyaert (2000) suggests that there are information and services on municipal council web sites that help support each dimension. This relationship helps identify the necessary content requirements of a web site if each resident role is to be supported.

Table 1. The type or dimension of government service for each resident role. (Adapted from Shand and Arnberg, 1996, p.17 and Steyaert, 2000.)

Resident	Category of Information/service	Example of information or Service Required
Consumer/Client	Government service	Home assistance for the aged
Receiver	Government funding	Grant to a sporting club
Prosumer (producer and consumer)	Government information/interaction	Parent volunteers in kindergarten.
User/Citizen	Community information/ interaction	User of public parks and facilities
Purchaser	Government information or service	Hire of bin service
Taxpayer	Government interaction	Payment of rates
Regulatee	Government information or regulation or interaction	Statutory town planning
Voter	Governance information	Voting in council elections

Table 1 shows the seven different resident roles, as outline by Shand and Arnberg (1996), and the different categories of Government services as outlined by Steyaert (2000). Examples of the type of local government service required are also provided.

Increasingly Victorian municipal councils are expected to be more responsive to the needs of their communities. The Victorian State Government has recently outlined four pillars of e-Government, primarily at the state level, that include a desire for improved participatory democracy (DTLR, 2001; Mulitmedia Victoria, 2002). Although it is often seen as the final stage in a transition to the Internet, it is the potential of the WWW to alter the relationship with communities that has *citizen-focused government* or *e-Democracy* as a comparatively new platform in e-Government policies (CITU, 2000; Mulitmedia Victoria, 2002).

4. MODELS OF THE STAGES OF E-GOVERNMENT MATURITY

A number of models have been proposed describing the stages of e-Government maturity. The United Nations describe a typical five stage model of e-Government service maturity from online presence to full integration that was used to benchmark government web sites at a national level (United Nations, 2002).

Musso, Weare et al's (2000) model of *metropolitan reform* outline stages of electronic maturity within two activities of municipal governments in the USA, *entrepreneurial* and *participatory*. Entrepreneurial activites emphasize the provision of services to residents and businesses to facilitate economic development. In their outline of a more mature electronic presence, changes to municipal web sites advance activities of providing *participatory* or *civic* reforms such as facilitating the formation of interest groups and improving access to the decision making process.

Riley (2001) details stages of e-Government maturity incorporating both service provision and community engagement. The model contains three progressive stages where governments move from net presence (e-Government), through to service provision and representative democracy (e-Governance), to a final stage of active community engagement (e-Democracy).

These models suggest a linear progression to final maturity. It is Stamoulis et al. (2001) who offers an alternative suggesting that governments and their agencies mature in various *spaces* rather than in distinct *stages*. Building on work by Angehrn (1997) they outline four spaces for a government revenue agency: Virtual Information Space, Virtual Communication Space, Virtual Transaction Space, Virtual Distribution Space.

Although Quirk (2000) offers a four stage model with "Information Giving" at the lower end and "Empowering Citizens" as the final stage, he outlines different *spaces* of e-Government for local authorities (Figure 2). Quirk's (2000) model best represents the implementation of e-Government amongst local councils because it emphasizes the disparate range of functions and services provided by governments at the local level.

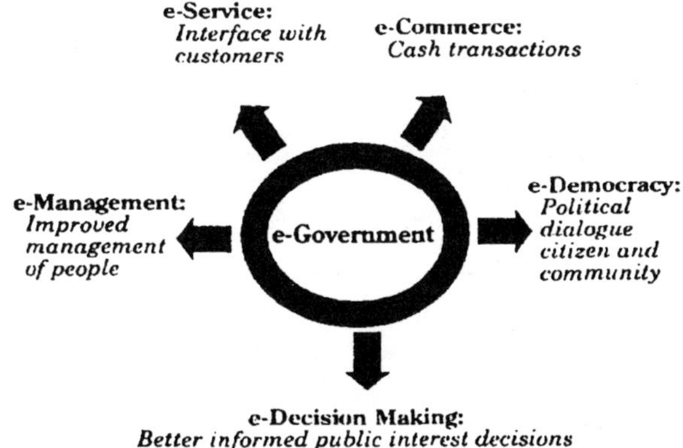

Figure 2. e-Government for Local Authorities (Adapted from Quirk, 2000)

5. RESEARCH APPROACH

5.1. Research Objectives

The motivation for this study is that although attempts have been made to apply e-Commerce or e-Business maturity models to e-Government development and implementation these models have not proven successful. It is becoming increasingly clear that the issues facing local governments are such that current e-business maturity models are inappropriate for describing or explaining what is happening in local government. The proposition, therefore, is that research is needed to better understand what is happening in the move to e-government in order to identify appropriate characteristics which should be embedded in a representative e-government maturity model. The study's objective reported in this paper is to provide rich qualitative data from an in depth case study to supplement data already collected from a study of Victorian local government web sites (Shackleton 2002). The data from both studies will be used to develop an e-government maturity model grounded in empirical data.

The earlier study examined the content and level of maturity of different aspects of Victorian council web sites, the outcome of this research is summarised in Table 2. The research found that while e-Government services for national governments are to a large extent consistent and follow a linear path (United Nations, 2002), the same is not true for municipal councils where community engagement and participation is more prevalent. Although many individual municipal councils lack the financial resources and expertise compared to higher levels of government, many councils have a strong web presence and it is both relevant and important to examine the stages of e-Government maturity at this level of government. The evaluation of the web sites established that the focus for local government was on aspects that reflect their strong community links. The emphasis therefore tends to be on e-governance issues and information while genuine e-service provision is often lagging.

Table 2. Summary of main characteristics by category (Shackleton, 2002)

Category & Feature	Percentage of Web sites
e-management	
Basic Information	95%
News and coming events	25%
Email address	95%
e-service	
service details	90%
Service tracking	0%
FAQs	25%
Email support	0%
e-Commerce	
On-line payments	23%
Ordering facility	5%
Email payment/ordering	5%
e-Decision Making/e-Governance	
Community information	20%
Links to other organizations/businesses	65%
Bulletin boards	0%

The second phase of this research is intended to further contribute towards the development of a representative maturity model for local e-government based on an ethnographic case study which collected detailed empirical data about one municipal council's move towards e-government.

5.2. Case Study Methodology

The major component of the research involved an intensive ethnographic case study of a moderately sized progressive Victorian municipal council. Ethnographic case studies, where the researcher becomes part of the case being observed, enables the researcher to "observe, interview, record processes as they occur naturally" (McMillan and Schumacher, 1993). This study involved working with staff over a period of six months, observing and interviewing them as they developed and implemented the council's latest web page in March 2003. A strength of this interactive research methodology is that prolonged engagement in the natural setting allows the researcher to observe and record processes that would be difficult to observe by the use of other methods (Leedy, 1997). Fourteen interviews were conducted with a range of council staff such as section managers, communications personnel, web co-ordinator, councillors and associated council support staff. Documents were collected and collated, while detailed observations were made both of formal and informal meetings and other settings.

The municipal council was chosen as historically its web development reflects that of other municipal councils in Victoria, however, it is more advanced than the vast majority in what it has achieved to date. It was important to select a municipal council that had made significant progress in its e-Government strategy. Since its first introduction in 1999 the council has not only changed the format and content of their site but on two occasions they have completely replaced the old web site.

5.2.1. Background and early web experience

The municipal council selected is located on the fringe of Melbourne in the state of Victoria and is classified as an "interface" council, the population is concentrated in a number of large suburbs while also serving a sparsely populated rural constituency. The council serves 19,000 households. Recent census data showed 47.6 % of the council population use the Internet (ABS, 2002) and the council web site receives 100,000 hits per month, a comparatively large number of hits. Historically the community has a strong commitment to environmental protection, arts and local history and is actively involved in council governance.

Details about the first web page of the council in this case study are vague. There are virtually no records of when it commenced although early 1999 was nominated by several people. It was developed by one person (described as an enthusiastic communications staff member) and the site was placed with a local ISP. The site provided information but did not engage the community. More importantly, staff within the council saw it as a project of one person who liked working with computers. When that person left the council the site virtually remained unchanged until early 2001 when it was removed and replaced with an under construction notice.

5.2.2. External Factors and Internal Initiatives

The investigation found that a number of disparate and interrelated external and internal factors impacted on the council's attitude to web-based service delivery.

During this period, a number of external factors were working in the background to change the way council staff were thinking about electronic service delivery. State and federal governments were establishing policies on electronic service delivery that included municipal councils. External performance measures were also benchmarking Victorian councils forcing them to re-assess the effectiveness and cost of their service delivery. In addition, a larger number of councils were going on line establishing lighthouse examples for others to follow. Although there was no evidence to suggest extensive community pressure for electronic service delivery, there was a perception that the council needed to have more than just a basic static web site. Communities could access electronically an increasing number of federal, state and semi-government authorities and there was increasing political pressure for councils to "catch up". The council in this case study was cited as an example in a critical article in July, 2001 by one of the large syndicated papers again highlighting the low level of web-based service delivery in the council at that time.

Within the council two important projects were underway. The first project was undertaken by the Communications Branch under the new manager to establish a new council web page. Extensive consultation with divisions within the council was undertaken. The site contained a large amount of rich but static information that was well organized and functionally easy to access and download. A major aim was to demonstrate a future commitment to web-based delivery rather than to provide online services at that time. The site was again seen by staff as the domain of one area, Communications Branch, rather than the entire council and as a result of restrictive updating procedures the static information dated quickly.

The second project involved an innovative web site developed for the By Laws division (responsible for parking, animal and pet management, fire permits) within the council. It was developed by one enthusiastic staff member and was launched in January 2002. Although this was the initiative of one staff member it had the support from the innovative division manager. Regular updates to the functions and content of the site were made. The division experimented with digital photos, email requests, form downloads on their site. Other areas within the large division were trained and included in new initiatives. The division won external recognition for its innovative work in that year. The site brought about 3 major changes:

- Despite less functionality on the main council site, the By Laws site was used by the rest of council to demonstrate its commitment to electronic service delivery
- It demonstrated the use of the Internet to the community and council
- It provided an achievable benchmark for the rest of the council

In the background the small IT section of only seven staff were providing technical support. More importantly, however, an IT Manager of 20 years experience in local government was lured from early retirement and joined the council. The IT manager was well respected, engaged staff in discussion of issues, involved other divisions in new programs but more importantly was committed to using technology to support and then change business processes. An extensive blueprint outlining these ideas was established called Business, Information and Technology Strategy (BITS) with a working group of staff from all divisions.

5.2.3. Outcomes for the Council and future directions

By the start of 2002, the council had an extensive council wide web page that mirrored information available over-the-counter. Moreover, in the background it had an innovative By Laws branch experimenting with new uses of Internet technology, and a strategic plan outlining a direction for change. Interviews with staff revealed that they saw web-based service delivery as important for improvements in the quality of service provision, indeed they wanted it to be incorporated but they lacked the knowledge on how to proceed. Their existing practices did not significantly utilize the available web technology.

A number of events occurred in 2002 that radically changed the speed of web implementation. In March of that year council elections were to be held and the number of hits on the web page increased by 30% in one month as people sought information about candidates. For the first time, a large number of residents became aware of the council web page. In September, another critical article of the council web page in the local community paper appears to have changed the views of the Communications Branch who identified the web as a major communication tool. While agendas, minutes and council papers had been available on the site, other strategic plans requiring community feedback were added. An expensive colour booklet, previously distributed to all residents outlining waste collection procedures and dates was replaced with an interactive query database. The changes led the Communications manager to state:

> It is not a matter of whether I will use the web or not – the web is intricate to everything we do so it is about how best we use the web.

It is important to note that the site contain a large amount of information about services, which was often out of date but that improvements in the site were seen as focusing on governance issues. Council staff were, however, starting to question the type of material on the web and need for genuine services. A staff member observed:

> We need to go beyond the governance side and concentrate more on services. As a ratepayer I want to go to a web page and find out what services they can provide. Through the technology it gives me the opportunity to seek out the right people and it has confidentiality.

By the end of 2002 the council had a massive 55% increase in the number of visits to the site. In the later part of 2002, two other issues accelerated the implementation. The council received funding under the VLGOSD project to purchase a sophisticated purpose built web content management package and a separate payments package. This enabled more people to take responsibility for the development and implementation of a broader range of information and services in their division. This also enabled divisional staff to look for new and innovative ways to present council services. It is interesting to note that despite this new power, most staff in pre-implementation discussions identified many governance issues as important to the community. Many also viewed electronic service delivery as too hard to implement and maintain.

Around this time the IT Manager, working closely with the co-ordinator for web implementation, initiated a review of the BIT Strategy with the aim of moving onto the next stage. Community Engagement Through Innovation (CETI) was developed with an emphasis on changing existing processes to incorporate web-based service delivery.

Although in its early stages, this strategic change laid the ground for an accelerated implementation of web-based services in the future.

6. DISCUSSION

Municipal councils are much closer to and must work more closely with their local community than other levels of government. The evaluation of the web sites reflect this, with a significantly higher level of activity focused on the provision of information for the local community, e-Governance activities and little focus on e-Commerce activities. The research revealed that many municipal councils, while often unable to move to a transactional stage of e-Government, exploit the potential of the web to enhance the participatory side of their activities. The cost of technology, software and resources, together with the lack of experience within municipal councils has impacted on their ability to move to electronic service delivery to any great extent. This has meant that for many councils the web has been used to focus on issues of governance and information provision with less emphasis on e-Commerce activities. Governance issues such as strategic planning, and reporting of council meetings, draws the community into the decision making process.

The research found that municipal councils are more likely to mature at different rates in different functional areas than at higher levels of government suggesting that a different web-based service maturity model for local government is required. Even at higher levels of e-Government maturity, municipal councils appear to emphasize governance issues before enhanced electronic service delivery. This would be an important area for investigation in future research.

Research is needed to better understand what is happening in the move to e-government by local councils. The case study suggested that for municipal councils the approach has been somewhat ad hoc, with little attention to an overall strategy particularly in the early stages. Councils have tended to see electronic service delivery more as an independent project driven by one enthusiast within the council rather than part of an overall broad strategy. This research indicates that new e-Government maturity models need to be developed to truly reflect how local governments are implementing successful online web services. Moreover, the research suggests that neither the e-Business maturity models nor the e-Government models are appropriate for evaluating or understanding local government approaches to electronic service delivery. It would appear that municipal councils do not follow a linear model of electronic maturity in all their areas of information and service delivery.

7. CONCLUSION

The focus of much of the research on e-Government has concentrated on the electronic service delivery at a national or state level. Municipal councils are relatively new and sometimes reluctant participants to this new form of service provision. In Victoria Australia, municipal councils are under pressure to continually improve the quality of services while reducing costs and fees to residents. Moreover, municipal councils are faced with higher levels of accountability and they must maintain close contacts with their communities. Web-based information and service delivery can both engage and disenfranchised different sections of a community thus providing local governments with a dilemma. The research found that the web sites of Victorian municipal councils focus heavily on governance matters. The case study showed that at early to middle levels of web maturity, web development is viewed as the domain of one division rather than an ongoing process for the entire organization. While all higher levels of government have been relatively uniform in their progress towards e-Government, local governments have been spasmodic in their approach suggesting a different model to describe stages in web maturity.

REFERENCES

ABS., 2002, *2001 Census community profile and snapshot*, Australian Bureau of Statistics, Canberra, Australia.

Angehrn, A., 1997, Designing mature internet business strategies: the ICDT model, *European Management Journal,* **15** (4), 361–368.

CITU, 2000, *E-Government: A strategic framework for public services in the information age*, Central IT Unit, Cabinet Office, London, United Kingdom.

Cochrane, A., 1993, From financial control to strategic management: the changing faces of accountability in British local government, *Accounting, Auditing & Accountability Journal,* **6**(2), 30–51.

Department of Transport and Regional Services, 1999, Benchmarking for local government: a practical guide, Department of Transport and Regional Services, (1999, 3rd September): http://www.dotrs.gov.au/nolg/pub/module9/module9/html.

DTLR, 2001, Strong local leadership - quality public services, Department of Transport, Local Government and the Regions, United Kingdom.

Gerritsen, R, and D. Osborn, 1997, Reform of local government in Australia, in: *Comparative Study on Local Government Reform in Japan, Australia and New Zealand*, Japan Local Government Centre (CLAIR), ed, Japan Local Government Centre, Sydney Australia, pp. 51–112.

Jones, M., 1993, *Transforming Australian local government*, Allen and Unwin, St Leonards, Australia.

Kloot, L., 1999, Performance measurement and accountability in Victorian local government, *The International Journal of Public Sector Management,* **12**(7), 565–583.

Leedy, P., 1997, *Practical research: planning and design* (Sixth ed.), Prentice Hall, New Jersey.

Lenk, K., and R. Traunmuller, 2002, Preface to the focus theme on e-Government, *Electronic Markets,* **12**(3), pp. 147–148.

MAV., 1993, *A guide to performance indicators in local government*, Municipal Association of Victoria, Melbourne, Australia.

McMillan, J. H., and S. Schumacher, 1993, *Research in education; a conceptual understanding*, Harper Collins. New York.

Mulitmedia Victoria, 2002, *Putting people at the centre: government innovation working for Victorians*, Department of State and Regional Development, Melbourne, Australia.

Multimedia Victoria, 1998, *Online government 2001 – from vision to reality*, Department of State Development, State Government of Victoria, Melbourne, Australia.

Musso, J., Weare, C., and M. Hale, 2000, Designing web technologies for local governance reform: good management of good democracy?, *Political Communication,* **17**(1), 1–17.

Ninhim, E., 1999, Increasing the quality and range of services by delivering customer service online, Government Online 99 Conference, December, 1999, Sydney, Australia.

NOIE, 2001, *Government Online Survey Results*, National Office for the Information Economy, Commonwealth Government of Australia, Canberra, Australia.

OECD, 1996, *Responsive government: service quality initiatives*, Organisation for Economic Co-operation and Development, Paris, France.

Quirk, B., 2000, From managing change to leading transformation, E-Government Summit Conference, December, 2000, United Kingdom.

Riley, T., 2001, Electronic governance and electronic democracy: living and working in the connected world, Paper presented at the Commonwealth Heads of Government Meeting (Postponed), Brisbane, Australia.

Sanderson, I., 2001, Performance management, evaluation and learning in 'modern' local government, *Public Administration,* **79**(2), 297–313.

Shackleton, P., 2002, The evolution of local government electronic services in Victoria, Australasian Conference on Information Systems, 4th–6th December, 2002, Melbourne, Australia.

Shand, D., and M. Arnberg, 1996, Background paper in: *Responsive government: service quality initiatives*, Organisation for Economic Co-operation and Development, Paris, France, pp. 15–38.

SOCITM., and I&DeA., 2002, *Local E-Government now: a worldwide view*, Improvement & Development Agency, and the Society of Information Technology Management, United Kingdom.

Stamoulis, D., D. Gouscos, P. Georgiadis, and D. Martakos, 2001, Revisiting public information management for effective e-Government services, *Information Management & Computer Security,* **9**(4), 146–153.

Steyaert, J., 2000, Local government online and the role of the resident, *Social Science Computer Review,* **18**(1), 3–16.

United Nations, 2002. *Benchmarking e-Government: a global perspective - assessing the progress of the UN member states*, Division for Public Economics and Public Administration, United Nations, New York, United States.

Whitehore Strategic Group, 2002, Local Government Online Services Project Report, Online Services Demonstration Conference, Melbourne, Australia. ·

World Bank, 2003, E*Government, World Bank Group, (16th July, 2003), ;http://www1.worldbank.org/publicsector/egov/.

WEB AUCTIONS

An impact analysis for Baltic region SMEs

Stanisław Wrycza*

1. INTRODUCTION

This paper was elaborated as the report within the BITNET project, launched in January 2001 under the European Union initiative of the Vth Framework Project (Wrycza, 2001). The report attempts to review and disseminate findings regarding the use of B2B web auctions by SMEs in the Baltic region.

In the era of digital economy, new effective forms of supporting business by Internet have appeared. One such possibility is web auction. The idea of B2B web auctions came from the success and popularity of B2C and C2C marketplaces. Web auction (or e-auction) is the electronic platform which secures an advantageous price in the bidding process using electronic means. Bidding results in the seller receiving the highest price for the goods (services) offered to the buyers.

In practice there are four types of web auctions (e-marketplaces) operating in day-to-day business: buyer-driven, sell-driven, independent and technology provider. In addition to price, there are other factors which can be taken into account as an option along with price when selection B2B e-auction, e.g. quality of the product/service, terms of guarantee governing the product, and the period and other conditions of delivery. Usually, B2B web auctions offer some additional services, like pricing of the product and services, their insurance, opening of a bank account or delivery of the commodity.

Web auctions are developing very quickly in Europe. According to EITO - European Information Technology Observatory (EITO, 2001) - there were in the year 2000 over 650 web auctions (e-marketplaces) in Europe and 2000 worldwide.

Elaboration of the methodological basis of analysis and the monitoring of B2B web auctions for SMEs is the first stage of the research. The task has been performed with the use of the following methods:

---

* Stanisław Wrycza, Department of Information Systems, University of Gdańsk, 81-824 Sopot, Armii Krajowej 119/121, Poland, e-mail: swrycza@univ.gda.pl

- comparative analysis;
- business panels.

The above methods allowed for the performance of the following tasks:

- comparative analysis of selected B2B web auctions;
- business panels performed in cooperation with selected Baltic subregions from different countries and in accordance with the general uniform model proposed by the author.

The first task, which was accomplished without the cooperation of the subregions, was to carry out quantitative research; the latter is based on qualitative research.

For the purposes of comparative analysis, the following criteria were taken into account: the name of the web auction, branch, specialization of the web auction, software platform used for web auction operation and maintenance, functions (standard and additional) incorporated into the web auction, additional notes about specific features of the web auction, and finally the region in which the web auction operates. The results are presented in tabular form.

Guidelines for Panel Discussion of B2B web auction impact analysis were proposed as inspiration to and as a means of assisting business panels. To carry out the qualitative research, a number of problems connected with effective use of web auctions were identified and than taken up in the discussion within business panels. This procedure made it possible to draw basic conclusions. The final survey results were supported by making a comparison between B2B web auction development in Germany (Schleswig-Holstein) and Poland (Pomerania). The results were related to the proposed three stages model of web auctions used in SMEs.

The paper is arranged in the following sections: after a brief introduction, the second section of the paper sets out to identify the basic functions and principles of a B2B web auction. The evolution of web auctions in Europe, based on statistical data, is addressed in the third part of the report. The methodological basis of web auctions analysis and monitoring are defined in chapter four, which includes a detailed specification of both quantitative and qualitative research. Special attention was given to the elaboration of guidelines for panel discussion of B2B Web auctions and their impact on B2B. In section five, a comparative analysis of an inventory of selected, characteristic B2B auction tools is presented. Here, both general and SME-directed tools have been selected and examined. Section six analyses the results of the survey carried out and concludes with a discussion of the impact of web auctions on SMEs in the Baltic Sea Region countries. Special attention is paid to Germany (Schleswig-Holstein) and Poland (Pomerania), of which a comparison is made. On the basis of the results received, a model of stages in B2B web auctions used in SMEs was both proposed and verified.

2. B2B WEB AUCTIONS – DEFINITION AND FUNCTIONS

The current business applications of Internet create many opportunities for SMEs. It is not, of course, a simple procedure for SMEs to adopt Internet applications as there are a number of barriers which must be overcome, including:

- The relatively high costs of hardware and software purchases;

- Payments for telecommunication services;
- The relatively low awareness of the practical capabilities offered by Internet business applications.

Nevertheless, a very high percentage of SMEs have included Internet resources and services in their business strategies. The most popular services to date have been:

- Electronic mail;
- A firm website – just promotion on the Internet;
- Selling and buying (e-shop);
- E-procurement of materials.

However, new, effective forms of supporting business by Internet have recently appeared. One such possibility is web auction. The idea of B2B web auctions came from the success and popularity of B2C and C2C marketplaces. There are a number of well known web auctions of this kind, e.g. the internationally well-known and broadly used e-Bay (http://www.ebay.com), where about half a million items are auctioned each day. The success of such platforms has inspired a new way of thinking: how to apply web auctions in the sphere of B2B markets for SMEs. This may prove a highly effective way of promoting electronic business development as around 90% of firms in many European countries are SMEs. According to Forrester Research, in the coming five years the most successful firms will be the B2B platforms for SME consumer goods.

Web auction (or e-auction) is an electronic platform which allows an advantageous price in bidding using electronic means. As a result of bidding, the seller receives the highest possible price for his or her goods (services). The basic precondition for successful web auction is a relatively high number of auction participants. Multiple buyers and sellers using appropriate software – search engine may undertake business transactions; they can buy and sell commodities and services. Internet creates a specific, extensive sphere and broad scale which acts as a highly competitive platform for both buyers and sellers.

Different classifications of web auctions are proposed. In general, there are two types of web auctions:

- forward auctions;
- reverse auctions.

The definition of a forward web auction, also commonly called simply web auction is presented above. In a reverse auction, the buyer offers the products/services which he/she wants to buy. Sellers make bids in the auction, offering the lowest price for an offer.

Web auctions which serve one specific homogenous branch or consortium of business organisations are called horizontal auctions, while web auctions crossing branch or business divisions are called vertical auctions.

In practice there are four types of web auctions (e-marketplaces) in operation in day-to-day business activities:

- buyer-driven;
- sell-driven;
- independent;
- technology provider.

The above are described in greater detail under point 3 of the paper.

There is one basic difference between web auctions of the B2C and B2B type. In the first case, there is in practice only one parameter which is of interest to web auction users, i.e. price. B2B auctions are more complicated. In addition to price, there are other factors which can be taken into account along with price, including:

- The quality of the product / service;
- The terms of guarantee governing the product;
- The period and other conditions of delivery.

B2B web auctions usually offer additional services, e.g. pricing of the product and services, their insurance, opening of a bank account or delivery of the commodity. In such cases there is a need for the mechanisms for multiparametric bidding and for negotiating the conditions of sale supported by the relevant software platform.

The technical components of the typical web auction are the product and services database, as well as the software, which is integrated with the database performing the bidding process. The logical components of the software itself are:

- Authorization of sellers and buyers;
- Acceptance of the offers according to the web auction database branches;
- Management of the bidding;
- Provision of information about the current state and final result of the auction;
- Information, newsletters about running offers and products structured in a systematic way;
- Optional additional utilities like invoicing, electronic payments, starting an account etc.

It is worth mentioning that if the web auction software is too complicated, the number and magnitude of transactions will decrease.

3. DEVELOPMENT OF WEB AUCTIONS IN EUROPE

Web auctions are developing very quickly in Europe. According to EITO - the European Information Technology Observatory (EITO, 2001) – in the year 2000 there were 650 web auctions (e-marketplaces) in Europe, and 2000 worldwide. Forecasts predict a substantial increase in the number of web auctions, rising to 2700 by 2002.

The operation and maintenance of web auctions is frequently outsourced: 80% of European web auctions are hosted by external suppliers. Both the decline in the digital economy and the process of web auction consolidation verify the accuracy of this prediction. The participation of web auctions in global European e-business services (in total, 11,4 bln euro) is still not high. It is on the level of 6% and in the last position of three main sectors of e-business service sectors. The numbers are detailed as follows:

- One-to-many e-commerce – 55%;
- Web auctions – 6% (664 million euro);
- Marketing/information websites – 39%.

The bulk of web auctions' services value – up to 91% – is generated by customization and consultancy; maintenance due to small number of web auctions before 2002 is still on a low value.

It is worth mentioning that the forecasts prepared in 2000 were too optimistic. The dot.com boom, finished dramatically at the beginning of 200, substantially verified the above predictions. According to different sources, cited by EITO (EITO, 2003, p.277), the number of e-marketplaces at the beginning of 2003 has been stabilized at the level of 1200 worldwide and 530 in Europe.

The use of web auctions is assessed according to the following classifications : buyer-driven, sell-driven, independent and technology provider. Further details of these classifications are included in Table 1. Buyer-driven web auctions are B2B, while others are also applied to B2C. Independent e-marketplaces in particular are dedicated to C2C marketspaces – they constitute as such the most important sort of web auctions. Buyer-driven and independent web auctions seem to be the most appropriate auction forms for SMEs.

Table 1. Types of web auctions

Web auction	Description	Marketspace	Percentage	Examples
Buyerdriven	Consortium of buyers to purchase products and services from their suppliers	B2B	29%	Covisint (car industry), GlobalNextExchange (retailers), Transora (consumer products)
Selldriven	Consortium of suppliers / sellers looking to sell their products online	B2B, B2C	2%	Global Healthcare Exchange, MetalSite
Independent	Operating the marketplace on behalf of buyers / sellers	B2B, B2C, C2C	64%	Achilles, Alibaba, eBay
Technology provider	Web auction established by technology providers to support their products and services among clients	B2B, B2C	5%	SAP, Oracle

4. METHODOLOGY OF WEB AUCTIONS ANALYSIS AND MONITORING

Elaboration of the methodological basis of analysis and monitoring of B2B web auctions is the first stage in accomplishing the research. The task has been performed using the following methods:

- comparative analysis;
- business panels.

The above methods assisted in the performance of the following tasks:

- comparative analysis of selected B2B web auctions;
- business panels operating within selected BITNET regions according to the general uniform model proposed by the Gdansk region partner.

The first task constitutes quantitative research, while the second task is based on qualitative research. The list of web auctions can be found under URL:

http://www.business2.com/webguide/0,1660,5407,FF.html
or:
http://www.canpol.pl/astronet/exporter/linki/linki.html

The synthesis of this survey is presented in chapters 4 and 5 of this report and represents the completion of the first task.

In the course of the performance of the second task, the BITNET partners have been asked to carry out the panel discussions (in the business panels which include the SMEs created in the specific regions) in accordance with the model proposed, thereby allowing assessment of the web auctions impact analysis. In the model proposed for the panel discussion, the guidelines for such an evaluation are formulated. Due to differences in the level of digital economy development, the survey is general and does not need to be uniform. The exceptional situations in the specific regions can not to be excluded. The proposed model should thus inspire and order the discussion during the panel meeting. It was expected that there would be several participants: 4–9 SME representatives taking an active part and with competence in carrying out web auctions. Several days before the panel meeting its participants received the model for panel discussion – Guidelines for Panel Discussion on Web auctions Impact Analysis. The discussion was planned to last about 3–4 hours. The panel moderator - BITNET partner was expected to prepare the summary of the discussion. Finally, the summary of the research has been prepared. The guidelines and the specific criteria for the panel discussion are presented below:

A. Specialization

- Business branch of the firm.
- Virtual or hybrid.
- Number of employees.
- Turnover or profit (if acceptable).

B. Use of Web auctions

- What kind of web auctions (type, brand name of the platform) are used by the firm?
- Payment for the web auction services - subscription, brokerage dependent on turnover, free of charge.
- Intensity of web auction use - rudimentary, frequent, occasional, seldom.
- For selling, buying or both.
- Web auction and/or reverse web auction (the ordering firm states the products/services which it wants to buy by dynamic pricing).
- Business reason for using B2B web auction.
- Number of offers per time period (day, week, month).
- Number of transactions per period (day, week, month).
- Turnover/ profit generated by web auctions (also in percentage of the general turnover/profit).

C. Preparatory phase

- Did regional development organizations, business associations inspire/train your firm in web auctions use?
- Did they help you to prepare a go-to-market plan or a business plan in relation to digital economy principles and web auctions in particular?
- Is contact with these organizations maintained?

D. Parameters of a web auction

- Is the price the only parameter to be taken into account?
- Do you use multiparametric software including the evaluation of product quality, guarantee, term and conditions of delivery?
- Does your web auction perform additional services, such as pricing, insurance, starting the account, organization of product deliveries?

E. Advantages of web auctions

- Better prices.
- Lower customer acquisition and promotion costs.
- Increase in the firm's competitiveness
- Reduced telecommunication costs.
- Wider access to new markets.
- Extension of the number of buyers and sellers.
- Comparison of offers.
- Online negotiations.
- Automatization of the decision process.
- Saving of time.
- Increase in turnover and profit.
- Growth of staff competence.
- Better organization of the firm's processes.
- Other.

Which of the above advantages are the most important?

F. Disadvantages of web auctions

- Uncertainty of sales and purchases.
- Price uncertainty
- Lower safety in making transactions.
- Lower information security.
- Effectiveness of information /telecommunication infrastructure.
- Other

Which of the above disadvantages are the most important?

5. COMPARATIVE ANALYSIS OF B2B AUCTIONS

During the research quite a number of web auctions were found and analyzed. A summary of the most typical B2B web auctions for SMEs is provided in Table 2. For the summary included in Table 2, the following **criteria** were taken into account:

- name of web auction;
- branch, specialization of the web auction;
- software platform used for web auction operation and maintenance;
- functions (standard and additional) incorporated into the web auction;
- additional notes about specific features of the web auction;
- region in which the web auction operates.

6. THE EVALUATION OF B2B WEB AUCTIONS' IMPACT ANALYSIS ON SMEs

Rather dynamic but versatile development and use of web auctions were observed in all Baltic subregions surveyed. Both firms and individuals were aware of the role of web auctions, particularly in the C2C marketspace. The intensity of web auction use varied greatly. The guidelines elaborated for assessment of web auctions on SMEs enabled a number of general conclusions to be formulated. It is worth stressing that there is still little interest in web auctions in the Baltic countries. Only a few firms use web auctions for their business activities. It thus appears that the application of web auctions to rudimentary activities within SMEs is minimal. On the other hand, the Scandinavian countries have one of the highest rates of informatization. Information about the use of all forms of web auctions described in the earlier sections of this report was available from secondary sources. The survey was carried out first and foremost in Poland and Germany. The answers regarding specific points are summarized below. It is mainly the qualitative aspects of the survey which are presented. The respondents were not willing to reveal their quantitative data, particularly when it came to financial results.

6.1. Specialization

All branches of SMEs were included. The number of employees ranged from several till fifty persons.

6.2. Web Auction Use

All types of web auctions such as forward, reverse, universal, specialized, domestic, regional, practical and experimental were of interest to SMEs. Two types of payments were used in the main: subscription and brokerage dependent on turnover. Where specific projects were financed by public sources, the web auction services were free of charge. Business interest in using B2B web auctions was closely related to an increase in profits. Other reasons are explained in point e.

Table 2. B2B Web auctions for SMEs

Name	Branches	Software	Functions	Region
Acequote http://www.acequote.com	IT / Telecommunications	Independent, own	Standard functions	UK
ECEurope http://www.eceurope.com	multibranch	ASP (Microsoft)	Bulletin board - acts as a matchmaker between international buyers and sellers	Europe / world
Eu-supply http://www.eu-supply.com	construction	Independent, own	Sourcing & Suppliers, Tender Management (estimating, procurement), document management, knowledge management reporting	Europe
Getin http://www.getin.pl	multibranch	Independent, own	Branch catalogue, e-mail account, SME website, consulting	Poland
Goodex http://www.goodex.com	Industrial equipment and supplies	independently developed eSourcing platform	Standard	Germany
Marketplanet http://www.marketplanet.com.pl	multibranch	SAP / CommerceOne (mySAP, Marketset)	Consulting	Poland
Mondus http://www.mondus.com	IT Hardware, IT software, Office Equipment (Furniture, Supplies), Telecommunications	StreamServe	Standard	UK / Germany / France / Italy
Openkontakt www.openkontakt.com	multibranch	PHP	Information about auctions, marketplaces	World
Serio.pl http://www.serio.pl	multibranch	Independent, own	Legal and financial advice electronic catalogue, sending information of new offers for the selected branches	Poland

6.3. Preparatory Phase

In Scandinavian countries and Germany national and local governments devoted substantial financial resources to the promotion of web auctions among B2B firms. Besides seminars and workshops, professional training was offered to potentially interested persons and firms. The support of regional organizations went even further by proposing consultation in drawing up the business plan and go-to-market plan. Some of the regional organizations developed incubators for start-ups. Due to financial barriers rather than a lack of awareness of the challenge entailed such initiatives were not taken up in Poland and the Baltic countries, with the exception of limited forms of consultancy on electronic business for SMEs.

6.4. Parameters of Web Auctions

It was, as was expected, proved that the price is the main parameter which is taken into account when bidding at SME web auctions . But in some cases the multiparametric software, including the evaluation of product quality, guarantee, terms and conditions of delivery were applied. Some web auctions performed additional services such as pricing, insurance, starting an account or organizing product deliveries - services of interest for the SMEs surveyed.

6.5. Advantages and Disadvantages of Web Auctions

The full list of advantages and disadvantages was confirmed. The most important advantage was a better price, while uncertainty of sales and purchases was perceived as the main disadvantage.

When analyzing the development of web auctions in different countries three phases can be proposed:

1. Emerging awareness of web auctions;
2. Extended use and intensive learning about web auctions;
3. Maturity.

The prerequisites, activities and effects of the above three stages are presented in Table 3. As already stated, the most detailed analysis was carried out in Germany and Poland. Some additional sources, e.g. Hussla (2001), were used to make a more precise analysis. According to the classification presented in Table 3, Germany (Schleswig-Holstein) achieved the third phase of web auction use, while Poland (the Pomeranian region) is approaching the second phase. The impact of web auctions on German SMEs is substantial. The critical mass in web auctions use in Germany was achieved by means of activities within policy, technology and skills development. All three factors are connected and support each other. The great awareness of the role of the digital economy for regional development was achieved 2–3 years ago. The local government of Schleswig-Holstein in cooperation with German Telekom started the project b2b-Markt-sh which was directed at 3000 SMEs. Using seminars, workshops, training and consultancy the project inspired several hundred SMEs to go digital. Cooperation with centers of excellence or innovation centers, in collaboration with universities and incubators resulted in dissemination of web auctions in small businesses in the region of Schleswig-Holstein. The development of the relevant technology was supported by project resources, German Telekom and local government.

In Poland the resources for web auction development were more scanty; however, awareness of the function of web auctions was quite common, and their role understood. The limited number of promotional activities for associations of SMEs were taken up. Private capital rather than public institutions paid for the development of web auctions. There was a barrier for many SMEs of software and hardware purchases to access the web auctions service. The firms which decided to use web auctions did so for two reasons:

- quicker sales of their products and services;
- promotion of the firm by including its offer in the web auction.

The web auctions promoted their service by phone calls to potentially interested SMEs.

Table 3. The stages of B2B web auctions use in SMEs

Prerequisites	Activities	Effects
	Phase I: Emerging awareness of web auctions capabilities	
• Understanding the business model of web auctions • The offer of different types of web auctions for a specific country • Sufficient infrastructure and access to Internet services and resources	• Participation in seminars, workshops • Reading materials in journals and Internet • Discussions with users already competent in web auctions	• Growing competence and interest in web auctions • First transactions • Elaboration of business plan and go-to-market plan
	Phase II: Extended use and intensive learning about web auctions	
• Growing number of web auctions is available • Investments in hardware and software	• Intensive training • Support of regional institutions • Participation in private – public projects • Establishment of centres supporting digital economy development such as Bitnet houses	• Growing number of transactions • Growing number of SMEs using web auctions
	Phase III: Maturity	
• Diversity and wide availability of branch, regional, domestic and international web auctions • Continuous improvement of hardware and software	• Rudimentary use of web auctions • Daily sales and purchases	• Critical mass of web auctions use by SMEs in the region • Web auctions use is part of a firm strategy • Web auctions are becoming one of several alternative ways of making sales and purchases making (sometimes auctions are the dominant form)

7. CONCLUSIONS

The results obtained show that the success of web auctions in SMEs depends on:

- High standards of Internet infrastructure;
- The skill and motivation of the staff of IT firms developing web auctions;
- The existence of a staff with a heightened awareness of the advantages of web auctions for SMEs;
- Awareness of among local government employees and those employed in telecommunication of the significance of regional policy providing financial support to the digital economy;
- Undertaking joint projects of regional authorities, the telecommunication industry and businesses with a special focus on digital economy initiatives.

The survey confirmed that the use of web auctions was varied in Baltic region countries. There is still little interest in web auctions in the Eastern Baltic countries, and only a few firms use there web auctions in business. These countries are in the initial stages of B2B web auction use, i.e. there is a growing awareness of the opportunities offered by web auctions. Poland, with its own B2B web auctions and growing interest in SMEs, is heading towards the second stage: the extended use of and intensive learning about web auctions. The third stage – maturity – has been achieved by Scandinavian countries (which have one of the highest rates of information technology and systems dissemination in the world) and Germany, which took up many of the original initiatives for promoting B2B web auctions among SMEs. As an overall conclusion, SMEs in the Baltic region show a growing awareness of the role of web auctions for their business activities, and are becoming increasingly active in the practical implementation of such auctions.

REFERENCES

EITO, 2001, Report, European Information Technology Observatory, Frankfurt.

EITO, 2003, Report, European Information Technology Observatory, Frankfurt.

Hussla. I., and Thiemann. A., 2001, From business community towards btob commerce, in: *E-work and E-commerce. Novel solutions and Practices for a Global Networked Economy*, Stanford-Smith B.,Chiozza E., eds., IOS Press, Venice, p.832.

Kalakota R., and Robinson M., 2001, E-business – Roadmap for Success, Addison-Wesley

Stanford-Smith B.,Chiozza E., eds, 2001, *E-work and E-commerce. Novel solutions and Practices for a Global Networked Economy*, IOS Press, Venice.

Wrycza S., 2001, *Web Auctions – An Impact Analysis for SMEs*, BITNET project of EU, report 12, Blekinge.

EXPERIENCES IN USING A WEB-BASED GDSS TO COORDINATE DISTRIBUTED GROUP DECISION-MAKING PROCESSES

Patrick P. Cao, Jocelyn C. San Pedro, and Frada Burstein*

1. INTRODUCTION

As modern organizations shift from vertical hierarchy to networked structure, distributed group decision-making becomes more prevalent. Distributed mode has the potential to not only reduce the costs of meetings but also improve the outcomes of group decision-making processes. However, as the group decision-making process takes place more asynchronously in time and dispersedly in proximity, coordination of group activities becomes more critical to the success of the process.

The need for coordination is inherent in all group decision-making activities (Schmidt and Simone, 1996). However, it may be more difficult to coordinate group decision-making processes in asynchronous and distributed mode than those in face-to-face meeting mode. Due to asynchronicity, group members have to agree upon how often and when communication should occur in order to keep the process going smoothly. In addition, lack of social cues such as voice and gesture in distributed environments may prevent the group from conveying information efficiently, which may result to group process losses (Johnson, 1999).

One approach of dealing with these difficulties is to provide structuring mechanisms for groups to organize their communication, and sequence the decision-making process (Ocker et al., 1995–1996). The advent of group decision support systems (GDSS) brings about the features to facilitate the distributed group decision-making processes. GDSS provide computer-mediated means to remove communication barriers. Meanwhile the utilization of decision-making modeling techniques embedded in GDSS can structure the group decision-making process in such a way that group members systematically evaluate various decision alternatives. The combination of communication support and modeling techniques may enhance the outcome of these processes (DeSanctis and Gallupe, 1987).

* School of Information Management and Systems, Monash University, PO Box 197, Caulfield East, VIC 3145, Australia, Tel: +61 3 9903 2735, Fax: +61 3 9903 1889.

It is clear that the GDSS design should reflect the requirements of communication and modeling support in order to improve the effectiveness and efficiency of distributed group decision-making processes. According to the *task-technology-fit theory* (*TFT*) (Zigurs and Buckland, 1998), the technology used in performing the group decision-making task should be consistent with the task in order to achieve high group decision-making performance. To address the communication needs in the design of GDSS, selection of an appropriate medium used in the GDSS is critical. In addition, *media richness theory* (Daft and Lengel, 1986) suggests that tasks with high equivocality demand the use of rich media to facilitate the group communications. GDSS research in general proves that the computer-mediated communication is effective to support group decision-making tasks. Meanwhile, it may be less efficient in performing group decision-making tasks than face-to-face meetings (Pervan, 1998). Questions remain open, however, as to whether computer-mediated communication is sufficient to coordinate the distributed group decision-making process involving the use of modeling techniques with respect to the effectiveness and efficiency of the process. In our research, we were particularly concerned with the adequacy of using GDSS technology based upon discussion databases in coordinating distributed group decision-making process.

This paper describes our experiences with a Web-based GDSS in coordinating distributed group decision-making process in light of the selection of communication media used in the GDSS. We begin with a brief review of media richness theory and task-technology-fit theory. These theories have significantly influenced the design and use of GDSS. We then describe the infrastructure and features of *CyberGDSS*, a Web-based GDSS prototype we developed for our study of coordination in the context of distributed group decision-making processes. We proceed with illustration of the use of *CyberGDSS* in a laboratory experimental environment where participants were coordinated to make a group decision. The qualitative data collected from a post-experimental questionnaire are presented. The implications of our experiences with the use of *CyberGDSS* are discussed at the end of the paper.

2. THEORETICAL FOUNDATION

2.1. Media Richness Theory

One of the widely applied theories in GDSS use is *media richness theory* (*MRT*) (Daft and Lengel, 1986). Media richness refers to "the amount of emotional, attitudinal, normative, and other meanings that the information carries beyond the literal denotations of symbols" (Hollingshead et al., 1993, p. 310). The media used in GDSS design tend to reduce uncertainty and equivocality in order to accomplish the group decision-making tasks. MRT argues that the improvement of task performance will depend on the match between the task needs and richness of the medium. Daft and Lengel (1986) argue that media capable of sending "rich" information (e.g., face-to-face meetings) are better suited to equivocal tasks, while media that are less "rich" (or lean media, e.g., computer-mediated communication) are best suited to tasks of uncertainty. A poor fit between medium and task will negatively affect member's perceptions of the medium (Chidambaram and Jones, 1993).

McGrath and Hollingshead (1993) have applied the notion of task-media fit in the MRT to the domain of GDSS. They present a framework that shows the potential best fit between the task and richness of information transmitted. For example, an intellectual task requires a leaner medium than a decision-making task, as the latter needs to rely on more information to reconcile different attitudes and opinions, and to reach consensus. Thus the clear implication from MRT is that the selection of media depends on the fit between information requirements of the task and the capacity of the medium considered (George and Carlson, 1999).

However, several researchers have pointed out the theoretical limitations of MRT (Suh, 1999), and the difficulty in satisfactorily explaining the controversial findings (see Carlson and Davis, 1998). A recent study conducted by Mennecke, Valacich, and Wheeler (2000) reported mixed support for the MRT. As a result, a number of variations, for instance, *media synchronicity theory* (Dennis and Valacich, 1999), based on the MRT have been developed.

Dennis and Valacich (1999) argue that all tasks are composed of two fundamental communication processes, *conveyance* and *convergence*. Conveyance is the exchange of information, followed by deliberation on its meaning. Convergence is the development of shared meaning for information. Media synchronicity theory argues that media have a definite set of capabilities that are able to support each communication process. Communication effectiveness is enhanced when processes are aligned with media support capabilities. Media synchronicity theory focuses on electronic communication media (Dennis et al., 1998).

2.2. Task-Technology Fit Theory

Task-technology fit can be defined as "ideal profiles composed of an internally consistent set of task contingencies and GSS elements that affect group performance" (Zigurs and Buckland, 1998, p. 323). The greater the degree of adherence to an ideal profile, the better the performance of the group.

The task-technology fit theory (*TFT*) postulates that an appropriate task-technology fit should result in a higher group performance. In particular, it predicts that decision tasks should result in the best group performance when using a GDSS configuration that emphasizes information processing and process structuring (Zigurs and Buckland, 1998). In a follow-up study, Zigurs et al. (1999) further developed a coding scheme to test the effects of TFT based on various GDSS studies.

The TFT provides a broad framework for the advancement of research in GDSS. It also provides a set of conceptual tools for GDSS practitioners to define a fit between task and technology. The conceptual architecture of TFT is based upon a functional paradigm. According to the functional perspective, the task activities primarily enable the desired outcome. The technological features and their ideal appropriations are seen as facilitators of the desired task and decision activities (Rana et al., 1997).

A number of studies have been conducted empirically to examine the effects of the TFT. For instance, Shirani, Tafti, and Affisco (1999) investigated the interaction between task structure (less and more structured) and communication technology (email and a group idea generation tool). They found that GDSS groups generated more ideas, while the email groups performed a deeper problem analysis capability. Straus and McGrath (1994) revealed that computer mediated groups performed better in collaborative and additive tasks but no different from face-to-face groups in the intellectual task. Murthy and Kerr (2000) found that face-to-face groups performed better in a decision-making task than GDSS groups, while the reverse occurred when performing an idea generation task. The findings generally suggest the task-technology fit enhances the group performance.

2.3. Experimental Research in Distributed Group Decision-Making Processes

Experimental research methods have dominated GDSS research (Nunamaker et al., 1993; Pervan, 1998). It appears that this dominance follows the experimental tradition of psychology in small group research. Although experimental research methods have drawn criticism due to their incapability of dealing with contextual variables and lack of generalizability of the results (Frey, 1996), they are deemed to be legitimate for exploratory type of studies, in which the casual relationship between variables intended to investigate is unknown.

In early experiments with distributed groups, Hiltz et al. (1991) found that distributed groups were significantly poorer than face-to-face groups on measures of amount of shared information and members' perception of decision-making progress. The distributed groups made worse decisions than their face-to-face counterparts, and did not participate regularly. Cass et al. (1992) used location and synchronicity as independent variables in their experiment with groups. They concluded that although GDSS could be used in distributed groups, there might be serious impediments to users' acceptance.

In contrast, Chidambaram and Jones (1993) found that GDSS might improve distributed groups in performing tasks effectively and satisfy group members. Contrary to MRT which posits that richer medium should produce better performance for the group undertaking an equivocal task, Burke and Chidambaram (1999) found the distributed groups using synchronous GDSS performed and felt better than face-to-face groups.

3. *CYBERGDSS* – A WEB-BASED GDSS PROTOTYPE

3.1. Architecture of *CyberGDSS*

Distributed group decision-making is different from traditional face-to-face meetings, because it allows group members to act in independent ways, and meanwhile share interdependence among them (Boland et al., 1992). In a distributed environment, participants have more flexibility to contribute to the group decision-making process at any time and any place, which may allow them to explore thoroughly about all decision alternatives. This may lead to the enhancement of the decision-making outcomes.

To reflect this requirement based on the TFT, which asserts that technology used in performing group decision-making task should be consistent with the characteristics of the task, we developed *CyberGDSS*, a Web-based GDSS prototype in a Lotus Notes environment. In the design of *CyberGDSS*, we implemented a three-tier architecture (see Figure 1). The first tier comprises a Web browser that handles user's input and presents information to the user. A group of decision-makers can be located in different places interacting with each other through the Internet. The second tier is the Domino server, which functions as the server and the application container. It functions as a server to the Web browser, where group members can use the modeling techniques to perform individual evaluation, or to interact with others during the group decision-making process. The Domino server also functions as an application container, accommodating the third tier components, such as the facilitation support component, the discussion database and the modeling application. The discussion database stores all interactive information among group members during the decision-making process, which can be accessed at any time.

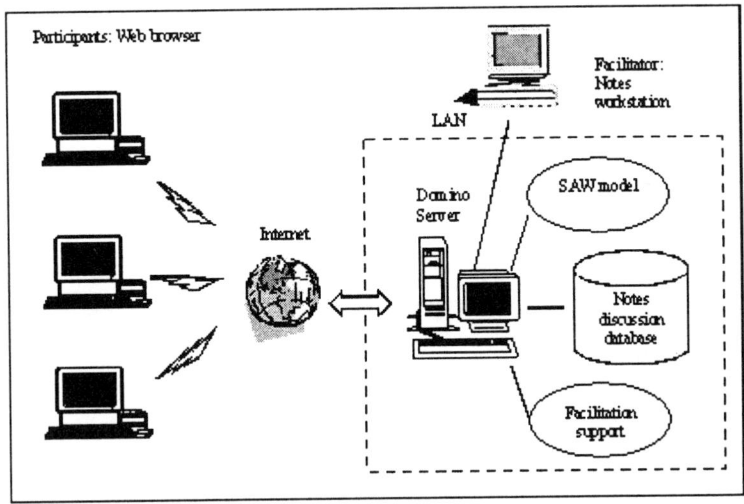

Figure 1. System architecture of *CyberGDSS*

CyberGDSS also uses a client/server concept in synchronizing the communication between facilitator and group members and in handling facilitation support via a local area network (LAN). Because the speed of LAN is much faster than the Web, facilitation support is designed to communicate with the Domino server via a LAN through Lotus Notes internal infrastructure and interface. This design allows us to control over the whole system.

3.2. Discussion Database

Database technology has been used to serve as group memory in GDSS applications (Hoffer and Valacich, 1993). Group members can readily access information that helps them make effective decisions. For example, a member can post a message to raise an issue for group discussion, or respond to others with his or her argument or preference. In *CyberGDSS*, the discussion database serves as an information repository in which all group interactions during the decision-making process are captured and organized. It acts as a vehicle which accommodates various models to support different requirements of group decision-making processes. The facilitator can also track and monitor the progress of decision-making process and create task assignment through the discussion database.

In *CyberGDSS*, users interact with others and the facilitator via the browser; all their individual activities are accomplished through the Internet, such as acquiring task requirements, uploading their preference models, viewing other members' preferences, and seeking consensus with all members. Figure 2 depicts an interface of *CyberGDSS*.

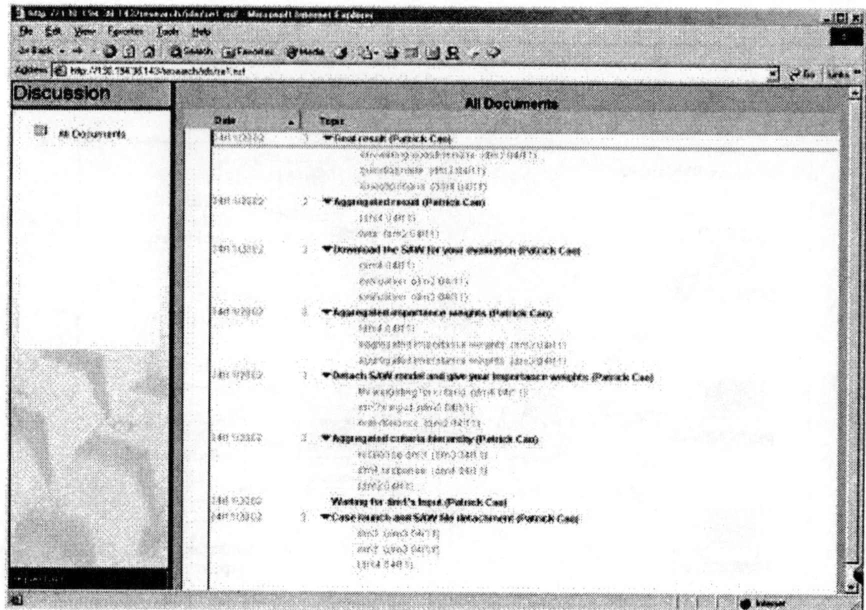

Figure 2. Web-based interface of CyberGDSS

3.3. The Modeling Technique

In *CyberGDSS*, we used the *Simple Additive Weighted method* (SAW, see Yoon and Hwang, 1995) as a decision-making modeling tool to facilitate the problem structuring for group members. We implemented the SAW model in a spreadsheet form. Individuals in the group can download the SAW model from the discussion database, and can then develop the criteria, weight those criteria, and assess the decision alternatives. Individuals can also upload the SAW models onto the discussion database, so that others in the group can view and share these models. The facilitator may use the SAW model as a means to carry aggregated information for further assessment. Figure 3 shows the main interface of the SAW model.

As shown in Figure 3, the interface of the modeling tool has four areas: (1) the left upper corner box displays the alternatives available for the evaluation; (2) the functional options box lets users choose from the development of criteria, allocation of weights, and assessment of alternatives with respect to each criterion; (3) the criteria input space allows users to input the hierarchy of criteria, which can be automatically displayed in the evaluation space; (4) the evaluation space is used to display assessment results; users can rate alternatives by entering scores in the evaluation space.

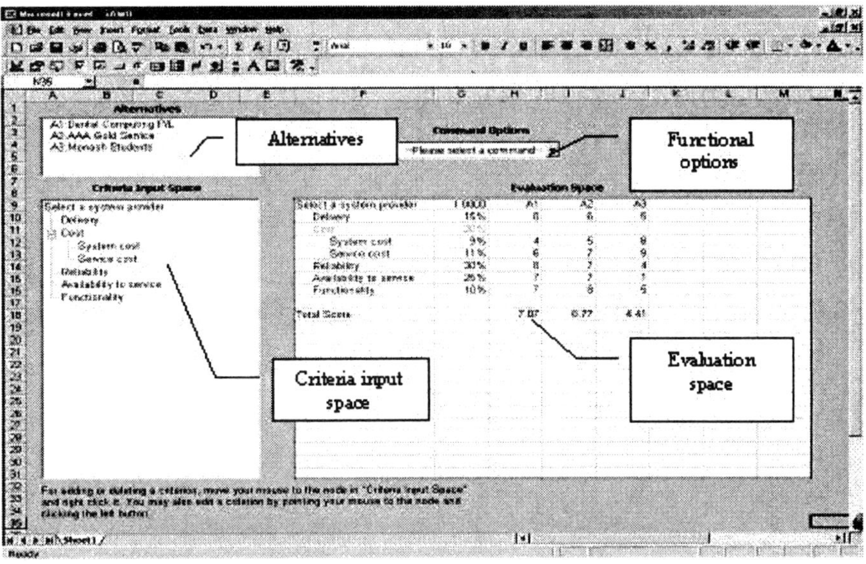

Figure 3. Model component in CyberGDSS

4. USERS' RESPONSES

The preliminary evaluation of the *CyberGDSS* was conducted in a laboratory experimental environment with 84 senior undergraduate students. Participants included 57 male and 27 female students, with the average age of 22.86 and 5.42 years of experience with computers (see Table 1).

Table 1. Descriptive statistics of subjects in terms of age and computer experience

	N	Minimum	Maximum	Mean	Standard Deviation
Age	84	21	26	22.86	.89
Computer experience	84	3	8	5.42	1.08

During the experiment, participants were coordinated with the *CyberGDSS* to carry out a designated group decision-making task. The task required the group of subjects to act as a group of expert IT consultants who were requested to select a suitable computer system provider for a local dentistry business (Cao et al., 2003). The experiment aimed at exploring the effects of different coordination methods in group decision-making processes using *CyberGDSS* as supporting GDSS technology. Results of quantitative analysis of this experiment showed that user's satisfaction on decision-making process and decision outcome vary according to the coordination method used to coordinate the group decision-making task. To elicit the participants' attitude towards technology employed in the *CyberGDSS*, in a post-experimental survey, the participants were asked to respond to three open-ended questions. Responses to these questions display some interesting patterns. Effectiveness of the coordination procedures supported by *CyberGDSS* was addressed in the responses to open-ended questions.

Comments made in response to the question: "In your opinion, what are the valuable aspects in the structured group decision-making process that assisted you to reach a group decision?" included:

> It was very effective. Some of the reasons for this assessment are the ability to get all participants together, to capture their thoughts being shared by others, the ability to evaluate the data for making the decision, and the ability to step through the entire decision-making procedures without stumbling at what to do.

> It provides a very organized way to do things, especially necessary for this kind of decision-making task.

Participants' responses to the open-ended questions appeared to confirm the theories of MRT and TFT. A simple combination of discussion database and the modeling techniques might not be efficient and flexible enough to suit the needs of different group decision-making situations, because the bandwidth of communication media provided by *CyberGDSS* might be too lean to reduce the equivocality of the task. In responding to the question: "*In your opinion, what improvements could be made to the decision-making process, in order to reach a better group decision in a more convenient and effective way?*" participants made the following comments:

> I would like to see the system being integrated with NetMeeting as well as ICQ kinds of stuff.

> It would be nice to see the system capable of handling more complex situations. Often, non-real time discussion facility is not enough to do what needs to be done. I would like to have the responses made available immediately. NetMeeting could do, but I'm not sure if it supports WAN.

> The lack of more advanced technologies in the system made the process cumbersome. The group discussion needed to be "live". Getting the quick responses from facilitator and my partners was crucial. I wouldn't wait fifteen minutes or more for others' inputs. It simply wastes time! We could have used ICQ stuff to make discussion "go live".

> Hey, why don't you use video-conferencing? It must be very cool!

It should be noted that, although some expressed their desire for the ability to accommodate more state-of-art technologies such as video-conferencing, real time discussion and workflow systems, satisfaction with present communication technology used in the CyberGDSS was a point of agreement among most of the participants. This apparent contradiction may be explained by noting that their general satisfaction with existing technology was strong but not absolute.

Some comments made by participants in responding to open-ended questions provide support for the argument that minimal technology is sufficient for satisfaction with the process, and the major criterion for media choice is convenience (Johnson, 1999). Face-to-face communication mode seems more preferable than the GDSS technology for a number of participants. The following comments profiled such responses:

> "Why didn't we just sit together and work the thing out. I bet it must be quicker than using Internet!"
>
> I like the whole idea about this kind of group decision-making. It was an eye-opening experience. But I didn't feel I was working in a group. I guess only would face-to-face meetings make me feel like that way. You should develop something like MIRC to support meetings.
>
> I'd like to have cameras in the front us, which allow us to talk to each other. It would save time.

This phenomenon was manifested in a study of collaborative writing in a GDSS environment (Horton and Biolsi, 1993–94). Given the right tools, face-to-face collaboration may be more efficient, and may reduce some of the coordination difficulties of working asynchronously, such as delays due to cycling work between group members and insufficient consensus. Several lines of research point to the advantages that face-to-face mode offers groups. Daft and Lengel (1986) argue that the richness of face-to-face communication is critical for decision-making tasks where uncertainty and equivocality are involved.

5. DISCUSSION AND CONCLUSION

The users' responses towards the use of *CyberGDSS* in our study have following implications for communication media used in coordinating distributed group decision-making processes.

- *Distributed group decision-making requires the reduction of equivocality of the task. Therefore, a lean medium provided by GDSS may not fully satisfy the communication needs of distributed group decision-making processes, especially in tightly coordinated groups.*

  The users' responses show that the Web-based discussion database did not efficiently support the coordination of distributed group decision-making tasks. In such an environment, users seem to rely on a richer medium to convey information to reduce the equivocality of the task. A Web-based discussion database might not be efficient for decision analysis. This result supports media richness theory, which argues that performing a decision-making task with high equivocality should be matched by rich media.

- *For effectively supporting distributed group decision-making processes, GDSS should provide a spectrum of media that suit the varied communication requirements of the tasks. Among them, face-to-face interaction or its technological alternative, such as video-conferencing is deemed to be critical for the acceptance of GDSS in performing distributed group decision-making tasks.*

  Although the *CyberGDSS* used in our study is generally perceived to be effective, many participants demonstrate their preference for face-to-face interaction or other synchronous multimedia technologies, such as real-time chatting, video-conferencing, NetMeeting, and so on.

According to Olson and Teasley (1996), GDSS should be able to provide support for a variety of decision-making tasks. The increasing sophistication and availability of various technologies imply that groups are not likely to be satisfied with one medium in performing their tasks (Burke et al., 1999). GDSS should provide a variety of communication media to match the needs of various tasks (Cockburn and Greenberg, 1993).

Dennis and Valacich (1999) decompose the group task into conveying information and converging on decisions. Verbal communication or face-to-face interaction is critical when the group task moves to converging on decision. Therefore, the discussion database type of GDSS technology appears not to be an adequate substitute for face-to-face interaction.

- *The choice of medium should be left for users to decide. GDSS should provide the capability of switching between media based on the requirements of task structures.*

  Both findings from this research and other studies suggest that the choice of communication medium depends upon a number of factors such as the complexity of task, technology used, the requirements of group interaction, and so on. Thus it is not wise to impose a certain kind of media on users. Rather, GDSS should allow users to choose an appropriate communication media (Cockburn and Greenberg, 1993). It is likely that different stages of the group decision-making process will require different media to meet the requirements of sub tasks. For instance, when aggregating individual criteria, it requires more focus on conveying information. In such cases, face-to-face interaction may be more desirable than an electronic communication means. On the other hand, when aggregating individual assessments, it is likely that convergence on decisions is more desirable. In this case, there is no need to use a rich medium of communication.

Our findings in this study provide some guidelines for GDSS designers and practitioners. In summary, our experiences with the *CyberGDSS* suggest that a lean medium such as distributed discussion database does not fully suffice the requirements of coordinating distributed group decision-making tasks, especially with respect to the efficiency of the process. In order to resolve the equivocality of the group decision-making task, a rich medium such as face-to-face meeting or its technical alternative (e.g., video conferencing) is demanded. Our experiences indicate that in the design of GDSS, a range of communication media should be provided to suit for different stages of the group decision-making processes. Selection of media bound in the GDSS design may be a decision made by the users.

Inevitably, this research was bound by a number of limitations. First, as with any experimental study, it shares drawbacks associated with the experimental research methodology, such as the use of students as surrogates for real world managers and limited applicability of results to other settings. Second, we were unable to explore other technologies that may be used in supporting the coordination of distributed group decision-making tasks. Third, our data collection seems inadequate to fully capture the meaningfulness of technological support in distributed group decision-making processes.

In this paper we merely describe our experiences with the discussion database type of GDSS in coordinating distributed group decision-making tasks, in which we feel the adequacy of this type of technology in supporting group decision-making especially involving modelling techniques needs to be addressed. Future research lies in using other research methods such as case studies or field tests, in which more state-of-art technology combining discussion database and real-time decision-making tools such as video conferencing can be tested in a real group decision-making environment. This may increase the generalizability of the results that are applicable to other settings.

REFERENCES

Boland, R. J., Maheshwarl, A. K., Te'enl, D., Schwartz, D. G., and Tenkasi, R. V., 1992, Sharing perspectives in distributed decision making, in: *Proceedings of the ACM Conference on Computer-Supported Cooperative Work (CSCW'92)*, The ACM, pp. 306–313.

Burke, K., Aytes, K., Chidambaram, L., and Johnson, J.J., 1999, A study of partially distributed work groups: The impact of media, location, and time on perceptions and performance, *Small Group Research*, **30**: 453.

Burke, K., and Chidambaram, L., 1999, How much bandwidth is enough? A longitudinal examination of media characteristics and group outcomes, *MIS Quarterly*, **23**: 557.

Cao, P. P., Burstein, F. V., and San Pedro, J., 2003, Coordinating distributed group multiple criteria decision-making processes: Preliminary results from a laboratory experiment, Proceedings of the Seventh International Conference of the International Society for Decision Support Systems (ISDSS'03), Poland.

Carlson, P., and Davis, G. B., 1998, An investigation of media selection among directors and managers: From "self" to "other" orientation, *MIS Quarterly*, **22:** 335.

Cass, K., Heintz, T. J., and Kaiser, K. M., 1992, An investigation of satisfaction when using a voice-synchronous GDSS in dispersed meetings, *Information & Management*, **23**: 173.

Chidambaram, L., and Jones, B., 1993, Impact of communication medium and computer support on group perceptions and performance: A comparison of face-to-face and dispersed meetings, *MIS Quarterly*, **17**: 465.

Cockburn, A., and Greenberg, S., 1993, Making contact: Getting the group communicating with groupware, in: *Proceedings of the Conference on Organizational Computing Systems (COOCS'93)*, The ACM, pp. 31–41.

Daft, R. L., and Lengel, R. H., 1986, Organizational information requirements, media richness and structural design, *Management Science*, **32**: 554.

Dennis, A. R., Valacich, J. S., Speier, C., and Morris, M. G., 1998, Beyond media richness: An empirical test of media synchronicity theory, in: *Proceedings of the 31st Annual Hawaii International Conference on System Sciences*, IEEE, pp. 48–57.

Dennis, A. R., and Valacich, J. S., 1999, Rethinking media richness: Towards a theory of media synchronicity, in: *Proceedings of the 32nd Annual Hawaii International Conference on System Sciences*, IEEE.

DeSanctis, G., and Gallupe, R. B., 1987, A foundation for the study of group decision support systems, *Management Science*, **33**: 589.

Frey, L. R., 1996, Remembering and "re-membering": A history of theory and research on communication and group decision making, in: *Communication and Group Decision Making*, R. Y. Hirokawa and M. S. Poole eds., Sage, Thousand Oaks, CA, pp. 19–51.

George, J. F., and Carlson, J. R., 1999, Group support systems and deceptive communication, in: *Proceedings of the 32nd Annual Hawaii International Conference on System Sciences*, IEEE, CD ROM.

Hiltz, S. R., Dufner, D., Holmes, M., and Poole, S., 1991, Distributed group support systems: Social dynamics and design dilemmas, *Journal of Organizational Computing*, **2**: 135.

Hoffer, J. A., and Valacich, J. S., 1993, Group memory in group support systems: A foundation for design, in *Group Support Systems: New Perspective*, L. M. Jessup and J. S. Valacich eds., Macmillan, New York, pp. 214–229.

Hollingshead, A. B., McGrath, J. E., and O'Connor, K. M., 1993, Group task performance and communication technology: A longitudinal study of computer-mediated versus face-to-face work groups, *Small Group Research*, **24**: 307.

Horton, M., and Biolsi, K., 1993–94, Coordination challenges in a computer-supported meeting environment, *Journal of Management Information Systems*, **10**: 7.

Johnson, J. J., 1999, A field study of partially distributed group support, in: *Proceedings of the 32nd Annual Hawaii International Conference on System Sciences*, IEEE, CD ROM.

McGrath, J. E., and Hollingshead, A. B., 1993, Putting the "group" back in group support systems: Some theoretical issues about dynamic processes in groups with technological enhancements, in: *Group Support Systems: New Perspective,* L. M. Jessup and J. S. Valacich eds., Macmillan, New York, pp. 78–96.

Mennecke, B. E., Valacich, J. S., and Wheeler, B. C., 2000, The effects of media and task on user performance: A test of the task-media fit hypothesis, *Group Decision and Negotiation,* **9**: 507.

Murthy, U. S., and Kerr, D. S., 2000, Task/technology fit and the effectiveness of group support systems: Evidence in the context of tasks requiring domain specific knowledge, in: *Proceedings of the 33rd Annual Hawaii International Conference on System Sciences,* IEEE, CD ROM.

Nunamaker, J. F., Dennis, A. R., Valacich, J. S., Vogel, D. R., and George, J. F, 1993, Group support systems research: Experience from the lab and field, in *Group Support Systems: New Perspective,* L. M. Jessup and J. S. Valacich eds., Macmillan, New York, pp. 125–145.

Ocker, R., Hiltz, S. R., Turoff, M., and Fjermestad, J., 1995–1996, The effects of distributed group support and process structuring on software requirements development teams: Results on creativity and quality, *Journal of Management Information Systems,* **12**: 127.

Olson, J., and Teasley, S., 1996, Groupware in the wild: Lessons learned from a year of virtual collocation, in: *Proceedings of the ACM Conference on Computer-Supported Cooperative Work (CSCW'96)*, The ACM, pp. 419–427.

Pervan, G. P., 1998, A review of research of group support systems: Leaders, approaches and directions, *Decision Support Systems,* **23**: 149.

Rana, A. R., Turoff, M., and Hiltz, S. R., 1997, Task and technology interaction (TTI): A theory of technological support for group tasks, in: *Proceedings of the 30th Annual Hawaii International Conference of System Sciences*, IEEE, pp. 66–75.

Schmidt, K., and Simone, C., 1996, Coordination mechanisms: Towards a conceptual foundation of CSCW system design, *Computer Supported Cooperative Work,* **5**: 155.

Shirani, A. I., Tafti, M. H. A., and Affisco, J. F., 1999, Task and technology fit: A comparison of two technologies for synchronous and asynchronous group communication, *Information & Management,* **36**: 139.

Straus, S. G., and McGrath, J. E., 1994, Does the medium matter? the interaction of task type and technology on group performance and member reactions, *Journal of Applied Psychology,* **79**: 87.

Suh, K. S., 1999, Impact of communication medium on task performance and satisfaction: An examination of media-richness theory, *Information & Management,* **35**: 295.

Yoon, K. P., and Hwang, C.-L., 1995, *Multicriteria Attribute Decision Making: An Introduction.* Sage, Thousand Oaks, CA.

Zigurs, I., and Buckland, B. K., 1998, A theory of task/technology fit and group support systems effectiveness. *MIS Quarterly,* **22**: 313.

Zigurs, I., Buckland, B. K., Connolly, J. R., and Wilson, E. V., 1999, A task of task-technology fit theory for group support systems, *DATA BASE,* **30**: 34.

WHISPERS FROM A DISCOURSE

Digital television in Australia

Cate Dowd*

1. INTRODUCTION

The digitization of Australian television is situated in a context of emerging contemporary digital technologies. Traditional free-to-air television services in Australia in the early phases of digitization at the start of the 21st century have involved controversial and costly developments especially for transmission infrastructure and digital reception devices.

This paper highlights important strategic developments for digital broadcasting in Australia, including the sale of Australia's national transmission infrastructure, as a formative stage of development that had to precede the possibility of any new values associated with spectrum, which are anticipated by the Australian Government by 2006. However, within less than two years of the Australian Government, the Australian Broadcasting Corporation (ABC) and an international company, with a three-letter name, signing a fifteen-year contract for transmission services, the contract was broken as the new owner/operator sold their "unprofitable" Australian investments to a major bank

Several new types of services and standards that enable digital broadcasting are identified in this paper with brief discussions about technical characteristics including aspect ratios, visual dimensions, streaming media and the capacity for multi-channels, the latter notably offered by the ABC for a limited period between 2002–2003. Digital content development issues are introduced, in particular via emerging cultural production means. The standards for enabling digital broadcasting technologies provide insight for the release of digital reception devices as evolutionary "versions", in spite of open systems.

Although a requirement for HDTV in Australia has created a serious problem, this paper places a focus on the sale and resale of the national transmission infrastructure network, particularly as it raises competing public and private interests that continue to require better knowledge management and discussion that is not "closed". This complex arena of digital broadcasting can be partly understood via technical perspectives, but its multidisciplinary nature suggests that knowledge is only a whisper from any given discourse, and simply cannot be available to any discourse where information itself is not available.

---

* Cate Dowd is an Academic in the Department of Information Systems at the University of Melbourne, Australia, with a Master of Information and Management Systems thesis via Monash University.

2. DECODING FREE-TO-AIR DIGITAL TELEVISION IN AUSTRALIA

The advent of digital television in Australia is perhaps just another application of digital technology, but its impact has not reached the consumer. At the start of the 21st century advances in computing power and communication methods, including the world-wide web, have spawned ubiquitous technologies and platforms such as mobile video phones and wireless lap-taps, which have been tagged with a euphoric "anywhere, any time" identity. By contrast, the television remains a reliable piece of analogue technology that sits in the corner of a living room in homes throughout the world, yet it has emerging digital characteristics and a potential for *connectivity* that could transform the traditions of television.

The progress of "digital television" is a complex and dynamic arena that is still being understood even by those who dare to embrace theory and practice and "read (almost) everything and know all the institutions and practices" (Foucault, 1970, p. 262). Understanding the *invisible* qualities of the *visible* medium of television is best matched with a belief in an emergence of "that which cannot yet be seen, but that which will be guaranteed by a commercial deal".

Digital Free-to-air television (FTA) services, such as those offered by the Australian Broadcasting Corporation (ABC) can be distributed as Digital Terrestrial Television (DTTV), although transmission in regional areas and retransmission may involve satellite and cable systems. Various broadcasting standards for Australia are regulated by a broadcasting authority based in Geneva[1] and include standards across three tiers of broadcasting, from production and transmission to digital reception devices.

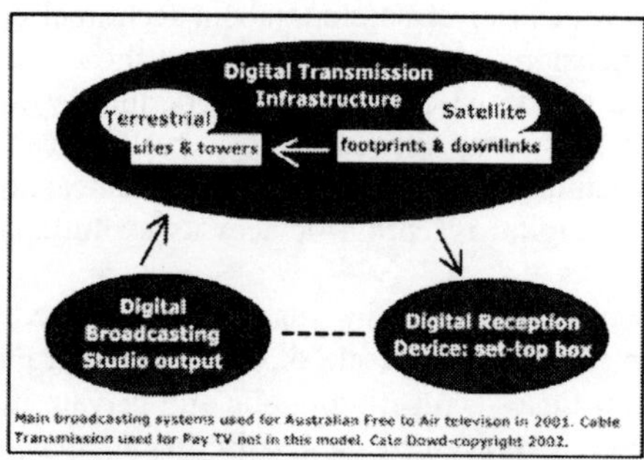

Figure 1. The flow of signals between studio, transmission facilities and reception devices. The broken line represents a potential flow for interactive services.

---

1 Standards set by the Digital Video Broadcasting organisation (DVB) can be recognized by the acronyms of the committees working with particular standards, such as DVB-C (cable), DVB-S (satellite) and DVB-T (terrestrial). "The DVB (Digital Video Broadcasting Project) is an industry-led consortium of over 300 broadcasters, manufacturers, network operators, software developers, regulatory bodies and others in over 35 countries committed to designing global standards for the delivery of digital television and data services" (http://www.dvb.org/latest.html, 2002)

Some early developments in Australia for digital broadcasting services began with negotiations for digital transmission facilities involving the ABC, the Australian Government and the private sector. Various strategies for digital services actually began as early as 1996 (including satellite developments) and were followed by the Digital Conversion Act of 1998,[2] which marked a major turning point for television systems and technologies that included a controversial change of ownership of Australia's National Transmission Network.

The rollout of terrestrial digital transmitters across Australia is not due in regional Australia until 2004,[3] however there is still a need for quality dialogue. The important issues involve the future of spectrum and directions for transforming flawed legislation, which continue to imply high costs for Australian consumers, even though services remain some distance from most Australians.

3. THE VALUE OF TRANSMISSION TOWERS AND SPECTRUM

Complete digital broadcasting services in Australia are anticipated by 2008[4] at which time analogue signals should cease. However the potential of progressive interactive services may be dominated by spectrum issues including management and the commercial value of spectrum which is likely to emerge before 2006 (see ABA timeline) when new broadcasting services could begin.

In early 1999 the Australian Government sold Australia's network of Commonwealth Transmission Towers,[5] which passed almost without notice. In July 1999 the Australian Broadcasting Authority (ABA) published technical plans for approaches to Digital Terrestrial Television Broadcasting, which included digital channel plans (DCP)[6] for the nation. Then, from mid 2000 until January 2001 transmitters and digital signals for the ABC were tested in a period of consolidation. The digital rollout was bestowed upon an international company, which made Australia's national broadcasting infrastructure an object of international corporate whim, resulting in unexpected issues for Australian broadcasting and the Australian Government, matters which are discussed later in this paper.

Digital compression technologies have already enabled multi-channels in Australia however the potential for other new broadcasting services, including a new usage of spectrum,[7] could not begin to be achieved without digital infrastructure systems in place.

An ethos of "profits" from broadcasting appears to have begun with a "loan" approach for FTA broadcasters for spectrum, matched by "payments" to the

[2] See the Digital Conversion Act at http://scaleplus.law.gov.au/html/pasteact/2/3156/0/PA000070.htm

[3] The ABA (Australian Broadcasting Authority) timeline for digital television is located at http://www.aba.gov.au/tv/digitaltv/industry/timeline.htm

[4] See ABA timeline at http://www.aba.gov.au/tv/digitaltv/industry/timeline.htm

[5] The sale of Australia's national transmission network took place in March 1999 and is listed in the government asset sales register located at http://www.finance.gov.au/assetsales/Website_Information__Asset_Sa/website_information_-_asset_sa.htm

[6] Details of UHF & VHF channel assignment numbers are located at the Australian Broadcasting Authority's web site at http://www.aba.gov.au/tv/digitaltv/industry/timeline.htm

[7] Issues on the sale of spectrum as noted by the Productivity Commission are contained in section IV of the Productivity Commission's Inquiry into Broadcasting Report on "Opening up the Spectrum", located at http://www.pc.gov.au/inquiry/broadcst/finalreport/index.html

Government for particular "usage" of digital technology for multiple streams, or datacasting, as outlined by the productivity commission.[8] The new approach to spectrum issues, as a *commodity,* does not seem to offer any guarantees for "public" broadcasting or genuine alternative services beyond 2006.

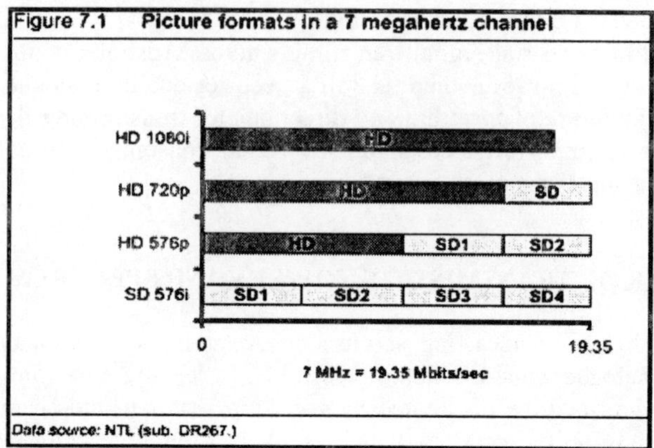

Figure 2. Possible multi-channels within a 7 MHz channel. Source: Productivity Commission[9] – copyright Commonwealth of Australia reproduced by permission.

In a transition period broadcasters may not be concerned about future competitors, as they are pre-occupied by immediate problems. The potential use of a given digital channel appears to be a technical choice between offering a few alternative services or offering varying degrees of high definition quality images via a single channel, however legislation partly determines how broadcasters should use their allocated 7MHz of spectrum. The problems then involve oscillations between Standard Definition Television (SDTV) and High Definition Television (HDTV) that are bound in "legislation". The problem is really HDTV and a quota requirement of around 20 hours of HDTV per week for FTA broadcasters, which involves high costs for production and consumption.[10] As noted by the Productivity Commission, "Australia has mandated a unique, high cost system" (See Productivity Commission's Broadcasting Enquiry Report Executive Summaries p.15).

Even if high definition images benefit some existing media players, the HDTV requirement continues to thwart the progress of digital television especially for set-top box manufacturing and investment in creative content. In addition, progress is impeded

---

[8] A payment for spectrum ethos is evident in the Productivity Commission's Enquiry into Broadcasting Report, with a note on spectrum being "lent" to broadcasters on p.199, located at http://www.pc.gov.au/inquiry/broadcst/finalreport/chapter06.pdf

[9] Extract from the Broadcasting Enquiry Report p 228 located at http://www.pc.gov.au/inquiry/broadcst/finalreport/chapter07.pdf

[10] Consumers need a wide-screen television in order to view HDTV. However only a limited number of hours of HDTV are offered, which is little incentive to buy an expensive wide-screen television.

by the uncertainty of standards and products for *more* or *less* interactive services in a complex and risky cycle of developments.

4. DIGITAL CONTENT FOR TELEVISION AND MULTI-CHANNELS

Digital content in a high definition format can offer a wide screen image with an aspect ratio of 16:9 compared to a standard television aspect ratio of 4:3, the latter fitting into the traditional space of 'the box'. Most content for television has been filmed in a standard format and until substantially new content is shot in 16:9 the old 4:3 standard dominates the broadcasting screen. Even if consumers buy a wide screen television, broadcasters are only producing and purchasing a limited amount of content in wide-screen and 'live' television is the cheapest to produce.

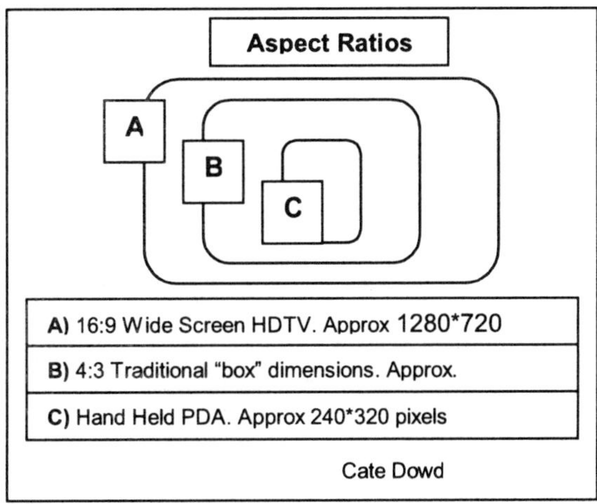

Figure 3. Comparative aspect ratios that indicate different "frame" dimensions for content deployed across multiple platforms, highlighting 'design' problems in terms of physical space differences.

In 2003 the visual dimensions via wide screen television, as experienced by a privileged few, show more variations in size than the traditional "box" as noted by Hillery in a review of the first set-top box for Australia (Hillery, 2002). Although the visible "seams" of digital television may last for years, they are not intentional. The variations in picture size exist even in the wide screen environment, even without a set-top box, however a digital reception device is still necessary to experience the emerging features of digital broadcasting services. A set-top box, or a digital television, can enable new services offered by FTA broadcasters including one-way interactivity[11]

[11] Multi-camera angles are used in several Australian programs notably by channel 10 Sports. See http://www.ten.com.au/main_idx.aspx?section=digitalTV

and multi-channel services, the latter offered for a brief period by the ABC as per legislation.[12]

The ABC multi-channels between 2002-2003 consisted of two streams on a limited basis, including a children's television channel called ABCKids™, and a youth stream called Fly™ TV.[13] The services were also available as retransmissions via Pay TV, including OPTUS channel 37 and AUSTAR Channel 14, however the ABC cut these services in June 2003, due to funding problems.

Multi-channels are a "natural" alternative use of bandwidth that provide a means for specialized content for targeted audiences. Multi-channels also suggest fragmented markets, which will not necessarily benefit commercial broadcasters. By contrast, public broadcasters could have an opportunity to meet "community' obligations in new ways via multi-channels.

In order to generate progressive digital content scripts need to go beyond "conjuring up a fictional person or persons" (Ong, 1982, p.177) as a convention of linear narrative, indeed scripts need to be revised in the context of the new medium. Non-linear scripts used for interactive games are unlikely to be appropriate for digital television as interactivity via television is recognized as 'lazy interactivity', as coined by Bernoff (Krebs, 2000, pp. 4–5), and partly due to its history as a passive medium. Nonetheless, as sophisticated set-top boxes and hybrid peripheral devices, such as small keyboards progress, functionality for multi-media content involving 'input and output modalities for visual, auditory, and tactile interfaces' (Elsom-Cook, 2001, p.132–134) is likely to increase.

Television ideas continue to be "reliant on scripts for story-telling and the development of characters" (Nielson, 1997) but new approaches to content have begun via strategic partnerships, including the Australian Film Commission (AFC) and the ABC.[14] Although these developments have been for a "broadband" context they also act as a testing base for interactive television and are designed to "ensure that Australian audiences and user groups have access to a range of Australian content" (Dalton, 2002). These initiatives may have cultural significance in so far as they provide opportunities for extending understanding of mediated communication via broadcasting in the 21st century, extending a 'Secondary Orality'[15] of the earlier electronic age (Ong, 1982, p.136), into contemporary cultural spaces and communications.

At the end of the 20th century broadcast media used high levels of "syndicated" services, which resulted in limited "local" production. For a major cultural organisation such as the ABC the 'syndicated' approach could only diminish "reflections of Australian communities" (see the ABC charter on representation of diverse communities[16]), but digital systems presented an opportunity to optimize network resources. Some early ideas included "regional radio networks using digital cameras for new local content" (Johns, 2001, pc), a production approach that goes beyond the

---

[12] See http://www.aba.gov.au/tv/digitaltv/index.htm

[13] See: http://abc.net.au/flytv/

[14] The ABC and the AFC in June 2002 formed a partnership for a broadband production initiative. Press release details are located at http://www.abc.net.au/corp/pubs/s574441.htm

[15] Ong refers to the telephone, radio and television age as belonging to a culture of "Secondary Orality", which has "striking resemblances to the old in its participatory mystique, its fostering of a communal sense, its concentration on the present moment and even its formulas" (Ong, p.136)

[16] See http://scaleplus.law.gov.au/html/histact/10/5029/0/HA000100.htm for the ABC charter.

limits of regional television studios, as the ABC operates more regional radio stations than television studios.

5. INFORMATION SYSTEMS FOR DIGITAL RECEPTION DEVICES

Digital television involves multiple standards that will impact on the information and content available at the interface of digital television. In the forthcoming decade a hybrid "viewer", even if not a conventional "user" may emerge as the viewer/user functionality progresses via specifications for devices beyond reception devices.

The Industry agreed standards for a free-to-air digital reception device is based on the DVB Multimedia Home Platform[17] system architecture, commonly referred to as the MHP. Some MHP compliant set-top boxes were manufactured during 2001 and by early 2002 a third set-top box[18] was available on the Australian market. However each box had different levels of functionality.[19]

The MHP even though it is an *open* set of standards, may be used for progressive stages of manufacturing closed "version" based devices for targeted markets. "Versioning" involves strategies for the "delay" and "release" of products (Shapiro and Varian, p.53–57) and factors that might add or detract value to products, as recognized in "different capabilities for different versions of a core product such as that seen in software development" (Shapiro and Varian, p.58–75).

The closed systems developed for Pay TV[20] are a contrast to the MHP standards which are "open" to change and "technological convergence" involving protocols of the World Wide Web and other standards that are transformed for Free-to-air broadcasting applications. Closed systems also have a potential for redundancy.

The MHP documents provide insights into the potential of digital television via the MHP system architecture, protocols, scripting and standards for interoperability. The basic system architecture indicates a relationship between the MHP system, which is akin to an operating system, and an MHP application in which there are three core application areas based on profiles, for either 'enhanced broadcasting, interactive broadcasting, or internet access' (DVB MHP 1.2.1, 2003, p. 55). Each profile actually consists of two levels in order to accommodate evolutionary stages of the standards, affirming the potential for "versioning" and the possible evolution of a hybrid viewer/user.

Digital broadcasting has so far limited its use of content coming together in the same screen space, however streaming provides wider choices for the future. A television production that successfully utilized streams for interactive content was the BBC documentary "Walking with Beasts". It contained digital features such as

---

17 The draft MHP1.0 was published in July 2000 by ETSI[17] (European Telecommunications Standards Institute). Works in progress related to MHP can be located via http://pda.etsi.org/pda/queryform.asp

18 The DGTEC model includes operability for HDTV, surround sound, multiple views, closed captions and other features. See http://www.dg-tec.com.au/homepage.html for specifications.

19 See Hillery p 37-40 on Thompson's first Set-top Box for Australia. The storage capacity in subsequent boxes enabled only simple "enhancements". DGTEC's box in early 2002 had 16 Mbytes of Flash Memory and a 32-bit RISC CPU.

20 Closed systems might include Liberate technologies for interactive solutions for television operators including AOL TV (America on Line and Time Warner) for cable services, and Open TV standards or Canal+ Technologies.

resizable video windows and alternative narrative streams. This level of functionality is possible due to the communication channels and other protocols[21] of an MHP system and the networks that the system connects with (MHP 1.1, p. 55), particularly for interactivity and Internet connectivity. An important protocol is the broadcast channel protocol based on a "user to user object carousel" (DVB MHP 1.2.1, p. 483), which enables the retrieval of programs via transmission streams and downloads (see Figure 4).

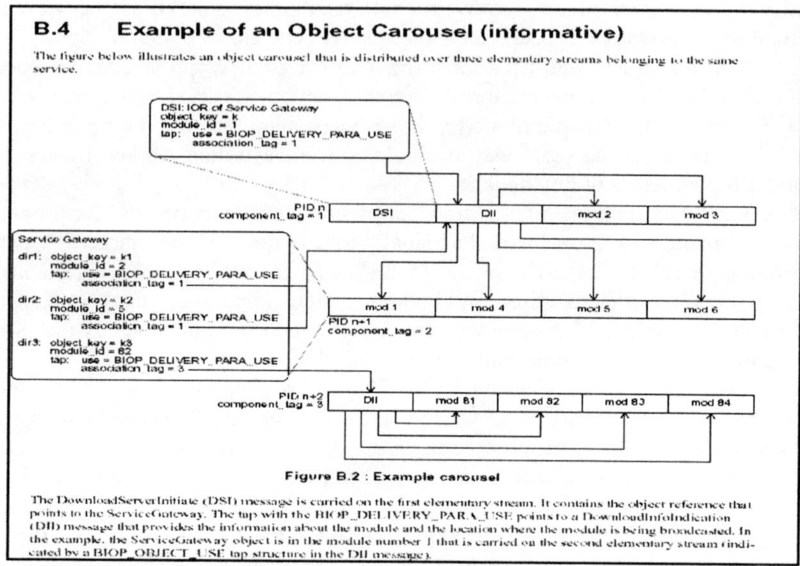
B.4 Example of an Object Carousel (informative)

The figure below illustrates an object carousel that is distributed over three elementary streams belonging to the same service.

Figure B.2 : Example carousel

The DownloadServerInitiate (DSI) message is carried on the first elementary stream. It contains the object reference that points to the ServiceGateway. The tap with the BIOP_DELIVERY_PARA_USE points to a DownloadInfoIndication (DII) message that provides the information about the module and the location where the module is being broadcasted. In the example, the ServiceGateway object is in the module number 1 that is carried on the second elementary stream (indicated by a BIOP_OBJECT_USE tap structure in the DII message).

Figure 4. An example of an object carousel using three streams for programs as set by the DVB-MHP standard. Programs belonging to the same service can be identified, located and availability determined, and "download" messages initiated. © ETSI 2003. Further use, modification, redistribution is strictly prohibited. The standards are available from http://pda.etsi.org/pda/, and http://www.etsi.org/eds/.

The broadcast protocols illustrated in figure 4.1 apply across all three profiles of an MHP system, which means it is mandatory (DVB MHP 1.1, p. 364) for all digital receiver products, whether basic or advanced, to use these, and other specified protocols, if they are to conform to MHP standards. Such uniformity is critical for broadcast content to be retrieved, alongside uniform metadata standards, and appropriate input devices for retrieval.

The capacity of the MHP is remarkable in that it is designed to be hardware independent, and the systems use of 'user agents' (or support applications) within multiple areas of the MHP specifications is the technical base of communications[22],

[21] The MPEG 2 Transport stream is the common standard for all profiles of an MHP system, whether it is for enhanced, interactive or Internet profiles. See the broadcast Channel Protocol stack on page 56 and the platform profile definitions on p.362 of the MHP 1.1 draft document via http://pda.etsi.org/pda/queryform.asp

[22] An "actor" communicates the "runtime" of applications between a user agent and the API. See page 73 of the DVB-MHP 1.1 document via http://pda.etsi.org/pda/queryform.asp

enabling the system to function across a variety of platforms. Theoretically, these features nudge Digital television into the euphoric zone of "anywhere, anytime" technologies of the early 21st century, but one hesitates to put digital television in a contemporary basket of ubiquitous digital toys.

6. THE SALE AND RESALE OF AUSTRALIA'S NATIONAL BROADCASTING TRANSMISSION INFRASTRUCTURE

The Digital Transmission infrastructure changes for Australia were evident in The Digital Conversion Act of 1998.[23] During 1997 The Department of Communications and the Arts (DOCA) began to implement a series of strategies that changed the role of the National Transmission Authority (NTA),[24] who were the central agency of the government for administration of Commonwealth broadcasting transmission facilities, administering contracts for a network of Broadcasting Towers and sites located all over Australia, notably used by the ABC and of other broadcasters for a modest fee.

By December 2000 The National Transmission Network was sold to an international company, by the brief name of "Ntl". Ntl entered into a contract[25] for 15 years with the Australian Government and the ABC for the provision of digital transmission services. They would own and operate the national transmission network, previously controlled by the Commonwealth government agent, the NTA. The management of Ntl in Australia were pleased with a long-term contract to deliver digital broadcasting for Australia.

> Ntl's services to the ABC covering a whole network of analogue TV and radio and digital television transmission services, is probably the largest out-sourced transmission contract in the world. (Ntl, 2000)

The sale of broadcasting assets has been a key feature of entry into digital broadcasting in several countries and continues to present risks for "national-public" services that depend on large networks now operated by private operators with primary interests in making profits. Companies such as "Ntl" generate their revenue from a range of media related services at several international levels and the provision of digital transmission services in Australia was just one of Ntl's services. Ntl's expansion into telecommunications[26] via global satellite operators may have meant possibilities beyond transmission services, but any benefits for interactive services in Australian broadcasting would not be realized.

To the amazement of only a few observers, in the middle of 2001 an Australian newspaper reported that, "transmission specialist Ntl, is bedeviled with old technology . . .and crippling debts of almost $40 billion" (Day, 2001). By the end of 2001 Ntl announced a series of 'cost cutting initiatives' (Ntl, Dec 2001).

[23] See http://scaleplus.law.gov.au/html/pasteact/2/3156/0/PA000070.htm

[24] The National Transmission Authority later became known as the NTN (National Transmission Network).

[25] The contract appears to be inaccessible for "Commercial in Confidence" reasons.

[26] In early 2001 Ntl entered into contracts with Cable & Wireless Optus for satellite downlink services for the ABC's regional services in Australia (Ntl. 2001, ref 24).

In February 2002 Ntl announced that it would sell its Australian broadcast business for $850 million dollars to Macquarie Bank and focus on its core business in Europe (Ntl, Feb 2002).

7. CONCLUSION

Australian public broadcasters such as the ABC and the Specialist Broadcasting Service (SBS)[27] who are dependent on "private" infrastructure for transmission services appear to have only benefited in the short term for commencement of digital broadcasting services. The costs to the public for digitisation seem high for *something* that is barely *visible* or *accessible* to the average consumer. The change of ownership of former Commonwealth transmission infrastructure suggests problems for sustainability, which must not transfer to public broadcasters, who have the least capacity to address business solutions, should a situation of rising costs related to infrastructure occur in the future.

Broadcasters, and the Australian public, need to remain vigilant about the nation's broadcasting issues. Likewise, the forthcoming sale of spectrum in Australia should be "open" to at least industry experts in order to understand the potential problems, however the use of "Commercial in Confidence"[28] clauses in contracts, as applied to the National Transmission Network negotiations, could barely be regarded as effective "knowledge management" of Australian *public* assets, whether visible or invisible. A "closed" approach to key issues of digitisation of Australian Broadcasting makes any epistemology of significant contemporary "technological progress" less than a whisper from any discourse, but Information Systems may provide a starting point for some clarity and comprehension of the issues.

REFERENCES

Australian Broadcasting Authority, 2002, Timeline for Digital Television implementation, (2002); http://www.aba.gov.au/tv/digitaltv/industry/timeline.htm

Australian Broadcasting Authority, 1998, Television Broadcasting Services (Digital Conversion) Act 1998, (Retrieved 2001); http://www.aba.gov.au/tv/digitaltv/legislation/

A.B.C., 2000, *Going Digital.* (Retrieved June 2000); www.abc.net.au/digital/

A.G.P.S., 1994, *Style Manual*, Fifth Edition, Australian Government Publishing Service. Canberra. p 165.

Dalton, K., 2002, 5 June, AFC and ABC New Media announce Broadband Production Initiatives,. ABC press release (Retrieved July 2002); http://www.abc.net.au/corp/pubs/s574441.htm

Day M., 2001, 5 July, Ridgy-digital TV, *The Australian IT.*

D.C.I.T.A., Department of Communications, Information Technology and the Arts, 2000, Digital Broadcasting,. (August 2000); http://www.dcita.gov.au

---

[27] SBS entered into a contract with Ntl in July 2000 in order to extend its "analogue" services to regional Australia, using the national infrastructure as a means of extending its services beyond metropolitan areas. See Press Release from ntl web site 17 July 2000 ref:92 http://www.ntl.com/locales/au/en/media/press/locate.asp?yearlist=2000

[28] Commercial-in-Confidence has been described as " a confidentiality provision, which enables companies to put details of research and development, tenders or other deals off limits to both public and parliament. It doesn't have to be approved, but once it's applied, any flow of information abruptly ceases and appeals can result in long, drawn-out legal battles" (Pelly, 1999). This quote was published by Aid Watch, but was no longer available via the web at the time of writing this paper.

DVB Digital Video Broadcasting, 2002-2003, Digital Video Broadcasting (DVB);Multimedia Home Platform (MHP) Specification V1.1.(withdrawn) and V1.2.1. (revised June 2003); http://pda.etsi.org/pda/queryform.asp

Elsom-Cook, M., 2001, *Principles of Interactive Multimedia*, McGraw-Hill, UK. p.132–134

Foucault, M., 1970, *The Order of Things. An archaeology of the human sciences*, Routledge. London.

Gillchrist, M. ,2000, (November 25-26, 2000). Rescue deal for digital TV boxes, *The Australian*. p 1.

Gillchrist, M. and Shanahan, D., October 11, 2000, TV's not ready in time for digital, *The Australian*. p. 3.

Hillery A. ,2001, The Box Seat, in: *Sound and Image*. Hillery A., ed., Horwitz Publications. St Leonards NSW, pp. 37–40.

Johns, B., 2001. Former Managing Director of the ABC & Academic, pc.

Krebs P. et al., 2000, *Building Interactive Entertainment and E-Commerce Content for Microsoft TV*, Microsoft Corporation. USA. pp.4–5

Mackenzie, K., 2001, (24 July) Interactive TV battle heats up, *The Australian IT*.

Mitchell, S. and Grayson, I., 2001, (9 January), Public Tunes out to Digital Set-top Boxes, *The Australian*, p. 25.

Neuman L., 2000, *Social Research Methods: Qualitative and Quantitative Approaches*. Allyn & Bacon, Boston.

Negroponte, N., 1995, *Being Digital*, London, UK: Hodder and Stoughton.

Nielson, J., 1997, TV meets the Web, (July 2002); www.useit.com/alertbox/9702b.html

Ntl Group., 2000, Broadcast, (October 16, 2000); www.ntl.com

Ntl Group, 2001, Ntl wins Cable & Wireless Optus ABC TV contract for satellite downlink services Ref 24. Press. (February 2001); http://www.ntl.com/mediacentre/press/

Ntl Group, 2001, NTL announces series of cost cutting initiatives, Press. (10 December 2001); http://www.ntl.com/mediacentre/press/

Ntl. Group, 2002, NTL to sell Australian Broadcast Business for A$850 million, Ref 8. Press. (21 February 2002); http://www.ntl.com/mediacentre/press/

Ong, W., 1982, *Orality & Literacy: The Technologizing of the Word*, Routledge. London.

O'Regan, M., 2000, The Outlook for Public Broadcasting, is it Bright or Bleak? (Part 2). Media Report, Australian Broadcasting Corporation, (October 12, 2000);http://www.abc.net.au/rn

Pelly J., 1999, Commercial in Confidence and the rise of Secret Government. (Retrieved 2001); http://www.aidwatch.org.au/news/18/12.htm. This article was inaccessible at time of print.

Productivity Commission, April 11, 2000, Productivity Commission's Inquiry into Broadcasting. (2002); http://www.pc.gov.au/inquiry/broadcst/index.html

Shapiro, C. and Varian, HR., 1999, *Information Rules*. Harvard Business School Press. Massachusetts.

Shulze, J., July 2001, Aunty First off the mark, *The Australian IT*.

Schulze, J., June 2002, Year of living digitally, *The Australian*, p 7

Note: The abbreviation "pc" has been used in this paper noting personal communication, which would otherwise be stated as pers comm. The expert cited here was interviewed in 2001 by the author.

WALKING THE WALK OF eTEACHING AND eLEARNING:

Enhancing teaching and learning using the new technologies

Dr Josie Arnold *

ABSTRACT

Today, the overarching goal of all Universities is to develop excellence in flexible eLearning and eTeaching. Such excellence grows from and upon the rich offerings of traditional teaching and learning: it is not opposed to it. This paper investigates some of the opportunities offered by the multimedia experiences of cyberlearning and embeds those in traditional learning and teaching experiences. In doing so it utilises feminist postmodernist techniques, particularly that of telling the unfocussed story that is a descriptive narrative wandering across the text.

Just as print led to universal education and the distribution of information which could be utilised as knowledge and even wisdom, so electronic information systems deliveries are influencing our educational deliveries not only content-wise but also conceptually. This paper takes an overview of the resultant social, cultural and educational issues from the story of teaching over 3,000 undergraduate and postgraduate students over 7 years using and developing a "Quadripartite System of eTeaching and eLearning" involving a balance in virtual reality/cyberspace of people, print, WWW and CD Rom. (Arnold and Vigo, 1996)

1. INTRODUCTION

The major aspect of online deliveries that academics need to explore is the alteration in mindset that needs to occur if the dynamic nature of online teaching and learning is truly to be explored. The dominance of print upon the western mindset has been well documented. Less well acknowledged is the reliance the academy places upon the various templates that have developed in the academic teaching and learning processes that have

* Dr Josie Arnold, Principal Lecturer, Writing, Media and Multimedia, Swinburne University of Technology, Lilydale Campus, Locked Bag 218, Lilydale Vic 3140, Australia. jarnold@swin.edu.au. Phone: 613 9215 7147, Fax: 613 9215 7070, isd2003@sims.monash.edu.au. 2003

occurred within those frameworks. The most obvious of these is the focus upon a sortive, taxonomic and epistemological framework which is as identifiable in the PhD process as in the first year one.

It is these spaces which interest me theoretically. This involves an understanding of the practical implications of such areas of critical and cultural theory as: rhizomatic text (Deleuze and Guattari, 1981); mystories (Ulmer, 1989); writerly-reading (Derrida, 1978); signs and signification (Barthes, 1977); feminist theories (Cixous; Irigary, 1989; Kristeva; Flax); curriculum discourse (Giroux, 1990); orderly disorder (Hayles, 1991.); the tyranny of philosophy on Western thought (Lyotard); metaphor and thought (Miller, 1982); text and context: construction and deconstruction (Poovey, 1988); cultural ideologies (Spivak, 1988); social semiotics (Scholes); Australian cultural construction (White, 1981); globalisation (Waters, 1995); cartographies (Benterrick et al., 1984); teaching theories and practices. (Arnold and Vigo, 1996); and textuality and discourse in the emergent electronic culture. (Arnold and Vigo, 1996). This paper is written as an exploration of such alternative research textuality and discourse in its own presentation as well as content.

2. TURNING INFORMATION INTO KNOWLEDGE

As teachers and learners, we are involved in the growth and development of knowledge for ourselves, our students, the Academy and the broader community. It may be said that knowledge takes information and makes it our own. A less tangible asset than information, knowledge makes information useful to the individual and to the group, to the culture and to its organisations. Whilst knowledge is encultured, it also transcends the culturisation process, for it offers the opportunity to make something new and personal from information. (Wang and Sleeman, 1993)

Each of us as individuals comes to understand information in a different way from the way in which it is first presented to us. (Willets, 1992) We take aspects of information and put them together again in new and essentially individual ways. In this way, knowledge becomes revolutionary use of information; an aspect of change and personal and cultural development. Information that becomes knowledge can develop attributes of wisdom from the people who make up our culture and enable it to change and develop rather than to stand still. (Ahn-Sook, 1996, 384–350)

If we value information and knowledge and its capacity to build human wisdom, then we must value people and not just information systems. Students learn well when they relate concepts to real-life activities and experiences. (Cunningham et al., 1993, 24) At the same time, we should not ignore new knowledge systems. We must endeavour to see cybertools as complementary to the human dimensions of knowledge in the same ways as print has contributed literacy to oral knowledge processes. This means considering how students and teachers can construct multimedia learning experiences, scenarios or complex models. (Hackbarth, 1996, 23; Milheim, 1993, 171.)

The teachers' roles in this are central to the facilitation of the students' learning journeys. Constructions of knowledge and wisdom by the individual student are developed through the co-construction of the teachers' interactions with them and the curricula. The freedom and flexibility of their own learning journeys means that they can express their own ideas, responses and cognition and reflect upon them. (Friere, 1970; Gardner, 1993, 357–358; Kauchak and Egan, 1998, 184–188)

There are, in this context, two givens we may consider: one is that information is not knowledge. Think about how the print based library offered information that could be turned into knowledge. The great libraries of the past and present offer us a useful analogy for the WWW and its endless information sources which have easy and immediate access for those who are able to go online.

The other given is that the past influences the present. Although the new technologies are a deeming cultural moment, they do not totally displace what has gone before. In education, this means that the people and print that have underpinned our pedagogy are still part of an enriched on and off campus experience. Learning has long been seen to be something other than pouring from the big bucket to the small thimble. Passive recipients are not learners, they are replicators. (Lander et al., 1995; Schank and Cleary, 1994) This is as true of learning and teaching in the virtual reality spaces of the cyber as it is the geographic reality spaces of the traditional.

3. THE PAST LEADS TO THE PRESENT

We come to this present period of the emergent electronic culture from a long period in Western society which we have nominated "literacy". This period took us away from the vis-à-vis of the preceding period which we call "oracy". For example, it took us away from producing Shakespeare live on stage to "The Collected Works" and from the chained Bible interpreted by the priest in the church to the international best seller available to all readers. It emphasised the power of knowledge and of information and legitimised a "master narrative". (Orner, 1992)

Print endeavoured to rise above the necessity of presence for communication to occur. In doing so it provided the basis for Western culture to become the dominant culture of the late 20th century. This occurred because the local became able to move into the national and the international. Now cybertexts are moving it into the global and the new virtual but nevertheless real arena of cyberspace.

Some contributing factors to the production of the dominant Western Culture (Lines, 1994; Braudel, 1986; Cocker, 1999) that underpins cyberspace include: Western European colonisation between the 16th and 20th centuries of much of the globe; the western alphabet of 26 figures has led to the easy representation of ideas, stories and directions in moveable type; the success of the development of print itself has been supported by the development of machinery; the publication of multiple copies of specialist books; mass education; the dispersal of knowledge throughout all groups in the community; many specialist scientific and instructional texts are written in English; the industrial revolution occurred in Europe and especially in England as a powerful force in the reconstruction of culture from agriculturally-based to industrially-based; the introduction of writing machines (the typewriter, telegraph, word-processors) that preceded more sophisticated computers; and the transference of wealth from the Americas to Europe. This material world has provided us with the bases of the world of Interactive Multi Media, which I call "The IMMaterial world of cyberspace". It also prefigures Western cultural dominance of that space.

4. TOWARDS AN ELECTRONIC PEDAGOGY: THE QUADRIPARTITE METHOD OF TEACHING AND LEARNING

The "Quadripartite model of teaching and learning" has as its four component parts the traditional or virtual reality of "people" and "print" and the new electronic technologies of the "WWW" and "CD ROM". The relationship of the learner with the teacher is always complex and personal. Currently, students who have an on-campus experience are enriched by the "real geographic" presence of researchers who are teachers and of teachers who are up-to-date with the cutting edge research in their subject areas. Off-campus students (who may be "distance" or who may choose a more flexible mode of delivery) experience "virtual electronic" teacher contact. It is true that the distinctions between the "real" or geographically present and the "virtual" or electronically present are continually blurring. Shortly, they may disappear.

We are already beginning to understand that the electronically present person is as real as the geographically present person. There are already programs and computer-eye cameras which enable us to interact visually in real time as well as chatrooms and discussion threads which allow us to interact synchronously or a-synchronously. These prefigure the more complex aspects of virtual and real interactions which the cyber will deliver to us in these early years of the new millennium.

5. TRADITIONAL AND ONLINE LECTURES

The traditional face to face lecture is still the central presentation in most universities today. There need be no apologies made for this if we are sure that it is one of the most effective methods to assist student learning. However, the fact that it is traditional is an inadequate reason for its continuation. Research indicates that this is not the most effective learning model. It has grown as a most effective delivery model. It's not hard to see how this delivery can be more effective online, even in its present form. Indeed, many Universities have audios and/or videos of lectures for students to borrow. These prefigure online delivery although they do not take advantage of any of the interactivity and multimedia that are the defining features of ePedagogy.

Bringing traditional lecture material online may be as simple as putting print online. Indeed, this is how many academics use electronic technology. Doing so means that you are only transferring print technology to electronic technology. Multimedia presents you with the opportunity to extend this significantly.

The new technologies enable us to retain the core values of lecturing. They do, however, challenge us to do something *other* than print or the audio/video of the lecture as presented in a lecture theatre with limited extended visual and audio referencing and no 3D animation or interactivity.

What qualities do lectures have, and what needs to be retained in the new electronic delivery format?

From the lecturers' point of view, lectures, per se, may or may not appear to contain deeply challenging intellectual content, or to develop complex arguments. They are, however, best viewed as the tip of the iceberg. They arise from lecturers' academic knowledge accrued from experience, research, debate, discussion, review, revision, and problematisation. Moreover, they are a valued and public face of the lecturers' knowledge of teaching and learning, of focussing tone, register and sense of audience; of delivery as well as content and intellectual background; of reception as well as preparation.

From the students' point of view, lectures are very often the first step students make in a sustained intellectual experience. They provide students not merely with information, but also with: models of how academics develop papers and ideas for the extension of knowledge and its application in their areas; the concept of delivery and its relationship to knowledge development; an ambience in which they share a common experience with their peers which aims to develop their own intellectual lives and lifelong learning skills. Lectures extend their private understanding, contribute to discussions with peers and experts, and enable application in/to the wider world. They provide a common body of knowledge for focus and equity of access as well as opportunities to identify and discuss intellectual points with lecturers and class members.

These core values are not under threat when we turn from print-based materials to interactive multimedia materials, or when we turn from geographically present lecturers to electronically present ones. For the virtual and the real are drawing closer together in virtual reality.

6. TRADITIONAL AND ONLINE TUTORIALS

How can what is offered by geographically based tutorials be retained and/or enriched by online interactions between student and student and student and academic?

Students who are on-campus, particularly students straight from school, seem to value the small group interaction and to derive a great deal of support from face to face tutorials. Our practical experience indicates, however, that students quickly begin to feel at home in online tutorial situations which begin as class spaces in computer labs and end as flexible deliveries according to the students' own needs.

7. REAL AND VIRTUAL INTERACTIONS BETWEEN TEACHERS AND LEARNERS

Once we enable ourselves to blur "real" interactions with "real" people with the further enabling teaching and learning layer of "virtual" tutorials and lectures with "virtual" teachers and "virtual" learning communities we provide a quite flexible delivery mode that is neither distance nor on-campus but encourages the student and teacher to select the most appropriate mix of virtual reality.

The specific situation of the individual course and/or student will indicate the balance of the 4 aspects of the Quadripartite method of eTeaching and eLearning: people, print, CD Rom and WWW. Sometimes virtual or real people will dominate, at others paper or electronic print, at others CD Rom and then again WWW sites. Or there might be any other computation of these 4 aspects of ePedagogy.

As students are becoming more and more e-literate, they will expect that the new learning modes will be able to be accessed at any time or place they institute connections. This flexible model places different expectations on the "people" aspect of the learning experience. It asks teachers to look at curriculum construction, development and deliveries in new as well as traditional modes. It provides a very flexible pedagogy.

In such a vital eCommunications context, the role of the teacher will inevitably change, as will the ways in which learning occurs. It is probable that the traditional model of face to face lectures and tutorials supported by on campus access will become a smaller and smaller percentage of the whole delivery system. At the same time, the role of the learner is changing to a more interactive one in which students have more control over the depth, pace and time of their learning experiences.

8. DISCUSSION THREADS AS VIRTUAL TUTORIALS AND VIRTUAL COMMUNITIES OF PEOPLE

Our undergraduate and postgraduate subject websites have a week by week module online for each subject. Students can, in their own time and space and at their own pace or in laboratory times set aside for them, see quite clearly what they are expected to do each week. These virtual tutorials have hotlinks to relevant sites which enrich the student's journey. They also have a button for Discussion Threads. Once students hit this they are taken to the discussion area where they login. This provides evidence of the students' attendance and work. It also provides them with the opportunity to enter into threaded discussions. Sometimes we pose a question and students can reply to it or to one another, sometimes students pose questions or enter into small groups to "talk" about their opinions. They express these in print online asynchronously. It's not too hard to see how this could become a multimedia community group: a tutorial.

9. THE VIRTUAL TUTORIAL

Thus, the possibilities of a virtual tutorial can be explored when students can enter into discussion with one another and their virtual tutor through electronic spaces. Questions can be posed and students can answer them; students can pose questions and answer one another; virtual communities can be formed by small groups of students and individuals can enter into dialogues with one another. The tutor may play a role which distances her or him or may play a more definitive and formative role about the direction of the tutorial discussions. Such tutorials may occur in chatrooms which have been constructed for the occasion and which may be visited synchronously or asynchronously as desired. An eTutor, eMentor, peer student or critical friend might meet you there.

10. ORACY AND ELECTRONIC DISCOURSE

This electronic form of textuality and discourse relies on the drawing together of oracy or the spoken word with electronic forms of print. It is not formal writing as in an essay or presentation, but is like written speech with all of its speculative and interactive nature. There are errors of spelling and grammar; there are signs of a lack of reflection; there are spaces in the linear argument itself; and there is some lack of cohesion and even coherence. There is a very great interaction here with the increasing communication of "texting" on mobile phones. The purpose of the discussion threads and chatrooms is to provide students with the flexibility of the virtual tutorial. It is, we think, important not to confuse this with an evaluation of their performance as writers of well structured written discourse.

11. PRINT

Traditional teaching and learning has been dominated by books, articles and reading and writing in the non-electronic mode. This traditional book/print discourse offers linearity and authority and is available in electronic as well as book form. Much of the material on the WWW is in the form of print and many books and journals are available in this way. As most academics have developed their teaching and learning styles in this mode, as well as their research methodologies, this discourse dominates academic studies. The role traditional print discourse will play in eLearning in the future will probably be considerably less than it does now.

Print itself is a powerful and dominant technology which has underpinned the advances of the Western world and which will continue to do so. Simply transposing print from paper to electronic form is merely a change in publication procedures. An electronic set of lecture notes is, in essence, no different from a handout even if it's in powerpoint and has flashing arrows and moving multicoloured type.

It is a very important principle in making an electronic text to ask the question: "*What am I doing here that I cannot do in print?*". This focuses the mind beyond the "gee whiz" of technology which might occur if you were to come from the technology end and to ask "*what do the new electronic programs offer me*?".

The new attributes of reading and writing consist of: storage; immediacy, interactivity; three dimensionality; virtuality; flexibility and user-inclusiveness. The concept of the stable platform of the CD Rom with the dynamic peripherals of WWW provides us with a huge amount of electronically delivered material which can take advantage of the very lively textuality and discourse offered by the new technologies. The CD Rom means that you have ever-ready accessibility to electronic interactions which might be difficult or too dense to download directly from the WWW. This enables students to experience virtuality, three dimensionality, interactivity and multimedia as the basic components of new reading and writing spaces.

12. STORAGE

Books have a small storage capacity yet take up considerable space in any number. The new technology presents us with the capacity to take large amounts of text and store them in a very economic and accessible way. As long as the computer is working, of course. If, however, we merely transfer books or printed text into a digitised form, we are not taking any advantage of the new possibilities offered by electronic textuality and discourse other than that of storage and perhaps immediacy.

13. IMMEDIACY

Although stored print text is immediately accessible, immediacy has different connotations for digital textuality and discourse. It enables the use of interactive multi media and it also enables the user to change given notations into different orders according to their needs. Interactive multi media means the use of the various single attributes of sound, vision, movement and print in any combination. Immediacy in this context means that the reader clearly takes on attributes of the writer. That is, becomes the "writerly-reader" identified by Roland Barthes. (Barthes 1997)

14. INTERACTIVITY

A multi-layered text has opportunities for the readerly-writer to make choices about the ways in which the material comes to life. For example, via the computer, a story might be read in the traditional print fashion through digitised words. Hotwords might lead to definitions or explanation or even visual enactments; film clips could be chosen or could run on a split screen; the impact of voices, background sounds and musical interpretations could flesh out the possibilities of the words making the story. The ways in which the reader might organise her or his tour through such a text highlight the power of interactivity. The story might never be read in its original print form. This is no less important a technique for non-fiction texts and engineering sites or science laboratories.

15. THREE DIMENSIONALITY

Print, photography, the visual arts, television and film, have all pre-figured the ways in which we can actually enter into a given text to experience it as we would had we been at the place it is describing. The whole point of recording information is that it will be subsumed into another's experiences, knowledge and self-constructions.

New computer software has enabled us to build three dimensional images which can be manipulated by the Barthian "writerly-reader". Already we can put on gear that enables us to enter into the three dimensional experience that is the subject of the textuality and discourse. This is a first move towards an electronic future which we are barely entering in 2003.

The filmic camera has aimed at recreating the 3 dimensionality of reality. It has point-of-view shots, for example, which make it seem as though we are viewing the experience as/with the characters. Compared to the flat vision of photography and the outside camera of TV it gives readers of the text a particular view of the discourse. This is an experiential view. Three dimensionality in digitised texts is an experience of reality which brings the discourse very close to that reality itself.

16. VIRTUALITY

This three dimensional experience, along with the sound and vision of interactive multi media, has come to be called "virtual reality". At first glance, this is a contradiction in terms. Certainly only 10 years ago it would have been understood by few. Now it is a commercial and everyday reality.

It means that we can experience in a virtual sense a life which might otherwise be closed to us. We might be a rally driver or have sex with Madonna the mother of Lourdes; we might play golf with Greg Norman or re-order the AFL final so that Collingwood always wins. That is, we enact or do.

17. ANIMATION

Computer textuality is enlivened by animations which can be made more and more complex and interactive with readily available programs such as Macromedia Director. An essential part of interactive multi-media, animation is often restricted to typefaces, arrows and diagrammatic representations closely related to print. Electronic animation packages offer academics the opportunity of entering into novel methods of envisualisation and pictorial representation. These can be particularly applicable in the "hard" disciplines such as the virtual science laboratory, the virtual engineering site, aeronautics, mathematics or medicine.

18. WRITING FOR THE WWW

The capacity to connect with virtual learning communities, supervisors, mentors, experts, "critical friends" and colleagues is a unique feature of the WWW. It offers students a breadth and depth of learning communities not available otherwise. It has effects on the ways in which traditionally discrete oracy and literacy come together. Genre and associated "rules" of academic communication are challenged by it. The WWW offers a dynamic place for curriculum to develop and change frequently and for the most up-to-date applications and information to be available to academics and students as they turn information into knowledge.

Education itself is being identified more and more as part of the "knowledge industry" and also the "new economy". Thus, the 21st century can't just be the "Information Era': it must also be the era in which loads of information that is readily available can be converted into knowledge that can be applied, used or seen as the basis for our theoretical, philosophical and ethical understandings. The World Wide Web provides an extremely useful virtual library, an extraordinarily rich resource tool at our fingertips for us to find out information: but how can we turn this into useful knowledge and even wisdom?

Visual representations are a powerful method of reinforcing verbal information. Feeling at ease with utilising and resourcing the WWW as a research tool is the first and most significant step to take in utilising this incredibly rich global information tool.

19. WRITING FOR CD ROM

This technology offers a stable eLearning product which is able to be accessed readily, to be connected to relevant dynamic websites and to provide an eLearning product for marketing.

It enables academics to think beyond traditional print based curricula and to begin to develop interactivity, virtuality, immediacy, animation, multimedia as an integral part of their teaching programs. The CD Rom offers a large storage area and can include print as well as the electronic aspects of discourse. The most exciting part of making CD Roms has been to use the new forms of textuality and discourse that we have mentioned: immediacy, interactivity, virtuality, three dimensionality and multimedia.

20. LINKING THE CD ROM AND THE WWW

The WWW sites can be related to the subject areas on a subject-based CD Rom and print guides. As eEducators this provides us with: an ever evolving tool for immediate updated information for all students to links to newly discovered sites as well as live links for the best research materials available on the web in this subject area; a virtual tutorial site in which discussion threads can be placed and replied to by students; virtual exams, learning hurdles or tests which can be electronically entered and can provide immediate feedback; a space in which students can access and tour the many levels of the learning materials in their own time and either on or off campus; links with the CD Rom to extend and enrich materials and interactions which occur there; a method of familiarising students with confident learning in the new online deliveries; ways of turning information into knowledge as students reflect upon, analyse, criticise and report upon electronic information; and new ways of enabling students with a variety of physical and intellectual disabilities.

21. eCURRICULUM DEVELOPMENT

Preparing eCurriculum materials is a challenging and time consuming task, even if it's only touring the WWW looking for relevant links. Setting up the website so that it is not just a pathetic imitation of a book text means taking web design into account as well as having relevant live links which students can use to answer the hurdle questions or to develop the learning topics. Making a subject CD Rom that is multimedia based calls upon educational expertise and a willingness to work with a team of expert designers and programmers to expand academics' print-based knowledge and information into the textuality and discourse offered by electronic deliveries. Relating them to print-based texts means a consideration of their different strengths and weaknesses.

Assuming that interactions with students via email replaces and is more economic than vis-à-vis is a deeply flawed assumption. Over-use of email will make teachers collapse. A more economical system of virtuality was the bulletin boards and discussion threads that we instituted on the WWW sites.

22. WRITING FOR FLEXIBLE eTEACHING AND eLEARNING

The delivery of courses to students, the exchange of scholarly information and the undertaking of scholarly research no longer depends on face to face interactions or print materials alone. The new deliveries provide eEducators with new ways of exploring flexible delivery of curriculum as well as flexible learning opportunities for students.

Flexibility 1: The ways in which virtual eTeaching and eLearning occur in relationship to traditional methods can vary. Courses can be constructed so that the quadripartite concept can be explored traditionally with, for example, print being 50% and people being 50% with the WWW and CD Rom being references or add-ons. The other end of the scale might see an emphasis on working from an enriched website with navigational nodes set for student application, virtual lectures, interactions and activities on CD Rom, and tutorials available online. There are clearly many opportunities in between.

Flexibility 2: Academics can review their time spent face to face and replace actual interactions with virtual interactions with students and curriculum. The new deliveries provide academics with a new path for leadership in conceptualising curriculum and teaching methodologies and bringing them to successful delivery to students and reception by them. Obviously, this takes time. The time comes from the traditional lecture/tutorial methods being replaced by other ways of reaching students: virtually through discussion threads, bulletin boards, chatrooms and e-mail; with face to face consultations, presence, dropins or seminars; through CD Roms which provide multi-media presentations of enriched lecture materials through hypertext links and jumping-off points to relevant websites.

Flexibility 3: Students can work from any station which connects them to the electronically delivered curriculum and the virtual lectures and tutorials. Students are increasingly e-literate. The provision of computer access through libraries and laboratories is being matched by the number of students who have WWW and CDROM access from home. Flexible subject deliveries mean that students can work from wherever they choose at the times they choose. The organising of their educational experience will be more firmly in the hands of those undertaking it. This is particularly pertinent as students' work hours increase as they support themselves through their studies.

Flexibility 4: Curriculum can be devised by academics from different institutions and delivered nationally or internationally. The singularity of the journey taken by students in one subject, school or campus can be enriched by academic partnerships across campuses and Universities to produce the best possible materials in subjects or courses.

Flexibility 5: Virtual travel: Academics and students can attend a variety of campuses through electronic means. Agreements can be made between Universities to recognise this. Parts of courses may be supplied by different Universities, or sections of subjects could be shared.

Flexibility 6: Assessment: Assessment procedures can be tailored to individuals. New ways of conceptualising the relationship of the course content and structure to the assessment procedures can be explored. The ways in which assessment drive the teaching and learning experience can be articulated. Online assessment can be utilised. to enable students to self-assess as well as to make academics' marking loads lighter.

Flexibility 7: Virtual Learning communities arise when students are placed in groups such as tutorial groups, or when they have the opportunity to select the groups which they feel would enhance their learning opportunities. Electronic deliveries offer students a global choice of chatrooms as well as specified discussion thread areas. Real learning communities set up by students to peer group themselves can arise from virtual tutorials and online learning communities.

Flexibility 8: The new technologies offer outstanding support to students with a large range of disabilities. This aspect has hardly been investigated but our students who have sight, hearing and learning disabilities have reported that learning at their own pace and in their own chosen spaces has been enabling.

23. THE KNOWLEDGE INDUSTRY

Print information and knowledge culture is on the cusp of becoming the electronic information and knowledge culture. In the 21st century, immediate access to information via computers will change forever the social and economic structures of technological cultures. Educational practices and writing will be particularly strongly affected by globalisation. As students will be able to undertake courses globally and flexibly, educators will have to develop strategies that enable them to interact with new methodologies and constructions of knowledge.

This period of time is an exciting and open one which provides academics with the opportunity to take the area of study with which you are most familiar and explore new dimensions related to its presentation.

Technophiles have dominated online projects and they tend to undervalue the content asset which is the reason for doing any of this. Academics have that asset. They do not need to learn how to do the technological implementation of expanding that asset into an online production. By thinking about academics' own knowledge as a script for an electronic production rather than as a script for a lecture with overheads or a book with pictures, footnotes, etc, teachers can take into account the contribution of electronic modes of delivery.

This paper has broadly surveyed the Quadripartite Model of eTeaching and eLearning as a model and gateway to developing online deliveries for tertiary subjects. Enhancing learning and teaching through utilising the new technologies has resulted in a great deal of talk and in putting some materials online in a basically traditional and often very templated way. We have walked the walk as well as talked the talk. This paper is as the result of that exhausting but enchanting journey.

REFERENCES

Ahn-Sook, Hwang, 1996, Positivist and Constructivist Persuasions in Instructional Development, *Instructional Science*, 24(5), pp. 343–56.

Arnold, J. and Vigo, K., 1996, Hyperteaching in the Immaterial World, *Media International Australia*, 81. August, pp. 77–84.

Arnold, J. and Vigo, K., 1999, Electronic Delivery of Curriculum: Preproduction to Cyberscripts, in: *Systems Development Methods for Databases, Enterprise Modeling, and Workflow Management*, Wojtkowski et al., eds, Kluwer Academic/Plenum Publishers, NY, pp. 441–454.

Arnold, J., 1999, The Machine is not the Woman: Cyberfeminism and the Techno-determinism of Information Systems, Kluwer Academic/Plenum Publishers. N.Y.

Arnold, J., Feminist Poetics and Cybercolonisation, in: *Cyberfeminism*, Hawthorne, S and Klein, R., eds., Spinifex Press, Melbourne.

Arnold, J. Vigo, K. and Green, D., 1996–2000, *Oz 21: Australia's Cultural Dreaming*, CD Rom.

Barthes, J., 1977, *Image-Music-Text*, Fontana Collins, London.

Boyle, T., 1997, *Design for Multimedia Learning*, Prentice Hall, UK.

Braudel, F., 1986, *Civilization and Capitalism 15th-18th century*, 3 vols., William Collins and Co. London.

Cixous, H., *Writing Differences. Readings from the Writings of Helene Cixous*, ed. S. Sellers, Open University Press, Milton Keynes.

Cocker, M., 1999, Rivers of Blood, Rivers of Gold: Europe's Conflict with Tribal Peoples, Pimlico, London.

Cunningham, D. J., Duffy, T. M. and Knuth, R., 1993, The Textbook of the Future in: *Hypertext: a Psychological Perspective*, McKnight, C. et al., eds., Ellis Horwood.

Deleuze, G. and Guattari, F., 1981, Rhizome, Power and Desire, Diagrams of the Social, *I&C*, Spring no.8.

Derrida, J., 1978, *Writing a Difference*, Routledge and Kegan Paul.

Flax, J., Thinking Fragments. Psychoanalyses, Feminism and Postmodernism in the Contemporary West, University of California Press, Berkeley.

Diprose, R. and Ferrell, R. 1991, Cartographies. Poststructuralism and the Mapping of Bodies and Space, Allen and Unwin, Sydney.

Druckery, T., ed., *Electronic Culture*, Aperture Foundation, NY.

Benterrick, K., Muecke, S., Roe, P., 1984, *Reading the Country: Introduction to Nomadology*, Fremantle Arts Centre Press, Fremantle, WA.

Friere, P., 1972, *Pedagogy of the Oppressed*, Penguin, Great Britain.

Gardner, H., 1993, *Multiple Intelligence: The Theory in Practice*, Harper and Collins, USA.

Giroux, H., 1990, Curriculum Discourse as Postmodernist Critical Practice, Deakin University, Geelong.

Hackbarth, S., 1996, The Educational Technology Handbook, A Comprehensive Guide, Englewood Cliffs, NJ.

Hayles, N. K., 1991, Chaos Bound. Orderly Disorder in Contemporary Literature and Science, Cornell University Press, Ithaca, N.Y.

Hoffman, D. D., 1998, *Visual Intelligence, How We Create What We See*, Norton and Co. New York.
Kauchak d. P.and Egan, P. D., 1998, *Learning and Teaching Research-Based Methods*, Allyn & Bacon, Boston.
Lander, D., Walta, A., McCorriston, M. and Birchall, G., 1995, A Practical Way of Structuring Teaching for Learning, *Higher Education Research and Development*, 14, 47–59.
Lines, W. J., 1994, An All Consuming Passion: Origins, Modernity and the Australian Life of Georgiana Molloy, Allen and Unwin, NSW Australia.
Lyotard, J., *The Lyotard Reader*, Benjamin, A.. ed., Basil Blackwell, Oxford, UK.
http://webreference.com/greatsite.html
http://www.cybergeography.com/atlas/atlas.html
http://wwwasu.murdoch.edu.au/eddesign/resources/onlinelearning/ways.html
Irigary, 1989, The Language of Man, *Cultural Critique*, No.13, Fall, Special Issue.
Kristeva, J., 1984 *Revolution in Poetic Language,* Columbia University Press. NY.
Milheim, W. D., 1993, How to use Animation in Computer Assisted Learning, *British Journal of Educational Technology*, Vol 24 No 3, pp. 171–178.
Miller, D., 1982, Metaphor and Thought, *Et Cetera*, Fall, pp. 249.
Poovey, M. 1988. Feminism and Deconstruction, *Feminist Studies*, Vol.14, No.1, Spring, 51–67.
Schank, D. A., 1994, *Engines for Educators,* Lawrence Erlbaum, NY.
Scholes, R., 1982, *Semiotics and Interpretation*, Yale University Press, New Haven.
Shousan, W., 2000, Multimedia and some of its Technical Issues, *International Journal of Instructional Multimedia*, Vol 27 No 4, pp. 303–314.
Spivak, G., 1988, *In Other Worlds. Essays in Cultural Politics*, Routledge, London.
Ulmer, G., 1989, *Teletheory: Grammatology in the Age of Video*, Routledge, NY.
Wang and Sleeman, 1993.
White, R., 1981, *Inventing Australia: Images and Identity, 1688-1980.*

EFFECTIVE TEACHING OF GROUPWARE DEVELOPMENT

A conceptual model

Adel M. Aladwani*

1. INTRODUCTION

GroupWare is a system(s) that helps workgroups share information and coordinate work-flows (Zigurs et al., 1988). It handles the access, manipulation, and sharing of data, information, and knowledge among a group of people, and in some cases it provides mechanisms by which the user(s) can query the system for a recommendation, given a particular problem. These group activities can be carried out in both centralized as well as distributed configurations.

The above described potentialities of GroupWare pushed many organizations to adopt this technology in order to promote the performance of organizational workgroups (Fjermestad and Hiltz, 2000). In a direct response to this interest, GroupWare courses are beginning to appear in the Information Systems curriculum of many universities to prepare their students for the future responsibility of designing, implementing, and managing this important technology.

Unfortunately, little is currently known about the pedagogy of GroupWare development principles; and for this reason university professors worldwide are left with little help with regard to understanding the right mix of skills and knowledge necessary to prepare university students to become future GroupWare professionals. Accordingly, this paper proposes a conceptual model identifying some of the basic determinants of effective teaching of these principles.

2. BACKGROUND

GroupWare development is an area of knowledge concerned with the delivery of GroupWare functions that meet predefined users' requirements. This definition highlights three major points:

* Adel M. Aladwani, Department of QM & IS, College of Bus. Admin., Kuwait Univ.

(1) the development process necessitates an interaction between three major parties – the user, the developer, and the problem;
(2) in order for the above interaction to be acceptable, it must result in a "quality" learning process; and
(3) in order for such a learning process to be successful, it ought to produce a "quality" design.

The nature of GroupWare development necessitates the cognizance of several factors affecting the outcome of the interaction among the user(s), the developer(s), and the problem/task. GroupWare development is not as an easy task as it may first seem (Hender et al., 2002). Persons involved in the development effort can be as much as few people in small GroupWare systems or as much as several hundred individuals in large projects. In such a case, a group-level effort may suit better the GroupWare development task than individual-level effort does (Jarvenpaa et al., 1988). Also, given the unique nature of GroupWare development, allocating adequate time periods to finish the task is of a great value. This is especially true since the shape of the product of an information system project team keeps changing with the advent of a clearer understanding of users' requirements. Moreover, GroupWare development can follow either an evolutionary approach or a traditional approach. The evolutionary method is concerned with speed of delivery and users' requirement definition and satisfaction. The traditional method, on the other hand, emphasizes functional decomposition, clarity of the development process, and technically robust solutions.

According to the learning hierarchy by Bloom et al. (1956), the learning process spans six levels: knowledge, comprehension, application, analysis, synthesis, and evaluation. Knowledge refers to remembering previously accumulated ideas. Comprehension is simply the understanding of the content of a communication message. Application is the ability to implement concepts to new situations. Analysis entails identifying the underlying structures and relationships of the problem. Synthesis emphasizes the linkage between the basic structures found in the previous stages to construct formations that have not been done before. Evaluation alludes to the ability to decide, given a set of criteria, whether the material is appropriate or not for a particular situation.

What constitutes a "quality" GroupWare development? The literature on quality of software development provides a wide view for this construct. McCall, Richards, and Walters (1977) and Vincent et al. (1988) maintain that system development quality can be viewed as a collective effect of eleven different factors: correctness, reliability, efficiency, integrity, usability, maintainability, testability, flexibility, portability, reusability, and inter-operability. Many authors have emphasized the importance of specific sub-characteristics that constitute the above-mentioned factors (e.g. Juergens, 1977).

3. CONCEPTUAL MODEL AND PROPOSITIONS

Based on the above discussion, the author proposes a model relating three sets of independent, intermediate, and outcome variables (Figure 1). Four factors are proposed to explain the GroupWare Learning Quality: the focus of development the effort (individual versus group), type of development methodology, task complexity, and assignment time constraints. GroupWare Learning Quality, in turn, is hypothesized to affect GroupWare

Development Quality. In addition, the role of computer experience is neutralized for reasons discussed later. The following is a discussion of each of three sets of variables.

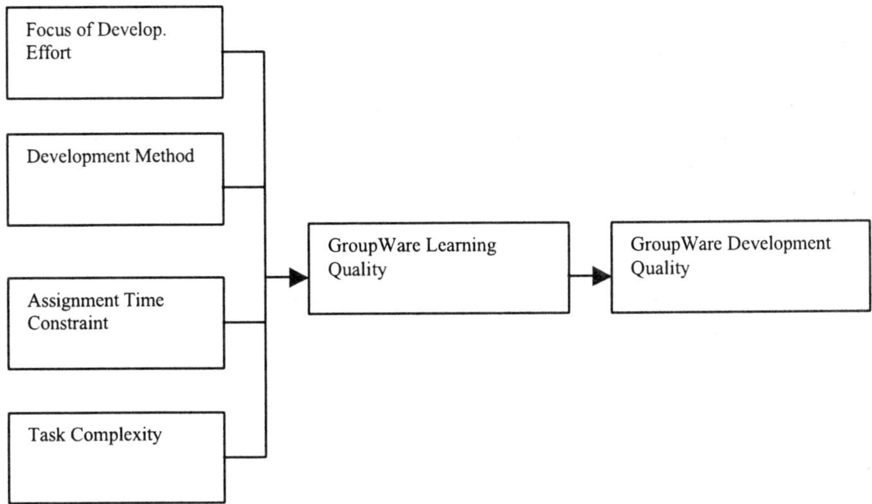

Figure 1. Conceptual Model

3.1. Outcome Variables

There is no empirical evidence to support or otherwise dispute the assertions regarding the relative importance of the different development quality factors. Consequently, the author will combine the above mentioned eleven factors (i.e., correctness, reliability, efficiency, integrity, usability, maintainability, testability, flexibility, portability, reusability, and interoperability) to come up with an index representing an overall GroupWare Development Quality.

3.2. Intermediate Variables

Following Bloom et al.'s (1956) model, the author defines intermediate variables as consisting of knowledge, comprehension, application, analysis, synthesis, and evaluation. Together, the six variables can form an index of GroupWare Learning Quality.

3.3. Independent Variables

3.3.1. The Focus of the Development Effort

The benefits of group learning over individualized learning in expanding students' knowledge bases and inventory of skills, and in enhancing the outcome of the task, are widely recognized. In an GroupWare research environment, Leidner and Fuller (1997) reported that students working collaboratively in either small or large groups were more interested in course material and perceived themselves to learn more than students that worked individually.

Proposition 1: Group projects contribute more to GroupWare Learning and Development Quality than individual projects do.

3.3.2. Type of the Development Method

Many methodologies and techniques were proposed for GroupWare development. Prototyping is simple to teach and it promotes greater understanding (comprehension) of requirements; whereas structured methods enhance systematic thinking, modularity, and synthesis. Therefore, it would be interesting to know how the choice of a specific methodology for teaching purposes would affect the effectiveness of the pedagogy of GroupWare development.

Proposition 2: There are differences in the contribution of the types of the development method to GroupWare Learning and Development Quality.

3.3.3. Task Complexity

Jeffery and Lawrence (1985) ascribed lower productivity of some software development teams to the algorithmic complexity associated with the developed application. In the context of GroupWare development pedagogy, the choice of a particular GroupWare development project (task) would place an obvious mental burden on students. A teacher's choice of a complex assignment to express his or her ideas may limit the ability of students to understand the subject matter and to meaningfully relate to stored development knowledge.

Proposition 3: Simple illustrative projects contribute more to GroupWare Learning and Development Quality than complex projects do.

3.3.4. Constraints on Development Assignment Time

Some authors contend that a project schedule constraint is one determinant of productivity (1981). In addition, development time is also found to be associated with programming tasks (Chrysler, 1978). These facts suggest that the time frame of a development assignment could have major consequences in the final outcome of the pedagogy of GroupWare development.

Proposition 4: Longer design assignment time contributes more to GroupWare Learning and Development Quality than short design assignment time does.

4. SUGGESTED RESEARCH DESIGN

The next phase of this research project will try to examine the research propositions described in the present study. An attempt will be made to use both the qualitative and quantitative methods to collect data. The author will start with a qualitative study, which is to collect some preliminary evidence from interviews of a small number of GroupWare developers/students. Soon afterward, based on the feedback obtained from the participants, the author will try to design and implement an experimental task to examine the specific propositions presented in the conceptual model.

5. CONCLUSION

A theoretical model of effective GroupWare development pedagogy was proposed. Four factors were hypothesized to associate with the GroupWare learning and development quality (the surrogates for pedagogy effectiveness). These factors are the focus of the development effort (individual versus group), the development method (traditional versus prototyping), task complexity (high complexity versus low complexity), and assignment time constraint (high versus low).

There are three major avenues for future research efforts. First, the proposed model needs to be empirically validated using an appropriate research methodology. Second, the model may need to be refined to incorporate other important determinants, for example, teacher characteristics, software/hardware characteristics, etc. Third, future research efforts may need to consider how one independent variable would perform depending on the performance of another variable(s). Therefore, interactions among the different independent variables could be considered in the future. To control the complexity of explaining the results of higher-order (3x and above) interactions, one may focus on fewer independent variables.

REFERENCES

Bloom, B. et al., 1956, *Taxonomy of Educational Objectives: The Classification of Educational Goals: Cognitive and Affective Domains*, McKay Company, New York., NY.

Boehm, B., 1981, *Software Engineering Economics*, Prentice-Hall, Englewood Cliffs, NJ.

Chrysler, E., 1978, Some Basic Determinants of Computer Programming Productivity, *Communications of the ACM,* V.21, 472–483.

Fjermestad, J. and Hiltz, S., 2000, Group support systems: A descriptive evaluation of case and field studies, *Journal of Management Information Systems*, v. 17, 115–132.

Hender, J., Dean, D., Rodgers, T., and Nunamaker, J., 2002, An Examination of the Impact of Stimuli Type and GSS Structure on Creativity: Brainstorming versus Non-brainstorming Techniques in a GSS Environment, *Journal of Management Information Systems,* v. 18, 59–82.

Jarvenpaa, S., Rao, V., and Huber, G., 1988, Computer Support for Meetings of Groups Working on Unstructured Problems: A Field Experiment, *MIS Quarterly,* v. 12, 645–666.

Jeffery, D. and Lawrence, M., 1985, Managing Programming Productivity, *The Journal of Systems and Software*, v.6, 34–42.

Juergens, H., 1977, Attributes of Information System Development, *MIS Quarterly*, v.1, 31–41.

Leidner, D. and Fuller, M. 1997, Improving Student Learning of Conceptual Information: GSS Supported Collaborative Learning vs. Individual Constructive Learning, *Decision Support Systems,* v.20, 149–163.

McCall, J., Richards, P. and Walters, G., 1977, Factors in Software Quality Assurance, RADC-TR-77-369 (Rome: Rome Air Development Center), I, November n.p. [cited in Vincent et al., 1988]

Vincent, J., Waters, A. and Sinclair, J. 1988, *Software Quality Assurance: Volume I: Practice and Implementation*, Prentice Hall, Englewood Cliffs, NJ.

Zigurs, I., Scott-Poole, M., and DeSanctis, G., 1988, A study of influence in computer-mediated group decision making, *MIS Quarterly,* v. 12, 625–644.

APPLICATION OF SYSTEM ENGINEERING METHODS IN INFORMATION SYSTEMS CURRICULA DEVELOPMENT

Albertas Caplinskas and Olegas Vasilecas*

1. INTRODUCTION

The paper proposes a systematic approach to the development of the curricula in information systems. The main idea beyond this approach is to adapt systems engineering methods to curricula engineering. A curriculum under development is thought as a system that is intended to meet market requirements. Requirements are transformed into design using localisation and flow-down techniques. The proposed approach has been applied to develop modern curriculum in information systems at master level in the project MOCURIS.†

Curricula development is a difficult and complicated task. It is a process by which an educational institution decides what is to be taught (the content) and how it will be taught (teaching and assessment methods) (Holzl, 2000). In order to develop curricula, many aspects should be taken into account including labour market needs, career tracks, body of knowledge, compulsory and optional units, courses of introductory and fundamental level, trained abilities, credits, etc. Typical curriculum includes dozens of units with numerous staff is involved in its development process. Amount of potential workload needed for the complete curriculum design is too large to cope with informally. However today engineering methods are not applied directly in curricula development. As far as we know, such methods are used only in lean-ISD methodology (Wallace et al., 2002). This methodology provides three-level engineering process: Curriculum Architecture Design (the rough equivalent of System/Architectural Design), Modular Curriculum Development (the rough equivalent of Product Design), and Instructional Activity Development (the rough equivalent of Component Design). This approach has been developed in 1982 and is used for industrial curricula development. However university curricula typically still are designed using informal or semi-formal techniques. A

* Vilnius Gediminas Technical University, Sauletekio al. 11, LT-2040 Vilnius, Lithuania; alcapl@ktl.mii.lt, olegas@fm.vtu.lt

† MOCURIS-modern curriculum in information systems at master level, SOCRATES/ERASMUS project, contract number **69077-IC-1-2001-1-LT-ERASMUS-PROG**

Constructing the Infrastructure for the Knowledge Economy
Edited by H. Linger *et al.*, Kluwer Academic/Plenum Publishers, 2004

university curriculum reflects usually the research traditions of a particular university and aims to respond to local challenges. As a result many curricula suffer from narrow specialisation, lack of integrity, and lack of interdisciplinarity. This paper is based on the view that any curriculum can be seen as a system and that curriculum development process may be considered as a kind of system engineering process called curricula engineering (Caplinskas, 2001). It discusses how to adapt general systems engineering techniques, mostly requirement engineering to curricula engineering.

The rest of the paper is organised as follows. Section 2 overviews briefly systems engineering techniques required to develop the complete set of system requirements. Section 3 discusses concepts of curricula engineering and curriculum architecture, curricula engineering techniques, and tools to support curricula engineering process. Section 4 concludes the paper and describes shortly the experience gained in application of proposed techniques in MOCURIS project.

2. REQUIREMENTS DISCOVERY AND ENGINEERING

Although systems engineering techniques are widely applied in many fields, no generally accepted agreement exists for the boundaries within which they can be applied. The main assumptions are that properties of a system under development can be described by set of requirements and that the aims of engineering process are to design architecture of the system and implement the system. In other words, the systems engineering process is a process by which a set of objectives is transformed into an operational system (Sailor, 1990). It can be also defined as "an interdisciplinary process that ensures that the customer's needs are satisfied throughout a system's entire life cycle" (Bahill and Dean, 2002). System engineering techniques are very general and should be adapted for different industries, products and customers.

The term *architecture* is used in systems engineering to describe design elements, which are characteristic of a system, and of a class of systems to which it belongs (Beam, 1990). Architecture is most often a measure of a system's commonality with other representatives of its class, rather than a measure of uniqueness. System designer can create also new architectures. Improvements of traditional design are recognised as architectural innovations. However, architectural innovations are related always with major risk and should be well grounded.

Another important term is *system hierarchy* (Sailor, 1990). Systems are organised into a hierarchy to facilitate their development and management. A hierarchy is the organisational structure established by dividing the system into functional areas at lower levels until the component level is reached. One should differ between the system architecture and system hierarchy. The architecture is composed of components that may have hierarchical structure. The system hierarchy provides abstraction levels of design. It means that both decomposition and abstraction principles are widely applied in system engineering.

The first phase of the systems engineering process is called discovering system requirements. It begins with the definition of user objectives and results in a complete set of requirements for the system together with the system configuration of the proper size and capability to meet those requirements. Requirements are identifiable capabilities or functions that the system must possess to meet the mission objectives. They are divided into functional and non-functional requirements.

Requirement discovering process combines *requirements partitioning, requirements allocation, requirements flowdown, interface definition*, and *requirements review* techniques. User objectives are described firstly by a mission statement. The data related to mission are either gathered or developed, analysed, and, finally, meaningful mission-related system requirements are derived from those data. Once the mission-related requirements are defined, requirements can be placed on the functional areas that make-up the total system. This process is called requirement allocation. Functional areas, combined with the mission-related requirements, form out the total set of system requirements. It should be noted that only a part of requirements is allocable. Non-allocable requirements refer to environment, operational, and design standards, which apply to unchanged across all elements of the system (Sailor, 1990).

Requirements allocation is an iterative process, leading eventually to a complete allocation of the system requirements. The results are described by so-called requirements *localisation matrix*. The process proceeds mainly in top-down manner through the system hierarchy. Each system-level requirement is allocated in one or more of its components; each component-level requirement is allocated in one or more subcomponents, etc. It means that system is decomposed (partitioned) into finer and finer elements, while the requirements start at a highly abstract level and become more and more concrete for the lower-level elements (Dorfman, 1990). The level of detail increases as we move down in the hierarchy. System-level requirements are general in nature, while requirements at low levels of hierarchy are very specific. System's decomposition can be done in several ways. So various system concepts that can be postulated and different operational concepts defining general system goals, functions, and components can be developed (Lane, 1990). Trade-off studies are performed to select the architecture that best satisfies the system requirements. However a top-down approach is relevant only to the part of process and usually is combined with other approaches.

The purpose of requirements flowdown process is requirements rewriting in terms of functional areas where they are allocated (Dorfman, 1990). The lower level requirements are called *derived requirements*. The derived requirement may closely resemble the higher-level one or may be quite different. It may be derived from one high-level requirement or from a group of such requirements. New requirements may be also added to the set of requirements at each level of hierarchy. They are called *additional requirements*. Additional requirements cannot be derived from the system-level requirements. They are derived from the system decomposition into the major functional areas that must communicate with one another (Nelsen, 1990). The results of requirement flowdown process are described by so-called *requirements traceability matrix*.

As each level of partitioning, allocation, and flowdown takes place, the interface of each element to the rest of the system must be specified. Errors in previous steps can be discovered when interface definition is taking place.

The final step is the review of developed requirements. Validation and verification of partitioning, allocation, flowdown, and interfaces are as important as their generation (Dorfman, 1990). All derived requirements should be written in such a manner that they are verifiable. The developers must keep in mind a method of verification for each requirement (Nelsen, 1990).

It should be noted that systems engineering techniques are only tools supporting system development process. The most important element of this process is conceptualisation of the system (Beam, 1990). It is produced by the developer. So central role is played by system engineer and project success depends on his skills and abilities. The developer must determine, often from indirect evidence, how the systems of certain class operate, or why they fail. In complex system design experiences of other persons should be involved as well because no single individual can have personal experience in all aspects of the problem. Experiences of other persons can be explored either by reading or by the personal interaction.

3. CURRICULA ENGINEERING

3.1. Curriculum development as a requirements discovering process

A curriculum is a plan for a particular area of study, which includes also a statement of underlying philosophy, assumptions, goals, objectives, strategies, instructional teaching materials, and time frame. Study program is an implementation of a curriculum. It meets requirements defined by implemented curriculum. Curriculum implementation includes:

- scheduling;
- staffing;
- planning of exercises, presentations, courseworks, practices in industry, and other forms of individual or team learning;
- definition forms of assessment; and
- other actions needed to be performed before to put the program in operation.

Thus a curriculum can be seen both as requirements specification and a design of a study program, and a study program can be seen as a system under development or, in other words, as a group of interacting parts (components) functioning as a whole and distinguishable from its surroundings by recognizable boundaries (Lucas, 2002). Components of a study program are some units of study called courses or disciplines. Typically a study program has modular architecture. It means that courses are divided in smaller components called module. Although module requirements specification is stand-alone learning package including competencies that must be validated to demonstrate mastery certification of the skills, abilities and knowledge, a module itself is inter-dependent with regard to overall course requirements and must be completed regardless of prior knowledge and skills. In other words architecture of a study program should be designed with conceptual integrity (Ellis et al., 2000) of this program in mind and module specifications should be derived from program requirements. Consequently curriculum development deals with the module specifications and may be treated as a requirement engineering process.

We propose to apply standard systems engineering techniques to curricula engineering in a following way:

- to formulate the mission of the curriculum and to gather or/and to develop mission-related materials,
- to analyse mission and mission-related materials, and to formulate curriculum requirements,
- to define curriculum architecture,
- to define a system hierarchy for the curriculum,

- to allocate curriculum requirements in modules by applying requirements allocation and flow-down techniques in top-down manner iterative,
- to do verification and validation of allocated requirements and, in bottom-up manner, to propagate changes up to the top-level of hierarchy.

Let us discuss the proposed approach in more detail.

3.2. Curricula engineering and instructional design

Traditionally, curricula developers use terminology borrowed from instructional design (ID) discipline. The terms *instructional design* and *curriculum development* in practice often are used as synonyms. In industry most often is used the term instructional design, while in academic word most often is used the term curriculum development. However to be precise the term instructional design is wider as the term curriculum development.

The underlying theoretical basis of instructional design discipline is behavioural, cognitive, and constructivist theories. There is also a close relationship between epistemology, learning theory and instructional design theory. A number of particular instructional-design theories and models have been described in literature (Reigeluth, 1999; Seel, 1997). Modern instructional-design theories and models emphasize learning by doing. These theories suppose that learners should be active, do things, and construct a sequence of operations to reach some goal.

According to (Seel and Dijkstra, 1997), instructional design as a science aims at detailed and theoretically well-founded specifications for effective learning situations. From a technological point of view, it mainly consists of creating concrete instructional materials and environments in which students can learn effectively. More exactly, instructional-design theory consists of assumptions and explanations why specific instructional designs will support specific kinds of learning and instructional design model puts that theory into a set of heuristics that can effectively guide instructional planners in developing instructional designs. In other words, instructional design as an enterprise involves some theoretical backgrounds as well as an engineering discipline. So the question what is the relationship between curricula engineering and instructional design rightfully arises.

Instructional design sees a curriculum as a particular instructional system or, in other words, as an arrangement of resources and procedures to promote learning. The development of instructional system is seen as a particular instructional problem. Systematic process of developing instructional systems is called instructional design. It is thought as a process of translating general principles of learning and instruction into plans for instructional materials and learning. Process of implementing of instructional systems is called instructional development. Development of a module is seen as a part of the overall instructional development process. Finally, the systematic application of strategies and techniques to the solution of instructional problems is called instructional technology (Smith and Ragan, 1993). In this context we see curricula engineering as a particular instructional technology for instructional design and instructional development.

3.3. Curriculum architecture

The term "curriculum architecture" is not new. For example, Svenson and his colleagues claim (Svenson et al., 1984) that "Curriculum Architecture identifies the modular structure and typical, logical paths an individual would follow in the formal process of acquiring the knowledge and skills required to perform the assigned tasks of a job." In similar mining this term is used also by other authors. Although no one uses explicitly the term "architecture style", different styles (learner-centred architecture, problem-centred architecture, subject-centred architecture (Ornstein and Hunkins, 1998), performance-based architecture (Svenson et al., 1984), competence-based architecture, etc.) also are described in literature. However both concepts as defined are vague and imprecise. In more precise way terms "curriculum architecture" and "curriculum architecture style" can be defined adapting definitions of similar terms done in software engineering.

According to (Shaw and Garlan, 1996), software architecture style **St** may be specified by a four-tuple

$$\mathbf{Arch}_{\mathbf{St}} =< \delta, \eta, \omega, \gamma >, \quad (1)$$

where

δ - types of primitive components,
η - types of primitive constructors,
ω - types of higher-order constructors,
γ - types of semantic constraints.

Then architecture of the style **St** for particular system is defined as four-tuple

$$\mathbf{arch}_{\mathbf{St}} =< \mathbf{pr}, \mathbf{c}_1, \mathbf{c}_2, \mathbf{cnstr} >, \quad (2)$$

where

pr - the set of instances of primitive components, allowed by the specification δ,
$\mathbf{c_1}$ - the set of instances of primitives constructors, allowed by the specification η,
$\mathbf{c_2}$ - the set of instances of higher-order constructors, allowed by the specification ω,
cnstr - the set of constraints, allowed by the specification γ.

We argue to apply this concept to curricula architecture, too. Our idea is to define curricula architecture in an UML (Muller, 1997) oriented way, because such approach allows applying in curricula engineering case-based object-oriented modelling techniques (Cockburn, 1997). Further, we suggest to follow software engineering tradition and to consider modules as primitive components, although sometimes modules can have sufficient complicated own internal structure. Depending on architecture style, different kinds of modules (introductory, fundamental, advanced, elective, career-oriented, etc.) may be used. Similar as in software engineering such approach enables separate concerns of architectural and detailed design.

UML-oriented approach requires using UML dependencies as primitive constructors. For example, "*extends*" dependency may be used to describe relationships between fundamental and advanced modules, "*refine*" – to describe relationships between introductory and fundamental modules, "*uses*" – to describe prerequisites of a module, etc. Using stereotypes it is possible to define any required additional architectural relationships including higher-order constructors.

We believe that concept of style may be useful in curricula engineering in many aspects. First at all a number of curricula architecture styles (Burnett, 1999; Gorgone and Gray, 1999; McBeath and Atkinson, 1992) are in use already many year but typically they are described only in a vague and imprecise way. Explicit definition of architecture styles will facilitate comparative analysis and evaluation of different styles. Secondly, it enables to prepare style and architecture catalogues, describe curricula design patterns, etc. Using architecture catalogue, curricula designer can either choose one of described architectures or decide to develop new architecture or even new architecture style. It should be noted, however, that architectural innovations may cause a major risk and for this reason always should be well grounded.

3.4. Mission statement

In our approach curricula development starts with the formulation of mission statement. The mission statement should describe the main curricula objectives. The mission statement of a modern European curriculum in information systems should postulate, at least, the following objectives (Sailor, 1990):

- to reflect current and future labour market needs,
- to support both traditional and emerging career opportunities,
- to ensure graduates are prepared for positions in all European area,
- to remove employers uncertainty by providing all degree holders with a core set of knowledge,
- to ensure that graduates leave university with enough capacity and the motivation to continue their learning throughout life,
- to allow international student mobility.

In order to extract meaningful top-level curricula requirements, mission-related data should be either gathered or developed, and then analysed. The most important data are as follows:

- definition of the main subject of curricula,
- list of career opportunities,
- main trends in the study field,
- rules of student mobility.

The subject definition should describe the state of the art and reflect current labour market needs. For example, information system (subject of the curriculum) in the MOCURIS project has been defined (Caplinskas, and Vasilecas, 2001) as "a computer-based system that aims to support the business and to enhance the work and the results by means of using of information technology as an integral part of daily operation of one or more (may be distributed) organisations. It includes not only technologies, but people, processes and organisational mechanisms as well. Information system provides and maintains an integrated information flow throughout the enterprise, so that the right information is available whenever and wherever needed, in the quality and quantity needed. Advanced information systems support operations at multiple locations and different time zones, are distributed, multimedia, network- and agent-based, use multidimensional data analysis, data warehousing, data mining and knowledge discovery, knowledge management, mobile computing, and other advanced technologies. The software used to implement an information system can be designed as a number of custom applications, purchased as off-the-shelf standard solution, or assembled from componentware. Information Systems, as an academic discipline, encompasses two broad areas: (1) acquisition, deployment, and management of information technology resources and services and (2) development and evolution of technology infrastructures and systems for use in business processes."

This definition reflects the state-of-the-art in a given field. The future needs of labour market should be also predicted on the basis of the known trends in the study field.

3.5. System hierarchy

We propose to define curricula system hierarchy as a four level hierarchy, which provides following abstraction levels:

- curricula requirements,
- exit requirements for graduates,
- refined exit requirements for graduates,
- module requirements.

The first two levels of hierarchy are domain-oriented and the rest two levels are implementation-oriented. It means that at two first levels the requirements should be formulated in terms of labour market needs, and at third and fourth levels requirements should be formulated in terms of teaching point of view.

Let us describe each level of abstraction in more detail.

The systems engineering approach suggests that the top-level requirements shall be partitioned into functional and non-functional ones. This way of requirements partition is reasonable for curricula, too. However, curricula developers as a rule do not use the terms "functional" and "non-functional" requirements. So, we prefer to use the terms "*content requirements*" (an analogue of functional requirements) and "*additional requirements*" (an analogue of non-functional requirements).

Content requirements should be derived from mission statement and related materials.

Additional requirements include curricula quality, curricula development, curricula implementation, curricula maintenance, and curricula application requirements.

Quality requirements depend on curricula quality model. Examples of curricula quality attributes are understandability and learnability. The details of curricula quality model are out of scope of this paper so this issue is not discussed here.

Additional requirements should be derived from mission statement and mission-related materials, too. They are not allocable. It means that they apply unchanged to all components of the curricula.

The next level of abstraction is general exit requirements for graduates. We propose to decompose this level into four functional areas: professional requirements, self-development requirements, personality requirements, and socio-cultural requirements.

Professional requirements at very general level define the professional abilities and skills, which should posses a graduate, and knowledge areas in which he or she shall be knowledgeable. An example of a professional requirement is the requirement that states: "*Graduates shall have comprehensive knowledge about the state-of-the-art in curriculum subject area*".

Self-development requirements define abilities and skills needed to ensure career-long learning. An example of a self-development requirement is as follow: "*Graduates shall cultivate an interest and desire for life-long learning*".

Personality requirements define capabilities, which should posses a graduate as a person. The following is an example of a personality requirement: "*Graduates shall posses leadership capabilities*".

Socio-cultural requirements define the capabilities, which should posses a graduate as a member of the society. An example of a socio-cultural requirement is the statement: "*Graduates shall gain ethic and professionalism*".

Exit requirements for graduates are derived from content requirements. They are very general and should be refined. We propose to decompose this level of requirements into four functional areas, too. The functional areas are as follow:

- required knowledge,
- required experience, abilities, and skills,
- required motivations and capabilities,
- required person properties.

Refined requirements are partitioned in another way as general exit requirements for graduates. The reason to change the partition is that general exit requirements for graduates are domain-oriented and refined requirements are implementation-oriented. Thus, the refined requirements are formulated in the form of required knowledge, experience, abilities, skills, motivations, capabilities and person properties.

Each portion (functional area) of refined requirements for graduates should be partitioned further into requirements for bachelor degree and requirements for master degree. The criteria of decomposition depend on the definitions of bachelor degree and master degree in a given country or even in a given university.

The requirements for graduates are not homogenous. Some requirements are more important, others are less important. It means that we need some measure to estimate the degree of required knowledge, abilities, and capabilities. We propose to use the following scale:

- be aware,
- to apply concepts,
- be able to do or to behave,
- be skilled,
- have rich experience.

The last level of curricula system hierarchy is the module level. All refined exit requirements for graduates (bachelors and masters) should flowdowned to the module level. It is proposed that each module description should include the following sections:

- philosophy which describes the type of the module (core module, elective module, etc.), its purpose (introductory, fundamental, advanced), the auditory (career track), the main approach taken in module, and prerequisite abilities and knowledge,
- objectives that describe what a person having studied the material covered in the module is expected to be able to do,
- prerequisite modules,

- content, which describes topics covered in the module,
- teaching considerations which describe suggested schedule, trained abilities, capabilities, motivations, and person properties,
- annotated list of recommended literature.

Required knowledge should flowdowned to modules as topics, other requirements as objectives or teaching considerations.

Using techniques described above the curricula is developed in a top-down manner. Top-down techniques are helpful to keep sight of objectives in the curricula development process. However, these techniques do not ensure homogeneous granularity nor completeness of the bottom-level requirements.

Additional sources (experts, other curricula, etc.) should be also used to ensure curricula completeness. Curricula evaluation report should be prepared and completeness and integrity of the curricula should be evaluated. To ensure homogeneous granularity of the bottom-level requirements standard review techniques (Beam, 1990) may be used. All levels of system hierarchy should be reviewed in bottom-up manner and bottom-level modifications should be propagated up to mission level.

3.6. Tools to support the curricula engineering process

Many tools, such as performance models, curriculum matrix, etc., are used to support curricula development process. We argue that the following additional tools are helpful to facilitate the curricula engineering process (Caplinskas, 2001):

- localisation matrix,
- traceability matrix,
- cross-reference matrix.

The localisation matrix shows where (in which functional area) each requirement is allocated. The cells of matrix should be filled with appropriate weight coefficients. The matrix should be developed for each level of system hierarchy.

In order to show how requirements are partitioned into exit requirements for bachelors and masters, and what degree of knowledgebility is required, at the third level of hierarchy the localisation matrix may be slightly modified.

Traceability matrix shows the source requirements and weight coefficient for each derived requirement. This matrix should be prepared for each flowdown level.

Cross-reference matrix shows what knowledge is needed to develop required experience, abilities, skills, motivations, capabilities, and person properties. It should be used for the refined requirements for graduates. Similar cross-reference matrix may be prepared to show references between co-requisite modules.

Sophisticated software tools used in requirement engineering, for example, Rational RequisitePro®‡, are very useful in curricula engineering, too.

‡ Rational RequisitePro is a registered trademark of Rational Software Corporation.

4. CONCLUSIONS

The proposed approach has been used successfully in the Socrates/Erasmus curriculum development project MOCURIS. In this project a modern master degree generic curriculum in information systems has been developed. It was designed to serve as a set of standards upon which individual universities can base their individual curriculum. Universities may vary in the master's programs they offer, with each university offering its own unique alternative, determined by faculty skills and local needs. Generic curriculum specifies core body of knowledge and includes resource requirements, teaching materials, and guidance on tailoring individual curriculum. The curriculum development starts from mission statement and follows above described approach. The mission statement has been formulated as follow (Caplinskas and Vasilecas, 2001):

> The integration trends and the extension of EU allow intensive international student mobility. The global trends of Information Society as the transformation of industrial economics into knowledge- and information-based service economics as well as the increasing role of global networks and new information technologies pose a number of new challenges. The objectives of the project are to develop Master Degree curriculum in order to meet new challenges, and to adapt it to labour market needs and needs of international student mobility.

The resulting generic curriculum is described in details in (Caplinskas and Vasilecas, 2002) and the experience in curricula engineering gained in the project MOCURIS is described in (Caplinskas and Vasilecas, 2001). This experience demonstrates a number of advantages of proposed approach. It systematises the curriculum development process, facilitates ensuring of the conceptual integrity of the curriculum under development, and enables to explain the reasons why some abilities or/and knowledge are required from graduates. However, several important problems also have been discovered: the requirement specification is difficult to look through because of its size; no clear criteria exist to separate different aspects of the topics; the methods proposed to ensure the homogeneity of the granularity of the requirements are quite time-consuming.

REFERENCES

1. T. Bahill, and F. Dean, 2002, What Is Systems Engineering? A Consensus of Senior Systems Engineers, University of Arizona (May 10, 2002); http://www.sie.arizona.edu/sysengr/whatis/whatis.html
2. W. R. Beam, 1990, Systems Engineering. Architecture and Design, McGraw-Hill Publishing Company.
3. D. Burnett, 1999, Pedagogical Alternatives for Web-Based Instruction, Proceedings of AusWeb99 Fifth Australian World Wide Web Conference, Southern Cross University; http://ausweb.scu.edu.au/aw99/papers/burnett/paper.html
4. A. Caplinskas, 2001, Curricula engineering: application of systems engineering methods to the development of university curricula, *Information Technology and Control*, **22**(1), 53–58
5. A. Caplinskas, and O. Vasilecas, 2001, Modern curriculum in information systems: a case study. *Information Technology and Control*, **22**(1), 59–63
6. A. Caplinskas, and O. Vasilecas, 2002, MOCURIS – modern curriculum in information systems at master level, in: *ECIS 2002. Information Systems and the Future of the Digital Economy.Proc. of the Xth European Conference on Information Systems, Gdansk, Poland, 6-8 June, 2002,* Vol. 1, S. Wrycza, ed., Wydawnictwo uniwersitetu Gdanskiego, pp. 184–193
7. A. Cockburn, 1997, Structuring use case with goals, *Journal of Object-Oriented Programming*, part 1, September-October, 1997, part 2, November-December, 1997.

8. M. Dorfman, 1990, System and software requirements engineering, in: *System and Software Requirements Engineering,* R. H. Thayer, and M. Dorfman, eds., IEEE Computer Society Press, Los Alamitos, California, Washington, Brussels, Tokyo, pp. 4–16
9. R. A. Ellis, R. Calvo, D. Levy, J. Kay, and R. J. Kummerfeld, 2000, *Conceptual Integrity in Web-Inclusive Curriculum Design*; http://ausweb.scu.edu.au/aw02/papers/refereed/ellis/paper.html
10. J. T. Gorgone, and P. Gray, eds., 1999, *MSIS 2000: Model Curriculum and Guidelines for Graduate Degree Programs in Information Systems,* Association for Computing Machinery
11. A. Holzl, 2000, A Strategic Approach to Curriculum Design at the University of Queensland, Proceedings of the Duchesne College Conference for University Teachers on Effective Teaching and Learning, The University of Queensland, 9 and 10 November 2000; http://www.tedi.uq.edu.au/conferences/teach_conference00/papers/holzl-1.html
12. R. J. Lane, 1990, A structured approach for operational concept formulation, in: *System and Software Requirements Engineering,* R. H. Thayer, and M. Dorfman, eds., IEEE Computer Society Press, Los Alamitos, California, Washington, Brussels, Tokyo, pp. 48- 57
13. Ch. Lucas, 2002, Self-Organizing Systems (SOS) FAQ. Frequently Asked Questions Version 2.8 May 2002. For USENET Newsgroup comp.theory.self-org-sys; http://www.calresco.org/sos/sosfaq.htm
14. C. McBeath and R. J. Atkinson, 1992, Curriculum, instructional design and the technologies: Planning for educational delivery, *Australian Journal of Educational Technology,* **8**(2), 119–131; http://cleo.murdoch.edu.au/gen/aset/ajet/ajet8/su92/p119.html
15. P. A. Muller, 1997, *Instant UML,* Wrox Press Ltd.®
16. E. D. Nelsen, 1990, System engineering and requirement allocation, in: *System and Software Requirements Engineering,* R. H. Thayer, and M. Dorfman, eds., IEEE Computer Society Press, Los Alamitos, California, Washington, Brussels, Tokyo, pp. 60–76
17. A. C. Ornstein, and Hunkins, F. P., 1998, *Curriculum Foundations, Principles, and Issues,* Third Edition, Boston: Allyn and Bacon.
18. C. M. Reigeluth, ed., 1999, *Instructional design theories and models: A new paradigm of instructional theory. Vol. 2.* Mahwah, NJ: Lawerence Erlbaum Associates
19. J. D. Sailor, 1990, System engineering: an introduction, in: *System and Software Requirements Engineering,* R. H. Thayer, and M. Dorfman, eds., IEEE Computer Society Press, Los Alamitos, California, Washington, Brussels, Tokyo, pp. 35–47
20. N. Seel, 1997, Models of Instructional Design: Introduction and Overview, in: *Instructional Design: International Perspective. Theory, Research, and Models. Vol.1,* R. D. Tennyson, F. Schott, N. Seel, and Dijkstra, S., eds., Mahwah, NJ: Lawrence Erlbaum Associates, pp. 355–360
21. N. Seel, and S. Dijkstra, 1997, General introduction, in: *Instructional Design: International Perspective. Solving Instructional Design Problems. Vol. 2.* S. Dijkstra, N. Seel, F. Schott, and R.D. Tennyson, eds., Mahwah, NJ: Lawrence Erlbaum Associates, pp. 1–13
22. M. Shaw, and D. Garlan, 1996, *Software Architecture: Perspectives on an Emerging discipline.* Prentice-Hall, Englewood Cliffs, NJ.
23. P. Smith, and T. Ragan, 1993, *Instructional design.* Upper Saddle River, New Jersey: Prentice-Hall, Inc.
24. R. A. Svenson, D. D. McKenna, K. M. Kennedy, and G. W. Wallace, 1984, Developing Performance-based Curriculum Architecture Using a Group Process to Create Performance Models and Knowledge/Skill Matrices, Presented at Chicago NSPI Cracker Barrel, July 20, 1984; http://www.eppic.biz/resources/res_articles_files/A-1006%20%20(original)%20How%20to%20Build%20a%20Training%20Structure.PDF
25. G. W. Wallace, P. R. Hybert, K. R. Smith, and B. D. Blecke, 2002, lean-ISD - Designing for the Life-cycle. CADDI, Inc., 2002; http://hobsongroup.com/pdf/lean-ISD%20Designing%20for%20the%20Life-cycle.pdf
26. K. F. Zuga, 1989, Relating Technology Education Goals to Curriculum Planning, *Journal of Technology Education* **1**(1); http://scholar.lib.vt.edu/ejournals/JTE/v1n1/zuga.jte-v1n1.html

CONSIDERATIONS IN SYSTEMS DEVELOPMENT OF APPLICATIONS FOR MOBILE DEVICES

A case study

Linda Dawson and Julie Fisher*

1. INTRODUCTION

Mobile devices differ from PCs because of their size, input device limitations, the mobility provided to users and their potential to be context aware. Because of usability, and implementation issues designing applications for mobile devices may require a different approach to systems development from that used for system development for PC applications. This study explores these issues by examining usability, implementation in the development of an application for a hand held device, a Palm Personal Digital Assistant (PDA), in a health care environment.

2. BACKGROUND AND RELATED WORK

Research priorities in mobile systems development to date have focused on the technology, networking and communications and generic applications particularly for WAP based devices such as mobile phones. Research on usability and mobile devices has focused primarily on the technology limitations and display size (Chan et al., 2002). There is little in the current literature that discusses development of applications for mobile or handheld devices particularly from either the implementers' or the users' perspective. The main areas potentially affecting approaches to system development for mobile applications which are explored in the study reported in this paper are: usability issues, technical and implementation issues, and specification and development issues.

* Linda Dawson, the School of Information Management and Systems, Monash University. Julie Fisher the School of Information Management and Systems, Monash University.

2.1 Usability Issues

The ISO standards on usability define it as "Usability: the extent to which product can be used by specified users to achieve specified goals with effectiveness, efficiency and satisfaction in a specified context of use." (Bevan, 2001, 537). Shneiderman (1998) argues that for those developing systems usability must go beyond "user-friendliness" to include an understanding of the diverse needs of users and what they are trying to accomplish. Users continue to face usability problems with PC based applications (Shneiderman, 2000). These problems are further exacerbated when applications are developed for mobile devices (Shneiderman, 2001; Chan et al 2002). Two key mobile device limitations issues, impacting on usability are discussed below.

2.1.1. Interface design and size

The design approach taken for standard PC software interfaces cannot be applied to mobile or hand held devices. Size of the display, resolution, and colour options require rethinking what is possible in terms of interface design. Screen brightness and backlighting are areas of common concern to users. Increasing brightness results in a corresponding loss of battery life. The tradeoffs tend to be a gain in portability and compactness versus a degradation of functionality. Small screen size has a dramatic effect on user effectiveness, reducing it in some cases by 50% (Albers & Kim, 2000).

2.1.2. Input Device Types

Significant progress has been made over the last decade in the development of innovative methods for interacting with PC based applications. We cannot assume however that the same input devices are appropriate for mobile device applications (Bellotti et al., 2002). Current input options for mobile devices include small numeric keyboards (mobile phones), stylus entry on screen based alphanumeric keypads, and handwriting recognition (or stylised writing - graffiti on PDAs). These input methods can be difficult and error prone severely limiting device usability (Abowd & Mynatt, 2000).

2.2. Implementation Issues

2.2.1. Technical and Infrastructure Environments

As people move around there will be a growing expectation of continuous use of devices across a range of systems and locations, office, car, home. The increasing use of mobile devices means that it cannot be assumed that people working collaboratively are using the same technology and so are able to support the same software. Mobile users will need to communicate with servers and each other using different devices, software and file formats (Huang, et al., 2001). Software transparency will be an important issue as will be the supporting infrastructures and architectures for providing truly ubiquitous environments and encouraging widespread use.

The underlying infrastructure supporting a wireless environment impacts on the quality of the user's interaction with a mobile device. Timely user feedback from the interface has come to be expected. "The need to consider the overall functionality of the application and design structures that provide appropriate access to different levels of functionality is amplified in the case of mobile applications where the infrastructure may vary dynamically as the application is in use." (Dix et al., 2000, 290). In a wireless environment where an application is distributed over a wide area delays in the transmission of data and information to users are likely. Battery life is also a constraint. Further, "The mobility of nomadic users implies that the users might connect from different access points through wireless links and might want to stay connected while on the move, despite possible intermittent disconnections." (Pierre, 2001, p 118).

2.2.2. Management Issues

Business deployment of mobile devices will require careful consideration. Organisations must decide which devices and architectures are most suitable for the organisation's core business. The lack of available applications currently hinders uptake for many organisations. Organizations who do implement a mobile work environment need to consider training and implementation issues, including user acceptance (Smith & Kulatilaka, 2002). Introducing mobile devices may entail a change in company culture or the way businesses is done and acceptance by users will be critical (Siau, et al. 2001).

2.3. System Development Methods and Issues

A system development methodology (SDM) has been defined as "...a systematic approach to conducting at least one complete phase (e.g. requirements analysis, design) of system development, consisting of a set of guidelines, activities, techniques and tools, based on a particular philosophy of system development and the target system." (Wynekoop & Russo, 1997, p. 48) It is generally recognised that the use of some kind of methodology is necessary to facilitate successful system development (Avison & Fitzgerald, 1995; Fitzgerald, 1998b).

In examining system development approaches for mobile devices it is useful to consider *non-functional requirements* (Loucopoulos & Karakostas, 1995; Sommerville & Sawyer, 1997). Loucopoulos and Karakostas (1995) define non-functional requirements as "...the constraints that can be placed on the system, its environment, or its development [and include aspects such as] security, availability, portability, usability, performance etc.". Somerville and Sawyer (1997) provide a simple definition "Very roughly, functional requirements describe what the system should do and non-functional requirements place constraints on how these functional requirements are implemented." For application development on mobile devices these non-functional requirements are much more pronounced because of the usability and technical constraints such as screen size, battery life and data entry methods on the implementation environment.

The identification of mobile-specific issues in systems development approaches should lead to a better understanding, documentation and improvement of methods, techniques, and tools for the development of mobile-specific applications.

3. MOBILE DEVICES IN HEALTH CARE

Most health-care workers could be described as "nomadic" in their daily working environment spending considerable time moving around with little opportunity to interact with a PC. Recent evidence suggests increasing interest in PDAs in health care however the health-care sector is a challenging environment in which to develop and implement mobile devices/applications (Shipman &Morton 2001). Such devices and applications however have the potential to provide users with a vast array of patient information, data can be immediately updated and overall patient treatment is improved. There are a number of issues, apart from those mentioned, relating to the use of mobile devices specific to the health-care sector, these include:

- Designing to maximise device mobility. In a hospital environment applications "sensitive to the identity of the user of the device" (Dix et al. 2000, 291) would be of great value.
- Data entry and the impact on data integrity is another concern. The use of mobile devices by volunteers in a clinical trial reported by Koop and Mosges (2002), found problems users had with data entry resulting in missing values, exacerbated because the system did not notify the users of the missing values. High error rates occurred because the application could not handle the speed of users' data entry.
- In health-care paper records have a value, Luff and Heath (1998) see the paper record supporting both "synchronous and asynchronous collaboration." This collaboration is between doctors, patient, and other medical staff. Paper records can be moved around within a hospital or clinic, this they argue is part of its success (Luff & Heath, 1998). Anderson (1997) argues that paper records when stored electronically place limitations on how data is recorded and organised. Replacement of paper records may not be widely accepted.
- Interaction with the devices by users differ depending on the context of use, hospital contexts are many and varied, this impacts on design (Dix et al, 2000).
- In the health-care area there are specific application development challenges including storage and transfer of data, how easy devices are to use and building applications to suit the work environment (Shipman and Morton, 2001; Dix, 2000).

Identification of these, among other issues, indicates a need for rigorous research into all aspects of introducing mobile devices and mobile information environments into the health-care sector.

4. RESEARCH APPROACH

4.1. Research Objectives

This study sought to investigate how professional systems developers develop applications for mobile devices. The following broad research question arises from this objective:

Are there special considerations for professional developers when building applications for mobile devices?

This broad research question can usefully be broken down into three sub questions,

How are mobile-specific ***usability issues*** *accommodated by mobile system development methods?*

How are mobile-specific ***technology constraints*** *and other mobile-specific implementation issues dealt with in mobile systems development approaches?*

Are the ***requirements analysis****, specification and design methods used for the development of applications for mobile devices "****mobile-specific****"?*

The research project described here explored the development of a mobile application in a health care environment from the implementers' perspective in order to address the research questions.

4.2. Participants

The unit of analysis in this project is an individual implementer including the project leader who was also a director of the organization undertaking the project. Interviews with users are part of the project but are yet to take place and so are not reported here.

All the participants were professional systems developers working for an organization which was developing an application for trainee anaesthetists in a large metropolitan teaching hospital. The application is a simple logging application implemented on a Palm PDA and based on CUSUM Charts (Page, 1954; Shewhart, 1931) which allows the trainee anaesthetists to monitor their use of various procedures.

The five developers interviewed for this study work for a company which is experienced in the development of mobile technology products including applications in the health-care industry. The mobile application investigated has been recently deployed as a pilot project with six registrars in three hospitals in Australia and New Zealand. The application is designed to record anaesthetic procedures and incidents occurring during the procedure. Most of the data is recorded by selecting options from drop-down menus or check boxes, however, users may also record information using the free text facility available. A report on the application of the devices, from a medical perspective, has recently been published by anaesthetists involved in the project (Bent, et al., 2002). Figure 1 is a snapshot of the application and opening screen. The application was developed around an existing paper-based system, users who had experience with the existing system therefore knew the primary purpose of the device.

4.3. Data Collection Method

Data in this project was collected by face-to-face and email interviews. Interview questions addressed issues of usability, implementation and system development methods.

Donald Norman (1988), a renowned cognitive psychologist in his book "The Design of Everyday Things", focuses on the design of everyday devices suggesting seven questions which should be asked when systems are designed. Norman's questions are built from what he describes as the "Seven stages of action" (p 48), the first is for goals, the next three relate to execution and the final three for evaluation. In the interviews usability issues were explored using questions based on adaptations of Norman's seven questions (Research Question 2). Other interview questions addressed technical and implementation issues (Research Question 1) and the system development process (Research Question 3). The Project Leader was interviewed in depth separately. The interview with the Project Leader was intended to draw out more detailed data about the philosophy behind the organisation's approach to system design and implementation. After all responses were received follow up questions for clarification were asked.

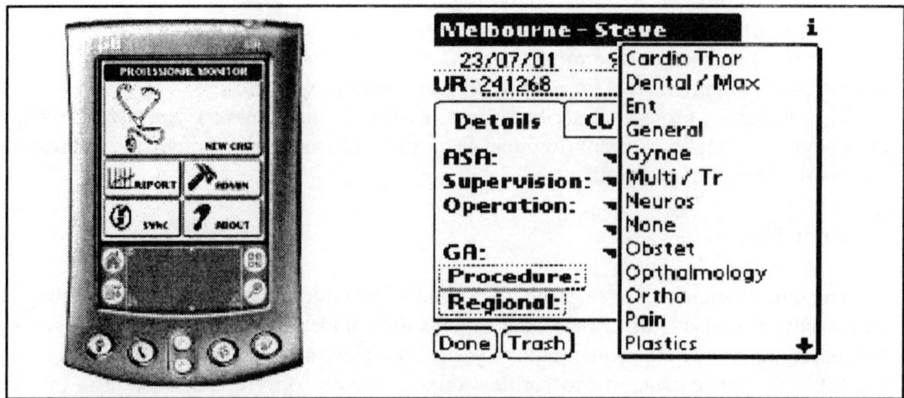

Figure 1. Application screens

5. FINDINGS

The following sections describe the case study findings with particular reference to usability, technical and implementation issues the research questions addressed. The presentation is based on illustrated narrative style, or an oral narrative told in the first person, as described by Miles and Huberman (1994) and Myers (1999) and as used in Fitzgerald (1997) and Urquhart (1998). This approach is described as "..each part of the sequence is followed by a series of illustrative excerpts [quotes from the transcripts]" which does not resort to explicit coding but looks for "..key words, themes, and sequences to find the most characteristic accounts." (Miles & Huberman, 1994, p 87) Where transcript data is quoted directly the researcher's questions or interactions are shown as bold italic and the participant's as plain italic.

5.1. Usability Issues

The implementers believed that the device was easy for users to understand. The reason being was because it had been built using specifications from the users. "*It was designed with the specific users in mind, they had a vested interest in knowing the application.*" The opening screen the user clicks once and they are into the application so it is very clear to the users what the device is for.

As the application was based on an existing paper-based system the developers believed that it was easy to identify the functionality. Providing obvious and intuitive icons and controls, supported by on-board context sensitive help, users are able to identify the functionality.

Although developers believe the system is "intuitive" and that it is easy to identify functionality, "intuition" seems to be confused sometimes with "tacit knowledge". Information and device functionality seems to be conveyed through training, suggesting the application is not intuitive. For example, decision rules dictate the pathway through the application, one decision dictates the next screen or drop down menu. What drives functionality is federal government regulations stored in tables that drive decision rules, this is not obvious to the users. The system relies on the users' tacit rather than explicit knowledge. Users need a very good high-level understanding of their own clinical behaviour to adequately and accurately record data in the application.

The project leader believed that *"... new users readily understand the application and how to use it ... because it mirrors their workplace."* The development team had also spent some time testing and training users and it was clear from this that *" ... even recently graduated anaesthetists could pick up the application quickly."* The project leader did acknowledge that to some extent the functionality was dependent on the user's medical knowledge and expertise.

When asked "***Can users easily determine how to achieve their goals using the device/application?***" the implementers agreed the system *".. validates data and produces accurate presentation quality reports and" ... "much of this [determining how to achieve goals] is firmly established through training and induction with the device.*"

The project leader described how significant validation rules were built into the system *"These rules guide the user to the next stage of the application"*. If an entry is made that contradicts a previous entry a dialog box will appear prompting the user to change what has been entered. Validation also occurs at the end of a data entry session.

The implementers were asked what had been done to make the application "user-friendly" and whether usability tests had been conducted. Each developer believed user-friendliness was important however no usability testing had been conducted. Users were however involved in the prototyping process. One of the developers suggested that the selection of a particular operating system was because it helped non computer literate users. Another developer responded that *"... user acceptance is paramount and intuitive GUI "wizard style interfaces 'lead' the user through pathways in response to users input as governed in configurable business rules"*.

Implementers generally agreed that users could tell if the device and application were ready to perform the task and that the status of the application was indicated on the screen of the device. Responses included: *"Yes, following from the above our 'rules-driven' engine ensures that the user is guided through the data entry process and is aware of the 'state of completion' of the task. The users cannot exit without completing the task."* and "*Yes, users know that this is the first stage of development, and can tell what stage of the application they are in, this is indicated on the screen."*

The anaesthetists so far have used neck straps that plug into the synch port of the Palm and standard carrying cases for carrying the devices around. The users are encouraged to see the devices as sophisticated electronic devices/computers like a mobile phone which "*don't like to swim.*"

When asked to suggest questions that should be asked regarding usability implementers nominated user expectations, "*How does the organisation expect to get all participants 'up to speed' with using the device and make it an integral part of the work process?" "How will the organisation tackle issues of technical literacy and/ or phobia in order to optimise the use of the device? "*

5.2. Implementation Issues

The project leader mentioned that many managers still see PDAs as *"calculators on steroids"*. Through the applications they are developing they are able to demonstrate more extensive functionality than most people are aware of.

The device starts at power up at the Palm system Home screen. The user must tap the application icon to start the application, this is followed by a wizard style decision tree prompting users through the application. The application is ended by tapping the final DONE key which triggers the final validation process described above. The paradigm for the device is based on turning it on 50 times a day compared with turning on a PC once or twice a day.

The project leader acknowledged it was difficult to design a system using such a small screen, to deal with this the implementation team had used a number of techniques. Where text data was to be entered a series of layered "sub-screens" with clickable tabs were used so details could be on a separate overlaid pages rather than all presented on the one screen at the same time.

The business rules are embedded in data not in code, they can be configured using a browser interface to an Internet site connected to a database by a "local" administrator (ie local to the client organization) independently of the implementers. This also allows for synchronisation via the Internet for users using their own business rules. The database also allows logging of online change requests ("field trouble reports"). User data management and synchronisation uses the secure web server pages for download and upload of data including individual user data that had been synchronised, documentation, user manuals, and system updates including rules updates. One implementer explained *"They can track their data collection and input, which is aggregated once it is synchronised. Discussion and training about what happens with the data takes place during training."* At the end of a data entry session users click the DONE button on the screen that completes the process. *"If as part of the final validation check there is something that needs to be changed, a dialog box will appear. If not the user can assume the entry is complete."*

Anaesthetists do not have hard synching deadlines. The nature of their work means that hard deadlines are not feasible or useful. The potential long lead times to synching in this environment has led to problems when the battery has gone flat before synchronisation has taken place. The Palm does have a "low battery" alarm which becomes increasingly insistent and the device will go into "life-support" mode when really low. It was recognised that specific "nagging" by on screen messages could be implemented to facilitate synching.

There is currently no user prompting for synchronising the mobile device, it is up to individual users. Status and system information such as battery level, signal strength and location are only available at operating system level not within the application. This has led to some implementation problems. Synchronisation is a problem with users not synchronising frequently enough. It is possible to modify the application to include regular prompts reminding users to synchronise. However a decision has been made that to ensure users are comfortable and avoid a "Big Brother" feel to the system a minimum number of reminders are built-in. However the project leader thinks it is likely that in the near future this will be included.

The implementation process for mobile devices and applications from the implementer's perspective was discussed and several issues were raised. Several implementers saw training as a specific issue: "*Training of the typically 'non-IT' literate users is vital to successful deployment. Keep the training simple but effective and get feedback and monitor any field problems closely.*" and "*Users seldom read the device manual let alone any application instructions. We find that when a user can identify some part of the application with their normal work practice the adoption is faster.*" Another issue raised was user participation in the development process: "*Ownership of the process, good training and induction are essential for uptake and ongoing use. Users need to feel like they are being listened to in the process, that we are accommodating their concerns and being responsive to needs. Getting champions in the workplace is important so that there is some support (informal) when we leave after training. Quick follow-up after initial implementation can help with sorting out problems, and for the next iteration of the application.*"

5.3. System Development

The method used by the implementing organization was an in-house method rather than a formal approach such as the Rational Unified Process (RUP) (Jacobson, Booch, & Rumbaugh, 1999) or Object Modelling Technique (Rumbaugh, et al., 1991). This concurs with published findings which suggest that the use of formal system development methodologies in many system development projects is low (Bansler & Bodker, 1993; Chatzoglou & Macaulay, 1996; Dawson & Darke, 2002; Fitzgerald, 1998a). Early work undertaken by the implementation team involved project scoping and determining trainee anaesthetists' needs. The developers worked closely with a hospital representative. Once there was a broad plan and scope defined, a full requirements/business analysis was done - "*the full A to Z*" according to the project leader - and from that a full prototype was developed. This prototype represented the general logic of the system design and how the decisions were made within the application eg, menu content, decision order. The logical design was based on a decision-tree approach where the user is prompted through the tree based on their last response. Real-time validation takes place throughout the process and also at the end of the process when the user taps the DONE key. Validation at the DONE step may require the user to clarify or provide further information based on the business rules that underlie the application.

Significant time was spent in user consultation once the overall application logic was determined. The identification of champions within the user group during prototype development was important. Champions are used in conjunction with "domain experts" to channel feedback between the implementation team and the users. The project leader believed that it was important for the users to explain to the development team exactly what it was that they wanted and where the current system did not meet their requirements. From the development team's perspective it was very important to capture user input effectively as they were unfamiliar with the medical field.

To ensure a high level of acceptance the implementation team spent time making the trainee anaesthetists feel comfortable with the application. The developers also expected sign off from the users but were prepared to accept minor changes and encouraged the users to come forward with new ideas or improvements they thought were necessary.

Device testing with the users was undertaken at two levels. Data was gathered by one hospital contact from the users about the application and any feedback relating to use. This was then fed back to the development team. The key developers through the hospital contact would demonstrate application changes. The development team did not want to include functionality that was not directly relevant to the trainee anaesthetists. At times there were requests for administrative functions to be included but these were not seen as directly relating to the anaesthetists' work.

Another approach taken by the development team to ensure wide acceptance was to make sure that the different aspects of the system were explained in detail to the users.

The development team are very aware that system success depends very much on user acceptance and this has been a driving consideration throughout the development process. The application had to be simple, effective and easy-to-use.

6. DISCUSSION

The research objective was to investigate how professional developers build systems for a mobile device application focusing on usability and implementation constraints.

6.1. Usability Issues in Mobile Systems Development

The results highlighted a number of critical issues related to usability that are likely to impact on the acceptance and successful implementation of mobile devices, those issues are:

- Whilst developers clearly believe the function of the device is obvious there have not been any specific design considerations made to ensure this. Explicit links between hardware and the application have not been made clear.
- Training and induction with the devices is still essential to ensure users are able to effectively use the application. What happens to users who do not receive training after implementation? Norman (1988) would argue that use should be transparent; the user should be able to see what it is the device does and how to use it.
- The development team is depending heavily on what they believe is a very intuitive interface to ensure usability. However, without conducting usability testing it is difficult to assess ease-of-use. The current screen design displays a significant amount of information (given the screen size) and requires users to input data into seven different fields on one screen, five of these fields require the user to select from a drop-down menu. Developers would be advised to consider usability testing as part of future application development.
- In some areas "intuition" seemed to be being confused with "tacit knowledge".

Many of these issues still need to be addressed in this application. Usability testing and training is still necessary to increase acceptance and ongoing use of the application.

6.2 Implementation Issues in Mobile System Development

Implementation issues centre on the following:

- The small screen size requires the use of tabbed, layered screens to deal with all the data that would logically belong on one screen.
- A decision tree approach where users are prompted to tap specific buttons, boxes or parts of the screen deals with the limited – single stylus rather than keyboard – design of the interface.
- Lack of integrated storage media on the PDA has been dealt with by using secure web sites for data storage and download. To obtain information about data users however, must log back into the system; the application does not provide users with information about their data whilst work/data input is in progress.

- Information relating to battery level is only provided on the first screen. The batteries in the devices are going flat because users are not aware of the need to recharge.
- Synchronisation and its enforcement is still a problem that needs to be resolved.

All these mobile specific issues must be dealt with in the design and implementation.

6.3. System Development Methods in Mobile System Development

There is evidence in this case of the use of standard system development approaches in the design of mobile-specific applications. These methods and phases include full business requirements analysis, requirements, and business rules are embedded in the data stored on a secure web site for download at appropriate times. There is evidence of standard prototyping using emulations and user champions and also a standard approach to acceptance testing and sign off. None of these areas appeared to be mobile-specific.

There was also evidence of the use of mobile-specific approaches. Most of these mobile specific approaches relate directly to the usability (screen size, data entry methods, portability in the hospital environment), and technical implementation constraints (data management, synchronisation, battery life etc) outlined above which need to be taken into account in the analysis and design phases.

This study highlights the importance of considering non-functional requirements such as battery-life, screen-size, and other usability issues in system development for mobile devices. As previously discussed, usability has not always had the prominence it deserves in system development.

7. CONCLUSION

This paper presented the findings from an exploratory research study motivated by the need to understand the considerations in developing applications for mobile applications. The findings show that although many standard approaches to system development are appropriate for mobile-specific applications there are some areas that require special consideration in the development process. Usability, specifically with respect to the user interface, usability testing and training, and dealing with technical and operational constraints such as battery life, synchronisation procedures, and data management. Longer term research following this exploratory study aims to understand mobile information environments as they are currently being implemented from both the implementers and the users' perspectives and to gather information about the implementation process which will assist in future developments of mobile information and application environments in the health care industry.

REFERENCES

Abowd, G., and Mynatt, E., 2000, Charting past, present, and future research in ubiquitous computing, *ATM Transactions on Computer-Human Interaction,* 7, 1: 29–58.

Albers, M. J., and Kim, L., 2000, User Web browsing characteristics using palm handhelds for information retrieval, *Proceedings of IPCC/SIGDOC 2000 Technology & Teamwork*, Cambridge, MA, pp. 125-135.

Anderson, J., 1997, Clearing the way for physicians' use of clinical information systems, *Communications of the ACM*, 40, 8: 83–90.

Andreou, A., Chrysostomou, C., Leonidou, C., Mavromoustakos, S., Pitsillides, A., Samaras, G., and Schizas, C., 2002, Mobile commerce applications and services: a design and development approach, Proceedings of the First International Conference on Mobile Business, Athens

Avison, D. E., and Fitzgerald, G., 1995, *Information Systems Development: Methodologies, Techniques and Tools*, (2 ed.), McGraw Hill

Bansler, J., and Bodker, K., 1993, A reappraisal of structured analysis: design in an organizational context, *ACM Transactions on Information Systems*, 11, 2: 165–193.

Bellotti, V., Back, M., Edwards, K., Grinter, R., Henderson, A., and Lopes, C., 2002, Making sense of sensing systems: five questions for designers and researchers, Proceedings of the Proceedings of the SIGCHI conference on Human factors in computing systems, Minnesota, USA, 415–422.

Bent, P., Bolsin, S., Creati, B., Patrick, A., and Colson, M., 2002, Professional monitoring and critical incident reporting using personal digital assistants, *Medical Journal of Australia*, 177: 496-499.

Bevan, N., 2001, International standards for HCI and usability, *International Journal Human-Computer Studies*, 55: 533–552

Chan, S., Fang, X., Brzezinski, J., Zhou, Y., Xu, S., and Lam, J., 2002, Usability for mobile commerce across multiple form factors, *Journal of Electronic Commerce Research*, 3, 3: 187–199.

Chatzoglou, P. D., and Macaulay, L. A., 1996, Requirements capture and IS methodologies, *Information Systems Journal*, 6, 209–225.

Dawson, L., and Darke, P., 2002), The adoption and adaptation of object-oriented methodologies in requirements engineering practice, Proceedings of the Tenth European Conference on Information Systems, Gdansk, Poland, 406–415.

Dix, A., Rodden, T., Davies, N., Trevor, J., Friday, A., and Palfreyman, K., 2000, Exploiting space and location as the design framework for interactive mobile systems, *Communications of the ACM*, 7, 3: 285–321.

Fitzgerald, B., 1997, The use of systems development methodologies in practice: a field study, *Information Systems Journal*, 7: 201–212.

Fitzgerald, B., 1998a, An empirical investigation into the adoption of system development methodologies, *Information and Management*, 34: 317–328.

Fitzgerald, B., 1998b, An empirically-grounded framework for the information systems development Process, Proceedings of the Nineteenth International Conference on Information Systems, Helsinki, Finland, 103–114.

Huang, A. C., Ling, B. C., Barton, J., and Fox, A., 2001, Making computers disappear: appliance data services, *ACM SIGMOBILE*, 7: 108–121.

Jacobson, I., Booch, G., and Rumbaugh, J., 1999, *The Unified Software Development Process*, Addison Wesley Longman, Reading, MA.

Koop, A., and Mosges, R., 2002, The use of handheld computers in clinical trials, *Controlled Clinical Trials*, 23, 4: 469–480.

Loucopoulos, P., and Karakostas, V., 1995, *Systems Requirements Engineering*, McGraw-Hill, London, UK.

Luff, P., and Heath, C., 1998, Mobility in collaboration, *Proceedings of the CSCW '98*, Seattle, Washington, 305–314.

Miles, M. B., and Huberman, A. M., 1994, *Qualitative Data Analysis: An Expanded Sourcebook*, (2nd ed.), Sage Publications Inc, Thousand Oaks, CA.

Myers, M., 1999, Qualitative Research in Information Systems; http://www.auckland.ac.nz/msis/isworld/.

Norman, D. A., 1988, *The Psychology of Everyday Things*, Basic Books, New York.

Page, E. S., 1954, Continuous Inspection Schemes, *Biometrika*, 41.

Pierre, S., 2001, Mobile computing and ubiquitous networking: concepts, technologies and challenges, *Telematics and Informatics*, 18, 109–131.

Rumbaugh, J., Blaha, M., Premerlani, W., Eddy, F., and Lorensen, W., 1991, *Object-Oriented Modeling and Design*, Prentice-Hall, Englewood Cliffs, NJ.

Shewhart, W. A., 1931, *Economic Control of Quality Manufactured Product*, Nostrand-Reinhold, New York.

Shipman, J. and Morton, A., 2001, The new black bag: PDAs, health care and library services. *Reference Services Review* **29**(3): 229–238.

Shneiderman, B., 1998, *Designing the User Interface: Strategies for Effective Human Computer Interaction*, Addison Wesley.

Shneiderman, B., 2000, Universal usability, *Communications of the ACM* **43**(5): 85–91.

Shneiderman, B., 2001, CUU: bridging the digital divide with universal usability. *Interactions*_(March–April): 11–15.

Siau, K., Lim, P., and Shen, Z., 2001, Mobile commerce: promises, challenges and research agenda, *Journal of Database Management*, 12, 3: 4–13.

Smith, H., and Kulatilaka, N., 2002, Developments in IS practice III: riding the wave: extracting value from mobile technology, *Communications of the Association for Information Systems,* 8: 467–481.

Sommerville, I., and Sawyer, P., 1997, *Requirements Engineering: A good practice guide*, John Wiley and Sons, Chichester.

Urquhart, C., 1998, Analysts and clients in conversation: cases in early requirements gathering, *Proceedings* of the Nineteenth International Conference on Information Systems, Helsinki, Finland, 115–127.

Wynekoop, J. L., and Russo, N. L., 1997, Studying system development methodologies: an examination of research methods, *Information Systems Journal,* 7: 47–65.

OUTSOURCING: AN INFORMATION SYSTEMS DEVELOPMENT CASE STUDY IN AN INDONESIAN SME

Mira Kartiwi and Helen Hasan*

1. INTRODUCTION

Small Medium Enterprises (SMEs) comprise the vast majority of businesses throughout Asia. Indeed, in the last twenty years, there has been a considerable growth in terms of the number of SMEs throughout Asian economies, and Indonesia in particular. The importance of SMEs to the Indonesia economy is further highlighted by their contribution to national development and by the fact that, as a sector, they provide and create jobs especially during time of recession.

Information Systems (IS) have made considerable inroads into large organizations and the majority of such organizations are heavily relying on IS for their day-to-day operations. This diffusion of technology has been credited with significant cost reduction, gains in productivity, organizational effectiveness plus, in some cases, a definite competitive advantage (Laudon and Laudon, 1996; Morell and Ezingeard, 2002; Oz, 2002; Watson et al., 1997).

In order to enhance the benefits of IS adoption in organizations, many researches on IS and management field has concentrated on the examination of large and successful corporations (Doukidis, 1996). Furthermore, it is often the case that these corporations operate in well-established economies, where formal structures and processes are common. As a consequence, all proposed solution for IS implementation are based on data collected from large, well-established and well-managed firms operating in the above-described environments

However, very few scientific studies have been made in the specific context of SMEs, especially in the area of IS adoption and implementation through outsourcing in developing countries, where different socio-economic and business structures are common. This paper will analyse the experience of an Indonesian SME and its difficulty in applying an outsourcing approach to IS. Several key points will be identified and discussed which appear to improve the implementation of IS in SMEs, especially when they adopt an outsourcing solution.

* Mira Kartiwi and Helen Hasan, University of Wollongong, Wollongong, NSW, Australia 2500.

2. SMALL AND MEDIUM SIZED ENTERPRISES IN INDONESIA

Small and Medium Enterprises are promoted in developing countries as providing a seedbed for economic growth (Hall, 1995). In Indonesia, SMEs form the backbone of the Indonesian economy. The growth of SMEs in Indonesia has been dramatic (see Tables 1 and 2). Currently there are a total of more than 40 million SMEs in Indonesia – in 2001, they accounted for 99.99% of the total number of enterprises. Based on the latest data, the largest percentage is in the agriculture sector (59.10%), followed by trade (24.13%) and manufacturing (7.18%) sectors with transportation and services also significant. In other sectors for the SMEs represent a relatively insignificant contribution as determined by the number of employees (see Table 2).

Table 1. Number of Small Medium Enterprises in Indonesia
(Adapted from Central Bureau Statistics, 2003; Ministry of Industry and Trade, 2003)

Sector	Year				
	1997	**1998**	**1999**	**2000**	**2001**
Agriculture	22,513,131	23,099,433	23,176,320	23,518,616	23,757,762
Mining	204,917	137,839	133,081	135,219	141,059
Manufacturing	2,827,874	2,114,401	2,536,221	2,724,662	2,885,827
Electricity, gas and water	13,804	7,694	4,887	5,336	5,711
Construction	207,064	130,042	108,246	116,551	117,986
Trade	10,013,454	8,347,432	8,710,068	9,236,072	9,698,204
Transportation	1,854,833	1,509,693	1,709,846	1,869,566	1,998,162
Financial Institution	77,357	22,938	29,464	31,025	31,938
Services	2,052,676	1,444,106	1,503,590	1,539,740	1,558,867
Total	**39,765,110**	**36,813,578**	**37,911,723**	**39,176,787**	**40,195,516**

Table 2. Number of Employees of Small Medium Enterprises in Indonesia
(Adapted from Central Bureau Statistics, 2003; Ministry of Industry and Trade, 2003)

Sector	Year				
	1997	**1998**	**1999**	**2000**	**2001**
Agriculture	29,891,389	34,224,109	32,523,873	34,525,866	34,833,986
Mining	467,942	374,740	334,528	339,902	354,582
Manufacturing	10,067,165	8,329,527	10,135,523	10,708,423	11,363,761
Electricity, gas and water	134,615	112,810	90,603	99,011	105,953
Construction	1,012,215	705,586	448,854	483,288	489,234
Trade	16,064,421	14,783,478	16,328,856	17,314,962	18,181,324
Transportation	2,662,379	2,146,424	2,411,378	2,636,631	2,817,988
Financial Institution	689,987	323,772	354,664	373,448	384,436
Services	4,218,843	3,313,127	4,541,565	4,650,757	4,708,529
Total	**65,208,956**	**64,313,573**	**67,169,844**	**71,132,288**	**73,239,793**

In reference to the data above, it can be identified that SMEs play a significant role in the economic development of Indonesia and have become one of the key reasons that Indonesian SMEs has been recently given greater attention by the government. With this crucial position in the economy, the development of SMEs should result in increased employment opportunities and new business startups. This would contribute to economic and social development through economic diversification and accelerated structural changes that promote stable and sustainable long-term economic growth.

Although the government of Indonesia has introduced several policies to improve the performance of SMEs in the economy, Indonesian SMEs continue to face many problems and the implementation of these SME policies has not been successful. There are two main issues regarding the development of SME in Indonesia. Firstly, SMEs lack of staff with Information Systems (IS) knowledge which results in the lack of the use of IS within their businesses. Secondly, most SMEs are known to be lacking in managerial skills (ASEAN, 1997). With these limitations the environment of SMEs is unconducive to a sustained and successful existence in the current globally competitive marketplace.

3. ROLE OF INFORMATION SYSTEMS IN SMES

Information Systems now play a vitally important role in almost in all organisations. By implementing IS, organisations usually achieve efficiency, savings in costs and time, quality and avoidance of errors, as well as long term benefits; the collection of experience, organisational learning and positive relationships with customers. In other words, many IS reserachers describe these benefits as a "competitive advantage" (Laudon and Laudon, 1996; Morell and Ezingeard, 2002; Oz, 2002; Watson et al., 1997).

The number of IS applications used in SMEs has grown rapidly since the beginning of nineties. However, with reference to the use of IS in organisation, Heikkila et al. (1991) asserts that there are three major differences between SMEs and large organisations:

1. SMEs tend to use computers more as tools and less as a communication medium;
2. The small number of stakeholders involved in an SME means that there are likely to be fewer problems in terms of organisational politics;
3. SMEs have considerably fewer resources available to implement IS solutions.

Furthermore, there are a variety of potential benefits for SMEs in making use of IS because they are able to complete the transition process to IS much faster, and they possess greater flexibility to undertake any reorganisation required to realise the full benefits of IS (Wroe, 1987). The potential benefits of IS usage within SMEs are (Robert et al., 2002; CII, 2001; Morell and Ezingeard, 2002):

1. Increased productivity and performance within the organisation;
2. The possibility of new ways managing activity;
3. Better relationship with partners;
4. Better customer service;
5. Greater internal control of operations;
6. Improved quality in order to delivery a high quality package of product and services;
7. Cost savings.

Despite the attractive benefits that SMEs may obtain from adopting IS into their business, SMEs possess significant problems IS adoption caused by the lack of staff with adequate knowledge of IS as mentioned in the previous section. As a result, the only available option to overcome this obstacle is by assigning their staff into IS training session or purchases those skills in marketplace (outsourcing).

4. CASE STUDY

4.1 PT. Amartex: Initiation of IS adoption

Amartex was established in 1993 as a textile manufacturing industry. Its main business is to supply the needs for canvas fabric of more than 10 large industries, such as garment and furniture makers. It has grown steadily and increased its turnover every year.

Prior to undertaking the IS development project in the organization, the hardware was initially comprised of a standalone PC and an inkjet printer together with packaged software in the form of a word processor, spreadsheet and a database packaged. The organisation mainly utilised the spreadsheet application for day-to-day operation. It allowed financial reports to be created, stored for later use, and/or printed for immediate use by the director as a reference for decision-making. Word processing, on the other hand, was used for creation of any correspondence in the form of documents.

However, the growth of the business has resulted in an increased expectation for faster and more efficient information processing. Unfortunately, the use of the computer with spreadsheet and word processor only, cannot meet this demand. The need for special software for financial, inventory, and payroll packages are now being identified. Another reason for a IS transformation is to improve organisation competitive position and long-term growth.

Table 3. Advantages and Disadvantages of Three Approaches

Approach	Advantages	Disadvantages
Develop In-house	• More secure in maintaining internal information. • Easier for resolving the problem, since the developer is within the company. • Softwares can be built in Indonesian language • The software can be built to suit the organisational needs	• There is no available human resource for managing and developing the project. • Difficulty in hiring appropriate person with adequate skills, since most of them would prefer working with large companies. • Usually it takes a longer time to implement
Ready made software	• Faster for implementation • Many software available to choose from • More variation in prices and features.	• Language, since most of the software is built in English. • Difficulty in obtaining appropriate training for certain software. • The available training for some International software could be expensive
Outsourcing	• Software can be built in Indonesian language • The software can be built to suit the organisational needs • Training could be included as part of the outsourcing agreement	• Revealing internal information could be a security risk • Usually it is much more expensive • Usually it takes longer time to implement

There are three approaches that the company were considering in order to acquire the required software capability; develop new applications in house, buy ready-made software, or outsourcing. The details of the considerations made to determine which approach is more suitable for the organisation are described in Table 3.

After considering the above advantages and disadvantages of each approach, the director decided to employ outsourcing as a possible and feasible approach for acquiring the required software solutions to meet their expectations.

4.2 Outsourcing: The Possible and Feasible Solution?

Amartex started their outsourcing process on January 2001. The director believed that he had a very limited knowledge of IS and had limited ability in gaining information about the available outsourcing provider. Therefore, there was no provider selection process that would enable the director to choose and compare the cost and features offered. As a substitute, the director merely depended on the information given by his accountant. The accountant proposed that a colleague of his would be able to undertake the software development and implementation process.

During the outsourcing process, a numbers of problems were identified. The first problem was the use of IS jargon and terminology that become a barrier when communicating the requirements that should be included in the software. Consequently, in most cases the provider assumed what the requirements of the company were instead of further clarifying the requirement details with the company.

Secondly, due to the inefficiency caused by the above process – that is difficulty in communicating the requirements – the time to complete the project was longer time than the estimated time. It was initially proposed that it would only take six months to complete the two software applications (inventory control and general ledger). In reality, it took one and half years to complete the general ledger software and another half year to complete the inventory control software.

The third problem identified was the lack of adequate training that would enable the end-users to fully understand the software. Based on the contract, the provider should provide the necessary training until the end-users could perform their daily tasks. However, from end-user perspective, the one training session, which was deemed sufficient by the provider, proved insufficient for the end-users. Furthermore, no written manual or built in help was produced by the provider to facilitate the end-users' operation of the software and to resolve any problem that might occur.

Moreover, the forth problem concerning outsourcing in this case study was the interpretation of 'lifetime warranty' term as written in contract. Due to the first problem above, many features, which were actually required by the end-users, were not provided. Instead when the user reported this to the outsourcing provider, complaining that some of the features required were not provided, the outsourcing provider ask for an additional charge to fix the software. This becomes a serious problem especially when the end-user urgently needed the solution.

Last but not least, the director believed that all of the problems described above were simply caused by his lack of knowledge in IS. This perception has put him in a weaker position in respect to bargaining power, especially when it came to the contract agreement which was full of IS jargons and terminologies. As the result, the overall outsourcing process was more provider-driven rather than user-oriented.

5. DISCUSSION

Two key points have emerged from the analysis of the IS outsourcing experience in the Amartex case study as depicted above and will now be discussed.

The first key point is the importance of a feasibility study in any project involving IS adoption. In spite of the classical problem that Indonesian SMEs are suffered from – lack of capable and skilled human resources – it is important to ensure that the process of a feasibility study for IS adoption is serious taken into account. In this matter, the entrepreneur may first investigate whether or not there is any government body that may assist them in recognizing what factors should be taken into consideration before the IS adoption process. If, finally, outsourcing become the only solution for the organisation to implement IS, then the next important steps are to gather as much information on the available outsourcing providers and comparing their cost against the features offered.

The second key point is the importance of continuing support from the government through any initiative such as providing standardised guidelines, free consultation, training, seminars on IS in SME, and so on. In order to be effective in helping SMEs, it is also important for the government to assure that the information on what kind of services provided to SMEs is distributed equitably. It is relevant to note that information provided by ASEAN (1997) shows that less than 20 per cent of the entrepreneurs of SMEs have received assistance from their governments in the form of training.

6. CONCLUSION

An information system development case study in Indonesian SME has been presented in this paper. It portrays an analysis of the difficulties that an SME experienced in IS adoption through outsourcing, mainly due to a lack of knowledge assistance. Further research is required to establish better processes for identifying methods or approach to support the SMEs as they implement more advanced IS. The process of such IS implementation can be viewed as an organizational learning process. The results of this study are useful not only for managers of SMEs but also for government bodies, in developing countries such as Indonesia, that have economic reasons to be concerned about the development of SMEs. The authors also believe that the results will also provide some insights to outsourcing providers, including software vendors, with SME customers in order to improve their service and customer satisfaction.

ACKNOWLEDGMENT

The authors would like to thank Teddy Surya Gunawan for the consistent encouragement and insightful comments to improve this paper.

REFERENCES

ASEAN (Association of South East Asian Nations), 1997, Small and medium enterprises in Indonesia, (March 16, 2003); http://aeup.brel.com/sme/sme1.html

Avison, D. E and G. Fitzgerald, 2003, *Information Systems Development: Methodologies, Techniques, and Tools*, 3rd Ed., McGraw Hill, Sydney, pp. 133–137.

Doukidis, G. I., Panagiotis, L. and Robert D. G., 1996, Information systems planning in small business: a stages of growth analysis, *Journal of Systems Software*, **33**, 189–201.

CII (Confederation of Indian Industry), 2001, *Third survey on usage of information technology by SMEs*, (March 16, 2003); http://www.ciionline.org/busserv/ssi

Fink, D., 1998, Guidelines for the succesful adoption on information technology in small medium enterprise, *International Journal of Information Management,* **8**:4, 243–253.

Hall, C., 1995, *APEC and SME Policy Suggestions for an Action Agenda*, Monash Asia Institute, Clayton.

Heikkila, J., Saarinen, T., and Saaksjarvi, M., 1991, Success of software packages in small business: an explanatory study, *European Journal of Information Systems*, **1**:3, 159–169.

Laudon, Kenneth C. and Jane P. Laudon, 1996, *Management Information Systems: Organization and Technology*, 4th Ed, Prentice Hall, New Jersey, pp. 43–47.

Morrell, M. and Jean-Noel Ezingeard, 2002, Revisiting adoption factors of inter-organisational information systems in SMEs, *Logistics Information Management*, **15**:1, 46–57.

Oz, Effy, 2002, *Management Information Systems*, 3rd Ed., Course Technology, Boston, pp. 53–87.

Robert, J., Buhman, C., Garcia, S. and David Allinder, 2002, Bringing COTS information technology to small manufacturing Enterprises, *Dynamic Business*, July/August.

Watson, R. T., Kelly, G. G., Galliers, R. D. and Brancheau, J. C., 1997, Key issues in information systems management: an international perspective, *Journal of Management Information Systems*, **13**:4, 91–115.

Wroe, B., 1987, *Successful Computing in Small Business*, NCC Publications, Manchester.

CURRENT STATUS AND TRENDS IN CUSTOMER RELATIONSHIP MANAGEMENT

The case of Slovenia

Boštjan Kos and Jože Zupančič[1]

1. INTRODUCTION

Winning new customers is becoming more and more important for organizations worldwide, and keeping the loyalty of existing customers is becoming increasingly difficult. In the times of e-economy often only a mouse click separates the customer from a competitor. This means that organizations must build relations with customers and focus on satisfaction of their customers. Customer information has always been one of the most important elements for building a stable and profitable relationship; therefore it is essential that organizations capture, integrate and store all the available customer related data.

Companies differentiate themselves less and less through products and prices only, but through additional information and services for the customer. Business transactions are becoming an outcome of relationships between the business partners. CRM focuses on providing quality service on the long run, attempting to assure that appropriate customers will stay with the firm for a long run. E-business means not only buying and selling products and/or services over the Internet, but entails strategic use of information and communication technology (including but not limited to the Internet) to interact with customers and partners through multiple communication and distribution channels.

The purpose of this investigation[2] was to assess the status and the expected development of CRM in companies in Slovenia. Goals of the study were also to collect and analyse opinions of top managers about CRM, opportunities and challenges for implementation of CRM, factors that promote or hinder implementation, and about

1. Boštjan Kos, IBM Slovenia, 1000 Ljubljana, Slovenia. Jože Zupančič, University of Maribor, School of Organizational Science, 4000 Kranj, Slovenia

2. The study presents an outline of the master thesis of the first author. IBM not involved in the study. Only the two authors are responsible for the results presented in the paper.

incentives and obstacles in implementation of CRM. A goal of the study was also to survey activities related to implementation of CRM in Slovenia.

There is no commonly accepted definition CRM. In an overview article discussing CRM implementation cycle and theoretically analysing critical success factors in implementing CRM (Ling and Yen, 2001) the authors collected several definitions of CRM, depending on different perspectives from the users of this concept. The most important aspects in a definition of CRM are the value of the customer, holistic approach, and technology empowerment. The authors describe CRM as "a set of processes and enabling systems supporting a business strategy to build a long-term profitable relationship with specific customers. ... CRM comprises acquisition and deployment of knowledge about customers to enable a company to sell more of their product or service more efficiently".

A conceptual framework for eCRM organizational architecture, including alternative eCRM models, was presented in (Kotorov, 2002). The author defines eCRM as "application of information and communication technology to increase the scale and scope of customer service". The framework emphasizes that successful eCRM projects are not narrowly departmental but instead organizations-wide initiatives.

For the needs of our investigation we defined CRM as coordinated set of processes and organizational measures supporting a customer centric business orientation (business model) that attempts to create the highest possible level of customer satisfaction and customer loyalty while achieving the highest possible level of profitability.

CRM related technologies, such as customer relationship portals, data mining, intelligent call centres, promise profound changes, but they bring no conceptual change. The concept of customer relationship management is as old as the concept of the competitive market. Customers have been patrons of the producers and merchants, and customers' goodwill rests on the quality, timelines and convenience of the service that they receive. While the objectives of CRM remain the same, the development of information and communication technology allows for significant increase in scale and scope of the service (Peppard, 2000; Kotorov 2002).

Little academic work has focused on CRM with much of the published work in business papers, magazines and web sites. This is a valuable source of data, but is usually presenting the perspective of the management. This can be problematic and highly likely to miss or ignore other important views and subsequent issues, strategic or otherwise (Light, 2001). Lack of academic research, and the fact that no academic study focusing on CRM has been done in Slovenia before, were among the initiatives for our work.

Our study focuses on Slovenia, a country in Central Europe with total population about 2 million and GDP per capita around US$10,000. The country achieved independence in 1991 after seceding from the then Socialist Republic of Yugoslavia. Socialism in former Yugoslavia was less dogmatic than in other Central and Eastern European Countries. Even during the socialist period, companies enjoyed a modest degree of economic freedom and practiced a policy of self-management. Our study may also show how managers who mostly started their careers in the socialist period, characterised by strong product orientation, adopted the customer oriented management approach adapted to the current globalised and deregulated business environment. The authors believe that finding of our study may be generalized to other East and Central European countries with comparable levels of economic activity an application of IT.

2. RESEARCH APPROACH

To collect relevant data for the investigation, we developed three questionnaires for three distinct target groups of respondents: (1) general managers (CEOs), (2) IT managers (CIOs) and (3) marketing and/or sales managers. Several sections of the three questionnaires overlapped. All of them consisted of the following five parts:

1. Demographic characteristics of respondents and organizations
2. Development of various types of strategies and relations among them
3. Organization and CRM
4. Information technology and CRM
5. Organization and information technology, and
6. CRM and Slovenia.

In addition to closed type questions, at least one open ended question was added at the end of each section, allowing the respondents more freedom to state their own opinions. A limited number of selected respondents reviewed the initial versions of questionnaire and suggested several improvements.

Data for the investigation was collected in May and June 2001. The target respondents were managers of large organizations (total employees 500+). Addresses of organizations were first obtained from the Chamber of Commerce of the Republic Slovenia. A test of 100 randomly selected addresses showed that 25% of them contained errors. Therefore, we gathered e-mail addresses from other publicly available sources such as the telephone directory, web pages of organizations and published business directories (such as info@CompanyName.si, Sales@CompanyName.com, etc.). A mail was sent to these addresses, explaining the purpose and goal of the investigation, expected results etc. We asked for names and e-addresses of individual managers to whom we intended to mail the questionnaire.

In the first action in February 2001, 769 e-mail letters were sent, and 64 of them bounced back because of errors in the addresses. About one quarter of the organizations (188 – 24.5%) provided us with relevant information about top managers. A few organizations (20 – 2.9%) asked for more detailed information about our study and the participating researchers. Only two organizations explicitly refused to participate with an explanation that their managers have no time for this type of studies. In a second action two weeks later, identical e-mail letters were sent to 706 organizations, and response rates were nearly the same as in the first action.

Sales, marketing and IT functions overlapped in some organizations. In many of the responding organizations, one department covered sales and marketing and was managed by one person. In such cases, only one questionnaire was sent to the manger responsible for more than one of the business functions.

A paper version of the questionnaire, together with an accompanying letter explaining the purpose and goals of the investigation, was sent to 1829 general, sales, marketing and IT managers in 573 organizations from different industries. In the accompanying letter, the web address (URL) of an identical electronic version the questionnaire was given, and managers were asked to respond only to one questionnaire. To increase the response rates, reminders were sent by e-mail two and three weeks after the questionnaires were mailed. The web site was open from April 4 to May 15, 2001.

Table 1. Response rates by business function

Business function	*Mailed*	*Responded*	*Response rate*
General management (MAN)	573	68	11.9 %
Information technology (TECH)	502	75	14.9 %
Sales and Marketing (MAR)	754	80	10.6 %
Total	1829	223	12.2 %

Response rates presented by business function are given in Table 1. More than a half (54.5%) of respondents filled the electronic version of the questionnaire. More then two thirds (69.1%) of all respondents were males with the highest portion among IT managers and the lowest among marketing and sales managers. One third (64 – 34.2%) of organizations were primarily service oriented.

To check the comprehension of the term CRM, we asked the respondents to write a short definition of CRM. More than a half of them (123 – 55.2%) provided their definitions. Because several different elements constitute CRM, it is not surprising that the responses were rather different. We categorized them into four groups, depending on the emphasis in the responses. Most frequently (32 responses) respondents emphasized that CRM represents satisfaction of customer needs in a way that is profitable for the company. The second group (31 responses) emphasized the support of IT for management of relations with customers. The third group (20 responses) included responses that were basically some translation of the term CRM, the fourth group (20 definitions) focused on understanding the customers, and 8 definitions combined the characteristics of the previous four groups. Eleven responses were non-specific.

Because it is easier to describe CRM than provide a definition in one sentence, all the responses were correct, but incomplete. Therefore, we assumed that most of the respondents were familiar enough with the idea and essence of CRM to provide relevant responses to most of the questions in the questionnaire.

3. THE FINDINGS

To estimate the customer centricity of the organizations, respondents were asked to rate the importance of customers and product/service for the firm (Table 2). Although customer was the most important component in their business orientation for the majority of respondents, considerable differences can be observed between the groups of respondents: nearly one third of IT managers considered the product/service as the most important component, which may indicate lack of business orientation among relatively many IT managers. Differences among responses of the three groups of managers may indicate lack of up-to-date business knowledge among IT managers, which may hinder the cooperation among IT and Sales & Marketing departments.

The customer centric focus is the essential theoretical foundation of the CRM strategy. More and more, executives and managers have realized that CRM is not just the responsibility of marketing department or customer service department, it is a fundamental business strategy carried out within the whole organization and across different business functions. This requires a central corporate CRM strategy.

Table 2. The most important component in the business orientation

Business component	*MAN*		*TECH*		*MAR*		*Total*	
	No.	*%*	*No.*	*%*	*No.*	*%*	*No.*	*%*
Customer	55	80.9	50	66.7	73	91.3	178	79.8
Product/service	10	14.7	23	30.7	3	3.8	36	16.1
Other	0	0.0	2	2.7	1	1.3	3	1.3
Undecided	3	4.4	0	0.0	3	3.8	6	2.7
Total	68	100.0	75	100.0	80	100.0	223	100.0

We asked respondents in our study to rate the status of CRM strategy in the organization. Their responses are summarized in Table 3. CRM strategy was described as a strategy focusing on how to meet challenges and take advantage of the opportunities of CRM. CRM strategy focuses on the organizational implementation of CRM.

Table 3. The status of CRM strategy in the organizations

The organization has a CRM strategy	*MAN*		*TECH*		*MAR*		*Respondents*	
	No.	*%*	*No.*	*%*	*No.*	*%*	*No.*	*%*
Yes	12	17.6	4	5.3	19	23.8	35	15.7
No, but we would need it today	26	38.2	31	41.3	26	32.5	83	37.2
No, we plan to develop it in the next 2 years	13	19.1	17	22.7	18	22.5	48	21.5
No, we plan to develop it in more than 2 years	2	2.9	4	5.3	1	1.3	7	3.1
No, it is not planned	4	5.9	7	9.3	5	6.3	16	7.2
I don't know	4	5.9	11	14.7	5	6.3	20	9.0
Undecided	7	10.3	1	1.3	6	7.5	14	6.3
Total	*68*	*100*	*75*	*100*	*80*	*100*	*223*	*100.0*

Considerable differences between target groups of respondents are evident: for example, 23.3% of marketing and sales executives and only 5.5% of IT executives indicated that the organization had a CRM strategy. A possible explanation for this is that marketing and sales departments had their own departmental strategies that were not adequately supported by IT, and IT executives were not involved in the creation of the strategy. Relatively large percentage of executives from all the three groups did not respond the question or selected "I don't know". This indicates that they may have not considered a CRM strategy yet.

Most of the respondents (65.8%) positioned the CRM strategy as part of business strategy, 20.3% of them as marketing and sales strategy, and 2.1% as a part of IS strategy, while 10.1% were undecided. No significant differences between the responses from the three target groups were found.

Table 4 summarises the responses to the question "Is the organization implementing CRM"? The term "implementation" refers to organizational implementation and may include implementation of some kind of CRM software. Again, considerable differences among groups of participants are evident. A possible explanation for this is that some marketing departments were implementing their own departmental strategies that were apparently not adequately supported by the IS, and that some IS managers were not fully informed about the CRM strategy in the organization. There were more organizations implementing CRM then organizations that have a CRM strategy; apparently some organizations are introducing CRM without a strategy.

Table 4. CRM implementation in organizations

Is has the organization implemented	*MAN*		*TECH*		*MAR*		*Respondents*	
or is implementing CRM?	*No.*	*%*	*No.*	*%*	*No.*	*%*	*No.*	*%*
Yes	16	23.5	5	6.7	25	31.3	46	20.6
No, implementation is planned	15	22.1	11	14.7	17	21.3	43	19.3
No, and initiative has been adopted	6	8.8	16	21.3	7	8.8	29	13.0
No, an initiative is planned	9	13.2	7	9.3	6	7.5	22	9.9
No	18	26.5	27	36.0	15	18.8	60	26.9
I don't know	0	0.0	8	10.7	7	8.8	15	6.7
Undecided	4	5.9	1	1.3	3	3.8	8	3.6
Total	68	100.0	75	100.0	80	100.0	223	100.0

The initiative for implementations of CRM in most cases came from the top management or from the marketing department. More than 80% or respondents agreed that the team for CRM strategy planning must consist of representatives of the top management, marketing, sales and IT departments.

Table 5. The estimated importance of communication channels

Communication channel	*Rank*	*Rating*	*The most important channel*
Personal contacts	1	4.3	43
Internet	2	4.0	29
Telephone	3	3.7	15
Fax	4	3.0	5
TV	5	2.7	6
Standard mail	6	2.6	2
Radio	6	2.6	3
Other	8	3.4	0

A comparison with the study (Firth and Swanson, 2001) that analysed opinions of top managers in 55 organizations in USA showed that organizations in Slovenia lagged behind the organizations in USA: 55% of the US companies have implemented or were implementing CRM, 16% were considering the implementation, 18% were waiting and observing what others will do, and 15% showed no interest in CRM.

The CRM concept requires that companies use multiple channels to communicate with customers. Table 5 presents the average ratings of the importance of the listed communication channels on scale 1 to 5.[3] The last column gives the number of respondents that rated a particular channel as the most important. Five respondents added other communication channels: newspapers, magazines, specialized journals, posters, SMS messages and professional journals.

Integrating data from different communication channels into the computerised information system is particularly important for the success of CRM to personalize the relationship with the customer and to broaden the organizational response to customer's needs. Therefore we asked the respondents the following question: "Are the communications channels (data sources) integrated into the company's information system in such a way that it is possible to obtain a complete and consistent view of the customer?" Table 6 presents a summary of the opinions of the 223 respondents. Most of the organizations (77%) have integrated, are integrating, or plan to integrate the communication channels.

Table 6. Integration of communication channels

Yes	*Partly*	*Integration is planned*	*No*	*"I don't know" or undefined*
10,7%	47.6%	18.7%	17.6%	6.3%

One of the goals of CRM is to determine and maintain loyalty of a particular customer. Table 7 summarises responses of the 223 participants in the survey to the question "What is the most important factor for developing and keeping the customer's loyalty?" We found no major differences among the three groups of respondents. In contrary to findings of some studies (Dussart, 2001), Slovenian managers expect that the importance of consumer brands will increase in the future. Somewhat surprising is the low rating of the importance of the location.

Table 7. The most important factors for developing and keeping customer loyalty

Quality	*Price*	*Consumer brand*	*Location*	*Other*	*Undefined*
57.8%	22.0%	7.6%	1.8%	2.2%	8.5%

Table 8 presents the respondents' evaluation the factors hindering implementation of CRM. No significant differences among the opinions of respondents from top management and marketing were found, but the opinions of IT managers diverged considerably from the group average: they indicated lack of money as the most important factor hindering CRM implementation. Table 9 shows the ratings of challenges promoting CRM implementation. The last column gives the percentage of respondents who rated a particular factor or challenge as the single most important. It is evident that all the listed factors were rated as rather important for CRM implementation.

3. 1 = not important at all, 2 = not important, 3 = neutral, 4 = important, 5 = very important.

Table 8. Ratings of factors hindering CRM implementation (in % of responses)

Factors that hinder CRM implementation in the organization	*Disagree or strongly disagree*	*Neutral*	*Agree or strongly agree*	*The most important hindering factor*
Resistance to changes in business processes	14.5	13.5	72.0	17.4
Lack of time	16.2	15.2	68.6	21.7
Lack of expertise	18.2	14.2	67.6	18.8
Lack of money	26.5	24.5	49.0	5.8
Operational business processes	15.8	35.5	48.7	
Existing information technology	29.0	22.7	48.3	
Organizational culture	19.7	33.0	47.3	
Advantages of CRM are not clear	32.5	25.5	42.0	
Business environment	23.7	34.5	41.8	
Insufficient management involvement and support	34.7	26.3	39.0	5.8%
Rapid changing in business	32.1	31.0	36.9	
Employees	25.1	38.9	36.0	
Rapid changes in IT	41.5	24.8	33.7	
Reluctance to take risks	34.6	34.7	30.7	
Poorly defined responsibility for customer satisfaction	52.0	28.1	19.9	
No business needs	67.5	21.0	11.5	

Table 9. Evaluation of factors promoting CRM implementation (in % of responses)

Challenges that promote implementation of CRM in the organization	*Not important*	*Neutral*	*Important or very important*	*The most important factor*
Keeping existing customers	3.9	5.8	90.4	16.4
Better data management (integration, ...)	1.0	8.9	90.2	5.1
Attracting customers	3.9	7.7	88.5	15.8
CRM brings competitive advantage	4.3	8.5	87.2	25.6
New communication channels	1.9	11.5	86.7	
Challenges in sales and marketing	2.9	13.0	84.1	
Business process reengineering	2.5	17.2	80.4	
Growth of electronic markets	5.8	20.8	73.5	
Globalisation of customers	7.8	20.0	72.2	10.7
Internet	5.3	22.7	72.0	
Technological challenges (CRM SW, data warehousing)	6.4	25.5	68.1	
CRM represents competitive threat	24.5	33.0	42.5	

A list of 20 CRM software and service vendors with the highest shares of CRM market in Europe (source: European Centre for Customer Strategies, October 2001, http://www.eccs.uk.com/markets/) was included in the questionnaire for IT managers. Respondents were asked to indicate the vendor names that they recognized and knew what was their area of business activity. A summary of results is presented in Table 10; the last column indicates the percentage of IT managers who recognized a particular company (brand name) as CRM vendor.

Table 10. Recognisability of CRM vendors by Slovenian IT managers

	CRM vendor	*Rank*		*Market share (%)*		*Recognisability in Slovenia*	
		Europe	*World*	*Europe*	*World*	*Rank*	*%*
1	Siebel	1	1	34.3	28.9	8	13.3
2	Nortel/Clarify	2	2	9.2	7.4	11	10.7
3	Remedy	3	4	5.2	5.5	17	2.7
4	Oracle	4	5	5.0	5.4	1	96.0
5	Peoplesoft/Vantive	5	7	4.6	4.9	4	25.3
6	SAP	5	15	4.6	1.8	2	88.0
7	Broadvision	7	3	4.2	6.7	13	5.3
8	Vignette	8	6	2.5	5.3	19	1.3
9	Prime Response	9	22	2.1	0.7	24	0.0
10	Chordiant	9	23	2.1	0.7	24	0.0
11	Pivotal	9	16	2.1	1.5	19	1.3
12	Dendrite	12	9	1.8	3.8	24	0.0
13	Point	13	25	1.7	0.5	8	13.3
14	Update.com	14	-	1.5	-	16	4.0
15	Open Market	14	11	1.5	2.2	10	12.0
16	Onyx	14	10	1.5	2.4	12	9.3
17	Sales Logix	17	14	1.4	2.1	17	2.7
18	Baan	18	-	1.3	-	3	80.0
19	Microstrategy	19	8	1.0	4.2	6	14.7
20	Kana	19	13	1.0	2.1	24	0.0

Four out of the 20 leading CRM vendors were unknown to all the 75 IT managers in companies surveyed: Prime Response, Chordiant, Dendrite in Kana. Only 13.3% of IT managers recognized Siebel, the company with the far highest market share in Europe and worldwide. On the other hand, ERP vendors were highly recognizable among managers in Slovenia, although they cover only a small portion of the CRM market.

The aim of our investigation was also to determine the opinions of participants regarding development of CRM solutions, availability and knowledge of experts in Slovenia. We asked all the three groups of respondents the same questions regarding development of CRM solutions. Table 11 presents the summary of results.

Table 11. Developing CRM solutions in Slovenia

Question	*Strongly disagree*	*Disagree*	*Neutral*	*Agree*	*Strongly agree*
»Experts in Slovenia are competent to implement CRM solutions«	1.0%	10.4%	27.7%	54.5%	6.4%
»There are not enough experts in Slovenia to implement CRM solutions"	4.1%	22.4%	35.3%	33.2%	5.1%

No major differences among the three groups of respondents were evident; IT managers were somewhat more confident about knowledge and skills of experts in Slovenia. The average estimated the growth rate for CRM software market in the next few years was 36.5%, and for CRM services 46.9%. Most (68.4%) of organizations have implemented are implementing, or planing data warehouse.

4. DISCUSSION

A recently published exhaustive literature overview on Electronic Commerce CRM (ECCRM)[4] tried to evaluate the current state of research in the field (Romano and Fjermestad, 2002). The study showed that researchers have applied a wide range of methods and studied a broad range of topics. Exploratory surveys dominate in the literature; most of the survey instruments were not validated. There has been little theoretical development, and only a few empirical studies used hypothesis testing. Cumulative tradition has hardly emerged, with each study developing a new conceptual model, new constructs, and new instruments. On the other hand, many texts dealing with CRM have been published in trade magazines and web sites, often based on single case studies or interviews with one or a few executives, and usually present the perspective of the management.

The primary goal of our study was to evaluate the current status and expected development of CRM in Slovenia. Therefore, we decided to carry out an exploratory survey to analyse opinions of a relatively large sample of competent managers from companies in Slovenia. In general, our investigation showed that companies mostly are aware of CRM and its impact on the competitive environment. We can expect that most companies will start introducing CRM soon after the implement data warehousing and business intelligence, which are considered as a precondition for CRM implementation. Although companies in Slovenia are relative small in comparison to large organizations in European Union and USA they need all the segments of CRM, to be in command of customer relations. Respondents in our investigation mostly understood the CRM concept correctly and took a sound approach to its implementation.

While CRM vendors were hardly known to most of IT managers in companies, ERP vendors were highly recognizable (also) as CRM vendors among managers in Slovenia, although they cover only a small portion of the CRM market. This may mislead organizations implementing CRM: while most ERP vendors included CRM modules into

4. ECCRM was described as a sub field of CRM in management information systems (MIS) and particularly electronic commerce which rests on a variety of technological opportunities for acquiring and maintaining extensive data about customers, establishing customized extranets to serve other businesses, and exploiting purely digital commerce, such as XML.

their products, they are not specialized in CRM. Superficial or missing knowledge of CRM vendors and their products/services may be a major reason for the failure of a CRM project.

ERP systems are becoming increasingly more complex, aspiring to provide support for business functions that were previously offered by third party vendors. Extended ERP software includes such applications as supply chain management (SCM), and CRM and decision support systems. Applications, such as SCM and CRM, can be considered as applications additional to ERP (Stefanou, 2001). CRM is one of the subject areas that link to ERP: performing internal operations for customer relationship that make CRM more efficient and effective. Integration of front-end CRM and back-end ERP may create new business architecture for an enterprise that places the customer in the centre. Now ERP vendors have positioned themselves to enter the CRM market. This situation will allow one vendor to offer fully integrated enterprise application architecture to business community (Yen et. al., 2002). Therefore, mayor ERP vendors are aggressively forming alliances with or taking over other software firms that have been operating on the CRM market. When considering implementation of CRM, managers should take this into account and consider other approaches, for example implementation of a stand-alone CRM software package and its integration into the corporate IS, or the best-of breed approach.

CRM has been defined as a project that integrates processes across marketing, sales and customer-service functions, in order to leverage each other's strengths. But this means standardization of business processes, the enemy of innovation. Some analysts observed that CRM is developing more like ERP – very rigid. While rigidity may work when dealing with business functions such as accounting and human resources, a marketing campaign has to be more flexible and dynamic. Separating data from processes can make CRM more flexible (Kaneshige, 2002). Best of breed approach, based on integration of standard software components from different vendors and/or custom software, instead of implementing a standard ERP application suite, has been successfully used to develop enterprise systems that are more closely aligned with business processes of an organization (Light et al., 2001). So, best-of-breed CRM strategy may be a viable alternative to ERP/CRM systems and single vendor CRM systems.

Many standard package based CRM systems do not offer integration with back-office functions to fully support a relationship management strategy (Light, 2001). Neither large CRM suite providers nor best-of-breed approach offer a complete solution. CRM suite providers may offer relatively broad tightly integrated basic functionality but lack depth of functionality. Best-of-breed CRM vendors deliver needed depth of functionality, but only for a relatively narrow range of functionality (Marcus and Close, 2002).

5. CONCLUSION

When we started with the investigation (end of 1999) the CRM market was in the beginning of its development, and many CRM vendors were emerging, each of them with an own definition or description of CRM. In the course of our study many changes occurred, particularly merges and takeovers of organizations. This process apparently is not at end yet, which indicates that the CRM market is still shaping. For example, AMR Research (http://www.amrresearch.com) expects, on one hand, linking and integration of

CRM vendors, and disappearance of many CRM companies from the market on the other hand: their number is expected to shrink from 500 in 2002 to around 75 by 2005.

Our study provided some overview of the attitudes and adoption of CRM in organizations in Slovenia. Further research could address questions related to implementation of CRM, such as:

- How do organizations approach to implementation?
- How are they satisfied with available CRM solutions and possibilities of its customisation?
- Help provided by external consultants: availability, satisfaction quality, cost
- Making certain parts of corporate database to business partners and customers
- How does CRM change core business processes?

Our investigation addressed organizations, not on the most important element of CRM, the customer. A further investigation focusing on the customer would provide a more comprehensive view of the implementation of CRM. It should address issues such as customer's perception of CRM and satisfaction with CRM, and how do customers feel if they know that all their actions and interactions with a company, purchases, calls, e-mail, even every click will be recorded and analysed.

REFERENCES

Bose, R., 2002, Customer relationship management: key components for success, *Industrial Management & Data Systems*, **102**(2): 89.

Dussart C., 2001, Transformative power of e-business over customer brands, *European Management Journal*, **19**: 629.

Chen, I. J., 2001, Planning for ERP systems: analysis and future trends, *Business Process Management Journal*, **7**: 374.

Davis, R., 2002, The wizard of Oz in CRMland: CRM's need for business process Management, *Information Systems Management*, **19**(4): 43.

Firth, D. R. and Swanson, B. E., 2001, Customer relationship management: a diffusion snapshot, Information Systems Working Paper 1-01, The Anderson School at UCLA.

Kaneshige, T., 2002, CRM's fatal flaws, (June 28, 2002); http://line56.com/articles

Kotorov, R. P., 2002, Ubiquitous organization: organizational design for e-CRM, *Business Process Management Journal*, **8**: 218.

Light, B., 2001, A review of the issues associated with customer relationship management systems, Global Co-Operation in the New Millennium, The 9th European Conference on Information Systems, Bled, Slovenia, June 27-29, 1232–1241.

Light, B., Holland C. P. and Wills, K., 2001, ERP and best of breed: a comparative analysis, *Business Process Management Journal*, **7**: 216.

Ling, R. and Yen, D. C., 2001, Customer relationship management: an analysis framework and implementation strategies, *Journal of Computer Information Systems*, **XXXXI**(3): 82

Peppard J., 2000, Customer relationship management in financial services, *European Management Journal*, **18**: 312.

Romano, N, C. Jr. and Fjermestad, J., 2001–2002, Electronic commerce customer relationship management: an assessment of research, *International Journal of Electronic Commerce*, **6**:61.

Stefanou C. J., 2001, A framework for the ex-ante evaluation of ERP software, *European Journal of Information Systems*, **10**: 204

Yen, D. C., Chou, D. C. and Chang J., (2002), A synergic analysis for Web-based enterprise resource systems, *Computer Standards and Interfaces*, **24**: 337.

INFORMATION SYSTEM DEVELOPMENT FOR DEMOLITION MATERIAL MANAGEMENT

Chunlu Liu and Sung Kin Pun*

1. BACKGROUND

In recent years, the increasing pressure of environmental requirements, including the reduction of waste, has widely challenged various industries worldwide. Most industrialised countries, including Australia, have achieved high levels of consumption and correspondingly high levels of waste disposal. Australia has the second highest domestic waste production per capita among all member nations of the Organization for Economic Co-operation and Development as published in the web page of the New South Wales Environment Protection Authority (2003). Nearly one tonne of solid waste is sent to landfill per person each year as the total waste stream in Australia is about 14 million tonne of which somewhere between 16% and 40% is construction and demolition *waste* (Reddrop and Ryan, 1997). This number was 33% in the Barwon region of Victoria in 2002. The demolition of building structures produces enormous amounts of materials that in most countries result in significant waste streams. The construction industry, particularly in the demolition of constructed facilities, is the top contributor among all industry sectors to these levels of waste.

In most current demolition projects, a great number of demolished materials are directly sent to landfill after the primary usage due to the difficulties to find their next usages immediately. On the other hand, because of lack of supply of second-hand materials, new and high quality materials are used in construction projects whose design standards can be fitted by the secondary or used materials. Waste-Exchange System is an increasingly widespread solution to this problem (Chen et al., 2003). However, because of the flow nature of the current Waste-Exchange systems and the demolition procedure, they are inefficient to achieve the goal of waste reduction. The recently created concept of deconstruction rather than destruction for demolishing a constructed facility fails to achieve widespread understanding or acceptance due to various practical limitations (Liu et al., 2003). This research aims to develop a Web-based information system for envisaging the deconstruction implementations in practice and promoting cascading

* Chunlu Liu and Sung Kin Pun, School of Architecture and Building, Deakin University, Geelong, Australia

usages of construction materials in order to mitigate the increasing environmental pressure by the construction industry.

2. THE REQUIREMENT OF A WASTE MATERIAL MANAGEMENT SYSTEM

In reviewing some current Waste-Exchange Systems, it is found that their impracticality and inefficiency is caused by the fact that there is no communication before the waste is actually created. Because the site of demolition activity is very likely to be cleaned up due to the preparation of new construction project, waste materials can only be kept in the site for a short period. It is certainly hard for both waste material producer and demander to find each other in a narrow time span. Also, the waste materials are likely to be reworked to satisfy the potential demander because there are no negotiations before the demolition project and thus no requirement to comply. Instead of information exchange happening after the waste materials are produced, information can be delivered before the waste is actually produced. As a result, negotiations are enabled between the material producer and the material demander. This gives great flexibility and time to both parties. They therefore can change plan to suit the situation of each other and produce detailed specification on waste materials so that the demolition project, construction project and transportation can be adjusted to connect to each other tightly.

This model gives flexibility and convenience to material producer and demander; however, there are also potential obstacles. The demolition material producer has to estimate the amount and classification of the waste produced before the project is undertaken. This imposes some difficulties to the material producers who do not have engineering background. The proposed system will address this problem with the assistant of intelligent applications. The material producer should only be asked to provide simple information regarding to the project, including the dimension of the building and the material used, and then gets estimated data on the material the project produces. Same as other Waste-Exchange System, the proposed system, Demolition Materials Management System (DMMS), is built on the Internet using the form of interactive web page. Also, it does not provide online transaction due to numerous flexibilities and possibilities during the information exchange process.

Different from most conventional waste management systems, DMMS deals with both construction and demolition waste, particularly the latter for the purpose of the promotion of deconstruction. Generally speaking, compared to the demolition waste, construction waste is relatively easy to be reused or recycled due to the singleness of waste materials. Instead of the conventional second-hand construction material exchange, DMMS aims at the generation, exchange and disposal of demolition materials. The providers of demolition materials may seek the potential demanders of second-hand materials and the construction projects before the implementation of demolition so that the demanders may involve in the demolition activities and the demolition may be oriented to reuse or recycling of demolition materials. In addition, DMMS supports the information exchange of demolition projects and construction projects for a long term so that a demotion project may be scheduled in consideration with the construction projects which need demolition materials and vice versa. In the proposed system, the main participants take part in four categories of roles as demolition project providers, demolition materials demanders, general web visitors and system managers. For the purpose of information accuracy, membership is required before providing demolition or demand information. Besides the systems managers, general web visitors may participate in SDMM positively such as navigating the education module, discussing on visiting board, or browsing system information. The current URL for demonstration of DMMS is: http://www.deakin.edu.au/~chunlu/dmms/.

3. INFORMATION SYSTEM DESIGN

3.1. Structure Design of the Proposed Information System

After identification of the major change to current system, a logical design of the whole system is provided. Similar to most web-based database application, the system uses three-tier client-server architecture. As shown in Figure 1, the database server manages the databases that describe projects, materials and user profiles. The server side script program is a part of Web server, and given the privileges of retrieval and modification of database by the system program. In addition, it generates and sends back HTML code for the client side according to various data sources. The web server acts as a client when it request service from database server, which is to access the data. On the other hand, it acts as a server when it sends back web page to client side.

Client side program runs inside Web browser, the most available tool to access Internet (Kurose and Ross, 2001). Its application entities include HTML, Java Script and Java Applet. HTML gives the appearance and formation of the Web page, while Java Script helps in formation of the Web page and validating the data inputted by the user. These two elements communicate to the server using get and post methods from HTTP protocol. They formed main application part of database access, including demolition project provider inserting project into database, material demander inserting material demand into database and all user retrieving project information from the database.

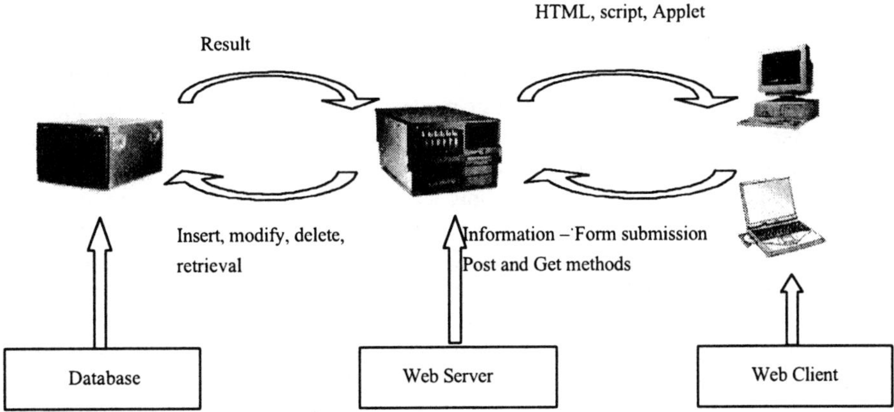

Figure 1. System structure

While HTML form is insufficient to describe the object to be submitted to Web server, Java Applet performs important part. It provides genuine graphical user interface to user contrasting raw HTML form. It is also dynamic in one single Web page without needs to refresh the page. More importantly, supporting of standard protocol allows Java Applet retrieval information from server side script program and transmits information user inputs at client side back to server side script program. This feature is very useful while the system needs a user to draw simple sketch of their building to be demolished. The characteristics of the drawing are sent to server, and the whole drawing is saved in server as an image file. This customer drawing approach will help the users to gain the knowledge of the building that is retrieved from the database under the search.

3.2. Data Processing in DMMS

Database is the core of the system. It provides a convenient and transparent way to access raw data. Data are mainly divided into four tables. The user table is used to store the authentication information for users. For users are registered with their contact information, the contact information is also stored in this table. One user can hold multiple projects, while project table is used to hold the information of its type, its time span of available and its location. Project table also holds the data related to project, such as the dimension of the building and structure factors of the building. A demolition project provides multiple kinds of materials; also a material can appear in multiple projects. As a result, a new table called product is generated that keeps references to both project table and material table, and the amount of the materials in particular project.

In the practical implementation of the system, database grows to more complex. Project has many child tables because different data are held representing different type of project, while they are still sharing some attributes such as location and available date. Other table might also be created. The system will allow user to upload multiple photos to help to describe the project, thus the photo table is needed to store the information of filename and directory of the image file related to a particular project. Among these tables, material table are predefined and maintained from system administrator according to the market information. Information in other tables, such as project and product, are generated during the practical use of the system.

Database table that is to describe the features of all kinds of materials is predefined in database server and accessible only to system administrator. Other tables are accumulated from the operation of the system. Because conventional web page form submission can only transfer simple text-based information or existing file to the server (Strahl, 2002), a web-based drawing tool is developed to allow users to draw graphics and submit to server. The needed information is acquired. And the graphics drawn is saved in server that can be viewed by other people in the future. Figure 2 shows the information flows implemented in DMMS. The information retrieved from the graphics can be the dimension of the building to be demolished and the structure features of the building. After obtaining all physical dimension characteristics and descriptive engineering characteristics, all information is put into an intelligent and knowledge aided calculation component. The additional parameters used in this intelligent system might be gained form past experience and scientific calculation. This system then outputs all the volumes of all kinds of materials. Volumes are then transferred into weights according to physical features of the particular material. Unit values, including unit price for new material and suggested unit price for used material, are used to produce the value of the materials, both categorized and summarized. Information about the values is shown on web page. This enables user to make selling and purchase decision based on the value. Information about products, which is the amount particular materials produced in one project, is saved in database for supporting the search and list activities.

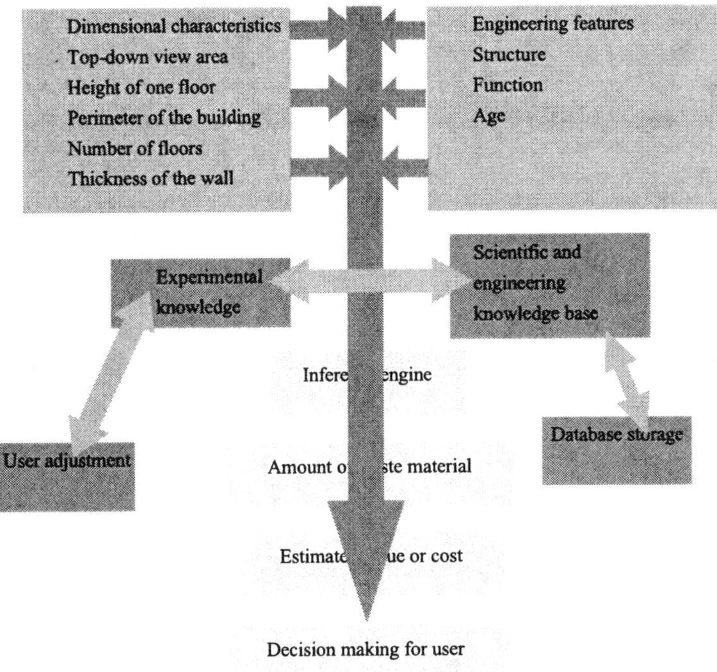

Figure 2. Information flow diagram

3.3. Drawing Data Acquisition Technique

In the development of the demolition material management system, a great amount of diversified information on projects should be acquired from users, which is better to be presented in graphics. Especially in the circumstance of construction industry, graphics materials such as draft and model are used more commonly then text. There is a need for the system to collect graphical information from user in an efficient way. To achieve this, the system adopts a specially designed drawing data acquisition toolkit. The multimedia data acquisition toolkit can be divided into server component and client component. Between them, the Internet is used as the communication channel.

Java Applet is used to construct the client component of the distributed drawing toolkit. Java is naturally distributed and is ideal for developing the Internet-based application. The main functionalities of the toolkit are to draw the graphics, save back to the server and analyse the graphics. Among these processes, drawing on a canvas runs on the client side only. Java provides rich Application Programming Interface (API) to support graphics processing (Moller and Schwartzbach, 2003). It includes drawing lines, rectangles, circles and other customized shapes. It is relatively simple to develop a tool that allows users to draw simple lines and shapes on the screen. Uses are also allowed to add comment to the drawn draft.

In the communication between the client and the server, large amount data need to be sent from the client to the server, including the drawn graphics. Traditionally, the HTTP protocol supports information transmission between the client and the server through both GET and POST methods. However, the pure POST method of HTTP protocol cannot be applied in this case due to the data exchange between the Java Applet and HTML code. Instead, Java Applet can initialise the connection to the server and send data along the connection. This mechanism actually deploys the HTTP POST method without submitting the HTML form. The server component adopts conventional server side techniques. It is composed using server side script language. In the system, we used PHP. The task of the server component is to receive the data from the client and store them on the server as an image file. The image file can then be shown to other users as a part of Web page. The image file can be further processed on the server side, including image analysing, recognition and manipulation. In the development of the toolkit, computation load is selectively loaded to the client side, which can eliminate potential bottleneck in the system.

4. DEVELOPMENT OF A PROTOTYPED SYSTEM

Due to the limitation of resources, the selection of tools, systems and programming languages is tightly related to the circumstances. HyperText Preprocesser (PHP), which is a mature programming language for server side, is chosen for the development of the server component of the system. The database is stored in an Oracle database server. The Java Applet is developed in Java Developer Kit (JDK) 1.4. The Web page is divided into three frames. Upper frame does not carry any actually function. It gives the title banner to the page. The left side frame is main menu area. Content regarding to particular menu item appears in right side frame. The first and default menu item is notice board. It gives up-to-date information about the change of the Web page to the users. The member area is the core of the system and main source of database. If user has not logged into the system, the login screen will be showed to authenticate member by username and password. User also has the choice of register as a member, which needs contact information. After logging into the system, submenu items are shown. Changing profile and changing password allow member to change personal contact information and password.

Adding project provides a wizard style procedure to members, allows them to add a project into database step by step. The data needed for the process includes the type of the project, the location of the project, the earliest available start date and the latest, photos that help to describe the project, the dimensional features and structure features of the project and an user custom drawing tool, which allows user to draw lines and shapes to further describe the project. Figure 3 shows the interfaces when a user provides information of a demolition or construction project into DMMS.

After all necessary data is collected. Potential materials produced or needed are categorized and quantified then listed. These numbers are available to modification from the user, considering user is able to gain more precise data through other mechanisms. The date is then stored into database. User is able to remove projects from his or her list in case the exchange is completed and the materials are not available any longer. User can also modify the quantity for a particular item or items from the list.

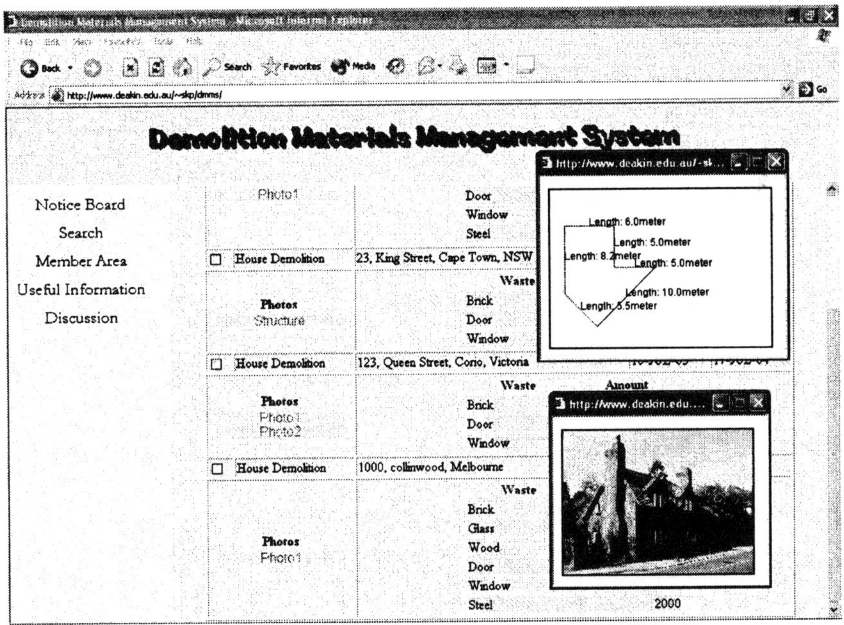

Figure 3. Interface of demolition project information acquisition

Project Search

Project type: House Demolition
Location:
Date: July 18 2003
Material type: Minimum amount:
Choose–
Choose–
Choose–
Search
Brick Glass Wood Steel Door Window

Figure 4. Screen shot of search component

Search function is also an important part of the system. As shown in Figure 4, users can search the catalogue using single or combined criteria, including project type, date, location, the type and amount of materials. There are also predefined categories for quick access. The result of search returns as a list of projects. Users can browse the details of individual project, including the photo that the project owner uploaded and the draft that the owner drew. Member who has logged into the system can obtain the contact information regarding to every project in the search results. This enables the communication to be made outside the system through the conventional channels such as phones and facsimiles. Furthermore, electronic communication manner is available through Email.

Useful information section gives user, both member and non-member, educational information on deconstruction and environment protection. One of the reasons that general construction practitioners do not want to actively involve in waste material reuse and recycle is that people are lack of motivation of doing so. Information of environmental figures and knowledge on the Internet is ideal for the education of general users. Finally, a discussion board is constructed to allow users to discuss issues of material reuse and recycle. It also provides a channel for system manager to answer questions from users.

5. CONCLUSIONS

The current waste exchange systems are relatively impractical and inefficient, due to the information flow in their system architecture. A new structure and design for waste-exchange system is proposed, named Demolition Material Management System (DMMS). Different with current system, DMMS allows user to provide information ahead of the waste materials are actually produced. The research identifies the components of the new system, its potential defects and possible solutions for them. A prototype of the system is provided and implemented. Technologies applied in the system such as multimedia information acquisition and intelligent system are verified.

Although waste reduction in construction industry involves lots of human factor such as attitude and knowledge, a user-friendly, realistic and efficient waste information exchange system can well support and educate environmental care over the industry.

REFERENCES

Chen, Z., Li, H., and Wong, C., 2003, Webfill before Landfill: An e-commerce model for waste exchange in Hong Kong, *Construction Innovation*. 3(1), 27–43.

Kurose, J. and Ross, K., 2003, The World Wide Web: HTTP, in: *Computer Networking – A top-down approach featuring the Internet*, 84–103.

Liu, C., Pun, S., and Itoh, Y., 2003, Technical development for deconstruction management, Proceedings of the 11th Rinker International Conference on Deconstruction and Materials Reuse, Gainesville, U.S.A., 186–203.

Moller, A and Schwartzbach, M, 2002, Interactive Web services with Java (May 10, 2003); http://www.brics.dk/amoeller/WWW/javaweb/http.html.

New South Wales Environment Protection Authority, 2003, Human Settlement, (May 10, 2003); http://www.epa.nsw.gov.au/soe/soe2000/ch/.

Reddrop, A. and Ryan, C., 1997, *Housing Construction Waste: A Research Study by the National Key Centre for Design*, Australian Government Publication Service, Canberra.

Strahl, R., 2002, The diminishing importance of HTML (May 10, 2003); http://www.west-wind.com/presentations/Editorials/ DiminishingImportanceOfHTML.asp.

A DISTRIBUTED LOGISTIC SUPPORT COMMUNICATION SYSTEM

V. Gruhn, M. Hülder, R. Ijioui, F.-M. Schleif,* and L. Schöpe†

ABSTRACT

This paper presents a communication architecture to provide an optimized support for communication within a logistic company. Truckage companies need continuous and up-to-date information about their business processes in order to respond quickly to customers' needs and problems emerging during transport processes. A reliable and user-friendly communication system is required, which improves the relationship between drivers and dispatchers. The main goals are integration with legacy logistics software and the possible use of new telematics and communication techniques. To achieve the goals above, a component based architecture allows the exchange and extension of components, making it possible to add new features to the system as they become available. The individual adjustment of business processes is supported by a distributed workflow engine.

1.INTRODUCTION

Truckage companies take advantage in business, when they can perform transports fast, securely, economically, and in time. "Time more and more becomes a critical component in freight transportation" (Ernst and Walpukis, 1997). This advantage is even more important, as due to globalisation and the extension of the European Union the number of truckage companies rises. Truckage companies that can achieve the named goals more efficiently due to the use of mobile communication can gain more trust as well as a better customer relationship.

* Chair of Applied Telematics / e-Business, Computer Science Faculty, University of Leipzig *E-Mail:{gruhn, huelder, ijioui, schleif}@ebus.informatik.uni-leipzig.de*

The chair for Applied Telematics / e-Business is endowed by Deutsche Telekom AG.

† *Informatik Centrum Dortmund e.V., Abt. Softwaretechnik*

E-Mail: lothar.schoepe@icd.de

1.1. Communication Problems within a Truckage Company

The following problems can appear during communication and cooperation between the different roles within a truckage company (drivers, dispatchers, customers) and thus stand in the way of reaching the required goals (Erkens and Kopfer, 2001).

Problems for the dispatcher:

- Discontinuous, oral information interchange between dispatcher and drivers leads to delays and mistakes.
- From the company's point of view drivers are a main source for information, but the information pooled at a driver cannot be transmitted into the logistics software without further manual work.
- Because of missing knowledge abut the transport progress the dispatcher can hardly reschedule transports.
- Calculations of transport costs can only be performed with a great delay.

Problems for drivers:

- Drivers can communicate problems only by mobile phone most of the time.
- Drivers have little influence on the scheduled tours and possible rescheduling.
- Data transmitted by the papers is often incomplete or even wrong.
- Dispatchers may not be available for questions.

Problems for customers:

- Transport progress is not known to the customer.
- Delays are not to be calculated.

By the development from location based acquisition towards a mobile acquisition and transmission of information and data, important information can be made available in time. This information may provide solutions to the named problems, and these solutions may not only help for the dispatching processes but also for the strategic fleet management.

Ideally such a communication system ought to provide a generic interface to logistics software systems and thus provide the advantage of being integrated into different logistics software systems. That way a clear cut between logistics software and communication system is made, proving the opportunity for truckage companies to extend their logistics software system rather than investing into a new monolithic system.

1.2. Realistic Usage Scenario

In order to plan the transports the dispatcher makes use of a logistics software system. To communicate with the drivers, the dispatcher usually uses paper forms or telephones. Using these means of communication exclusively can lead to loss of information or delays which prevent the dispatcher from reacting appropriately to events that happen to the drivers. The communication system introduced in this paper helps to overcome these problems.

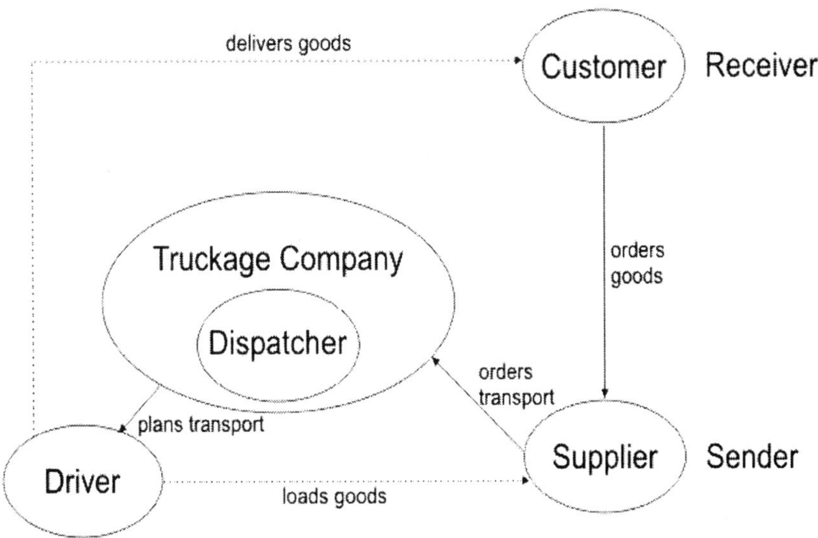

Figure 1. Transport scenario

The communication system described in the following chapters is based on the following scenario (see Figure 1): The dispatcher asks the driver to perform a transport. The driver then loads the freight and delivers it to the customer. This scenario differs from other parcel or express services in so far as there are very few private people but rather business customers involved who typically get freight with several tons of weight delivered.

To support the communication between drivers and dispatchers, the drivers are provided with mobile devices (e.g. PDAs). On one hand these devices can inform the drivers about the scheduled transports and on the other hand they enable the drivers to report back about each transport's status and problems that might appear during the delivery.

2. ARCHITECTURE OF THE COMMUNICATION SYSTEM

The communication system's architecture consists of three components: mobile devices (e.g. PDAs), stationary devices (e.g. PCs), and an application server. The mobile devices connect to the application server via a wireless telecommunication system (GSM, GPRS, HSCSD, UMTS), whereas the stationary devices use a wired connection (Ethernet, FastEthernet) to connect to the server.

The software architecture of the communication system follows the client/server paradigm (Lewandowski, 1998). The business logic for working on business objects is provided by an application server (Baker and Geraghty, 1998), which itself takes advantage of other server components: a workflow server, a communication server, and a database server (see Figure 2). The services provided by the server according to the business processes are used by the clients to deliver data to the targeted user.

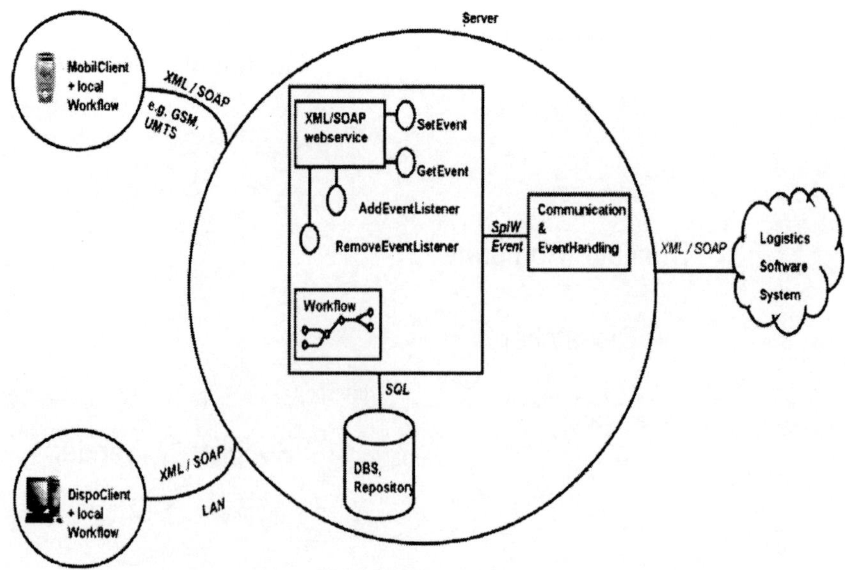

Figure 2. Architecture of the proposed communication system showing the involved components, there relations and access to the legacy system

The kind of data that is supplied by different clients may differ to a great extend, according to the users' roles and needs. While a driver mainly needs transport data, the dispatcher needs to have not only transport data but also the appropriate managing data as well. Depending on the kind of device used and its particular technical possibilities (e.g. display size) the different clients do not only render the data differently but also the amount of data displayed is adjusted. Similarly the usage of the user interface is realised in a different way (e.g. preconfigured hardware keys on PDA or mouse control on a PC).

If business logic is not only supplied by an application server, but parts of the business logic are realised on a client, clients are called "thick clients" (Lewandowski, 1998). On the other hand so-called "thin clients" (e.g. web browsers) do not have business logic on their own, but exclusively use services provided by an application server. Although thin clients generally need fewer resources, and therefore appear to be especially suited for devices with limited memory and processing power, thick clients are used on the mobile devices. This is due to the fact that a wireless connection cannot be guaranteed to be available or even stable. But to take care of the requirements mentioned in the introduction, parts of the business logic need to be executed even when the communication link is temporarily unavailable. After re-establishing the connection, data synchronization has to take place.

It is rather unlikely that the communication link over the wired medium in a local area network (LAN) breaks down for a long time, so that this line of argument is not valid for stationary devices. Still, a thick client is used for the stationary devices, for this client being the logistics management software which contains the complete business logic for rendering and working with the data. For more information on the advantages and disadvantages of thin and thick clients (Lewandowski, 1998). and (Orfali and Harkey, 1996) can be named.

The communication system defines interfaces for exchanging data with logistics management software. The data structure for the data exchange between clients and application server is described by a Document Type Definition (DTD) (Tolksdorf, 1999; Böhnlein and Ulbrich, 1999) and transmitted according to the XML-format.

For this purpose attributes of objects need to be transformed into XML data and then send over the communication link. During the transmission additional compression and cryptographic techniques may be used. The receiver then has to search the transmitted XML-document (parsing) and reproduce copies of the original data from the structure and the contents of the document.

This process is necessary because the development of application server and clients is based on a component model (Gruhn and Thiel, 1998; Szyperski, 1998) used in conjunction with an object-oriented programming language. Due to this, a later extension of the system does not require the data transmission part to be developed again, because only the required classes and the extended DTD have to be deployed on the system. According to the object-oriented paradigm the parser itself can use the objects' methods to produce an XML-code representation of the objects and vice versa reconstruct an object from the XML representation.

3. DISTRIBUTED WORKFLOW SUPPORT

Business processes that are to be supported by the communication system are described by so-called workflows. A workflow consists of a number of single actions, which can be simple or complex in themselves again. The actions of a workflow can be carried out in either a sequential, or parallel way, or as alternatives to each other. Workflows can be connected, i.e. initiate or depend on one another.

For any component in the architecture (see Figure 3) there are one or more workflows which deal with the creation, manipulation, and visualisation of business objects that are connected with it.

According to dependencies between components, workflows of different components may also be dependent on each other. Such dependencies are not always fixed but can evolve after creation or modification of data. Any class of a component contains a so-called display-method which is used to visualize data of that class according to a style-guide and the user interface. This way it is made sure that rendering of data is consistently done in the same way and the user is directed to his goal in the same manner.

In addition to the global workflow which describes business processes, there is local workflow which describes method collaboration within a class. This local workflow can be realised by implementing the display-method of a class.

Any component of the architecture consists of several classes. The components themselves possess a specified interface. The components shield data and store it permanently in a database. Realisation of components is done using an object-oriented programming language (such as Java or C#).

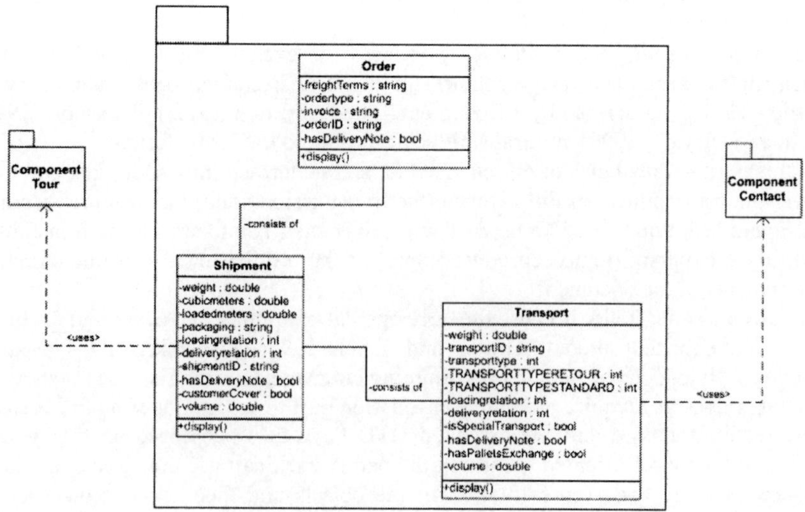

Figure 3. Components of the communication system

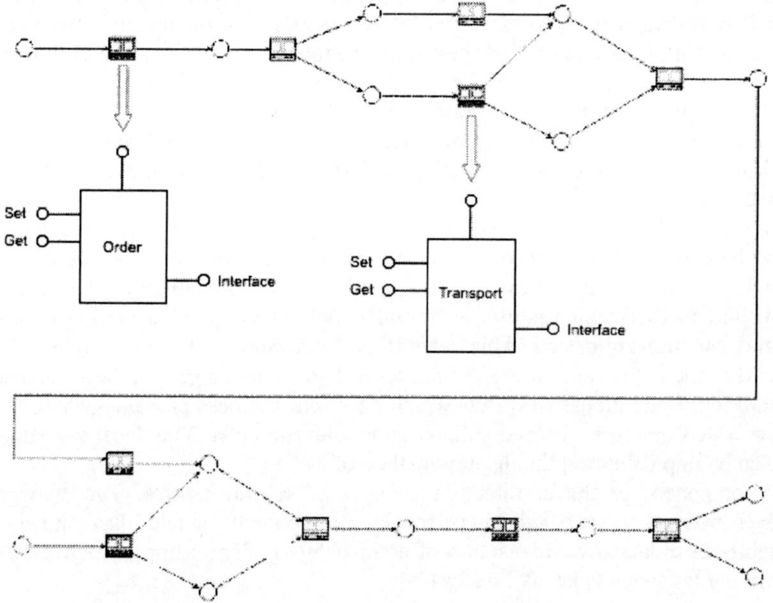

Figure 4. Realised and associated components establishing a workflow between different business objects

Components are associated with actions of a workflow (see Figure 4). In general there should only be one component associated with each action, but in exceptional cases there can be an association with several components. Such a complex association may only be allowed if changing the workflow is not possible or does not solve the problem. In this case workflow between associated components has to be described explicitly.

If there is a decision to be made depending on the data during the course of an action which defines the following course of the action, there has to be a decision table (see Figure 5).

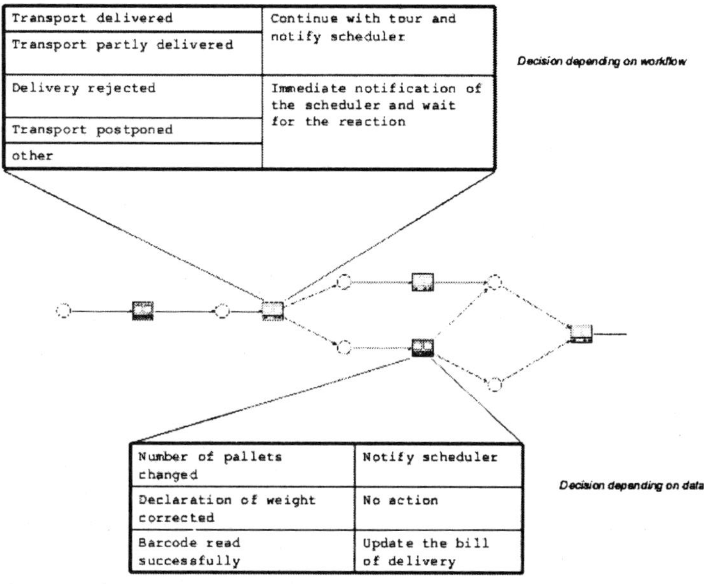

Figure 5. Decision table for actions modifying the workflow process

The course of workflows is controlled by a workflow server which is part of the application server. Due to the fact that parts of the business processes need to happen in a mobile and therefore distributed environment – on the clients as well as on the application server – the workflow server has to support the distributed execution and is responsible for data consistency and integrity. Distributed execution may be achieved by either a centralised or a decentralised approach. Considering the wireless connection between mobile clients and application server, and the problems originating from this (loss of connection, network availability, etc.), a decentralised solution appears to be suitable. That means that there is a central workflow server available as well as local workflow servers on each of the clients, although they may differ in the amount of functionality they provide.

Depending on the environment and equipment of the mobile devices the mobile workflows have to be adjustable. For example it is possible to attach a barcode scanner to the mobile device. In this case, the workflow has to handle scanner and read barcodes appropriately, e.g. when delivering goods. In another case, when there is no barcode scanner installed, the delivery process has to leave out the scanning and proceed accordingly, e.g. prompting the driver to confirm that he has delivered the appropriate goods. This mechanism of modelling different workflows for different user and device profiles, and then executing the workflows in the workflow server, allows for fine grained adjustment of the software without changing the source-code.

Whether components may be loaded dynamically at runtime from the server according to the workflow executed or whether all components have to be deployed statically on the clients, depends on the communication techniques (HSCSD, GPRS, EDGE, UMTS) available.

4. RELATED WORK

The complexity of the transportation field is reflected by the richness of research areas, methods, and software. The future of truckage companies, however, lies in providing a more efficient and cost effective transport service. The objective is to use modern technology in order to exploit the full potential of saving costs. More and more goods have to be moved efficiently, quickly and cost effectively by service and transport companies. In order to survive, transport companies must respond quickly to their customers' needs and focus on cost control. Continuous and up-to-date understanding of business processes is essential and requires a reliable and user-friendly system for mobile data communication (Frediani, 2003).

Researchers have already developed a number of techniques to solve the communication and fleet management problems of truckage companies. For example, researchers at the University of Bremen proposed a concept for controlling truck fleets through cellphones and the Internet (Erkens and Kopfer, 2001; Siek et al., 2003). Economists at the University of Koblenz are also working on a prototype for supporting logistics processes (Jung, 2001). The main goal of these research efforts is to provide flexible fleet management and introduce new kinds of services that truckage companies could offer in the future (e.g. location-based services).

There is no universal solution that is suitable for any truckage company, and the systems available today still have a few weaknesses.

5. CONCLUSION

Electronic support of transport execution is barely integrated with conveyance systems. Communication during the transport process and afterwards is done either on paper documents or by telephone, both of which require additional work to receive an electronic representation later on. This additional work is not only time consuming but also error prone. The scheduler is not informed well enough about the progress of the transport, and needs to acquire additional information actively himself.

Therefore we see the need for bidirectional communication to exchange transport information in time on one hand, and on the other hand unidirectional communication between mobile devices and other backend software systems to exchange data over a wireless yet stable medium.

Most of the systems available today do not focus on the need of small conveyance companies. Those companies often cannot invest into a completely new software system. Employees would have to get used to the new software and the market situation is so unclear that no one can say which systems are going to last for enough time to secure the investments. Systems that are based on application service providing concepts put up another barrier, because they require hosting vital company data about customers and lorries on the service provider's side. Thus the company becomes dependent on a third party's accessibility and reliability.

The project "Mobile Spedition im Web (SpiW)" which is supported by the German Ministry of Education and Research, aims to reach the two main goals of integration with legacy logistics software and the possible use of new telematics and communication techniques. The component based architecture of the communication system allows the later change and extension of components, making it possible to add new features to the system, as they become available (such as transmission of video data or data gained from board sensors).

Within the project consortium it is not possible to reach these goals completely, especially for the integration with legacy software the interface defined has to be supported by the legacy software developers.

Although the benefit of such a communication system is obvious, it also depends on the costs of acquisition and operation which is even more important. The industrial partners in the project consortium are to ensure that the benefit exceeds those costs.

REFERENCES

Baker, S. and R. Geraghty, 1998, Java For Business Objects, in: *Developing Business Objects,* Carmichel, Andy, ed., SIGS, Cambridge University Press, pp. 225–237.

Böhnlein, U. and A. Ulbrich vom Ende, 1999, XML – Extensible Markup Language, in: *Wirtschaftsinformatik, Band 41, Heft 3,* Vieweg Verlag Wiesbaden, pp. 275–277.

DaimlerChrysler, 2003, *Fleetboard - fleet management.* (available online from: http://www.fleetboard.info/show_page_t1.php4?advantages,e, Last accessed 07 Mar 2003).

Datafactory A. G., 2003, *Webfleet - Fahrzeug und Personenortung im internet,* (available online from: http://www.webfleet.de/en/doc/datafactory_Webfleet-Brochure.pdf, last accessed 07 Mar 2003).

Erkens, E. and H. Kopfer, 2001, WAP-LOG: Ein System zur mobilen Fahrzeugeinsatzsteuerung und Auftragsfortschrittkontrolle, in: *Logistik Management - Supply Chain Management und e-Business* (Grünert, S.), Teubner Verlag, Stuttgart, pp. 293–303.

Ernst, M. and D. Walpukis, 1997, *Telekommunikation und Verkehr*, Verlag Franz Vahlen, München.

Frediani, J., 2003, *Fleet management via the internet,* (available online from: http://www.daimlerchrysler.de/environ/report2001/pdf/fleet_e.pdf, last accessed 07 Mar 2003).

Gruhn, V. and A. Thiel, 1998, *Komponentenmodelle*, Addison Wesley, München.

Jung, J. S., 2001, *Flottenmanagement im Handwerk durch integrierte Telematikdienste*, (available online from: http://www.uni-koblenz.de/~flotthit/Project/overview.html, last accessed: 07 Mar 2003).

Lewandowski, S., 1998, Frameworks for Computer-Based Client/Server Computing, in: *ACM Computing Surveys,* Vol. 30, No. 1, ACM Press, 3–27

Orfali, R., D. Harkey, and J. Edwards, 1996, *The Essential Client/Server Survival Guide*, Wiley Publ.

Siek, K., Erkens, E., and H. Kopfer, 2003, Marktübersicht über Systeme zur Fahrzeugkommunikation im Straßengüterverkehr, Submitted to *Logistik Management, 5. Jahrgang, Ausgabe 1*, Germa Press Verlag GmbH, Hamburg.

Szyperski, C., 1998, *Component Software – Beyond Object-Oriented Programming*, Addison-Wesley, Reading, MA.

Tolksdorf, R., 1999, XML und darauf basierende Standards, in: *Informatik Spektrum, Band 22, Heft 6,* Springer Verlag, Heidelberg, pp. 407–421.

AUTHOR INDEX

Aarons J. 393
Abramowicz W. 555
Aisbett J. 169
Aladwani A. 643
Arnold J. 629
Bajec M. 141, 317
Beekhuyzen J. 507
Box I. 223
Burstein F. 405, 443, 605
Cao P. 605
Caplinskas A. 649
Cecez-Kecmanovic D. 1
Ceddia J. 569
Chen P. 455
Croll P. 179
Cybulski J. 331
Dampney C. 169
Dawson L. 581, 661
Dowd C. 617
Finkelstein C. 43
Fisher J. 581, 661
Flitman A. 293
Fuller A. 179
Gasston J. 281
Gedge R. 569
Gregor S. 83
Gruhn V. 705
Hakkarainen S. 305
Hall W. 443
Hansen B. 127
Hasan H. 379, 675
Hawryszkiewycz I. 467
von Hellens L. 507
Hobbs V. 519
Holck J. 187
Howard S. 155
Hulder M. 705
Ijioui F. 705
Ivanov S. 103
Jacobsen D. 127
Jennex M. 355
Jones D. 83
Jørgensen M. 187
Kaczmarek T. 555
Kartiwi M. 675

Kautz K. 127, 495
Khan K. 367
Kirikova M. 481
Knapp G. 431
Kos B. 555
Kowalkiewicz M. 141, 317
Krisper M. 543
Ledington P. 695
Liu C. 431
Lowe M. 267
Madsen S. 495
Magyar G. 431
Marshall P. 507
McKay J. 481
Metcalfe M. 443
Milton S. 519
Mussio P. 27
Németh G. 431
Nielsen S. 507
Nikiforova O. 481
Owen J. 443
Pigott D. 519
Pokorny J. 531
Pun S. 695
Richta K. 209
Roy S. 545
San Pedro J. 605
Sarkar P. 331
Satchell C. 417
Schleif L. 705
Schoepe M. 705
Shackleton P. 581
Shanks G. 155
Sheard J. 569
Singh S. 417
Strasunskas D. 305
Tansley E. 155
Taylor P. 237
Terrill B. 293
Unold J. 115
Valatkaite I. 199
Vasilecas O. 199, 649
Vavpotic D. 141, 317
Vrazalic L. 341
Wrycza S. 593
Zupancic J. 683
Zyngier S. 405